Rereading Cultural Anthropology

Rereading

Cultural

Anthropology

Edited by George E. Marcus

Duke University Press   Durham and London 1992

Contents

Introduction

This selection of articles from *Cultural Anthropology*'s first six years, 1986–1991, is meant to provide one access to the prominent interests that shaped cultural anthropology in the United States during the 1980s and define its current end-of-the-century predicaments and possibilities. It is perhaps supremely ironic that anthropology in the United States, so long identified with the concept of culture, has had so little to do, until very recently, with the emergence of the lively inter-disciplinary arena of research, discussion, and thought now known as cultural studies.

This arena has largely been shaped within the humanities by developments over the past two decades in literary studies, history, philosophy, and academic feminism. While French poststructuralist theories have been the primary intel-lectual capital, the example of British cultural studies, an intellectually eclectic critical movement of the 1950s and 1960s, has been the institutional inspiration for the emergence of cultural studies in the United States. In Britain, as in the United States, anthropology, still perhaps identified with the fine-grained, merely descriptive study of primitive, exotic peoples, had little role to play in the develop-ment of cultural studies as an interdisciplinary field. Still, in the desire of cultural studies scholars to "world" themselves, to be politically and globally relevant, and to find alternatives to strictly textual frames of cultural analysis, anthropology has much to offer. And in anthropologists' search for different, more intellectually complex, and relevant contexts for their practice of ethnography, cultural studies provides a vast, largely unknown terrain to explore.

A major agenda, then, of *Cultural Anthropology* has been to provide a much-needed register of the current traffic in the borderland between cultural studies and anthropology. While mostly rooted and identified within the tradition of anthro-pological research, the pieces collected in this volume might reveal for cultural studies scholars in general, and anthropologists in particular, the tensions and possibilities that currently exist for grounding cultural analysis in the details of everyday life in the many places and situations in which anthropological ethnog-raphy constructs and focusses its gaze, and, reciprocally, for reshaping that gaze in terms of a set of provocations and a complex intellectual history of theory and practice in the study of culture that anthropologists are now all too aware that they had isolated themselves from.

The journal was founded as the organ of the Society for Cultural Anthropology within its larger, historic organization, the American Anthropological Association. This new society was the inspiration of a number of leading senior cultural anthropologists (for example, David Schneider, Roy D'Andrade, and Clifford Geertz) who had developed their reputations during the 1960s and who sought a different forum for discussion and debate of ideas in anthropology than was then available within the AAA. The formation of this subsociety was a part of a general trend of fragmentation into specialized groups within the AAA during the 1970s and 1980s. The founders of the SCA were clearly concerned about the absence of a coherent vision in contemporary anthropology, or even any focussing debates. They looked to the activities and the journal of the new society to overcome a sense of malaise since the decline in enthusiasm for a number of 1960s theoretical initiatives, including French structuralism, Marxism, and cognitive studies.

When the SCA was formed in the mid-1980s, several internal critiques of Anglo-American anthropology were taking hold among cultural and social anthropologists in the United States. One critique derived its power from an exposure of the conventions, tropes, and rhetoric of anthropological writing. Making transparent the narratives or scripts by which the production of anthropological knowledge had proceeded, rather than suggesting a new, alternative narrative, seemed for most anthropologists to be an important move to make, however strongly or unsympathetic they were to such an effort. I suspect that I was offered by the SCA board the task of creating and editing its journal because of my association (through the publication in 1986 of [with James Clifford] *Writing Culture* and of [with Michael Fischer] *Anthropology as Cultural Critique*) with stimulating the discipline's own internal critique, which seemed to be at the moment the modicum of focussed intellectual dynamism. This was logically one point from where cultural anthropology's revitalization might occur.

The mid-1980s critique can only be partly explained as the culmination of an evolving internal critique within the discipline. Its power, in fact, derives from a much broader process of transformation that has been affecting the practices of all of the disciplines in the humanities and social sciences, of which the critique of anthropological writing is one variant. Yet, the critique and debate about the production of knowledge in anthropology are particularly important cases of the more general trend: First, because unlike most other disciplines affected, the debate in anthropology has occupied a central focus of attention in which the identity of the discipline itself is at stake for its practitioners. And second, the critique of knowledge in anthropology was produced by a working alliance of scholars inside and outside of anthropology, that is, of historians and critics, focusing upon the discipline, and of practitioners within it. This alliance across the boundaries of the discipline made the critique both more provocative and more difficult to dismiss or marginalize among anthropologists.

One of the main vehicles for promoting cultural studies in the United States has been the founding of new journals that often distance themselves from, if not reject, disciplinary origins and traditions. Indeed, *Cultural Anthropology* has partaken of the same manifesto-like self-characterizations as journals like *Representations*, *Public Culture*, *Transition*, *Diaspora*, *Cultural Critique*, and *Contention*, requiring a break with the past, and in which a new world must be confronted that demands changes in practices of questioning and representation. Yet, it remains resolutely a disciplinary journal in identity, the property of a long-established "professional" society (the AAA)—and not one of this society's central journals at that (rather, the *American Anthropologist* and the *American Ethnologist* define the central tendency). This publishing situation of the journal has had its disadvantages: as one of the several publications of a professional society, ambitions for its promotion and circulation beyond its own subsociety's membership are very modest indeed, compared to the broad-gauged efforts of university and commercial presses to distribute their journals. Also, while having a free hand as editor, I (as well as officers of the SCA) had to deal with the complaints of more conservative, or orthodox, elements among readers of the journal, who receive it as a function of membership in the SCA, who are suspicious of the "new" as "fashionable," and who think that the journal should be representative of the society's membership rather than having a distinctive profile and purpose, as it did under my editorship.

Nevertheless, I consider these same mundane, limiting circumstances of *Cultural Anthropology*'s publication to be also the source of its distinction among the wave of new or revitalized journals concerned with critiquing and transforming knowledge production in the human sciences. It is one of the few "officially" published journals, associated with the professional identity and organization of a discipline, that so clearly represents and allies with the broad-based critique that is now occurring. *Cultural Anthropology* has not promoted interdisciplinarity from a space outside disciplinary apparatuses, enabled by university press or commercial publication. Rather, at a time when the new journal initiatives have been fleeing from identification with disciplines, *Cultural Anthropology*, while making common cause with those in cultural studies broadly conceived, nonetheless has recognized the importance of siting critique and exploration of other possibilities within the frame of given disciplinary traditions. Initiatives within disciplines are as important as those that apparently float free in self-styled interdisciplinary space. This positioning of the unofficial, merged within the official, was the unusual space that *Cultural Anthropology* occupied under my editorship. The critical engagement with a specific disciplinary tradition and practices at a particular historic moment has also been specific and direct—just as the production of ethnographic knowledge itself has been.

The following selection of papers is personal, but not idiosyncratic. In the eight categories that I have invented to organize the papers selected, I have tried to reflect the major trends of movement within cultural anthropology toward engagement with the broader interdisciplinary stream of cultural studies. I have chosen papers both for their interest and for the way they represent particular categories. Of course, there were several other outstanding and unusual papers published during the first six years that could not be included. Some of these would have fit within my categories; others reflect the diversity of interests and work, not represented here, but that anthropology still encompasses. Also, of course, there are a number of dimensions of the emergent field of cultural studies that the journal did not represent well in its first years. Nonetheless, the following selections do register the shifts and jolts within the anthropology of the 1980s that account for styles of work that are now being more fully explored.

I.   Critiques

It is perhaps not surprising that the largest category of papers chosen for inclusion in this reader concern the variety and situations of internal critiques of anthropology that occurred in force during the 1980s and still continue, but most usefully now as a threshold for reworking styles, definitions of subject matter, and rhetorics in research and writing.

Stephen Tyler's short paper was the introduction to a special issue on the hermeneutics of orality and literacy, and in extremis, reflects the critique of representation that raised the specter of the limits of language (particularly, as writing) to achieve the aims of a scientific, descriptive anthropology.

Michael Taussig's equally short paper also poses the limits of conventional discursive forms by an appeal to and lapidary explanation of Walter Benjamin's sense of the modern, cognitive experience of urban life as tactile and distractive. Like Tyler, Taussig suggests that language without the sensorial impoverishes anthropology, limiting it finally and repetitively to the sole task of disclosing social constructions of meaning. But unlike Tyler who valorizes the oral and the aural at the expense of the visual (especially, as domesticated in writing), Taussig exalts mimesis, performance, and the strongly emotive and physical power of images.

Robert Thornton's paper, which was to have appeared in *Writing Culture*, reflects the critique of ethnographic rhetoric and convention at the level of the monograph. In its mission to evoke cultures as "wholes," ethnography has worked less by narrative than by classification. Thornton displaces the encyclopedic practice of holism in classic ethnographic writing, and thus opens the way for the use of actual narrative techniques.

Arjun Appadurai's paper, included in a special issue on "Voice and Place in Anthropological Theory," extends the critique of ethnographic rhetoric from texts to ethnographic areas and regions—how particular places have come cumulatively to be represented and discussed in terms of strong tropes, such as hierarchy for India, thus obscuring the complexity and multiplicity of other themes, possibilities, and representations.

Alcida Ramos' review of the ethnographic caricaturing of the Yanomamo, the favorite contemporary "exotic people" in the teaching of undergraduate anthropology, examines the circulation of ethnographic portrayals as a desire for the violent, the erotic, or the noble in the idea of the exotic. She disturbingly finds these motivated distortions to originate in the ethnographic accounts themselves.

Ted Swedenburg's paper moves critique to fieldwork experience and deepens the well-established genre of fieldwork accounts by giving his experience a critical, poignant edge, exposing the difficulties, if not impossibility, of doing a self-controlled fieldwork project in highly charged political contexts.

The inclusion of Geoffrey White's report on the transformation of an academic conference by the action of indigenous people present is intended to show that the so-called critique of ethnographic writing has not been a strictly academic exercise. In contexts where subjects confront anthropological representations of them, they certainly "speak for themselves." On such occasions, the critique of anthropology is a "happening" in which academic authority and purposes become unexpectedly and unpredictably transformed. Such events are occurring with more frequency, and they signal the changing contexts of the creation and reception of anthropological knowledge.

White's paper incidentally reflects the effort of the journal during its first years to encourage reports of events, conferences, seminars, and informal groups, stimulated by the idea that a number of the shifts in anthropology might be occurring on such occasions that go usually unreported in any formal way, and awareness of which otherwise circulates only anecdotally as corridor talk.

The final two papers included in this category are intended to reflect a broader context in academia for the specific internal critiques of anthropology. Postmodernism, of course, has been the elusive figure for both the condition of society and the style of knowledge in regard to it that has held attention for so long in the current broad wave of critiques of disciplines. Now there are many efforts to reflect on postmodernism, even in a retrospective mode as the velocity and scale of its influence still continue. Vincent Crapanzano's paper is one such effort out of anthropology, and with a special interest in intellectual discourse beyond the Western world. This paper fixes well anthropology's ambivalence toward postmodernism, and the realm of interdisciplinary discussion in the West for which it stands. At once liberating, stimulating, ethnocentric, and parochial, the postmodern constitutes a not completely definable object of desire in the present critical efforts of anthropologists to remake their discipline.

My paper is a playful and personal effort to ground, sociologically, recent interdisciplinary trends which I term a humanities revitalization movement. Couched as both a travel account and amateur ethnography, this piece is still one of the few that tries to come to terms with the appeal and prestige of the literary, and its theories of textual representation, as the source of the critical probes that have undone or challenged given practices of inquiry and theory in so many fields.

II.   Reaction

Melford Spiro's paper is included to reflect the worried, but reasoned, response to shifts in cultural anthropology with which the journal came generally to be associated. Coursing through his paper is a warning of the possible delegitimation of anthropology in the attitudes of its past sponsors, which departures from the path of its commitment to (social) science might cause.

III.   Witnessing

Much recent anthropology has been done in regions and areas of the world experiencing traumatic political change and violence. Increasingly, anthropologists are writing out-of-genre to witness events around them that have only awkwardly fit into conventional anthropological scholarship. This emerging genre of witnessing/reportage is well represented by two pieces that concern protracted guerrilla war in the Andes region of Peru, one of those "culture areas" that is the focus of increasingly sophisticated and complex ethnographic and historical scholarship. Orin Starn's paper takes anthropologists to task for being oblivious in their writing to the social and cultural sources of political violence and the guerrilla movement in Peru. Enrique Mayer's paper disagrees with Starn, but, more broadly, it constitutes itself as a form of reportage based on considerable background knowledge of the aftermath and investigation surrounding the sensational murder of a group of journalists.

IV.   Poetics

In the continuing, strong tradition of the study of peoples still existing in their own distinctive cosmological life worlds, Keith Basso's paper represents the move from the longstanding concern with language and cognition in cultural anthropology to a deeper involvement with issues of poetics. This does not mean just more attention to tropes, to the figural qualities of language, long the staple of symbolic analysis in anthropology, but to an interest in how language and cognition are tied to the senses and emotions in cultural context. Basso's paper exemplifies the transition from the heavily linguistic emphasis of earlier approaches to poetics in anthropology to a poetics of the senses, which in the Apache case, focusses upon the visual imagination relating to place and landscape.

V.   What's Left, What's Emergent

A major trend that the journal has reflected is an interest in the historic (colonial) and contemporary incorporation of "peoples" as working classes or in the apparent reduction of local cultures by the macro processes associated with capitalist political economy in the many forms that it has taken. This has led to refined examinations of resistance and accommodation, a concern with the dynamics of encapsulation, focussed upon the relationships, language, and objects of encounter and response from the sides of both local and cosmopolitan groups and persons, who, although in very different relative power positions, experience a process of being mutually displaced from what has counted as culture for each of them.

On the one hand, anthropology has been very good at developing an understanding about "what's left" in cases in which once undeniably vibrant cultures appear to have been devastated. Kathleen Stewart's paper shows where to look in such situations, amid the ruins, so to speak, and in so doing establishes a basis for a renewed attention to the cultural analysis of objects and material life.

On the other hand, anthropology has been good at showing how newly formed working classes and others in subaltern situations have renewed themselves by participating creatively in dominant institutions and processes of commodification, especially in relation to the expressive forms of popular, mass culture. Forms of culture that such encapsulated "peoples" as ethnic minorities and working classes do not own are nonetheless claimed by them through popular artistic practice as is shown in David Coplan's paper on music, song, and dance among the Basotho migrant proletariat of southern Africa. The stuff of cultural analysis is not in the reclamation of some previous culture state or its subtle preservation despite changes, but in the new cultural forms that changes in colonial subaltern situations have given rise to. There is both a politics and poetics to this process that are nicely woven into Coplan's paper, an exemplar of a whole genre of work that not only focusses the research of much current anthropology, but also defines a major set of interests in contemporary cultural studies. The attention to the culture and political economy of diverse subaltern situations in past colonial and present postcolonial worlds is thus one major site for exchanges between anthropology and the broader interdisciplinary trend of cultural studies.

VI.   Circulations

The other major related trend that concerns contemporary global transformations is a move out from local situations to understand how transcultural processes themselves are constituted in the world of the so-called "system" (modern interlocking institutions of media, markets, states, industries, universities—the worlds of elites and middle-classes) that has encapsulated, transformed, and sometimes obliterated local cultures. This work examines the circulation of cultural meanings, objects, and identities in diffuse time-space. It shows how the global arena is itself constituted by such circulations. John Russell's paper argues a fascinating point about how the apparent open racism in Japanese culture entered through its style of relationship with other large nation-state societies, especially the United States. Fred Myers' paper, rooted in a deep ethnographic knowledge of a local people of the classic sort studied in anthropology, moves beyond this context to an arena of their contemporary appropriation in the global, cosmopolitan art world's desire for aboriginal painting. The Pintupi now circulate and are constructed by worlds they never imagined locally, yet, they are an integral part of these other worlds. Myers' paper is an application of an ethnographic sensibility moving from its traditional disciplinary moorings and offers a glimmer of the necessary creative changes in the way anthropologists conduct research and write about not only the contemporary situations of their classic subjects, but also about new subjects such as worldly art markets, tastes, and collecting. Most importantly, it shows impressively what can be done analytically, in a grounded empirical frame of inquiry beyond the critiques and arguments for alternatives, under the signs of poststructuralism, postmodernism, deconstruction, heteroglossia, and the like.

VII.   Media

Another opening of anthropology to different and more complex worlds of engagement and practice are the relevant media beyond the book and the film in which it might operate, such as video and television. Most transformative is the increasing extent to which anthropological subjects are being fully integrated as reception classes for work by anthropologists and vice versa. This process is far more than a matter of bookishness: this new meeting ground is likely to be constituted in terms of rapidly developing media technologies that create different communicative spheres altogether. Faye Ginsburg's piece on the diverse media that shape cultural politics as these concerning Australian aborigines outlines the dimensions of this new emergent arena in the positioning and composition of anthropological work.

VIII.   Experiment

Finally, one of the most controversial, provocative trends from the critique has been the idea of anthropological writing as being in an experimental phase. How self-conscious experiments are, how new they really are, how appropriate they are—these are some of the issues that form the ethos of experimentalism, which threatens to transgress the kinds of boundaries on which the professional and espistemological identity of anthropology depends. The most radical forms of experimentation tend to be seen within anthropology as self-indulgent, if not excessive and dangerous to the rectitude of the discipline.

But there are serious issues at stake in trying to write differently. For example, to what degree is experimentation not just a question of writing in a different analytic jargon, but rather of developing through a shift in discursive form novel arguments that, in effect, perform their theoretical implication? Or, is there a sense in which writing involves not just interpretive translation, but the appropriation and incorporation of subjects' forms of writing and speaking in one's own—a kind of literal transformation of the anthropologist's conventional identity? Feminist genres of autobiography, for example, have most openly tolerated and sanctioned such experimentation. Reflecting this kind of provocative experimentation is the short piece by Julie Taylor, which moves from a distanced, analytic treatment of tango as a seminal cultural form in Argentina to a personal enactment of tango narrative, a literary form developed by Argentines in exile, parallel to the dance. Such experimental writing, for all its risks (not the least, of ambivalent, hostile reception among anthropologists), represents the vitality of the critiques that began the current revitalization of work in cultural anthropology.

Rereading Cultural Anthropology

On Being Out of Words

Stephen A. Tyler

"Yes, I know but . . ."

The papers in this collection are part of a larger discourse that takes discourse itself as the object and means of understanding. As in that wider discourse, they are more concerned with the means of sentiment than with the structure and means of knowledge. They resonate to the discourse that questions the hegemony of representation and epistemology in Western thought and they echo its concerns with the tropes that legitimate and justify thought and action (cf. Rorty 1979; Lyotard 1979).

As in that discourse, the discourse on orality and literacy resounds with the clash of two master tropes. One is the modernist trope of "loss and liberation," of "the past surpassed"; the other is the post-modern trope of "resistance and recovery," of "the past recuperated." The first tells the tale of how speech was overcome and surpassed by a writing that, though it destroyed the warmth, intimacy, passion, and spirit of the participatory oral world, created a powerful new form of consciousness capable of ever-increasing abstraction and precision (Ong 1982; Goody 1977; Barfield 1985). It is the modernist fable of technology triumphant, of the creativity-in-destruction of the technology of the alphabet, of the rise of civilization from savagery, and the surpassing of the life-world of common sense and oral mnemonics by science and technology. This story of the glory of the eye is also an elegy that tells of loss and alienation, for the price of civilization is the fragmentation of the wholeness of a form of life, and liberation from nature is paid for in alienation from nature. The kingdom of the liberated, autonomous cogito is a lonely place where others are only ghosts out of a romanticized past, summoned like natives from far off places to justify and legitimize alienation by their outlandish otherness. The difference that is the past is overcome in a utopian future still to come, but surely just around the corner.

The post-modern trope of resistance and recovery tells a different tale. It speaks of the irony of representation, of that inescapable difference between appearance and reality, and exposes writing as the means that makes reality accessible only by occulting it in a simulacrum that substitutes itself for the reality it pretends to represent. It parodies the sign that seeks to become speech by cannibalizing the reality it represents. It stigmatizes writing as the enigma that seeks to enclose within itself both the representation and what the representation represents. It speaks of writing as the identity of means and ends that overcomes its object by becoming it (cf. Derrida 1974).

Paradoxically, orality is also the name of the counter discourse that resists the hegemony of the written word by recuperating the past, by reminding us that speech and communication ground all representation, not in the sign's alienation of the world, but in commonsense practices when word and world meet in will and deed. This part of the story is told polyphonically in fragmentary episodes in the writing of Heidegger, Wittgenstein, Gadamer, and Habermas.

"On the other hand . . ."

So long as we write as we do, we can never understand the world as a non-literate might. That is the real message of Derrida's *Of Grammatology* (1974). It asserts again and again the necessary priority of writing to orality. Writing encompasses, precedes, and grounds orality. And if, as Ong declares (1982:78–117), literacy means a change in consciousness, we must ask how writing then could describe that consciousness it replaces, except as it recreates it in its own image.

The discourse on orality and literacy reflects this conundrum. Having posited the absolute difference between orality and literacy in the writing of Parry, Havelock, Ong, and others, the writing of that difference must necessarily seek to erase the difference by comprehending it within the understanding that writes the difference. Predictable dialectical responses seek to soften or obliterate the distinction between orality and literacy by questioning the difference of the difference (cf. Tannen 1980). This reduction of difference never quite succeeds; a stubborn, residual orality resists final absorption into the literature that created it, and engenders a suspicion about writing, for each attempt to erase the difference recreates it and encourages suspicion about the instrument and purposes of reduction.

This riddle is effectively expressed in the phrase "oral literature," which conveys exactly this sense of irreducible duality. Oral literature is not oral, but neither is it exactly literature, as the adjectival sense of "oral" clearly tells us. So long as we write alphabetically, so long will the world or orality seem to us at once strange and familiar, for orality and literacy are correlatives, the one unthinkable to us without the other. Our thinking is projected out of a con-text that presupposes writing and must necessarily render occult whatever proceeds from another presupposition. At best, we only mark and remark the difference in a writing that presupposes the possibility of the difference and seeks to relativize it to its own project.

The point of Derrida's exercise is not that orality is at last overcome by a writing that no longer presupposes it, but that so long as we write as we do, we will only re-establish the difference we seek to extirpate. All our efforts to represent it tell us only of the re-presenting and mark the absence of the represented by pointing to the difference between the representation and what it is a representation of. This is the contradiction at the heart of the idea of the sign—that it has a meaning that is other than itself.

One way out of this dilemma is to get rid of meaning by transforming the sign into a sign of itself, as the sign of another sign. Signs, and writing too, would then become simulacra that portend no beings beyond themselves or their combinatory possibilities. Semiotics, the combinatory possibilities of signs would overcome and obviate the semantic and representational aspects of the sign (cf. Derrida 1974:45–65). Not only would signs represent no thing—which would be only a failure of reference—they would not represent at all; they could only represent themselves; they would fill up their hinterland.

This move establishes at once the impossibility of "de-scribere" as realities "out of" writing, and the absolutism of "de-scribere" as realities out of "writing." Writing makes realities out of writing but those realities are not outside of writing, which means that we are out of writing in at least one of these ways. Paradoxically, we could no longer speak (if ever we could) of the arbitrariness of the sign, for it would have no other of which it could be the arbiter. Its only other would be other signs from which it differed, but which it could not represent. It would be a new kind of natural sign to parallel a new kind of nature. We could thus erase the otherness of the sign just as we have erased the otherness of the cultures it writes about. Having destroyed otherness in the rest of the world, we rend the otherness in the bosom of its creator.

If there could be no prior being for which signs could substitute and thus make the possibility of representation, how, but for sound, would this differ from speech? Would it not be the "pure being" and "self presence" of the monad wrapped in the self-evidence of its own incorruptible essence—the veritable spirit of speech as the simultaneous co-presence of word and world in the sign, the alpha and the omega of the Derridean reading? Derrida's deconstruction of the sign does not call being into question, it destabilizes the idea of the sign and ultimately undermines the whole system of alphabetic writing. Derrida finds the sought for full presence of the word by a kind of negative capability, by not seeking it, but by *inventio,* coming upon it in its denial. He retrieves orality not by appropriating or representing it, and not by describing it, but by a misrepresentation that amounts to a "de-scribing." He confirms that when we turn a deaf ear to speech we also turn a blind eye to writing.

"How can you . . ."

The neologism "computer literacy" seems to adumbrate some new kind of writing that will spell the end of the alphabet's magical spell, even as it impends its apotheosis, but the computer's artificiality and its uncompromising literalness are parodies of the fictions writing conceals, for they show us how writing was always a discourse shaped more by the demands of its technology than by the demands of production.

The computer is the sign of the triumph of parology, but it does not overcome writing any more than did moveable type. It undermines the meaning of writing, but it does not alter the means writing represents, for the alphabet is the model, source, and means of analysis and representation. It is not just the facilitation of reason and the instrument of abstraction, it is that reason and abstraction. What is abstraction that is not already the idea of the letter-as-sign, and what is reason beyond the idea of rules for combining letters-as-signs? Analysis is a kind of applied alphabetism, a decomposition of wholes into elementary units-as-signs and the reconstitution of totalities synthesized by recombining elementary units. Representation is the substitution of one appearance for another, of the sign for the thing. It is the idea of mimesis that mimics the substitution of the letter for the sound.

Because it takes over, virtually unchanged, these fundamental features of alphabetic writing, the computer cannot overcome writing. It merely carries forward writing's project of the "matrix mind" (Hartog 1985). It emulates, even though parodically and often without vowels, the basic operations of alphabetic writing. Its arrays, columns, and rows are a verbless text that recapitulates writing's aversion to narrative, time, movement, change, and mutation. It provides metaphysical foundation to the post-modern suspicion of meta-narratives that have beginnings, middles, and ends or "heavy" characters whose acts have moral consequences, but it does not portend the end of writing.

Only a writing that gave up analysis and representation could overcome alphabetic writing and that is why speech and the heiroglyph have always been writing's occult others and symbols of another form of life and way of knowing. Whenever we question representation or the analytic presupposition of discontinuous, autonomous, interacting parts, we look to some analogue of speech or the heiroglyph, and so today when analyticity and representation seem more and more inappropriate in disciplines concerned with continuous, non-discrete processes and events, or with change, mutation, creation, and destruction, it is not surprising to find people searching for some new holographic writing (cf. Bohm 1980:27–64, 111–157). In other words, when we seek to understand "kinesis" in its full Aristotelian sense as something more than just local motion, then analysis and representation are inappropriate, for they are fitted to the matrices of mimesis, to static, spatial structures consisting of discontinuous, discrete, autonomous, interacting parts.

In the history of Western thought, speech, not writing, has rightly been associated with the "lively" aspects of kinesis, and it is worth remembering that it was this changeable, impermanent character of speech that led Saussure to reject speech *(parole)* as the basis of semiology. We can thus understand why, for some, interest in orality, rhetoric, and dialog implies a rejection of the easy totalitarianism of Platonist semiology and a recuperation of Heraclitus.

Orality then, is not just a counter discourse that can be co-opted and surpassed by the computer, as Ong and others seem to think. It is part of the larger resistance to what Habermas has characterized as the "colonization of the lifeworld" by scientism and the creaky futurist ideology of modernism. Orality is a discourse that articulates post-modernism with a different nuance.

"Really . . ."

"So long as we write as we do," could we write differently, could we change the conventions of writing, could it be other-wise? Something of this sort is imagined above and in the idea of dialogical anthropology as a kind of "re-oralization" of writing, but inasmuch as dialog is understood as a better representation of native thought and culture it is still trapped in the allegory of alienation, for it is the anthropologist who represents native speech within the context of anthropological writing for his/her own reasons. So too, with the idea of *poesis* in anthropology where the exaltation of reflexivity merely reconfirms that anthropologists write of the native not for the native's sake, but for themselves, out of their own interests or as an act of contrition or atonement (per contra Prattis 1985:266–281). Their elegies confirm the right to write and remind us that from Longfellow to Diamond the right of representation is the means of a morality.

Anthropologists invoke native speech out of nostalgia, a guilty longing for a past before writing and the corruption of civilization that writing creates and symbolizes. Their "in memoriam" in the incorruptibility of writing is the corruption of speech. Anthropologists play out the myth of the "letter that killeth," for they play the role of tricksters who out play the natives and spirit away the spirit of speech in a played out writing that hides the theft and exculpates them from any complicity in corruption (Derrida 1974:101–140; Swearingen this issue).

The post-modern world countenances no surpassing or overcoming, those peculiarly modernist motives. Our interest in orality tells us that writing suppresses but does not surpass speech. Speech irrupts again and again in one or another of its Adamic guises as we tell and retell the tale of origin-al-ienation. We can neither leave this past behind nor overcome it through a critique of writing that dismisses it as a mere correlative of a necessary future. We can neither forget the past that is speech nor represent it as other than past. Except in our speaking, speech is withheld from us. Writing puts everything in the past; it has no future. The past is the incurable illness of writing, for the myth tells us that writing is only our way of remembering something that never happened. That too, is why we turn to speech as a kind of therapeutic from an overdose of the past, from a writing that promised a truth it could not deliver.

Writing is an illness we cannot treat but only recover from. Our interests in dialog, poetry, and orality are vectors of a single urge to recover a sounding sense deadened by algebraisms without the sense of sound or the sound of sense. Our recovery of rhetoric and poetry, those writings marked by the presence of speech, signifies our discontent with plain style, with a form of writing defined by the absence of voice and the pretense of an absence of interest. We acknowledge not so much the presence of speakers and hearers as the presence of interest evoked by the presence of speakers and hearers. Our recovery of this past is our recovery from the illness of writing.

Discontent with the form of writing is nothing new. Writing reform has been the hallmark not only of modernism, but of the whole modern age from Bacon and Descartes to the present, but the plain style that separated itself from rhetoric and rhetoric from poetry in order to make itself more transparent to the independent order of things is snared by representation. It was the economy of style that mirrored the economy of things, but in a world where things have been swallowed up by their signs, who needs a style of writing that pretends to represent something other than itself? Our recovery of orality is our recovery from a kind of writing that more and more gets in the way of what we want to say.

The text of orality implicates participation, common action, common sense, reciprocity, communication, and the *communis* as key concepts in place of our "letterized" epistemology of being, knowing, and representation founded on the distanced, alienated, and impersonal observation of a transcendental, panoptic ego. Speaking implicates a reality that constantly remakes itself, a reality whose total structure is never realized and cannot be known, yet can be participated in as if it were known or as if participation grounded itself. Our understanding, growing within participation, is autotelic; it develops its own standards of rightness and interpretation from within itself rather than from an exterior, transcendental method. In place of the metaphor of seeing and observing it encourages a metaphor of saying, hearing, and doing that undermines the primacy of reason and apodictic proof as the work of an autonomous cogito. It relativizes knowledge and representation to communication, to the purposes, interests, and agreements of the *communis* which creates them as aesthetic fictions, after-the-fact by-products of making, doing, and acting. Being and knowing are situated within the world of work and are not its means, justification, or foundation. Orality makes us think of many voices telling many tales in many tongues, in contrast to the inherent monologism of texts that only tell different versions of the one true tale, each version recapitulating—even unwittingly—the founding allegory of Q.E.D., which is its source, terminus, and standard.

"Tell?"

Orality is the difference alphabetic writing invents for itself as the ground of the arbitrariness of the sign. It is the difference that enables the sign's origin and justifies its other-ness. Without it, the whole possibility of arbitrary and unnatural signs collapses. Signs become once again marks of a determinate natural order. Orality is the obstacle writing creates and seeks to encompass and overcome, for orality is to it the symbol of all that is chance, passion, mutability, and indeterminateness in writing's story of its own origin and essence. It is the miraculous residue of time in the all-memory of the timeless text. It is the remainder of nature, reminder of that past before civilization that civilization both disdains and eulogizes. It is the lack that is source, justification, and obstacle.

Orality and literacy are contemporary reflexes of an ancient argument between the ear/mouth and the eye, between "saying" and "seeing," between *kinesis* and *mimesis*. Ever since the Greeks learned to write, the eye has dominated the ear/mouth in the West. The argument reemerges now because writing, the instrument of domination, has undermined itself and is being challenged by new technologies of representation. The whole idea of writing and literacy, at the very moment when this hegemony seemed most assured, is now suspect in a way that it has not been for many centuries in the West. There is no need here to reiterate all the formidable cliches that intone the futuristic possibilities of computerization and their implications for literary's key notions of "book," "word," "reading," and "writing," except to note that these further triumphs of the eye portend the end of the domination of the eye, for they imply a logographic writing that will entail a pattern of sensorial integration different from that of the alphabet. They will engender a new struggle for domination, not just between the eye and the ear/mouth, but between the eye and the hand that will finally end the hegemony of mimesis over kinesis in a consicousness that does not overcome orality but recovers, without repetition, the miraculous, the mutable, the chance, and the passion of speech.

But this age of ours, the one just before the age of the new writing, is a stage in which not even the eye can long survive. In order for the new writing to be born, it must first be disconnected not only from the voice, but from the eye as well. It must break the whole spell of representation and project a world of pure arbitrariness without representation. It must be disconnected from any world that is not built into its own circuitry and programs. The new writing will be preceded by this writing that closes upon itself and no longer pretends to represent the voice or the eye, or anything but itself. For us, "orality" is the name of the resistance to this algebraism—this soundless shuffling of meaningless signs. Our redemption in/from this tale of loss and liberation is not in sight, nor at hand. Could it be just on the tips of our tongues?

References Cited

Barfield, Owen
 1985   Saving the Appearances: A Study in Idolatry. New York: Harcourt Brace Jovanovich.
Bohm, David
 1980   Wholeness and the Implicate Order. London: Ark.
Derrida, Jacques
 1974   Of Grammatology. Baltimore: Johns Hopkins University Press.
Goody, Jack
 1977   The Domestication of the Savage Mind. New York: Cambridge University Press.
Hartog, Curt
 1985   Matrix Mindsets. Datamation July:201–204.
Lyotard, Jean-Francois
 1979   The Postmodern Condition: A Report on Knowledge. In Theory and History of Literature, Vol. 10. Minneapolis: University of Minnesota Press.
Ong, Walter
 1982   Orality and Literacy: The Technologizing of the Word. London: Methuen.
Prattis, J. Iain, ed.
 1985   Reflections: The Anthropological Muse. Washington, DC: American Anthropological Association.
Rorty, Richard
 1979   Philosophy and the Mirror of Nature. Princeton: Princeton University Press.
Tannen, Deborah
 1980   Implications of the Oral-Literate Continuum for Cross-Cultural Communication. In Georgetown University Round Table on Language and Linguistics. James E. Alatis, ed. Washington, DC: Georgetown University Press.

Tactility and Distraction

Michael Taussig

> Now, says Hegel, all discourse that remains discourse ends in *boring* man.
> —Alexander Kojave, *Introduction to the Reading of Hegel*, 1969

Quite apart from its open invitation to entertain a delicious anarchy, exposing principles no less than dogma to the white heat of daily practicality and contradiction, there is surely plurality in everydayness. My everyday has a certain routine, doubtless, but it is also touched by a deal of unexpectedness, which is what many of us like to think of as essential to life, to a metaphysics of life, itself. And by no means can my everyday be held to be the same as vast numbers of other people in this city of New York, those who were born here, those who have recently arrived from other everydays far away, those who have money, those who don't. This would be an obvious point, the founding orientation of a sociology of experience, were it not for the peculiar and unexamined ways by which "the everyday" seems, in the diffuseness of its ineffability, to erase difference in much the same way as modern European-derived notions of the public and the masses do.

This apparent erasure suggests the trace of a diffuse commonality in the commonweal so otherwise deeply divided, a commonality that is no doubt used to manipulate consensus but also promises the possibility of other sorts of nonexploitative solidarities which, in order to exist at all, will have to at some point be based on a common sense of the everyday and, what is more, the ability to sense other everydaynesses.

But what sort of sense is constitutive of this everydayness? Surely this sense includes much that is not sense so much as sensuousness, an embodied and somewhat automatic "knowledge" that functions like peripheral vision, not studied contemplation, a knowledge that is imageric and sensate rather than ideational and as such not only challenges practically all critical practice across the board of academic disciplines but is a knowledge that lies as much in the objects and spaces of observation as in the body and mind of the observer. What's more, this sense has an activist, constructivist, bent; not so much contemplative as it is caught in *media res* working on, making anew, amalgamating, acting and reacting. We are thus mindful of Nietzsche's notion of the senses as bound to their object as much as their organs of reception, a fluid bond to be sure in which, as he says, "seeing becomes seeing *something*" (1989:119). For many of us, I submit, this puts the study of ideology, discourse, and popular culture in a somewhat new light. Indeed, the notion of "studying," innocent in its unwinking ocularity, may itself be in for some rough handling too.

I was reminded of this when as part of my everyday I bumped into Jim in the hallway of PS 3 (New York City Public School Number Three) where he and I were dropping off our children. In the melee of streaming kids and parents he was carrying a bunch of small plastic tubes and a metal box which he told me was a pump and he was going to spend the morning making a water fountain for the class of which his daughter, aged eight, was part. She, however, was more interested in the opportunity for the kids to make molds of their hands and then convert the molds into clamshells for the fountain. I should add that Jim and his wife are sculptors and their home is also their workplace, so Petra, their daughter, probably has an unusually developed everyday sense of sculpting. It turned out that a few days back Jim had accompanied the class to the city's aquarium which, among other remarks, triggered off the absolutely everyday but continuously fresh insight, on my part as much as his, that here we are, so enmeshed in the everydayness of the city that we very rarely bother to see any of its sights, such as the aquarium. "I've lived here all of 17 years," he told me, "and never once been there or caught the train out that way." And he marveled at the things he'd seen at the station before the stop for the aquarium—it was a station that had played a prominent part in a Woody Allen film. He was especially struck by the strange script used for public signs. And we went on to complete the thought that when we were living in other places, far away, we would come to the city with a program of things to see and do, but now, living everyday in the shadow and blur of all those particular things we never saw them anymore, imagining, fondly, perhaps, that they were in some curious way part of us as we were part of them. But now Jim and Petra were back from the visit to the aquarium. He was going to make a fountain, and she was going to make molds of hands that would become clamshells.

"The revealing presentations of the big city," wrote Walter Benjamin in his uncompleted *Passagenwerk,* "are the work of those who have traversed the city absently, as it were, lost in thought or worry" (1973:69). And in his infamously popular and difficult essay, "The Work of Art in the Age of Mechanical Reproduction," written in the mid-1930s, he drew a sharp distinction between contemplation and distraction. He wants to argue that contemplation—which is what academicism is all about—is the studied, eyeful, aloneness with and absorption into the "aura" of the always aloof, always distant, object. The ideal-type for this could well be the worshiper alone with God, but it was the artwork (whether cult object or bourgeois "masterpiece") before the invention of the camera and the movies that Benjamin had in mind. On the other hand, "distraction" here refers to a very different apperceptive mode, the type of flitting and barely conscious peripheral-vision perception unleashed with great vigor by modern life at the crossroads of the city, the capitalist market, and modern technology. The ideal-type here would not be God but movies and advertising, and its field of expertise is the modern everyday.

For here not only the shock-rhythm of modernity so literally expressed in the motion of the business cycle, the stock exchange, city traffic, the assembly line and Chaplin's walk, but also a new magic, albeit secular, finds its everyday home in a certain tactility growing out of distracted vision. Benjamin took as a cue here Dadaism and architecture, for Dadaism not only stressed the uselessness of its work for contemplation, but that its work "became an instrument of ballistics. It hit the spectator like a bullet, it happened to him, thus acquiring a tactile quality." He went on to say that Dadaism thus promoted a demand for film, "the distracting element of which," and I quote here for emphasis, "is also primarily tactile, being based on changes of place and focus which periodically assault the spectator" (1969:238). As for architecture, it is especially instructive because it has served as the prototype over millennia not for perception by the contemplative individual but instead by the distracted collectivity. To the question How in our everyday lives do we know or perceive a building?, Benjamin answers through usage, meaning, to some crucial extent, through touch, or better still, we might want to say, by proprioception, and this to the degree that this tactility, constituting habit, exerts a decisive impact on optical reception.

Benjamin set no small store by such habitual, or everyday, knowledge. The tasks facing the perceptual apparatus at turning points in history, cannot, he asserted, be solved by optical, contemplative, means, but only gradually, by habit, under the guidance of tactile appropriation. It was this everyday tactility of knowing which fascinated him and which I take to be one of his singular contributions to social philosophy, on a par with Freud's concept of the unconscious.

For what came to constitute perception with the invention of the 19th-century technology of optical reproduction of reality was not what the unaided eye took for the real. No. What was revealed was the *optical unconscious*—a term that Benjamin willingly allied with the psychoanalytic unconscious but which, in his rather unsettling way, so effortlessly confounded subject with object such that the unconscious at stake here would seem to reside more in the object than in the perceiver. He had in mind both camera still shots and the movies, and it was the ability to enlarge, to frame, to pick out detail and form unknown to the naked eye, as much as the capacity for montage and shocklike abutment of dissimilars, that constituted this optical unconscious which, thanks to the camera, was brought to light for the first time in history. And here again the connection with tactility is paramount, the optical dissolving, as it were, into touch and a certain thickness and density as where he writes that photography reveals "the physiognomic aspects of visual worlds which dwell in the smallest things, meaningful yet covert enough to find a hiding place in waking dreams, but which, enlarged and capable of formulation, make the difference between technology and magic visible as a thoroughly historical variable" (1979:44).[2] Hence this tactile optics, this physiognomic aspect of visual worlds, was critically important because it was otherwise inconspicuous, dwelling neither in consciousness nor in sleep but in waking dreams. It was a crucial part of a more exact relation to the objective world, and thus it could not but problematize consciousness of that world, while at the same time intermingling fantasy and hope, as in dream, with waking life. In rewiring seeing as tactility, and hence as habitual knowledge, a sort of technological or secular magic was brought into being and sustained. It displaced the earlier magic of the aura of religious and cult works in a pretechnological age and did so by a process that is well worth our attention, a process of demystification *and* reenchantment, precisely, as I understand it, Benjamin's own self-constituting and contradictorily montaged belief in radical, secular, politics *and* messianism, as well as his own mimetic form of revolutionary poetics.

For if Adorno reminds us that in Benjamin's writings "thought presses close to its object, as if through touching, smelling, tasting, it wanted to transform itself" (1981:240),[3] we have also to remember that mimesis was a crucial feature for Benjamin and Adorno and meant both copying *and* sensuous materiality, what Frazer in his famous chapter on magic in *The Golden Bough,* coming out of a quite different and far less rigorous philosophic tradition, encompassed as imitative or homeopathic magic, on the one side, and contagious magic, on the other. Imitative magic involves ritual work on the copy (the wax figurine, the drawing, or the photograph), while in contagious magic the ritualist requires material substance from the person to be affected. In the multitude of cases that Frazer presented in the 160-odd pages he dedicated to the "principles of magic," these principles of copy and substance are often found to be harnessed together, as with the Malay charm made out of body exuviae of the victim sculpted into his likeness with wax and then slowly scorched for seven nights while intoning, "It is not wax that I am scorching, it is the liver, heart, and spleen of So-and-so that I scorch" (Frazer 1911:57), and this type of representation hitching likeness to substance is borne out by ethnographic research throughout the 20th century. This reminder from the practice of that art form known as "magic," second only to advertising in terms of its stupendous ability to blend aesthetics with practicality, that mimesis implies *both* copy and substantial connection, *both* visual replication and material transfer, not only neatly parallels Benjamin's insight that visual perception as enhanced by new optical copying technology, namely the camera, has a decisively material, tactile, quality, but underscores his specific question as to what happens to the apparent withering of the mimetic faculty with the growing up of the Western child and the world historical cultural revolution we can allude to as Enlightenment, it being his clear thesis that children, anywhere, any time, and people in ancient times and so-called primitive societies are endowed by their circumstance with considerable miming prowess.[4] Part of his answer to the question as to what happens to the withering away of the mimetic faculty is that it is precisely the function of the new technology of copying reality, meaning above all the camera, to reinstall that mimetic prowess in modernity.

Hence a powerful film criticism which, to quote Paul Virilio quoting the New York video artist, Nam June Paik, "Cinema isn't I see, it's I fly," or Dziga Vertov's camera in perpetual movement, "I fall and I fly at one with the bodies falling or rising through the air," registering not merely our sensuous blending with filmic imagery, the eye acting as a conduit for our very bodies being absorbed by the filmic image, but the resurfacing of a vision-mode at home in the pre-Oedipal economy of the crawling infant, the eye grasping, as Gertrude Koch once put it, at what the hand cannot reach.[5]

And how much more might this be the case with advertising, quintessence of America's everyday? In "This Space For Rent," a fragment midst a series of fragments entitled "One Way Street," written between 1925 and 1928 (1978), Benjamin anticipated the themes of his essay on mechanical reproduction, written a decade later, claiming it was a waste of time to lament the loss of distance necessary for criticism. For now the most real, the mercantile gaze into the heart of things, is the advertisement, and this "abolishes the space where contemplation moved and all but hits us between the eyes with things as a car, growing to gigantic proportions, careens at us out of a film screen." To this tactility of a hit between the eyes is added what he described as "the insistent, jerky, nearness" with which commodities were thus hurtled, the overall effect dispatching "matter-of-factness" by the new, magical world of the optical unconscious as huge leathered cowboys, horses, cigarettes, toothpaste, and "perfect" women straddle walls of buildings, subway cars and our living rooms via TV, such that sentimentality, as Benjamin put it, "is restored and liberated in American style, just as people whom nothing moves or touches any longer are taught to cry again by films." It is money that moves us to these things whose power lies in the fact that they operate upon us viscerally. Their warmth stirs sentient springs. "What in the end makes advertisements so superior to criticism?" asks Benjamin. "Not what the moving red neon sign says—but the fiery pool reflecting it in the asphalt" (Benjamin 1978:85–86).

This puts the matter-of-factness of the everyday on a new analytic footing, one that has for too long been obscured in the embrace of a massive tradition of cultural and sociological analysis searching in vain for grants that would give it distance and perspective. Not what the neon says, but the fiery pool reflecting it in the asphalt; not language, but image; and not just the image but its tactility and the new magic thereof with the transformation of roadway parking-lot bitumen into legendary lakes of fire-ringed prophecy so that once again we cry and, presumably, we buy, just as our ability to calculate value is honed to the razor's edge. It is not a question, therefore, of whether or not we can follow de Certeau and combat strategies with everyday tactics that fill with personal matter the empty signifiers of postmodernity, because the everyday is a question not of universal semiotics but of capitalist mimetics. Nor, as I understand it, is this the Foucauldian problem of being programmed into subjecthood by discursive regimes, for it is the sentient reflection in the fiery pool, its tactility, not what the neon sign says, that matters, all of which puts reading, close or otherwise, literal or metaphoric, in another light of dubious luminosity.

This is not to indulge in the boring game of emotion versus thought, body versus mind, recycled by current academic fashion into concern with "the body" as key to wisdom. For where can such a program end but in the tightening of paradox; an intellectual containment of the body's understanding? What we aim at is a more accurate, a more mindful, understanding of the play of mind on body in the everyday and, as regards academic practice, nowhere are the notions of tactility and distraction more obviously important than in need to critique what I take to be a dominant critical practice which could be called the "allegorizing" mode of reading ideology into events and artifacts, cockfights and carnivals, advertisements and film, private and public spaces, in which the surface phenomenon, as in allegory, stands as a cipher for uncovering horizon after horizon of otherwise obscure systems of meanings. This is not merely to argue that such a mode of analysis is simple-minded in its search for "codes" and manipulative because it superimposes meaning on "the natives' point of view." Rather, as I now understand this practice of "reading," its very understanding of "meaning" is uncongenial; its weakness lies in its assuming a contemplative individual when it should, instead, assume a distracted collective reading with what I call, by way of shorthand, a tactile eye. This I take to be Benjamin's contribution, profound and simple, novel yet familiar, to the analysis of the everyday, and unlike the readings we have come to know of everyday life, it has the strange and interesting property of being cut, so to speak, from the same cloth of that which it raises to self-awareness. For above all his writing, which is to say the medium of his analysis, is constituted by tactility, by the objectness of the object. This I take to be not only the verbal form of the "optical unconscious," but a form that, in an age wherein analysis does little more than reconstitute the obvious, is capable of surprising us with the flash of a profane illumination.

And so my attention wanders away from the American Museum of Natural History on Central Park, upon which so much allegorical "reading," as with other museums, has been recently expended, back to the children and Jim at the aquarium. It is of course fortuitous, overly fortuitous you will say, for my moral concerning tactility and distraction that Jim is a sculptor, but there is the fact of the matter. And I cannot but feel that in being stimulated by the "meaning" of the aquarium to reproduce with the art of mechanical reproduction its watery wonderland by means of pumps and plastic tubes, Jim's tactile eye and ocular grasp have been conditioned by the distractedness of the collective of which he was part, namely the children. Their young eyes have blended a strangely dreamy quality to the tactility afforded the adult eye by the revolution in modern means of copying reality, such that while Jim profers a fountain, Petra suggests molds of kids' hands that will be its clamshells.

Notes

Acknowledgments. This essay was written for the conference "Problematics of Daily Life," organized by Marc Blanchard, Director, Critical Theory, University of California, Davis, November, 1990.

[1]In stressing the tactile in the reorganization of the human sensorium under conditions of early 20th century, Benjamin was echoing not only Dada but even earlier statements such as that of the Russian Tatlin in 1913 that "the eye should be put under control of touch." Benjamin Buchloh, from whose article (1987:81) I take this quotation, adds to it Marcel Duchamp's "famous statement," that he wanted to abolish the supremacy of the retinal principle in art.

²Note that more than one English translation exists of this essay and they vary considerably.

³I have used Susan Buck-Morss's translation of this passage from her *The Origin of Negative Dialectics* (1977:83).

⁴Take the opening paragraph of Benjamin's 1934 essay, "On the Mimetic Faculty," which reads:

> Nature creates similarities. One need only think of mimicry. The highest capacity for producing similarities, however, is man's. His gift of seeing resemblances is nothing other than a rudiment of the powerful compulsion in former times to become and behave like something else. Perhaps there is none of his higher functions in which his mimetic faculty does not play a decisive role. [1978:333]

Adorno had much to say about the relation between alleged origins of mankind, mimesis, and magic, in his posthumously edited *Aesthetic Theory* (first published in German in 1970). A good place to begin is with the Appendix II, "Thoughts on the Origins of Art— An Excursus" (1984:447–455).

⁵Gertrude Koch, "Mimesis and the Ban on Graven Images," paper distributed in Department of Cinema Studies, New York University, 1990, forthcoming in *October*. See also Sergei Eisenstein's 1935 lecture, "Film Form; New Problems," in his *Film Form* (1977:133–145).

References Cited

Adorno, T. W.
  1981   A Portrait of Walter Benjamin. *In* Prisms. Cambridge: MIT Press.
  1984   Aesthetic Theory. London: Routledge & Kegan Paul.
Benjamin, Walter
  1969   The Work of Art in the Age of Mechanical Reproduction. Illuminations. Pp. 217–252. New York: Schocken Books.
  1973   Paris of the Second Empire in Baudelaire. *In* Charles Baudelaire: Lyric Poet of High Capitalism. Pp. 9–106. London: New Left Books.
  1978[1934]   On the Mimetic Faculty. *In* Reflections. Pp. 333–336. New York: Harcourt, Brace, Jovanovich.
  1979   A Short History of Photography. *In* One Way Street. Pp. 240–258. London: New Left Books.
Buchloh, Benjamin
  1987   From Faktura to Factography. *In* October: The First Decade; 1976–1986. Annette Michelson, ed. Pp. 76–113. Cambridge: MIT Press.
Buck-Morss, Susan
  1977   The Origin of Negative Dialectics. New York: Free Press.
Eisenstein, Sergei
  1977   Film Form. Jay Leyda, trans. New York: Harcourt, Brace, Jovanovich.
Frazer, J. G.
  1911   The Golden Bough, Part 1: The Magic and the Evolution of Kings. 3d edition. London: Macmillan.
Nietzsche, F.
  1989   On the Genealogy of Morals. Walter Kaufman, ed. New York: Vintage.

The Rhetoric of Ethnographic Holism

Robert J. Thornton

Memory provides the soul with a kind of consecutiveness which resembles reason, but which is to be distinguished from it.

—G. W. Leibniz
The Monadology

If seeming is description without place,
The spirit's universe, then a summer's day
Even the seeming of a summer's day,
Is description without place. It is a sense
To which we refer experience, a knowledge
Incognito, the column in the desert,
On which the dove alights. Description is
Composed of a sight indifferent to the eye.
It is an expectation, a desire,
A palm that rises up beyond the sea,
A little different from reality:
The difference that we make in what we see

—Wallace Stevens
"Description Without Place"

Classification as Rhetorical Trope

The fundamental and motivating problem of ethnography is how to use writing to bring the "everyday" into relation with "history" and "environment." Since writing is a work of the imagination, it is in the imagination that the crucial synthesis between the microcosm and the macrocosm takes place. Unlike the zoologist who describes the mollusc before him, the ethnographer must imagine the "whole" that is society, and convey this imagination of wholeness to his reader along with the descriptions of places seen, speech heard, persons met. The description of wholes, however, is "description without place . . . a sight indifferent to the eye." For this, the ethnography needs a special kind of rhetorical technique. Both the rhetoric and the imagination essential to it are founded on classification employed as rhetorical figure. The ethnography's use of classification constitutes a use of language outside of its normal syntactic and semantic sense that point to or suggest other levels of meaning—that is, it functions as a trope that I shall call the rhetoric of classification.

The understanding of ethnographic writing that I present here focuses on the apparently pragmatic way in which the text is organized into chapters and sub-headings within which is embedded the "verse" of daily life as it is encountered in the fragmented rhythms of existence. I argue that the imagination of wholes is a rhetorical imperative for ethnography since it is this image of wholeness that gives the ethnography a sense of fulfilling "closure" that other genres accomplish by different rhetorical means. The rhetoric of classification is the means whereby this closure is achieved, since it structures the descriptions of "items" that derive ultimately from the experience of research in the field. Where the narrative achieves closure by a successful conclusion to the plot, the ethnography achieves it by a successful *description* of a social structure. Social structure, then, like plot, is the image of coherence and order that writing creates.

Certainly, there are a number of other ways of conceiving the relationship between text and social reality. One way of conceiving this relationship is to say that it is a "dialectic" one (Webster 1982), or that it is "dialogic" (i.e., like a dialogue—Clifford 1983). But these approaches are unsatisfactory because of their claim that the cognitive and the social are both entities of equal logical (or ontological) standing, and that the entities can interact in a way that is analogous to a dialogue or a dialectic (literally "two readings"). Both approaches assert that reality is somehow "negotiated" between the cognitive and the social, and both neglect the fact that "society" and "cognition" are processes whose historical/temporal and spatial scales are radically different.

In fact, these claims can be critically dissolved into the problem of whether the dialectic itself is ultimately social—and therefore an emergent or transcendent property of social "formations" independent of individual will and of meaning—or whether it is a property of cognitive processes themselves, and thus intrinsic to meaning. Before Hegel, the idea of a dialectic meant simply "two readings" and was one way of determining the true meaning of apparently contradictory sacred scriptures. After Hegel, the idea of a dialectic meant the resolution of "contradictions" between the individual and society, but even then it requires an image of two realities that can interact. After Marx, "the dialectic" took on the sense of struggle between "classes," but here one must accept that such social parts are entities capable of autonomous social action. All of these dialectical or dialogical approaches imply that there can be a negotiation over a reality outside of the text itself, and that the ethnography (or other genres of social description) merely presents the results.

Alternatively, the narrative has been employed as a model for analyzing the rhetoric of ethnography (Bruner 1982). This is problematic, however, since narrative is frequently suppressed in the monograph. Narratives exist, but they are restricted to the narration of the anthropologist's own entry into the field (e.g., Pratt 1986, Thornton 1985) or are the included fragments of informants own narratives—the "verses" subsumed in chapters. Pratt has suggested that where narrative does persist in ethnography it does so "because it mediates a contradiction between personal and scientific authority.'' While this is probably true, it does not seem appropriate to analyze the whole of the ethnographic monograph in terms appropriate to narrative alone. It is not unreasonable to suppose that ethnography has come up with a few tropes of its own.

The Nature of Trope in Sociological Writing

In narrative, tropes may create a feeling of tragedy or a sense of humor; in ethnography they generally evoke an image of "a society" or "a culture." Literature may be classified in terms of poetic types or narrative forms. Generic labels for these tropes include metonymy, synecdoche, irony, ellipsis, metaphor, and so on. Secondly, types of narrative may be distinguished as tragedy, comedy, satire, realistic, romantic. We may also classify by discursive "types," known as genres, which include the novel, the travelogue, the confession, the diary, the monograph, the ethnography, and many others, some general, and some specific to particular intellectual or technical disciplines and practices. When the tropological classification is combined with a classification of genres and narrative types, a multi-way classification allows us to talk about an elliptical poem, the tragic drama, the ironic novel, a metaphorical travelogue, and so on. Some of these combinations may be more likely than others: an ironic monograph on bivalve molluscs would be of little scientific use.

A full multidimensional matrix of tropes and genres would be impossible, however, since the criteria for each tropological, generic, or narrative category are logically incommensurable. Moreover, genres, narrative types, and tropes may be associated with particular historical epochs, activities, individuals, or social classes: the bourgeois novel, modern poetry, the scientific monograph. This sort of classification of types allows us to begin to comprehend the variety of written expression, and to explain them through recourse to (usually) sociological, psychological or historical aspects of the author, his context, and that of his audience. It may also help us to understand why, for example, the diary was common in the 19th century, and virtually absent in contemporary times.

Hayden White (1973), for instance, has taken this approach in his investigation of European 19th-century historiography. He demonstrates that the major historical works of this century (e.g., those by Hegel, Michelet, Ranke, Marx, Tocqueville, Croce) were framed in terms of one of four "generic plot structures" (metaphor, synecdoche, metonymy, irony), derived from the "tropes" of literature. These tropic formulae were familiar to the readers, though not in the specific forms of the histories that these men wrote, and thus "pre-figured the field" in such a way as to make the historical narrative morally compelling, emotionally evocative, and often politically and socially provocative. The sense of "closure" or satisfactory "explanation" achieved by the historian depends, according to this view, on the portrayal of history (the sequence of events) as coincident with one or another generic plot structures in either comic or tragic modes. Thus Hegel's historical apprehension can be described as ironic (the human condition is one of contradictions and paradoxes) in the comic mode (humanity will win the struggle), while Marx's presentation of history was synecdochic in the structure of its plot ("the parts merged into a whole which is qualitatively superior to any of the entities which comprise it" [White 1973:283]) but apprehended in the tragic mode ("attempts to construct a viable human community are continually frustrated by the laws that govern history" [1973:287]).

It has been argued (Bruner 1982; Marcus and Cushman 1982; Webster 1982) that the ethnographic monograph is susceptible to exactly these same kinds of analysis. But, since most tropological classifications have been elaborated in response to, and are most appropriate to, narrative and poetic types of writing, it may be that this approach will yield little in the consideration of ethnography. In any case, Nietzsche destroyed once and for all "the notion that the historical process has to be explained or emplotted in any particular way" (White 1973:371).

Our questions about how ethnography "works," then, become questions about the rhetorical construction of the text since it is at the level of rhetoric rather than of descriptive detail that the peculiarly ethnographic view and knowledge emerge. The details that it presents are almost always available elsewhere without creating the "effect" that is peculiar to ethnography.

This "effect," like the effect of the novel or the narrative in general, is to produce a sense of wholeness and order that, if we are convinced, we believe did or could or might *happen*. We believe, after reading a good ethnographic monograph or a novel or a play about a social situation, that it is (or it might be) "real," or that it "reflects" back to us memories of our own experience, tinged with their proper emotions. Thus, the structure of the Nuer lineage (Evans-Pritchard 1951), or the wanderings of Ogotemeli's pale fox (Griaule 1965) is more than a little bit like Bob Cratchet's Christmas (Dickens 1843) or the death of the salesman Willy Loman (Miller 1949). Whether things really happened exactly that way or not, they could have—we might say, "It wouldn't surprise me if it did," or some such phrase. But they don't. Criticism must deal with precisely this disjuncture between the sense of "it could happen" that writing creates, and what does in fact happen.

The notion of a specifically ethnographic trope leads us away from using narrative, dialogue, and dialectics as models for the criticism of ethnography. Ethnography deals with social wholes, of which narratives are only a part. Dialogues and dialectics are also subsumed as theoretical propositions or as "data" in the overall framework of the monograph. It is a genre in which the description of economy exists side by side with the personal confession, the myth and the well-worn fireside tale. It attempts to lead the reader to believe that the myth or the personal confession has a definite relation to the way the economy works. It attempts to establish the reality of the connections it describes. The vast apparent gap between the person who "confesses" and the economy that "works" must be bridged. This is the work of the ethnographic trope. The nature of the connection between the text itself and that reality remains, however, a perennial problem.

Imagination of Wholeness and Rhetorical Necessity

Social wholes can not be directly experienced by a single human observer. The vision of the scope and scale of social life that extends beyond what we can experience must be imagined. But this imagination of social wholes never includes *only* that one which is being described. The ethnographic imagination inevitably includes those realities that are or have been realized in historical or present time, and those that exist as possibilities, dreams or nightmares. For European thought since the time of the Eleatics, the possible, the imagined, and the future have been treated as though they possessed the same status in reason as the realized, the observed and the past. There are historical as well as rhetorical reasons for this, but most important perhaps is the fact that anthropology—indeed any science that attempts to say what man "really is," what he is "in essence"— must necessarily be a moral science. Some have called anthropology a "reformer's science," as did E. B. Tylor (1871) or Henri-Alexandre Junod (1927 vol. I:9). For others it has been the choice between "being history or being nothing," as the constitutional historian F. W. Maitland once claimed. It has been defined as a "natural science of society" by Radcliffe-Brown (1925), or as many contemporary ethnographers seem to agree, as a never-ending unraveling of textile-like meanings, morals, and messages through hermeneutic interpretation of texts.

In other words, reference to some ulterior entity is always implicit in holism: we merely choose between the moral imperative of society, the "spirit" of history, the textile-like "text" which is no text in particular, or the "nature" of Man. Like the imaginary "frictionless space" in Newtonian mechanics, these ulterior images of wholes are not directly accessible to either the author's nor his subject's experience. They can only exist in the imaginations of the author, his informants, and his readers. This is the "essential fiction" of the ethnographic text.

The fiction of wholes, however, guarantees the facticity of "fact." The imagination is an essential part of this rhetorical process for several reasons. Inhabiting the minds of all writers of ethnography is an ideal vision of society— existing in states of utopic grace or absolute horror, positive harmony or debasement and negation of all value—or the vision of the imagined past of the classics, the images of distant, different lands of travelers.[1] These images, scenarios, or counterfactuals have served as the templates against which reality, and the description of reality, has been compared and judged. In fact, these images may well be archetypes, the sort of thing a possible pidgin sociology would constantly resort to, or which exist framed in some deep-structure of the human mind.

Indeed, it may be that it is impossible to conceptualize society,[2] except in terms of holistic images. But, while we can experience social relationships in which we are involved, and witness a few of those in which others are involved, it is manifestly impossible to witness or experience society. We may only experience parts of what we today call "society," and somehow bring these experiences into relation with a larger entity that we can not directly experience. Phrased in this way, the question about the relationship of ethnography to social reality becomes a more general one about the role of the image and the imagination and the cognitive process by which such images come into being. The rhetoric of ethnography presents these ulterior images against which description makes sense, and within which microcosm may be wedded to macrocosm.

All explanations eventually make reference to these ulterior images. The scientific, or nomothetic-deductive method achieves explanation through appeal to formulae that are regarded as "established" through either empirical or logical means. As Kuhn (1970) has shown, this appeal to truth is only effective within scientific communities who share certain beliefs and formulae whose proof is beyond the range of "ordinary science." The laws of nature serve as one such ulterior whole. Similarly, a moral understanding consists of making a connection between a moral problem and the universe of absolute and ultimate values. A theoretical understanding connects the description with the partition of the universe into discrete but related parts and assigns it a place in this world. The scientific understanding depends on the existence of natural order, the moral understanding depends on the cosmological image of ultimate moral truth, and the theoretical account acquires its truth-value from the belief that such connectivity must exist. As the quasi-religious speculation of contemporary astronomers and physical cosmologists demonstrates, an absolute dissolution of the universe into mystery or indeterminacy is intolerable (Toulmin 1982).

An ethnographic description, then, is a work, in the sense of an effort, *un travail* as opposed to *un oeuvre*, because it cannot offer in itself the understanding that it seeks. Ethnography cannot be replicated as a test of its validity or truth precisely because it is always in the process of achieving an understanding of an object that can never be completely understood. Description conveys its understanding through multiple levels of analogy, and, for ethnography, the classificatory mode of description does this best.

Social Wholes, Social Parts and Classification

Today, after MacLuhan (1962), Foucault (1974) and Derrida (1976), the text itself is no longer taken to be just a medium for communicating what is discovered elsewhere by other means. We see it now as an object, a practice and a form that communicates ideas in its own right, independent of whatever its "content" might be. In anthropology (and social sciences generally) this content—social or cultural wholes—is nevertheless still taken to be constituted elsewhere and by other means. Is ethnography "just description" of these objective wholes? Or, does such description merely "resemble reason" as Leibniz claims memory does? It seems to me that the heart of the problem may be the very *concept of wholes themselves*.

Indeed, "social wholes" may be seen as an artifact of rhetoric. The notion of "social wholes" and the doctrine of "holism" has long been taken to be the hallmark of anthropology, and the broadly classificatory or "classified" way in which ethnographic monographs are presented is central to the idea of "wholes." By understanding classification as itself a kind of trope, attention is directed to the problematic nature of the idea of "holism" or "social wholes" for the entire ethnographic project.

Social wholes are conceptualized against a background of other possible "wholes" within which, and compared with which, the ethnographic doctrine of holism makes sense. In fact, the notion of the whole is heavily overdetermined in anthropology and in other social sciences as well. The history of the Judeo-Christian religion, philosophy, modern politics, biology, and psychology all contribute to the notion of "the whole." The Kingdom of God, Eden, the concept of truth, the nation-state, language, ecology, and mind are all thought of as wholes, chiefly as a consequence of a particular intellectual history. It could scarcely be different for anthropology, which has interacted closely with the other disciplines of the sciences, and with literature and politics, and ever since Tylor spoke of "culture or civilization as that complex whole," anthropology has taken it for granted. The classification, however, provides a rhetorical means for bringing any number of "wholes" into play at one time. In doing so, however, it may have confused us somewhat about how these wholes actually "work."

Parts and Wholes

An anatomy of ethnography's essential fiction reveals that the "social whole" consists of parts, and it is in terms of the part-whole relationship (formally called the mereological relation) that many theoretical arguments within ethnographic writing are phrased. Whether the parts are taken to be persons, groups, institutions, symbols, combinations of these or something else entirely, it is usually asserted that the "social whole" is made up of just these parts. Furthermore, the ethnographic text is made up of parts or "chapters" that are compilations of many disparate observations of behavior, language, ritual, dance, art and other aspects of expressive culture, spatial dispositions, reports of these, and so on. These small fragments of patterned, usually formalized behavior and thought are the elements of the fieldwork record, that is, they are "real" (given to experience), and more importantly here, necessarily shared by the ethnographer and his interlocutors. But once we have begun to collect and combine these records they are no longer given to experience in quite the same way. The "experience of fieldwork" is both the experience of social life and the experience of the textual fragments in which it is recorded.

Chapters and divisions of books reflect an idea of society as a "sum of parts." As the social whole is held to be composed of mutually determining parts, the textual whole is composed of these textual fragments. The apparent wholeness of society, then, emerges from this process of collection and combination, and may have more to do with the manifest and concrete wholeness of the book that is itself constructed from parts.

But, this assumed relationship between social wholes and what are taken to be their parts—namely, social entities such as individuals, clans, age-grades, hospitals, nations, factories, etc.—is founded on a mistaken analogy with the text whose parts—namely chapters, titles, subheadings, paragraphs and so on—are truly constitutive of the textual whole. This relation of constituency does not hold true of "social wholes": they are not composed of parts in this way at all; they do not "add up." Again, the elusive "replicability" of ethnographic data demonstrates this pervasive but mistaken analogy: replicability is only elusive at the level of text. Individual events observed, stories heard, phrases remembered, formulae recited, artifacts seen, etc. are repeated again and again, often monotonously across epochs and cultures. It is the writing, collection, and compilation of these into books that cannot be replicated.

There is a further difficulty arising from the fact that there are two types of wholes. On the one hand a whole may be conceptualized mereologically, as a relationship between a concrete whole and its parts, as a cake and its slices, the Leviathan and its organs, a graph and its bars. On the other hand, the social whole may be held to be constituted by a rule of class-inclusion or it may be defined as the class of instances of specific attributes. E. B. Tylor's famous definition of culture as "that complex whole," is just such a set of elements selected according to some more or less specific criteria of which there are many possibilities (e.g., all human behaviors, all thoughts, all customs). The problem is that these two logically distinguishable holisms are almost always confused in sociological thought.

First of all, all organic and mechanistic metaphors of society imply that there is a mereological relationship between the parts of society and the whole that they are said to constitute. These images of social wholes are usually framed in terms of metaphorical images of organic bodies (function, functionalism), texts (signs and symbols, hermeneutics), trees (branches, evolution), rivers (flow, history), geological and architectural formations (strata, structuralism and Marxism) or machines (process, economics). Since the mereological relationship holds for the metaphorical image (i.e., an arm or head is clearly a part of the whole body, the branch a part of the whole tree, and so on), it is accepted that the same relationship holds for the social whole and its parts. That is simply the way good metaphors work. The matter is further complicated by the fact that class-inclusion relationships are often represented in graphic images. When the analysis is developed and elaborated in writing, it is done by recourse to terms for these images of branches, organs, strata, links and nodes, bodies and flow, that is, in terms of the same spatial or graphic images that are employed as metaphors for society. And finally, the words category, kind, class, genus, type are all used more or less interchangeably, and all conceived as parts of a classification (Manley Thompson 1983:342). But the class-inclusion rules that make categories members of classifications must be carefully distinguished from the mereological part-to-whole relationship.

In ethnography, this distinction is usually confused, especially since the material text is composed of (true mereological) parts and since the image-like metaphors of body/text/tree/river etc. are rarely far from the surface.

In fact, it appears that the confusion is almost essential to the achievement of what must be one of the chief aims of ethnography: to convince the reader of the existence of an initially unperceived coherence, a surprising meaningfulness, a covert rationality, or (merely) a history. This aim could not be carried out were it not for the writer's appeal to an ulterior image of wholeness or individuality, of organic or mechanical orderliness that transcends both the Author and the Other.

Inasmuch as classification functions as rhetorical trope, it is the chief means for evoking the imagination of wholeness. Roughly speaking, the tropes of synecdoche and classification are two sides of the same coin. On the one side, synecdoche suggests the whole through reference to one of its parts; on the other, a classificatory trope refers to an imagined whole in order to assert that the parts compose it. In writing, this takes the form of an assertion that if the whole (society, culture, *conscience collectif,* etc.) exists, then the evidence presented must constitute it.

Rhetorical Wholes Are Not Social Entities

The problem lies, in part, in the confusion of the different kinds of wholes that can be imagined. It should be clear that in a *logic* of classification we may distinguish between a class and a class that contains itself as its only member, or we may specify a class and then derive from this a class that contains all subsets of its members. *No such relations hold for a material or spatial (mereological) whole and its parts.* In the first case, the (mereological) whole and the whole that contains only itself must be identical. In the second case, a mereological whole cannot be itself and all subsets of itself. These propositions are intuitively obvious but can also be rigorously proved. Furthermore, we may conceive of an empty class, a class that has no instances of a given attribute, or for which no items satisfying a given criterion could be found. An empty mereological whole is a transparent contradiction (Korner 1983:355). Arguing along these lines, Ruben (1983) has claimed that any social philosophy is seriously misconceived if it holds that the relations between "at least some social entities and the human beings who are their members is the relation of the whole to its parts." This belief, however, appears to underlie much social philosophy since ancient times.

Ruben argues that either social wholes have parts that are not people, or they do not exist as such, and if people are parts of something then these entities cannot be social wholes conceived in mereological terms. His arguments rest on the material and spatial properties of the mereological relation of being parts of wholes, and the differences between this relationship and the class-inclusion relation holding between members of social wholes. An example illustrates his argument.

If the queue waiting for the 38 bus forms itself into local branch 38 of the bus-users association, the individuals in the queue are parts, not the members, of the queue, and the members, not the parts, of the local branch of the bus users' association. Each of the individuals in the queue is a material entity and so is the queue that they make up. No material entity can completely occupy the same total spatial position occupied by the queue at the same time unless it is just identical with the queue. On the other hand, the local association of bus-users is a social entity, and if it did have parts, perhaps committees, they would also be social entities. Some other entity can completely occupy precisely the same total spatial position at the same time, if indeed an association of this sort has any spatial position at all, for the same individuals might form themselves into any number of analogous associations they care to create. [Ruben 1983:237]

Rhetorical wholes, then, are not social entities. They are cognitive constructs that are relative to the scale and scope of the observer's view and to the rhetoric that constitutes them in the imagination. Some fondly held images of social wholes may be little more than a property of the argument that social wholes exist.

Emile Durkheim, for instance, says in effect that the social wholes *must* exist because the text that describes them does.

> There can be no sociology unless societies exist, and societies cannot exist if there are only individuals . . . [There will] emerge . . . from every page of this book, so to speak, the impression that the individual is dominated by a moral reality greater than himself. [Durkheim 1966:38]

Durkheim's "so to speak" seems ingenuous, but it directs attention away from "every page of this book," where the force he speaks of clearly lies, to the social whole that he endeavors to construct. He ignores the differences in scale between the observer, the analytical "individual," and the rhetorically constructed concepts of "societies" and "moral reality." These concepts are essential to the Durkheimian imagination that lives in so much 20th-century ethnography, but an argument for their *validity as concepts* does not prove the existence of their ostensible object.

The parts of texts—of books and articles—achieve their reality not from correspondence to reality but from coherence with the rest of their text and the rest of texts in general. We may see the problem in a different light when the rhetorical whole is dissected into its "parts," which achieve their reality not from their bearing on experience, but rather from the degree to which they are consistent with the image of the whole. Henri Bergson's commentary on religion, for instance, which is closely tied to Durkheim's own notion of the collective, illustrates this by unself-consciously confusing textual and social "parts":

> The future of a science depends on the way it first dissects its object. If it has the luck to cut along the lines of the natural joints, like Plato's good cook, the number of "cuts" is of little importance; as the cutting up into pieces will have prepared the way for the analysis into elements, we shall be finally in possession of a simplified representation of the whole. [Bergson 1935:96]

Here an image of a simple "cutting" of the whole is asserted to be identical with analysis, and the parts are not the elements of experience, but the decomposition of the imagined whole. Textual parts are confused with social "parts."

In a similar way, language is taken as a single holistic reality. The unity of language is, however, quite clearly created by texts which make language*s* (plural) out of language. This holism is asserted despite the fact that continuums of dialect, phonology, lexicon, degree of elaboration or reduction (pidginization) exist at all levels and in most languages. The concept of lexicon, is after all, a concept of text: a dictionary. The impact of dictionaries and grammars on the concept of linguistic units for most of world's languages that have only been written for the first time by European linguists has been considerable. In the field, every ethnographer has constant reference to dictionaries and grammars as he tries to come to grips with the always elusive "wholeness" of social experience. If they don't exist, they are created. Malinowski's "corpus inscriptionum agriculturae Quiriviniensis" (Malinowski 1961:24; 1978, vol. 2:77–210) is a clear example. The analogy with the text *(inscriptionum)* and with the body as a metaphor of organization and classification *(corpus)* are clear in this example.

From Rhetoric to Social Structure

One of the most characteristic differences between narrative and ethnographic description is that the ethnography is compiled over a relatively long period and from a range of discrete, disparate, and fundamentally incommensurate experiences, and expressed in terms of a classificatory schema or image. It is in terms of this schematization, rather than in terms of a discursive argument, plot or narrative flow, that the ethnographic (more generally: social) description achieves a closure that is intellectually satisfying. Chapters have special rhetorical significance in this regard since it is under their "headings" that data are classified. This format alone suggests another level or kind of meaningfulness that is not given by the facts themselves.

A monograph classified in chapters and subheadings must convey to the reader, by virtue of the classified discontinuity of chapters, citations, quoted discourse, case studies, and so on, that a connectedness does exist on another level. Simply a numbering of chapters and subheadings suggests a rationalized and higher-order logic than that which exists in the continuous narrative itself. The Bible, divided minutely into "chapters and verses" is the paradigmatic case of this form of arbitrary classification. The Bible, too, is profoundly self-referential, and was, moreover, prominent in the minds of most 19th-century ethnographers and some 20th-century ones as well.

Evans-Pritchard's ethnographic trilogy on the Nuer—*The Nuer* (1940), *Kinship and Marriage among the Nuer* (1951) and *Nuer Religion* (1956)—is a case in point. The three volumes express a tripartite division of social life into "environment," "social relations" and "belief." Once this partition has been made, further reference to one of these categories—let us say, kinship—is no longer a reference to kinship in general but to that variant of kinship which is specifically Nuer. In fact, patterns of kinship, such as they are, are varied and grade off into other patterns (which until they are written about remain kinship in general). Now, "Nuer kinship" refers as much to the book in which it is described as to the ostensible (though now historical and unrecoverable) reality that it described. Similarly, the existence of "prophets" among the Nuer is confirmed by the chapter that defines them in opposition to "priests," and that deliberately evokes the image of biblical priests and prophets. Although Evans-Pritchard himself declared it was no more than a matter of taste whether one considered "prophets" to be "political actors in a religious context or religious actors in a political context," the textual identification of them with the prophets of the Bible effectively resolves the issue. A chapter entitled "Nuer Priests and Prophets" refers in multiple directions to the Bible, the ethnographic monograph (the book) itself, and to some individuals who may or may not have understood themselves in this way at all.

Unlike discourse, and unlike narrative, the ethnography is compiled from "items"—notes, observations, texts, commentary (themselves compiled from items)—that are all subordinate to an encompassing classifying framework. The ethnographic text never really escapes from this "item-level." There are two related classificatory procedures: the practical, technical classification that takes place "in the field" and the intellectual (rhetorical) classifications that emerge most clearly in chapter and subheadings, and in textual keywords. While these are related processes, they differ in their conceptualization as "technique" on the one hand, and as "format" or "style" on the other. Both conceptualizations, however, disguise the rhetorical nature of the classificatory mode of exposition.

Meyer Fortes expressed this clearly in *The Web of Kinship among the Tallensi:*

> I was fortunate in that both my chief teachers on [the subject of kinship], the late Professor Bronislaw Malinowski and Professor Radcliffe-Brown, approached it with working hypotheses founded on the realities of field observation. Their theories have the merit of being adapted to the methods of observation available to the anthropologist in the field, and to the kind of data within his reach. [Fortes 1949:1]

One of the problems that emerges is how are the descriptive or experiential "items" of behavior and thought to be recognized or defined. For our consideration of ethnographic rhetoric, the nature of the units of description determines the way in which the descriptive text is able to relate the microcosmic level—the "items" of the field notebook, and the "evidence" of the ethnographic presentation such as a person met, a mask seen and sketched, a ritual attended—to the macrocosm of economy, culture, society, or cosmos.[3]

Again, this feature is especially marked in Fortes's books on the Tallensi. Indeed, Fortes can not define either his subject ("The Tallensi") or the structure of their society without reflexive references to his own writing and to other textual resources such as maps:

> The "tribal unity" of the Tallensi is, in general terms, the unity of a distinct sociogeographical region. This region can be demarcated only by dynamic criteria. The Tallensi have more in common among themselves . . . than *the component segments of Tale society have with other like units outside of what we have called Taleland. This characteristic of Tale society has a special relevance for the investigation we are undertaking in this book.* For, like the network of clanship ties and the bonds of common custom and of politico-ritual association analysed in our first book, the web of kinship spread far beyond the social frontiers of the Tallensi. [Fortes 1949:2; emphasis added]

For Fortes, the "component segments" are clearly parts of a whole. Despite claims that the social ties he writes of extend "far beyond the social frontiers," cross-link in countless ways, and form endlessly *ambiguous* categories, he concludes that

> Tale society is an organic society. . . . Taking Tale social structure as a whole, it can be visualized as a complex structure of different categories of social relations. [Fortes 1949:341–343]

In fact, it would be more apt to describe the books he wrote in these terms than to attribute this "structure" to the "Tale." The chapters of the two volumes, *The Dynamics of Clanship* (1945) and *The Web of Kinship* (1949) comprise detailed lists of categories, while the text throughout refers both to itself—that is, to the titles and contexts of other sections—and, in the footnotes, to the other of the two volumes for support.

Thus, the items of the field notebook, the so-called units of description appear to be prefigured by the technical practice of data collection in the field. The person met on the path that morning was simply a contingent event—contingent on a trip to the shop for salt, or being *en route* to the next interview. The mask described, among all possible masks, was the one that just happened to be seen while pencil and paper were ready to hand, one that belonged to a "best informant." But mere contingency cannot account for the text that eventually results. Reflection shows that even merely counting implies a rhetorical project. By counting, listing, summing, averaging, and other numerical manipulations we begin to construct macrocosmic entities (volume of petroleum shipped, total population of China, the average distance traveled by a Bushman hunting party) that are representative of some aspects of social reality, but only insofar as those aspects are part of a textual argument. The same is true of measurement. The "rate of suicides" is an example of one such measure (Durkheim 1966) that makes sense only in the context of Durkheim's moral project, and could be realized only through textual methods of compilation, analysis, graphical display, and exposition. Total yam yields compared with total pig yields in a New Guinea village is another such example. The derived ratio (yams to pigs), moreover, when considered as a changing quantity over time, exhibits a periodic rise and fall characteristic of "ideal" market economies or of population trends arising from predator-prey interactions in closed, near-equilibrium ecologies (Rappaport 1968:153–167ff; Michael Thompson 1979:184ff).

Numerical regularities such as these, and the arguments that depend on them, are types of holism that are critically dependent on textual argument. A "rate of suicide" or a pig-to-yam ratio are conceptually distant and even irrelevant to the experience of a suicidal depression or feeding pigs. Nevertheless, within an appropriate numerically constructed holism both suicide and pig-raising can be encompassed. Incommensurate experiences become commensurate within the domain of a rhetorical project through which they are defined, isolated, and rendered discrete.

Numerical methods in ethnography achieve their rhetorical effectiveness in sociological writing by permitting one to itemize and classify in order to relate small-scale entities to macrocosmic entities. Experienced reality is immediately translated, first of all, into a domain of symbolic tokens such as numbers, or ratios or formulae. These formalisms may translate or express a sense of coherence, but not meaning. By isolating specific interactions from the ramifying complexities of social life, they focus attention, and permit reductive propositions to be stated. There is also an undoubted appeal to physical-scientific methods that contributes an aura of legitimacy. But most important, any such sociology relies on the assumption that the entities it counts are both discrete and finite, an assumption that must be made in order to begin counting at all. Thus, it is not surprising that any statistical sociology easily achieves a sense of "finiteness" or "closure" which discursive and narrative methods must achieve by other rhetorical means.

The classificatory rhetoric may also subsume many other rhetorics, and thus encompass a range of expressive forms that are otherwise incommensurate. The classificatory rhetoric is a "macro-structure," which because it subsumes other rhetorics within an imagined or image-like "whole" is able to transcend the requirements of linguistic or propositional logics. Such "macrostructure" must be accorded as much cognitive and grammatical reality as other aspects of grammatical structure in linguistic analysis if larger-scale (i.e., larger than the sentences, phrases, words, and morphemes) features of discourse, tone, anaphoresis, etc. are to be comprehended linguistically (van Dijk 1983). Unlike most common narrative tropes that are closely tied to signs, simple reference, sentence-level syntax, poetics and prosody, the classification, as rhetorical trope, relies on macro-structures, comprehensive images, and a commitment to inclusivity and analogy.

Similarly, an outline order of chapters, heads, subheads, and paragraphs imparts an architectural pattern that may be rhetorically useful in legitimizing the text as reasoned or scientific, or which may serve to frame it in order to hold the reader's attention, or, may suggest the part-to-whole relationship that is crucial to the satisfactory closure of this kind of discourse. In fact the vocabulary of the classification of the physical book is nothing more than extended metaphors of the body ("chapter,"[4] "heading," "footnote," "spine"), of the landscape ("verse,"[5] "strophe") of trees ("leaves," "page"[6]), buildings ("tables"), and streets ("margin").

Finally, the discursive classification is powerfully evocative of time and space, especially as these are imagined as interpenetrating categories of knowledge that may stand for one another (Fabian 1983). The social-evolutionist paradigms of Auguste Comte, James Cowles Pritchard, Lewis Henry Morgan, Edward Burnett Tylor, James Frazer and others collapse time and space into a single manifold of categories that not only serve to classify types of society, but classify the text as well. In these paradigms of evolution, temporal priority (causation, or time asymmetry) is confused with logical priority (entailment/implication). The logically simpler social form is assigned, by the classificatory logic, a temporal priority. All of this has the function, as Foucault has pointed out, of establishing a "ground" and a "site" in which it is possible to juxtapose empirical and imaginary realities (Foucault 1974).

The ethnography relies on the fact that it is an object, a text, radically removed from the initial experiences and perceptions on which it is based. The representation of reality, whether on note cards or in chapter headings is confused with reality and manipulated as objects in ways that culture or society can not be. The text itself is the object of knowledge.

Social Structure as Rhetorical Closure

Ethnography must confront the radical continuity of life. With a number of modern novelists who assert the infinity of even individual consciousness, and with recent linguists who assert the relatively unlimited productivity of language (Langendoen and Postal 1984) we might ask if there are "units" (experiential or descriptive quanta) at all. Is social life radically continuous, only broken by the periodicity of text? Perhaps we must agree with the historians F. Pollock and F. W. Maitland who wrote, "Such is the unity of all history that anyone who endeavors to tell a piece of it must feel that his first sentence tears a seamless web" (Pollock and Maitland, 1898, vol. 1:1). Apparent boundaries, then, such as those that define nations, ethnic groups, age-grades, or classes, are seen to be relative to time, the observer, or to each other, and thus not "really" there at all. In any case, we cannot always assign them unambiguous ontological status.

For the ethnographer, however, this is not an acceptable solution to his rhetorical problem. A text, to be convincing as a description of reality, must convey some sense of closure. For the ethnography, this closure is achieved by the textual play of object-reference and self-reference that the classificatory imagination permits. The discreteness of social entities, it appears, is chiefly an artifact of textual description that classifies them and substitutes the logic of classification for the experience of the "everyday."

The ethnographic monograph presents us with an analogy between the text itself and the "society" or "culture," that it describes. The sense of a discrete social or cultural entity that is conveyed by an ethnography is founded on the sense of closure or completeness of both the physical text and its rhetorical format. In this it shares features with the novel or the travelogue. The novel rounds out a plot by bringing events to expected conclusions, a rhetorical method that is shared by prophecy in religious and epic narratives. The travelogue achieves closure as a result of an actual itinerary with a definite start and finish: The traveler comes home in the end to write of his journeys. (Otherwise, it is an "origin myth"—a travelogue without a return sequence—or a "Roots" type of narrative, told from the other end, as it were, with only the expectation of an imaginary or emotional "return.") The ethnographic monograph, however, presents "society" through the order of its chapters which do not unfold temporally but spatially and logically.

But while the novel cannot pretend to be comprehensive, the ethnography often attempts to maintain the pretense. The outline of chapter headings is often designed to suggest exhaustive coverage, like a catalog, or an encyclopedia. Models for this exist in J. G. Frazer's, Karl Marx's, or Malinowski's compendious treatments of their fields of knowledge. Malinowski, for example, wrote to Frazer in October while on board the S. S. *Makambo* bound for Kiriwina that

> As far as the subject matter of my investigation is concerned, I am endeavoring to cover the whole field, and not neglect any aspect that really matters. [letter 25 October 1917, Trinity College Library]

Herbert Spencer expressed this goal most eloquently in a way that could serve as the motto of the sort of sociology he outlined and which Frazer attempted:

> If intellectual progress consists largely, if not mainly, in widening our acquaintance with this past and this future [of the world] it is obvious that . . . [our knowledge] is

imperfect so long as any past or future portions of their sensible existence are unaccounted for. . . . Only by some formula combining these characters can knowledge be reduced to a coherent whole. [Spencer 1863:280]

The chapters of the ethnographic classics are meant to be encyclopedias of social life, and attempt to achieve a sense of closure by means of brute force. A quick glance at reviews of ethnographies shows that the ''comprehensiveness'' of an ethnography is one thing that is almost certain to be remarked upon. If the claim to comprehensive treatment is widely accepted, then the text becomes the established ''truth'' of the society. The text, rather than the society, becomes the object of knowledge. Perhaps this is why one of the most popular contemporary analogies for culture and societies is that they are ''like texts,'' or even that, culture *is* a text (Geertz 1973).

Closure is achieved by the gradual limitation of possibilities when the plot is resolved, the traveler returns home, the clues of the mystery receive definitive interpretations, or the suspense of the uncompleted is brought to its eventual end. For the ethnography, as for other descriptive genres of science, the physical text provides a physical analog of closure. This relationship between the text (ethnography) and the social reality has been prefigured as a kind of mirror: to close the book is to achieve a ''closure'' since the text itself, irrespective of how many ''readings'' it may be given, is discrete, finite. This analogy, however, also contributes to another sense of closure by defining the limitation of social possibilities. In other forms of narrative description it is the ending that gives meaning to the whole, the resolution of conflict that assuages anxiety, the return that makes sense of the ''venturing forth.'' In the travelogue, the ''ending'' is prefigured by virtue of the very definition of the genre itself. The traveler is striving toward a goal, even if it is ''unknown'' in the sense that the source of the Nile was once ''unknown.'' There is always an image of a limited space, a definite itinerary. The missionary's narrative, likewise, told a story whose end was foretold, and that, through the ever-present analogy with the scriptures, was both the end of his story, and the end of history.

The monographic ethnography, on the other hand, substitutes a representation of limited social possibilities, often called ''social structure,'' for the ''closure'' that the other genres strive to achieve through plot, itinerary, or other customary narrative formulae.

A text we should be born that we might read
More explicit than the experience of the sun
And moon, the book of reconciliation,
Book of a concept only possible
In the description, canon central in itself
The thesis of the plentifullest John.

—Wallace Stevens
''Description Without Place''

Notes

[1]Naturally, I mean here travelers who *write,* who travel as such, ultimately in service of the texts they create.

[2]Here society as the object of ethnographic and sociological description, must not be confused with the social, the experience of other people and our relationships with them.

[3]The old "unit of analysis" problem, unlike that which is raised here, was concerned with methods of comparison between societies, and was derived from a natural history model for anthropological inquiry.

[4]"Chapter," from *caput* (Latin), "head," via Old French *chapitre.*

[5]"Verse," from Old English *vers,* from Latin *versus,* "furrow," literally "a turning," from *vertere,* "to turn."

[6]"Page," from Latin *fagus,* "tree," "wood."

References Cited

Bergson, Henri
  1935   The Two Sources of Morality and Religion. R. A. Audra and C. Brereton, trans. New York: Doubleday.
Bruner, Edward
  1982   Ethnography as Narrative. *In* The Anthropology of Experience. Victor Turner and Edward Bruner, eds. Pp. 139–158. Urbana: University of Illinois Press.
Clifford, James
  1983   On Ethnographic Authority. Representations 1(2):118–146.
Derrida, Jacques
  1976   Of Grammatology. G. C. Spivak, trans. Baltimore: Johns Hopkins University Press.
Dickens, Charles
  1843   A Christmas Carol. London: Chapman and Hall.
Durkheim, Emile
  1966[1897]   Suicide: A Study in Sociology. J. A. Spaulding and George Simpson, trans. New York: The Free Press.
Evans-Pritchard, E. E.
  1940   The Nuer: Description of Modes of Livelihood and Political Institutions of a Nilotic People. Oxford: Oxford University Press.
  1951   Kinship and Marriage among the Nuer. Oxford: Oxford University Press.
  1956   Nuer Religion. Oxford: Oxford University Press.
Fabian, Johannes
  1983   Time and the Other. New York: Columbia University Press.
Fortes, Meyer
  1945   The Dynamics of Clanship among the Tallensi. Oxford: Oxford University Press.
  1949   The Web of Kinship among the Tallensi. Oxford: Oxford University Press.
Foucault, Michel
  1974   The Archaeology of Knowledge. Sheridan Smith, trans. London: Tavistock.
Geertz, Clifford
  1973   The Interpretation of Cultures. New York: Basic Books.
Griaule, Maurice
  1965   Conversations with Ogotemeli. Oxford: Oxford University Press.

Junod, Henri-Alexandre
    1927   The Life of a South African Tribe. 2 volumes. London: Macmillan.
Korner, Stephen
    1983   Thinking, Thought and Categories. The Monist 66(3):353–366.
Kuhn, Thomas
    1970   The Structure of Scientific Revolutions. Chicago: University of Chicago Press.
Langendoen, D. Terence, and Paul M. Postal
    1984   The Vastness of Natural Languages. London: Basil Blackwell.
MacLuhan, Marshall
    1962   The Guttenburg Galaxy: The Making of Typographic Man. London: Routledge & Kegan Paul.
Malinowski, Bronislaw
    1978[1935]   Coral Gardens and Their Magic. 2 volumes. New York: Dover Publications.
    1961[1922]   Argonauts of the Western Pacific. New York: E. P. Dutton.
Marcus, George, and Dick Cushman
    1982   Ethnographies as Texts. Annual Review of Anthropology. Palo Alto: Annual Reviews Press.
Miller, Arthur
    1949   The Death of a Salesman. New York: Viking Press.
Pollock, Frederick, and Frederic William Maitland
    1898   The History of English Law before the Times of Edward I. Cambridge: Cambridge University Press.
Pratt, Mary Louise
    1986   Fieldwork in Common Places. *In* Writing Culture: The Poetics and Politics of Ethnography. James Clifford and George E. Marcus, eds. Pp. 27–50. Berkeley: University of California Press.
Radcliffe-Brown, A. R.
    1925   Structure and Function in Primitive Society. New York: The Free Press.
Rappaport, Roy A.
    1968   Pigs for the Ancestors: Ritual in the Ecology of a New Guinea People. New Haven: Yale University Press.
Ruben, David-Hillel
    1983   Social Wholes and Parts. Mind 92:219–238.
Spencer, Herbert
    1863   First Principles. London: Williams and Norgate.
Thompson, Manley
    1983   Philosophical Approaches to Categories. The Monist 66(3):336–352.
Thompson, Michael
    1979   Rubbish Theory: The Creation and Destruction of Value. Oxford: Oxford University Press.
Thornton, Robert James
    1985   "Imagine Yourself set down . . . " Mach, Conrad, Frazer, Malinowski and the Role of the Imagination in Ethnography. Anthropology Today 1(5):7–14.
Toulmin, Stephen
    1982   The Return to Cosmology: Postmodern Science and the Theology of Nature. Berkeley: University of California Press.
Tylor, Edward B.
    1871   Primitive Culture. 2 volumes. London.

van Dijk, Teun A.
   1983   Macrostructures: An Interdisciplinary Study of Global Structures in Discourse. Hillsdale, N.J.: Erlbaum.
Webster, Steven
   1982   Dialogue and Fiction in Ethnography. Dialectical Anthropology 7(2):91–114.
White, Hayden
   1973   Metahistory. Baltimore: Johns Hopkins University Press.

Putting Hierarchy in Its Place

Arjun Appadurai

In the essay that follows, I shall be concerned with the genealogy of an idea. But before I put forward this genealogy, I need to make two preliminary arguments. The first involves the anthropological construction of natives. The second involves a defense of one kind of intellectual history.

The Place of the Native

On the face of it, an exploration of the idea of the "native" in anthropological discourse may not appear to have much to do with the genealogy of the idea of hierarchy. But I wish to argue that hierarchy is one of an anthology of images in and through which anthropologists have frozen the contribution of specific cultures to our understanding of the human condition. Such metonymic freezing has its roots in a deeper assumption of anthropological thought regarding the boundedness of cultural units and the confinement of the varieties of human consciousness within these boundaries. The idea of the "native" is the principal expression of this assumption, and thus the genealogy of hierarchy needs to be seen as one local instance of the dynamics of the construction of natives.

Although the term *native* has a respectable antiquity in Western thought and has often been used in positive and self-referential ways, it has gradually become the technical preserve of anthropologists. Although some other words taken from the vocabulary of missionaries, explorers, and colonial administrators have been expunged from anthropological usage, the term *native* has retained its currency, serving as a respectable substitute for terms like *primitive*, about which we now feel some embarrassment. Yet the term *native*, whether we speak of "native categories," or "native belief-systems" or "native agriculture," conceals certain ambiguities. We sense this ambiguity, for example, in the restricted use of the adjective *nativistic*, which is typically used not only for one sort of revivalism, but for revivalism among certain kinds of population.

Who is a "native" (henceforth without quotation marks) in the anthropological usage? The quick answer to this question is that the native is a person who is born in (and thus belongs to) the place the anthropologist is observing or writing about. This sense of the word *native* is fairly narrowly, and neutrally, tied to its Latin etymology. But do we use the term *native* uniformly to refer to people who are born in certain places and, thus, belong to them? We do not. We have tended to use the word *native* for persons and groups who belong to those parts of the world that were, and are, distant from the metropolitan West. This restriction is, in part, tied to the vagaries of our ideologies of authenticity over the last two centuries. Proper natives are somehow assumed to represent their selves and their history, without distortion or residue. We exempt ourselves from this sort of claim to authenticity because we are too enamored of the complexities of our history, the diversities of our societies, and the ambiguities of our collective conscience. When we find authenticity close to home, we are more likely to label it *folk* than *native,* the former being a term that suggests authenticity without being implicitly derogatory. The anthropologist thus rarely thinks of himself as a native of some place, even when he knows that he is from somewhere. So what does it mean to be a native of some place, if it means something more, or other, than being from that place?

What it means is that natives are not only persons who are from certain places, and belong to those places, but they are also those who are somehow *incarcerated,* or confined, in those places.[1] What we need to examine is this attribution or assumption of incarceration, of imprisonment, or confinement. Why are some people seen as confined to, and by, their places?

Probably the simplest aspect of the common sense of anthropology to which this image corresponds is the sense of physical immobility. Natives are in one place, a place to which explorers, administrators, missionaries, and eventually anthropologists, come. These outsiders, these observers, are regarded as quintessentially mobile; they are the movers, the seers, the knowers. The natives are immobilized by their belonging to a place. Of course, when observers arrive, natives are capable of moving to another place. But this is not really motion; it is usually flight, escape, to another equally confining place.

The slightly more subtle assumption behind the attribution of immobility is not so much physical as ecological. Natives are those who are somehow confined to places by their connection to what the place permits. Thus all the language of niches, of foraging, of material skill, of slowly evolved technologies, is actually also a language of incarceration. In this instance confinement is not simply a function of the mysterious, even metaphysical attachment of native to physical places, but a function of their adaptations to their environments.

Of course, anthropologists have long known that motion is part of the normal round for many groups, ranging from Bushmen and Australian aborigines, to Central Asian nomads and Southeast Asian swidden agriculturalists. Yet most of these groups, because their movements are confined within small areas and appear to be driven by fairly clear-cut environmental constraints, are generally treated as natives tied not so much to a place as to a pattern of places. This is still not quite motion of the free, arbitrary, adventurous sort associated with metropolitan behavior. It is still incarceration, even if over a larger spatial terrain.

But the critical part of the attribution of nativeness to groups in remote parts of the world is a sense that their incarceration has a moral and intellectual dimension. They are confined by what they know, feel, and believe. They are prisoners of their "mode of thought." This is, of course, an old and deep theme in the history of anthropological thought, and its most powerful example is to be found in Evans-Pritchard's picture of the Azande, trapped in their moral web, confined by a way of thinking that admits of no fuzzy boundaries and is splendid in its internal consistency. Although Evans-Pritchard is generally careful not to exaggerate the differences between European and Azande mentality, his position suggests that the Azande are especially confined by their mode of thought:

> Above all, we have to be careful to avoid in the absence of native doctrine constructing a dogma which we would formulate were we to act as Azande do. There is no elaborate and consistent representation of witchcraft that will account in detail for its workings, nor of nature which expounds its conformity to sequences and functional interrelations. The Zande actualizes these beliefs rather than intellectualizes them, and their tenets are expressed in socially controlled behavior rather than in doctrines. Hence the difficulty of discussing the subject of witchcraft with Azande, for their ideas are *imprisoned in action* and cannot be cited to explain and justify action. [Evans-Pritchard 1937:82–83; emphasis mine]

Of course, this idea of certain others, as confined by their way of thinking, in itself appears to have nothing to do with the image of the native, the person who belongs to a place. The link between the confinement of ideology and the idea of place is that the way of thought that confines natives is itself somehow bounded, somehow tied to the circumstantiality of place. The links between intellectual and spatial confinement, as assumptions that underpin the idea of the native, are two. The first is the notion that cultures are "wholes": this issue is taken up in the section of this essay on Dumont. The second is the notion, embedded in studies of ecology, technology, and material culture over a century, that the intellectual operations of natives are somehow tied to their niches, to their situations. They are seen, in Lévi-Strauss's evocative terms, as scientists of the concrete. When we ask where this concreteness typically inheres, it is to be found in specifics of flora, fauna, topology, settlement patterns, and the like; in a word, it is the concreteness of place. Thus, the confinement of native ways of thinking reflects in an important way their attachment to particular places. The science of the concrete can thus be written as the poetry of confinement.[2]

But anthropologists have always known that natives are not always so incarcerated. The American anthropological tradition, at least as far back as Boas, and most recently in the voices of Sidney Mintz (1985) and Eric Wolf (1982), has always seen cultural traits as shared and transmitted over large cultural areas, as capable of change, and as creating shifting mosaics of technology and ideology. The French tradition, at least in that part of it with roots in Herder and Vico, and more recently in Mauss, Benveniste and Dumézil, has always seen the links, at least of the Indo-European "linguaculture" (Attinasi and Friedrich 1987), across many geographically scattered places. Even in British anthropology, there have been minority voices, like those of Lord Raglan and A. M. Hocart, who have seen that the morphology of social systems and ideologies is not confined by single, territorially anchored groupings. It is now increasingly clear that in many instances where anthropologists believed they were observing and analyzing pristine or historically deep systems, they were in fact viewing products of recent transregional interactions. Diffusionism, whatever its defects and in whatever guise, has at least the virtue of allowing everyone the possibility of exposure to a world larger than their current locale.

It is even more evident that in today's complex, highly interconnected, media-dominated world, there are fewer and fewer native cultures left. They are oppressed by the international market for the objects once iconic of their identity, which are now tokens in the drive for authenticity in metropolitan commodity cultures. They are pushed by the forces of development and nationalization throughout the world and are attracted by the possibilities of migration (or refuge) in new places. Natives, as anthropologists like to imagine them, are therefore rapidly disappearing. This much many will concede.

But were there ever natives, in the sense in which I have argued the term must be understood? Most groups that anthropologists have studied have in some way been affected by the knowledge of other worlds, worlds about which they may have learned through migration, trade, conquest, or indigenous narratives. As we drop our own anthropological blinders, and as we sharpen our ethnohistorical tools, we are discovering that the pristine Punan of the interior of Borneo were probably a specialized adaptation of the larger Dayak communities, serving a specialized function in the world trade in Borneo forest products (Hoffmann 1986); that the San of Southern Africa have been involved in a complex symbiosis with other groups for a very long time (Schrire 1980); that groups in Melanesia have been trading goods across very long distances for a long time, trade that reflects complex regional relations of supply and demand (Hughes 1977); that African "tribes" have been reconstituting and deconstructing essential structural principles at their "internal frontiers" for a very long time (Kopytoff 1987).

Even where contact with large-scale external forces has been, till recently, minimal, as with some Inuit populations, some populations in lowland South America, and many Australian aboriginal groups, these groups have constituted very complex "internal" mosaics of trade, marriage, conquest, and linguistic exchange, which suggests that no one grouping among them was ever truly incarcerated in a specific place and confined by a specific mode of thought (see, for example, Myers 1986). Although assiduous anthropologists might always discover some borderline examples, my general case is that natives, people confined to and by the places to which they belong, groups unsullied by contact with a larger world, have probably never existed.

Natives, thus, are creatures of the anthropological imagination. In our dialogic age, this may not seem like a very bold assertion, but it ramifies in several directions. If anthropologists have always possessed a large amount of information that has militated against the idea of the native, how have they succeeded in holding on to it? How have places turned into prisons containing natives?

The answer lies in the ways that places have been married to ideas and images, and here I resume an argument initiated elsewhere (Appadurai 1986a). Anthropology has, more than many disciplinary discourses, operated through an album or anthology of images (changing over time, to be sure) whereby some feature of a group is seen as quintessential to the group and as especially true of that group in contrast with other groups. Hierarchy in India has this quality. In the discourse of anthropology, hierarchy is what is most true of India and it is truer of India than of any other place.

In the subsequent sections of this essay I shall show that ideas that become metonymic prisons for particular places (such that the natives of that place are inextricably confined by them) themselves have a spatial history, in the evolving discourse of anthropology. Ideas and images not only travel from place to place, but they periodically come into compelling configurations, configurations which, once formed, resist modification or critique. By looking at Dumont's conceptualization of hierarchy in India, I shall explore the archaeology of hierarchy as an image that confines the natives of India. In the last part of the article, finally, I shall propose a theory about the circumstances under which such resilient configurations tend to occur in the history of anthropological discourse.

The Genealogy of Hierarchy

The recent wave of reflexivity among anthropologists, especially those practicing in the United States, has already created a backlash, founded on many reservations, including temperamental and stylistic ones. But one of the reasons for the backlash has been the suspicion that the self-scrutiny of ethnographers and fieldworkers might be a prologue to the extinction of the object of our studies. Faced with the disappearance of natives as they imagined them, some anthropologists run the risk of substituting reflexivity for fieldwork. I belong to that group of anthropologists who wish neither to erase the object in an orgy of self-scrutiny, nor to fetishize fieldwork (without carefully rethinking what fieldwork ought to mean and be in a changing world), in the way that Victorian educators fetishized cold baths and sport as character-building devices for the public-school elite. So why engage in any sort of genealogy?

All genealogies are selective, as any good historian of ideas would recognize. They are selective, that is, not through sloppiness or prejudice (though these could always creep in), but because every genealogy is a choice among a virtually infinite set of genealogies that make up the problem of influence and source in intellectual history. Every idea ramifies indefinitely backward in time, and at each critical historical juncture, key ideas ramify indefinitely into their own horizontal, contemporary contexts. Nontrivial ideas, especially, never have a finite set of genealogies. Thus any particular genealogy must derive its authority from the moral it seeks to subserve. The genealogy I have constructed in the case of Dumont's conception of hierarchy is one such genealogy, which subserves my interest in the spatial history of anthropological ideas. Thus my genealogy, like any other genealogy, is an argument in the guise of a discovery.

There is another way to characterize my position. The sort of genealogy I am interested in has something in common with Foucault's sense of the practice he calls "archaeology," a practice which, when successful, uncovers not just a genetic chain, but an epistemological field and its discursive formations. The discursive formation with which I am concerned, at its largest level, is the discourse of anthropology over the last century, and within it the subdiscourses about caste and about India. This sort of genealogizing is intended to occupy the middle space between the atemporal stance of certain kinds of contemporary criticism (especially those affected by deconstruction) and the exclusivist and genetic assumptions of most standard approaches to the history of ideas.

In Dumont's (1970) conception of *hierarchy* as the key to caste society in India, we see the convergence of three distinct trajectories in Western thought. These separate trajectories, which come together in recent anthropological practice, are threefold. First there is the urge to *essentialize,* which characterized the Orientalist forebears of anthropology. This essentialism, which has a complicated genealogy going back to Plato, became for some Orientalists the preferred mode for characterizing the "other." As Ronald Inden has recently argued (Inden 1986a), this led to a substantialized view of caste (reified as India's essential institution) and an idealized view of Hinduism, regarded as the religious foundation of caste. The second tendency involves *exoticizing,* by making *differences* between "self" and other the sole criteria for comparison. This tendency to exoticize has been discussed extensively in recent critiques of the history of anthropology and of ethnographic writing (Boon 1982; Clifford and Marcus 1986; Fabian 1983) and has its roots in the "Age of Discovery" as well as in the 18th-century "Age of Nationalism," especially in Germany. The third trajectory involves *totalizing,* that is, making specific features of a society's thought or practice not only its essence but also its totality. Such totalizing probably has its roots in the German romanticism of the early 19th century and comes to us in all the variations of the idea of the *Geist* (spirit) of an age or a people. Canonized in Hegel's holism, its most important result was the subsequent Marxian commitment to the idea of totality (Jay 1984), but it also underlies Dumont's conception of the "whole," discussed below. In this sense, the dialogue between the idealistic and the materialistic descendants of Hegel is hardly over. In anthropology and in history, particularly in France, it is to be seen in Mauss's idea of the gift as a *total* social phenomenon and in the Annales school's conception of *histoire totale.*

Hierarchy, in Dumont's argument, becomes the essence of caste, the key to its exoticism, and the form of its totality. There have been many criticisms of Dumont's ideas about hierarchy. I shall be concerned here to deconstruct hierarchy by unpacking its constituents in Dumont's scheme and by tracing that aspect of the genealogy of these constituents that moves us out of India and to other places in the ongoing journey of anthropological theory. As we shall see, this genealogy is in part a topographic history of certain episodes and certain links in the history of anthropological thought in the last century. Since my argument is concerned largely with the extra-Indian implications of Dumont's ideas, let me briefly place them in their Indian context.

Arriving on the scene in the late 1960s, when American cultural particularism, British structural-functionalism, and French structuralism had come to a rather dull standoff in regard to the study of caste, *Homo Hierarchicus* had a galvanizing effect. It was widely (and vigorously) reviewed, and it generated numerous symposia, an army of exegetes, acolytes, and opponents. For almost two decades it has dominated French structuralist studies of rural India, formed the intellectual charter of the influential journal *Contributions to Indian Sociology*, and generated much empirical and theoretical activity both in England and the United States. Dumont's ideas have been subject to careful and sympathetic criticism by a host of scholars who have pursued his French intellectual roots, his conception of ideology, his model of renunciation and purity, and the fit of his ideas with Indian facts (see, for example, Berreman 1971; Das 1977; Kolenda 1976; Marriott 1969; Parry 1980; Srinivas 1984; Yalman 1969).

While difficulties have been seen with almost every important aspect of Dumont's methodology and claims, most scholars working on the caste systems of South Asia (even the most obdurately empiricist critics of Dumont) will grant that Dumont's idea of hierarchy captures the distance between the value-assumptions of India and post-Enlightenment Europe like no previous characterization.

There are thus two trajectories within which *Homo Hierarchicus* fits. One is the trajectory that has to do with the history of Western values. Dumont, as early as the mid-1970s, had shown his concern with the dynamics of individualism and egalitarianism in the West. This latter concern has intensified since the publication of *Homo Hierarchicus,* and Dumont's latest collection of essays (Dumont 1986) makes it clear that the argument about hierarchy in India was an episode in a long-term exercise in the archaeology of modern Western ideology.

Yet, since *Homo Hierarchicus* also made a bold and sweeping structuralist argument about the ideology of the caste system, it demands assessment and critique in its areal context as well. This it has amply received. What is now called for is an effort to bring these two trajectories into a unified critical discussion, a discussion in which areal and theoretical issues are not invidiously separated and ranked. This essay is a preliminary contribution to this sort of unified discussion.

Pauline Kolenda (1976) has shown the ambiguities in, and polysemy of, Dumont's use of the word *hierarchy* in *Homo Hierarchicus,* and has provided a valuable basis for extending our understanding of the roots of his idea of hierarchy. Dumont owes a very large part of his understanding of caste society to Célestin Bouglé, about whom I shall have more to say shortly. Bouglé (1971) argued that the caste system was a product of the unique configuration of three relational properties of the castes: separation, hierarchy, and interdependence. Dumont's advance is to find a principle linking and underlying all three and developing a more sweeping and abstract conception of hierarchy than Bouglé's.

The ingredients of this conception of hierarchy, each of which has a different genealogy, are (1) a particular conception of the whole; (2) a particular conception of the parts; (3) a particular conception of the opposition of pure and impure; and (4) a particular commitment to the idea of the profoundly religious basis of caste society. I shall consider each of these in turn, starting with the idea of the whole.

Dumont's idea of the whole is consciously derived from Hegel, to whom he attributes the view that the hierarchy between castes is a matter of the relation to a *whole*. Hegel's *Philosophy of History* (1902), his most important contribution to German Orientalism, is the main link between Dumont and the tradition, going back to Plato, in which a conception of the social or collective whole is the primary source of values and norms.[3] India, in this Hegelian view, ceases to be a showcase for rank and stratification (which is a commonplace of foreign notices of India from the beginnings of the Christian era) and becomes instead a living museum of that form of social holism that has been lost to the West. Less conscious, but equally decisive for Dumont's idea of the whole, is the conception of the Années Sociologiques, in which certain archaic social forms, especially gift and sacrifice, are seen as *total social phenomena*. Although I shall have more to say on the topographic genealogy of Mauss's ideas, it is worth noting that they are the product of a particular French philological tradition that seeks to link the Indo-European world with the world of the primitive. Its *topos* is the spatiotemporal landscape of the vanished Indo-European heartland and the scattered islands of early ethnography. In Dumont's conceptualization of hierarchy, Hegelian *holism* and Maussian totalizing come together, and a decisive break is made with the earlier Western obsession with Indian stratification. The subordination of parts to the whole is at the heart of Dumont's understanding of the ideological basis of the system of castes. This whole ("the system of castes") is taken by Dumont to be complete, more important than its parts, stable, and ideologically self-sustaining. Dumont's idea of the whole represents one variant of the wider anthropological commitment to holism, a commitment that has elsewhere been opened to critical examination.[4]

So much for Dumont's conception of the "whole." What about his conception of the parts? Here the plot gets thicker. Dumont's understanding of *castes* as parts of a very particular type of hierarchical whole comes from two sources, both of which he acknowledges. The first is Evans-Pritchard, whose classic study of the *segmentary* nature of Nuer society influenced Dumont greatly (Dumont 1970:41–42). As Srinivas has recently emphasized, the topographic roots of the segmentary nature of Indian castes comes from Evans-Pritchard's analysis of the Nuer data, a special sort of African case (Srinivas 1984). In turn, Evans-Pritchard's view has complex, though obscure, roots. One aspect of the Nuer model doubtless goes back to Robertson Smith's classic work on Semitic religion, which contains a particular English Orientalist picture of Arabian society (Beidelman 1968; Dresch, this volume). On the other hand, the general roots of the classic British social anthropology of African political systems surely goes back to the 19th-century Anglo-Saxon tradition in studies of ancient law. Especially central here is the work of Henry Maine, who is a critical theorist of kinship as a basis for jural order.[5] Since Maine also worked on Indian law and society, in comparison with ancient Rome, we have here a wonderful circle. From the ancient village republics of India, via ancient Rome and comparative law, through African political systems and Nuer segments, back to Indian castes.

But the other source of Dumont's conception of the castes as "parts" is Bouglé's image of the "repulsion" of the castes toward each other, a fascinating Gallic precursor of Evans-Pritchard's conception of the fissive tendencies of Nuer segments (Bouglé 1971:22; Evans-Pritchard 1940:148).

It is not easy to trace the roots of Bouglé's emphasis on the "repulsion" of the parts for each other, except as a synthetic insight based on the ethnography and Indology available to him at the turn of the century. Since Bouglé was not (unlike Mauss) an Indologist, and since he was mainly concerned with the history of egalitarian values in the West, we can only guess that the areal interests of his colleagues in the Années Sociologique group had some effects on him. One such specific influence we shall note shortly.

Before we come to Dumont's critical contribution—the opposition of pure and impure as the axiom of the entire caste system—we need to ask about the larger view on which it is based, namely that in India, *religion* is the dominant shaper of ideology and values. Although this is something of a commonplace, and has been noted by centuries of observers from the West, Dumont places a special emphasis and interpretation upon the religious basis of Indian society. One source for this orientation again is Hegel. But more proximate are Bouglé, mentioned already, and A. M. Hocart. As to Bouglé, he attributed the hierarchical Hindu conception of castes to the utter predominance of the priesthood in India. On the one hand, this predominance was attributed to a weak state organization (and here we have a parallel to the link that leads from Henry Maine to Evans-Pritchard). On the other hand, Bouglé attributes it to the centrality of the *sacrifice* in ancient India. This, in turn, Bouglé derives from Hubert and Mauss's classic work on *sacrifice* and—you guessed it—Robertson Smith on the Semitic religion of sacrifice. So we are back in the shadow of Arabia.

But the other crucial source of Dumont's ideas about the religious basis of Indian society is the work of the English anthropologist-administrator, A. M. Hocart. Although Dumont makes many criticisms of Hocart's work on caste, he is explicit in acknowledging his debt to him on the centrality of religion to caste. What is interesting about Hocart's own anthropological career is that it began in the South Pacific, where he conducted anthropological researches in Fiji, Tonga, and Samoa. He was also Headmaster for some time of a native school at Lau (Fiji), and he wrote a learned monograph on the Lau Islands. It was this experience of the centrality of chieftainship and castelike specialization that was on his mind when, after World War I, he was appointed Archaeological Commissioner in Ceylon, where he further developed his ideas on caste and kingship. In fact, his entire model of Indian society—centered on the ritual of kingship—is based on his apperception of Ceylon, where the ritual of royalty remained a macro reality. When he finally wrote his comparative study of caste in the 1930s, it reflected an understanding of Indian caste that echoed a Ceylonese redaction of his understanding of rank, chieftainship, and religious order in the South Pacific, especially in Fiji.

An interesting variant on this genealogy can be seen in Dumont's understanding of the contrast between the pure and the impure. Dumont acknowledges the important but mistaken ideas of scholars like H. N. C. Stevenson (1954) (whose work on status evaluation in the caste system may have been influenced by his own earlier work on the Chin-Kachin group in Burma, whom Leach subsequently immortalized). But he must have also been greatly influenced by Hocart, whose comparative work on caste (Hocart 1950) contains an important, though tacit, emphasis on the problem of ritual separation and the purity of chiefs. Although Dumont does not explicitly attribute this part of his thinking to Hocart, there is a very interesting section in *Homo Hierarchicus* where he notes that his ideas about food prohibitions in India are owed to an unpublished course on sin and expiation taught by Mauss at the Collège de France, where Mauss partly drew his ideas from Hocart's work on Tonga (Dumont 1970:140). Thus, in the central matter of food prohibitions, which exemplify the contrast between pure and impure, which is in turn the cultural pivot of Dumont's ideas on hierarchy, the topographic genealogy leads back to Hocart on Tonga.

Let me conclude with a review of my findings. Dumont's conception of hierarchy leads from India in at least four major topological directions: Africa, in regard to its conception of the parts; ancient Arabia, for its conception of religious segmentation and solidarity; ancient Rome, for its conception of jural order in the absence of a powerful state; and the South Pacific (via Ceylon), for its conception of the power of *taboo* and the ritual implications of specialization. But, of course, there are two other discourses that mediate this one, discourses whose analysis lies outside the scope of this essay. One is the metropolitan discourse of anthropology, conducted at places like Oxford, the Collège de France, and the various sites of colonial administration. The other is the grander discourse of Orientalism, whose strengths and weaknesses are still with us in the anthropological study of India (Inden 1986a, 1986b).

Hierarchy in Place

It remains now to ask, more generally, about the circumstances under which certain anthropological images—such as hierarchy—become hegemonic in, and confined to, certain places. This question is inescapably both historical and comparative.

From the comparative point of view, ideas or images that become metonyms for places in anthropological discourse appear to share certain properties. First, for the nonspecialist they provide a shorthand for *summarizing* the cultural complexity that has already been constituted by existing ethnography. By extension, they provide a handy guide for navigating through new (or newly discovered) ethnographies without getting lost in the minutiae of the locality. Although some ethnographies become classics because they are compelling works of literature, most routine ethnographies profit from those summarizing metonyms that provide a point of orientation for the nonspecialist reader. Of course, this does nothing to increase the likelihood that the nonspecialist is likely to pick up the situational diversities of these local worlds.

Second, from the point of view of the specialists who work on a place, certain ideas or images are likely to become hegemonic because they capture something important about the place that transcends intraregional variations and that is, at the same time, *problematic,* because it is subject to ethnographic or methodological question. Thus, hierarchy is (at least in some of its Dumontian meanings) undeniably a striking feature of Indian society, but its exact status is profoundly debatable. For the specialist, images like hierarchy acquire their appeal not because they ease the labors of traveling through the jungles of other people's ethnographies, but because they are compelling ideas around which to organize *debate,* whether such debate is about method, about fact, about assumptions, or about empirical variations.

Finally, neither of the above properties is quite sufficient to guarantee that a particular idea (expressed as a term or a phrase) will become hegemonic in regard to the construction of a place. It is also important that the image provide a credible link between internal realities (and specialist accounts of them) and external preoccupations (and their larger discursive contexts). The most resilient images linking places and cultural themes, such as honor-and-shame in the circum-Mediterranean, hierarchy in India, ancestor-worship in China, *compadrazgo* in Hispanic America, and the like, all capture internal realities in terms that serve the discursive needs of general theory in the metropolis.

This hypothesis about the images of place in anthropology needs to be put into a historical perspective as well. Such hegemonic ideas not only come into being in specific conjunctures but are also liable to being pushed out of favor by other such ideas. What accounts for such shifts is not easy to talk about in a general way, or in a brief space, since it involves the gradual accumulation of small changes in metropolitan theorizing; in local, ethnographically centered debate; and in the relationship between the human sciences in (and in regard to) particular places.

Assuming that such topological stereotypes cost us more in terms of the richness of our understanding of places than they benefit us in rhetorical or comparative convenience, how are we to contest their dominance? Here three possibilities present themselves. The first, exemplified in this essay, is to remain aware that ideas that claim to represent the "essences" of particular places reflect the temporary *localization* of ideas from *many* places. The second is to encourage the production and appreciation of ethnographies that emphasize the *diversity* of themes that can fruitfully be pursued in *any* place.

The third, and most difficult possibility, is to develop an approach to theory in which places could be compared *polythetically* (Needham 1975). In such an approach, there would be an assumption of family resemblances between places, involving overlaps between not one but many characteristics of their ideologies. This assumption would not require places to be encapsulated by single diacritics (or essences) in order for them to be compared with other places, but would permit several configurations of resemblance and contrast. Such a polythetic approach to comparison would discourage us from thinking of places as inhabited by natives, since multiple chains of family resemblance between places would blur any single set of cultural boundaries between them. Without such consistent boundaries, the confinement that lies at the heart of the idea of the native becomes impossible.

Notes

Acknowledgments. Earlier versions of this article were presented at the panel on "Place and Voice in Anthropological Theory," at the 85th Annual Meeting of the American Anthropological Association, Philadelphia, December 1986, and at the Research Colloquium of the Department of Sociology, University of Delhi, in January 1987. I am grateful to colleagues present on each of these occasions for useful comments and suggestions. Comments by Paul Friedrich (on several drafts) and Paul Dresch (on an earlier draft) forced me to clarify key points and eliminate certain errors.

[1] For a fascinating account of the ironies in the historical evolution of such terms as *native, inlander, indigènes,* etc., in the context of Dutch colonialism in Southeast Asia, see Anderson (1983:112–128).

[2] Lest I be seen as excessively critical of the attention that anthropologists have paid to this poetry of confinement, I should add that some of the ethnography that best combines description and theorizing capitalizes on the enmeshment of consciousness in culturally constituted environments: Evans-Pritchard on Nuer time-reckoning (Evans-Pritchard 1940), Irving Hallowell on Saulteaux measurement (Hallowell 1942), Steven Feld on Kaluli poetics (Feld 1982), and Fernandez on the imagery of African revitalization movements (Fernandez 1986).

[3] Hegel's own ideas about Indian religiosity were greatly influenced by the romantic Orientalist treatises of Herder and Schlegel (see Inden 1986a and Schwab 1984).

[4] When I published my own critique of anthropological holism, in the context of a critique of Dumont's ideas (Appadurai 1986b), I had not had the opportunity to see Fernandez (1986). In this essay, Fernandez is concerned with the mechanisms that create "the conviction of wholeness" in African revitalization movements. He is thus able to propose a more optimistic solution to the problem of "cultural wholes" than I was. The time seems ripe for a full-fledged debate about the many dimensions of the problem of cultural wholes and the relationship between them.

[5] Evans-Pritchard seems to have been conscious of this debt, and has stated that one of Maine's most important generalizations was that "kinship and *not* contiguity is the basis of common political action in primitive societies" (Evans-Pritchard 1981:87). Of course, Dumont was also influenced by Maine, but I believe that in this regard, the influence was mediated by Evans-Pritchard.

References Cited

Anderson, Benedict
   1983   Imagined Communities. London: Verso.
Appadurai, Arjun
   1986a   Theory in Anthropology: Center and Periphery. Comparative Studies in Society and History 28(2):356–361.
   1986b   Is Homo Hierarchicus? American Ethnologist 13(4):745–761.
Attinasi, John, and Paul Friedrich
   1987   Dialogic Breakthrough: Catalysis and Synthesis in Life-Changing Dialogue. *In* Toward a Dialogic Anthropology. Bruce Mannheim and Dennis Tedlock, eds. Forthcoming.

Beidelman, T. O.
    1968   Review of W. Robertson Smith, *Kinship and Marriage in Early Arabia*, in Anthropos 63/64:592–595.
Berreman, Gerald D.
    1971   Review of *Homo Hierarchicus*. Man 4:515.
Boon, James
    1982   Other Tribes, Other Scribes: Symbolic Anthropology in the Comparative Study of Cultures, Histories, Religions, and Texts. Cambridge: Cambridge University Press.
Bouglé, C.
    1971   Essays on the Caste System. D. F. Pocock, trans. Cambridge: Cambridge University Press.
Clifford, James, and George Marcus
    1986   Writing Culture: The Poetics and Politics of Ethnography. Berkeley: University of California Press.
Das, Veena
    1977   Structure and Cognition: Aspects of Hindu Caste and Ritual. Delhi: Oxford University Press.
Dumont, Louis
    1970   Homo Hierarchicus: The Caste System and Its Implications. Chicago: University of Chicago Press.
    1986[1983]   Essays on Individualism. Chicago: University of Chicago Press.
Evans-Pritchard, E. E.
    1937   Witchcraft, Oracles and Magic among the Azande. Oxford: Clarendon Press.
    1940   The Nuer. Oxford: Clarendon Press.
    1981   A History of Anthropological Thought. New York: Basic Books.
Fabian, Johannes
    1983   Time and the Other: How Anthropology Makes its Object. New York: Columbia University Press.
Feld, Stephen
    1982   Sound and Sentiment: Birds, Weeping, Poetics and Song in Kaluli Expression. Philadelphia: University of Pennsylvania Press.
Fernandez, James
    1986   The Argument of Images and the Experience of Returning to the Whole. *In* The Anthropology of Experience. Victor W. Turner and Edward M. Bruner, eds. Pp. 159–187. Urbana: University of Illinois Press.
Hallowell, Irving
    1942   Some Psychological Aspects of Measurement among the Saulteaux. American Anthropologist 44:62–67.
Hegel, Georg W. F.
    1902[1837]   Philosophy of History. J. Sibree, trans. New York: Collier.
Hocart, A. M.
    1950   Caste: A Comparative Study. London: Methuen.
Hoffman, Carl
    1986   The Punan: Hunters and Gatherers of Borneo. Ann Arbor: UMI Research Press.
Hughes, Ian
    1977   New Guinea Stone Age Trade: The Geography and Ecology of Traffic in the Interior. Canberra: Department of Prehistory, Research School of Pacific Studies, The Australian National University.

Inden, Ronald B.
  1986a Orientalist Constructions of India. Modern Asian Studies 20(1):1–46.
  1986b Tradition Against Itself. American Ethnologist 13:762–775.
Jay, Martin
  1984 Marx and Totality: The Adventures of a Concept from Lukács to Habermas. Berkeley: University of California Press.
Kolenda, P.
  1976 Seven Types of Hierarchy in *Homo Hierarchicus*. Journal of Asian Studies 35(4):581–596.
Kopytoff, Igor
  1987 The African Frontier: The Reproduction of Traditional African Societies. Bloomington: Indiana University Press.
Marriott, M.
  1969 Review of *Homo Hierarchicus*. American Anthropologist 71:1166–1175.
Mintz, Sidney
  1985 Sweetness and Power: The Place of Sugar in Modern History. New York: Viking.
Myers, F.
  1986 Pintupi Country, Pintupi Self: Sentiment, Place and Politics Among Western Desert Aborigines. Washington, D.C.: Smithsonian Institution Press.
Needham, Rodney
  1975 Polythetic Classification: Convergence and Consequences. Man 10:349–369.
Parry, Jonathan
  1980 Ghosts, Greed and Sin: The Occupational Identity of Benaras Funeral Priests. Man 15(1):18–111.
Schrire, Carmel
  1980 An Enquiry into the Evolutionary Status and Apparent Identity of San Hunter-Gatherers. Human Ecology 8(1):9–32.
Schwab, Raymond
  1984 The Oriental Renaissance: Europe's Rediscovery of India and the East, 1680–1880. Gene Patterson-Black and Victor Reinking, trans. New York: Columbia University Press.
Srinivas, M. N.
  1984 Some Reflections on the Nature of Caste Hierarchy. Contributions to Indian Sociology 18(2):151–167.
Stevenson, H. N. C.
  1954 Status Evaluation in the Hindu Caste System. Journal of the Royal Anthropological Institute 84(1–2):45–65.
Wolf, Eric
  1982 Europe and the People Without History. Berkeley: University of California Press.
Yalman, Nur
  1969 Review of *Homo Hierarchicus*. Man 4:123–131.

Reflecting on the Yanomami: Ethnographic Images and the Pursuit of the Exotic

Alcida R. Ramos

In the world of ethnography certain images are created of entire peoples which remain undisturbed in the reader's memory. The lovely and companionable Pygmies, the proud and intractable Nuer, or the headhunting Jivaro are evocations that come easily to mind. Malinowski's Trobrianders still maintain the old magic of kula voyagers, even though Weiner (1976) has told another story. That each ethnographer produces a unique portrait of the people studied is neither news nor is it surprising, since field experiences are forged as much, or more, by the ethnographer as by the people. This becomes particularly evident when two or more anthropologists do research with the same people. In most cases pioneer ethnographers are followed by other researchers after long contact with the West has brought about fundamental changes in the people being studied. The result is a substantial historical leap and not merely a temporal distance separating the former from the latter. Apart from those cases of acrimonious accusations of incorrect research procedures (as in the Freeman-Mead affair), the divergences that emerge are most often attributed, with varying degrees of persuasion, to the discontinuity of time and events intervening between the two moments of fieldwork. However, when you have several ethnographers working simultaneously in the same general area, it is easier to appreciate the twists and turns of personal preferences in describing *a* culture.[1]

For two decades the Yanomami, at least in the United States, have been Napoleon Chagnon's Fierce People. They have caught the academic and popular imagination ever since Chagnon put them on the map with the publication of his monograph in 1968. For 30 years the Yanomami have been visited by film crews, linguists, anthropologists, geographers, not to mention missionaries, from a good many places: Germany, the United States, Britain, France, Brazil, Venezuela, Italy, Switzerland, Japan. Chagnon was neither the first nor the last among them, but his book has had more impact than all the others added together.

Being recognized as the largest indigenous group in the Americas still little touched by drastic changes from the outside world has been a mixed blessing for the Yanomami. They have been the object of fantasies both in film and book form, of journalistic sensationalism as well as of vast political campaigns in defense of their human rights. I want to discuss the phenomenon of image creating by taking the Yanomami as the focus of attention of three ethnographers who have done extensive fieldwork among them throughout the 60s, 70s, and 80s.

What are the Yanomami like? To such an apparently simple question there is no simple answer. Reading the three authors selected here one might be tempted to characterize these Indians as fierce people, or as erotic people, or as introspective intellectuals. Consider also Eric Michaels's comments on two specific instances of film recording: ''I was particularly impressed by the pervasive differences between the films and the tapes. The fierce people whom Asch recorded in a manner that made my students recoil became transformed into attractive human figures in the Downey tapes'' (1982:135). Add to this the superb photographic work by Claudia Andujar (Tassara and Andujar 1983), where the Yanomami are mostly depicted as contemplative mystics on an endless metaphysical quest, and we have as varied a gamut of representations as we might ever hope to get for a single people: brutal, amiable, mystical, macho, fun lovers, pornographers, sages, warmongers.

Are the Yanomami one of the above, all of the above, or none? The old story of knowing the elephant by piecemeal discovery of its parts by differently located observers does not seem appropriate here (nor perhaps anywhere). There is no such thing as an elephant out there, waiting to be put together as a jigsaw puzzle. The sum of the parts does not make up a positive totality acknowledged as such by all concerned. Rather, each ethnographer constructs his own Yanomami totality, and the tools for his construction are provided by his personal inclinations as much as by the specific tool kit of anthropology from which he draws.

Having done fieldwork myself among various subgroups of the Yanomami, I recognize in all of the ethnographic descriptions available a nagging sense of family resemblance. Yet none quite matches my own perception of the people I know. From 1968 to 1985 I spent 27 months among the Sanumá of the Auaris river valley, two months among the Shiriana of the Uraricoera river valley, and three and a half months among the Yanomam of the Catrimani river valley, all in Brazil. In each location I have found a different ethos, a greater or lesser tolerance toward foreigners, and a definite linguistic and social singularity. Nevertheless, I perceive them all as unquestionably Yanomami. One of the most fascinating intellectual games for me during my last stay with the Shiriana was to witness the transformations and permutations constantly displayed as I heard words and watched actions that were so similar and yet so different from the others I had known before. If there is such a thing as a Yanomami mode of being, such a field of ''Yanomaminess'' is so vast that many pictures can be made of it, each one the unique result of the combination of particular Indians with a particular ethnographer in particular situations.

My intention is not to do a biography of these ethnographers, a project for which I have neither the competence nor a special interest. What I am proposing to do is a personal reading of their works that would allow me to see them through the images they built of the Yanomami: their choice of genre and style, of themes, of emphases, of theoretical models, of conclusions, hoping to understand why it is that with each new book or thesis a new face of the Yanomami is drawn. It is, in short, a tricky exercise in seeing the ethnographer through the eyes of his own creation. Being a Yanomami ethnographer myself, my position is not that of an impartial onlooker, but what one might call a "privileged observer."

The opportunity for this exercise is the recent translation into English of Jacques Lizot's *Le Cercle des Feux,* and the appearance of Bruce Albert's important doctoral dissertation. The three texts discussed here are thus Chagnon's *Yãnomamö: The Fierce People,* Lizot's *Tales of the Yanomami: Daily Life in the Venezuelan Forest,* and Albert's *Temps du Sang, Temps des Cendres: Représentations de la Maladie, Système Rituel et Espace Politique chez les Yanomami du Sudest (Amazonie Brésilienne).*All three write on warfare, aggressiveness, and drama, but each one constructs a different world with these elements. They differ in their emphases on subject matter, on choice of rhetorical style, and on audiences aimed at. It should be pointed out that Lizot has worked in the same area as Chagnon with the Yãnomamö subgroup of the Orinoco-Mavaca region in Venezuela, whereas Albert has done fieldwork among the Yanomam subgroup (more often spelled Yãnomamë by Albert) of the Catrimani river valley in Brazil, many miles away from the other two.[2] All of them have had contact with the Yanomami for at least ten years. Each ethnographer appears as either the main protagonist, an omnipresent but invisible companion, or a diligent observer. Depending on how much each of them allows the curtain to be lifted, his Yanomami appear more or less visible, more or less tangible, more or less believable. The ethnographer is in control.

Fierce?

Waiteri is translated by Chagnon as "fierce." Other renderings both from the Yãnomamö and from other subgroups stress different features. Lizot glosses *wait^{h}eri* as "both physical courage—the capacity to bear great pain—and the ability to return blows" (1985:194). To Albert the term *waithiri,* as used by the Yanomam of the Catrimani region, ties together the virtues of humor, generosity, and bravery.

> The *waithiri* man must therefore be capable of showing himself fearless in battle and ready to publicly demonstrate the power of his determination when the situation so demands, but also to show little concern for his possessions and be a virtuoso in matters of irony and, better still, of self-derision. [Albert 1985:97]

Out of the multivaried complexity of this important concept, Chagnon chose the English word "fierce" as its sole translation. Actually, the innuendos one finds at several points in his book belie this oversimplification, for much of the proclaimed Yãnomamö fierceness is displayed tongue-in-cheek, which, in turn, is interpreted by the ethnographer as demonstrations of not quite trustworthy behavior, or plain mischief.

Chagnon's writing is vivid, dynamic, and at times very funny. Some examples: "Many amused Yãnomamö onlookers quickly learned the English phrase

'Oh, Shit!' . . . and, once they discovered that the phrase offended and irritated the missionaries, they used it as often as they could in their presence'' (Chagnon 1983:12).[3] On the interchange between him and a Yãnomamö man, first, when the anthropologist was being watched eating frankfurters: '' 'Shãki! what part of the animal are you eating?' . . . 'Guess.' He muttered a contemptuous epithet, but stopped asking for a share'' (Chagnon 1983:14); later, when the anthropologist was being watched eating honey: '' 'Shãki! what kind of animal semen are you pouring onto your food and eating?' His question had the desired effect and my meal ended'' (Chagnon 1983:15). *Waitheri* exchanges such as these occur often throughout his book in situations not always as lightweight as having a meal on stage.

His Yãnomamö society is a strongly emphasized male world. It is the men who tell stories, take drugs, kill people, hunt animals, do all the exciting things a Westerner would hope to find in the jungle. They are the quintessence of the primitive tribe in the wilderness of unspoiled lifeways. They are ''fierce'' in doing all those thrilling things and even in their domestic endeavors, when they occasionally chop an ear or two off their wives. In Chagnon's exuberant style the Yãnomamö come out as energetic, high-strung, vicious, and vivacious men. By contrast, his women, when at all visible, appear as overburdened, battered, meek, uninteresting, or worse: ''By the time a woman is 30 years old she has 'lost her shape' and has developed a rather unpleasant disposition. Women tend to seek refuge and consolation in each other's company, sharing their misery with their peers'' (Chagnon 1983:114). In Chagnon's analysis they are the cause of all the fighting and warfare of their men. And yet, somehow, women manage to press and impress the men enough to keep them on their toes:

> They are therefore concerned with the political behavior of their men and occasionally goad them into taking action against some possible enemy by caustically accusing the men of cowardice. This has the effect of establishing the village's reputation for ferocity, reducing the possibility of raiders abducting the women while they are out collecting firewood or garden produce. The men cannot stand being belittled by the women in this fashion, and are forced to take action if the women unite against them. [Chagnon 1983:114]

So much for female powerlessness.

In May 1976, *Time* magazine published the following:

> . . . the rather horrifying Yãnomamö culture makes some sense in terms of animal behavior. Chagnon argues that Yãnomamö structures closely parallel those of many primates in breeding patterns, competition for females and recognition of relatives. Like baboon troops, Yãnomamö villages tend to split into two after they reach a certain size. [*Time*, 10 May 1976:37]

That was before the second edition of *Yãnomamö: The Fierce People*. *Time*'s piece triggered off angry responses from anthropologists and missionaries (see *Time*'s Forum section of 31 May 1976:1), and probably overwhelmed Chagnon himself, judging by the considerable changes he made in the third edition, toning down or deleting statements that precipitated such embarrassing publicity.[4] Tone down he did, but readers of the 1983 edition still find reason to agree with the *Time* article in saying that Chagnon is "chronicling a culture built around persistent aggression—browbeating, goading, ritual displays of ferocity, fighting and constant warfare."

The third edition totally eliminated the discussion of what had been one of the main pillars of his argument for explaining aggressive behavior, that is, female infanticide, also picked up by *Time:*

> . . . the Yãnomamö practice female infanticide—on the grounds that males are more valuable to a people always at war. Yet infanticide sets up fierce competition for marriageable females, both within and among villages, and this in turn produces chronic warfare.

Throughout the years this vicious circle received decreasing attention in Chagnon's writings, starting with his doctoral dissertation in 1966, until it was dropped altogether in the latest edition of *The Fierce People.*

The reason for abandoning the female infanticide theme may not have been entirely due to the incredulity of critics or the use made of it by the news media, but perhaps to its having been adopted by Marvin Harris and his followers as a major prop to their protein theory of warfare. Chagnon takes issue with them in the third edition, not once confirming or denying the existence of female infanticide. It is as if he had never mentioned it in the first place. So, not only do the same people look different in the eyes of different observers, but the same observer, for whatever reason, can change his outlook about them as time goes by. Yesterday Yãnomamö women shocked the world by killing their baby girls. Today no one would know that ever happened, were it not for Harris's reminders from time to time.

The latest edition of the *Fierce People* also presents clearer theoretical stances than was the case previously. Paying lip service to structuralism via an unconvincing presentation of a Yãnomamö nature/culture dichotomy, Chagnon declares his allegiance to sociobiology, a trait already detectable in the first edition, but only implicitly so. Such a theoretical inclination is very consistent with his emphasis on aggression, demography, reproductive patterns, and territorial expansion. It is to Chagnon's credit that he succeeds so well in keeping an interest in the people, maintaining a constant relationship with their individuality, while working on such depersonalizing issues. At no time do Chagnon's Yãnomamö men show themselves to be boring, faceless, mere objects of research. They are full of life, verve, and humor, or unbearable at times, making the ethnographer wish he were doing fieldwork with someone else, such as the neighboring Yekuana.[5]

Chagnon is the uncontested boss of his text. He tailored it in such a way as to keep a constant counterpoint between the aggressiveness of the Yãnomamö and his own feats of daring. He is in full command. He never lets any of the proverbial and inevitable clumsiness, ignorance, and blunders of the incompetent neophyte impair his authority in the field. Once he masters his kitchen and laundry chores, under the entertained gaze of the forever joking Yãnomamö, he is in business: he makes canoes, he hunts, he dispenses medicines, he may or may not permit the Indians to share his food or his cigarette butts, he shouts back at them, he takes hallucinogens, chants to the *hekura* spirits and gets himself photographed by tourists, he even has a close encounter with a live jaguar. In fact, the more intractable the Yãnomamö and the jungle show themselves to be, the more exciting his life in the field becomes.

Especially in the now much longer introduction and in the new conclusion, it is as if the Indians are there for little more purpose than to provide the necessary local color and scenic backdrop for his adventures, be they negotiating clogged rivers, visiting hostile villages, or challenging the missionaries. Narcissus in the bush, Chagnon casts his own shadow too far onto the Yãnomamö *shabono* and onto his text. Like Evans-Pritchard (Geertz 1983), he involves the reader by choosing the right pronoun at the right time: "Once *you* are on good terms with *your hekura, you* can engage in sex without having *your* spirits abandon *you*" (Chagnon 1983:107, emphasis mine). Like Lizot, he pays a lot of attention to sexual matters, with the justification that "sex is a big thing in Yãnomamö myths . . . If I were to illustrate the dictionary I have been patiently collecting on my field trips, it would be, as one of my puckish graduate students once commented, very good pornography" (Chagnon 1983:94).

Between 1968 and 1983 prolonged contact with the Yãnomamö has mellowed his pen, to a certain extent. He now writes dearly of his Yãnomamö friends and shows other dimensions of their world besides violence: "Some Yãnomamö play with their rich language and work at being what we might call literary or learned" (Chagnon 1983:90). Or,

> Some of the characters in Yãnomamö myths are downright hilarious, and some of the things they did are funny, ribald, and extremely entertaining to the Yãnomamö, who listen to men telling mythical stories or chanting episodes of mythical sagas as they prance around the village, tripping out on hallucinogens, adding comical twists and nuances to the side-splitting delight of their audiences. [Chagnon 1983:93]

His engaging style, with imagery drawn from Western *waitheri* realms ("I was learning the Yãnomamö equivalent of a left jab to the jawbone" [Chagnon 1983:16]), is greatly responsible for the wide acceptance of his monograph, catching the imagination of undergraduates, journalists, and other exotica-hungry audiences.

Erotic?

Lizot's Yãnomamö don't just make love. They do it with a vengeance. A good part of his book is dedicated to descriptions of masturbating practices, amorous encounters between boys, between girls, between boys and girls, as well as descriptions of many adulterous trysts. Chapter 2, entitled "Love Stories," begins with the amusing remark: "The young Yanomami's sexuality is not repressed as long as it remains discreet and limited"! Moreover, "Everything here is very natural"! (Lizot 1985:31).

Discretion and naturality, however, are overridden by Lizot's voyeurism. For six years, as stated in the preface of this English edition, he was a go-between in most of the love stories he tells and sometimes a witness too. The results are passages such as this:

> She discovered then that prolonged fondling could give pleasure. She learned how to recapture the sensations she experienced with her friend: She could bring about her own body's enjoyment. She would go off alone to rub her vulva softly against a hump on a tree trunk, or she would invite her friend, or others whom she would initiate in turn. [Lizot 1985:68]

or this:

> Brahaima puts her leg on the young man's thighs, and his desire is aroused by that invitation. They go on with their conversation; Tōtōwë is excited and no longer knows what he is saying. Soon a hand is touching his groin; he wants to prevent the expected caress and protects himself with his hand. Intimidated by Rubrowë's presence, he wants to leave, but is asked to stay a while. He is about to make up his mind to make move when the bright disk of the sun slowly emerges, casting its light under the roof. [Lizot 1985:42]

Parenthetically, romantic as it may be, this passage would very likely get a chuckle of disbelief from the Yãnomamö, for no one in their right mind would remain in bed, or rather in hammock, by the time the sun is up (apart from the sick or the anthropologists). Healthy human beings are up and about while it is still dark; the loving couple would have been disturbed many times over before the bright disk of the sun emerged from behind the tall trees of the forest surrounding the village.

This brings us to an aspect of Lizot's book that is clearly its most striking feature, falling as it does into that fuzzy gray area between ethnography and admitted fiction. Unlike Chagnon, he does not impose on the reader the weight of his presence in the narrative, or the forceful assertion that he was there, really, factually, positivistically. Of course, Lizot is perfectly aware of all this: "I wanted to recede into the background as completely as possible. Nevertheless, it is an obvious fact that I am the one who is observing, reporting, describing, organizing the narrative" (Lizot 1985:xiv). His unorthodox way of resolving his experiences into ethnographic writing is explicitly acknowledged: "The way of presenting an incident or a story and of arranging it according to one's fancy is one form of ethnographic reality" (Lizot 1985:xiv). Be that as it may, his invisibility is his special tool for carving out of memory his image of the Yãnomamö, and he uses it to the full by taking liberties that would make many a conservative colleague cringe with discomfort.

An invisible observer, or absent participant, omnipresent and indiscreet with the sardonic eye of a voyeur, he takes the reader along to watch intimate encounters, listen to myth telling, probe into emotional states, or accompany devious acts. He does not tell us how he does it. But then, he doesn't need to; his style is self-revealing. His tense is the present, his narrative, being an amalgamation of multiple events, cannot be fixed in points of time. Past and present are fused; his denial of retrospection makes the present tense imperative. The following example has been picked at random:

> The others follow suit, walking on the bank. They come near the *rahara* [a water monster], and it is Hebëwë, who has been here before with his father, who first realizes it. They are going to cross on an enormous trunk spanning the stream. Around them spreads a tapir's feeding ground etched with countless hoofprints and trails that the big herbivores use to come here and forage in the earth. Fear and foreboding rise in Hebëwë as he recognizes the place more and more positively. He is thinking: "This is it, the monster lives here." He is about to speak and warn the others, when Frẽrema, who is walking ahead, suddenly turns back. He makes hand signals telling the others to squat down and, in a low voice, warns them of the danger. [Lizot 1985:151]

Having the ever-present narrator hovering over them has the effect of lending the Yãnomamö an unreal quality, as if they were characters in a play rather than people going about their daily lives. It also arouses cravings for the exotic. Even though hidden from view, Lizot is reflected on the Yãnomamö figures he creates. Here is an ethnographer who weaves a plot of characters where certain things are done: daily chores, quarrels in the village, raids against other villages, shamanism, magic spells, and a lot of sex. But rather than just letting the Yãnomamö do them, he makes them perform them, as if intent on amusing an audience that is always there, waiting for the next skit. Perhaps having Chagnon just across the river, at least some of the time, and missionaries all around would be enough to make anyone self-conscious and stage-oriented. Provoking as it is, nevertheless, Lizot's sometimes-belabored style has the effect of nearly stifling the Yãnomamö, who go about the text displaying their Yanomaminess as *dramatis personae* in a script. They seem to depend, more than usually, on the narrator to control their moods and actions. Yet, oddly enough, or perhaps for this very reason, his Yãnomamö are less adventuresome, less vivid, and somewhat more cynical than Chagnon's. The same could be said of Lizot himself, as mirrored on his own writing.

The interesting quality of his narrative is not diminished by these remarks; it is an engaging and lively piece of writing, as, for instance, in the village scene where visitors sojourn:

> The shelter hums with overflowing life. Long-sustained, shrill, and repeated cascades of laughter flare up everywhere, provoked by jokes or funny memories. News items are passed along, often amplified and distorted; tattletales take delight in gossip and scandalmongering. Plans are laid, never to be realized. Youths compete for the girls' attention, and jealous, suspicious husbands tighten their vigilance. Special friendships are strengthened, others are born. Personal alliances are formed, jealousness and hatreds are set off. What dominates, however, is the breath of friendship that circulates through the whole shelter, warm as a fire after a drenching rain. [Lizot 1985:127]

Picturesque prose such as this compensates for lack of depth. Lizot does not reveal any particular theoretical inclination when it comes to *Tales of the Yanomami*. Loosely woven, his narrative lets people in and out of view, leaving behind vignettes that succeed each other with no recognizable line of development, as if at random. With perhaps one exception, there are no portraits, only snapshots or camera sequences.

Lizot makes an effort (or so he claims) to minimize the image of the fierce Yãnomamö, which is laudable but not entirely successful. Women are still brutalized, at least some of them; men are still aggressive and warmongering, at least some of the time; youths are still a nuisance to adults, at least to some adults. What is especially disturbing is that Lizot's Yãnomamö seem to be so very whimsical in their nastiness, inflicting pain on others for no other reason than that it strikes their fancy. This, too, contributes to the impression of characters on stage. In the attempt to free his text of any cluttering academic jargon, Lizot falls into the other extreme, with the unfortunate result of making his protagonists seem rather inconsequential. In this respect it is interesting to point out that the English title captures the spirit of the book much better than the original, *Le Cercle des Feux: Faits et Dits des Indiens Yanomami*, as a series of stories, tales, where the deeds and words of the Yanomami are heavily filtered by an overdose of what Sperber has called "free indirect speech" (1985:18).

Like Chagnon, Lizot attributes to the women the aggressive behavior of the men: "Men fight first of all because they are competing for the possession of women" (Lizot 1985:114). Also like Chagnon, he finds war to be a constant. But unlike Chagnon, Lizot attempts to put violence into a more balanced perspective, even though his tales go a long way to undermine his initial claims:

> I would like my book to help revise the exaggerated representation that has been given of Yanomami violence. The Yanomami are warriors; they can be brutal and cruel, but they can also be delicate, sensitive, and loving. Violence is sporadic; it never dominates social life for any length of time, and long peaceful moments can separate two explosions. [Lizot 1985:xv]

He feels the need to assert that "these Indians are human beings" (Lizot 1985:xv).

If that is so, why do these two authors place so much emphasis on violence? They can hardly describe a trip to the garden without getting involved in stories of aggression, sometimes with gory details. Are the Yãnomamö of the Orinoco-Mavaca region forever giving each other a hard time, do they tailor their figures to impress their ethnographers, or could it be the other way around? Other tribal societies have been reported for their violent practices, such as the headhunting Jivaro and Mundurucu, or the Guaikuru, for instance, yet violence has not stuck to their ethnographic reputation in any outstanding way compared to the Yãnomamö. Chagnon claims that the sensationalism built around the Yãnomamö has to do with the fact that their aggressive behavior is not something of the past, but still goes on and can actually be witnessed by fieldworkers. Not entirely convincing, this argument raises some issues which will be expounded in the last section of this article.

Intellectual?

Bruce Albert rebels against what he calls lyric impressionism and the myth of violence. His long doctoral dissertation (833 tightly typed pages) departs drastically from both Chagnon's and Lizot's books. The nature of his text is more Malinowskian in its unrelenting ethnographic detail and realism than anything we find in the other two authors or, for that matter, in most ethnographies. His position is quite clear in this respect:

> The impressionism more or less lyric with which one might describe their way of life and its framework seems to me . . . to be much less satisfying than the theoretical effort to do justice to the complex intricacies of their intellectual universe. [Albert 1985:136–137]

It is possible to read this passage and, adding the impact of the plethora of ethnographic data that follows, interpret it to suggest that justice to the people studied is in direct proportion to the theoretical effort and the toiling of the ethnographer who attempts to unravel the tangle of ethnographic material. Following this line of reasoning, as a parenthetical remark, I would like to touch upon another dimension of ethnographic writing. Since reality can never be exhausted—some say it may not even be representable—anything that the ethnographer chooses to concentrate on, no matter how detailed, is always the result of a personal option. Ethnographic facts are not out there on the ground to be picked up by the competent anthropologist, but are the result of a complex process of give-and-take in the interaction between observer and observed. On the other hand, for whom he writes and what he writes about have immediate bearings on how the ethnographer writes. Rich ethnographies are always welcome, but a flood of ethnographic detail, although a valuable reservoir for anthropological thinking, may not necessarily do more justice to the people than an impressionistic piece, if all it does is bore the reader and pass unnoticed. Fortunately, this is not Albert's case.[6]

Guiding his remarkable ethnographic effort is the model of structuralism, the search for mental structures that would counteract catchy epithets and facile characterizations:

> "Fierce people" or "Amiable savages," the Yanomami appear all too often in the literature dedicated to them as lacking the taste for a *"pensée sauvage"* and cut a poor figure among lowland South American societies reputed for their profuse "idealism." In this work we hope, therefore, to also contribute to reestablish an image of their culture which can be more congenial with reality. [Albert 1985:137]

Reality in Albert's work is revealed in a long, highly elaborate and complex interlocking set of symbolic realms, which he chooses to cluster around the central theme of representations of disease. This rich, symbolic apparatus, in turn, makes sense of much of what goes on in political and social affairs. Since I am dealing with an unpublished dissertation, a summary of its major thrust must be provided, even at the risk of distortion and impoverishment. It is an intricate weaving of a lush symbolic world that defies any urge for brevity.

Like a Magister Ludi, Albert constructs a refined glass bead game, in which each pearl of information is expandable into a universe of its own. The Yanomam concept of blood is the thread holding the pieces together, be it the blood of enemies (in substance or in symbol), or of first menstruation. Too little of it makes time go too fast, too much of it makes time go too slowly. In the oscillation between prolonged immaturity and precocious senility resides the secret of keeping the world in order by obeying death and puberty rites. What causes disease and death is not a simple matter. It requires a long march through layer upon layer of esoteric and practical native knowledge.

Albert starts his analysis with a schematic account of village distribution, their historical interconnections, marriage networks, matters of residence and descent: a preliminary skeleton onto which much symbolic flesh will be attached in the remainder of the work. That is followed by a richly detailed presentation of how the Yanomam person is constructed and what its strengths and weaknesses are. It is the vulnerability of the human (that is, Yanomam) body that permits the formulation of an array of magical procedures designed to attack or protect various kinds of people, that is, coresidents of the same communal house, allies, actual enemies, potential enemies, and those totally unknown. Thus, there are five spheres of social cognition to which an intricate ideology of magical aggression is applied. Yanomam war, Albert says, is better for thinking than for killing (Albert 1985:98). And think they do, all the way from the practical business of cultivating and preparing magical plants to the endowment of supernatural powers to material and nonmaterial entities.

Of course, expressions of violence are not limited to warfare, which by Albert's account is relatively rare. Violence includes such things as physical and magical assault, but never in a blind or capricious fashion:

> . . . everything is done in Yanomam culture so as to channel violence by avoiding it or by providing it with formal frameworks: the rules for expressing anger, the ritualization of confrontation (duels, war), or its attendant loop-holes (humor, generosity). [Albert 1985:98]

The degree of virulence of magical formulas and attacks defines the tenor of political relationships between villages. Magical agents (what Albert calls "pathogenic powers") include the use of special plants, dirt with footprints, shaman's assistant spirits, and "alter ego" animals, the obligatory double of every human being (that is, Yanomam). Within the same residential unit there is no incidence of magical attack; among friendly neighbors "sorcery of alliance" is responsible for some illnesses, but not deaths; between enemies "war sorcery" can kill twice as much as it causes diseases; with distant villages ("virtual or ancient enemies") aggressive shamanism can do harm with little killing; and with unknown people, those who live in the outer limits of the social world, the killing of one's animal double is the only way of aggression, resulting in few casualties. It is important to emphasize that one's double is always located far away, in the territory of those people on the fringes of recognized humanity.

Most illnesses can be cured with shamanism, particularly if caused by sorcery of alliance. War sorcery is much more serious and may kill people. Deaths caused by human intention—and most of them are—send the killers into a state of extreme danger and pollution. While the deceased's body is decaying, hung from a tree somewhere in the forest, the killer has to "eat the trace" *(unokaimu)* of his victim. In seclusion, he fasts and remains silent for days, while going through the symbolic motions of cannibalism, eating the flesh, fat, and blood of the deceased. Before he consumes all that, and grease oozes out of his forehead, he cannot return to normal life. His ordeal ends with vomiting, by which time the cleaned bones of the corpse are ready for cremation. Cremation and burial or consumption of the bone ashes ensure the definitive separation of the dead from the living. This system defies, of course, concrete verification, for a killer in one village may not in fact have caused anybody's death. In turn, death in a particular village, when diagnosed as the result of war sorcery, or the killing of an animal double, presupposes the *unokaimu* rite by an alleged killer. The Yanomam do not need empirical proof to have their symbolic system in operation.

Should the killer fail to perform this ritual, he would shrivel away into premature old age. Of crucial importance here is the place of blood in the cosmic order:

> Blood *(iyē)* which irrigates the flesh *(iyēhikë)* thus constitutes for the Yanomamë the fundamental agent of physiological development and for that reason it is the privileged symbolic referent of biological time. [Albert 1985:349]

By the same token, the first menstruation is equally surrounded by ritual care. In seclusion, the young girl fasts and remains silent for days, just like her murderous male counterpart. Should she break the rules of the ritual, a cataclysm would ensue in the form of an ominous flood which, according to mythical lore, would destroy village, people and all, and, last but not least, bring about the Whiteman.

The combination of controlling the blood flow of humans with the care to separate the living from the dead by means of cremation is the backbone of normal life. On the one hand, male death rites maintain the normal time rhythm of the individual and the dead/living distinction; on the other, the female puberty ritual ensures both individual normal timing and an adequate cosmic periodicity.

A universe of intellectual elaboration is opened up by Albert, shedding unprecedented light into Yanomami ethnographic materials. Much of what seems spotty or whimsical in Chagnon's and Lizot's accounts make more sense in view of the symbolic articulations spelled out by Albert. Granting the fact that he has worked with a different subgroup, one can easily recognize within the bounds of family resemblance what would or would not be pertinent to the Yānomamö of the Orinoco-Mavaca region.

Death, cremation, puberty, magic, and specters are not only good for Yanomam thinking, they are also extremely fascinating for an anthropologist with structuralist inclinations. Albert's work is generous in matrices and tables demonstrating by permutations and combinations that murder and menstruation are transformations of each other, and are statements about the minds through which they are elaborated. To the extent that Albert allows his formalist vein to take charge, his Yanomam become pieces in a clever intellectual game. This game, however, is not the main gist of his work. The spirit, and often the letter of his study is to pay tribute to the inventiveness and creativity of the Yanomam, a far cry from the rather impoverished figure of Chagnon's "homo bellicosus" or Lizot's "homo/femina eroticus/a." The many contemplative moments in Albert's journey into Yanomam symbolism turn into lively action in the description of a death festival and in the myriad of colorful remarks in his footnotes. There is, however, the sensation of great redundancy in that intellectual universe, as if the Yanomam, or their ethnographer, could not risk having their point lost on others or on themselves.

A diligent and admiring observer, Albert probes into Yanomam minds and lets them talk through long quotations in their language. He only concedes to appear to his public in one short passage and in a footnote, once his credentials as a student of anthropology and assiduous fieldworker have been established in the introduction. In these brief moments he handles material that occupies many a page in Chagnon's book: being deluged with requests for his possessions:

> The ludic paroxysm of the *reahu* [death festival], and even the few instances of respite on that night, will be occupied, for want of something better, in driving to derision one last time (at least for the guests) an ethnographer who too often clings to his notebook: "aren't you asleep? lend me your flashlight! the enemy sorcerers will kill me if I go out for a piss in the dark!" . . . "give me your pen! my body paint is fading away!" . . . "I'm bringing a piece of meat . . . I want a piece of your manioc cake to go with it!" . . . "my thigh itches! I want medicine!" ". . . give me beads right away . . . I'm furious . . . the women refuse me their vaginas!" [Albert 1985:493]

and being reproached for meddling in the secret realm of personal names:

> The ethnographer, impudent and clumsy collector of names of the dead, is often threatened with death right after his blunders. "If you were a Yãnomamë I would have killed you long ago," concluded one of my informants regularly; a genealogist despite himself, he heroically attempted to change his extreme irritation into mere condescendence at the end of our interviews. [Albert 1985:399]

What is highlighted by Albert in these passages is not violence or obnoxious behavior, but the humorist ethos of hedonist men at the peak of a high-power festival, and the humility of an outsider who recognizes how his importune intrusion can drive to its limits the patience of his informants. It is noteworthy that throughout his long dissertation not once does Albert drop a single Yanomam name to identify people. All in all, Albert provides us with a profound, scholarly, and refreshingly new way of looking at the Yanomami, counterbalancing the appeal to exoticism that is present in so much that has been said and written about these Indians.

The Cost of Being Exotic

Popular visions of primitive peoples with bizarre customs are usually generated by travel writers, colonists, and the like, often exploiting cruelty and other shocking practices.[7] These are then followed by sobering, professional works by anthropologists who then attempt to cut down on the exotica and bridge the cultural gap between those primitives and Western audiences. Not so with the Yanomami. The sensationalism that has plagued them has been precipitated by the first publication of *Yãnomamö: The Fierce People* in 1968. A rare occasion in the history of anthropology, for ethnographic writing seldom achieves so much visibility outside academia. But, with the book's success goes the dubious merit of exposing the Yanomami people to a barrage of abusive imagery.

Following in Chagnon's footsteps, Lizot produced a collection of Yãnomamö tales (originally published in 1976), which was meant to counterbalance the stereotype of fierce people by then attached to the Yanomami. The 1970s and early 80s have been prodigal in outlandish stories told in film and book about these wild Indians of South Venezuela (for a number of reasons the Brazilian Yanomami have been spared much of this). A particularly hideous example was a film called "Canibal Holocausto," an Italian production with an all-white cast purportedly depicting Yanomami Indians engaged in extraordinary orgies of cannibalism and sadistic relish. Its pornographic content was so extreme that the Swiss government prohibited its exhibition, so the story goes; it was also denounced by the Interamerican Indigenist Institute during a meeting held in Ecuador in 1981.

Less delirious but also controversial is *Shabono,* a book authored by Florinda Donner, whose identity remains somewhat mysterious. At play in the fields of Amazonia, somewhere in a nonidentified piece of Venezuelan jungle, Donner tantalizes the reader with great adventures and love affairs with the Indians, thus detonating a minor scandal in the profession (Holmes 1983; Picchi 1983; see also Pratt 1986). Indeed, there seems to be no end to sensationalism when it comes to the Yanomami. Recently, another North American anthropologist, Ken Good, has made his debut into the Hall of Fame via *People* magazine (19 January 1987:24–29), by telling the story of his marriage to a Yãnomamö girl. Profusely illustrated, the article picks up on her newly acquired taste for Philadelphia's junk food. Good is quoted as saying:

> That's all she wants to eat [unsalted french fries]. That and plantains. Bananas won't do, so I spent half my time buying out the city's supply of plantains. Then there's all the tobacco leaves I buy. She rolls them in wads, then puts one behind her lower lip and that keeps her satisfied for hours.

As husbands go, it could be worse, or so Chagnon might perhaps say. At this Yãnomamö girl's expense, wild thing turned into a zoo attraction, much mileage is being made into the realm of exotica.

What is there about the Yanomami that so ignites white men's and women's imaginations? Bruce Albert calls it *"nostalgie de l'exotism"* (Albert 1985:3). Let us take a closer look at this idea. Exoticism is not created by a particular subject matter as such, but by the mode of expression used to describe it. The exotic, says Stephen Foster, "is thereby reified and institutionalized, no longer a metaphor for the culturally unknown." With rhetorical devices, one can create "the illusion that the exotic is in the world rather than of the imagination" (Foster 1982:27), a point magnificently demonstrated by Said in his *Orientalism*.

Granting that Chagnon or any of us "Yanomamists" must have appeared to the Yanomami as exotic in the extreme—eating phallic sausages or inserting contact lenses into one's eyeballs—neither he nor any of us have ever had to worry about the consequences of their judgment for the future of our lives or those of our compatriots. At the time of our first meeting them I am sure the Yanomami did not think of that either. It is when missionaries, government agents, and private entrepreneurs close in on them, demanding that they become more like us (whoever those "us" may be) that the awareness of themselves as being exotic dawns on them. There is no possible symmetry in the mutual disjunction that Indians and anthropologists feel in their first encounters. The consequences of exoticism may be cute for the latter but can become devastating for the former.

The idiom of exoticism has served the West in its crusades of conquest for a long time, but certainly ever since a feather-cloaked Tupinambá Indian was displayed at the French court in the 16th century. What that Tupinambá experienced then may not have been so very different from what Rerebawë, Chagnon's close informant, felt when the anthropologist took him to see Caracas to be convinced once and for all of the vastness of the white man's world (Chagnon 1983:192–198); a mind-boggling, sobering lesson on differential power.

In this day and age, when exotic customs are said to be in short supply, the Yanomami come in handy as scenarios for the projection of narcissistic fantasies which, in turn, are fed into the rhetoric of the "civilizers." From rhetoric to action there is but a short distance. In a world that sees Amazonia as one of the last frontiers to be tapped for its mineral and floral riches, there is little room for tolerance of quaint, unpalatable primitiveness. The more the Yanomami are represented as fierce, immoral and otherwise unchristian, the more easily it is to justify their subjugation, a measure deemed necessary by the powers-that-be if those riches are to be attained. Perhaps inadvertently—and here goes the benefit of the doubt—anthropologists have made their contribution to all that. Foster's timid suggestion that "it may at times have been a pursuit of the exotic rather than the pursuit of an understanding of human society which motivated and motivates anthropologizing" (Foster 1982:30) echoes through Yanomamiland with a disquieting ring of *déjà vu*.

When Bruner says that both anthropologist and Indian are coauthors of ethnographic writings because they are "caught in the same web, influenced by the same historical forces, and shaped by the dominant narrative structures of our times" (Bruner 1986:150), he is talking about a situation of long centuries of contact between North American Indians and whites. Even so, it is questionable whether even the acculturated North American Indian speaks the same ethical and political language as his white ethnographer; and becomes much less likely of indigenous peoples such as the Yanomami who have so far lived according to their own historical forces. They are caught in the same web only by the appropriation that the anthropologist makes of them. Not even the "unhappy conscience" of a self-perceived exotic Yanomami would make him automatically coauthor of, say, *The Fierce People*. Coauthorship takes more than being the subject of a narrative or contributing to the idiom that will be woven into it. I have no qualms against Bruner's assertion that "narratives are not only structures of meaning but structures of power as well" (Bruner 1986:144), so long as the authority of the writer is properly established and recognized. To attribute power where there is none may be as insidious as hiding behind the rhetoric of the exotic.

The consequences of what one writes can go much farther than one might have intended in the first place. Lizot (1970) was the first to point out the risks of exaggeration when he took Ettore Biocca (1971) to task for having edited an account depicting the Yanomami as brutes who, among other things, were in the habit of bashing the heads of little babies against tree trunks. The reputation that such writing generated, argued Lizot, would only supply the national (and international) powers with ammunition for the repression of the Yanomami.[8] Yet one does not assassinate character with impunity. Like Lizot, other anthropologists in Venezuela, Brazil, and elsewhere have objected to such manifestations of insensitivity and have positioned themselves in defense of Yanomami rights, aware of the commitment that goes with our profession.[9]

Much of the work by Anglo-Saxon anthropologists shows that they are not usually concerned with the ethical or political implications that their writings may have for the people they write about. The tradition of telling-it-like-it-is, which values truth above anything else, has downplayed the importance of the anthropologist's social responsibility. An unshakable faith in the notion that one can discover truth and truth shall make one free of responsibility has kept the limits of commitment quite narrow. Now aware of the power that ethnographic writing can have, Chagnon makes a belated and rather dubious as well as presumptuous attempt to call attention to the need for protection of the Yanomami:

> I also hope that my Brazilian and Venezuelan colleagues understand that there are still some very noble people in the remaining isolated and uncontacted Yãnomamö villages who are able to, as Dedeheiwä once proudly told me, teach foreigners something about being human. They are, as one of my anthropology teachers aptly phrased it, our contemporary ancestors. [Chagnon 1983:214]

Exotic indeed![10]

It might be worth remarking that the image of fierceness of the Yanomami has not reached Brazil—in part, no doubt, because Chagnon's book has not been translated into Portuguese and has, therefore, a very limited circulation. More important, however, than this perhaps not so fortuitous oversight, is a very different attitude with regard to the ethics of our métier. The anthropological profession in Brazil cannot afford to ignore the political implications of its own production, given that it is fairly visible as a social agent and thus rendered accountable to a wider and often critical public. To do anthropology in Brazil is already in itself a political act. Academic and politically critical matters are part and parcel

of the same professional endeavor where the quality of the former is not jeopard-
ized by the practice of the latter. This commitment to uphold the social responsibility of the anthropologist is all the more apparent in the field of Indian studies,
given the activism of most Brazilian ethnologists who study indigenous peoples.
The Indian question is a particularly privileged field for the exercise of a twofold
project of academic work and political action. There are reasons for this. Indian
peoples are the most dramatic example of oppression for the fact of being different. Also, until recently, they had neither place nor voice in the national arena, a
gap that was filled by committed whites, among them, anthropologists (see Ramos 1986a). One of the most imposing aspects of their lives is, naturally, contact
with the dominant Brazilian society. There are in Brazil studies of mythology,
ritual, kinship, and other matters considered nonpolitical, but virtually all of us,
Brazilian ethnologists, have also worked, either through writing or through action, or both, in the political arena of indigenous affairs. We might say that the
trademark of Brazilian ethnography has been its focus on interethnic contact with
its ramifications in the historical, dialectical, and political components of the fundamental asymmetry that characterizes Indian-white relations. In our view, no
Indian society can any longer be studied as if it were isolated, unaffected by the
surrounding populations. Even Albert's Yanomam, for all the autonomy of their
rich intellectual world, have to cope with invasions, epidemics, decimation, and
prostitution, and the authoritarian rule of the nation-state to which they are increasingly submitted. As shown by Albert, the Whiteman has already made his
entry into that world.

I do not wish to glorify the ethos of Brazilian anthropologists, for, if we look
for them, we can easily find what may be called ethical pitfalls and academic
weaknesses in their discourses. I simply want to point out the difference between
their posture and that found in other national anthropologies, particularly of the
so-called First World, vis-à-vis indigenous societies. Perhaps also because the
Indians are geographically, if not socially, closer to us, they are not burdened with
the same load of exoticism as one finds in anthropological writings elsewhere.
Books have been written by ethnologists (Melatti 1983; Ramos 1986b) for the
explicit purpose of informing the public about Indian societies, highlighting the
importance of knowing their customs beyond the packaged simplifications of stereotypes. Thus, they emphasize the legitimacy of different ways of life and point
out how dangerous cultural misunderstanding can be to indigenous peoples. The
time invested in the writing of such books, diverting us as it does from high-power
intellectual endeavors, is not regretted; publications of this sort reach a certain
slice of the public and do have an effect, small as it may be.

Far from being the savage baby killers depicted in the English language, the
Yanomami have become associated with the political struggle of indigenous peoples in that country. While Euro-American audiences, be they susceptible undergraduates or cocktail party small talkers, indulge in embroidering images of Yanomami fierceness, in Brazil a large number of people dedicate a lot of their energy
to pressuring the government to abide by the existing Constitution and legislation,
which guarantees these and other Indian peoples their rights to land, health care,

and cultural autonomy. Repeated measles epidemics and other contagious diseases have taken a heavy toll of Yanomami lives; the continuous incursions of miners, the tearing open of their territory by futile roads, the constant threat of colonist invasions have all contributed to the state of extreme vulnerability and insecurity in which the Yanomami are now living. Rather than being the epitome of primitive animality, the Yanomami have become a symbol of pristine good life endangered by the brutality of capitalist expansionism. Thus a different stereotype has been created; side by side with important and committed efforts to protect the land and freedom of choice of the Yanomami, there is a whole rhetoric of conservation that clings to the romantic idea that a good Indian is a naked, isolated Indian. Perhaps also inadvertently, Brazilian anthropologists have, no doubt, contributed to it. But that is another story that will some day be told.

Notes

Acknowledgments: My thanks to George Marcus for his comments and encouragement, and to Bruce Grant, Michael Fischer, Vincent Crapanzano, and Mariza Peirano for their careful reading and useful suggestions.

[1]Beverley Gartrell (1979) considers at length divergences between hers and Mariam Slater's ethnographic results from fieldwork in East Africa. See also Goldfrank (1956), Thompson (1956), and Bennett (1956) on this phenomenon. I am grateful to Bruce Grant and Vincent Crapanzano for having brought these articles to my attention.

[2]Chagnon's complaint that his colleagues misspell Yãnomamö is foreshadowed by his own persistence in ignoring subcultural variations. While Yãnomamö is the autodenomination of one language group (the other three, to the best of my knowledge, are Yãnomam, Sanumá, Shiriana or Ninam; see Migliazza 1972), some sort of consensus is beginning to gather around the term Yanomami as the designation for the language family as a whole. Chagnon's apprehension that spelling Yãnomamö as Yanomami runs the risk of becoming Yanomami is well founded, albeit for different reasons. It is unfortunate, however, that he gives the impression that his study applies to all of the nearly 18,000 Yanomami, both in Brazil and Venezuela. This is no mere quibble. The richness of this indigenous group resides, among other things, in the variation that exists among the subgroups. Being one of the first anthropologists to do intensive and prolonged research among them, Chagnon had initially no reason to suspect big differences. However, there is now a growing body of material from other parts of Yanomamiland that clearly shows considerable variation. It is tempting at times to pitch Chagnon's descriptions against one's own when we come across flagrant differences, but it would be as inappropriate to disagree on matters of substance as it is for him to insist on uniformity, as if the entire language family were one undifferentiated monad.

[3]Quotations from Chagnon's book refer to its 1983 third edition, unless otherwise stated.

[4]See, for instance, the last section of the third edition, subtitled "Balancing the Image of Fierceness."

[5]But see, for instance, what David Guss has to say about the Yekuana (1986). Having worked with both groups on the Brazilian side of the border, I can appreciate Chagnon's

admission, even though my inclination goes more easily toward the outgoing Yanomami than to the solemn, no-nonsense Yekuana.

⁶This raises another issue regarding audiences. Albert's work, being a doctoral dissertation, has much more freedom to be maximally thorough in building a *corpus inscriptionum* (Albert 1985:106) than Chagnon's and Lizot's books, directed to a lay audience. Nothing in Albert's dissertation is affirmed without the authentication of indigenous discourse. In sharp contrast with Chagnon and Lizot, where indigenous citations are precious few, Albert's work is laden with them. What can a nonspecialist do with them? On the other hand, his translation of Yanomam passages is free in the French language, which limits its value for the specialists. Albert's compromise may satisfy a doctoral dissertation committee but it does not serve either a strictly "Yanomamist" readership or a wider audience. However, this is a technical problem and should not be insurmountable.

⁷See, for instance, the Ilongot case examined by Rosaldo (1978).

⁸A similar point is made by Picchi (1983) about Donner's *Shabono,* and by Davis and Mathews (1976) about Chagnon's *The Fierce People.*

⁹There is a reasonably large body of papers written by anthropologists in Brazil, Venezuela, and elsewhere regarding the defense of Yanomami land rights and respect for their culture; for example, some documents published by the International Work Group for Indigenous Affairs (IWGIA) in Copenhagen by Lizot (1976), Ramos et al. (1979), and Colchester (1985).

¹⁰I cannot resist commenting on the fact that, sacrosanct as the secrecy on names seems to be for the Yãnomamö, Chagnon's and Lizot's books are strewn with them. Where does respect for the people studied begin?

References Cited

Albert, Bruce
  1985   Temps du Sang, Temps des Cendres. Représentations de la Maladie, Système Rituel et Espace Politique chez les Yanomami du Sud-est (Amazonie Brésilienne). Doctoral Dissertation, Université de Paris X (Nanterre).
Bennett, John W.
  1956   The Interpretation of Pueblo Culture: A Question of Values. *In* Personal Character and Cultural Milieu. Douglas C. Haring, ed. Pp. 203–216. Syracuse: Syracuse University Press [1946].
Biocca, Ettore
  1971   Yanoáma. The Narrative of a White Girl Kidnapped by Amazonian Indians as Told to Ettore Biocca. New York: E. P. Dutton. [Originally published in Italy in 1965].
Bruner, Edward M.
  1986   Ethnography as Narrative. *In* The Anthropology of Experience. Victor Turner and Edward Bruner, eds. Pp. 139–158. Urbana: University of Illinois Press.
Chagnon, Napoleon A.
  1983   Yãnomamö: The Fierce People. Third Edition. New York: Holt, Rinehart and Winston [1968].
Colchester, Marcus, ed.
  1985   The Health and Survival of the Venezuelan Yanoama. Copenhagen: IWGIA Document 53.

Davis, Shelton, and Robert O. Mathews
1976   The Geological Imperative. Anthropology and Development in the Amazon Basin of South America. Boston: Anthropology Resource Center.
Donner, Florinda
1982   Shabono. New York: Delacorte.
Foster, Stephen W.
1982   The Exotic as a Symbolic System. Dialectical Anthropology 7(1):21–30.
Gartrell, Beverley
1979   Is Ethnography Possible? A Critique of African Odyssey. Journal of Anthropological Research 35:426–446.
Geertz, Clifford
1983   Slide Show. Evans-Pritchard's African Transparencies. Raritan 3(2):62–80.
Goldfrank, Esther
1956   Socialization, Personality, and the Structure of Pueblo Society. In Personal Character and Cultural Milieu. Douglas C. Haring, ed. Pp. 303–327. Syracuse: Syracuse University Press [1945].
Guss, David M.
1986   Keeping it Oral: A Yekuana Ethnology. American Ethnologist 13(3):413–429.
Holmes, Rebecca B. de
1983   Shabono: Scandal or Superb Social Science? American Anthropologist 85:664–667.
Lizot, Jacques
1970   Les Indiens Yanoama et la Raison des Blancs. Critique 279/280:741–746.
1976   The Yanomami in the Face of Ethnocide. Copenhagen: IWGIA Document 22.
1985   Tales of the Yanomami: Daily Life in the Venezuelan Forest. Cambridge: Cambridge University Press.
Melatti, Julio C.
1983   Indios do Brasil. Fourth Edition. São Paulo: Hucitec.
Michaels, Eric
1982   How to Look at Us Looking at the Yanomami Looking at Us. In A Crack in the Mirror. Reflexive Perspectives in Anthropology. Jay Ruby, ed. Pp. 133–148. Philadelphia: University of Pennsylvania Press.
Migliazza, Ernesto
1972   Yanomama Grammar and Intelligibility. Doctoral Dissertation. Bloomington: Indiana University.
Picchi, Debra
1983   Review of Shabono by Florinda Donner. American Anthropologist 85:674–675.
Pratt, Mary Louise
1986   Fieldwork in Common Places. In Writing Culture. The Poetics and Politics of Ethnography. James Clifford and George Marcus, eds. Pp. 27–50. Berkeley: University of California Press.
Ramos, Alcida R.
1986a   Ethnology Brazilian Style. [Unpublished manuscript.]
1986b   Sociedades Indigenas. São Paulo: Atica.
Ramos, Alcida, Kenneth Taylor, Bruce Albert, Carlo Zacquini, and Claudia Andujar
1979   The Yanoama in Brazil 1979. Copenhagen: ARC/SI/IWGIA Document 37.
Rosaldo, Renato
1978   The Rhetoric of Control: Ilongots Viewed as Natural Bandits and Wild Indians. In The Reversible World: Symbolic Inversion in Art and Society. Barbara Babcock, ed. Pp. 240–257. Ithaca: Cornell University Press.

Sperber, Dan
   1985   On Anthropological Knowledge. Cambridge: Cambridge University Press.
Tassara, Marcello, and Claudia Andujar
   1983   Povo do Sangue, Povo da Lua. Film directed by Tassara based on still photo-
      graphs by Andujar. São Paulo.
Thompson, Laura
   1956   Logico-Aesthetic Integration in Hopi Culture. *In* Personal Character and Cultural
      Milieu. Douglas C. Haring, ed. Pp. 729–743. Syracuse: Syracuse University Press
      [1945].
Weiner, Annette B.
   1976   Women of Value, Men of Renown. New Perspectives in Trobriand Exchange.
      Austin: University of Texas Press.

Occupational Hazards: Palestine Ethnography

Ted Swedenburg

One of the first days after I had moved to Nablus, in November 1984, I had an experience that has now become a daily routine for Israeli settlers in the West Bank. I was driving downtown, when suddenly, bam! the car shook under the impact of a heavy blow to its side. A Palestinian youth, whom I never saw, had darted out of an alley, hurled a large stone, and rapidly vanished. He only managed, luckily, to put a large dent above my gas cap and did not break the windshield, the usual goal of hurled stones. I guess he singled out *my* car as a target from all the others on that busy street because its yellow license plates and my appearance led him to believe I was an Israeli settler. (As the holder of a tourist visa, I had to register my car in Israeli-annexed East Jerusalem, so its yellow plates stood out amidst the distinctive blue-plated vehicles driven by West Bank Palestinians.)

I was so shaken that I was ready to give up fieldwork and go straight home. My immediate thought was that *I,* of all people, should never have been stoned. After all, unlike those other Westerners one saw in the West Bank—the settlers, tourists, and embassy officials—I was a *good* foreigner, working in the best interests of the Palestinians. My response was typical of a mentality I shared with other Westerners who worked as teachers, journalists, or researchers in the occupied territories and sympathized with the Palestinians. This was a frame of mind that I shared but also, in calmer moments, criticized. We "good foreigners" practiced constant rituals of self-purification, designed to guarantee that we—unlike the settlers, tourists, and diplomats—were part of the Palestinian community. We spoke Arabic, dressed modestly (no shorts, low-cut blouses or wild haircuts), avoided tourist haunts, rarely ventured into Israel proper and, whenever possible, purchased Palestinian rather than Israeli products. We were often more obsessive about these latter practices than our Palestinian friends. My point is not that these actions were incorrect, but that insomuch as they demonstrated our radical difference from "other" Westerners, they allowed us to disavow our real connections to the centers of power.

My response to the stoning was emblematic of a reluctance to acknowledge my implication in the forces of domination in the West Bank. My Palestinian friends' reaction to the incident, which was much less sympathetic than I had expected, underscored their better understanding of my ambiguous position. Since they faced violence head-on virtually every day, they saw my experience as normal, not alarming. And my brush with violence was *much* preferable to being shot, beaten, arrested without charges, tortured, having one's house blown up for alleged "security" offenses, and all the other routine harassments of the occupation that Palestinians faced and I only felt at secondhand. Why should I make a fuss about a flying rock denting my car?

However, my friends made a useful suggestion, which I quickly took up. To guard against flying stones, they said, why didn't I put a *kufiya* (Palestinian headdress) on my dashboard and wear one as a scarf? By displaying the *kufiya* in this way, I was more or less guaranteed safe passage as I drove around the West Bank over the next year.[1] (I was stoned only once more.) But whenever I spotted an Israeli army roadblock, I quickly threw the *kufiyas* on the floor. My Palestinian research partner Sonia Nimr, a Ph.D. candidate in history at the University of Exeter, hid hers as well. The soldiers, taking me for an Israeli Jew or a Western tourist, usually waved us through. Unlike the drivers of cars with blue plates, I did not have to suffer searches or long lines. To avoid harassment by the forces of the occupation who—not without justification—saw a U.S. passport-holder as allied with them, my fieldwork trips required this constant shifting of position, between identification—symbolic and felt—with the Palestinians and its denial.

This perpetual cycle of putting on and taking off the *kufiya* could be taken as an allegory of the uncertainties of my position as a fieldworker under military occupation. Although for reasons of personal history, having chiefly to do with the 11 years I spent studying and working in Lebanon between 1964 and 1976, I identified strongly with the Palestinian cause, I now found myself identified, for historical reasons beyond my control, with the same forces of violence that I hoped my research might, in some small way, help undo. In the course of fieldwork, I learned that I could never escape that larger historical positioning.

My oscillation also had important effects on the results of my research. That project concerned Palestinians' memories of an anticolonial insurgency against British rule that took place between 1936 and 1939. The subjects of my interviews were primarily elderly male West Bank villagers who had fought as insurgents during that rebellion. Gripped tightly in the vise of violence, their memories were powerfully overdetermined by the (British and Israeli) colonial scene. Thus their memories were filled with circumspection and forgettings that were in part a function of my ambiguous positionality. Caught in its own way in existing networks of power, this article too will be marked by hedgings and tactical exclusions.

The aim of my research was to uncover a popular memory of the 1936–39 revolt, carried by elderly peasant insurgents, to ferret out the submerged, lower-class memory of revolt that was hidden by authoritative nationalist historiography. I hoped that this obscured, local remembrance might serve as a kind of corrective to the official Palestinian nationalist representations that tend to project a unified picture of the revolt and gloss over the important contributions of the popular classes.[2]

I was indeed able to find expressions of a popular memory of revolt buried beneath official discourse. But more significant, I eventually learned, was the extent to which popular views were always couched within a nationalist idiom. Under the pressure of Israeli colonial repression, the various strands of popular memory and official histories have been fused into a fairly unified picture. My elderly informants always took the unity of the Palestinian experience for granted. Their stress on Palestinian identity, which to someone not embattled might appear obsessive and verging on the xenophobic, must be understood as a response to the extreme measures Israeli authorities take to suppress all manifestations of Palestinian nationalism. Let me illustrate with a few examples of how repression impinges upon Palestinian cultural production. The Israeli censor has banned hundreds of books from the occupied territories, with the aim, according to Meron Benvenisti, of eradicating written "expression that could foster Palestinian nationalist feelings, or that suggests that Palestinians are a nation with a national heritage" (1983:1). In 1983 the West Bank writer Sami Kilani was put on trial for "incitement," the charge sheet citing the fact that he had invoked, in a volume of poetry, the name of Shaykh 'Izz al-Din al-Qassam, national hero and the chief instigator of the 1936–39 rebellion (al-Fajr, November 11, 1983). Official Israeli histories generally label the Palestinian hero Qassam as the leader of "the first Arab terrorist movement in Palestine" and a forerunner of the "terrorist" PLO (Lachman 1982:86). Sami Kilani was not convicted, but this act of poetic "incitement" and his trade union activity led to a series of town arrests and administrative detentions that have lasted almost without interruption from 1983 until today. (While under town arrest Sami collaborated with Sonia and me in the research project by transcribing and discussing our taped interviews. He intends someday to use the transcripts as the basis for a novel about the 1936–39 revolt.) Since the beginning of the uprising, the military authorities have closed institutions like the Society for the Preservation of the Family (In'ash al-Usra) of al-Bireh and the Arab Studies Society in Jerusalem, which have sponsored and published important studies of Palestinian folklore, society, and history, and have set up national archives. (Copies of the tapes and transcripts of the interviews I and Sonia Nimr conducted are housed in the Arab Studies Society, to which researchers have been denied access for two years.)

The old fighters we interviewed knew that from the Israeli perspective the revolt is a dangerous memory. All the men we interviewed who kept memorabilia from the revolt lost them during Israeli army searches, or destroyed their personal archives out of fear. Many had been interrogated about their part in the revolt by Israeli intelligence officers. Several veterans refused, for such reasons, to be interviewed by us at all. Those who consented generally needed considerable convincing that my research partner was trustworthy. The old villagers' fears were not due merely to my citizenship in the country that is Israel's main financial and military support, but also to the prevailing atmosphere of suspicion fostered by the Israeli intelligence network of spies and collaborators. The presence of a Palestinian coworker was no guarantee that an informant would speak freely (al-Ghazali 1986).

The former rebels were equally aware that Israeli policies aim not just at forcibly suppressing memories of revolt but at ideologically defacing and denigrating that symbol of national resistance as well. They are cognizant that official Zionist discourse labels the rebels of 1936–39 as criminals and terrorists, that it routinely refers to the revolt as "riots" and "pogroms" against Jews rather than as an anticolonial insurgency, and that it taints the rebel movement with Nazi associations. They know too that Israeli historians tend to view Palestinian society in the 1930s as a tribal and segmented entity given to internal fragmentation, as an "allochronic" (Fabian 1983) rather than a modern and national body.

Little wonder that elderly fighters hesitated at unveiling everything they knew about the revolt, especially when their stories would be carried back to the United States. Because Israeli policies concentrate so ferociously on disintegrating all cultural forms that evoke the national reality, Palestinians carefully protect the memory of those same symbols (see Fanon 1965:37). And it should come as no surprise that they try to project an image of Palestinian unity. The interviews we conducted were therefore punctuated by significant silences and resistances, the passing over of issues that might project the "wrong" image of the 1936–39 revolt and expose the faultlines of the society. The issues informants handled gingerly were precisely the ones that are the target of hostile official Israeli discourse. Those "facts" that are stressed in Israeli histories and that elderly peasants, in Nietzsche's formulation, "actively forgot," included: that some insurgents committed robbery in the name of the revolt, that differences between commanders fractured the rebel movement, that peasants sold properties to Zionist land purchasers, that rebels attacked *Jewish* settlements as well as British army patrols.

I will focus on this last area of silence, which relates to the charged question of anti-Semitism. Official Zionist discourse continues to associate the 1936–39 rebellion with Nazism, claiming that the Arab insurgents were aided and inspired by European fascism. And it makes much of the fact that the leader of the Palestinian national movement during the 1930s and 1940s, Hajj Amin al-Husayni, took refuge in Berlin during World War II and collaborated with the German war effort. A photograph of Hajj Amin and a letter he wrote to Ribbentrop are the only representation of a Palestinian Arab displayed at Yad Vashem, the holocaust memorial in Jerusalem. It is a powerful example of how Israeli discourse uses Hajj Amin as a metonym for the entire Palestinian people, implicating them wholesale in the Nazi crimes against the Jews. Given the global power of such representations, it is understandable that my subjects skirted around and rarely mentioned this facet of the career of their national leader. This also helps clarify why they stressed that their relations with the Jews prior to the founding of Israel in 1948 had been excellent, and why they generally avoided discussing rebel raids on Jewish settlements in 1936–39, focusing instead on their engagements with the British army. Let me emphasize, again, that these are not lapses in memory, but active forgettings situated in a complex set of determinants: colonialism, anti-Semitism, my presence, etc.

Because of my privileged position an investigator, it was not too difficult for me to find cracks in this constructed mnemonic edifice of national unity. By trav-

eling between different sites of memory and locating persons with opposing views
and interests, I could cross-check data and find various versions of the same story.
More important, perhaps, was the fact that the honorable, national memory of
revolt was often preserved on a very local or personal level. Memory tended to
operate through local condensation and displacement. Informants often told us:
other rebel bands may have engaged in robbery, but not ours. Members of our
village (or our *hamula*) did not sell any land to the Jews, but in *that* village (or
hamula) they did. There were no significant family splits in our village but that
one over there was wracked by division. (And in that other village, another person
might say the opposite.) And yes, I also found evidence of a kind of "negative"
class consciousness (Gramsci 1971:272–273), for many persons claimed that the
urban leadership was corrupt and timid, the city middle classes were insufficiently
active, but that the poor and the peasants were honorable and militantly nationalist. By such means, veterans preserved a dignified local memory of the revolt,
but at the cost of revealing difference.

We also elicited details from the younger generation, which was ready to
divulge more than their elders. A woman I knew as a fellow student at the American University of Beirut in the early 1970s, who now teaches at a West Bank
university, related a story she heard from her father, an officer in the mandate
police force during the revolt. It concerned the famous rebel commander 'Abd al-
Rahim al-Hajj Muhammad, whose fighters, on orders from Hajj Amin's headquarters in Damascus, assassinated two men from the rich Palestinian landowning
Irshayd family. After carrying out the attack, the rebels hoisted the underclothing
of the Irshayd women on their weapons, to rub in the humiliation. Farid Irshayd,
a prominent member of the clan, retaliated by informing the British as to 'Abd al-
Rahim's hideout, and the British army was able to locate and kill him. When my
friend told her father that she had related this and similar anecdotes to me, he
exploded: "How can you trust an American?! What do you think he might do
with such stories?" I should add that other persons disputed 'Abd al-Rahim's role
in the assassination, and that none mentioned the display of women's undergar-
ments.

By such means I was able to show that my informants' representation of Palestinian society as a timeless presence and of the revolt as a manifestation of national unity was an active reconstruction. I was able as well to uncover the evidence I had wanted in order to show that the revolt was to a considerable extent
popular and much more rooted in the villages than in the educated urban classes.
But thinking back, the old police officer's anger at his daughter makes me uncomfortable. By emphasizing class difference within Palestinian society, am I imposing my own agenda? Is this some essential truth that *I* desire as a democrat and a
socialist? Such an interpretation was not what was asked of me. For many Palestinians regarded me as a possible relay to U.S. public opinion, and they im-
plored me to convey their nationalist message. They urged that I write about their
current problems, which they saw as more urgent than those they faced in the
1930s. They emphasized the long Arab heritage in Palestine and their historical
rights to the land. We just want our rights, we just want to live in peace and for
the occupation to end, I was told again and again.

My study of these memories of revolt, related in an unstable present, has required an effort on my part to unlearn an academic training in anthropology and history that compels one to unveil the objective truth. The silences, resistances, dissimulations, avoidances, and hedgings about the past that I encountered in fact have a greater "truth" value than supposedly neutral historical facts. This truth lies in an unequal relation of power, between occupier and occupied, between researcher and subject. Furthermore, much of the real "truth" of the old rebels' tendentious memories and active forgettings can be traced *here* to the United States, the underwriter of Israel's capacity to efface all traces of Palestinian nationalism. As Edward Said puts it, here in the United States there is simply "no socially acceptable narrative to absorb, sustain and circulate" any Palestinian counterfacts to the hegemonic Israeli narrative (1984:34). Little wonder that when their existence as a people is so endangered, my informants wanted so urgently to convey an image of their insurgency that would preserve the national honor. We must understand the necessity for Palestinians to conceal some "truths," to forget others, and to embellish the positive, even if those operations might appear, to those of us who do not live under a state of siege, xenophobic or fanatical. Out of solidarity, therefore, I feel compelled to participate in those veilings and to resist a full revelation before the holders of power. Positioned where I am, part of my role is to help develop some "socially acceptable" narrative within which the Palestinian case might be argued in the West. Such a narrative, like all narratives, will necessarily be based on partial truths and strategic exclusions.

By way of example, let me offer a more positive instance of active forgetting than those discussed above. During the high point of the rebellion, in September 1938, the rebel leadership ordered all Palestinian males to put on the *kufiya,* which until then had been exclusively the headcovering of the peasant and the insurgent, and they banned the wearing of the urban effendis' *tarbush* or fez. This event is widely celebrated today as a great moment of national unity, and incidentally is the origin of the adoption of the *kufiya* as a national emblem. The population's mass donning of the *kufiya* allowed rebel insurgents to disguise their identities as they entered and occupied the cities. Today it is not very often recalled that this order was imposed, sometimes forcibly, upon the middle and upper classes and that it represented a symbolic initiative from below. But what no one ever told us was that in this same period, Palestinian women were ordered to veil (see Porath 1977:268). My compulsive search for archival data led me to the Central Zionist Archives, where I found the record of a manifesto by a rebel commander in the Nablus district ordering all women to cover themselves heavily and not to go about with light or transparent veils. Another manifesto warned peasant women not to bring their vegetables to sell in Nablus, under penalty of a £5 fine. The intelligence agent who wrote the memo noted that, on the day after the order was issued, men from the villages brought in vegetables to sell in the city (CZA/S/ 4960, July 21, 1938). What does it mean that everyone we spoke with was silent about such orders? Have I uncovered some essential fact that exposes the revolt as a traditional movement? I think rather that the absence of this story from collective memory is a sign of social development, another instance of the "active forgetfulness" without which, Nietzsche wrote, there could be "no cheerfulness, no hope, no pride, no *present*" (1969:58). When Palestinian women are increasingly mobilized in the current uprising and as they too now put on the *kufiya*, formerly an exclusively male property, we should see this forgetting of a dead tradition, this active breaking up of the past, as eminently healthy.

I conclude by noting that ever since I visited the West Bank at the age of 12 and became aware of the injustices suffered by the Palestinians, I have felt frustrated by the degree to which hegemonic institutions impinge upon our ability to speak openly about these issues. These pressures now seem to be lifting. At the 1987 AAA meeting in Chicago my dissertation adviser Robert Fernea chided me for wearing a *kufiya* as a scarf, afraid that this symbolic act of identification might upset my chances of landing an academic job. Only three months later, Bob informed me over the phone that he was wearing a *kufiya* all the time, out of solidarity with the uprising. I in no way want to suggest any opportunism on his part, for I share his feeling that these days, as a direct result of the *intifada,* we have much more freedom to speak out on the question of Palestine. It is in that spirit that I quote from an article by Anita Vitullo that appeared in the New York *Guardian* on October 19, 1988.

> In Yaabad, a 28-year-old trade union leader, Ahmad Kilani [the brother of Sami Kilani, mentioned above] was shot dead by an Israeli intelligence agent when troops entered the town to stop a memorial for the [five] Nablus victims killed [on October 6 and 7]. At least 25 other Yaabad residents were shot and injured in the assault, and 40 were arrested and taken away by helicopter to an unknown destination. West Bank trade union leaders called Kilani's killing "a willful murder" by security forces. Recently families have charged that Israeli snipers are waging an assassination campaign against specific Palestinian leaders, shooting them from rooftops in town or on the sidelines of demonstrations. Kilani . . . had been released from detention only three weeks before. He was killed by the same intelligence agent who had interrogated him in prison.
>
> Kilani's body, like that of every Palestinian martyr, was taken by soldiers for a military autopsy. But instead of returning the body to his family for burial, soldiers dumped it in a makeshift cemetery in a tiny village in the northern West Bank. Yaabad villagers, who reportedly had been told of the bulldozer burial by a Jewish ambulance driver, retrieved the body and buried Kilani in his hometown. [Vitullo 1988:14]

On October 26, the *New York Times* obliquely lent credence to the claim that Ahmad Kilani was assassinated when it stated that Israel had suspended the press credentials of two Reuters correspondents who had reported that Israel is using undercover death squads in the occupied territories. (Better confirmation has appeared in the Israeli press; see Be'er 1988 and *Ha'aretz* weekly edition, October 28.) According to Kilani's family, Ahmad was shot in the act of hurling a stone at the soldiers of the occupation. I think back to my first encounter with a flying Palestinian rock, which reminded me of my contradictory positioning. I remember the hospitality extended to me by the entire Kilani family (all four surviving brothers are currently in prison) and their generous support for my research. I try to hold the image in my mind of Ahmad throwing a stone, while I think of my comfortable academic position in a country that is silently underwriting death squads in Central America, and about what it means for Palestinians when those technologies of murder migrate, without fanfare or protest, to the West Bank.

Notes

Acknowledgments. Thanks to Ruth Frankenberg, Lata Mani, and Kristin Koptiuch for their careful readings and helpful comments on this article, and to Sandra Campbell, who pushed me to think about positionality.

[1]This tactic has now been adopted, during the *intifada,* by Israeli settlers.

[2]"[I]f the story of the rise of the national resistance to imperialism is to be disclosed coherently, it is the role of the indigenous subaltern that must be strategically excluded" (Spivak 1987:245).

References Cited

Be'er, Yizhar
    1988   The Killers Arrived in an Arab Van. Kol Ha'ir, 21 October. [Translation reprinted in al-Fair, 30 October, pp. 10, 15]
Benvenisti, Meron
    1983   Israeli Censorship of Arab Publications. New York: Fund for Free Expression.
Fabian, Johannes
    1983   Time and the Other: How Anthropology Makes Its Object. New York: Columbia University Press.
Fanon, Frantz
    1965   A Dying Colonialism. Haakon Chevalier, trans. New York: Grove Press.
Al-Ghazali, Said
    1986   Bir Zeit Center Revives the Memory of Ein Houd. Al-Fair, 28 February, p. 11.
Gramsci, Antonio
    1971   Selections from the Prison Notebooks. Quintin Hoare and Geoffrey Nowell Smith, eds. and trans. New York: International Publishers.
Lachman, Shai
    1982   Arab Rebellion and Terrorism in Palestine 1929–39: The Case of Sheikh Izz al-Din al-Qassam and his Movement. *In* Zionism and Arabism in Palestine and Israel. Elie Kedourie and Sylvia G. Haim, eds. Pp. 52–99. London: Frank Cass.
Nietzsche, Friedrich
    1969   On the Genealogy of Morals. Walter Kaufman and R. J. Hollingdale, trans. New York: Vintage Books.
Porath, Yehoshuah
    1977   The Palestinian Arab National Movement. From Riots to Rebellion. London: Frank Cass.
Said, Edward
    1984   Permission to Narrate. Journal of Palestine Studies 51:27–48.
Spivak, Gayatri
    1987   In Other Worlds. New York: Methuen.
Vitullo, Anita
    1988   Israelis 'Shoot to Punish' with Plastic Bullets. The Guardian, 19 October, p. 14.

The Politics of Remembering: Notes on a Pacific Conference

Geoffrey M. White

Conferences and symposia convened to examine areal issues are a standard event type in American anthropology: those who have done fieldwork in a region assemble to discuss its distinctive cultural patterns—whether Melanesian big-men, Indian castes, or Mediterranean honor. A standard part of this genre is the swapping of fieldwork stories, exchanged onstage as well as off. The conference provides a confirming occasion for validating key features of anthropological expertise and identity. Typically the subjects of this type of discourse have been at a geographically and institutionally "safe" distance. Ethnographers convene in one place (including opulent European chateaux); people remain in another, far from the academy in rural villages where an occasional published ethnography sometimes circulates among people interested mostly in the pictures. But this is changing. Increasingly the subjects are turning up in the halls of the academy and are finding other arenas in which to add their voices to the debates. The following discussion reports on a recent Pacific conference where the subjects not only turned up, but to a large extent set the agenda.

The author was the co-organizer for a conference on "Pacific Recollections of World War II" convened at the University of the South Pacific Centre in Honiara, Solomon Islands, from June 29 to July 3, 1987. Funded primarily by the Wenner-Gren Foundation and the East-West Center in Honolulu, the aim of the conference was to explore the sociocultural significance of wartime experiences as remembered by Islanders. Although broadly labeled "Pacific," the conference was in fact limited to Melanesia, primarily Papua New Guinea, Solomon Islands, and Vanuatu. The 22 invited participants included a mix of researchers from the southwest Pacific and the United States and a larger number of Solomon Islanders who played some role in the war. Reviewing the social organization of this event illuminates more general issues surrounding relations between anthropologists and informants, researchers and researched, representers and represented.

As the single most prominent historical epoch in the 20th-century Pacific, World War II provides grist for popular images of modern Pacific societies. This is so for Islanders as well as outsiders who regard the war as a critical era, a moment of intensified experience portending momentous change. As is the case well beyond the Pacific region, the war is widely regarded as a marker by which to locate past events relative to the present. The image of small insular societies thrust suddenly into a larger world has provided the storyline for a compelling War Epic—one which may be heard and read in most portrayals of the region. The Epic has many variants: loss of innocence, passage to independence, and, in anthropology, encounter with cargo-laden troops sowing the seeds for postwar cults and movements. For the author and other researchers involved in the conference, staging an international meeting offered an occasion in which to juxtapose and explore these variant representations of the war, particularly those versions currently circulating in Melanesia.

From its inception the conference was planned through dialogue (or perhaps cacophony) among academics and nonacademics, Islanders and non-Islanders. The initial impetus came from the East-West Center in Honolulu where a project coordinated by the author is exploring the social and cultural dimensions of Islanders' wartime experiences. The mission of the Center to foster international collaborative projects provided the rationale for discussions with Solomon Islanders to plan a jointly sponsored conference to be held in their country. The Solomons seemed a fitting place for such a meeting, as it was there that the Allies began their offensive in the Pacific with the battle for Guadalcanal.

The East-West Center's rhetoric of international cooperation converged in this instance with the assertive posture of postcolonial Pacific governments toward research and scholarship pertaining to their populations. Asking that social research in their countries be both relevant and beneficial to indigenous concerns, local officials and scholars seek to "re-center" the research enterprise by seeing that Islanders take roles other than that of informant. Jointly planning an "oral history" conference in the Solomons with mostly Islander participants was, for all parties concerned, one way of doing that.[1]

The selection of the Solomon Islands as a conference site determined more than geographic location. It also assured that Islanders (specifically, Solomon Islanders) would take a leading role in defining and organizing the event. Due largely to this somewhat unusual collaboration in planning, what started out to be a fairly typical international conference consisting solely of scholarly presentations became a meeting conducted almost entirely in Melanesian Pidgin with a substantial amount of storytelling by Solomon Islanders invited to relate their own wartime experiences.

In defining the purpose of the conference, all the organizers drew upon shared notions about the desirability of recording unwritten histories and documenting indigenous perspectives. In regard to the war era, this mission was lent urgency by the fact that the generation which experienced the war is rapidly dying off. These goals, however, also left plenty of room for a divergence of agendas— a divergence reflected in the division of labor worked out among the organizers. Following the usual conference script, the East-West Center organizers set about recruiting international participants to come and give presentations about the oral history of the war in particular Melanesian countries. The Solomon Islands organizers, for their part, formed a committee of the directors of various national institutions along with three prominent war veterans to determine their contribution to the conference. For this group, the stated purpose of the conference "was to assist Solomon Islanders record their personal experiences on the World, War II (sic) most of what was now available was written by non-Solomon Islanders." And so they went about recruiting Solomon Islanders who had experienced the war firsthand (hereafter called "veterans") to come and give accounts of those experiences.[2] Their original plan called for a conference ratio of four to one, Solomon Islands veterans to overseas participants. Due largely to limitations in financing, this was ultimately scaled down to about two to one.

The invitation of a relatively large number of Solomon Islands veterans framed the purpose of the conference in at least two ways. On the one hand, it implied that much of the proceedings would be cast in the mode of storytelling, of relating firsthand experiences. This, of course, contrasted with the standard model of academic presentations of materials digested through a research process. While vaguely disquieting to the anthropologist organizers responsible for producing a scholarly conference, this mode of organization offered us the prospect of recording important narratives directly relevant to our research interests.

Secondly, the large Solomon Islands contingent made the conference more of a national event than an international one. Clearly, this would be an opportunity, perhaps a final opportunity, to assemble and record the voices that speak of their role in a unique moment of national history. One of the New Guinean participants, the historian John Waiko, showed his solidarity with the objectives of his hosts and neighbors by stating in a meeting prior to the conference that his time on the agenda should be reduced so as to give priority to the older Solomon Islanders. The conference, he said, was their occasion, and it would be "immoral" to do otherwise. His remarks were a useful reminder that notions about "centering" the conference in "the Pacific" may be relative to multiple vantage points.

As a national event, the conference became something more than a forum for scholarly discussion. It was also a ceremonial occasion for the public reconstruction of collective history. Indeed, war stories, like the more visible war relics that dot the landscape, are now an acknowledged part of national heritage. A good example of the popular status of war history is a recent newspaper advertisement that attempted to entice tourists with the prospect of being regaled with local war stories:

> See this beautiful island . . . and hear the tales of the Japanese occupation and the Americans' bombing of Tulagi at the heart of World War Two.
> Tulagians can tell you these wonderful stories as if they were YESTERDAY.
> And it's always nice over a cold beer and a superb Chinese or European meal.
> [*Solomons Toktok,* August 28, 1987]

The Pacific Recollections conference promised something similar, only it framed the storytelling with the prestige of an international scholarly meeting, and recorded the proceedings with both audio and videotape so that the storytellers' performances could be replayed again and again to even wider audiences at home and overseas.[3]

The bifurcated roster of participants (researchers from overseas giving papers written in English, and Solomon Islands veterans giving oral presentations of personal experience) posed something of a challenge in working out an agenda that would facilitate interaction and discussion among them. The potential for a major gap emerging between English speakers and non-English speakers was solved fortuitously by the last minute withdrawals of participants from Fiji and New Caledonia—the only two who would not be expected to know some variety of Melanesian Pidgin. As a result, both researchers and veterans shared a common *lingua franca*. (Vanuatu Bislama, Papua New Guinea Tok Pisin, and Solomons Pijin are mutually comprehensible, especially given the educated dialects spoken by the overseas participants.)[4] The fact that the linguistic code shifted from English to Pidgin at the end of the first morning and remained so until the end proved to be a critical factor in the interactive dynamics of the meeting.

The program called for four days of discussion, with each morning beginning with two presentations by researchers, followed by storytelling during the remainder of the day. The last day, Friday, was reserved for the organizers and researchers to work out plans for a conference publication. So, despite the presence of innovative elements in conference planning, the script for academic conferences still affected decisions about agenda setting and allocation of time, with papers given temporal priority and the objective of publication underscored by a final caucus among researchers.

Early in its deliberations the local organizing committee had contacted 17 veterans recognized for their wartime experiences, and invited them to the conference without giving specifics of time. Just a week prior to the conference, a radio message was aired asking those invited to make their way to Honiara (the capital) for the conference the next week. Most of those invited did in fact arrive on time (some with harrowing stories to tell, such as old Martin Sebo with his failing eyesight who walked and hitchhiked 50 miles around the rugged coast of Guadalcanal, only to arrive in Honiara and have to ask a policeman how to find the conference). Other Solomon Islanders who had been involved in the war but were not invited to the conference also heard the radio message and interpreted it to mean that they should attend as well. In the planning session just prior to the conference, a well-known veteran on the organizing committee said that since the radio message, things had started to "boil up," that veterans were appearing at his house, some with old uniforms and medals, asking if they were supposed to report. In fact, eight or ten such men from Guadalcanal who could easily arrange their own transportation did in fact show up at the conference and joined in the week-long deliberations.

Advance publicity for the conference, including a brief radio interview with the organizers and a banner put up at the National Museum, turned the conference into a public event of some notoriety. Its national and international significance was underscored by a ceremonial opening planned by the organizing committee. A government dignitary, Francis Saemala, Secretary to Cabinet and former U.N.

Ambassador, gave the welcoming remarks, with representatives of the Australian, New Zealand, and U.S. governments in attendance. In his remarks the Secretary tapped yet another vein of meaning in the war's layers of significance. It is common in exchanges between the Solomon Islands and the United States for both sides to invoke the war as an emblem of a historical bond of friendship. In this conference, Saemala played upon this well-worn theme in his remarks, but did so to contemporary advantage by calling into question the wisdom of current U.S. policies that seem less than consistent with those symbolic bonds:

> I make these remarks on the importance of the Solomon Islands to the U.S. and the Allies during the war with one intention in mind, and that is that this conference will be able to formulate the message and send it forth from here to Washington, D.C., that Pacific Islanders fought yet as courageously for the future of democracy and that these efforts should not be forgotten in terms of our new relationships as a sovereign state in this ever interdependent world. Washington, I think with all due respect, has been lukewarm to the development needs of the Pacific Islands. But we are some of its best friends as a result of the comradeship established during the war.

As Saemala began his welcoming remarks, he looked around the room and quickly perceived a dilemma which the conference would itself soon face: what language to use? International conferences in the Solomons are usually conducted in English. But here the meeting room was filled almost entirely with Melanesians, the majority of them Solomon Islanders. Only a handful of white-skinned researchers and diplomats marked its non-Melanesian composition. Uncomfortable about speaking to such a group solely in English, he quickly began to mix Pidgin terms and phrases into the English speech, even adding a sentence of apology appropriately mixing both languages together: "*Mi no save* (I don't know) whether I should speak in English or Pidgin . . . *bikos mi priperem long Ingglis ia* (because I prepared in English)." He solved his dilemma by delivering the remainder of his speech with similar Pidgin interjections.

Following this diplomatic welcome, Hugh Laracy, a New Zealand historian, gave the first conference presentation entirely in English (a historical overview of events leading up to the war in the Solomons). His was also the last presentation given only in English. Laracy was followed by David Gegeo, a researcher and Solomon Islander who presented a paper dealing with Islanders' views of the war and their role in recording it. However he, like Saemala, faced a dilemma in choice of language code. He had prepared a paper in English, but Pijin would be the code of solidarity with fellow Solomon Islanders in the audience. The dilemma was exacerbated by murmurings from one of the anthropologist observers that some of his local friends in the audience couldn't follow the previous presentation in English. The complaint itself indicates the extent to which the composition of the conference had already framed its purpose for many, even as an orthodox conference paper was being read in English. Gegeo deftly solved his problem by reading the paper and interspersing Pijin paraphrases and elaborations. In so doing, he provided a useful bridge into the remainder of the proceedings, conducted in various dialects of Melanesian Pidgin.

This completed the first morning session. In the afternoon session chaired by one of the war veteran organizers, Pidgin established itself as the language of the conference as the Solomon Islanders began to tell their stories. (Each was given the same amount of time as paper presenters: 30 minutes followed by 15 minutes of discussion.) The following morning, two Papua New Guinean speakers, John Waiko and Patrick Silata, who had prepared papers in English spoke entirely in Pidgin, as did James Gwero of the Vanuatu Cultural Centre.[5] Gwero, who had labored for days with a colleague in Vanuatu to write his paper in English was much relieved by the codeswitch to Pidgin.

The emergence of Pidgin as the language for conference discussion facilitated the full involvement of the veterans. Not only was the storytelling natural and fluid (with some speakers more skilled at oratory than others), but the veterans easily questioned one another, joked, and exchanged anecdotes. When the group hit upon an interesting topic, the ease of interaction allowed for spontaneous participation. For example, when one of the speakers told a humorous story about some unfortunate soul who blew himself up when he unknowingly tampered with an unexploded bomb, others quickly chimed in with similar anecdotes. It appears that the story tapped a preexisting genre of "bomb stories" which rely upon the black humor and tension in islanders' unwitting encounters with the unfamiliar and deadly technology of modern warfare. The spontaneity of participation evident as speakers vied for the floor depended upon the use of Pidgin, a language well suited to storytelling and joking, and to the definition of an egalitarian situation. At times the conference took on the appearance of a testimonial as participants stood in succession to relate their own experiences and views.

The questions and answers that followed each veteran's narrative often went beyond simple clarifications to raise issues of meaning and motivation. For example, both academic and narrative presentations raised the question of why Islanders in many areas had so completely supported the British and Allies despite oppressive prewar relations with colonial officials and bosses. Numerous ideas and theories were offered (including the genetic: one of the half-caste veterans responded to this question by observing that a lot of Europeans produced Solomon Islands offspring).

Whereas the organizers shared a vision of the conference as an effort to document indigenous perspectives and oral histories, and politicians saw it as an opportunity to restate international relations in the rhetoric of wartime bonds, the veterans used it to publicize their roles in the war and to advance claims for compensation. For them, this was an occasion in which to put forward their accounts of wartime experiences in an authoritative and legitimizing context. Here they could be seen, heard, and recorded by an international audience. Like the conference organizers, they also wanted to "set the record straight," to rewrite colonial history. However, for them this was less a matter of pursuing truth or correcting ethnocentric histories, than a way of finally gaining the recognition and, more importantly, the compensation due them as active participants in the war. Of course, the former concern does not exclude the latter. For Melanesians, the issue of compensation signifies the key themes of native service and suffering omitted from colonial war history.

Although the veterans were a diverse group drawn from all over the Solomon Islands, most of them had been involved closely in active support of the Allied war effort. The selection of local participants by the organizing committee reveals a common attitude toward war history in the Solomons and elsewhere. Local histories of the war, like most of the books by the warring powers, tend to center upon the men who were closest to the fighting: members of the small Solomon Islands Defence Force, scouts, and coastwatchers who gathered intelligence and rescued pilots behind Japanese lines. Nearly all the participants invited by the local committee were individuals with these sorts of experience. No women were invited and none of those who "simply" evacuated their villages and struggled for survival were invited. Only a few participants were invited to talk about their work in the Labour Corps, which was by far the most common form of direct involvement in the war—over 3700 men recruited between 1942 and 1944, a huge proportion of the population of able-bodied men at that time.

The other Melanesian participants in the conference voiced their sympathy for the veterans' concerns about inequalities of pay and compensation. On the second day of the conference John Waiko stepped into an entrepreneurial role by giving an impassioned speech about the Papua New Guinean campaign to obtain compensation for war veterans, including soldiers, police, and carriers. Using oratorical skills no doubt gained from his home culture in the Northern Province, Waiko pointed out that he had actively pushed for recent legislation that obtained compensation for PNG veterans from their own government. Furthermore, he noted, he had just the previous evening at the conference reception spoken with the Solomon Islands Prime Minister about the importance of placing similar legislation before the Solomon Islands Parliament.

Many attitudes and evaluations were aired during the four days of conference discussion, reflecting considerable diversity in interpretations of the war and the unusual experiences it engendered. For some the war was full of excitement and new possibilities, especially that of racial equality. Numerous veterans noted the great infusion of cargo associated with the war and the many economic developments that followed. With tongue only partly in cheek, one speaker loudly proclaimed, "We should have another (war)!" Yet the themes of suffering, deprivation, and unfulfilled expectations surfaced repeatedly, offering a topic to which nearly everyone could subscribe. And so, when Sir Gideon Zoleveke, a veteran on the organizing committee, gave his concluding remarks, the theme of uncompensated sacrifice was the most prominent motif. The following is a translation of a passage excerpted from those remarks.

I would like to ask this conference to resolve that World War II was not our war. It was the war of two countries that came to fight on our land. . . . So they were victorious in the battlefield while we suffered from hardship, labor, loss of life and things like that. But their victory would not have occurred if it had not been for us and our bodies out there. So we should say something at this conference before it ends to make our government understand what our feelings are today. . . . First of all we must convince our government about this suffering, what you and I talked about today. What did we get from that war, from our friends who came here to fight? Goodness, they were "fully insured," everything, families at home, everyone got something, but for us nothing. If you agree with me, all I want you all to do is put forward some statement from this conference.

The conference in fact did not immediately produce the sort of statement Zoleveke was calling for, although nearly all participants were in agreement with him. Instead, the conference produced what academic conferences usually do: publications. True to the conference plan, the organizers met on the final day and worked out plans for publication that have resulted in a special issue of the local journal *'O'O: Journal of Solomon Islands Studies* (no. 4, 1988) and a book of longer narratives, *The Big Death: Solomon Islanders Remember World War II* (University of the South Pacific, 1988).[6] More in line with Zoleveke's plea, however, another veteran on the organizing committee later began a letter-writing campaign directed to the Prime Minister and other heads of government asking for recognition and compensation for former members of the Solomon Islands Defence Force. The conference may yet prove to have been useful in this effort. This individual stated that he intended to air a program about the conference produced by the Australian Broadcasting Commission on Solomon Islands radio to bring pressure on members of Parliament.

To some extent, the conference itself was regarded as a reward for wartime activities. Since all conference participants received a generous per diem for seven days, and most had only minimal subsistence costs, the cash differential could easily be seen as a lump-sum payment for knowledge or stories recounted at the conference. Also important as emblems of the veterans' identity were the conference name tags, T-shirts, and plastic zippered portfolios—all of which were received with considerable appreciation.

As an organizer, I was pleased that I had been able to recruit one of my principal informants from the island of Santa Isabel for the conference, offering him those same benefits in the spirit of reciprocity. However, when I later returned to that island I was chagrined to learn from that same informant that others from whom I was recording stories were asking why they weren't paid similar amounts of money. Indicative of problems pertaining to almost any type of fieldwork, the context for these questions is a local epistemology that regards knowledge as an exchangeable resource. Where knowledge is regarded as useful by others, such as genealogies or magical formulae, it usually circulates in very restricted channels, sometimes at a price. It may have surprised some people that anyone was "paying for" war stories, but there were clear indications from the outset of conference planning that war stories had commodity value. In its first meeting the organizing committee noted in its minutes, "some people might demand payment for their stories."

As a final comment about lessons to be drawn from these goings on in the South Pacific, it is useful to note parallels between some of the local understandings of this conference and views of anthropology generally in the region. As already mentioned, the local sponsors saw the major rationale for the conference as a way of recording oral history and promoting indigenous perspectives on wartime events. Implicit in this view is a conception of knowledge as fixed and finite, and of research (and conferences) as a way of recording it. In the case of old knowledge or *kastom,* research is useful as a way of "preserving" culture before it deteriorates, just as research on the oral history of the war "salvages" stories that might otherwise be lost like rusting relics.

In line with these premises, anthropology becomes social history, the rendering of a more enduring accounting of past events and practices. On the one hand, these understandings may legitimize the work of anthropologists with other research agendas. However, such understandings may also lead to other, less comfortable propositions such as "Researchers take (even 'steal') valuable resources without giving anything back," or "We provide the culture and researchers make money and careers." If one listens closely to the voices raised in the "Pacific Recollections" conference, one may hear an uncanny resemblance between these propositions and the veterans' claims that "We sacrificed and suffered for the war and received almost nothing in return," and "They couldn't have won the war without us."

For myself and other researchers involved in this event, the payoffs involved not only the good stories we anticipated, but a sense of having stepped outside the scripted patterns of academic discourse and listened to some of the things the subjects of that discourse have to say when they take part in composing the script.

Notes

Acknowledgments. I and the other conference organizers would like to thank the Wenner-Gren Foundation for Anthropological Research and the East-West Center for their generous support of the conference described herein. I am also grateful to John Kirkpatrick and Lamont Lindstrom for helpful comments on an earlier version of this report.

[1]The concerns of the Solomon Islands organizing committee regarding matters of definition and control were expressed clearly in several points listed in the minutes of their first meeting:

Concern was expressed that effort should be made to ensure that the project benefited the islanders and not overseas-based commercial interests.

It was clarified (sic) that publishing activities would be controlled by the Committee in the Solomons. Only editing aspects would be done in the East-West Centre, Hawaii.

[2]The local committee also stated initially its intention to collect war stories and songs themselves. This, however, was not carried out in any systematic way.

[3]One of the singular ironies of the conference, in which Japanese voices were noticeably absent, was the fact that the proceedings were recorded on videotape by a Japanese volunteer operator and equipment donated to the National Museum by the Japanese government.

[4]It is appropriate that Pidgin, a key feature of emergent notions about pan-Melanesian identity, would facilitate discussion of a period in regional history also regarded as a basis for common experience and identity.

[5]Their preparation of scholarly papers in English indicates that each of the Melanesian scholars adhered to some degree to the standard model for an academic conference. However, it is worth noting that in other ways their work departs from Euro-American assumptions. The fact that each reported on research in his own society indicates that they do not entirely subscribe to anthropology's romantic cross-cultural vision.

[6]The journal *'O'O* is available from the University of the South Pacific Centre, P.O. Box 460, Honiara, Solomon Islands; and *The Big Death* may be ordered from the Institute of Pacific Studies, University of the South Pacific, Suva, Fiji.

The Postmodern Crisis: Discourse, Parody, Memory

Vincent Crapanzano

> The process of making equal is the same as the process of incorporation of appropriated material in the amoeba.
>
> —Nietzsche
> *The Will to Power*

In writing about the baroque *Trauerspiel*, the mourning play, the play of melancholy, Walter Benjamin (1977:177–178) notes that the allegorical physiognomy of history conjoined with nature—"The word 'history' stands written on the countenance of nature in the characters of transience"—is present in reality in the form of the ruin. "In the ruin history has physically merged into the setting." Today, in an age that has been declared postmodern—indeed, by some, in Spain for example, as neo-Baroque—the ruin has been replaced by the quotation, the trace, really a pseudo-trace, a detritus, a re-ferent, a carrying back to/from a past, which is so completely decontextualized, so open to recontextualization, that it, the quotation, the trace, becomes at once an emblem of a past evacuated of history (history understood as a somehow meaningful account of the past) and a signal of the artifice of any such account, any history. Ironically, demonically, the denial of the possibility of a "real" mimetic account, of any master narrative, proclaimed by the relentless signals of artifice does in fact announce an overarching narrative of—a consuming obsession with—artifice. As baroque mourning—constituted on the experience of transience, death and the corpse—gives way (I need not pass, I suppose, through the defiles of neoclassicism and romanticism) to today's (ideologically bruited) *jouissances,* constituted on the experience of change, of difference, *différance,* of rupture, the bit, the flickering image, the digital sound, no doubt masking a postcoital emptiness, nostalgia, and the longing for repetition and reunion, so allegory, whose artifice, at least during the baroque, was mournfully relished, surrenders to artifice, whose allegorical possibility is playfully denied. There is in all play a danger that the truth alluded to (from the Latin *ludere,* to play) will break through and arrest the play.

I will be concerned with putative discursive changes associated with postmodernism and with their relationship to memory understood as a structural precipitate of any dialogical engagement in which a change of perspective, or the illusion of a change of perspective, occurs. This "new" discourse, at least in cross-cultural settings, is structured, I will argue, like parody. Parody, Linda Hutcheon (1988:11) writes, "is a perfect postmodern form, in some senses, for it paradoxically both incorporates and challenges that which it parodies." It stresses difference and, through the inscription of that difference in a literary or artistic tradition, masters it. Its assumption is imperial.

Many definitions of "postmodern" have been advanced, and, for the most part, as even the most superficial reading reveals, they are vague, over-generalizing, and contradictory.[1] Some stress epistemological skepticism, hyper-reflexivity, and the artifice of all accounts including those which articulate a perduring self. Others emphasize play, language games, the "logical operations of cultural terms" within a structure that seems independent of its medium of expression, indeed of reality itself. And still others point out the arbitrariness, the conventionality, of those temporal connections that give us the illusion of history and continuity and take ironic delight in a sort of promiscuous quotationalism that subverts history, continuity, and memory (Gaggi 1989). "Pouvons-nous aujourd'hui continuer à organiser la foule des évenéments qui nous viennent du monde, humain ou nonhumain," Jean-François Lyotard (1988:46) asks, "en les plaçant sous l'Idée d'une histoire universelle de l'humanité?"

Postmodern commentary, that is, commentary on postmodernism by contemporary postmodernist critics, stresses reflexivity. Commentary and its subject, criticism and *its* subject, metalanguage and primary language, are entangled and declared inseparable. There can, as such, be no external vantage point for commentary, criticism, indeed, reading and perception. We are caught within the play of arbitrary signs that are loosened from their referents and no longer systemically constrained by grammars of style, say, or narrative. (The postmodernist debt to Saussure, as understood by the deconstructionists, is enormous.) Not only is the arbitrariness of the sign in any act of signification paradigmatically proclaimed but so is the arbitrariness of its syntagmatic, its syntactic, placement. There is— there can be—no longer a "natural" or "naturalized" sequence. The concatenation of signs becomes an ironic montage, ultimately a self-subverting comment. In architecture, where a postmodern ideology has flourished, the juxtaposition of disparate styles is no longer justified on transcending aesthetic or decorative principles (as were the juxtapositions of Egyptian, Greek, Roman, and Oriental motifs on *Empire* furniture). When Philip Johnson couples immense vaults, reminiscent of Sabastiano Serlio and a stage setting for grand opera, with a Chippendale scroll that reminds one of the secretary back home, he is making a statement about the artifice of his project, about its place in the "history" of architecture, about history itself, and about the conventionality of aesthetic theory. So at least it can be read, and is read, by the postmodernist reader.[2]

Fredric Jameson (1984) has observed that postmodernism seems always to be understood in terms of some sort of "radical break" with *another* moment of socioeconomic organization and cultural and aesthetic orientation. It is defined against that which it is not, against conditions which no longer prevail or are somehow irrelevant. For Marxists like Jameson, it is rooted in a "consumer society" that differs structurally from other moments of capitalism (Jameson 1988).

I stress "another moment"—"other moments"—for postmodernist theorists seem to be particularly concerned with the relationship between postmodernism and modernism. Although some see postmodernism as simply following modernism, others, who are anxious not to succumb to "the illusions of history," attempt to describe the relationship between modernism, or romanticism for that matter, and postmodernism in some more complex, often dialectical way. The Italian philosopher Gianni Vatimo (1985) likens the "post" of postmodernism to Heidegger's *Verwindung* and *Überwindung*. According to Vatimo, *Verwindung* is analogous to *Überwindung*—to overcoming—and yet different from it. Unlike *Überwindung*, *Verwindung* has no relationship to *Aufhebung*. It is the leaving-something-behind of a past that has nothing to tell us. Postmodernism is then both part (an extension, a sublation) of modernism and, despite the modernist traces (the detritus) it exploits, wholly different from it.

This concern with the "post" of postmodernism, with the relationship between one period and another reflects a far-reaching discontent with—an epistemological anguish over—the conventions of historical, indeed, at times it seems, of any kind of, understanding. Sequencing, the causal assumptions that underlie that sequencing, continuity, the experience that fosters that sense of continuity, selecting and framing of events, the theoretical understanding that sanctions that selection and framing of events, the adoption of an appropriate vantage point and the authority that authorizes that vantage point, are all questioned. The skepticism appears here to be as thorough, but by no means as terse, as Hume's. It is clotted theoretically; it lacks Hume's ultimate confidence. It does take a certain delight—some critics would say nihilistic delight—in the impossibility of any universal understanding, any incontestable truth, any indefeasible argument, any ultimate authority. God is surely dead in the postmodernist world. There is, as Lyotard (1984) remarks, no faith in meta-narratives that legitimate science and other totalizing (emancipatory) visions of the world.[3] Included among these are the Marxist and the psychoanalytic, which in their causal over-determination, in their totalizing assumption, resemble the magical systems Lévi-Strauss describes. I would also include the quasi-articulate, commonsensical stories we tell ourselves about everyday life that assume meaning, totality, progress, and emancipation. These meta-narratives are as subject to deconstruction as their narratives of reference.

When I write that God is dead in the postmodernist world, I am at once playing with a popular postmodernist conceit—Nietzsche is of course a postmodernist hero—and making a very serious point about the world the postmodernist postulates. I am referring to the authoritative function, which I (1990a; 1990b) have called the Third, that mediates any interlocution. In any dialogue, conversation, or exchange there is always an appeal to a complex, stabilizing authority that authorizes a particular linguistic code, a grammar, a set of communicative conventions, allocations of power among the interlocutors, criteria of intra-, inter-, and extra-textual relevance, and appropriate interpretive strategies. This function is, in technical terms, meta-pragmatic, for it determines the way the communication indexes itself, its personnel, its context, and its possible interpretations. It is symbolized, I believe, abstractly by such notions as the law, grammar, or tradition,[4] more concretely by totems and fetishes. It may be embodied by father, king, or priest—more rarely by female figures—by spirits and deities, and even by a third person (the audience) in any dyadic exchange. It may be appealed to directly or indirectly in any of its symbolic guises. In ordinary exchanges, it is usually taken for granted or easily negotiated. In some extraordinary exchanges (cross-cultural exchanges before they are routinized, for example, or exchanges during periods of crisis or, less well understood, creative fervor), there is no mutually acknowledged Third to whom rhetorical appeal can be made. When the Third is simply an empty function, there can be no communication.

The postcolonial world has been called postmodern: an off-centering juxtaposition of contradictory styles that are not supported by any single, seemingly unified vision—or narrative—of the world. Observers stress surface; the spectacle; the multimedia nature of social life, its polyphony, its heteroglossia; the rapidity of change; the uncritical adoption of modern technology (from the pocket calculator to the submachine gun); the absence of historical awareness; the lack of compelling criteria for contextualization, interpretation, and understanding; the "protean" nature (to use an anachronistic term) of postmodern man, his lack of depth, his uncritical narcissism, his interminable quest for gratification. The description appears to be altogether too specular, too literary, like something out of Salman Rushdie, having more to do with the New York art scene, the Milan world of fashion, or the Paris bar in Berlin than with the pathetic conditions of a Bangkok slum where a man may wear a Woman's Lib T-shirt, enslave his wife, spend his evenings in a brothel listening to Michael Jackson on a cassette recorder made in Japan, and hope his daughter will win a Miss Thailand contest so that he can open a little restaurant for workers in the center of the city and have his teeth capped in gold.

The post of postcolonialism is not subject to the same play, not yet at least, as the post of postmodernism. The past of postcolonialism is not yet a repertory of self-referential citations. For the postcolonialist the past evokes the imposition of a history, no doubt in alien form, that has been used, paradoxically, in the failed struggle to overcome that history, that imposition. It calls attention to the absence of voice—and what is worse the absence of a responsive interlocutor. However real their source, fantasms, like ghosts, can never respond, not truly, for they can add nothing to what is already known. The past of postcolonialism is the past of the Aufhebung. It cannot be overcome. It cannot be controlled by citation. It cannot yet be reduced to trash, the trace, the pseudo-trace. It is too painful. Like the shoddy borrowings of that other culture, those cultures of reference, the polyester shirts, the tinny transistors, the expired penicillin, and the Mercedes Benz, it calls attention to difference—difference framed in equality—and the locus of power that perpetuates that artifice of equality.

There is of course considerable truth in the postmodern vision of the world despite its overgeneralizations, its literariness, and its loose associations. It challenges us. It can be neither simply accepted nor simply rejected. This results less perhaps from what it says than how it says it, and this we find particularly disturbing. Postmodern discourse, at least the discourse that comments on it, not only entangles primary level discourse with secondary or meta-level discourse but it also confounds description with prescription. Insofar as it is descriptive of a state of affairs, we are free to accept or reject it in terms of its accuracy, its truth value, but insofar as it prescribes (programmatically in the works and writings of architects like Paolo Portoghesi [1983], or in the commentaries of Hutcheon [1988], Foster [1983], and others) a particular orientation toward reality, including perhaps the rejection of those meta-narratives that justify our criteria of accuracy and truth, we can neither accept nor reject it in terms of accuracy and truth. We can take a moral, or even a political, stance toward its prescription, but, again, insofar as the prescriptive is confounded with the descriptive, we can neither accept nor reject fully the prescription. We are confronted with, more accurately, incorporated into, a totalizing hermeneutic—a sort of epistemological antinomianism—that rejects totalization, questions the authority of any hermeneutic, and refuses any transcendental position.

Now, let me do precisely what the postmodernist rejects. Let me take, arbitrarily, an *external* vantage point. They do, despite themselves. Let me suggest that what the postmodernist describes/prescribes is the result of a change in the manifest articulation of power relations—the result of a failure of hegemony—that creates the illusion, at least, of an anything-goes egalitarianism at the discursive level. (I stress "the discursive level" since I am not arguing that there is in fact today a "real" egalitarianism or a "real" hegemonic failure. It may well be—the Marxist would certainly argue—that discursive egalitarianism, hegemonic failure, and all this self-reflective talk about postmodernism are in fact contemporary mystifications, a bit decadent no doubt, of real class relations.) There is, in the terms I used earlier, no stabilizing Third in any dialogical engagement to which a final appeal may be made. The Third qua function is not rejected; rather, it is depleted, not completely, however, of its pragmatic force. Its symbols become rhetorical, but not fully. Depleted, symbolically reduced, the Third is still "required" for any successful communication. This is one of the sources of the tension we find in the commentaries on, if not the discourse of, postmodernism itself: the strained conflation of the prescriptive and the descriptive. It can also lead to a danger: assertions of sheer power, uncritical declarations of a correct version, if you will, of reality, fevered affirmations of maimed symbols. These are of course the characteristics of that other discourse, that other movement, that seems to accompany the postmodern: fundamentalism. I refer here not only to religious fundamentalism but also to ideological and scientific fundamentalism.

The evacuation of the Third and its symbolism, the breakdown of authoritative conventions of communication, and the consequences of this evacuation, this breakdown, if it does in fact occur, have yet to be examined on the ground. Many postmodernists, even in their descriptive mode, are given to largely unsubstantiated generalizations. From literature and the arts, they generalize to a "reality" and read that constituted reality as though it were empirically real or simply another "text." It seems likely that it is in declaredly egalitarian cross-cultural

contexts, particularly those that are not yet routinized or have resisted routiniza-
tion, that the discursive conditions reflected in the postmodern outlook are most
salient. As any good anthropologist knows, the communicative conventions of all
the participants in a sensitive cross-cultural encounter are always put into question, and the progression of such encounters is largely determined by the response
to this questioning. The threat may be denied. Established conventions may be
reaffirmed and enforced. New conventions may be negotiated. The communication may be ended. In most such encounters all of these responses occur over time.

By an egalitarian dialogue, I refer to an exchange between participants who
presume with whatever illusion, or pretend that they are equals and have equal
rights in the exchange. This dialogical egalitarianism may in fact be purely ideological, a mystification of "real" differences in power, and these real differences
may—certainly do—affect the plays of power that occur within the egalitarian-
framed dialogue. The framing—the convention, the pretense—of the dialogue is
not of course without its effect. No doubt determined by power relations exterior
to it, the framing constrains the way these external power relations are given or
denied expression. There is a double indexing that occurs within any exchange:
an intra- and extra-dialogical indexing of the participants, for example, as equal
within the dialogue but as unequal outside the dialogue, in real life, as we say.
The difference may be masked meta-pragmatically by the dialogue's pretense.
Court speech, diplomatic exchanges, conventional hypocrisy, and, of particular
interest to us, those cross-cultural exchanges "between equals" in this postcolonial era that just a few years ago, during colonialism, were manifestly hierarchical, are especially revealing of this double indexicality.

Despite their pretense, the declaredly egalitarian, yet to be routinized, cross-
cultural dialogues are never in fact between equals, for the absence of a fully governing convention, of a mutually acceptable Third, fosters hierarchy—a (silent)
assertion of authority over, an "understanding" of, the position of the interlocutor. (Or its opposite.) There is little to mediate—to attenuate—the challenge
each participant, coming, as it were, from somewhere else, poses to the other.
Whatever the reasons for the exchange and its continuation, whatever the source
of its egalitarian pretense, the challenge of a different orientation, of a different
cognitive outlook and a different set of values, which has to be reckoned with
among equals, threatens the respective orientation, the stability, the outlook and
values, of each participant. We are, in extreme cases, at the limit of relativist
artifice and can well understand the appeal of one fundamentalism or another.

There are many different responses each of the participants can have to this
challenge. One is to deny the challenge and play the game. A second is to seduce
the other into one's own orientation. A third is to succumb to the other's orientation. A fourth is to negotiate a shared orientation. A fifth is to suspend the game.
With the exception of the fifth, all of these have to be accomplished within the
egalitarian pretense. No doubt all of these (again excepting the fifth) occur within
any of these special exchanges. The danger of my formulation is that it presupposes a degree of lucidity and control that, I believe, is precluded by participation
within any dialogue. Our language is intentionalist and tends to weigh any de-

scription or analysis of interlocutory space, of the *Zwischenraum* or the *Zwischenzeit* of dialogue, in terms of the actors and their intentions.

Here, recognizing the dangers of intentionality, I should like, nevertheless, to discuss two types of response to the other that can occur in all dialogues but particularly in the cross-cultural ones I have been describing. I refer to what Mikhail Bakhtin (1973) calls *stylization* and *parody*. I will focus on parody. Both stylization and parody can be related to the challenge posed by the other and reveal the writing and, more often, I suspect, unwitting assertions or denials of power that occur in such exchanges. In postmodern discourse, there are times when it is impossible for the external observer—the audience, including perhaps the interlocutor's self-reflection—to determine the hierarchical relations that lie behind these two stylistic responses. We end up with something like what the literary critic Gary Saul Morson (1989) calls meta-parody and, I would add, meta-stylization.

For Bakhtin, parody and stylization are *double-voiced words,* that is, words that are to be interpreted as the expression of two speakers. The words of one speaker are appropriated by a second speaker as the words of the first speaker but used for the second speaker's own purposes "by inserting a new semantic orientation into a word which already has—and retains—its own orientation" (Bakhtin 1973:156). In other words, they are recontextualized or, in Hutcheon's (1985:11) terms, "transcontextualized"—revised, replayed, inverted. Such double-voiced words are—and here I quote Morson (1989:65)—"best described not simply as the interaction of two speech acts, but as *an interaction designed to be heard and interpreted by a third person* (or a second 'second person'), whose own process of active reception is anticipated and directed." For Bakhtin the difference between stylization and parody lies in the relationship between the two utterances. In parody the relationship is antithetical; in stylization it is corroborative. Both are evaluative; both objectify, more so perhaps in parody than in stylization, the stylized or parodied discourse; both attribute symbolic value to that discourse. Stylization can be read as either an indication of submission to the discourse, the position, the authority, of the other, or as a sign of mutuality. Parody is essentially hierarchical. It dominates its target. Unlike imitation, quotation, or allusion, it requires critical, ironic distance (Hutcheon 1985:34). Though it is incorporative, it calls attention to difference. (''Parody'' is derived from the Greek *parodia*, a countersong but also a song beside, a neighboring song [Hutcheon 1985:32; see Genette 1982 for a more complete discussion].)[5] It need not be comic. According to Morson (1989:67), it must evoke or indicate another utterance; it must be antithetical in some respect to that utterance; and it must have a clearly higher semantic authority than that utterance. Where the semantic authority cannot be determined, we have meta-parody. Where we cannot determine the relationship between stylized discourse and its reference, we have meta-stylization. This indeterminacy occurs, I suggest, when there are no shared conventions of interpretation and evaluation.

These criteria of parody also apply to egalitarian cross-cultural discourses. Insofar as the response is meant to engage with the other's ''in some meaningful way," it has to evoke or indicate that response. The speaker has to use the other's language (as he understands it) to engage with him for whatever ends. But insofar as the speaker does not share the other's orientation and may well resist that orientation, his response is antithetical to the other's. It may in fact be marked as such or it may only be "understood" as such (though I suspect that careful stylistic analysis will reveal some sort of antithetical marking where the response is only *understood* by the speaker as being antithetical). Insofar as the speaker accommodates to the other's language for his own purposes, his response has "higher semantic value" for him and may well be marked as such, that is, within the parameters set by the egalitarian pretense. In other words, at least at the level of understanding, the target is recontextualized and in its new context (ironically) evaluated.

More specifically the other is recontextualized, most often, I suspect, stereotypically, and his words are treated as symptoms of that stereotyped contextualization. We understand and evaluate his words because we know "where he is coming from." This process leads to a practical engagement with, or manipulation of, the other (justified often enough on crude utilitarian grounds) and precludes a real engagement with the other's point of view. In blatantly non-egalitarian cross-cultural exchanges, during the colonial period, for example, the hierarchically inferior other's response presented, so to speak, only an administrative challenge. He was expected to respond, often did respond, was certainly taken to respond by accepting, as best he could, the outlook, the language, of the speaker; that is, he was to respond—to learn to respond—corroboratively. That his response might well have been parodic was ignored. (Here, I should note that the response of South African blacks to South African whites is often understood by the black's parodically and only occasionally so by whites. They say the blacks are being cheeky. Indeed, the blacks have a tradition of parodying whites, on stage even, as in the play *Wozu Albert*.) Where the commitment to the egalitarian pretense is, for whatever reasons, very strong, it may well be that no participant to the exchange can admit that his recontextualizing response to the other has higher semantical authority. It is this meta-parodic situation that resembles the discourse the postmodernist postulates. It is, I believe, potentially a highly creative moment, one whose essential relativism forces us to recognize and reconsider the moral basis of our cognitive outlook that is so often masked by taken-for-granted communicative conventions. It is an equally dangerous moment for it can always stimulate backlash.

Here is an example of the type of exchanges I have been talking about abstractly. It is rather more complicated than, and certainly not as pristine as, I should like. It occurred over a year ago at an academic conference attended by American, Indian, and Chinese scholars. The Chinese, most from Beijing, had been active in Tiananmen Square and were in exile in the United States. One of them had just finished telling us about a greater individuation of the self in recent Chinese literature. After a somewhat disorderly discussion of her presentation, including frequent reference to the Chinese government's brutal reaction to the student protest, one of the Indian participants, a poet, spoke.

> Let me try to approach many of the things we have said this morning from a completely different angle. As you spoke, I have been thinking of the problem of violence and nonviolence in India. In many ways India faces, has faced, the same problems as China . . . and one of the things that we know in Indian literature and politics is the problem of—let me characterize it as Orientalism. Let me also say out right that it seems to me the way you presented the whole problem [of violence] seems to give in to the Orientalist paradigm set up for China by the West. This is constantly surprising to me coming from the Indian context. In a sense the self is one of the major themes of the Orientalist discourse about the Orient. Why pick up on this? Why concentrate on individualism? . . . In the Indian case, much the same thing happened but it happened in the Nineteenth century in alarming ways. Once India opened up, it picks up prepacked ideas from the West, jumps on the bandwagon, and repeats, as it were, the history of the West . . . and loses its own cultural identity. . . .

The Chinese reaction to his observations was immediate, violent, emotional. (Most of the Chinese participants were not familiar with the debates on Orientalism that Edward Said's work has inspired. Most of them did not have the command of English that the Indian poet did.) The American participants listened for an unusually long time before entering the discussion. The first respondent was one of the principal leaders at Tiananmen Square. He spoke angrily.

> I don't think you will reform China according to Western patterns. . . . At the same time, I think no people can go their way only according to their own way, their own culture. Chinese can only develop in a Chinese way. But what we are trying to do, what we hope to do, is to introduce some concepts, some institutions [from the West] that will be useful to us—not all concepts and institutions.

The Indian poet interrupted with "a quick footnote"—one of his favorite expressions—about how in India, being modern meant being Western, being traditional meant being tribal. He was in turn interrupted by a second Chinese participant who just managed to utter, "On the surface you are right, but actually you are not," before he was interrupted by a third, highly articulate Chinese man—I'll call him Wenzhong—who reiterated the leader's comment while emulating (parodying), so it seemed to me, the style of the Indian poet. (He spoke slowly, ponderously, using the "we" as the Indian had, and turns of phrase like "up-to-the-minute" and "wholesale borrowing," reminiscent of the Indian's "bandwagon" and "prepackaged.") His discourse was, so to speak, triple voiced! It was very controlling.

> When we introduced these up-to-the-minute concepts, we were quite aware of the danger of wholesale borrowing, blindly borrowing, copying from Western models. We discussed their limitation. We were always aware of their [being] obstacles to Chinese culture. We see them on only a utilitarian basis or a basis of expediency. No, we study them, we scrutinize them for an essence that can hold out something for us, be healthily absorbed into the Chinese way, and play some positive role.

The Indian poet—he was now standing up—was irritated. A second Indian participant also stood up and tried to mediate, by paraphrasing, with some critical distance, his countryman's position. He concluded by contextualizing it, stereotypically, in terms of an Indian propensity toward the mimetic—"the quoting of passage after passage of a Western text, encapsulating it."

I cannot pursue the discussion in detail. The Indian poet asked the Chinese if there was a Chinese equivalent to the Indian mimetic tradition. No one answered. A fourth Chinese participant from Taiwan, an outsider among the Beijing intellectuals, argued that one could not speak of a single Chinese response, and saw his own participation in Tiananmen Square as a painful way of discovering his own selfhood. No one followed up on his observation. Wenzhong spoke again, offering the possibility of resolution by invoking the different historical traditions of China and India and their different relations with the West. But before anyone had time to respond to him, an American participant, the first to speak, seemingly oblivious to what was happening, offered a manifestly Orientalist view of how the Chinese often mistook the Western ideas they borrowed. He was ignored. The discussion turned to history and repetition, with references to Kierkegaard, without anyone noticing that "history" and "repetition," as understood by Kierkegaard at least, were distinctly Western. At one point, I intervened, noting that "Orientalism" was a Western category. Several Chinese agreed; several ignored my intervention. The Indian poet simply asked, "So what?" There was no final resolution, though an American political scientist, a Frankfurt school Marxist, tried to mediate by invoking the inevitable progression of social change. He said talk about Orientalism was a red herring. What was important was the discontinuity that was occurring or would occur in India and China as it had occurred in the West with the development of modern capitalism (or some other economic arrangement), and that this discontinuity, this break with tradition, would be painful.

After the meeting, there was a lot of talk about what had happened, and although I was not privy to most of it, what I did hear and overhear from Chinese, Indian, and American participants was an attempt to reframe the argument in terms of different historical traditions and responses to the West. History, evacuated of content, served rhetorically to preserve the "egalitarian tone" of the meeting. No one wanted to talk, for example, about notions of cultural confidence and cultural superiority, or about feelings of losing one's cultural identity by being identified with another culture. No one took an ironic stance, noting that despite all the critical talk about, and the resistance to, "prepackaged," "up-to-the-minute" Western ideas, the discussion was in fact couched in distinctly Western terms.

The violence of the encounter stemmed, I believe, from the Indian poet's failure to preserve its egalitarian tone and thereby exposing its pretense. He revealed the "superiority" of his own parodic response and broke the meta-parodic illusion of egalitarianism. He also revealed his own vulnerability, for though he made use of Western categories in a structurally parodic fashion, he did not have, so it seems to me, a critically ironic distance from them. The Chinese response, at first angrily confrontational, was in its own way parody-like insofar as it evoked, and was antithetical to, the Indian's comment and assumed a higher semantical authority. There was, however, no compelling authority—not even Orientalism, and certainly not the Westerners present—that could be appealed to, to mediate, to reconstitute the egalitarian pretense. So serious was the betrayal that ironic understanding of the meta-parodic situation was precluded, even in the retrospective accounts. No one wanted to analyze, at least semi-publicly, the dynamics of the encounter. Only one alternative was left if the meeting was not to break off completely and if any claim to egalitarianism was to be preserved: namely, the appeal to a symbol, *history,* that was so empty as to pose no threat to any position. "Orientalism played itself out differently in India and China," one of the Chinese participants observed toward the end of the discussion, and was seconded by the Indian poet and the Americans. History here becomes one of the maimed symbols of that meta-pragmatic function that I have referred to as the Third.

That history was the chosen symbol for preserving the egalitarian pretense of the meeting is significant. It is history—memory, I would prefer—that has been radically altered by the changes in discourse that the postmodernists have postulated. History—that is, *narratio rerum gestorum* and not *res gestae,* whatever that may be[6]—is a positioned narrative that affirms, among other things, its position. Hence its importance in nationalism, territorialism, and group and individual identity. History or memory or some objectification—some emblem or monument that stands for it—can serve as an authoritative reference point, whose artifice has been traditionally denied, in dialogues within one culture or across cultures when one of the cultures is manifestly dominant. Where there is a failure in hegemony, history can no longer serve as such a reference point, for each of the parties to an encounter has his own "legitimate" position, his own history, his own memory. The artifice of historical assumption—the incorporation of multiple positions into a single, consuming narrative—is revealed. The strain—to share or not to share, to be incorporated into, or to remain independent of, any historical tradition—is enormous. (Hutcheon stresses the ex-centricity of the postmodern outlook and the play between incorporation and differentiation in parody.) When universalist narratives, like the Marxist, lose their legitimacy as meta-narratives, then history becomes an evacuated symbol of only rhetorical or pragmatic interest. Or again, there is always the possibility of some nationalistic, religious, racial, or ethnic appropriation—or invention—of an historical narrative whose encompassing authority is affirmed through ritual, through the sacralization of chosen, iconic events. We are of course familiar with these in the fascist states of the Thirties and Forties, in white South Africa today, and in many contemporary fundamentalisms.[7]

As a speculative coda, I should like to consider the relationship between new discursive—parodic and meta-parodic—forms (or perhaps more accurately, the privileging of existent forms) and memory, understood as a precipitate of these forms. (Hans-Georg Gadamer [1975:16], writing in a different vein, asks us "to rescue the phenomenon of memory from being regarded as a psychological faculty and to see it as an essential element in the finite historical being of man." "Memory must be formed," he writes, "for memory is not memory for anything and everything.") I suggest that insofar as memory is articulated in conventional forms, it, or at least its expression, is constrained by these forms, and that when there is a change in a conventional discursive form, there will be a corresponding change in memory or its expression. In other words, memory is determined by the meta-pragmatic function, the Third, that determines how various communicative *Einstellungen,* or functions, including, notably, the intra- and inter-textual, are indexed.

Traditional, empirical approaches to dialogue have assumed the continuous identity of the participants and have regarded dialogue as simply an alternation of speakers and hearers (Tedlock 1983). They have ignored what the Viennese poet Hugo von Hofmannsthal (1973) called the *allomatish* (the allomatic), the *gegenseitige Verwandlung* (the "mutual change"), that occurs between two or more persons who are engaged in some way, say dialogically, with each other.[8] They have assumed, in other words, that Speaker A before hearing Speaker B's response is the same as Speaker A after hearing Speaker B's response, and no doubt this assumption can safely be made for most conventional conversations—for what Heidegger calls *Gerede,* or idle talk. But, there are of course occasions, often dramatic ones, like conversion, a sudden insight, an epiphanous experience, a new way of seeing things, triggered by Speaker B's words, that radically change Speaker A's perspective, his understanding, his sense of self, his identity even. The dialogical situation becomes far more complicated—more productive of the selves in the encounter (Crapanzano 1990b). Speaker A and, in another way, Speaker B now have to reckon with Speaker A's previous dialogical incarnation, all that that incarnation symbolizes, and the challenge to (the artifice of) personal continuity it poses. (It may indeed become a symbol of the Third.) We ought perhaps to regard any conversation as an exchange not between Speaker A and Speaker B but between Speaker A prime, double prime, et cetera, and Speaker B prime, double prime, et cetera. It is the gap between the dialogical incarnations of each speaker that affords the space of memory—and forgetting. We must remember Nietzsche's (1956) observation: "Forgetting is no mere *vis inertiae . . .* it is rather an active and in the strictest sense positive faculty of repression [*positives Hemmungsvermoegen*]. . . ." Forgetting as well as memory are implicated in the perduring self.

Hofmannsthal was writing about the allomatic, or more correctly trying to capture it, in *Andreas*—a novel he was never able to complete—and in *Die Frau ohne Schatten* (1920), which took several forms, during a period of great discursive turmoil and invention. In this discursively troubled period, another Viennese was developing a new speech genre of revolutionary import, the psychoanalytic, and was also elaborating the most systematic theory of memory and forgetting we have ever had. Freud's theories of screen memories, of distortion, condensation, displacement, repression, foreclusion, and sublimation, which were largely discovered from within this new genre, can all be seen as ways in which an individual negotiates the gap between his present self and his previous ones. Freud provided a compelling master narrative for preserving the sense of continuity, which, paradoxically, was subverted, altered certainly, by the discursive form he invented.

We should ask what is happening today to memory, and by extension to history, if there is in fact a radical change in discursive forms and practices of the sort I have been describing and the postmodernist has been postulating. We do not live easily with our ghosts—with the traces of the past. We talk about a loss of history among young people, for example, as though it can be regained. We try desperately to preserve—and pass on—the memory of events, so often traumatic events, which we once found significant and perhaps still do, in another way, we know grudgingly, as they enter our personal and our collective rhetoric. We document them, commemorate them, memorialize them, to the point even of sacrificing ourselves to them. And particularly where we have no narratives that support our memory, we are left with only the truth of its evacuation, its rhetorical reduction, and the certainty of the artifice of our documentation, commemoration, and memorialization. We understand despite ourselves the enchantment of retrogressive movements, like the fundamentalism, the racism, and the nationalism to which I have referred obliquely, and we know the risks of such enchantment. We have to recognize the inescapable dangers—and the extraordinary creativity—of those discursive changes that trouble our complacency, and we have to resist the facility (the cant) with which they can be described and ultimately reduced.

There are those who argue that postmodernism does not reject history and those who argue that it does miss the point. *History* is no constant. It is a discursive practice, subject to change, that presupposes a particular temporal organization and bears a particular symbol (existential) weight. It changes as discursive practices change. If there is any truth in Lyotard's (1988:115) contention, for example, that the citations of past architectural forms in postmodern architecture are like day residues in the dream, then it follows that the "history" that arises from such citations has a radically different temporal organization than that of our traditional narrative histories. It is autonomous, closed in on itself, frozen. The unconscious, the dream, knows no time, Freud tells us. We are not particularly comfortable with this history. Nor are we comfortable with the Roshomon effect of the dialogically open, self-questioning, multi-perspectival histories that are appearing today (e.g., Rosenstone 1988). We may delight in the artistry of their montage, but underlying this delight is, I believe, an anxious nostalgia for the modernist preoccupation with the wounded tales of emancipation. Benjamin (1977:178) observed that it was "common practice in the literature of the baroque to pile up fragments ceaselessly, without any strict idea of a goal, and, in the unremitting expectation of a miracle, to take the repetition of stereotypes for a process of intensification." Benjamin's words can also be applied to the postmodern, that is, if one erases but does not expunge "in the unremitting expectation of a miracle." Would this erased miracle be the return of the Third—*our* Western hegemony—and the capacity to escape meta-parodic indeterminacy by knowing whose parody is empowered? The parody and meta-parody I have described are serious.

Notes

Acknowledgments. In accordance with the dialogical approach I take, I should note that this article was first delivered as a paper to the Israeli Anthropological Association in the winter of 1990. Its political message, however allegorical, or better displaced, was no doubt appreciated by that audience. I wish to thank the Association for their invitation. It was revised during the Bush-Hussein war. Its allegorical dimension seemed as relevant. Its displacement, I'm afraid, a bit obscene.

[1]See Hutcheon 1985 and 1988 for extensive discussion and bibliography.

[2]Unlike the quotationalism of much postmodern architecture in which the "historical referent" is simply a marker of the postmodern—an architecture that quickly degenerates into kitsch—Johnson's elegant citations of the past, in the AT&T building for example, respect the cited past, tradition, however artificial it may be. His citations are not self-referential. They do not proclaim membership in a school.

[3]I should note that since the publication of *The Postmodern Condition*, Lyotard (1988) has modified his position slightly, giving critical attention to his model of the narrative.

[4]Ought I to write here law or "law," grammar or "grammar," tradition or "tradition"? Our system of punctuation insists upon a distinction between use and mention that may be analytically productive but masks the rhetorically potent slippage between the two that occurs in nonanalytic discourse. This same problem of punctuation occurs below in my use of history/"history," as when I write about "history evacuated of meaning."

[5]By calling attention to the two meanings of *para*, against and beside, Hutcheon (1985:35, 1988:57) underlines the fact that parody is "a personal act of supersession and an inscription of literary-historical continuity." Like Genette (1982), she does not consider the importance of parody's domination of its target by both superseding it and affirming its position in tradition or context. In the nonliterary instances I am discussing, this inscription of continuity is one of the devices for imposing a set of conventions on the exchange.

[6]See note 4. There is of course a rhetorical slippage between *narratio rerum gestorum* and *res gestae*.

[7]Similar strains and similar responses, including the retrogressive, can be seen in family and personal histories where, for whatever reasons, their assumption is questioned and their incorporation of multiple positions revealed. (Deconstructionist and certain psychoanalytic readings of life historical texts reveal their multi-voicedness, their several narrative positions, which are ideologically encompassed by the governing personal pronoun—the I.)

[8]See also Miles (1972) and Bennett (1988) for discussions of the allomatic.

References Cited

Bakhtin, Mikhail
    1973   Problems of Dostoevsky's Poetics. Ann Arbor, Mich.: Ardis.
Benjamin, Walter
    1977   The Origin of German Tragic Drama. London: NLB.

Bennett, Benjamin
  1988   Hugo von Hofmannsthal: The Theaters of Consciousness. Cambridge: Cambridge University Press.
Crapanzano, Vincent
  1990a   On Dialogue. *In* The Interpretation of Dialogue. Tullio Maranhao, ed. Pp. 269–291. Chicago: University of Chicago Press.
  1990b   On Self Characterization. *In* Cultural Psychology: Essays on Comparative Human Development. J. W. Stigler, R. A. Shweder, and G. Herdt, eds. Pp. 401–423. Cambridge: Cambridge University Press.
Foster, Hal, ed.
  1983   The Anti-Aesthetic: Essays on Postmodern Culture. Port Townsend, Wash.: Bay Press.
Gadamer, Hans-Georg
  1975   Truth and Method. New York: Crossroad.
Gaggi, Silvio
  1989   Modern/Postmodern: A Study in 20th Century Arts and Ideas. Philadelphia: University of Pennsylvania Press.
Genette, Gérard
  1982   Palimpsestes: la littérature au second degré. Paris: Seuil.
Hofmannsthal, Hugo von
  1920   Die Frau ohne Schalten; Erzahlung zon Hugo Hoffmannsthal. Berlin: S. Fischer.
  1973   Ad me ipsum. *In* Aufzeichnungen. Pp. 211–244. Frankfurt am Main: S. Fischer.
Hutcheon, Linda
  1985   A Theory of Parody: The Teachings of Twentieth-Century Art Forms. New York: Methuen.
  1988   A Poetics of Postmodernism: History, Theory, Fiction. New York: Routledge.
Jameson, Fredric
  1984   Foreword. *In* The Postmodern Condition: A Report on Knowledge, by Jean-Francois Lyotard. Pp. vii–xxi. Minneapolis: University of Minnesota Press.
  1988   The Politics of Theory: Ideological Positions in the Postmodern Debate. *In* The Ideologies of Theory: Essays 1971–1986, vol. 2. Pp. 103–113. Minneapolis: University of Minnesota Press.
Lyotard, Jean-François
  1984   The Postmodern Condition: A Report on Knowledge. Minneapolis: University of Minnesota Press.
  1988   Le postmoderne expliqué aux enfants. Paris: Galilée.
Miles, D. H.
  1972   Hofmannsthal's Novel: Andreas. Princeton: Princeton University Press.
Morson, Gary Saul
  1989   Parody, History, Metaparody. *In* Rethinking Bakhtin: Extensions and Challenges. Pp. 63–86. Evanston, Ill.: Northwestern University Press.
Nietzsche, Friedrich
  1956   The Birth of Tragedy and the Genealogy of Morals. Francis Golfing, trans. Garden City, N.Y.: Doubleday.
Portoghesi, Paolo
  1983   Postmodern: The Architecture of Postindustrial Society. New York: Rizzoli.
Rosenstone, Robert A.
  1988   Mirror in the Shrine: American Encounters with Meiji Japan. Cambridge: Harvard University Press.

Tedlock, Dennis
  1983   The Spoken Word and the Work of Interpretation. Philadelphia: University of Pennsylvania Press.
Vatimo, Gianni
  1985   La fine della modernità: nihilismo ed ermeneutica nella cultura post-moderna. Rome: Garzanti.

A Broad(er)side to the Canon: Being a Partial Account of a Year of Travel Among Textual Communities in the Realm of Humanities Centers, and Including a Collection of Artificial Curiosities

George E. Marcus

Current issues about canons, or "the" canon, are, of course, more generically about the constitution of authority and tradition in social groups. At present, the canon is the specific referent or object, constructed not by those who wish to defend tradition and authority, but by those critics who wish to conceptually circumscribe authoritative knowledge so as to delegitimate not only the specific items to which it refers, but also the category of authoritative knowledge itself in the interest of some not as well conceptualized, but certainly more open and pluralist, conditions for producing knowledge. Why the critique of authoritative knowledge should be so vocal and pervasive across the disciplines of the humanities, the arts, and, to a lesser degree, the social sciences, is a complex and interesting situation, which I mostly stipulate in this paper, so as to focus on the other related question that interests me: the specific formulation and rhetoric of this critique focused on the term *canon*.

Canon itself connotes sanctity, orthodoxy, and discipline in a church context, and this lends ideological intensity to critique, but the broader referent is that of authority embodied in the selection and reading of *literal* texts. Thus, the rhetoric of critique has been formed and its terms defined specifically within literary theory, and has spread from there as "the issue of the canon" to other related fields. My purpose in this paper, after a brief, speculative inquiry into the significance of the canon issue for contemporary literary studies, is to explore comparatively how this particular formulation of critique, with its emphasis on textuality and the act of reading, has settled into the critique of other disciplines.

What this comparative inquiry will clarify are the unexamined assumptions about how authority is constituted through the use of the canon-formulation developed within literary studies. For example, the assumption that the canon is embodied in texts and that it is primarily realized through the activity of reading is a major (largely unexamined) rhetoric of literary scholarship. One purpose of this paper is to question the adequacy of such a formulation to characterize the actual process by which authority is produced, not only in the disciplines to which it is applied by extension, but also in the discipline in which it originates, literary studies. That is, my approach here is intentionally and literally sociological or ethnographic, because it is needed in a compensatory way, given the power and privileging of the canon formulation developed in literary studies. Is emphasis on textuality and reading enough to describe how authority arises and is challenged in contemporary disciplinary or interdisciplinary communities?

My inquiry here is conducted within a particular sociological landscape distinctive of contemporary academic institutions. While disciplines, organized in conventional university departments, are indeed the framing institutional object of discussion—disciplines, after all, create and police textual canons at their core—the discussions themselves do not occur there. Rather, they take place in the cultural studies/humanities research centers that have been created in most American universities in the course of a veritable humanities revitalization movement, now occurring. Such centers are the new interdisciplinary spaces in which critical-minded scholars attempt to reimagine their disciplines under the influence of a number of signs—critical theory, feminism, postmodernism, the crisis of representation, poststructuralism, and, not least, challenges to canons. Most commonly, exchanges between history and literature are at the center of discussion with the major source of theoretical novelty entering through literary studies over the past two decades, but philosophy, anthropology, history of art, and architecture also prominently participate. The ultimate aim of the movement is some sort of disciplinary effacement—in the words of Roland Barthes, ''To do something interdisciplinary it's not enough to choose a 'subject' (a theme) and gather around it two or three sciences. Interdisciplinary consists in creating a new object that belongs to no one.'' While such a seductively unattainable object is not in sight, in the pursuit of it, the category ''disciplines,'' and the canons that stand for them, are objectified and constructed in such centers to refigure and blur the boundaries of the scholarly communities that are constituted by this pursuit.

While for the most part these humanities centers might be labeled left/liberal in the way just described, some are nativist and/or conservative. That is, they stand for totalities, traditions, canons. I spent the academic year of 1988–89 in one of the latter, the Getty Center for the History of Art and Humanities in Santa Monica, part of the $4 billion J. Paul Getty legacy. In contrast to the nativism as represented in, say, the popular writings of E. D. Hirsch, Jr., and Alan Bloom, and the ideology of the NEH under William Bennett and Lynn Cheney, the Getty Center is cosmopolitan, devoted to interdisciplinarity, but is definitely acknowledging of a canon—in this case, of the Western visual arts—within which it eclectically works. It is the best of establishment interdisciplinarity at the moment, which works under the sign of totalized knowledge. It is an interdisciplinarity that sustains the identity of disciplines in relation to the authority of a Western intellectual tradition.

The Getty is embodied in a corporately run organization whose atmosphere feels a lot different to the participating scholar than does the university environment. As such, it might suggest to the humanist, who works there, so close to capital, the hothouse insularity of politics and political gestures developed in cultural studies/humanities research centers of the university. After all, such centers are supported in the interstices of an organization whose ideology is not that much different from the corporate Getty, especially as one moves up the ladder of university administration to boards of trustees. Universities are committed firmly to a traditional table of departmental organizations as constituted for most of this century in the United States, and this table is another representation of an authoritative EuroAmerican knowledge tradition.

While I will hardly be able to escape the identity of an ethnographer in this paper, I would at least like to evoke the rhetoric for myself of a traveler, say, one of those writers of 18th- or 19th-century travel accounts who tell of events in lands strange to his readers. My intention in so evoking this rhetoric is only partly parodic. I indeed do want to ground what I have to say in my experience over the past couple of years, and particularly over my year based at the Getty Center, when I traveled, much like David Lodge's academic pilgrims in *Small World* (1984), to a number of conferences and seminars, occasionally in anthropology departments, but mostly in humanities/cultural studies centers, both here and abroad (especially during 1988–89 in Denmark and Australia). Like the classic traveler, I want the license, not granted the ethnographer wishing to distinguish himself as scientific sojourner, to write from anecdotes, overhearings, observations, impressions, chats on the road, in short, from soundings. In fact, I open each section below, which is named for a discipline but originates in what I have heard/seen/learned in cultural studies/humanities centers, with soundings from this traveler's experience.

There are two senses in which I feel that this parodic-serious evocation of the traveler is quite appropriate to the topic. First, in a postmodern age, the flexibility of the traveler's account in the variety of modes in which arguments, explanations, connections, and assertions can be made is ironically quintessential to the postmodern mode of pastiche. While the literal old-style travel account of civilized movement in a less civilized world can only still be achieved with great artifice (as in the writing of Paul Theroux), its parodic borrowing is true to the postmodern style of juxtaposition, collage, and associating those things that are worlds apart. Second, the traveler primarily listens, engages in conversation, and treats readings as if they were voices; he takes soundings, privileges experientially the power of the spoken over the textual in its most literal and metaphorical sense. Thus, in line with the critique that I want to offer here of the overly literacy-minded, text, and reading bias of the canon formulation of the problem of disciplinary authority, the notion of the travel account is quite appropriate—it is not a "reading" of an issue but a presentation of how authority is constituted in textual communities by equal attention to such things as gossip, corridor talk, charismatic oratory, and oracular self-presentation. Finally, then, I am trying to assert the value of looking at this issue of authority in knowledge-producing groups from a grounding in the ethnography of situations from which this quite academic issue emerges. Thus, the special contribution of ethnography to the canon debate is that it bridges the humanities and social sciences, and particularly gives the humanities a reflexive and empirical sense of its own practices. But since I was only a "sort-of" ethnographer in the world that I want to focus on, I plead as a traveler, offering myself more flexibility and latitude.

Before proceeding with a critical treatment of what I take to be the theory behind the canon issue in literary studies, I want to make two related observations about its appeal, primarily to literary studies, but also to other fields that this issue has touched.

First, it is worth noting that the canon issue seems to be a distinctively American one. While much was shared topically with their American counterparts in the Humanities Research Centers in Copenhagen and Canberra where I visited during 1988–89, the focus on specifically textual authority—of the canon—was absent. The canon issue is a particularly reflexive question of a sociology-of-knowledge sort concerning the nature of the institutions that generate humanities scholarship—the university, patronage by the state or foundations—and the fear of the withering away of a civilizing tradition from within and without by cultural forces that erode the viability of literacy and advanced literateness focused on the possibility of deriving truth from texts, as vessels of truth. This specific formulation of the authority issue has become focused in America, and its absence in two regions of the extreme periphery where the Humanities are nonetheless vibrantly practiced suggests just how parochially American this formulation is.

Second, the canon issue in the United States has something to do with the relationship of intellectuals, and scholars in particular, to politics and political debates outside the academic context. What is the position of the academic, particularly as humanist, in relation to domestic or even world politics? Academics identify with the politically aligned and legendary free-floating intellectual of earlier periods, most proximately, the 1920s–1930s and the 1950s. And the American image is in turn derived from the figure of the 20th-century European intellectual committed to political and social movements, left and right. However, his reputation has suffered by contemporary studies. Lionel Trilling, for example, stands as a model of the humanities academic made intellectual by his relationship as cultural critic to real-world politics. Now there is only nostalgia for this kind of position. As Russel Jacoby has lamented recently, the free-floating intellectual is indeed a figure of the past, the position having been completely absorbed into academic bureaucracies. More important, humanist intellectuals in the university, nostalgic indeed, perceive crises, unprecedented change, and social movements around them—domestically or internationally—for which the left-right orientations of liberal political theory are a very poor frame of reference. In short, academics, in seeking attachment to real-world events and politics, suffer from the same crisis of representation that affects them professionally. Their desire for political commitment lacks conceptual frameworks that they can take for granted. The American university academic is more vulnerable than the European in this regard, since the liberal model of intellectual political commitment had been borrowed from European experience and applied to American conditions anyhow. The fit was never good, but in the 1920s and 1930s, and 1950s, it was good enough. From the late 1960s, this liberally inclined orientation to real-world politics started to be undone, and there has been a vicarious, hermetic re-creation of traditional categories within the politics of the academy. So the cultural studies movement serves to create some substance to liberal-conservative, left-right distinctions that have no, or very uncertain, relations to any parallel process in real-world politics, domestic or international. In the face of confusion about the relevance of traditional political alignments in social movements, then, there has been an involution in relation to politics—from politics in the world to politics in the academy, as a screen for these confusions, and as a cypher for a variety of positions that do not communicate very well the relationship of academic intellectuals to the world. It might be remarked here that the social appeal and authority of academics thoroughly in *our* cultural studies/humanities world, but with Third World commitments and associations, lay precisely in that they appear to retain in other worlds the sort of classic relationship to politics for which American intellectuals are nostalgic. Thus, the power of such academics to shame their colleagues is remarkable in this regard.

Now this is all by way of saying that world politics and internal academic politics have become isomorphic, especially in the issue of the canon. Debate about the canon reproduces the fiction of the old categories, and has great nostalgic appeal. There is a conservative, orthodox authority, which various liberal/ left positions can resist. This is not to say that these ''hothouse'' nostalgic political struggles in the academy do not have real-world political implications. It is just that the relationship of academic politics to external politics is not very clear at the moment, given that a common vocabulary of political alignment has been rent asunder.

(I want to say here parenthetically that while ethnography has no special authority or privilege as a form of representation—indeed it is under thorough critique as such—it does nonetheless offer the humanities the means, in a piecemeal, grounded fashion, to remake the sociological landscape to which humanist intellectuals can relate politically—at least it can help to clarify such a landscape. This was the hope Mike Fischer and I had in *Anthropology As Cultural Critique* (1986), which tried to realign ethnography with the humanities, being the one kind of humanist story that reports empirically from direct experience outside the academic culture. However vulnerable is ethnography's own authority, it adds something missing, something that worlds the text in a way that can be debated and held accountable, and brings the longing for humanist political commitment at least in touch with other communities however problematically. The opportunity exists precisely because the available frameworks no longer work as well in marking position, and ethnography offers one kind of possibility away from the complete reproduction of political commitments, based on the old distinctions, hermetically within the politics of academic positions themselves.)

Finally, I want to argue that the appeal of the challenge to the canon in literary studies, and particularly within a feminist frame, is precisely that, in one of its basic dimensions and motivations, it promises to break with this insularity of political commitment and finds an issue in the real world leading directly and naturally into the academic community. It not only feeds the nostalgia for such old models of intellectual commitment but also provides an actual cause. What I am referring to, of course, are the conservative cultural policies of the Reagan years that have stirred well-publicized official and other attacks on recent trends in the humanities, which cultural studies/humanities revitalization predominantly represents. The popularity of the books by Bloom and Hirsch, Bennett and Cheney at the NEH, and the attack on those charged with education of basic skills, have resulted in the targeting of scholars in English directly in their function as educators, and more ideologically, in terms of their responsibly preserving the Western/American heritage against all sorts of perceived threats as the decline of American geopolitical power becomes more generally apparent. That is, in literary studies alone among disciplines, the issue of the canon is not just about the authority of disciplinary tradition, but it involves seamlessly an external political issue, which flows directly into real-world politics. Whether or not the old categories of liberal/conservative fit this situation well is not clear, but they do work in forming responses from the humanities. The "relevance" of literary studies in this regard gives it authority among the critical elements in other disciplines, which are also critiquing their central authorities as textual canons.

This kind of worlding of the humanities, while existentially powerful and involving, is superficial, however, because it arises from a turning inward of political involvement one level higher than the academy—that is, at the level of statecraft, which makes its own hermetic response to forces of change that it does not know how to come to terms with. Fear of Japanese efficiency and discipline, for instance, or the growth of non-English speaking populations within the United States are major geopolitical issues that stimulate an inward search for the roots of our own decadence and that find a natural object for Americans in the educational system, not scientific or technical education, but that aspect which inculcates cultural value and national will—the humanities. But the geopoliticians are as confused about the shifting processes as are the humanists. Thus, the humanists gain this real-world political relevance in which the liberal/left finally has a cause not only against academic conservatives, but against statist ones also, at the cost of the confusion about contemporary social changes being reproduced and embedded one level higher in state and society themselves. This means, all the more, that the humanities beyond the issue of the canon must participate in the clarification of the language for representing the social landscape, perhaps no longer an American one, that will allow them to have clearsighted political relevance once again, but in new forms and perhaps in different terms. To me this is the important task embedded within the often obscure debates about postmodernism and a crisis of representation that motivate the cultural studies/humanities revitalization movement.

Literary Theory: A Remaking of the Theoretical Foundation of the Canon Issue so as to Understand the Formation of Canonic Heresy in Contemporary Textual Communities Across Disciplines

In this section, I want to suggest the theoretical backing for the canon issue in American literary studies. Specifically, the concept I want to develop is one that focuses sociologically on both those groups that constitute and submit to the authority of textual canons as well as those that develop in opposition to them. This concept is textual communities, which for my purposes is a remaking of Stanley Fish's influential construct of *interpretive communities* (1980). To make his argument, Fish uses an inherently sociological construct but does nothing with it empirically as might a sociologist or ethnographer. Through a brief critique of this construct, I want to remake it into *textual communities* (after Brian Stock's use of this term in his book *The Implications of Literacy* [1982]) not only to demonstrate the limitation of Fish's construct in understanding the process of canon formation and resistance to it in his own field of literary studies, but also to create a more flexible framework to pursue the broader sides of the canon issue in other associated disciplines that participate in the cultural studies movement.

Why do I choose Fish? Along with a few others like Barbara Herrnstein-Smith, Charles Altieri, Myra Jehlen, Jane Tomkins, and Arnold Krupat, he has provided the generic theoretical conceptualization that grounds the issue of canon. Fish, in *Is There a Text in This Class?* (1980), has been so influential because his theory has been accessible, pragmatic, refreshingly uncomplicated, and, in some sense, so American. To an anthropologist, what Fish, Herrnstein-Smith, and others have gotten onto in the 1980s for their purposes is the sort of interpretive anthropology of cultural meaning that Clifford Geertz developed in the early 1970s, a renewed and sophisticated statement of the doctrine/practice of cultural relativism at the core of 20th-century liberal anthropology in the Boasian tradition. Fish has found his way to this without any attribution to Geertz or anthropology, but it is clear that his interpretive communities are like "tribes" or small-scale societies in which possible meanings in communication, literate and oral, are circumscribed by tacit knowledge and assumptions. It is this realm of tacit knowledge that has long been the object of description and explanation in American cultural anthropology. The whole purpose of Fish in evoking interpretive communities is to revitalize the field of literary studies so as to dissolve the encrustedness of canons, of meaning inherent in texts rather than communities. Instead of a standard of authoritatively correct readings (as argued by E. D. Hirsch, for example), the possibilities for interpretation rest in the community of readers, their tacit assumptions, debates, the complex cultural processes of their life as a community, in short, in their culture. It seems to me that this is the relatively simple but powerful argument that defines the enlightened position for evoking canons so as to challenge them. For instance, here Fish, in his introduction to *Is There a Text in This Class,* sets up the canon issue:

> Literature, I argue, is a conventional category. What will, at any time, be recognized as literature is a function of a communal decision as to what will count as literature.

> All texts have the potential of so counting, in that it is possible to regard any stretch of language in such a way that it will display those properties presently understood to be literary. In other words, it is not that literature exhibits certain formal properties that compel a certain kind of attention; rather, paying a certain kind of attention (as defined by what literature is understood to be) results in the emergence into noticeability of the properties we know in advance to be literary . . . the reader is identified not as a free agent, making literature in any old way, but as a member of a community whose assumptions about literature determine the kind of attention he pays and thus the kind of literature he makes. . . . The notion of "interpretive communities," which had surfaced occasionally in my discourse before, now becomes central to it. Indeed, it is interpretive communities, rather than either the text or the reader, that produce meanings and are responsible for the emergence of formal features. Interpretive communities are made up of those who share interpretive strategies not for reading but for writing texts, for constituting their properties. [1980:68]

While I am sympathetic to Fish's position, and he deserves great credit for evoking the sociological basis of interpretation and canon formation, his construction of what he labels "interpretive community" is itself biased by a set of assumptions that restrict its usefulness as a more general framework not only for examining the process of canon formation and resistance to it in other disciplines in which the literary formulation of the problem of canon has been adopted, but also for giving an account of the same process in Fish's own field. That is, how can we further sociologize or make more ethnographic the sociological construct that Fish evokes? Can the notions of the text and reading tell us all or even much about the tacit cultural processes that he wants to focus upon?

I find two major limitations within Fish's construction of interpretive community. While iconoclastic, he thinks only in terms of the channels of literacy—texts, and reading texts. This, for him, is what *primarily* goes on in interpretive communities of literary scholars. Largely omitted are the crucial forms of oral communication by which interpretations (of texts?) get constituted and spread with certain values attached to them. So, in Fish's construct, he needs at least a literary-oral continuum or interaction. To be fair to Fish, he does acknowledge corridor talk, gossip and the like (for example, he says, "it is only when readers become literary critics and the passing of judgment takes precedence over the reading experience that opinions begin to diverge. The act of interpretation is often so removed from the act of reading that the latter is hardly remembered" [1980:63]). But, nonetheless, the metaphor of the reader is dominant in Fish's construct to stand for the central activity in canon formation. Certainly, any scholar who lives in the information age knows there is something antiquated, nostalgic, not exactly right about such a formulation. Oral forms of communication are at least as important as reading in interpretive communities, even though the focus may emblematically remain upon literal texts. Much gets established by listening to interpretation, by reading reviews of books, by corridor talk, rather than literal reading of texts itself (and I do think that Fish in his sociologism of interpretive community does mean to refer literally to the scene of reading as a practice). In short, Fish does not take fully into account the importance of secondary orality that Walter Ong has evoked. In contrast to Fish's interpretive communities, David Lodge's *Small World* (1984) is a sociologically much better formulation—a world in which ironically Fish as Morris Zapp, and his theories, get encompassed—since it focuses on the readers/critics/theorists in literature tending to their own social processes, precisely how through talk in social action reputations, authority, get constructed, and how the medium for this is the discussion of certain texts. And in *Small World* textual canons themselves are provocatively put off center to give the emphasis to interpersonal processes by which their authority is constituted in *community*.

Why is this criticism of Fish consequential and why does putting at least as much emphasis on networks of gossip, opinion forming, et cetera, as on the conflict of interpretation based on literal reading, make a difference? This is the related, second limitation of Fish's construct. While he focuses on the canon as authoritative object of scholarly communities, thus clearing the way for altering this object, he evades the reflexive question of how canons of interpretation or criticism themselves (that is, counterauthority) are being formed at the very same time. And I argue that this dimension cannot be opened up without a thoroughgoing sense of how a canon is formed by processes of oral communication in the shadow of literacy—this would mean a perspective that is not dominated by the figure of the reader, or reading. Then the question is how certain texts come to serve an emergent canon of interpretation or criticism, and it is this secondary or countercanon that scholars adhere to in paying attention to their primary object: a canon of literary work that they do not produce, but focus upon and give value to; thus the special, wider political significance of literary studies. Now Fish argues something very close to this, but how the critical canon gets formed requires a more complicated understanding of the processes that constitute interpretive communities than just reading, and this is where Fish is undeveloped and inadequate in his discussion. Pace Lodge's satire, interpretive canons are not formed primarily by reading, but by off-center forms of socially embedded (mainly spoken, oral) discourse.

To adjust Fish's characterization of interpretive communities to this critique, I propose to substitute for my purposes the notion of textual communities, a construct that I borrow from Brian Stock who used it in his study of the impact of literacy on the essentially oral world of the 11th and 12th centuries. As he says,

> From reading, dialogue, and the absorption of texts, therefore, it is a short step to "textual communities," that is, to groups of people whose social activities are centered around texts, or more precisely, around a literate interpreter of them. The text in question need not be written down nor the majority of auditors actually literate. The interpreter may relate it verbally, as did the medieval preacher. It may be lengthy, as were, for instance, genealogies or monastic rules; but normally it is short enough that its essentials can be easily understood and remembered—a few proverbial maxims, let us say, of St. Paul, rather than an entire epistle. Moreover, the group's members must associate voluntarily; their interaction must take place around an agreed meaning for the text. Above all, they must make the hermeneutic leap from what the text says to what they think it means; the common understanding provides the foundation for changing thought and behaviour. [1982:382]

With appropriate changes in historical context then and now, Stock's formulation with the hybrid mix of texts and orality, but with the accent on oral communication, is much better than Fish's, with the focus on literacy and reading, to establish Fish's own position. Most important, Stock's formulation allows for the focus on how a canon of interpretation or criticism itself gets established through orality in the shadow of a textual canon. Fish elides this issue altogether, since he has no vehicle for reflexively understanding how these critical attitudes themselves get authoritatively shaped, independent of the reading of particular texts. This is the conceptualization that "textual" rather than interpretive community provides.

Furthermore, Stock develops his notion of textual community specifically in the context of his discussion of outbursts of heresy between A.D. 1000 and 1050 in which the central motor of change was a literate interpreter of a text working within a less lettered community: "Within smaller groups contact was informal and personal; in larger ones, or when the audience was dispersed, a more formal means of communication was adopted, normally preaching, through which a heretical or reformist text was transmitted and commented upon orally" (1982:384). Perhaps taken a little parodically, even in the Lodgean mode of small world, this description of textual communities in the 11th and 12th centuries could be taken as a better description of Fish's conception of interpretive communities within and between disciplines in the late 20th century, especially as it applies to heretical communities of cultural studies/humanities research centers.

Textual communities as a remaking of Fish by way of Stock will be our guide for reviewing the issue of canon in the disciplines of anthropology, history, and art history. For an extreme end comparison, I include "science," much written about in this regard by contemporary historians and ethnographers of particular scientific communities. There is a doubling of the notion of textual community in this enterprise. It can stand for how canons arise and function authoritatively in disciplines, and this will be the object of my commentaries. Textual communities as disciplinary communities are focused on texts and reading to greater or lesser degrees, and it is this "greater or lesser" that Stock's formulation addresses by his explicit attention to the literacy-orality mix in the understanding of how textual communities are constituted. This mix is of key importance in assessing comparatively how different disciplines constitute their internal authority, whether it depends on a literate reception of a textual canon or not. Textual communities can also stand for the heretical or reformist interdisciplinary communities where it is canons of critique (or countercanons) that are being formed, and for whom the state of canons itself in disciplinary communities is an object of critique. It is through these heretical communities in the cultural studies revitalization movement, which I traversed in 1988–89, that the state of canonic authority in disciplines is reflected upon.

Each section below begins with soundings, in my guise as traveler, with things I overheard, fragments I read, quotes I made special note of on my way through various textual communities of the cultural studies movement. Then, I provide a commentary on them that addresses how canons are presently constituted in the disciplines that are objects of discussion in the heretical environments of humanities centers/cultural studies events and conferences. The semiliterate practices that ground the interpretation of focal texts, at the core of Stock's notion of textual communities, characterize canon formation in both the textual communities of the disciplines and those of their heretical counterpoints in the cultural studies/humanities centers movement. In setting up this metaphorical traversing of disciplines (through my literal traversing of the cultural studies world), literary studies stands at one extreme and science (high energy physics, for example) stands at the other with respect to the significance in each field of its canon residing in the literal materiality of print texts, of writing, and thus in the solitary literate practice of reading.

Anthropology: After the Ethnographic Canon of Malinowski, Evans-Pritchard, et al.

Soundings:

"How do you write polyphonic ethnographies?" (question from the audience to a panel at a recent American Anthropological Association meeting, which featured Edward Said's "mau-mauing the anthropologists" with responses from Renato Rosaldo, Paul Rabinow, among others. The question was not merely evaded; it was ignored.)

"How do I make my dissertation reflexive?" (revealingly naive question I have received more than once in my talks at various anthropology departments. I answer by critiquing the question.)

****

(Pierre Bourdieu overheard at an address to the senior chieftains of American sociology on his visit to the University of Chicago during my year at the Getty and reported in a letter to George Stocking, my neighbor at the Getty):

". . . which reminds me that Bourdieu made several notably caustic comments about George Marcus, from whose brand of 'nihilistic' and 'narcissistic self-criticism' he clearly wanted to distinguish himself. 'Reflexivity is [meant to be] a means to understand and refurbish the tools you will use.' In addition, he cited Marcus as an example of the trans-national distortion effect. They [Rice] take ideas 'from people they don't know, things they don't understand, and put them in an atmosphere of campus radicalism. . . . They think they are Parisians, but they are nothing.' To think you can be an American Habermasian is necessarily to forget [and paradoxically so] that there are social modes of production affecting those ideas. . . .''

The note I did not send to Bourdieu:

Dear Pete,

Heard about your performance in Chicago. Thanks for making us a part of the canon, and sharing your cultural capital.

Salut,
Georges from Houston

****

Comments:

Until recently, well-trained social/cultural anthropologists, whatever particular peoples they studied, shared a working knowledge of the facts of life of particular "classic" peoples such as the Nuer, Trobriand Islanders, Tikopians, Ndembu, et cetera, through discussions of which, many of the theoretical points about such matters as kinship, ritual and religion had been established. These "classic" peoples were in turn represented for anthropologists at large by a canon of classic ethnographic works, that the British in particular had pioneered. Not only were they exemplary works, signifying much about how anthropologists should conduct research, but they also shaped the questions and problems that oriented the discipline for over 50 years. So anthropology has operated with a rather rigid and circumscribed canon of ethnographic works that had a great impact on the training process, how fieldwork was conducted, how routine ethnographies as dissertations and then books were written, and how the object of anthropology—the primitive or some variant thereof, once the term became unmentionable—was constructed. A separate fieldwork literature, much of it confessional, repeated attempts to tell the history of anthropology in the context of Western colonialism. And finally, the critique of ethnographic writing, similar to that earlier conducted by Hayden White in history, but done at a moment when world conditions, at least perceived from an Anglo-American perspective, were forcing a shift in the way the traditional subject matter of ethnography was constituted—all these factors considerably weakened, if not demolished, the tightness and sharedness of this canon, at least in America.

Being very text-centered ideologically, anthropology is now obsessed with the cult of the new and ephemeral. New ethnographies are read for their novelty and then pushed aside for the next innovation. Texts per se do not serve as models any longer. The classic ethnographies are in the general education of anthropologists relegated to the history of the discipline. This is regretted by many older anthropologists, and brings about charges of nihilism directed toward those who have undertaken the critique of the discipline, particularly those who have focused on the critique of writing practices, and who have seemed to undercut the possibility of authoritative works as such. Tradition in anthropology thus depends now more than ever on oral transmission, in courses, corridor talk, teacher-student relations, seminars; on specialized exegetes reading classic work for the only partly literate in this regard; and on those who are reading/listening in other directions. The tradition is now largely, then, an oral one in which classic texts are evoked, but only lightly read. It is the job of teachers to establish the relevance of the tradition, just as the ethnographic frame itself becomes experimental.

Where is the canon here? It exists primarily nostalgically as "truth in texts." New texts are produced all the time, but are received in an anti-canonic vein. What is exciting about anthropology at the moment is that new objects of study are being constructed without the operation of canons, either those that conservatively establish discipline or those that organize and dominate lines of critique and challenge. There are shared myths, legends, stories, a history in anthropology, a method, but no canon and no canonical rendering of method. Yet, the discipline manages to retain a distinctive identity despite the absence of internal policing at the moment. More than any of the other disciplines discussed around the issue of canon, anthropology exudes a state of emergence, indeterminateness in its current projects, both possibility and danger, and this is probably the source of interest it has as a discipline for contemplation from within the frame of cultural studies/ humanities centers.

History: The Critique of the Canon Moves in from the Margins

Soundings:

(Eric Hobsbawm, commenting in a *TLS* of June 1989, shortly after a stay at the Getty Center during my own sojourn there. From a brief response to a survey of 15 historians asking them what books or projects would they most like to see undertaken):

"The history I should like to see written is the one which probably cannot be written adequately yet: that of the world since the Second World War, and more particularly, during the third quarter of the 20th century. There are two powerful reasons why we need it. The first, and by now the most obvious, is that this was the most revolutionary era in the recorded history of the globe. . . . The second reason for seeing this period in historical perspective is that those who lived through it plainly failed utterly to understand, or even—if politicians—to be fully aware of, what was happening. . . . What has taken place in the world since the war really has been extremely hard to understand. . . . It is rather important for those about to enter the 21st century to see the second half of the 20th in historical perspective. Whether we can, is not yet clear. However, some of the advantages of trying to can now be seen. First, it forces a genuinely global perspective upon us. 'World history' is no longer the Western scholar's polite concession to UNESCO, but the only history that can be written. Second, it will also force historians to reconsider earlier periods, and notably the era of global catastrophe from 1914 to the aftermath of the Second World War, which marked the breakdown of 19th-century liberal society, whose heritage is slowly vanishing. . . . Thirdly, a Marxist historian cannot resist pointing out that, whoever writes that history . . . will have to start with what the old man called 'the mode of production in material life' and go on from there to 'social, political and intellectual life-processes in general.' Try it any other way, and see where you get. But those of us who belong fully to the 20th century are probably too deeply rooted in it to see its extraordinary transformation in historical perspective. Or, perhaps, to recognize a history that gets it into perspective, if we should live long enough to see one."

****

(Three connected incidents at "cultural studies" events during my year in Los Angeles):

Carlo Ginzburg attended the first meeting of our informal Wednesday night discussion group among the visiting scholars at the Getty Center, which focused upon, session by session, the nature of the ongoing internal critiques of human science disciplines. This first session we were focusing on anthropology and the critique of its central practice of ethnography developed in the volume *Writing Culture,* edited by Jim Clifford and myself. Based on my familiarity with his previous work, I had expected Ginzburg, unlike others present, to be sympathetic to the critique of ethnographic rhetoric. Not so. I found myself uncomfortably positioned by Ginzburg to defend some of Jim Clifford's statements in the introduction to this volume that concerned the possibility of descriptive realism after a thoroughgoing exposure of the construction of ethnographic objectifying rhetoric and authority. Ginzburg himself took a surprisingly hard-nosed, polarizing position that there is a really real, which is the object of historical (and ethnographic) research and that the critique in the way that Clifford has posed it is dangerously diverting from the practice of historical scholarship.

The next evening, when I attended the inaugural sessions of a three-day conference sponsored by the Critical Studies and Human Sciences Group at UCLA, I perceived a context for Ginzburg's intervention the evening before. The opening addresses were given by Hayden White ("Plot, Character, and Event in Historical Writing") and by Carlo Ginzburg ("The Inquisitor as Anthropologist"). Following Ginzburg's address, there was an extended exchange between White and Ginzburg that was acerbic, and even bitter. White claimed that he was interested in language, discourses, and representation, that Ginzburg was interested in a reductionist, and objectified power at the root of human affairs. Ginzburg reasserted a strong reality position that was essential for those who actually *do* this work—that is, producing actual histories from arduous archival work—implying that White, the historian-become-critic had become effete and irrelevant to the practice of historical scholarship. In retrospect, I could see that, for Ginzburg, the Getty discussion was a rehearsal for the UCLA event, and that Clifford, White's colleague in the History of Consciousness Program, was the stalking horse for White. But the hardline, ideological character of Ginzburg's position (and *not* the realist position itself) remained a mystery to me.

Finally, I was invited to speak to an informal History Workshop group that had been organized among younger faculty and graduate students of the UCLA history department, primarily as a forum to discuss the role of history in the interdisciplinary cultural studies movement. I spoke about the various reactions that I had registered both inside anthropology and out to the critique of ethnography articulated, for example, in the volume *Writing Culture*. Given the preceding Critical Theory conference, a comparison between the ongoing critique of the ethnographic canon and a very similar one introduced much earlier by Hayden White directed to history became the center of discussion. It was readily acknowledged that White's critique of the discipline had been thoroughly marginalized in history (as in Ginzburg's retorts to White), while a similar critique in anthropology seems to have stimulated debate at the very core of this discipline. And furthermore, only through the "backdoor" of the critique of ethnography in the context of the cultural studies movement has the sort of critique White had earlier made been renewed with some force in history. Tangential to these discussions was a wondering about Ginzburg's hardline realism against White/Clifford/ the critics of disciplinary canons, the reasons for which Ginzburg had not seemed to make clear to his UCLA students.

****

Comments:

History is perhaps the canonical case for the existence of disciplinary canons as truth in texts—texts being the literal accounts that "working" historians produce. That is, the ideology of internal textual canon is strongest in history, and any attempt to relativize this, by making it "literary," or by demonstrating the theoretical underpinnings of historical writing as writing is relegated to the legitimate, but marginal, and lower rank subspecialty of historiography. This is of course where Hayden White's work conventionally belonged and was placed, but because it wouldn't stay there due in turn to the broader crisis of representation that challenged the very adequacy of the historian's function, as interestingly registered in Hobsbawm's remarks, White's work has been especially controversial—sharply resisted, or dismissed by most historians, emblematically defended by a minority. There is much in common with anthropology in the way that a set of exemplary works as model and practice have been necessary for the discipline of history. It is just that anthropology has lost its specificity of canon, has absorbed the critique, while the ideology of the textual canon remains strong among historians.

Just as in literary studies or any other disciplinary textual community, in history too, the canon is constructed not only by reading but also by the influence of particular works, arguments, and styles of expression through corridor talk, speeches, and prophesy. But "reading" as such is not a major trope for historians; instead, the argument is to be distilled from a complex explanatory/narrative text and then debated free of the text. But how arguments develop is definitely text-centered, and focused on a canon as to what counts as the product of approved historic research (usually archival). So the textual canon of historians will not include that which is produced by anthropologists or literary historians who have made a recent claim to be doing history. The discipline rests on the history done by the historians, and the reputation of the work depends not on intense or alternative readings of it, but on debating the arguments that are distilled from it. And these arguments often have a life in conferences, seminars, and discussions quite separate from the text itself. For the debates and arguments to continue, it must be presumed that the texts contain realist truth—facts and interpretations that can be argued as right or wrong. Any effort to see the historical work as literature threatens this activity. Unlike the literary theorist, but like the ethnographer, the canon is composed of works that the professional historian produces guildlike—an internal literature.

Art History: Producing European High Culture in Los Angeles

Soundings:

(From Hans Belting's, *The End of the History of Art?* (1987), which served as a reading for the Wednesday scholars' seminar at the Getty Center that concerned itself specifically with the contemporary internal critique of the discipline of art history):

"We have heard before of the end of the history of art: the end both of art itself and of the scholarly study of art. Yet every time that apparently inevitable end was lamented, things nevertheless carried on, and usually in an entirely new direction. Art is produced today in undiminished volume; the academic discipline, too, survives, although with less vitality and more self-doubt than ever. What does stand seriously in question is that conception of a universal and unified "history of art," which has so long served, in different ways, both artist and art historian. Artists today often decline to participate in an ongoing history of art at all. In so doing they detach themselves from a tradition of thought, which, after all, was initiated by an artist, Giorgio Vasari, and in many ways for artists, a tradition that provided artists with a common program. Art historians appeared on the scene only much later. Today they either accept a model of history that they did not themselves devise, or shun the task of establishing a new model because they cannot. Both the artist and the art historian have lost faith in a rational, teleological process of artistic history, a process to be carried out by the one and described by the other."

****

What became very clear in the Wednesday evening scholars' seminar at the Getty Center was the consistent effort of the European scholars (of the ten scholars in my year, only two of us were American; the Europeans were mainly art and social historians) to assert an authority over or else express a condescension toward the critiques of various disciplines developed in an American context (but crucially informed of course by European social theorists). Thus, in our first session, the suspicion and dismissal by Carlo Ginzburg of the critique of ethnographic representation. And in our second session, an almost derisive attitude toward Richard Rorty's misreadings of the Western philosophic tradition. Then, the concerted and noticeably vehement demolition of Belting's essay by four prominent European historians of art who were present at the Center. Belting is an acknowledged leading German historian of art, who holds a professorship at Harvard. His essay was viewed at the seminar as an aberration, a "crowd-pleaser" for his American constituency. If the seminar is an index, from a European point of view, the issue of humanities canons that extend to and depend on European cultural productions lack legitimacy or authenticity in their American context. For Europeans, the critique of disciplinary authority in the U.S. signals a distinctly American cultural crisis, rather than a Western or European one.

Comments:

Art history is by reputation and, I think, by conviction the most conservative of the disciplines that unapologetically constructs its authority in terms of a canon, but it is a visual canon, rather than a print one, as ultimate object. The critical canon that grows up around this tends to be more mystified and potentially more dogmatic. Good and tireless historic scholarship participates in the aura of taste and connoisseurship—the scholar takes on something of the ethos of the collector. Value judgments go hand-in-hand with scholarly ones in a way that is much more explicit than in other humanities disciplines. Also, in the American context, authority for the canon originates in Europe and its own sense of high culture. The European-American split that was quite prominent in the Getty seminar merely strengthens the mystification of the canon, as something that art history in America, at least, can never fully possess unless in total devotion to it. Thus, any effort to relativize the art historical canon as in the Belting essay meets with a much more concerted resistance than one perhaps finds in literature or history.

However much the textual metaphor may be extended and used in referring to the canonic objects of art history, art history does not have a canon in this sense. While like the literal book or text, the object of art historical authority is material, still art historical objects are not "read" but appreciated through a mystified hierarchy of taste that while it motivates scholarship does not describe itself. The "canon" in art history is mystified, not available to be read, exists, at best, as a philosophy of aesthetics, and remains both unwritable and unspeakable. More than literary studies in relation to what is literature or great works, art history in its alliance with connoisseurship, cocooned in high culture, is responsible for valorizing what is art as a cultural object beyond the discipline.

Finally, what art history does share with literary studies, and what distinguishes these two disciplines from history and anthropology, is that the canons that they construct materially—what named works are to count as great literature or art—are shared with the world beyond disciplinarity; they spill over into it.

While anthropologists and historians have broader social functions—to circumscribe otherness and to tell the past—the literal texts by which this is done are only canonic for and within the disciplines. But for art historians and literary specialists, their canonic objects are literally shared with the public—thus they have a different role in relation to the public (the state?) than do anthropologists and historians. The former are the guardians of sacred cultural artifacts, and thus they have a political import, and a possible conservatism that anthropologists and historians do not have as much. The canons of the latter are more insular to disciplinary concerns although they are held accountable for the kinds of general stories they produce, but these are not texts except in the most metaphorical sense. The literal canonic texts of literary critics and art historians are the sacred property of a much larger community than just the discipline.

Science (with Special Reference to High-Energy Physics): The Case of the Literary Formulation of the Canon Issue

(While I did not pass through any centers devoted to the history and social study of science that tangentially could count as part of the heretical wing of the cultural studies/humanities centers trend, I think a consideration of science offers a useful contrast and extremity for any comparative consideration of canon formation at the heart of disciplinary authority, or rather the adequacy of the canon metaphor, by route of literary studies, for understanding this process generically.)

Soundings:

> Bruno Latour, in *Science in Action* (1987), concluding his generic discussion of the role of the "literature" among scientists. I became aware of Latour's work, in part, through my network of cultural studies associations, for whom he is a major representer of "science," particularly in this book and more specifically in his work on Pasteur, recently published in translation as *The Pasteurization of France,* (1988):
>
> ". . . It should be clear now why most people do not write and do not read scientific texts. No wonder! It is a peculiar trade in a merciless world. Better read novels! What I will call fact-writing in opposition to fiction writing limits the number of possible readings to three: giving up, going along, working through. Giving up is the most usual one. People give up and do not read the text, whether they believe the author or not, either because they are pushed out of the controversy altogether or because they are not interested in reading the article (let us estimate this to be 90 percent of the time). Going along is the rare reaction, but it is the normal outcome of scientific rhetoric: the reader believes the author's claim and helps him to turn it into a fact by using it further with no dispute (maybe 9 percent of the time?). There is still one more possible outcome, but such a rare and costly one that it is almost negligible as far as numbers are concerned: re-enacting everything that the authors went through. This last issue remains open because there is always at least one flaw even in the best written scientific text: many resources in it are said to come from . . . things out of the text. The adamant objector could then try to put the text in jeopardy by untying these supply lines. He or she will then be led from the text to where the text claims to come from: nature or the laboratory. . . . The peculiarity of the scientific literature is now clear: the only three possible readings all lead to the demise of the text. If you give up, the text does not count and might as well not have been written at all. If you go

along, you believe it so much that it is quickly abstracted, abridged, stylised and sinks into tacit practice. Lastly, if you work through the authors' trials, you quit the text and enter the laboratory. Thus the scientific text is chasing its readers away whether or not it is successful. Made for attack and defence, it is no more a place for a leisurely stay than a bastion or a bunker. This makes it quite different from the reading of the Bible, Stendhal or the poems of T.S. Eliot.''

****

(personal communication from Sharon Traweek, who has done ethnographies of high-energy physics communities in the United States and Japan):

"If you have to read about it in journals you are out of the loop of research. Communications among researchers move in very quick day-to-day, even hour-to-hour, electronic networks. Considerable amounts of time are spent in such communications, but publication in the print medium is definitely a by-product of the knowledge production processes that is of minimal concern to the main actors.''

****

Comments:

Science as generically discussed by Latour, and as specifically discussed with reference to high-energy physicists by Traweek, is clearly the null case of focusing the issue of authority in knowledge production on a canon, especially a textual canon. No such referent is constructible for scientists, at least as researchers rather than educators, or the notion of canon does not seem to be a useful way to understand the dimension of authority in the production of scientific knowledge (this does not mean of course that there might not be methodological canons, but it would hardly be a topic of discussion in the practice of research, rather than education). The "literature" is an artifact in many scientific disciplines. Orality, or its electronic analog, is primary, and textualization in print or print analog is clearly secondary. What a canon is in this quickly changing situation, or if the notion applies at all, is posed by this case. The idea of the reader is, finally, irrelevant here.

The Final Broad(er)side to the Canon:
The Rushdie Affair and Emergent Literatures

Soundings:

(From Aijaz Ahmad's response in *Social Text* (1987) to Fredric Jameson's "Third-World Literature in the Era of Multinational Capital." Specifically he reacts to Jameson's claim that "all third-world texts are necessarily . . . to be read as . . . national allegories.")
"But one could start from a radically different premise, namely the proposition that we live not in three worlds but in one; that this world includes the experience of colonialism and imperialism on both sides of Jameson's global divide . . . ; that societies in formations of backward capitalism are as much constituted by the division of classes as are societies in the advanced capitalist countries; that socialism is not restricted to something called the second world but is simply the name of a resistance that saturates the globe today, as capitalism itself does; that the different parts of the

capitalist system are to be known not in terms of a binary opposition but as a contradictory unity, with differences, yes, but also with profound overlaps. One immediate consequence for literary theory would be that the unitary search for 'a theory of cognitive aesthetics for third-world literature' would be rendered impossible . . . many of the questions that one would ask about, let us say, Urdu or Bengali traditions of literature may turn out to be rather similar to the questions one has asked previously about English/American literatures. By the same token, a real knowledge of those other traditions may force US literary theorists to ask questions about their own tradition which they have heretofore not asked . . . I want to insist that within the unity that has been bestowed upon our globe by irreconcilable struggles of capital and labour, there are those texts which cannot be easily placed within this or that world. Jameson's is not a first-world text, mine is not a third-world text. We are not each other's civilizational Others.''

****

(From Michael Fischer's and Mehdi Abedi's account (1990) of the Rushdie affair and interpretation of *Satanic Verses*):

"*Satanic Verses* stands in two sociologically distinct currents of writing, corresponding to the two arenas of cultural class-warfare. On the one hand, it stands within the stream of modernist writing that attempts to find a home within Islamic countries for modern sensibilities, the tradition in Iran of Sadeq Hedayat, Bozorg Alavi, Jamalzadeh, Gholam Hosain Sa'edi, Sadeq Chubak, Jalal Al-e Ahmad, Simin Daneshvarin; in Egypt of Taha Husain, Tawfiq al-Hakim, Naqib Mahfuz, Nadwa al-Sadaawi; and many others in North Africa, the Levant, and Mesopotamia. On the other hand, *Satanic Verses* stands within the stream of the postmodern comic novel, the tradition of James Joyce, Thomas Pynchon, and Gunter Grass (with roots going back to *Tristram Shandy, Don Quixote,* and *Gulliver's Travels*) that has done so much to re-envision the contemporary world and revalue the narratives of the past. Although Rushdie is the first major postmodern comic novelist for the Muslim world, he does not stand alone even here in Middle Eastern and South Asian writing. He is part of a gathering stream of writing and film-making by Jamil Dehlavi, Amitav Ghosh, Elias Khoury, Hanif Kureishi, Parviz Kimiavi, Rustam Mistry, Bharati Mukherjee, Mira Nair, Anton Shammas, Bapsy Sidwa, Sara Suleri, Adam Zameenzad, and the ''Decentrist'' poets of Beirut (Ghada al-Samman, Hana al-Shaikh, Emily Nasrallah, Laila Usairan, Daisy al-Amir, Calire Gebeyli, and Etei Adnan). Few of these latter, except Dehlavi and Rushdie, are concerned with Muslim belief structures. But all are concerned with the psychic transformations that living in or with the modern West has wrought for those of non-European background—themes central to *Satanic Verses* more than Islam per se.'' [109–110]

Comments:

Rushdie's *Satanic Verses* engages with canonic authority in the most canonic, fundamental(ist) sense of the term, Islamic church authority. Whether it itself is canonical or heretical depends upon how one reads, or more accurately reacts (since in the recent controversy, which has centered on it, few have read it) to *Satanic Verses,* based on its own many-leveled complexity. In the Stock/Fish sense of textual/interpretive community, it constitutes one on a global scale in which a literal text is fetishized at its core, but it is precisely not canonical, but rather challenges the very notion of such authority. Thus *Satanic Verses* looks like what Fish and Stock are conceptualizing, but it exceeds it as a phenomenon. As such, it is the ultimate broad(er)side to the idea of canon, and as such, is the appropriate note on which to end this paper. Contra to the canons of disciplines within national contexts (as surveyed in this paper for the United States), *Satanic Verses* represents emergence, a resistance to authority in the production of art and knowledge, and a phenomenon in spite of itself—thanks to the voice of orthodoxy and authority in the interest of realpolitic (that of the late Ayatollah Khomeini).

What *Satanic Verses* more broadly represents is emergent literatures that Fischer and Abedi characterize above by their list of names. Suddenly, there is a whole complex world that is not accessible to the average American scholar but that partakes wholly of our disciplinary traditions. The list of names confronts us and relativizes our debates, showing that there is indeed a broader world of the text and in the text, that is not our world, like no mere making of the argument about the relative nature of interpretive communities could ever communicate as effectively.

So, as the traveler within the strange realm of cultural studies/humanities centers, the identity I evoked for myself, I end this account having seen myself operating in quite a parochial milieu. *Satanic Verses* faces me with a cosmopolitan subject that challenges the very notion of disciplines and their internal authority, conceived in terms of the issue of the canon or otherwise. The problem of the canon in Anglo-American disciplines is a national struggle that indeed must be addressed, but only in the parochial frame that the Rushdie affair, and the emergent literatures that stand behind it show it to be. The Rushdie affair shows finally that while identity struggles go on globally and locally with great power and substance, the "national" for which canon debates stand is in doubt. This is the ultimate broad(er)side to the canon issue, which its formulation in terms of disciplines and national traditions in the West masks.

References Cited

Ahmad, Aijaz
    1987   Jameson's Rhetoric of Otherness and the "National Allegory." Social Text 17:3–25.
Belting, Hans
    1987   The End of the History of Art? Chicago: University of Chicago Press.
Clifford, James, and George E. Marcus, eds.
    1986   Writing Culture: The Poetics and Politics of Ethnography. Berkeley: University of California Press.
Fish, Stanley
    1980   Is There A Text in this Class? The Authority of Interpretive Communities. Cambridge: Cambridge University Press.
Fischer, Michael M. J., and Mehdi Abedi
    1990   Bombay Talkies, the Word and the World: Salman Rushdie's "Satanic Verses." Cultural Anthropology 5(2):107–159.
Latour, Bruno
    1987   Science in Action: How to Follow Scientists and Engineers Through Society. Cambridge: Harvard University Press.

1988   The Pasteurization of France. Cambridge: Harvard University Press.
Lodge, David
    1984   Small World. New York: MacMillan.
Marcus, George E., and Michael M. J. Fischer
    1986   Anthropology As Cultural Critique: An Experimental Moment in the Human Sci-
        ences. Chicago: University of Chicago Press.
Stock, Brian
    1982   Implications of Literacy. Toronto: University of Toronto Press.

Cultural Relativism and the Future of Anthropology

Melford E. Spiro

Unlike old generals, the debate regarding cultural relativism neither dies nor fades away, as a spate of recent publications indicates (for example, Brown 1984; Geertz 1984; Gellner 1985; Hatch 1983; Hollis and Lukes 1982; Jarvie 1984; Lloyd and Gay 1981; Meiland and Krausz 1982; Shweder 1984). If the present contribution to this debate is not entirely redundant, it is because it has somewhat different aims.

The first aim of this article is to clear away some of the intellectual underbrush that has served to obfuscate some of the controversies surrounding this perennial debate. These controversies, I hope to show, have been beset by two conceptual muddles. The first derives from the frequently committed fallacy of confusing cultural relativism with cultural variability or diversity. The second derives from the fact that in contemporary anthropology there are not one, but three types of cultural relativism—descriptive, normative, and epistemological—which, because they are designated by the same term, are often conflated. These three types of cultural relativism are not merely analytically separable but historically distinct.

The second, and more important, aim of this article is to explicate the adverse consequences of epistemological relativism—arguably the dominant contemporary type of cultural relativism—for anthropological theory and research.

On the Three Types of Cultural Relativism

Descriptive Relativism

Descriptive relativism (a judgment concerning the fact of cultural variability) is based on the theory of cultural determinism. Since, according to that theory, human social and psychological characteristics are produced by culture, then, given the fact of cultural variability, descriptive relativism is its obvious corollary: the variability in social and psychological characteristics across human groups is relative to—depends on—cultural variability.[1]

Since, however, different theorists make different assumptions in respect not only to the magnitude of cultural variability, but also the scope of cultural determinism, there are actually three forms of descriptive relativism. We shall refer to them as the strong, moderate, and weak forms respectively. Although, as we shall observe below, the differences among them are fundamental, we shall postpone their explication until we have had an opportunity to discuss the other two types of cultural relativism, normative and epistemological.

Normative Relativism

Building on descriptive relativism, normative relativism actually consists not of one, but of two judgments, one regarding culture itself, the other regarding its putative social and psychological products.

Regarding culture, the claim is as follows: because all standards are culturally constituted, there are no available *trans*cultural standards by which different cultures might be judged on a scale of merit or worth. Moreover, given the fact of cultural variability, there are no universally acceptable *pan*cultural standards by which they might be judged on such a scale. In short, since all judgments regarding the relative merit or worth of different cultures are ethnocentric, the only valid normative judgment that can be made about them is that all are of equal worth. That judgment holds in respect to total cultures (German as compared with Hopi); single cultural systems, such as religion (Judaism as compared with Mithraism); and particular cultural propositions (monotheism as compared with polytheism).

Since any cultural system (religion, kinship, science, ethics, and the like) consists of both *descriptive* and *evaluative* propositions, when a cultural proposition of one group is judged to be better or worse than an alternative proposition of some other group, that judgment is perforce based on a different dimension of merit or worth, depending on whether the paired propositions are descriptive or evaluative. Thus, while descriptive propositions (for example, "the earth is round," "witchcraft causes cancer," etc.) are judged along a *true-false* dimension, inasmuch as evaluative ones (for example, "stealing is immoral," "atonal music is beautiful," etc.) are statements of value, preference, and the like, they are judged along a *right-wrong* dimension. That being the case, normative cultural relativism comprises for the most part two subtypes, usually designated as "cognitive" and "moral" relativism, respectively (Jarvie 1984; Meiland and Krausz 1982).

According to cognitive relativists the truth claims of descriptive propositions are relative to the cognitive standards of the cultlures in which they are embedded. In short, all science is ethnoscience. Hence, since modern science is Western science, its truth claims (and canons of proof) are no less culturally relative than those of any other ethnoscience (Scholte 1984).

According to moral relativists, the claims of ethical propositions are relative to the moral standards of the cultures in which they are embedded. Just as in the case of food preferences or aesthetic canons, so also in the case of moral codes, there are no universally acceptable standards by which the latter might be validly judged on a scale of relative merit or worth.

Turning now to the putative social and psychological products of culture, the claim of normative relativism is as follows: since there are no universally acceptable evaluative standards, any judgment regarding the behavior patterns, cognitions, emotions and the like of different social groups—judgments such as good or bad, right or wrong, normal or abnormal, and the like—must be relative to the variable standards of the cultures that produce them. Thus, for example, although the Kwakiutl exhibit a constellation of characteristics which, according to Western standards, are paranoid, the latter judgment is invalidly applied to the Kwakiutl constellation because, according to Kwakiutl standards, it is judged to be normal (Benedict 1934). Similarly, if the logical processes underlying Azande magic violate normal canons of logic, it is nevertheless impermissible to judge it as irrational because logical canons, like anything else, are culturally variable. In short, since all logic is *ethno*logic or *socio*logic, the judgment that Azande magic is irrational merely reflects an ethnocentric preference for Western logic (Barnes and Bloor 1982; Winch 1958. For detailed discussion, see Finnegan and Horton 1973; Hollis and Lukes 1982; Lloyd and Gay 1981).

Epistemological Relativism

The point of departure of epistemological relativism is the strong form of descriptive relativism. Adopting the Lockeian view that the mind of the human neonate is a *tabula rasa,* the strong form of descriptive relativism claims—now departing from Locke—that everything that is eventually found on that blank slate is inscribed by culture. Thus, if "culture patterns provide the template for *all* human action, growth and understanding" (M. Rosaldo n.d., emphasis mine), and if moreover "culture does not dictate simply *what* we think but how we feel about and live our lives" (M. Rosaldo n.d., emphasis in original),[2] then virtually all human social and psychological characteristics are culturally determined.

This wholesale theory of cultural determinism is not in itself, however, the distinguishing feature of the strong form of descriptive relativism. Rather, it is distinguished by the conjunction of wholesale cultural determinism with an all but limitless view of cultural diversity. That conjunction produces—what might be called—the particularistic, in contrast to the older generic theory of cultural determinism which is associated with a less sweeping view of the magnitude of cultural diversity.[3]

According to generic cultural determinism, culture is man's species-specific mode of adaptation, analogous to those biological specializations that characterize the adaptive modes of nonhuman animals. From that perspective, every culture is a variant of a universal culture pattern (Wissler 1923), and therefore any culture produces a common set of *uniquely human* psychological characteristics which comprise what is called the psychic unity of mankind. Hence, man's phylogenetically determined biological unity combined with his culturally determined psychic unity produce a pancultural human nature.

By contrast, particularistic cultural determinism, the version which is held by the strong form of descriptive relativism, holds that inasmuch as cultures are radically different from each other, each culture produces a set of *culturally particular* human characteristics. The degree of particularity, and, therefore, the magnitude of cultural diversity which is postulated by this version of cultural determinism may be gauged from Geertz's comments on the academic world. The various subgroups that comprise that world (scholars, artists, scientists, professionals, and administrators) are, he writes, "radically different not just in their opinions, or even in their passions, but in the very foundations of their experience" (Geertz 1983:160).

Now if the subcultures *within* a single society are so different that they produce radically different psychological characteristics, then the magnitude of the differences that separate cultures *across* societies must be even larger, and the degree of psychological differences that they produce must be correspondingly large. And that is precisely what is claimed by the strong form of descriptive relativism.

As for cultural diversity, its magnitude is held to be all but limitless. Each culture, it is claimed, is unique, not in the trivial sense in which, for example, every snowflake or crystal may be said to be unique, but in the fundamental sense of being incommensurable with any other (Schneider 1984). That being the case, particularistic cultural determinism explicitly rejects the concept of the psychic unity of mankind, arguing instead that human nature and the human mind—the two components of the psychic unity concept—are culturally variable (Geertz 1984; M. Rosaldo 1984). That is why some advocates of this view—following contemporary French thinkers like Ricoeur and Foucault—refer to persons and groups whose cultures are different from our own as the "Other" (Rabinow 1977), their "fundamental Otherness," of course, being culturally, not biologically, determined.[4]

From this strong construal of descriptive relativism, epistemological relativism draws two conclusions. First, panhuman generalizations regarding culture, human nature, and the human mind are likely to be either false or vacuous; only if their provenance is confined to particular groups are generalizations likely to be both true and nonvacuous (Geertz 1973:25–26). By the same token, any general theory that purports to explain culture, human nature, and the human mind is likely to be either invalid or trivial; only if its explanatory scope is restricted to the characteristics of a particular group—and even then, only if it incorporates the latter's cultural assumptions regarding those characteristics—is a theory likely to be both valid and nontrivial (Barnes and Bloor 1982; M. Rosaldo 1984).

Put differently, significant generalizations and theories can be true and valid, respectively, if and only if they are both group-specific and culturally relative. Thus, since the "science" of psychology is Western ethnopsychology "disguised in weighty tomes" (Lutz n.d., quoted in M. Rosaldo 1984:142), its theory of aggression, for example, might explain aggression in the West, but it cannot explain aggression among the Ilongot because they make very different cultural assumptions regarding the vicissitudes of hostility and anger (op. cit.). Similarly, because the "science" of anthropology is Western in its assumptions, its theories of culture and society cannot explain Muslim social institutions; the latter can only be explained by an "Islamic Anthropology," one based on Islamic cultural assumptions (Ahmed 1984). In sum, anthropology has the choice—to modify the famous dictum of F. W. Maitland—between being emic ethnography or nothing.[5]

That brings us to the second conclusion that epistemological relativism draws from its strong construal of descriptive relativism, a conclusion that entails no less than a sea change in the conception of anthropology as a scholarly discipline. Since cultures are incommensurable and all science is ethnoscience, the very notion of cultural explanation is misplaced. Explanations are based on general theories, causal laws, and the like, which pertain to classes or types of phenomena, whereas the radical pluralism of cultures precludes the establishment of classes or types without doing violence to the "particularity and complex texture" of each culture (Rabinow and Sullivan 1979:4). In short, since in the nature of the case, "anthropology is the study of particular cultures" (Schneider 1984:196), the explanatory paradigm of scientific inquiry, though entirely appropriate for the study of the physical world, is misconceived when applied to the study of cultural worlds.

Hence, embracing the older Continental dichotomy between the *Naturwissenschaften* and the *Geisteswissenschaften*[6] and viewing anthropology as a discipline of the latter type, epistemological relativism regards the aim of anthropology to be not the *explanation* of culture, but rather the *interpretation* of particular cultures. Since, according to this view, culture is conceived as a symbolic system, the interpretation of a culture consists of the elucidation of its symbolic meanings. That aim is achieved not by the application of general principles or theories (of culture, behavior, mental functioning, symbolic processes, whatever) to the subject under investigation, but by the ethnographer's empathy, *Verstehen*, insight, imagination, understanding, and the like. (Geertz 1973; Habermas 1971; Rabinow and Sullivan 1979; Ricoeur 1970; Winch 1958).

Although epistemological relativism is viewed by epistemological relativists themselves as both logically entailed by descriptive relativism, and as itself entailing normative relativism, that is a decidedly modern view. In fact, each of these types arose independently in separate historical periods.

The Relationship Among the Three Types of Cultural Relativism

Although 19th-century cultural anthropologists were descriptive relativists—for them diversity in beliefs and customs was a function of cultural diversity—none of them so much as contemplated epistemological relativism, and they all explicitly opposed normative relativism. Thus, with respect to the latter, the diversity in culture which they documented over space and time was construed by them as supporting not only the unilineal stage theory of social and cultural evolution, but also the theory of progress, according to which Victorian culture—their own—was better by far than any of the cultural stages that preceded it.

It was only with Boas, and the rise of the American Historical School, that anthropologists came to believe that descriptive relativism entailed normative relativism. Boas and his followers rejected not only the theory of social and cultural evolution, but also—and more important for the present discussion—the notion of progress as well. Since the latter is a value judgment, and since values, they argued, are culturally relative, the judgment that Western culture is more advanced than, and therefore superior to, primitive cultures is only an expression of Western ethnocentrism (Herskovits 1972). In the service of this egalitarian view, the very term "primitive" was expunged from the anthropological lexicon and replaced, first by "preliterate" and then—because that, too, seemed invidious—by "nonliterate."

For those still not convinced that descriptive relativism does not entail the other two types, it might be observed, first, that not all of Boas's students accepted normative relativism. Kroeber, for example, rejected his teacher's views in this matter (Kroeber 1948:597–607), even while supporting his opposition to cultural evolution and extending the range and scope of his cultural determinism (Kroeber 1917). Second, just as the cultural evolutionists, though adopting descriptive relativism, did not espouse normative relativism, similarly most Boasians adopted normative relativism, but none espoused epistemological relativism.

To be concrete neither Boas himself, nor any of the pioneering normative relativists who followed his lead, held that because of the diversity of culture, anthropological generalizations and theories are necessarily culturally relative, and that consequently anthropology cannot or ought not be a scientific discipline. On the contrary, they all affirmed the obverse of these propositions.

Melville Herskovits, for example, perhaps the most polemical—if not the most radical—of the early normative relativists, was simultaneously the most insistent upon the scientific status of anthropology (Herskovits 1949). Moreover, it was precisely because he viewed all cultures as of equal value that he held, contrary to epistemological relativism, that empirical cultural generalizations and lawlike cultural theories could be sought. And it was because he believed in the "psychic unity of mankind" that he expected that search to be successful. Indeed, for Herskovits, anthropology had the choice (to now reverse the dictum of Maitland) between being science or nothing.

It was not until the 1960s, some 30 years following the development of normative relativism, that epistemological relativism, a creation of a new, post-Boasian, generation of anthropologists—known as "symbolic anthropologists"—entered upon the anthropological stage. Although the relationship between them is by no means perfect (cf. Turner 1978), it is not inaccurate to say that, in general, epistemological relativism is the philosophical and methodological concomitant of the principle tenets of symbolic anthropology (the symbolic constitution of social reality, the radical diversity of symbolic worlds, the essential arbitrariness of symbols, and the like).[7]

It should now be evident that although normative and epistemological relativism alike take their point of departure from descriptive relativism, they are otherwise historically and analytically independent of each other. That is because, in addition to their shared agenda, each also has its separate agenda. Their shared agenda—the agenda of descriptive relativism—is to challenge the validity of *noncultural* theories of social and psychological variability. But whereas the separate agenda of normative relativism is to challenge the validity of *ethnocentric* theories of variability (particularly, in the case of Boas and Herskovits, those that are racist in inspiration), that of epistemological relativism is to challenge the validity of *scientific,* that is, universalistic-explanatory, theories of variability.

Given their separate agendas, it is no accident that while epistemological relativism takes its departure, as we have seen, from the strong form of descriptive relativism, normative relativism, in its Boasian version, takes its departure from the moderate form. Although agreeing with the former that (1) virtually all social and psychological characteristics are culturally determined, the moderate form departs from it in holding that (2) many of those characteristics are universal because (3) despite the wide diversity in culture, there is also a significant degree of cultural universality. In short, this form espouses the notion of the psychic unity of mankind.

That the moderate form of descriptive relativism should have served as the scientific charter for the agenda of Boasian normative relativism is not difficult to understand. Rejecting biological, that is, racial, diversity as the explanation for social and psychological diversity, and replacing it with cultural diversity, Boas and his students then made two crucial moves. First, all cultures are equally valuable; second, the nonwhite races that preponderantly make up nonliterate societies are as capable as any other of inventing and acquiring the technologically more complex cultures of literate societies (Boas 1938).

To support the latter claim they invoked the traditional anthropological axiom that all races, whatever their culturally determined psychological diversity, share a "psychic unity." In order, however, to reconcile that axiom with, on the one hand, the fact of cultural diversity and, on the other hand, the theory of wholesale cultural determinism, they adopted a moderate view of cultural diversity, one which allowed for a certain degree of cultural universality (which then accounted for psychic unity).

Epistemological relativism by contrast not only espouses the theory of wholesale cultural determinism, but it also holds a maximal view of cultural diversity; a combination, so it contends, that precludes both nonvacuous cultural generalizations as well as the axiom of psychic unity. Hence, that combination—that is, the strong form of descriptive relativism—constitutes its charter for the claim that anthropology is an interpretive, ("hermeneutic"), not an explanatory ("scientific") discipline. (That same combination, of course, also constitutes the charter for the normative agenda associated with epistemological relativism, whose target is not a racially inspired ethnocentrism—which is no longer scientifically problematic—but a socially and culturally inspired one.)

A Critique of Epistemological Relativism

The Claim of Radical Cultural Diversity

Espousing the strong form of descriptive relativism, epistemological relativism takes its point of departure, it will be recalled, from the premise that the range of cultural—and, therefore, social and psychological—diversity is virtually limitless. Hence, before assessing its specifically epistemological claims, it is perhaps useful to assess this premise from which they are derived. There are, I believe, two grounds—theoretical and empirical—for rejecting that premise. The theoretical ground rests on a set of considerations derived from human biological and behavioral evolution, the empirical on the epistemological entailments of ethnographic research. We shall begin with the former.

Since, as a species, we are the product of biological (including behavioral) evolution, it is not necessary to subscribe to the program of sociobiology to acknowledge—together with our colleagues in biological anthropology—that as a result of selective evolutionary pressures, our hominid ancestors acquired a set of species-specific biological characteristics, many of which are socially and culturally relevant. I would mention, for example, the relationship between the evolutionary development of bisexual reproduction, prolonged infantile dependency, and the suppression of estrus, on the one hand, and the universality of the biparental human family and the parent-child incest taboo, on the other, as only one instance of that rather elementary proposition (cf. Fox 1980; Symons 1979:ch. 4).

Given this causal (but ultimately feedback) relationship between a set of evolutionary biological characteristics, on the one hand, and a set of universal social and cultural characteristics, on the other, we might then expect to find, in accordance with even the weak form of cultural or social determinism, a set of universal psychological characteristics attendant upon that relationship. And to this set, let us add a second which is the direct product of biological evolution (unlike the former, which is socially or culturally mediated). In this second set I would include such characteristics, for example, as pain avoidance, object constancy, attachment behavior, and the like, which, of course, are rooted in our mammalian heritage.

To these two sets of universal psychological consequences of biological and behavioral evolution, we may now add a third—one consisting of the products of the interaction among the putative biological, social, and cultural universals mentioned above. Thus, for example, it would not be incautious to assume that everywhere the violation of strongly internalized cultural norms and values arouses some type of emotionally painful reaction such as shame, guilt, the lowering of self-esteem, and the like. Given, moreover, the universal tendency to avoid pain, we might expect to find that everywhere psychological defenses of some form—repression, displacement, etc.—are found as cognitive resources for coping with these types of emotional pain (Hallowell 1955:ch. 1, 4).

Many more items might be added to this brief inventory of cultural, social, and psychological universals. But these few are perhaps sufficient to support my contention that it is only by rejecting human biological evolution that the premise of radical cultural pluralism—the incommensurability of cultures—can be sustained. Contrariwise, the acceptance of human evolution, together with its highly probable social and psychological consequences, all but assures the universality of many nontrivial cultural universals.

Put differently, although the impressive degree of cultural, social, and psychological variability renders either the weak or moderate forms of descriptive relativism inevitable, human biological evolution renders the strong form unimaginable. In my view, however, it is not the moderate form (with its wholesale cultural determinism) that is inevitable, but rather the weak form.

Briefly, the latter form can be outlined as follows: (1) because the range of cultural diversity, though formidable, is constrained by adaptive evolutionary imperatives, cultures also display universal features; (2) although human social and psychological characteristics are culturally determined to some (but to, as yet, an empirically unknown) degree, they are also determined by other variables, such as ecology, biology, subsistence economy, social structure, socialization, and the like; consequently, (3) although the diversity in human social and psychological characteristics is large, to the degree that their determinants, both cultural and noncultural, display universal features, their diversity is constrained to the same degree; therefore, (4) although much of the diversity in those characteristics is culturally relative, much of it is also relative to the diversity in noncultural variables; moreover, (5) to the extent that many social and psychological characteristics are (to, as yet, an undetermined degree) universal, they are not relative at all.

Lest I be misunderstood, it should be emphasized that cultural "universals" refers not only to cultural "content"—which is what the strong form of descriptive relativism refers to in claiming that cultures are unique—but also to cultural function. This qualification has two theoretical consequences.

On the evolutionary argument that many cultural, and social, characteristics of human groups are responses to a set of species-specific needs, it follows that cultural variability is constrained by the adaptive and integrative prerequisites of any viable social group. This is the functionalist assumption of "functional prerequisites" (Merton 1957:19–84).

The latter assumption, however, does not entail that for every prerequisite there is only one viable social or cultural response for its satisfaction. On the contrary, in view of the remarkable degree of human plasticity (also a product of human evolution), for any prerequisite there exists a wide range of potentially viable alternative responses; and, for reasons peculiar to their historical circumstances, different groups have actualized some, rather than others, of those potential responses. In consequence, many differences in kinship systems, religious doctrines, and the like may be properly viewed—but to, as yet, an empirically unknown degree—as structural alternatives for satisfying one and the same prerequisite. In sum, although differing in content, these different social and cultural structures serve the same function. This is the assumption of "[structurally alternative] functional equivalents" (Merton 1954:19–84).

Rejecting this functionalist view of cultural and social systems and directing its interpretations exclusively to the emic meaning of cultural content, it is hardly surprising that epistemological relativism holds that cultures are incommensurable. Given this limited and limiting perspective, how could it be denied, for example, that the doctrine of karma is unique to the religious tradition of India? Or that, even within that tradition, its meaning in Buddhism may be different from that in Hinduism. Or, for that matter, that even within Buddhism (Spiro 1982a) and within Hinduism (Keyes and Daniel 1983) it again has different meanings.

If, however, the concept of karma is understood in the context of Hindu and Buddhist praxis—that is, functionally—it is then apparent that, at only a slightly more abstract level, it bears a striking family resemblance to concepts found in many other cultural traditions. Consider, for example, such concepts as luck, fate, predestination, God's will, kismet, fortune, destiny, or, for that matter, cultural determinism! Although formally and semiotically different from each other, and they in turn from karma, all of those concepts, just like karma, provide an explanation for the vagaries of an actor's "life chances" (as Weber called it) without recourse to the agency (and therefore the responsibility) of the actor himself.

Let us turn, now, to the empirical, or epistemological, challenge to the premise of radical cultural—hence social and psychological—diversity. That challenge is simply put: if cultures are incommensurable and if the characteristics of human nature and the human mind are predominantly culturally determined, how is it at all possible for an ethnographer to understand a group that is different from his or her own?

For ethnographers to understand an alien people, it is a *sine qua non,* as epistemological relativists among others rightly claim, that they be able to exploit their own powers of empathy and insight. But how can the ethnographer participate to any degree in the thoughts and feelings of others—which is what empathy means—if their psychological makeup is radically different from the ethnographer's? Moreover, how can the ethnographer make any sense of their thoughts and feelings—which is what insight means—if their culture, or conceptual framework, is also radically different from the ethnographer's? As Sperber has tellingly put it,

> If members of other cultures live in different cognizable worlds and if one thing we can take for granted is that these worlds are more complex than that of cats [then, since we cannot intuit what cats feel or think] how can we get to know them? Shouldn't we conclude with Rodney Needham that "the solitary comprehensible fact about human experience is that it is incomprehensible"? [1982:157]

Nevertheless, it is an anthropological fact, as Gellner has stressed, that every ethnographer, without exception, has been able to comprehend the "human experience" of alien peoples.

> It is an interesting fact about the world we actually live in that no anthropologist, to my knowledge, has come back from a field trip with the following report: *their* concepts are *so* alien that it is impossible to describe their land tenure, their kinship system, their ritual. . . . As far as I know there is no record of such a total admission of failure. [1981:5, emphasis in original]

In short, since the "human experience" of all those alien peoples *is* comprehensible to ethnographers, it can only be assumed that although culture, human nature, and the human mind are diverse enough, they are not all *that* diverse. In other words, if alien peoples are comprehensible to ethnographers (and the ethnographers to them), it is because the characteristics which they share—the universal characteristics of culture, human nature, and the human mind—are at least as prominent as those in which they differ.[8] To be sure, ethnographers may be deluded in their belief that they understand all those alien peoples; but if that is the case, that delusion is shared by epistemological relativists, as well, for they also claim to understand the peoples they study.

In fact, if cultures were truly incommensurable, then (as I have observed elsewhere [Spiro 1984:345]) the ethnographer not only could not understand, but could not even describe a culture unless the ethnographer himself or herself had been enculturated in it. Moreover, to accurately convey its meanings, the ethnographer would have to describe it in the native language for, *ex hypothesi*, the conceptual system of one culture cannot be adequately rendered by the concepts of another.[9] Consistent with that conclusion, Schneider (1984:ch. 31), in his "Second Description" of the Yapese kinship system, refrains from translating Yap kin terms, just as he refuses to designate it as a kinship system.

In sum, epistemological relativists can't have it both ways. They can't at one and the same time argue that cultures are incommensurable while also claiming that ethnographers (themselves included) are able to understand the cultures and minds of alien peoples. That they have been able to achieve such understandings is itself sufficient to refute the premise of radical cultural diversity from which epistemological relativism derives its epistemological claims.

Can Anthropology be a Science?

Given the premise of radical human diversity, epistemological relativism, it will be recalled, makes two fundamental claims: (1) panhuman generalizations and theories (cultural, social, and psychological) are in general either false—because ethnocentric—or trivial and vacuous. Hence, anthropology neither is nor can it in principle become an explanatory—a scientific—discipline. Rather, (2) it is, or it should constitute itself as, an interpretive—hermeneutic—discipline. We shall examine these claims *seriatim*.

That any or all of the generalizations and theories of the social sciences (including anthropology) may be culture-bound is the rock upon which anthropology, conceived as a theoretical discipline, was founded. But the proper scholarly response to this healthy skepticism is not, surely, their a priori rejection, but rather the development of a research program for their empirical assessment. And that is precisely what I take anthropology to have been attempting among other things, to do over the past 70 or 80 years of its existence. Altough these attempts have not been as successful as we might have wished, given the formidable conceptual and operational difficulties of such an enterprise, our studies have nevertheless yielded some not inconsiderable results (for example, Levinson and Malone 1980).

This achievement has been possible precisely because of the wide range of human diversity (cultural, social, and psychological). That is, far from constituting an insurmountable obstacle to the establishment of generalizations and theories, such diversity, I shall now argue, is, paradoxical though it may seem, its necessary condition.

A scientific generalization, whether in the physical or the human sciences, is a statement not to the effect that some object or event is universal—though it might be—but that, the world being lawful, its occurrence (whether universal or singular, frequent or infrequent) is governed by a *principle* that is universal. In other words, a scientific generalization states that whenever and wherever some object or event occurs, its occurrence sustains a systematic—that is, a predictable—relationship to some other object(s) or event(s).

Consider, for example, religion. Although by almost any definition religion is a universal cultural system, in light of the bewildering variety of religious belief systems, that generalization is in itself of only limited intellectual interest. It is the kind of generalization that epistemological relativists quite properly call trivial. Hence, a nonvacuous generalization regarding religion is a generalization not about religion in general, but about concrete types of religious-belief systems: monotheism, polytheism, and the like. And in this regard, a scientific generalization is a statement of the kind not that monotheism is universal—and not only because it is false—but that wherever and whenever monotheism occurs, it sustains a systematic relationship to the occurrence of some other specified social or cultural condition.

By the application of Mills's canons of similarity and difference, ethnographic studies of different religious belief systems can ascertain to what degree, if any, such regularities obtain.

Taking these generalizations as paradigmatic, it will now be noticed (as I argued above) that (1) scientific generalizations regarding society or culture are statements not of frequencies but of *regularities* and (2) although these regularities are of universal scope, they pertain not to universals but to *differences* in social and cultural conditions (in this case religious belief systems).

Both propositions apply to psychological generalizations in anthropology as well. Thus, the traditional postulate of the psychic unity of mankind does not claim that the content of the human mind is everywhere the same—of course the Ifaluk and Ilongot, for example, differ in respect to aggression and they, in turn, from the French and the Fulani—but that the working of the mind is everywhere the same. In short, psychic unity is a generalization to the effect that despite the wide differences in the form and frequency of aggression, wherever and whenever aggression occurs, it is governed by the same set of principles.

If, then, anthropological generalizations are statements of regularities in respect to group differences, anthropological theories are statements that purport to explain or account for such differences.

Suppose, for example, that differences in religious belief systems have been shown to be related to differences in family systems. If that were the case, it might then be proposed that the latter generalization might be explained by the theory that the belief in supernatural beings is a projection of the conceptions of parents that are formed in childhood. Thus, since children's conceptions of parents are formed in large part as a result of the parent-child relationship, such a theory can (in principle) explain not only the universality of religious belief systems, but also their diversity—the association of different types of religious belief systems with different types of family and socialization systems. Again, this theory like the previous generalization can be tested by employing Mills's canons in comparative ethnographic investigations.

We may now briefly summarize this discussion. Scientific generalizations take the form of "if . . . then . . ." propositions, and scientific theories purport to explain generalizations of that form. That being the case, in the absence of a wide range of diversity in the social, cultural, and psychological characteristics of human groups, generalizations of that form could not be discerned in the first instance, theories that purport to explain them could not be formulated, and empirical tests of those theories could not be conducted. In short, if *pace* epistemological relativism, nonvacuous generalizations, and nontrivial theories have been discovered by anthropology, it is because of—not in spite of—cultural, social, and psychological diversity.

If it may be now concluded that human diversity does not preclude anthropology from being or becoming a scientific discipline, epistemological relativism opposes that conclusion on still other grounds; not descriptive but prescriptive.

Should Anthropology be a Science?

Even conceding that nontrivial generalizations and nonvacuous theories are discoverable, epistemological relativism rejects the conception of anthropology as a scientific discipline not so much on pragmatic as on principled grounds. The proper aim of anthropology, it contends, is not explanation but interpretation— the elucidation of symbolic meanings—and that aim requires that anthropology be conceived and practiced not as a scientific but as a hermeneutic discipline.

Actually, many epistemological relativists, following the Continental tradition mentioned previously, prefer another set of locutions. Although anthropology, like the other disciplines that study man and culture, is a science, it is not, they say, a natural science but a human science *(science humaine),* one whose mode of inquiry is hermeneutic not positivistic (Rabinow and Sullivan 1979).

To be sure, if "science" is conceived substantively—as a *subject* of inquiry—there are then, of course, many kinds of science, from the study of atoms and galaxies to that of mind and culture; and it might then be agreed that at the most inclusive level of classification, it is useful to distinguish the class of human sciences (anthropology, history, psychology, etc.), on the one hand, from that of the physical sciences (physics, chemistry, astronomy, etc.), on the other.

It will be noticed, however, that I refer to the members of the latter class not as natural, but as physical, sciences, in order to explicitly reject the dichotomy between nature and culture. The notion that somehow atoms, trees, and stars are part of nature whereas mind, culture, and human experience are not is a notion which, I would have thought, had been laid to rest many years ago by John Dewey (1929) among others. To place culture outside of nature is an anthropological conceit reminiscent of the creationist conceit that places man outside of nature. To say that mind and culture are part of nature does not, however, entail the reductionistic fallacy that they can be explained by the laws and principles of the physical sciences.

If, now, physical is not synonymous with natural, the physical science/human science dichotomy does not entail, as the hermeneutic tradition claims, the natural science/hermeneutic science dichotomy, for the former dichotomy is substantive, the latter epistemic.

If science is conceived epistemically, I would then submit in agreement with many logicians and philosophers of science (for example, Dewey 1938; Grunbaum 1984; Hempel 1965; Popper 1963; Rudner 1966) that there is only one kind of science. For whatever the subject (whether atoms and galaxies or man and culture) if the aim of scientific inquiry is reliable (replicable) and public knowledge, only one method is properly designated as scientific. That method consists in the formulation of explanatory theories in respect to that subject, and the employment of both empirical and logical procedures which, at least in principle, can lead to their verification or falsification.

The hermeneutic tradition (including now epistemological relativism) rejects that view, arguing that the substantive differences between the physical (what they call the "natural") sciences and the human sciences entail a critical epistemic difference as well.

Because, it is argued, the aim of the physical sciences is *explanation,* they offer causal accounts of the subject under investigation, for which the scientific method as defined above is entirely appropriate. Inasmuch, however, as the aim of the human sciences is *interpretive,* that method is inappropriate because interpretive accounts have reference to meanings, not causes. Consequently, the human sciences require a hermeneutic method of inquiry (whose characteristics will be described in the following section). Let us now evaluate this argument.

When it is claimed that interpretive accounts have reference to meanings, what is usually meant[10] is that culture, mind, action, social institutions, and the like—the subjects comprising the human sciences—are to be understood in terms of intentions, reasons, purposes, motives, and the like (Vendler 1984). Inasmuch as that claim explicitly opposes meanings to causes, it rests on the presumption that the concept of cause, on the one hand, and the conceptual set comprising, *inter alia,* intentions, reasons, and motives, on the other, are mutually exclusive.

Now that presumption would be entirely convincing if, as its proponents contend, the scientific concept of cause referred to material conditions alone (Habermas 1971; Ricoeur 1981; Vendler 1984). For by that conception of cause, a causal account of culture could only have reference to ecological niches, modes of production, subsistence techniques, and the like, just as a causal account of action could only have reference to the contraction of muscles, the firing of neurons, the secretion of hormones, etc.

But the contention that the scientific conception of cause is restricted to material conditions is hardly self-evident. To be sure, psychological behaviorists deny that purposes, motives, and intentions serve as causes of human action, just as cultural materialists dismiss their causal relevance for the creation and persistence of culture. But such views are rejected even by tough-minded philosophers of science (Grünbaum 1984:69–94; Hempel 1965:225–258). For by the most rigorous conception of cause—any antecedent condition in the absence of which some stipulated consequent condition would not occur—purposes, motives, intentions, and the like, for all their being nonmaterial, are no less causal than hormonal secretions and subsistence techniques.

It is only on the assumption that motives, intentions, and the like *are* causes that it is not only important, but crucial to study meanings; crucial in order to offer not just any old interpretation, but rather a valid interpretation, for the actions, customs, and institutions under investigation.

Indeed, that is precisely why, beginning with Sapir (Mandelbaum 1949:part III), psychological anthropology has made the study of meanings, both cultural, as well as noncultural, and unconscious as well as conscious, the centerpiece of anthropological inquiry. For in addition to their representational functions, cultural meaning systems, as D'Andrade has observed, also have three causal properties: they "create cultural entities, direct one to do certain things, and evoke certain feelings" (1984:96–101).

If, however, cultural meanings, as epistemological relativism claims, have no causal relevance, what then *is* their relevance for the understanding of society and culture? And since, under that circumstance, meanings could only be, as behaviorists and cultural materialists claim, epiphenomena, why should they be the focus of inquiry?

Indeed, I would claim that the opposition that the hermeneutic tradition has erected between interpretation and explanation is yet another false dichotomy. For if the interpreter is concerned with formulating a valid interpretation of some particular case, not just any old interpretation, then (as I shall argue below) his idiographic interpretation must be consistent with, if not derived from, a nomothetic (theoretical) explanation which it instantiates.

In any event, since the study of meaning does not entail that anthropology cannot be a scientific discipline, when epistemological relativists claim that a focus on meaning requires that it is, or ought to become, a hermeneutic (interpretive) discipline, that claim is made not by default, but by choice. That choice, I now wish to argue, has adverse consequences for the anthropological enterprise.

A Critique of the Hermeneutic Agenda
of Epistemological Relativism

The Subjective Methodology of Hermeneutic Anthropology

According to the hermeneutic tradition, two characteristics in particular, in addition to the differences in their aims, distinguish a hermeneutic from a scientific discipline. First, whereas the former employs insight, imagination, empathy, Verstehen, etc., the latter relies on objective methods of inquiry. Second, because a hermeneutic discipline is interested in the particular, interpretation is always concerned with individual cases, which it addresses in all of their particularity. A scientific discipline, on the other hand, is concerned with principles, laws, theories, and the like, so that even when explanation is applied to individual cases, it addresses them as instances of the general. We may now examine each characteristic separately.

The proposition that the study of man and culture requires a subjective method of inquiry including empathy, intuition, Verstehen, imagination, and the like, rather than the objective methods employed in the study of natural phenomena is a fallacy, one which is based on the confusion of method with techniques (see Rudner 1966:4–7).

A scientific technique consists of any empirical procedure—observation, experimentation, instrumentation, interviewing, and the like—that is employed for obtaining or eliciting data. Now few, surely, would dispute the claim that the techniques that are available to or required by different subjects of inquiry are different one from another. Indeed, seeing as the various disciplines comprising the human sciences themselves employ different techniques—the techniques employed by anthropology, for example, are different from those employed by history or psychology, and they, in turn, differ from each other—it is not to be wondered that the techniques employed by any or all of them may be different from those employed by the physical sciences.

Although it is pluralistic in technique, scientific inquiry is not, however, pluralistic in method. If scientific techniques consist of the empirical procedures employed for obtaining or eliciting data, the scientific method consists of the logic or rationale according to which those data are judged to be evidentially relevant, adequate, or sufficient for the acceptance or rejection of hypotheses, whether explanatory or interpretive.

Attending to that distinction, I shall now argue that when the hermeneutic tradition claims that insight, imagination, empathy, and the like mark a watershed between the human and the physical sciences, it confuses their proper role as techniques in the context of discovery with their improper role as methods in the context of validation.

That insight, imagination, empathy, and the like are indispensable in the human sciences as techniques of inquiry is a proposition, surely, with which almost everyone (except for unregenerate or born again behaviorists) would agree. Indeed, as techniques they are also, with the exception of empathy, indispensable in the physical sciences as well. If not by insight and imagination, how else might an investigator, whatever the subject of inquiry, arrive at a hypothesis—a guess, a hunch, a speculation—regarding the proper explanation or interpretation of his observations and data? Indeed, how else could certain kinds of data be obtained, if not by means of those same techniques? (Though in the latter regard, these subjective techniques play a more important role in the human than in the physical sciences.)

Nevertheless, however indispensable these subjective procedures may be for the formulation of interpretations and explanations, in the scientific mode of inquiry they are entirely disqualified as a method for their validation. It is in the latter context—and in the latter context only—that scientific inquiry requires objective (public and replicable) procedures. That requirement is rejected by the hermeneutic mode of inquiry. According to the latter, empathy, Verstehen, and the like are indispensable not only as techniques in the context of discovery, but also as methods in the context of validation. From a scientific perspective such a procedure can only be characterized as intellectually irresponsible.

The reason for such a characterization is obvious. Suppose, to take an anthropological example, an ethnographer has formulated an interpretation of a religious rite, a myth, a marriage custom, whatever. He must then decide whether and to what degree his interpretation (hypothesis) is valid. But having already employed his insight and empathic understanding for arriving at an interpretation, to then accept that interpretation because it is empathetically, intuitively, or insightfully grounded is hopelessly circular. In sum, short of a public and replicable method, there is no way by which the validity of the interpretation can be evaluated. However acute his insight or powerful his empathy, when they are employed both as a technique, as well as a method of inquiry, there is no escaping the "hermeneutic circle," as it is called.[11]

In justification of this method hermeneutic anthropology has taken literary criticism as its model. Adopting the metaphor of culture (or society or action) as "text" (Ricoeur 1971), any interpretation is said to be a "reading." And since, according at least to one construal of textual analysis, there may be as many readings as there are interpreters, the question of validating any particular reading does not have to be confronted; either because that question is irrelevant, or because it is impossible of resolution. "Ultimately," so the argument goes,

> a good explanation [that is, interpretation] is one which makes sense of the behavior; but then to appreciate a good explanation, one has to agree on what makes good sense; what makes good sense is a function of one's readings; and these in turn are based on the kind of sense one understands. [Taylor 1979:35–36]

That argument, of course, is unexceptionable. Indeed, I would take it much further. Not only does every observer understand and make sense of behavior from his own perspective, but his very perception of that behavior is a function of that perspective. Thus, the ethnographer's theoretical orientation, psychological conflicts, ideological biases, narcissistic investment, personal values, scientific ambitions, cultural background, and many other subjective factors, at least guide (when they do not determine) both his perception, as well as his interpretation, of the behavior.[12]

But that fact which, among others, precludes the possibility of a logic of discovery, is precisely what requires a logic of validation. For if ethnographic interpretations are processed through all those subjective filters,[13] an objective— a public and replicable—method is required for deciding whether an interpretation should be accepted or rejected. The scientific method, which assesses the validity of interpretations by the logical procedure of testing their predictive or retrodictive consequences, constitutes such a method.

If that method or some functional alternative is rejected, and if consequently competing interpretations are merely variant "readings," then anything goes. And if anything—well, almost anything—goes, a scholarly discipline is not intellectually responsible.

It might be argued that in large measure that is the way that, in fact, it has usually been. But to adopt the hermeneutic method is to ensure that, in principle, it is also the way it must always be. For while the boundary in all of the social sciences between theory and ideology, fact and value, objective and subjective, evidential constraint and personal preference is often blurred, the hermeneutic method guarantees that those boundaries will never be clear.

The Ethnographic Particularism of Hermeneutic Anthropology

An anthropology which abdicates the search for explanatory theories of culture and society in favor of particularistic interpretations of specific cultures and societies exclusively is an anthropology whose attraction will (in my opinion) become confined to scholars whose intellectual curiosity is limited to, and whose intellectual appetite is nourished by, strange customs of exotic peoples. For the rest—and from the increasing grumblings one hears at the annual meetings of the American Anthropological Association, that would seem to include more than a few—that aim produces (if I may be forgiven, a neologism) anorexia curiosa; in a word, boredom.

Now I have no doubt that as a consequence of our traditional focus on social and cultural particularities "we have with no little success sought to keep the world off balance; pulling out rugs, upsetting tea tables, setting off firecrackers" (Geertz 1984:275). Nor can it be doubted that "it has been the office of others to reassure; ours to unsettle. . . . We hawk the anomalous, peddle the strange. Merchants of Astonishment" (Geertz 1984:275).

The problem, however, is that nothing fails like success. Having already documented the entire range of cultural differences, we no longer astonish, the strange is jejune, there are no anomalies. Hence, if even today, some fifty years after Malinowski and one hundred after Tylor, not to mention twenty five hundred after Herodotus, our aim is to document the fact of cultural variability (without ever, however, explaining it) and to offer interpretive accounts of particular cultures—but never, however, explanatory accounts of culture—such an aim may be of value on many counts, but intellectually it has become trivial.[14]

That judgment is perhaps best supported by contrasting that hermeneutic aim, the intellectual child of epistemological relativism, with the aims that informed ethnographic inquiry during the hegemony of descriptive and normative relativism.

When cultural relativism was confined to the descriptive type—not, however, in its contemporary (strong) form, but its original (moderate) form—ethnographic inquiries were harnessed to the idea of progress. Thus the purpose for studying all manner of societies, including and most especially primitive societies, was to document the stages, and to discover the processes of unilineal cultural and social evolution. That enterprise may have been (as most, but not all, anthropologists believe it to be) abortive, but few would deny that its aim was scientifically important, or that it conferred intellectual importance on the study of primitive peoples.

When, however, the idea of progress, together with the unilineal stage theory of cultural evolution, was discarded, and when concomitantly cultural relativism came to include the normative type, the aim of ethnographic inquiry and the rationale for concentrating on primitive peoples were transformed. Because the diversity of cultures was now viewed as comprising not a scale of cultural evolution, but rather the range of cultural variability, its aim was taken to be the discovery of principles and theories that might explain the diversity in cultural and social systems.

With that change in aim, the rationale for focusing on primitive peoples correspondingly changed. No longer viewed as similar to one another—each being an instance of an archaic type of society—they were now chosen for study precisely because (as Margaret Mead observed) they were viewed as different, each different from every other, and all, in turn, from Western peoples. Hence, since every culture was now conceived in Ruth Benedict's famous metaphor as one "segment" of "a great arc" (Benedict 1934:24) and since the other social sciences studied only one of those segments (Western), the unique function of anthropology, and its rationale for focusing on primitive cultures, was to fill in the rest of—that is, most of—that "great arc." It was no accident that Ralph Linton, writing at the zenith of that period, titled his book, not *The Primitive World*, but *"Most of the World"* (Linton 1949).

Given, then, that this was the era of Boasian normative relativism, which viewed all cultures as equally valuable, and given, too, that every society was conceived, as the saying went, as an "experiment of nature," ethnographic studies of primitive peoples were viewed as contributing not only to a substantive (particularistic) aim, but also to a scientific (theoretical) aim. That is, they were viewed as a means not only for expanding our knowledge of the range of social and cultural diversity, but also for arriving at valid theories and principles that might explain society and culture.

The latter aim, it was believed, could not be achieved by the study of Western culture alone because the latter represents only one segment of the arc of culture. To express it in the cultures-as-natural experiments metaphor, primitive cultures were viewed vis à vis Western culture as experimental control groups.

To be sure, given the philosophy of science of that era—radical empiricism and naive inductivism—it was believed that only when the descriptive and classificatory aims of ethnographic inquiry were completed—"when all the facts are in"—could that scientific aim be accomplished (Boas 1940:243–289). In the meantime, the typical anthropological response to the typical generalization in sociology or economics or psychoanalysis—"But the Hopi . . ." or "But the Kwakiutl . . ."—was intended to hold up a mirror not only for man (Kluckhohn 1957), but also for the other social sciences whose theories of society and culture were essentially based on a sample of one.

Admittedly, in the execution of that inductively conceived scientific aim, many anthropologists, concerned as they were with the immediate task of ethnographic description and classification, lost sight of the forest for the trees. Nevertheless, a surprisingly large number never lost sight of that aim, and for them ethnographic inquiry was more often than not theoretical in aim and comparative (if only implicitly) in method. Thus, whether fieldwork was conducted among the Trobrianders, Samoans, Navajo, Nuer, or Saulteaux (to take some obvious examples), it was in the service of some general theory of ritual exchange (Malinowski 1961 [1922]), adolescence (Mead 1928), witchcraft (Kluckhohn 1967 [1944]), segmentary lineage systems (Evans-Pritchard 1940), or cultural psychology (Hallowell 1955) respectively.

It should be emphasized, moreover, that many of these studies were, in the best sense of the word, interpretive. Beliefs and customs were described in their full ethnographic context, and they were interpreted (as Malinowski put it) from the "natives' point of view."

Nevertheless, for the influential anthropologists just mentioned the interpretive understanding of the cultures of particular tribal groups was only the first step—an intellectual way station—to the theoretical understanding of cultural systems. For them it was axiomatic that, conceived as a science, anthropology transcended the ethnoscience of any and all cultures—including Western culture— and that, consequently, it was capable both in principle and in fact of discovering theories that might explain the social and cultural systems of any society—including, once again, Western society.

It is by contrast with the latter two aims that, in my judgment, ethnographic particularism is intellectually trivial. For if, in principle, ethnographic studies cannot contribute to the formulation of nontrivial explanatory theories of society and culture, nor even to the discovery of nonvacuous empirical generalizations about them; if, on the contrary, they can only contribute to unique understandings of this or that belief or custom of this or that primitive or peasant culture in all of its particularity, what possible intellectual relevance might such studies have?

Put differently, if cultures are texts and the aim of ethnographic inquiry is interpretation, then in choosing *our* texts, we ought to adopt the criteria that literary critics employ for choosing *theirs*. Rather than wasting their time on any old text, literary critics, in contrast to book reviewers, devote their energies to the interpretation of exemplary ones—not, for example, the novels of Jack Kerouac and Herman Wouk, but those of Jane Austen and Dostoevsky. An interpretive understanding of the latter texts is intellectually important because, being exemplary, they speak to issues of general, sometimes perennial, human concern.

Analogously, if interpretation is our aim, then we should choose exemplary cultures—cultures whose interpretation can contribute to an understanding of the "great arc" of culture. But if, as epistemological relativism claims, the incommensurability of cultures precludes in principle the very possibility of such a contribution, then it is indeed difficult to discern how the particularistic interpretation of this or that belief or custom in this or that primitive or peasant culture might be of intellectual importance.

If, now, this judgment were idiosyncratic, or if, though widely shared, it had little practical import for the status of anthropology, it could be ignored as the expression of one scholar's intellectual preference. Unfortunately, it is neither the one nor the other; that judgment is widely shared and it does have such import, as I now wish to indicate by reference to three warning signals.

Item: Recently, the National Research Council (the research arm of the National Academy of Sciences) constituted a blue ribbon committee to evaluate the "status of the behavioral and social sciences." The committee identified 32 research areas in which, according to a survey it conducted among leading researchers, the most important "basic research" in those disciplines is currently being pursued. Of the 32, only 3 might be considered as having some degree of anthropological input. If that were not bad enough, of the 75 persons appointed by the committee to chair or cochair subcommittees to evaluate research in those areas, only 2 are anthropologists. It would appear that contemporary anthropological research is not viewed by distinguished colleagues in the social and behavioral sciences as having much to contribute to "basic research."

Just as distressing, however, is the fact that while "culture and ideology" was identified as an area of basic research—which might be taken as a favorable sign—all the members (including the chairman) of the subcommittee appointed for its evaluation are anthropologists, in contrast to almost all the other subcommittees whose members represent a range of disciplines. In short, anthropologists are viewed or view themselves as inhabiting a kind of intellectual ghetto whose main resource—culture and ideology—has little to contribute to the intellectual capital of the collective social science enterprise.

Item: Recently, that same body (the National Research Council) appointed another blue ribbon committee to evaluate the status of black Americans. The original roster of that committee did not include even one anthropologist. When a protest was registered, it was dismissed on the grounds that anthropological studies of race relations are typically conducted overseas. But, it was countered, it is precisely for that reason that anthropological representation is important: the anthropologist can bring to the work of the committee a crucial comparative perspective. Ironically enough, that argument was dismissed on the very grounds adduced by epistemological relativists for denying that anthropology is a scientific discipline: every culture being unique, the study of race relations in non-Western contexts can contribute little to the understanding of race relations in the United States. (As it happens, under pressure, a highly accomplished anthropologist was eventually appointed to the committee.)

Item: It is an open secret that the National Institutes of Health (NIH), formerly the most important source of funding for sociocultural anthropology, has all but phased out its support for foreign area research, although anthropologists are still funded for research in the United States. In case there is any doubt regarding the reason for this policy change, consider the following colloquy between an NIH review committee and a department of anthropology whose training grant on culture and mental health the committee declined to renew on the grounds that training and research on non-Western societies—the focus of the program—would not contribute to an understanding of mental health problems confronting American society.

The counter argument of the Department—that the validity of any theory of mental health or mental illness can only be evaluated by evidence from a variety of different sociocultural contexts—was simply not grasped, either by the NIH staff or by its social science advisory panel. Research in non-Western societies might be relevant (their argument went) for understanding mental health and illness in the latter societies, but inasmuch as it has no relevance for the understanding of mental health and illness in the United States, it cannot be supported by a governmental agency whose mission, mandated by Congress, is the welfare of American society.

Thus it is that an unchallenged axiom of only a generation ago—the axiom that comparative ethnographic research is indispensable for the advance of knowledge in the human sciences—is now rejected as false. And it would be a transparent rationalization to attribute that change solely to an increasing parochialization of American social science. For if a large and distinguished group of anthropologists together with other social scientists claim that ethnographic research has no generalizability and that cross-cultural theories are, in principle, impossible to attain; and if, moreover, the bulk of current ethnographic research instantiates that claim, we can hardly expect nonanthropologists to accept as axiomatic a proposition that anthropologists, themselves, reject both in principle and in practice.

Recall that when, beginning in the 1930s, that axiom was regnant, it was hardly by accident. Rather, it was because a distinguished group of anthropologists—Sapir and Benedict, Murdock and Hallowell, Mead and Kluckhohn, Whiting and Linton, Eggan and Redfield, to name only a few—preached and practiced an anthropological agenda that would exploit the fact of cross-cultural diversity for the creation of a comparative "science of man." Moreover, some members of that group took the lead in institutionalizing that agenda at three prestigious universities—Yale (in the Institute of Human Relations), Harvard (in the Department of Social Relations), and Chicago (in the Committee on Human Development).

That combination of distinguished scholars and prestigious universities had a powerful influence on the creation of a climate of opinion, both within and outside of anthropology, that would acknowledge the importance of ethnographic knowledge as one of the cornerstones for human understanding. With the death of Margaret Mead, the most distinguished and tireless public advocate (popularizer) of that view and in the absence of a contemporary advocate of equivalent stature, ethnography is again perceived as the study of strange customs of exotic peoples. Although, one hears it said, it may be important for our government to know about such peoples during times of international crises—when Miskitos or Shi'as or Hmong, though hardly household words, are yet pertinent for the national interest—the study of their customs is not the stuff from which a science of man is to be constructed. It would seem that Kroeber's warning, 66 years ago, has been confirmed:

> As long as we continue offering the world only reconstructions of specific detail, and consistently show a negative attitude toward broader conclusions, the world will find very little profit in ethnology. [Kroeber 1920:380]

In conclusion, if we continue to pursue the aim of ethnographic particularism, it would be better, if only for our enlightened self interest, to focus our studies on Western culture. Short of that, we have one other alternative. We can adopt or return to a generalizing-explanatory mode of ethnographic research, while focusing on the comparative study of non-Western cultures. Although either alternative would assure our vitality as a discipline, from the foregoing discussion my own preference should be obvious.

Notes

Acknowledgments: This paper is an expansion of a discussion paper presented to the Symposium on Ethical Relativism at the 1984 annual meeting of the American Anthropological Association. I wish to express my appreciation to Alan Fiske for his invitation to serve as a discussant, and to the participants on the Symposium—Caroline Edwards, James Fernandez, Alan Fiske, Robert LeVine, Joan Miller, Brad Shore, Richard Shweder, and David Wong—whose papers stimulated the present effort. I wish especially to acknowledge the helpful criticisms of Aaron Cicourel, Roy D'Andrade, A. K. Epstein, Michael Meeker, Robert Paul, Fitz John Porter Poole, Richard Shweder, Marc Swartz, Donald Tuzin, and Aram Yengoyan.

[1]It will be noted that the judgment that I have designated as "descriptive cultural relativism" must be distinguished from the judgment—which might be designated as "contextual relativism"—that the meaning or significance of some social or psychological variable is relative to (depends on) the total context in which it is embedded.

[2]In the published version of Rosaldo's paper, which was first presented and discussed at the Conference on Culture Theory, this passage was changed to "culture *makes a difference that concerns not simply* what we think but how we feel about and live our lives" (Rosaldo 1984:140, changes italicized). Because the published version is not only inconsistent with the main thrust of Rosaldo's paper, but is one to which any opponent of cultural relativism would assent, I have quoted the original version as a representative expression of the strong form of descriptive relativism.

[3]For a detailed comparison of these two theories of cultural determinism see Spiro 1978:350–358.

[4]This culturally grounded notion of "Otherness" is to be distinguished from the politically grounded notion according to which the Third World Other is a construction of the Western Self in the service of colonial and other forms of political domination (Dwyer 1982:253–287). Since, however, that notion takes us out of the realm of theoretical and into the realm of ideological discourse, I shall not address it in this paper.

[5]The sweeping claim that social science theories merely reflect Western ethnoscience would have to be qualified in respect, at least, to some of the most influential ones. The Darwinian, Marxian, and Freudian theories, for example, were, and are, rejected by scientists and laymen alike on the grounds that they violate common sense or are counterintuitive, and the like; in short, because they contradict the prevailing ethnoscientific theories. Conversely, those who have accepted them have done so in spite of the fact that they were, or are, in conflict with prevailing ethnoscientific theories. Moreover, if that sweeping

claim is correct, why is it that those three theories—among others—have found acceptance by non-Western social scientists when they clearly contradict their *own* ethnoscientific theories?

[6]Substantively—but not necessarily methodologically—this dichotomy parallels the contemporary American distinction between the physical sciences, on the one hand, and the social sciences and humanities, on the other. Originating in mid-19th-century German philosophy, it achieved prominence among contemporary social scientists as a result, most notably, of the influence of Wilhelm Dilthey (1833–1911). For an explication of Dilthey's views of the *Geisteswissenschaften,* Makkreel (1975) is an excellent introduction.

[7]Needless to say, these tenets were part of an intellectual *zeitgeist* which both influenced the rise of symbolic anthropology and was, in turn, influenced by it. Among the influences, I would only mention such obvious names—each for a somewhat different reason—as Cassirer, Langer, and Wittgenstein in philosophy, Garfinkel, Goffman, and Schutz in sociology, Saussure and Whorf in linguistics. For a sample of the work and thought of the first generation of symbolic anthropologists, see Basso and Selby 1976, Dolgin, Kemnitzer and Schneider 1977, Spencer 1969.

[8]When Renato Rosaldo, following a remarkably courageous act of insight, came to understand that his own feelings of grief and anger were identical with those of the Ilongot—a view that he had rejected in his previously published work on the Ilongot—he characterized the theory of psychological incommensurability (to which he had formerly subscribed) as the "pernicious doctrine that, my own group aside, everything human is alien to me" (R. Rosaldo 1984:188).

[9]Compare Putnam's critique of the relativistic views of Kuhn and Feyerabend regarding the history of western science (1981:114–115).

[10]It is not always easy to stipulate what hermeneutic anthropologists understand by "meaning" because that term is all too often obscure, if not opaque, in their work.

[11]Contemporary hermeneutic interpreters of psychoanalysis usually emphasize, with Ricoeur (1970), that the title of Freud's most important work is "The Interpretation of Dreams," and that (with some few excursions) its title accurately reflects its focus. True enough. But that claim overlooks the fact that the dream interpretations proposed in that book are derived from a general theory, a theory which purports to offer a causal explanation of dreams and dreaming.

[12]It is because self-conscious awareness of one's own biases is an important means for controlling for (if not reducing) perceptual distortions and the like that some anthropologists (Bateson, Kluckhohn, LaBarre, and Mead, among others) have recommended that ethnographers undergo a personal analysis.

[13]The most important of these filters derive perhaps from those unconscious anxieties aroused in the ethnographer in his encounter with an alien society. Since in this regard the emotional situation of the ethnographer is analogous to that of the psychoanalyst in his encounter with a patient, Devereux (1967) refers to these distortions as "counter-transference" reactions. Since Devereux's is perhaps the most trenchant analysis of the subjective factors in observer bias in the social sciences (including anthropology), it is regrettable that his book is little known, or at least infrequently cited in the growing literature on this topic.

[14]That judgment would also be shared by Max Weber, although, ironically, that towering figure is uniformly claimed by hermeneutic social scientists as a central actor and founding

father. Although Weber was a leading proponent and theorist of Verstehen, his agenda and work, alike, are otherwise in dramatic opposition to the current hermeneutic approach. Hence, it is perhaps desirable at this juncture to place him in respect to the argument of this paper.

First, while for Weber Verstehen was a crucial technique in sociocultural inquiry, he explicitly abjured its use as a method. For him, hypotheses formulated in respect to one culture or society, though arrived at by means of Verstehen cannot be accepted until they are tested in other sociocultural settings whose characteristics are evidentially relevant. And this methodological injunction was brilliantly implemented in his own work as, for example, in his famous thesis concerning the relationship between Calvinism and the rise of capitalism (Weber 1930), a magisterial undertaking involving ancient Israel (Weber 1952), India (Weber 1958), and China (Weber 1951).

Second, although stressing the actors' point of view, Weber explicitly rejected the epistemological relativism of hermeneutic social science. Denying that different historical groups are incommensurable and that consequently generalizing theoretical categories are impossible to achieve, he argued instead for the very opposite tenets, both in his theoretical statements (Weber 1957:87–123) and in their implementation in the comparative studies just mentioned.

Third, while he emphasized that the social sciences differed from the physical sciences in their need to attend to meanings, Weber was especially and explicitly concerned with meanings because of their causal relevance, which, of course, is his main thesis in his comparative study of the "economic ethics" of the great religions mentioned above. Finally, he insisted (as Parsons [1937:ch. 16] has shown in detail) that despite their differences in respect to techniques, the social and physical sciences must employ the same methodology: "logical schema." That, now, Weber should be claimed by the interpretive social sciences as a founding father is rather puzzling.

References Cited

Ahmed, A.
  1984   Defining Islamic Anthropology. RAIN 65:1–2.
Barnes, D., and B. Bloor
  1982   Relativism, Rationalism and the Sociology of Knowledge. *In* Rationality and Relativism. M. Hollis and S. Lukes, eds. Pp. 21–47. Cambridge: MIT Press.
Basso, K., and H. Selby, eds.
  1976   Meaning in Anthropology. Albuquerque: University of New Mexico Press.
Benedict, R.
  1934   Patterns of Culture. Boston and New York: Houghton Mifflin.
Boas, F.
  1938   The Mind of Primitive Man. New York: Macmillan.
  1940   Race, Language and Culture. New York: Macmillan.
Brown, S., ed.
  1984   Objectivity and Cultural Divergences. Cambridge: Cambridge University Press.
D'Andrade, R.
  1984   Cultural Meaning Systems. *In* Culture Theory. R. Shweder and R. LeVine, eds. Pp. 88–122. Cambridge: Cambridge University Press.
Devereux, G.
  1967   From Anxiety to Method in Behavioral Sciences. The Hague, Paris: Mouton.

Dewey, J.
   1929   Experience and Nature. New York: W. W. Norton.
   1938   Logic: The Theory of Inquiry. New York: Holt.
Dolgin, J., D. Kemnitzer, and D. Schneider, eds.
   1977   Symbolic Anthropology: A Reader in the Study of Symbols and Meanings. New
           York: Columbia University Press.
Dwyer, K.
   1982   Moroccan Dialogues. Baltimore and London: The Johns Hopkins University
           Press.
Evans-Pritchard, E.
   1940   The Nuer. Oxford: Clarendon Press.
Finnegan, R., and R. Horton
   1973   Modes of Thought: Essays on Thinking in Western and Non-Western Societies.
           London: Faber and Faber.
Fox, R.
   1980   The Red Lamp of Incest. New York: E. P. Dutton.
Geertz, C.
   1973   The Interpretation of Cultures. New York: Basic Books.
   1983   Local Knowledge. New York: Basic Books.
   1984   Distinguished Lecture: Anti Anti-Relativism. American Anthropologist 66:263–
           278.
Gellner, E.
   1981   General Introduction: Relativism and Universals. In Universals of Human
           Thought. B. Lloyd and J. Gay, eds. Pp. 1–20. Cambridge: Cambridge University
           Press.
   1985   Relativism and the Social Sciences. Cambridge: Cambridge University Press.
Grünbaum, A.
   1984   The Foundations of Psychoanalysis. Berkeley and Los Angeles: University of
           California Press.
Habermas, J.
   1971   Knowledge and Human Interests. Boston: Beacon Press.
Hallowell, A.
   1955   Culture and Experience. Philadelphia: University of Pennsylvania Press.
Hatch, E.
   1983   Culture and Morality: The Relativity of Values in Anthropology. New York: Co-
           lumbia University Press.
Hempel, C.
   1965   Aspects of Scientific Explanation. New York: The Free Press.
Herskovits, M.
   1949   Man and His Works. New York: Alfred Knopf.
   1972   Cultural Relativism. New York: Random House.
Hollis, M., and S. Lukes, eds.
   1982   Rationality and Relativism. Cambridge: MIT Press.
Jarvie, I.
   1984   Rationality and Relativism: In Search of a Philosophy and History of Anthro-
           pology. London: Routledge & Kegan Paul.
Keyes, C., and E. Daniel, eds.
   1983   Karma: An Anthropological Inquiry. Berkeley and Los Angeles: University of
           California Press.

Kluckhohn, C.
   1957   Mirror for Man. New York: Premier Books, Fawcet World Library.
   1967[1944]   Navaho Witchcraft. Boston: Beacon Press.
Kroeber, A.
   1917   The Superorganic. American Anthropologist 19:163–213.
   1920   Review of "Primitive Society." American Anthropologist 22:377–381.
   1948   Anthropology. New York: Harcourt Brace.
Levinson, D., and M. Malone
   1980   Toward Explaining Human Culture. New Haven: HRAF Press.
Linton, R., ed.
   1949   Most of the World. New York: Columbia University Press.
Lloyd, B., and J. Gay, eds.
   1981   Universals of Human Thought. Cambridge: Cambridge University Press.
Makkreel, R.
   1975   Dilthey: Philosopher of the Human Studies. Princeton: Princeton University
      Press.
Malinowski, B.
   1961[1922]   Argonauts of the Western Pacific. New York: E. P. Dutton.
Mandelbaum, D., ed.
   1949   Selected Writings of Edward Sapir. Berkeley, Los Angeles, London: University
      of California Press.
Mead, M.
   1928   Coming of Age in Samoa. New York: Morrow.
Meiland, J., and M. Krausz, eds.
   1982   Relativism: Cognitive and Moral. Notre Dame: University of Notre Dame Press.
Merton, R.
   1957   Social Theory and Social Structure. New York: Free Press.
Parsons, T.
   1937   The Structure of Social Action. Glencoe, IL: Free Press.
Popper, K.
   1963   Conjectures and Refutations. New York: Basic Books.
Putnam, H.
   1981   Reason, Truth and History. Cambridge: Cambridge University Press.
Rabinow, P.
   1977   Reflections on Field Work in Morocco. Berkeley and Los Angeles: University
      of California Press.
Rabinow, P., and W. Sullivan, eds.
   1979   Interpretive Social Science: A Reader. Berkeley and Los Angeles: University of
      California Press.
Ricoeur, P.
   1970   Freud and Philosophy. New Haven and London: Yale University Press.
   1971   The Model of the Text: Meaningful Action Considered as a Text. Social Re-
      search 38:529–562.
   1981   Hermeneutics and the Human Sciences. New York: Cambridge University Press.
Rosaldo, M.
   n.d.   Toward an Anthropology of Self and Feeling. (In manuscript.)
   1984   Toward an Anthropology of Self and Feeling. In Culture Theory. R. Shweder
      and R. LeVine, eds. Pp. 137–157. Cambridge: Cambridge University Press.

Rosaldo, R.
1984 Grief and a Headhunter's Rage: On the Cultural Force of Emotions. *In* Text, Play, and Story. E. Brunner, ed. Pp. 178–195. Washington, DC: Proceedings of the American Ethnological Society.
Rudner, R.
1966 Philosophy of Social Science. Englewood Cliffs, NJ: Prentice-Hall.
Schneider, D.
1984 A Critique of the Study of Kinship. Ann Arbor: University of Michigan Press.
Scholte, Bob
1984 Reason and Culture: The Universal and the Particular Revisited. American Anthropologist 86:960–965.
Shweder, R.
1984 Anthropology's Romantic Rebellion Against the Enlightenment, or There's More to Thinking Than Reason and Evidence. *In* Culture Theory. R. Shweder and R. LeVine, eds. Pp. 27–66. Cambridge: Cambridge University Press.
Spencer, R., ed.
1969 Forms of Symbolic Action. Proceedings of the 1969 Annual Meeting of the American Ethnological Society. Seattle and London: University of Washington Press.
Sperber, D.
1982 Apparently Irrational Beliefs. *In* Rationality and Relativism. M. Hollis and S. Lukes, eds. Pp. 149–180. Cambridge: MIT Press.
Spiro, M.
1978 Culture and Human Nature. *In* The Making of Psychological Anthropology. G. Spindler, ed. Pp. 330–360. Berkeley and Los Angeles: University of California Press.
1982 Buddhism and Society (Second Expanded Edition). Berkeley and Los Angeles: University of California Press.
1984 Some Reflections on Cultural Determinism and Relativism with Special Reference to Meaning and Emotion. *In* Culture Theory. R. Shweder and R. LeVine, eds. Pp. 323–346. Cambridge: Cambridge University Press.
Symons, D.
1979 The Evolution of Human Sexuality. New York: Oxford University Press.
Taylor, C.
1979 Interpretation and the Sciences of Man. *In* Interpretive Social Science: A Reader. P. Rabinow and W. Sullivan, eds. Pp. 25–72. Berkeley and Los Angeles: University of California Press.
Turner, V.
1978 Encounter with Freud. *In* The Making of Symbolic Anthropology. G. Spindler, ed. Pp. 557–583. Berkeley and Los Angeles: University of California Press.
Vendler, Z.
1984 Understanding People. *In* Culture Theory R. Shweder and R. LeVine, eds. Pp. 200–213. Cambridge: Cambridge University Press.
Weber, M.
1930 The Protestant Ethic and the Spirit of Capitalism. New York: Scribner.
1951 The Religion of China. Glencoe, IL: Free Press.
1952 Ancient Judaism. Glencoe, IL: Free Press.
1957 The Theory of Social and Economic Organization. Glencoe, IL: Free Press.
1958 The Religion of India. Glencoe, IL: Free Press.
Winch, P.
1958 The Idea of a Social Science. New York: Humanities Press.
Wissler, C.
1923 Man and Culture. New York: Thomas Y. Crowell.

Missing the Revolution: Anthropologists and the War in Peru

Orin Starn

On 17 May 1980, Shining Path guerrillas burned ballot boxes in the Andean village of Chuschi and proclaimed their intention to overthrow the Peruvian state. Perhaps playing on the Inkarrí myth of Andean resurrection from the cataclysm of conquest, the revolutionaries had chosen the 199th anniversary of the execution by the Spanish colonizers of the neo-Inca rebel Tupac Amaru. Chuschi, though, prefigured not rebirth but a decade of death. It opened a savage war between the guerrillas and government that would claim more than 15,000 lives during the 1980s.[1]

For hundreds of anthropologists in the thriving regional subspecialty of Andean studies, the rise of the Shining Path came as a complete surprise. Dozens of ethnographers worked in Peru's southern highlands during the 1970s. One of the best-known Andeanists, R. T. Zuidema, was directing a research project in the Río Pampas region that became a center of the rebellion. Yet no anthropologist realized a major insurgency was about to detonate, a revolt so powerful that by 1990 Peru's civilian government had ceded more than half the country to military command.

The inability of ethnographers to anticipate the insurgency raises important questions. For much of the 20th century, after all, anthropologists had figured as principal experts on life in the Andes. They positioned themselves as the "good" outsiders who truly understood the interests and aspirations of Andean people; and they spoke with scientific authority guaranteed by the firsthand experience of fieldwork. Why, then, did anthropologists miss the gathering storm of the Shining Path? What does this say about ethnographic understandings of the highlands? How do events in Peru force us to rethink anthropology on the Andes?

From the start, I want to emphasize that it would be unfair to fault anthropologists for not predicting the rebellion. Ethnographers certainly should not be in the business of forecasting revolutions. In many respects, moreover, the Shining Path's success would have been especially hard to foresee. A pro-Cultural Revolution Maoist splinter from Peru's regular Communist Party, the group formed in the university in the provincial highland city of Ayacucho. It was led by a big-jowled philosophy professor named Abimael Guzmán with thick glasses and a rare blood disease called policitimea.[2] Guzmán viewed Peru as dominated by a bureaucratic capitalism that could be toppled only through armed struggle.

A first action of his guerrillas in Lima was to register contempt for "bourgeois revisionism" by hanging a dead dog in front of the Chinese embassy. Most observers initially dismissed the Shining Path, Sendero Luminoso, as a bizarre but unthreatening sect. This was fiercely doctrinaire Marxism in the decade of *perestroika*.

What I will claim, though, is that most anthropologists were remarkably unattuned to the conditions which made possible the rise of Sendero. First, they tended to ignore the intensifying interlinkage of Peru's countryside and cities, villages and shantytowns, Andean highlands and lowlands of the jungle and coast. These interpenetrations created the enormous pool of radical young people of amalgamated rural/urban identity who would provide an effective revolutionary force. Second, anthropologists largely overlooked the climate of sharp unrest across the impoverished countryside. Hundreds of protests and land invasions testified to a deep-rooted discontent that the guerrillas would successfully exploit.

To begin accounting for the gaps in ethnographic knowledge about the highlands, the first half of this essay introduces the concept of Andeanism.[3] Here I refer to representation that portrays contemporary highland peasants as outside the flow of modern history. Imagery of Andean life as little changed since the Spanish conquest has stretched across discursive boundaries during the 20th century to become a central motif in the writings of novelists, politicians, and travelers as well as the visual depictions of filmmakers, painters, and photographers. I believe Andeanism also operated in anthropology, and helps to explain why so many ethnographers did not recognize the rapidly tightening interconnections that were a vital factor in the growth of the Shining Path.

Andeanism, though, was not the only influence on anthropologists of the 1960s and 1970s. The growing importance of ecological and symbolic analysis in international anthropology theory of the period also conditioned ethnographic views of the Andes. In the second half of the essay, I argue that the strong impact of these two theoretical currents produced an intense preoccupation with issues of adaptation, ritual, and cosmology. This limited focus, in turn, assists in accounting for why most anthropologists passed over the profound rural dissatisfaction with the status quo that was to become a second enabling factor in Sendero's rapid rise.

My mapping of Andeanist anthropology starts with Billie Jean Isbell's *To Defend Ourselves: Ecology and Ritual in an Andean Village* (1977). Through a close reading of this synthetic and widely read ethnography, I begin to outline the imprint of Andeanism on anthropological thinking and to explore how the heavy deployment of ecological and symbolic approaches led to the oversight of political ferment in the countryside. Isbell's book has a special significance because its Andean village was Chuschi, the hamlet where the Shining Path's revolt would explode just five years after Isbell's departure.

I juxtapose *To Defend Ourselves* with a remarkable but little-known book called *Ayacucho: Hunger and Hope* (1969) by an Andean-born agronomist and future Shining Path leader named Antonio Díaz Martínez.[4] *Hunger and Hope* proves it was possible to formulate a very different view of the highlands from that of most Andeanist anthropology. While Isbell and other ethnographers depicted discrete villages with fixed traditions, Díaz saw syncretism and shifting identities. Most anthropologists found a conservative peasantry. Díaz, by contrast, perceived small farmers as on the brink of revolt. Passages of *Hunger and Hope* foreshadow the Shining Path's subsequent dogmatic brutality. Yet the man who would become the reputed "number three" in the Maoist insurgency, after Abimael Guzmán and Osmán Morote, discovered an Ayacucho that escaped the voluminous anthropology literature, a countryside about to burst into conflict.

Through criticism of Andeanist anthropology, my account points to alternatives. I press for recognition of what historian Steve Stern (1987:9) calls "the manifold ways whereby peasants have continuously engaged in their political worlds"; and I argue for an understanding of modern Andean identities as dynamic, syncretic, and sometimes ambiguous. Finally, I seek to develop an analysis that does not underplay the Shining Path's violence yet recognizes the intimate ties of many of the guerrillas to the Andean countryside and the existence of rural sympathies for the revolt.

I feel a certain unease about writing on the Andes and the Shining Path. "Senderology"—the study of the guerrillas—is a thriving enterprise. In my view, a sense of the intense human suffering caused by the war too often disappears in this work. The terror becomes simply another field for scholarly debate. This essay is open to criticism for contributing to the academic commodification of Peru's pain. But I offer the account in a spirit of commitment. No outside intervention—and certainly not by anthropologists—is at present likely to change the deadly logic of the war. I hope, though, that sharper anthropological views of the situation will help others to understand the violence and to join the struggle for life.

Isbell wrote *To Defend Ourselves* from fieldwork in 1967, 1969–70, and 1974–75. Closely observed and richly detailed, the book presents the village of Chuschi as divided into two almost caste-like segments: Quechua-speaking peasants and Spanish-speaking teachers and bureaucrats. An intermediate category appears more peripherally, migrants from Chuschi to Lima. Like other Andeanists, Isbell positions herself firmly with the Quechua-speaking *comuneros*. The *mestizos,* even the dirt-poor teachers, figure as the bad guys, domineering and without Isbell's knowledge or appreciation of Andean traditions.

Isbell's analysis revolves around the proposition that Chuschi's peasants had turned inward to maintain their traditions against outside pressures. The comuneros, she argued, had built a symbolic and social order whose binary logic stressed their difference from the *vecinos,* Chuschi's mestizos. Melding the then-popular structuralism of Lévi-Strauss with Eric Wolf's concept of the closed corporate community, Isbell (1977:11) made her mission to document "the structural defenses the indigenous population has constructed against the increasing domination of the outside world."

Isbell registered that Chuschi was a regional market center with a church, school, and health post. She noted that trucks plied the dirt highway between Chuschi and the city of Ayacucho. We learn of the constant traffic in people and goods between Chuschi and not only Ayacucho but also Lima and the coca-growing regions of the upper Amazon. More than a quarter of Chuschi's population had moved to Lima. Many others migrated seasonally. Even the "permanent" migrants maintained close ties in their native village, returning periodically and keeping animals and land.

When it came to representing Chuschino culture, however, Isbell downplayed mixture and change. Instead, she concentrated on how the ritual, kin relations, reciprocity, cosmology, and ecological management of Chuschi's comuneros embodied the "stability of traditional customs" (Isbell 1977:3). She draws parallels between the annual ritual cycle of the Incas according to the 16th-century chronicler Guamán Poma de Ayala and the calendar of modern Chuschinos. A long section presents marriage practices as if they were unchanged since the Incas. Another elucidates the Santa Cruz harvest festival in the same ahistorical language. The photographs reiterate the feeling of stasis. Two farmers till with oxen. Men drink at a ritual cleaning of irrigation canals. A woman offers corn beer to Mama Pacha. Cultural identity in *To Defend Ourselves* appears as a matter of preservation. Despite change, villagers had conserved their distinctly Andean traditions, "maintain[ing] the underlying order of their society and cosmology" (Isbell 1977:105).

Isbell's emphasis on continuity and non-Western "otherness" in Chuschi needs to be situated in relation to the tradition of representation that I want to call "Andeanism." In Orientalism, as James Clifford (1988:258) deftly summarizes Said, the tendency is "to *dichotomize* the human continuum into we-they contrasts and to *essentialize* the resultant 'other'—to speak of the oriental mind, for example, or even to generalize about 'Islam' or the 'Arabs.' " Andeanism has a similar logic. It dichotomizes between the Occidental, coastal, urban, and mestizo and the non-Western, highland, rural, and indigenous; it then essentializes the highland side of the equation to talk about *"lo andino,"* "the Andean worldview," "indigenous highland culture," or, in more old-fashioned formulations, "the Andean mind" or "the Andean Indians." The core of the "Andean tradition" is presented as timeless, grounded in the preconquest past. Words like "indigenous," "autochthonous," "native," and "Indian" are attached to modern peasants.

Of course, Andeanism represents only one face of what Johannes Fabian (1983:147) calls "the ideological process by which relations between the West and its Other . . . [are] conceived not only as difference but as distance in space and Time." Like other discourses about the Third World, though, Andeanism also has its own special history. It emerged in the early 20th century. Amidst the decline of evolutionism, the intellectual and political movement called *indigenismo* attacked earlier views of Andean peasants as degraded subhumans and argued that highland farmers were instead the bearers of a noble precolonial heritage. Thanks to indigenismo, wrote a leading figure in the movement, historian

Luis Valcarcel (1938:7), "no longer does anyone doubt that the Indian of today is the same Indian who, a millennium ago, created dynamic and varied civilizations in the vast cultural area of the Andes."[5]

Questions of national identity spurred the writing of *indigenistas* like Valcarcel and Manuel Gonzalez Prada. A view of Andean peasants as stewards of the Inca past fit the desire of many intellectuals and politicians to see a potential alternative to the discredited legacy of Spain and the capitalist culture in the north. Socialists such as Hildebrando Castro Pozo and José Carlos Mariátegui hoped "Inca socialism"—which they took to be embodied in contemporary Andean institutions—could be the foundation for a more just postcolonial order.

By the 1930s, the concept of an unbroken Andean heritage had expanded beyond the label of indigenismo to become common sense across art, politics, and science. The powerful novels of Ciro Alegria and José María Arguedas celebrated the "pure" traditions of mountain farmers. Documentaries like *The Spirit Possession of Alejandro Mamani* (1974) and *In the Footsteps of Taytacha* (1985) gave visual expression to Andeanism with their images of a ritualistic, nature-loving, and tradition-bound peasantry. Wilderness Travel Company in Berkeley plays on Andeanism to advertise treks for 1990 that answer to the hunger of Western travelers for authenticity:

> In our newest Andean escapade . . . [we encounter] splendidly dressed Quechua Indians, herds of llamas and alpacas decorated with brightly colored ribbons grazing in idyllic alpine meadows . . . local inhabitants speak no Spanish . . . and maintain(ing) a mystical attachment to the land.

A tour leader assures us that:

> You feel you've stumbled into a time warp when you sit in a sleepy village plaza and realize it's . . . remained virtually unchanged since Inca times.[6]

This is Andeanism in pure form. Nowhere does the ten-page text disclose that a major war is raging in Peru's highlands.

The rhetoric of Wilderness Travel signals a key irony. On one hand, Andeanism has an egalitarian and antiracist thrust. Writers from Castro Pozo to Isbell want to show the richness of Andean culture and the exploitation of Andean people under colonial and postcolonial rule. On the other, residues of paternalism and hierarchy persist in Andeanist discourse. Middle- and upper-class city people retain their unquestioned privilege to speak for poor farmers in the mountains; and evolutionism recurs with the depiction of 20th-century peasants as the holders of premodern beliefs. Luis Valcarcel believed in racial equality. Yet in 1950 he could still invoke evolutionist thinking to proclaim that within Peru's "rugged confines, people of occidental background live together with others who belong to epochs long submerged in the tide of history" (1950:1).

It would be a mistake to overstress the coherence or reach of Andeanism. In *Orientalism,* Said expends his critical energy to demonstrate the dependence of Western representations of the Middle East on tropes of distance, exoticism, and timelessness.[7] The pathbreaking yet overly tidy polemics of the book do not explore variations and tensions across and within the partly autonomous Orientalist discourses of travel writing, fiction, history, ethnography, and journalism. As many critics have observed, Said performs the same essentializing operation of which he accuses Orientalists.[8] All Western representations of the Middle East from Homer to Flaubert are swept into the category of Orientalism.

Andeanist ethnographers of the 1960s and 1970s often cut against the paradigm. The late 1960s had brought the beginnings of criticism against synchronic models of social analysis, and new attempts to put history into ethnography. By the early 1970s, some anthropologists carried the attack on ahistoricism into Andean studies. Frank Salomon's (1973:465) insightful work on Otavalo, for example, spoke against the "stereotype of Indian societies as hermetically sealed, static, and historically doomed." From a Marxist perspective, ethnographers like Thomas Greaves (1972) and Rodrigo Montoya (1979) showed the transformations that capitalist expansion had wrought on the lives of mountain peasants. By the mid-1970s, a sense of history's importance had spread into most anthropology on the Andes.

But Andeanism also remained very much alive in Andeanist ethnography. Images of a timeless Andean tradition continued to appear across anthropological writing on all aspects of mountain life. Isbell's graduate adviser R. T. Zuidema and Quispe (1973:362) used an old farm woman's dream to show that modern highland social structure was "still similar to that of indigenous communities of the XVIth century . . . essentially the same as the Incan one." Giorgio Alberti and Enrique Mayer (1974:21) described Andean economics in similar fashion: "In spite of the passing of four centuries many of the forms of symmetrical reciprocity existing in the times of the Incas and even before . . . continue to work in the present."[9] J. V. Nuñez del Prado (1974:250) concurred about religion: "We find that the supernatural world has characteristics very similar to those it had during the Inca Empire." "Many of the private and domestic observances of the old religion survived and are still practised today," confirmed Hermann Trimborn (1969:145).

The juxtaposition of Western and Andean also persisted. Andeanism tended to plot the contrast in terms of the presumed individualism and alienation of the West against the communal ideals and closeness-to-nature of Andean culture. Many anthropologists followed suit. "What we have possessed, we have also destroyed," as Joseph Bastien (1978:xxv) concluded the preface to *Mountain of the Condor*, "Andeans, in contrast, are in harmony with their land." Stephen Brush (1977:7) invoked the same vision of Andean closeness to the earth and collective values:

> Even though he may speak Spanish, a highlander is easily recognizable by a coastal person as such: a serrano. He comes from an area where the pace of life is slower, where a family's tie to the land is still primary, and where there is a sense of community derived from a certain homogeneity that has been lost in the cities.

Paul Doughty (1968:1) melded his formulation of the Andean/Western contrast with an assertion of Andean timelessness: "the Indians have survived in provincial aloofness, rarely affected by the vicissitudes of time, politics, society and technological innovations which have so stirred Western civilization."

Andeanism, I should stress, did not just inflect ethnographies primarily by and for area specialists. It also spilled into more broadly conceived anthropological writing about the Andes. Especially notable was Michael Taussig's influential *The Devil and Commodity Fetishism in South America* (1980). This original and passionate book attracted wide attention across the social sciences. But it, too, was loaded with Andeanism. In classic Andeanist fashion, Taussig insisted on portraying highland culture as a survival from precolonial times. Thus he could overlook almost five hundred years of constant change to argue that "preconquest institutions still flourish in the Andes" and that modern peasants live in 'precapitalist' communities" and possess "pagan" beliefs (Taussig 1980:159–160). Taussig (1980:27, 161) also recycled the standard juxtaposition of the Occidental and Andean traditions to contrast the "atomization and bondage" of Western capitalism with the belief in "the all-encompassing unity that exists between persons, spirits, and the land" in "Andean metaphysics." Fifteen million diverse inhabitants of a 3,000-mile mountain range became unspoiled "Andean Indians" for the purposes of a vastly oversimplified us/them dichotomy. In fairness, Taussig's (1987) recent book on terror and healing in southern Colombia moves away from *The Devil*'s romantic and essentialized view of a pure "Andean culture" and toward a picture of the Andes as a place of multiple, shifting, and synthetic identities all fashioned within the common context of colonial and neocolonial expansion. Yet Taussig's analysis in *The Devil,* from an ethnographer who has always viewed himself as a challenger of convention, reveals just how far Andeanism reached into anthropological imaginations.

Ethnographic visions of the perennial "otherness" of lo andino had a self-fulfilling logic. In their desire to study "indigenous" Andean culture, anthropologists searched out the most ostensibly traditional regions for their research. Most wanted, as Harold Skar (1982:23) frankly explained his choice of Mataquio in Apurímac, the places "where traditional Quechua culture seemed to be most intact." In Peru, ethnographers flocked to the southern mountains, where the peasants spoke Quechua or Aymara, had *ayllus* and prestige hierarchies, and lived in the historic heartland of the Inca empire. They largely ignored the entire northern highlands of Spanish-speaking and more "acculturated" rural people. The virtual elision of northern Peru from the ethnographic record helped maintain the image of the Andean countryside as the province of ayllus and speakers of native languages, a place little changed from the ancient past.

Arriving at their chosen field sites, most ethnographers again highlighted the most traditional-looking aspects of mountain life. Small farmers who could fit the part of "Andean Indian" captured most space in ethnographies. Schoolteachers, nurses, agronomists, teachers, bureaucrats, and priests were relegated to marginal roles. Thus Isbell devoted most of *To Defend Ourselves* to Chuschi's comuneros. The town's large mestizo population appears only in the brief passages that mark

them as evil foils to the peasants. Many of the mestizos must have spoken Quechua, a language common among not only rural people but the middle classes in
the Ayacucho region. Some were third-generation Chuschinos. But Isbell's use
of the "natives"—as in a section subheaded "The Natives' Conceptualization of
Their Ecology"—encompassed only the comuneros. Peasants became the only
real Andeans in Chuschi.

The strong grip of Andeanism was summed up in the insistent deployment
by ethnographers of the contrast between "Indians" and "mestizos." With *cholos* as an intermediate category, this classification placed ethnographers like Isbell
squarely in the pattern of seeing the lives of mountain peasants through lenses that
accented their pre-Columbian roots. Small farmers were herded into the category
of "Indian." This was a word seldom used by peasants in Peru. They identified
themselves, depending on the context, as Peruvians, *campesinos, agricultores,*
or by their region, village, or family. But the term that has always signified "otherness" in Western thinking was perfect for anthropologists who wanted to depict
Andean peoples as fundamentally non-Western. An Andean "Indian," Michael
Olien (1973:245) could write, is "a person who wears sandals, lives in a mud
walled, thatch roofed house, maintains 'pagan beliefs' and speaks Quechua or
Aymara." Cholos and mestizos were presented as progressively more Westernized, abject lessons of the corruption of authentic Andean culture.

It was precisely as a consequence of their emphasis on the isomorphism of
Andean traditions that anthropologists tended to ignore the fluid and often ambiguous quality of Andean personal identity.[10] The typology of Indian, cholo, and
mestizo suggested three separate spheres of personhood. This contravened the far
less clear-cut experience of hundreds of thousands of highland-born people. From
1940 to 1980, poverty drove at least a quarter of a million Andean farmers to settle
in the jungle and more than a million more to Lima (cf. Martinez 1980). Seasonal
migrations took thousands of others on frequent journeys between the mountains
and the Amazon and coast.[11] This mass mobility meant that many people in the
most "remote" highland hamlets had visited the bustling coast. Conversely,
many inhabitants of the sprawling shantytowns of Lima, La Paz, Quito, Ayacucho, Cuzco, and Huancayo kept strong bonds to the countryside. The distance
between thatch-roofed adobe Andean peasant dwellings and city shacks of tin,
cardboard, and straw mats was not that between "indigenous" Andean society
and "Westernized" modernity. Rather, it was the space between different points
on a single circuit that was integrated by family ties, village loyalties, and constant circulation of goods, ideas, and people. Indian, cholo, and mestizo were not
discrete categories, but partly overlapping positions on a continuum.

The rise of the Shining Path highlighted the continuities between different
locations along the city/country circuit. Urban intellectuals led by Abimael Guzmán founded the movement during the late 1960s at Ayacucho's University of
Huamanga. But university and high school students of mostly peasant origin were
the cadre of the revolution. These young people had friends and family in their
home communities; yet most had studied in the city of Ayacucho and been politically radicalized by exposure to a revolutionary discourse that answered to their

own experience of poverty and lack of opportunity. They became the guerrillas who fanned across the countryside during the 1970s to begin underground organizing, and then took up arms in the 1980s.

The ability of these cadres to start a major upheaval testified to the interpenetrations of different positions along the rural/urban loop. Education and the language of Marxism separated the young revolutionaries from peasants in the countryside. But most of the Senderistas were also poor people with dark skin, knowledge of Quechua, and familiarity with the physical geography and cultural textures of mountain life. "Sendero advances," as the Ayacucho-born historian Jaime Urrutía pointed out in a recent interview,

> because they are the ones there [in the mountains] who are the equal with the population. They aren't the middle class, they aren't physically different, they speak the same language and the people feel close to them.[12]

Urrutía underplays how the arrival of the Shining Path in a village by force of arms can be a sudden and often violent intrusion. Yet he also explodes the favorite counterinsurgency metaphor of the Peruvian authorities, familiar from Vietnam, El Salvador, and wherever governments fight guerrilla uprisings—that the Shining Path are "infiltrators" and "subversives," a force completely external to the peasantry. What distinguishes Sendero from the failed Peruvian guerrilla movements of the 1960s is precisely the close connections of so many Senderistas to the mountains. The Lima intellectuals of Luis de la Puente Uceda's Cuban-inspired National Liberation Army were quickly wiped out by the army. But the young women and men of the Shining Path know the hidden trails of the mountains, how to survive the cold nights, how to dodge army patrols, how to blend with the civilian population and regroup when the security forces withdraw. The guerrillas, in short, frequently have a double status in the peasant communities of Ayacucho. They are part "insiders" and part "outsiders."

The Peruvian director Francisco Lombardi captures this ambiguity in a scene from his recent movie *The Mouth of the Wolf*.[13] The film depicts the Army occupation of the fictional village of Chuspi, a play on the real-life Chuschi. After Senderistas surreptitiously raise the hammer-and-sickle over the police station, soldiers begin a house-by-house search. We watch as two young recruits kick down the door to a dirt-floored house, discover a small workshop for the beautiful carved *retablos* typical of the Ayacucho region, and a hidden plan of the police station. The two soldiers seize the poncho-wearing, dark-skinned young artisan as he tries to flee. They beat him, then proudly deliver him to their commanding officer. But the prisoner does not confess even under burns from a lighted cigarette. Disturbed by the torture and doubtful whether the prisoner even understands Spanish, the commander decides to take the captive by truck to Army headquarters. Senderistas, however, stage a bloody ambush of the pickup truck to commence a series of events that ends with the massacre by the army of more than thirty innocent campesinos.

The sequence not only calls attention to the brutality of the war, but also to the mixed identity of Sendero. For the viewer, like the soldiers, never really knows whether the suspect was a guerrilla. The evidence of the plan and the later ambush indicate involvement. Yet the apparent inability of the prisoner to speak Spanish—along with his peasant dress and retablo craft—clash with the popular image of Shining Path militants as propaganda-spouting university students in Western clothes and red bandanas. The line between indigenous villager and cholo revolutionary turns out to be difficult to establish. The Peruvian soldiers, like U.S. troops in Vietnam, confront an enemy that does not easily sort out from the rural population. Rather than doing the hard work of distinguishing Senderistas, the military wages an indiscriminate terror.

It was precisely the sense of ambiguous identities developed by Lombardi in his fictional Chuspi that is missing from Isbell's portrayal of the real-life Chuschi. Andeanist anthropologists carefully documented and analyzed the customs of highland communities. But they tended to gloss over the overlap and partial interchangeability of Andean personhood that were to become crucial in the spread of the Shining Path.

Born in the northern Andean town of Chota, Antonio Díaz Martínez graduated from the agrarian university near Lima in 1957.[14] Three years as a government development official gave the promising young engineer the opportunity to supervise a planned colonization in the Amazon and to travel briefly to Switzerland, Spain, Egypt, and Chile. But Díaz became disillusioned with state-sponsored development. By the mid-1960s, he had joined the agronomy faculty at the University of Huamanga where Abimael Guzmán was consolidating the pro-Chinese faction that would become Sendero Luminoso. It was from the charged political climate at the university that Díaz wrote *Ayacucho: Hunger and Hope*. Díaz built the book through a colloquial blend of description, dialogue, and anecdote from his travels across Ayacucho between 1965 and 1969. But *Hunger and Hope* also contained a clear message. The "obsolete colonial structure" of Ayacucho had to be overturned (Díaz 1969:33). The region would progress only through "social-economic change" and the recovery of "what's worthy in the art, music, and customs of our people" (1969:265).

Hunger and Hope refracts Andeanism. Like most anthropologists, Díaz believed in the survival of an age-old Andean tradition that could be juxtaposed with the Western culture of conquest. He, too, tended to divide between traditional peasants and corrupted mestizos. In Díaz's view, the labor exchanges of the *minka* and the collective structure of the ayllu testified that rural Ayacuchans had inherited a communal ethic from the Incas. Much like Peruvian socialists in the first decades of the 20th century, Díaz felt this tradition of cooperation could become the foundation of a new social order.

The Andeanist flavor shared by *Hunger and Hope* and so many ethnographies points to the important intersections that have always existed between socialist politics and anthropology research on the Andes. Ethnology and socialist writing—as well as journalism, archaeology, fiction, and travel writing—were tightly intertwined in indigenismo. In the small community of Peruvians and foreigners writing about the Andes during the 1920s and 1930s, the socialists José Carlos Mariátegui and Hildebrando Castro Pozo could quote historian Luis Valcarcel and archaeologist Julio Tello and in turn be cited by American anthropologists Wendell Bennett and Bernard Mishkin. Academic inquiry became more specialized as the numbers of Andeanist scholars expanded after World War II amidst the fast growth of European and U.S. universities. But traffic across different modes of urban discourse about the highlands also continued. The career of José María Arguedas was exemplary. He wrote poetry and fiction about the highlands, worked as a curator of Andean artifacts, and published ethnography. The southern community of Puquio became Arguedas's subject in a full-length ethnography (see Arguedas 1956) and also in his great novel *Yawar Fiesta* (1980). If anthropology and socialist politics were no longer so enmeshed as in Mariátegui's time, Andeanist ethnographers remained cousins to the politicians of the 1960s and 1970s who spoke of a return to the minka and ayllu.

Unlike most other socialists and many anthropologists, however, Díaz made a partial break from Andeanism. He recognized the sharp cultural and economic differences that separated a mountain-born farmer from a coastal bureaucrat. Yet he never lost a sense of mixture and movement. Everywhere in Ayacucho Díaz found people who resisted neat pigeon-holing as Indians, cholos, or mestizos. We meet poor mestizos who speak Quechua; comuneros who travel constantly to Lima; children in the Apurímac who are trilingual in Quechua, Spanish, and Campa. Díaz's rapid sketches of these individuals destabilize boundaries, questioning easy separations between "traditional" Andean society and "modern" mestizo culture. "José de la Cruz," he wrote (1969:142),

> is 45 years old, *mestizo*, speaks Spanish very well, having left the region early when he was little. . . . As a child he took care of the dog and garden for a gringo, then as a young man travelled to the jungle valley of Chanchamayo, where he worked as a peon. Hard years, he tells us. . . . Restless and roving, he later travelled to Ucayali. . . . He's bilingual, his wife monolingual in Spanish, his children are learning Quechua . . . eight years ago he returned to Cangallo where he inherited a small bit of land.

The nomadic De la Cruz spoke Quechua and lived for the moment as a campesino. He cut against the simplified presentation in *To Defend Ourselves* of mestizos as privileged Spanish-speakers. In a barren Cangallo village, Díaz (1969:144) met Anastasio Alarcón, a peasant who:

> has five kids, doesn't drink because he's an evangelical . . . works in construction in Lima from May to October, where he lives in the spareroom with his brother who's a permanent worker. Antonio has three hectares and plants wheat, corn, and barley.

Here a Quechua-speaking villager who should fit in the "Indian" category turned out to spend part of his time in Lima and to be a Protestant. Again our sure sense of authenticity, of who fits where, ends up in question. Instead of easily distinguishable Indians, cholos, and mestizos, we find an interconnected population shifting along positions in the busy circuit between city and country, lowlands and highlands, village and squatter settlement.

Part of Díaz's insight came from his wide-angled view. He visited apparently traditional communities like Quispillacta and Pomacocha. But he also spent much time in La Mar's feudal haciendas. Apurímac's jungle colonizations, Ayacucho's shantytowns, Huanta's dusty truck stops—places where the extent of Andean mobility and interconnection were impossible to ignore.

Just as importantly, Díaz wrote as an informed layman without the need to fix people in rigid analytical categories. Andeanist ethnographers of the 1960s and 1970s joined other Westernized anthropologists in deploying what Françoise Michel-Jones (1978:14) calls "absolute subjects" (the Nuer, the Hopi, the Dogon). Thus in *To Defend Ourselves* we do not encounter Chuschinos as individuals. Instead, Isbell (1977:73) talked about how "the *comuneros* participate in the [national] economy to a limited degree" or "the *vecinos* use village exogamy to secure upward mobility" as if the villagers and the mestizos could be considered homogeneous categories whose members shared identical beliefs.[15] Díaz, by contrast, always introduced unique characters. Some, like the tyrannical hacienda owner at Orcasitas, work simply as emblems of larger categories. But Díaz described others, like Alarcón and Cruz, with a sense of variation and individuality. He, too, spoke of "the *mestizos*" and "the peasants." But the plural voices and long dialogues between Díaz and different Ayacuchans convey a feel for the nuances and partial instability of the larger categories that is largely absent from Andeanist anthropology with its easy confidence about Andean social boundaries.

Finally, Díaz's socialism helped him to see the interlinkages of modern Peru. Side-by-side with their usually romantic view of the "purity" of Andean culture, socialists since Mariátegui had also deployed the concept of class to stress the common position on the bottom of Peru's economic pyramid of indigenous villagers, cholo migrants in the vast *barriadas* of Lima, and poor mestizo laborers. The concept of a broad coalition of the poor, bridging ethnic identifications and rural/urban divisions, would become the heart of organizing by the United Left party in the 1980s. Thus while Díaz retained an idealized view of lo andino, he also recognized that poverty connected peoples of disparate identity across Ayacucho. This economic nexus was one that most anthropologists—largely depending on the categories of "culture" and "community"—were unprepared to explore. The interest in political economy that began to emerge in North American anthropology in the 1970s—which might have led ethnographers to look more deeply at issues of class—arrived slowly to the Andes.[16]

The portrayal in *Hunger and Hope* of the community of Moya, 34 kilometers from the city of Ayacucho, typified Díaz's (1969:53) recognition of the profound interpenetrations of Andean life. He began with a description that emphasized the preservation of tradition and pastoral autonomy in Moya:

> There's no *hacienda* here, all are smallholders with tiny *chacras* that go from 1/6 to 1/2 hectare per family. They all call themselves part of the community . . . [and] sometimes practice the *ayni* and *minga*. . . . The houses of the village can be found

distributed on the gentle hillside; the red color of the roof tiles and the adobe walls blend with the dark green of the alders to give the landscape a very singular beauty.

But Díaz was not content to present Moja as a self-contained and stable community. He entered into conversation with a group of men working to build a school in a communal work-party. Instead of analyzing the event as a pure expression of Andean collectivity, however, he described the men smoking "National"-brand cigarettes and using lumber and cement solicited from a government development agency. We learn that Moya's population was constantly on the move. Without sufficient land, many had left for the cities or jungle. Others migrated between the village and coastal sugar plantations where they hired themselves out as temporary laborers. Though appreciative of the community's success in retaining a measure of communality and stability, Díaz (1969:56) ended with images of Moya's present fluidity and uncertain future:

> We keep walking, and we talk with a few old campesinos in their houses. Only the old stay permanently in the community, the young have become migrants, sometimes returning to help with the planting and harvests and then disappearing only to appear again for fiestas or the next harvest.

Here was the sense of the interconnections that would help make possible the spread of the Shining Path. And here, too, were the mobile young people with knowledge of both city and country that would form the pool from which Abimael Guzmán, Osmán Morote, and Díaz himself were about to begin recruiting a revolutionary cadre. Thirteen years later Moya would be part of the "Red Zone" named by Army intelligence as a stronghold of Sendero.

If the thick interchange between city and country made possible the spread of the Shining Path across Ayacucho from the gray-stoned University of Huamanga, the immediate successes of the revolutionaries in winning support in the countryside testified to the explosive discontent of many peasants. It is vital from the start to point out that the Shining Path also depends on violence. The revolutionaries have killed campesinos for reasons from breaking decrees against voting to participating in compulsory Army-directed civil patrols. In September 1984, guerrillas slaughtered 21 villagers in Huamanguilla, Ayacucho on the suspicion of "collaboration" with the government (Amnesty International 1989:5). "Violence is a universal law," as Abimael Guzmán himself proclaims, ". . . and without revolutionary violence one class cannot be substituted for another, an old order cannot be overthrown to create a new one."[17]

At the same time, though, persuasive evidence exists for a degree of genuine rural backing of the revolution. In mid-1982, inquiries about Sendero in Ayacucho by journalist Raul Gonzalez (1982:47) elicited a near unanimous reply: "It's a movement supported by the youngest peasants. The older ones are resigned to their lot, but do back their kids." In early 1983, peasant leaders in Huancayo told political scientist Cynthia McClintock (1984:54) "that substantial majorities [of peasants] were supportive.'' David Scott Palmer (1986:129) concluded that Sendero retained a ''substantial reservoir of support'' in rural Ayacucho. By 1985, Senderistas had also found a profitable new niche in the upper Amazon as the defenders of smallholding coca-growers, mostly migrants from the highlands, against rapacious Colombian buyers and government officials.[18] It was in part because of popular support that Sendero grew so fast in the 1980s. Nine of Peru's 181 provinces were declared military-controlled Emergency Zones in December 1982. The number had jumped to 56 by mid-1989 (Amnesty International 1989:2).

The Senderistas used a similar strategy in communities across Ayacucho, Huancavelica, Andahuaylas, and Junin.[19] They arrived preaching the overthrow of the government and often redistributing land and animals from state-administered cooperatives. The call for radical change appealed to many villagers. The young guerrillas, who sometimes had relatives in the communities where they went to organize, had the knowledge of Quechua and mountain life that enabled them to bear the revolutionary doctrine effectively. Executions of corrupt bureaucrats and cattle rustlers were generally greeted with enthusiasm. They bolstered the Shining Path's popularity. Torture and massacres by the security forces could scare off support. But it was also clear by the end of 1980s that the tactics of terror often backfired. Resentful villagers had another reason to back the Shining Path.

Signs of the discontent that Sendero exploited abounded in the southern highlands during the 1960s and 1970s. Growing pressure from peasants for the breakup of haciendas was one reason behind the decision in 1969 of the Velasco government to carry out agrarian reform. The 1960s brought an outpouring of land invasions, strikes, and the strengthening of regional and national peasant unions. In 1963 alone, political scientist Howard Handelman (1975:121) estimated that campesinos staged between 350 and 400 land seizures in Peru's southern mountains. Thousands of peasants continued to mobilize through the decade, even though police usually sided with landowners and many farmers died in invasions under fire from the security forces.[20] The reform did not stop the unrest. Many haciendas were not divided, and new cooperatives proved inefficient. The state failed to provide money for loans or technical assistance even as official rhetoric during the early Velasco years of equality and campesino pride further radicalized many peasants. In Ayacucho and Apurímac, peasant protest intensified (Isbell 1988:7). Campesinos now invaded not only undivided haciendas, but also the cooperatives. Agrarian leagues first formed by the Velasco government became independent, and by the late 1970s a mosaic of militant regional federations stretched across the highlands.

Andeanist anthropology, however, registered little sign of the immense discontent of peasants or their frequent recourse to action. *To Defend Ourselves* reflected the tendency to ignore rural political activity. Isbell depicted Chuschinos as unhappy about their relations with mestizos. But she stressed the conservatism of the villagers—their desire to retain continuity with their Andean traditions. Her argument rested on similes of defense. The peasants ''defend their way of life,'' ''maintain[ing] social closure,'' ''close[d] themselves socially and economically to strengthen their defenses against the encroachments of the outside world'' (Isbell 1977:97, 37, 243). Desires for change were ascribed only to the mestizo schoolteachers and the cholo Lima migrants. ''The peasants have chosen a strategy of protecting what they have,'' wrote Isbell (1977:237) in a passage that ignored rural interest in change, ''while the radical teachers have chosen strategies to gain what they do not have—better wages, increased social mobility, and the power to influence decisions.''

Only in the postscript to her 1975 visit did Isbell disclose signs of political initiative by Chuschino farmers. We learn that in February 1972 the villagers expelled the local priest, angry about the church's control over animals and property. In April 1975, Chuschinos organized a massive invasion of an unrepartitioned hacienda. After the occupation, 200 Chuschinos made the long journey to the city of Ayacucho to press for legal recognition of their claim.

All this suggested a willingness to take bold action. But Isbell held to her picture of the villagers as conservative. She presented cholo migrants as leaders of both movements, as if villagers would not take such aggressive steps on their own and even though the two actions had wide community support. Despite their aggressive thrust, Isbell (1977:243) ultimately glossed both events as more evidence of ''the comuneros . . . attempting to strengthen their mechanisms of defensive isolation.''

Isbell at least recorded evidence of peasant mobilization. Many other Andeanists entirely ignored the widespread strikes, invasions, and campesino unionism across not just the Peruvian Andes, but also in Bolivia, Colombia, and, to a lesser extent, Ecuador. Studying peasant movements was left largely to political scientists, journalists, and lawyers. The only well-known ethnography devoted to protest, June Nash's (1977) fine *We Eat the Mines and the Mines Eat Us,* dealt not with the countryside, but the proletarianized Bolivian tin mines. Of the 464 publications cited by Frank Salomon (1982) in his thorough review of Andean ethnology in the 1970s, only 5 dealt directly with peasant organizing. Anthropologists, in short, almost entirely bypassed one of the most crucial issues of the time.

Part of the explanation rests with the state of anthropological theory in the 1960s and 1970s. Until the florescence of political economy in the mid-1970s, much of the thinking in these years sorted into the general camp of either cultural ecology or symbolic anthropology.[21] This alignment carried into studies of the Andes. A large body of scholarship arose on issues of adaptation; another gathered around cosmology, kinship, and ritual. The analysis of mobilization and protest did not have a real place on either side.

The disappearance of politics was most marked in the work of ecological anthropologists. With the rapid growth of cultural ecology in North American anthropology during the late 1960s, anthropologists like Stephen Brush, Glynn Custred, Jorge Flores Ochoa, R. Brooke Thomas, and Bruce Winterhalder made the study of Andean ecosystems into popular specialty. These scholars recognized that modern highland life reflected the experience of Spanish conquest and contact with capitalism. A few, most notably Benjamin Orlove, combined interests in the environment and political economy to fashion creative historically sensitive ethnography. Most of the literature, though, followed the line of leading ecological anthropologists like Marvin Harris and Roy Rappaport. It emphasized the development by Andean people of stable adaptations to their rugged environment. The more biologically minded scholars documented the large lungs of mountain peasants, and their success in developing strains of grains and potatoes suited to the cold. Others, like Brush and Flores Ochoa, analyzed how highland land tenure and pastoral management in Andean villages were especially suited to the ecology. The precise nature of Andean "vertical ecology"—the term coined by John Murra to describe how pre-Inca states controlled lands at varying altitudes—became an issue of special debate. Stressing the self-regulating and distinctive character of Andean ecology, the ecological literature fit with the premise of Andeanism about a discrete and stable Andean tradition. The authors, in long collections like *Man in the Andes* (Baker and Little 1976) and *Pastores de Puna* (Flores Ochoa 1977), could discuss in painstaking detail the special character of adaptation in places like Puno, Ayacucho, and Huancayo even amidst political tumult and an imminent revolution.

There was marginally more interest in politics on the culturally focused side of Andeanist ethnography. The structuralism of Lévi-Strauss and interpretive anthropology of Clifford Geertz were variously brought to the classic Andeanist topics of ritual, reciprocity, kinship, and cosmology by ethnographers like Joseph Bastien, Leslie Brownrigg, Olivia Harris, Luis Millones, Tristan Platt, and R. T. Zuidema. New studies analyzed Andean cultures in terms of "structural oppositions," "ritual transformations," "webs of meaning." Where the ecologists made "vertical ecology" a particular concern, the nature of the ayllu became the focus for many of the scholars concerned with symbol and structure. Anthropologists such as Michael Taussig (1980) and Nathan Wachtel (1977) elucidated highland culture in the context of conquest or the arrival of capitalism. But they preserved a vision of unchanging beliefs that dovetailed with the assumptions of Andeanism. Like that on cultural ecology, debate over the structure of Andean culture became such an absorbing project that it was possible to miss the signs of the nearing upheaval. Efforts in the mid-1970s to join ecological and structural perspectives—Isbell subtitled her book "ecology and ritual" in the spirit of synthesis—only perpetuated anthropological insensitivity to the political agency of Andean peasants.

Beyond their narrow and partly distorting theoretical lenses, a further factor in the oversight of rural unrest was the general orientation of Andeanists toward their ethnographic subjects. In the 1950s, paternal views of Andean people as backward agriculturalists who would have to become modern farmers still prevailed. The renowned ecological anthropologist Julian Steward (1963:xxix) coupled Andeanist imagery of highlanders as non-Westernized "Indians" with the rhetoric of modernization typical of the 1950s:

> As the Indians' slight understanding of European systems leaves them poorly equipped to solve their own problems, great efforts are being made to rehabilitate them economically, through restoration of lands and improved farm methods, and to

reintegrate them culturally, through education and other means designed to facilitate their fuller participation in national life.

The conviction that peasants needed a dose of Western initiative and modern technology guided the Cornell anthropologists in the 1950s who bought the hacienda of Vicos in the central highlands to supervise the process through which the ex-serfs were to enter the modern age.

This unabashed paternalism had largely disappeared by the mid-1960s with the decline of modernization theory. The flavor of Andeanist anthropology in the 1960s and 1970s was increasingly redemptive. Some ethnographers highlighted problems of intracommunal feuding and conflict (Bolton 1973, 1974; Stein 1962). But most unilaterally stressed the resilience and value of Andean traditions. While often edging into a condescending presumption about their right to "speak for" highland people, anthropologists sent an important message to government bureaucrats and development administrators about the need to respect the practices and opinions of campesinos. Peasants were shown to possess sophisticated knowledge of their environment, to have elaborate ritual calendars and astronomical systems, to possess rich memories of their past. An entire literature sprang up on the physiological benefits of coca-chewing, a practice once considered a sign of Andean backwardness.

At the same time, though, the project of redeeming lo andino helped lead Andeanists to downplay the underside of highland life: the grinding poverty that led so many peasants into angry action. All Andeanists recognized poverty. But the stress on ecological adaptations and sophisticated symbolism had as a consequence a tendency to minimize the full extent of the economic suffering across the countryside. Ethnographers usually did little more than mention the terrible infant mortality, minuscule incomes, low life expectancy, inadequate diets, and abysmal health care that remained so routine. To be sure, peasant life was full of joys, expertise, and pleasures. But the figures that led other observers to label Ayacucho a region of "Fourth World" poverty would come as a surprise to someone who knew the area only through the ethnography of Isbell, Skar, or Zuidema. They gave us detailed pictures of ceremonial exchanges, Saint's Day rituals, weddings, baptisms, and work parties. Another kind of scene, just as common in the Andes, almost never appeared: the girl with an abscess and no doctor, the woman bleeding to death in childbirth, a couple in their dark adobe house crying over an infant's sudden death.

In sum, Andeanist anthropology did not recognize the explosive pain and discontent in the highlands. This anger did not, of course, neatly translate into backing for the Shining Path. Campesinos in the southern department of Puno and the northern departments of Cajamarca and Piura have rejected guerrilla overtures. Even in the Sendero strongholds of Ayacucho, Apurímac, Huancavelica, Junin, many rural people have refused to collaborate.

Isbell's Chuschi, though, was one of the many places where the Shining Path found a warm reception. Chuschinos almost universally approved of the Sendero execution of two cattle thieves, the public whipping of two others, and the expulsion of five corrupt bureaucrats.[22] In August 1982, many Chuschinos were among the 2,000 peasants from nine villages who joined a Sendero-led invasion of a University of Huamanga agricultural station. In December, the communities converged in Chuschi for an enthusiastic march to celebrate the birth of a Shining Path-organized popular army. Ten blocks of peasants waved red flags, shouting *vivas* to the revolutionary war.

In the short final section of *To Defend Ourselves* about Chuschi's future prospects, Isbell (1977:244–245) had written that "consumerism and new cultural values due to increased out-migration and education may in time cause changes in the perspective of the community." But her main contention was that change had not yet happened, and that villagers would in the near future "retain their conservative attitudes" and continue "efforts to resist incorporation into the national economy and culture." The impact of radical mestizos would "be minimal because, as discussed earlier, they do not share the political concerns of the comuneros, who are attempting to protect their cultural isolation."

Like other Andeanists, Isbell had drastically underestimated the desires of impoverished Ayacuchans for change. Far from rejecting radical ideology and "attempting to protect their cultural isolation," many Chuschinos and other Andean peasants proved ready to embrace the concept of revolution. The price Chuschinos would pay for welcoming Sendero proved incalculably high. In 1983–84, government forces disappeared 6 peasants from Chuschi and 46 from the neighboring community of Quispillacta. A detachment of Sinchis, black-sweatered police commandos who are the most self-avowedly savage of the counterinsurgency forces, blew apart an elderly Chuschino with hand grenades in the village square. By 1985, the Army had burned down much of Chuschi. Most of the comuneros fled to Lima's brown shantytowns.[23]

As the "hunger" in the title suggests, Antonio Díaz Martínez made the desperate conditions in Ayacucho a focal point of *Ayacucho: Hunger and Hope.* Díaz's explanation of the situation foreshadowed that of the Shining Path. He viewed highland poverty as the product not of incorporation into the world economy but of the region's stagnation in a semifeudal system dominated by big landlords and parasitic bureaucrats. But the Díaz of 1969 wrote with a subtlety that would disappear in Sendero's formulaic Maoism. The result was a close-grained and sensitive picture of the many sides of Ayacucho's poverty: rich farmers buying out smallholders in Cangallo, Apurímac plantation owners paying a pittance to day laborers, peasants with parcels too tiny for subsistence, communities in conflict with haciendas and each other.

Anthropologists like R. Brooke Thomas (1976:403) stressed that Andean people made a "successful adaptation to one of the most stressful regions inhabited by man." Díaz (1969:65–66), by contrast, saw lands that were "eroded, poorly irrigated, extremely divided . . . tired and deforested." Far from adapting to their mountain environment, peasants were forced onto the busy circuit between jungle, mountains, and coast:

> The Coast, the mines of Cerro de Pasco, the jungle of Apurímac serve them as an escape from the poverty of the land, giving them some temporary or permanent work and a bit of economic income. After the planting, they go to these centers of work and then return for the harvests, bringing with them a few clothes and a little money saved for the family that stayed to take care of the house and the fields. Others emigrate for good, taking their family with them and leaving their small plot to a relative. Sometimes they come back for the fiestas, or don't come back ever. [1969:65]

Díaz believed that some comuneros, like those in Moya, had maintained a semblance of equilibrium through the careful management of their limited resources. In general, though, *Hunger and Hope* eschews the language of "adaptation" and "balance" in favor of images of suffering and impoverishment.

Díaz shared the faith of anthropologists in the merit of Andean traditions. Yet this did not prevent him from coming to grips with poverty and injustice. Most Andeanist ethnography insistently celebrated. Díaz preferred to denounce. He found that "poverty, malnutrition, illiteracy are the common denominator" from the shantytowns of Ayacucho to the malarial jungles of Apurímac to the windswept heights of Huamanga (1969:33). Avoiding extensive statistics or Marxist jargon, Díaz chose to depict the harsh conditions through informal interviews and vivid vignettes of particular communities. One typical passage finds Díaz in conversation with José Hinostroza, a migrant from Cangallo to the humid Apurímac valley. Díaz used Hinostroza's words to extend our understanding of rural Ayacucho's predicament. The conversation is low-key. Yet we learn about the lack of schools, bad prices for crops, disputes with the government, and devastating diseases. Díaz ended not with grand pronouncements but mulling over Hinostroza's views as he walked down the muddy path from the house sucking on a papaya given him by Hinostroza's Amazon-born Campa wife.

Peasants, Díaz believed, wanted change. He portrayed Ayacucho as bubbling with political activity. "Communities, villages, and hamlets" were "fighting . . . to get rid of this obsolete and unworkable colonial structure" (1969:33). We hear about the complaints of an Apurímac laborer about his tiny wages, the angry words about government bureaucrats from a Cangallo farmer, a land invasion by 114 farm families in Huascahura, the takeover of another estate in La Mar, Cangallo farmers rejecting a government-administered cooperative to form their own association. This, for Díaz, was a region of "*campesinos* disenchanted with the public powers," of small farmers actively and consciously engaged with the larger world.[24] The "hope" of *Hunger and Hope* referred to what Díaz felt was the capacity of Ayacuchans to remake their society.

Disaffected by his own experience in the early 1960s, Díaz considered Western-sponsored development an unacceptable response to Ayacucho's problems. Engineers, agronomists, and administrators in development projects come under biting criticism in *Hunger and Hope*. They represented, for Díaz, not the prospect of change but the most recent face of government oppression. He repeatedly criticized development bureaucrats for their paternalism, insensitivity to local knowledge, inefficiency, and corruption; and he appends to *Hunger and Hope* a short essay by a visiting U.S. student that denounces a U.S. Agency for International

Development colonization project in Apurímac for its waste and elitism. It was the harsh view of development in *Hunger and Hope,* pushed to a rigid extreme, that would lead the Shining Path to make government development workers a target of assassination. In early 1989, a guerrilla communiqué also ordered private development groups out of Peru because "you give crumbs to the people to entertain them and fail to realize that the correct path is that of the people's war."[25]

Díaz (1969:34) summed up his dislike of development and belief in the revolutionary potential of Ayacuchan peasants in a passionate passage with strong Andeanist overtones:

> Here the man of the Andes lived under a centralized economy, until the white predator who lasted for 300 years and his successor the modern *mestizo:* governor, priest, congressman, public employee, propagandists and sellers of technology, who say they will achieve "development." "Development" of whom?, if they don't even stop to learn about the native culture, or even the economic structure, how will they be able to develop it? But nevertheless, this autochthonous people stands on its feet, with hope for the future, with faith in its efforts, and one day will break the chains that impede its development.

Díaz's language reiterates that Andeanism does not always accompany a vision of peasants as conservative. It did for anthropologists with their disinterest in politics. But Díaz, like the *indigenista* socialists of the 1920s and 1930s, connected his belief in the survival of "autochthonous" traditions with an assurance about the possibility of change. Lo andino became a seed of purity that would flower in a new social order.

Despite the heteroglot identity of its own cadre, the Shining Path would also invoke the concept of a return to uncorrupted Andean origins. In the "popular war" against the "reactionaries and their imperialist masters," certified an article in the semiofficial party newspaper *El Diario,* "the Andean people advance . . . the Quechua, aymara, and chanka advances."[26] Where Sendero differs from other socialist alternatives is the frightening rigidity of its vanguardism. The absolutism of the Senderistas about their views—and their own right to lead—provides the moral framework that justifies the murder of those perceived as opponents. *Hunger and Hope* contained some advance warning of this authoritarianism. Díaz (1969:34–35) directed the book not to poor people in Ayacucho, but to "young students and researchers" whom he hoped would recognize their "historical responsibility to study our problems and take an honest position in the search for new situations." While conserving a profound regard for peasant knowledge and militancy, he also mixed in phrases about the "miserable masses" and "illiterate peasants" that suggested their political consciousness to be less acute than that of an educated vanguard. The people would be at the heart of the revolution. But they would need to be organized in a "planned state" (1969:266).

On balance, though, Díaz's vision had a collaborative flavor very different from the dogmatism of the party he would help to organize in the next decade. The sharp-sighted passion of the young professor had not yet hardened into doctrine. The University of Huamanga, Díaz (1969:265) wrote, should avoid becoming a "producer of egotists and individualists" and "put itself at the service of the collectivity." But if it did not, Díaz (1969:24) believed Ayacucho's poor would make change on their own, "passing sooner or later right over [the university], and transforming its world." At the end of Díaz's (1969:266) vision was a powerful yet strangely innocent dream of a collectively fashioned utopia. The Andes have strong people and rich natural resources, he wrote in the last line of *Hunger and Hope*—"let's make them into a paradise."

Edward Said (1979:1) speaks of how the bloody civil war in Beirut of 1974–75 crashed against the imagery of Orientalism. It was no longer so possible to represent the Middle East as "a place of romance, exotic being, haunting memories and landscapes, remarkable experiences." Ayacucho marked a similar moment for Andeanism. No longer could the highlands so easily support interpretations where they appeared as a place of static cultures and discrete identities. Colorful posters of Andean peasants in ponchos posed next to llamas at Macchu Picchu still adorned the walls of travel agencies across the United States. But a different kind of image of the highlands also began to reach this country: pictures of mass graves, wreckage from explosions, soldiers in black ski masks, and farm families mourning their dead.

Far from the paradise imagined by Díaz, life in much of Peru's highlands has become a nightmare. More than fifty thousand people fled the terror in the countryside for Lima's slums over the 1980s (Kirk 1987). Senderistas murder not only representatives of the state, but political candidates and trade unionists. Government security forces have made rape and torture into standard practice. They have "disappeared" more than 3,000 people since 1982, and killed at least as many in mass executions and selective assassination (Amnesty International 1989:1).

One casualty of war was Antonio Díaz Martínez. Arrested in the early 1980s, he was one of the 124 prisoners in the terrorism wing of the cement-block Lurigancho prison in the sandy hills on Lima's periphery. In June 1986, Senderistas in Lurigancho, the island prison of El Frontón, and the women's detention center of Santa Barbara staged simultaneous takeovers to protest government plans to move them into a more secure facility. President Alan García refused to negotiate. He turned the prisons over to the armed forces. The police stormed Santa Barbara, killing two prisoners. At El Frontón, helicopters bombed the main pavilion. Troops killed at least 90 prisoners. At Lurigancho, the police fired bazookas, mortar, and rockets into the compound and then stormed the prison. Díaz was probably one of at least one hundred prisoners executed after surrendering, shot in the head or mouth as they lay flat on the ground (Amnesty International 1989:7). To prevent autopsies, the security forces secretly buried the bodies at night in graveyards around Lima. Díaz's body was discovered in a shallow grave in the Imperial Cemetery in Cañete province, just south of the capital.

Just five weeks before the prison uprising, Díaz gave one of the first interviews granted by a Shining Path leader. Journalist José María Salcedo (1986) passed from the chaos of the regular prison into the special terrorist cellblock where Senderistas maintained tight discipline. Salcedo attempted to paint Díaz as a half-hearted revolutionary. He concentrated on the young guerrilla who supervised the interview. The prison transfer was already announced. Díaz foresaw that the army might use opposition to the transfer to justify a massacre, but professed no fear. "Our morale is superior and we take death as a challenge," said Díaz (quoted in Salcedo 1986:64).

In the end, however, the interview undermines Salcedo's effort to depict Díaz as less than committed to the Shining Path. For Díaz had clearly evolved into a hard-liner. The answers were still concise and smart. But they had the uncompromising edge that had already emerged in Díaz's second book, *China: The Agrarian Revolution* (1978). Written after a 1974–75 stay in China and published a decade after *Hunger and Hope*, this book revealed Díaz's turn to the inflexible Maoism of the Cultural Revolution. "Since 1949 . . . the Dictatorship of the Proletariat against the bourgeoisie had grown even more intense," Díaz (1978:8) began the book, ". . . [and] with the Great Proletarian Cultural Revolution the red line of President Mao again becomes more vigorous." In Lurigancho, Díaz could now give emphasis to his commitment to communism ("we are all material for the transition to communism") and cite the cold-blooded Abimael Guzmán— "President Gonzalo"—as a maximum paragon of moral virtue ("the greatest affirmation of life over death"). The Shining Path must sometimes kill peasants, he explained in good Maoist-Stalinist language, because "the countryside is not flat but divided into classes."

As for anthropologists, most have retreated from Peru. Only a handful still work in the highlands, and none in Ayacucho's countryside. Only one remains of the more than ten major Andean archaeology projects that operated at the end of the 1970s. Graduate students interested in the Andes now opt for Ecuador or Bolivia.

To my knowledge, the only Andeanist to offer written public reflections on why anthropologists did not anticipate the Shining Path is Billie Jean Isbell. Her short introductory note to a 1985 reprinting of *To Defend Ourselves* mixes a frank admission of error with a confident rhetoric of continuing expertise. "My anthropological perspective," she writes, "blinded me from seeing the historical processes that were occurring at the time. . . . I did not adequately place Chuschi in a world system in which increasing violence and the breakdown of nation states in the Third World are becoming commonplace" (Isbell 1985:xiii–xiv).

But Isbell also conserves her same vision of Andean continuity and self-containment. She does not consider how the growth of Sendero has reflected peasant discontent or Peru's intensifying interconnections. Instead, she still speaks of an "increasing polarization of the Quechua-speaking masses and the national culture" and depicts the Shining Path as a "small leftist movement" external and different from the peasantry:

Sendero Luminoso has declared that they are prepared for a fifty year struggle in order to destroy the existing government and institute a new order. The peasants, on the other hand, are concentrating on preserving their lands and their way of life. [Isbell 1985:xiii]

Of course, this position has partial truth. It remains essential to understand that Sendero is no organic peasant uprising. But Isbell overlooks that many of Sendero's young recruits are the sons and daughters of peasants; and she ignores currents of sympathy for the guerrillas amidst the vast numbers of Peruvian campesinos who want change and not just to defend their traditions. If the Shining Path were only a group of violent leftist intellectuals, the movement would long ago have been destroyed. Instead, it has spread through much of the mountains and now presents a daily threat to Lima. The guerrillas are in parts foreign and homegrown, terrorist and popularly based.

I believe that anthropologists still concerned with the interpretation of highland life need to break decisively from Andeanism. Two related moves seem to me crucial. One is to dismantle the binary logic of Andeanism: Andeanism/European, indigenous/Western, precapitalist/capitalist, pagan/Christian, traditional/modern. Instead of presuming the separateness of the Andean and Western, we might begin to approach the plural identities in the mountains as particular ways of living built from inside far-reaching webs of power and meaning. Campesinos like those from Chuschi are not, as Isbell (1977:4) put it, "peasants approach[ing] degrees of national incorporation." Rather, they have lived for almost half a millennium under colonial and republican rule. Roads, radios, universal education, political campaigns, evangelization, military conscription, and the massive migration have tightened the links between the Andean countryside and big urban centers during this century. Recognizing these intricate ties does not mean downplaying the persistence of sharp cultural differences in the Andean nations. It does, however, require seeing difference not as the result of distance and separation, but as constructed within a history of continuous and multilayered connections.

A second key move is to stop representing modern Andean identity as a matter of continuity with the indigenous past. What Fabian (1983) calls "allochronism"—the presentation of a contemporary cultural tradition as if it were an artifact of an earlier era—underlies the assumption that today's Andean cultures derive from the precolonial era. Of course, it would be wrong to ignore the strong ties of Andean people to their past. To take the most obvious example, more than 5 million people still speak Quechua, albeit a Quechua now spiced with Spanish borrowings. At the same time, though, metaphors of "continuity" and "traditionalism" work poorly in the Andes (cf. Clifford 1988). On close inspection, chemical dyes color homewoven ponchos. Celebrations of harvest festivals come on Saints' Days. Japanese-manufactured MSG spices the ancient specialty of roast guinea pig. Mountain ballads to Inca melodies praise the building of new hydroelectric projects. Andean culture thrives even in Peru's tormented highlands. But it is never the expression of primordial mountain traits, so much as the product of visions that people continually rework in ongoing processes of innovation and recombination.

Active anthropological work for life and peace ought, I believe, to accompany the break from Andeanism. If the effects may be small, our efforts can at least help to bring Peru's situation to public attention and to build pressure on the Peruvian government to respect human rights. We can also support the courageous peasant federations, women's organizations, shantytown soup kitchens, mineworker unions, and human rights groups which stand between the fire of the Shining Path and the government.

Political engagement, after all, will not be new for Andeanists. As contributors to Andeanism, we have helped to construct a discourse that has conditioned not only how the rest of the world perceives the Andes but also how Andean people understand themselves. During this century, an idealized sense of Inca lineage, harmony with nature, and communal values has filtered across the mountains through schoolbooks, radio, TV, and political speeches. Many campesinos, in turn, reappropriate these Andeanist concepts—often in conjunction with parts of the also externally imposed discourses of Christianity, nationalism, and socialism—to articulate political identities that answer to contemporary needs. In Ayacucho, a wood cross, Peruvian flag, and anti-imperialist poster adorn the tin and straw-mat shelter of the Association of the Families of the Disappeared (ANFASEP). So, too, does a copy of a reverential ode by José María Arguedas to the "Andean spirit." Some of the mostly peasant women of the Association mention their "indigenous heritage" and "Inca culture" in their talk about human rights and lost relatives. In part, then, Andeanism has come full circle. What began as the imposition of outside observers now becomes redeployed by popular organizations. "We" and "they" connect not just through political economy but also across the more subtle channels of representation and self-imagination.

Let me end, then, with an appeal rather than a conclusion. ANFASEP and two other Peruvian human rights organizations have urgent need for support. They work under great danger to monitor violations and to assist victims of the terror. Please consider sending them a donation:

Committee for the Defense of Human Rights in Apurímac
CODEH, Apartado 26, Abancay, Apurímac, Peru

Association of the Families of Disappeared in Ayacucho
ANFASEP, Apartado 196, Ayacucho, Peru

Center for Research and Action for Peace
CEAPAZ, Costa Rica 150, Lima 11, Peru, tel. 63501

Notes

Acknowledgments. An abbreviated version of this article was presented at the American Anthropological Association meeting, November 1989, Washington, D.C. I would like to thank Ralph Bolton, George Collier, Miguel Diaz-Barriga, Robin Kirk, Charles Hale, Donald Moore, Lisa Rofel, Renato Rosaldo, Frances Starn, Randolph Starn, and Brackette Williams for their comments.

[1] In the Peruvian press, the best reporting on the Shining Path can be found in the quarterly *Quehacer*, especially by Nelson Manrique, José María Salcedo, and Raul Gonzalez. Berg (1988), Bourque and Warren (1989), Degregori (1986), McClintock (1984), and Palmer (1986) are among the best academic sources on Sendero. The collection of essays in *Resistance, Rebellion, and Consciousness in the Andean Peasant World, 18th to 20th Centuries* (1987) edited by Steve Stern is an excellent introduction to the longer history of protest and revolt in the Andes.

[2] A good piece in *Granta* by British journalist Nicholas Shakespeare (1988) discusses the personal background of Sendero's leader.

[3] My thinking owes a great debt to Said's (1979) controversial writing on Orientalism. For more on how my analysis of Andeanism partly diverges from Said's of Orientalism, see pp. 67–68, 85 below.

[4] Harding (1988) has written a short article that to my knowledge is the only study of Díaz.

[5] See Salomon (1985) for an excellent discussion of indigenismo and the representation of the Andes in the first decades of this century.

[6] The quotes come from the 1990 catalogue of Wilderness Travel, pp. 63–68. The catalogue of another trekking company, Mountain Travel, uses almost identical language.

[7] Clifford (1988) provides an excellent review of *Orientalism*.

[8] Clifford (1988:255–277) and Marcus and Fischer (1986:1–2) develop this criticism of Said.

[9] This and all subsequent translations from the Spanish are mine.

[10] See Rosaldo (1989) for a discussion of ''cultural borderlands,'' and their general disappearance in anthropology where people were assumed to inhabit bounded cultures that corresponded to a circumscribed geographical area.

[11] One ethnography that broke decisively with Andeanism to give a well-developed sense of mobility between city and country was *The Bolivian Aymara* by Hans and Judith-Maria Buechler (1971).

[12] The interview is in *Quehacer*, no. 57, February/March 1989, pp. 42–56.

[13] The movie is loosely based on the massacre by police in 1983 of 47 villagers in Soccos.

[14] This biographical information on Díaz comes from Harding (1988:66–67).

[15] Isbell does draw a division between three economic levels within the comunero category: the *apukuna, wachakuna,* and *tiypakuq*. But she always insists that the division between comuneros and vecinos is the most fundamental in Chuschi, and for most of the book speaks of these two groups as homogeneous entities.

[16] More work on the Andes informed by political economy began to appear in the 1980s (Collins 1989; Orlove, Foley, and Love 1989; Roseberry 1983).

[17] This comes from an interview with Guzmán in *El Diario*, 31 July 1988, p. 15. There remains some doubt about the interview's authenticity, as there is about whether Guzmán is still alive. But most Sendero-watchers in Lima believed the interview was indeed authentic; for their opinion, see *La Republica*, 31 July 1988, pp. 12–15.

[18]Kawell (1989) reports on the emergence of Sendero as a political force in the Upper Huallaga Valley.

[19]See Berg (1988), Isbell (1988), and Manrique (1989) for accounts of Sendero's arrival in peasant communities.

[20]The recent study of Huasicancha in Junin by anthropologist Gavin Smith (1989) provides a close look at the history of protest in one southern Andean community.

[21]Sherry Ortner's (1984) "Theory in Anthropology Since the Sixties" is the best introduction to the general shape of the discipline in the United States during the 1960s and 1970s.

[22]This information on the reception in Chuschi of the Shining Path comes from a paper by Isbell (1988) based on interviews with Chuschinos and outsiders familiar with the village.

[23]This information comes from Isbell's introductory note to the 1985 reprinting of *To Defend Ourselves*.

[24]The quote comes from the back cover of *Hunger and Hope*.

[25]Quoted in *Latin American Weekly Report* 5 October 1989, page 12.

[26]*El Diario*, 8 May 1988, p. 6 quoted in Mauceri (1989:21).

References Cited

Alberti, Giorgio, and Enrique Mayer
    1974   Reciprocidad andina: ayer y hoy. *In* Reciprocidad e intercambio en los andes peruanos. G. Alberti and E. Mayer, eds. Pp. 13–37. Lima: IEP.
Amnesty International
    1989   Caught Between Two Fires, Peru Briefing. London: Amnesty International.
Arguedas, José María
    1956   Puquio, una cultura en proceso de cambio. Revista del Museo Nacional 26:78–151.
    1980   Yawar Fiesta. Lima: Editorial Horizonte.
Baker, Paul, and Michael Little, eds.
    1976   Man in the Andes: A Multidisciplinary Study of the High-Altitude Quechua. US/IBP Synthesis Series, 1. Stroudsburg: Dowden, Hutchinson, and Ross Inc.
Bastien, Joseph
    1978   Mountain of the Condor: Metaphor and Ritual in an Andean Ayllu. St. Paul, Minn.: West Publishing Company.
Berg, Ronald
    1988   Retribution and Resurrection: The Politics of Sendero Luminoso in Peru. Paper presented at the annual meeting of the American Anthropological Association, Phoenix, Arizona.
Bolton, Ralph
    1973   Aggression and Hypoglycemia among the Qolla: A Study in Psychobiological Anthropology. Ethnology 12:227–257.
    1974   To Kill A Thief: A Kallawya Sorcery Session in the Lake Titicaca Region of Peru. Anthropos 69:191–215.
Bourque, Susan, and Kay Warren
    1989   Democracy Without Peace: The Cultural Politics of Terror in Peru. Latin American Research Review 24(1):7–35.

Brush, Stephen
   1977   Mountain, Field, and Family: The Economy and Human Ecology of an Andean
   Valley. Philadelphia: University of Pennsylvania Press.
Buechler, Hans, and Judith-Maria Buechler
   1971   The Bolivian Aymara. New York: Holt, Rinehart & Winston.
Clifford, James
   1988   The Predicament of Culture. Cambridge: Harvard University Press.
Collins, Jane
   1989   Unseasonal Migrations: The Effects of Rural Labor Scarcity in Peru. Princeton:
   Princeton University Press.
Degregori, Carlos Ivan
   1986   Sendero Luminoso. Lima: IEP.
Díaz Martínez, Antonio
   1969   Ayacucho: Hambre y Esperanza. Ayacucho. Ayacucho: Ediciones Waman
   Puma.
   1978   China: la revolución agraria. Lima: Mosca Azul.
Doughty, Paul
   1968   Huaylas: An Andean District in Search of Progress. Ithaca, N.Y.: Cornell Uni-
   versity Press.
Fabian, Johannes
   1983   Time and the Other: How Anthropology Makes Its Object. New York: Columbia
   University Press.
Flores Ochoa, Jorge
   1977   Pastores de Puna. Lima: IEP.
Gonzalez, Raul
   1982   Por los caminos de Sendero. Quehacer 19:39–77.
Greaves, Thomas
   1972   The Andean Rural Proletarian. Anthropological Quarterly 45(2):65–83.
Handelman, Howard
   1975   Struggle in the Andes. Austin: University of Texas Press.
Harding, Colin
   1988   Antonio Díaz Martínez and the Ideology of Sendero Luminoso. Bulletin of Latin
   American Research 7(1):65–73.
Isbell, Billie Jean
   1977   To Defend Ourselves: Ecology and Ritual in an Andean Village. Austin: University of Texas Press.
   1985   Reprinting of To Defend Ourselves. Prospect Heights, Ill.: Waveland Press.
   1988   The Emerging Patterns of Peasants' Responses to Sendero Luminoso. Paper presented at Patterns of Social Change in the Andes Research Conference sponsored by
   NYU and Columbia University LAS Consortium, New York City.
Kawell, Jo Ann
   1989   Going to the Source. NACLA 22(6):13–22.
Kirk, Robin
   1987   Refugees Rebuild Communities. NACLA 21(5–6):9–11.
Manrique, Nelson
   1989   Sendero en los andes centrales. Quehacer 60:62–83.
Marcus, George, and Michael Fischer
   1986   Anthropology as Cultural Critique: An Experimental Moment in the Human Sciences. Chicago: University of Chicago Press.

Martinez, Hector
1980 Migraciones internas en el Peru. Lima: IEP.
Mauceri, Philip
1989 The Military, Insurgency and Democratic Power: Peru, 1980–1988. Papers on Latin America, No. 11. New York: Columbia University, Institute of Latin American and Iberian Studies.
McClintock, Cynthia
1984 Why Peasants Rebel: The Case of Peru's Sendero Luminoso. World Politics 27(1):48–84.
Michel-Jones, Françoise
1978 Retour au Dogon: Figure du double et ambivalence. Paris: Le Sycomore.
Montoya, Rodrigo
1979 Produccion parcelaria y universo ideologico. Lima: IEP.
Nash, June
1977 We Eat the Mines and the Mines Eat Us. New York: Columbia University Press.
Nuñez del Prado, Juan Victor
1974 The Supernatural World of the Quechua of Southern Peru As Seen from the Community of Qotobamba. In Native South Americans. P. Lyon, ed. Pp. 238–250. Boston: Little, Brown.
Olien, Michael
1973 Latin Americans, Contemporary Peoples and Their Cultural Traditions. New York: Holt, Rinehart, & Winston.
Orlove, Benjamin, Michael Foley, and Thomas Love, editors
1989 State, Capital, and Rural Society: Anthropological Perspectives on Political Economy in the Andes and Mexico. Boulder, Colo.: Westview Press.
Ortner, Sherry
1984 Theory in Anthropology since the Sixties. Comparative Studies in Society and History 26:126–165.
Palmer, David Scott
1986 Rebellion in Rural Peru: The Origins and Evolution of Sendero Luminoso. Comparative Politics 18(2):127–146.
Rosaldo, Renato
1989 Culture and Truth: The Remaking of Social Analysis. Boston: Beacon.
Roseberry, William
1983 Coffee and Capitalism in the Venezuelan Andes. Austin: University of Texas Press.
Said, Edward
1979 Orientalism. New York: Vintage Books.
Salcedo, José María
1986 Con Sendero en Lurigancho. Quehacer 39:60–67.
Salomon, Frank
1973 Weavers of Otavalo. In Peoples and Cultures of Native South America. Daniel R. Gross ed. Pp. 463–485. New York: The Natural History Press.
1982 Andean Ethnology in the 1970s: A Retrospective. Latin American Research Review 17(2):75–128.
1985 The Historical Development of Andean Ethnology. Mountain Research and Development 5(1):79–98.
Shakespeare, Nicholas
1988 In Pursuit of Guzmán. Granta 23:149–197.

Skar, Harold
   1982   The Warm Valley People. New York: Columbia University Press.
Smith, Gavin
   1989   Livelihood and Resistance: Peasants and the Politics of Land in Peru. Berkeley:
           University of California Press.
Stein, William
   1962   Hualcan: Life in the Highlands of Peru. Ithaca, N.Y.: Cornell University Press.
Stern, Steve, ed.
   1987   Resistance, Rebellion, and Consciousness in the Andean Peasant World, 18th–
           20th Century. Madison: University of Wisconsin Press.
Steward, Julian
   1963   Preface. *In* Handbook of South American Indians, vol. 2. New York: Cooper
           Square Publications.
Taussig, Michael
   1980   The Devil and Commodity Fetishism in South America. Chapel Hill: University
           of North Carolina Press.
   1987   Shamanism, Colonialism, and the Wild Man: A Study in Terror and Healing.
           Chicago: University of Chicago Press.
Thomas, R. Brooke
   1976   Energy Flow at High Altitude. *In* Man in the Andes. P. Baker and M. Little, eds.
           Pp. 379–404. Stroudsburg: Dowden, Hutchinson, Ross Inc.
Trimborn, Hermann
   1969   South Central America and the Andean Civilizations. *In* Pre-columbian Ameri-
           can Religions. W. Krickeberg et al., eds. Pp. 83–114. New York: Holt, Rinehart &
           Winston.
Valcarcel, Luis
   1938   Los estudios peruanos. Revista del Museo Nacional 15:3–12.
   1950   Introduction. *In* Indians of Peru, a book of photographs by Pierre Verger. Pp.
           1–6. New York: Pantheon.
Wachtel, Nathan
   1977   The Vision of the Vanquished. Hassocks: Henson Press.
Zuidema, R. T., and V. Quispe
   1973   A Visit to God. *In* Peoples and Cultures of Native South America. Daniel R.
           Gross, ed. Pp. 358–373. Garden City, N.Y.: Natural History Press.

Peru In Deep Trouble: Mario Vargas Llosa's "Inquest in the Andes" Reexamined

Enrique Mayer

Instructive, fascinating. Condensed in a few striking images and objects, there is an essential ingredient, always present in the history of this country, from the most remote times: violence. Violence of all kinds: moral, physical, fanatical, intransigent, ideological, corrupt, stupid—all of which have gone hand in hand with power here. And that other violence—dirty, petty, low, vengeful, vested and selfish—which lives off the other kinds.

—Mario Vargas Llosa
The Real Life of Alejandro Mayta

In January 1983, a series of world-shaking emblematic events took place in a remote Andean community of Peru. One version was featured in the Sunday magazine section of the *New York Times* ("Inquest in the Andes") (Vargas Llosa 1983). In it, the prominent Peruvian writer Mario Vargas Llosa described how eight journalists, five from Lima and two from the city of Ayacucho, traveled to the highlands to investigate reports that *comuneros* of a small peasant community of Huaychao had killed seven *"terroristas,"* members of the insurgent Communist Party of Peru commonly known as Shining Path (*Sendero Luminoso,* after the phrase of Peru's Marxist philosopher José Carlos Mariátegui, that only Marxism-Leninism will provide the shining path to revolution).[1] News of the comuneros actions against terrorists had been jubilantly received in Ayacucho (the capital of one of Peru's departments, where the Shining Path insurgency was then in its third year). Especially happy were the newly installed military commander charged with eliminating the insurgency, General Roberto Clemente Noel Moral,[2] and the president of Peru, Fernando Belaunde Terry, who on television had congratulated the villagers (comuneros) and urged others to take up similar actions to rid the country of criminal terrorists.

However, events turned sour. As narrated by Vargas Llosa, the eight journalists arrived at Uchuraccay, one of the communities of the Iquicha ethnic group, en route to Huaychao. They had a dialogue with the local people, but then were suddenly and cruelly massacred with stones, sticks, and axes. The journalists' bodies had been horribly mutilated and buried upside down, two to a grave, in shallow pits away from the village cemetery. Anthropological testimony described these mutilations and burial practices as typical of the way local people treat their enemies. To the police patrol that came looking for the missing journalists two days later, the comuneros declared that they had killed eight Senderistas.

Reaction to this turn of events in Ayacucho and Lima was quick but divided. Conservative Lima circles found confirmation of their deepest prejudices against Indians; they were indeed savages. The leftist opposition did not believe the story and suspected some kind of cover-up by the military. A shaken President Belaunde appointed a commission to investigate the events and asked fiction writer Vargas Llosa to head it. Jurist Abraham Guzman Figueroa and journalist Mario Castro Arenas were also appointed members of the commission. Vargas Llosa requested additional help from a prominent group of experts—anthropologists, lawyers, psychoanalysts, linguists, and photographers. The Vargas Llosa Commission then set out to Ayacucho to investigate the murders.

The Vargas Llosa Report (Vargas Llosa et al. 1983) established a hierarchy of causes to explain the tragic event. The Commission asserted that they had absolute confidence in the following: (1) that the communities of the region had decided in communal assemblies to kill "terrorists of Shining Path," because they were exasperated by the abuses, exactions, and thefts as well as the assassination of two shepherds by Senderistas. The Iquichanos had already killed at least 25 "terrorists" before the journalists arrived; (2) that in making such a decision, the comuneros felt they were authorized to do so by the authorities, represented by the *sinchis* (Peru's crack but uncontrollable antisubversive police batallion), who had told them—as per testimony of the people in Uchuraccay—that "if the *terrucos* came through, they should defend themselves and kill them" (Vargas Llosa et al. 1983:21);[3] (3) that the comuneros mistook those journalists for a detachment of Senderistas. They believed the Senderistas were on their way to punish them for the lynching of two Senderistas, which had been carried out in the very same community only a few days previously; (4) that this massacre took place without there being any participation of the police forces.

As background causes that influenced these events, the Commission noted that Shining Path had a following, or some degree of control, among the lower lying agricultural communities, but not among the pastoralist highland Iquichanos. There, the guerrillas had not had much success in infiltrating or controlling the Iquichano communities because the agents of Shining Path who appeared in the highlands were identified with the valley people—their traditional exploiters and rivals.[4] The Iquichanos also accused Shining Path of stealing cattle and of two murders. They also resented the prohibition, which Shining Path had imposed on them, that forbade participation in marketing activities. This was part of the "starving the city" campaign imposed by the guerrillas.

The report went on to tell that the Iquichanos are a fierce people, proud of their independence and, therefore, despised by the valley agriculturalists. (Iquichanos had always supported the wrong side—the Spaniards during Indian rebellions, the Royalists during Independence.[5] In 1896 they had taken the provincial capital town of Huanta and lynched the subprefect and, more recently, they expelled agrarian reform officials.) Once the Iquichanos had declared war on the Senderistas they were in a feverish and excited state of mind because they feared imminent revenge by the guerrillas. "They were convinced—by their traditions, culture, the conditions in which they live, and by the practice of their daily lives—that in their fight for survival everything is valid and that it was a matter of killing first or be killed" (Vargas Llosa et al. 1983:33).

Vargas Llosa also posed a series of rhetorical questions. Is it possible, he asked, for the comuneros to make moral, constitutional, and juridical distinctions between the right and wrong of lynching and the due process of law (i.e., did they know they were doing wrong)? One answer was given through the opinion of the legal expert member of the Commission, Fernando de Trazegnies. His explanation used a favorite anthropological theme, the existence of customary law different from the nation's laws. This separate judicial system is "traditional, archaic, secret and frequently in conflict with official law"; it supposedly provides for the death penalty through lynching of cattle thieves after public trials (Vargas Llosa et al. 1983:32).

The second answer to Vargas Llosa's rhetorical question also appropriated favorite anthropological themes. It goes like this: The Iquichanos are a peculiarly isolated social group. They belong to a separate culture that has been exploited and pushed around for centuries. Its members do not understand the issues and complexities of the modern sector. Here is Vargas Llosa's statement: "They are part of a 'besieged nation' as José María Arguedas calls them, with thousands—perhaps millions—of compatriots who speak another language, have different customs, and who, under such hostile and isolated conditions, have managed to preserve a culture—perhaps archaic, but rich and deep [*profundo*]—that links up with the whole of our prehispanic past, which 'official' Peru has disdained" (Vargas Llosa et al. 1983:36).

In sum, the Commission concluded that the killings were a mistake that arose out of cultural misunderstandings and psychological stress during the heat of a war declared on their society by the Shining Path guerrillas and brought about through police encouragement.

Cover-Up or Simplification?

For a writer, it must have been fascinating to be able to ascribe the causes of a horrendous tragedy to a misunderstanding. If the context were not so morbid, we all would find in such language acceptable, contextualizing, actor-oriented, anthropological explanations. Wouldn't we? However, many skeptics and critics of this report said that Vargas Llosa had again excelled in telling another great story. To others, myself included, the fictional writings of Vargas Llosa reflect reality more closely than this report. Here are the issues for which Vargas Llosa was criticized.

Factual

During the investigation of the Commission, and continuing for about three years, the Peruvian press was engaged in the detective game of attempting to uncover new facts that would undermine the substance and gist of Vargas Llosa's report. Newspaper reporters and TV talk shows avidly pursued alternative explanations and looked for missing facts that would bolster other theories with as much sensationalist and morbid zest as when the U.S. news media and the Warren Commission sought to explain the assassinations of John F. Kennedy, Lee Harvey Oswald, and Jack Ruby in 1963. Although the Vargas Llosa Commission was given only some of the photographs captured by the police (others were leaked later), and these altered some of the initial assertions of the Commission, to date—eight years later—no new facts have come to light to significantly alter the logic of the story reconstructed by Vargas Llosa's Commission. There have, however, been numerous deaths and disappearances of key witnesses, which lead to strong suspicions that potentially damaging evidence must have been eliminated with those disappearances. Any potential witnesses would not have spoken up out of fear of certain death. Nor have there ever been candid press discussions with the police force most directly involved in the case, which leads to suppositions that there may be more to know than what the police chose to reveal.

Customary Law, Vigilantism, or War?

If comuneros are granted the privilege to exercise their customary laws, what are we to do when such rights are also claimed by revolutionary Senderistas? When Shining Path guerrillas occupy peasant villages, they conduct popular trials and execute people in plazas claiming to carry out "popular justice." Their favorite victims have been so-called well-known cattle thieves whom neither the comuneros nor the corrupt official judicial system were capable of bringing to justice.

The issue is, however, even more complex. In the first place we need to distinguish the practice of customary law from vigilantism, that is, when comuneros defend themselves against outside attack. Since their creation by the Spanish colonial administration, indigenous communities have been granted a certain degree of delegated autonomy to manage their own administrative and judicial affairs. There is a hierarchy of elected, nominated, officially recognized and non-recognized authorities that regulate many aspects of juridical life in the communities.[6] However, Peruvian law is strict in insisting that communities only deal with minor cases, and the comuneros know this curb on their autonomy.[7] Homicide must be referred to higher courts. Although the journalists talked with the comuneros of Uchuraccay, they do not appear to have been tried, found guilty, and then executed by any local system of customary law. Rather, their photographs show that they were victims of a surprise attack. Thus the Vargas Llosa Commission's appeal to customary law is invalid. The comuneros claim that they did conduct trials of a number of people accused of being terrorists before and after the journalist event, and that those accused had opportunity to defend themselves. The journalists thus received a different treatment than the terrorists.

On the other hand, the self-defense argument ("that in their fight for survival everything is valid" mentioned above) has more validity. Indigenous communities collectively defend themselves from outside attacks. Battles between rival communities over boundaries frequently take place and bloodshed occurs.[8] Violent community action is based on the collective decision, the complete participation of every member of the community, and the often futile efforts by comuneros to prevent authorities to single out any individual for official judicial reprisals. It is this kind of collective action that has been effectively used by peasants in land occupations and uprisings against abusive landlords and authorities. Comuneros and the nation know that these acts are illegal, but certain intellectual sectors of society occasionally give them moral and historical justification as the ultimate recourse against exploitation of Indians. Peruvian history is full of Indian rebellions savagely put down (Kapsoli 1987; O'Phelan 1988; Stern 1987). These are then carefully reconstructed by historians, celebrated by writers, and extolled in popular culture. The moral "right" to defend themselves is one of the consciously manipulated "weapons of the weak" (Scott 1986), and is known in Spanish as *"hacerse justicia"* ("to take justice into one's own hands"). It is, however, a moral or political action, not a judicially sanctioned aspect of customary law.

Within this distinction, a rather ambiguous situation arises concerning comuneros' treatment of cattle rustlers. Primarily because this is more often a crime that takes place across community boundaries and is more difficult to control, comuneros occasionally deal harshly with the cattle rustlers they catch. And they have collectively defended their right to do so when all attempts to bring these thieves under official judicial control have failed.[9] Moreover, Poole (1988) and Orlove (1980) show that this self-perceived "right" has been manipulated and used by armed groups, and promoted by landlords, gangsters, rural power brokers, and even some comuneros to justify the formation of armed groups seeking to enhance their power base. Comuneros, too, have used systematic rustling to weaken landlords, enemies, and rival communities.[10]

Either the comuneros of Uchuraccay or the Vargas Llosa Commission sought to equate the attack on outsiders with the supposed treatment of cattle thieves by comuneros. Thus, the report says, "In the meeting with members of the commission, they always designated them with the term *'terrorista sua'* ('terrorist thief')" (Vargas Llosa et al. 1983:34), but this comunero description sounds contrived.

Vargas Llosa states that the Iquicha groups, having collectively decided to battle the Senderistas, proceeded to ambush, beat, lynch, and execute people they identified as members of Shining Path. By his count, the Iquichanos killed 25 people before killing the journalists. One thing is a war of self-defense when attacked, another is an "authorized" war conducted on behalf of someone else. This is the comuneros position, and the Vargas Llosa Commission supports this view. Law professor de Trazegnies, much enamored of anthropological language states, "The comuneros of Uchuraccay declared themselves partisans of Belaunde and of the government. . . . But these are declarations of a tribe or nation that decides to ratify its alliance with another nation or tribe which is embroiled in a war. Hence they spontaneously feel that they have an obligation with their ally, *Señor Gobierno* [Sir Government], to capture the latter's enemies and to neutralize them using tribal strategems'' (de Trazegnies 1983:145).

The Commission uses all three argumentations in its report. They are mutually exclusive, and each carries different legal implications as to the guilt, or lack of it, of the comuneros.

Omissions

Re-reading the Commission's report and the critiques it produced, I am struck by the number of loose ends. For example, to my knowledge, no one has ever investigated the 25 deaths of ''terroristas'' that the Iquichanos together with the comuneros of Uchuraccay were allegedly responsible for. Who were the victims? Where were they from? How were they caught, and how were they sentenced and killed? Why spend so much effort to single out the circumstances in the death of eight journalists and not ask the same questions of the circumstances of the death of 25 other people, supposedly killed under similar circumstances, by the same people, and in the same context?

For many on the left of the political spectrum, fault is found with the Vargas Llosa Commission for not investigating the possibility of further, deeper, more incriminating involvement of the police force or other undercover operations. To them, the coincidence of increased comunero violence against ''terrorists'' and a newly installed military command with enhanced powers in Ayacucho is highly indicative of a change in tactics. Though the Commission does fault the police for their heavy-handed methods, it tends to be more careful in the language with which it describes them. There is a tendency to soft-pedal this aspect by citing the police force's lack of experience and inefficiency and unfamiliarity with the area and customs of the people. Another possible angle is never explored. Had there been a military or police presence in Uchuraccay the day the journalists arrived, perhaps the killing of the journalists could have been prevented.

There is a paradox in how the Left—often victims of police persecution and brutality—is more willing to ascribe to the police incredible capabilities. More likely the Peruvian police forces were then, and continue today to be, more ''underdeveloped'' than critics would like to believe. Gorriti (1990:80–93), for example, notes that, early on, the National Security Services had correctly informed and alerted Lima authorities regarding the activities of Shining Path, but no one paid attention. Moreover all the files disappeared when the Belaunde government took over. Initial perceptions of police incompetence and inability to deal with Shining Path actions had led Belaunde to entrust the counterinsurgency actions to the army that was then just getting established in Ayacucho. Their underdeveloped tactics, however, include the police's and the military's preference for torture, abuse of power, and viciousness toward the civilian population.[11] The military's antiterrorist tactics have included the teachings of U.S. sponsored counterinsurgency campaigns, applied elsewhere in Latin America, that massively terrorize uninvolved civilian populations. Arbitrary persecution is arbitrary persecution, even though in Peru these occurred to a lesser extent than in El Salvador or Guatemala.

Disbelief

Most of the criticisms centered around the issues in the anthropological account. Critics cried out that "comuneros are not like that!" In the national image of some intellectuals, comuneros are not supposed to be so violent, so ignorant or naive as the report makes them out to be. Emblematic of this debate was a careless remark made by General Noel that most probably the comuneros of Uchuraccay had confused the journalists' cameras with guns. This infuriated critics. Vargas Llosa addressed this question in his report. He asked, "Would the comuneros of Uchuraccay be able to identify a photographic camera and know what it is used for?" And answered, "Some of them, at least, without doubt. . . . But . . . this is not the first case of a society in which cultural primitivism and archaism can coexist with certain modern manufactured products" (Vargas Llosa et al. 1983:23). After the report was published, it became evident that the journalists talked to the comuneros. Two of them spoke Quechua and were known in the region. They certainly could have explained themselves to the comuneros. More cogently, in a later interview, Vargas Llosa speculated that the theories of Mao, or even Mariátegui, are esoteric to the comuneros of Uchuraccay, and that comuneros would regard the interference of Senderistas in community affairs as acts of "wanton *prepotencia* [arbitrary imposition]" (Vargas Llosa 1990:136). Millones (1983:97) points out that we do not know the contents of Sendero's message to the comuneros, nor how they appeal to their sympathies. To suppose comunero ignorance of the world's current ideological debates is simplistic, too. At the time of these events, evangelical pastors were spreading the Protestant gospel and preaching against the evils of Catholicism and communism, and active recruitment by peasant federations and left-wing parties was also taking place throughout the department of Ayacucho.[12]

Nor would the critics easily accept that the comuneros alone were capable of such unspeakable acts of cruelty and violence and morbid mutilations, despite the ethnographic explanations provided by the experts. But comuneros are known to have acted cruelly toward outsiders. For example, Canadian and Peruvian anthropologists Lionel Vallée and Salvador Palomino were tied up and held as prisoners overnight by the comuneros of the community of Manchiri in the Ayacucho region in the early 1960s. They saved themselves; as Palomino overheard heated discussions among the villagers as to how to kill them, he shouted across the room in Quechua that he understood everything they were saying. Being addressed in their own language caused some comuneros to vacillate in their decision, giving the anthropologists the opportunity to escape that night.

Vallée and Palomino were probably perceived as *pishtacos,* feared figures, believed to be white marauders who capture Indians and kill them to obtain human grease needed to cast specially sonorous bells for sale abroad, to run complex machinery (space craft, for example), or to pay Peru's international debt (Ansion and Sifuentes 1989:61–105). The widespread belief has encouraged people to actually become pishtacos. In 1969, two young men were caught by the police while trying to sell bottles of rendered human grease to a Yugoslav merchant in Tarma,

Junín. Once arrested, the men confessed and showed police the buried and mutilated bodies of several shepardesses they had killed and dismembered for what
they believed was a profitable crime. Pishtaco fears have increased remarkably
since political violence has reigned in the highlands. As recently as 1987, in one
of the refugee squatter settlements in the outskirts of the city of Ayacucho, a poor
merchant was cruelly stoned to death by a frenzied mob of residents who were
convinced that he was a pishtaco (Degregori 1989:109–114). In popular belief,
pishtacos are quintessential outsiders. They possess advanced technology with
which to perpetrate these crimes whose purpose it is to convert the bodies of Indians into monetary profits. Pishtacos are coherent and historically mythologized
versions of the real threat of externally perpetrated violence against which collective outrage is one possible outlet.

Perhaps to the comuneros of Uchuraccay the journalists represented not only
police, army, and guerrillas but also pishtacos. This alternative explanation,
known to the anthropologists who were members of the Commission (Ossio and
Fuenzalida 1983:70), was vaguely alluded to in the report. The Vargas Llosa report and, even more so, its critics are, at best, naive to ascribe moral virtues and
"meekness" to one segment of Peruvian society, and, at worst, manichean to
ascribe the capability for violence to only one or the other side of the great ethnic
divide.

Clearly, even before the events in Uchuraccay, collective violence has been
used by comuneros under circumstances of real or perceived external threat, and
this violence goes beyond that which is necessary to achieve one's goal, including
morbid atrocities committed against outsiders. There are, in these arguments, hidden dimensions of a double fallacy. One side ignores acts of irrational violence
even when the context and circumstances explain, but do not condone, them. The
other side of the fallacy is to point to historical evidence of cruelty, bloodthirsti-
ness, and ritual involvement with violent acts using pre-Hispanic iconography,
historical text, and hearsay as proof of the "inherent violent nature of the Indian"
a psychological or racially inherited trait. The only correct stance is to face the
facts in the context of each case and not to be ethnocentrically repelled, or mor-
bidly attracted, by them.

Nor is it that simple to counterpose, in moral terms, physical violence committed by peasants to "structural violence" committed by the "system" against
them as a justification for peasant or terrorist violence. In Peru, structural violence, which has come to mean poverty, abuse, discrimination, racism, and arbitrariness and/or indifference by the state, impedes the potential actions individuals may take. In daily debates on television and at home, a frequent response to
outrage against terrorists has been to counter this with examples of structural violence. Such debates may score points but do not lead to solutions. It confuses
cause with moral justification, and it confuses issues of individual guilt with collective guilt. The only way to face this problem is by treating structural violence
as a cause for political violence, and then resolve to do something about the former. Both kinds of violence undoubtedly exist—they may even explain one another—but they do not justify or excuse each other. Since Uchuraccay, very little

evidence exists that any actions have been taken to correct structural violence and thereby ameliorate real violence. Civilian society, by and large, has let the armed forces handle the problem, despite the criticisms its methods have repeatedly evoked. The state, too, has debated violence endlessly, but little significant legislative, reformist, or even political action can be listed as a rational response to this kind of armed uprising.[13] Vargas Llosa's treatment of this will be examined below.

Even more unbelievable to the critics of the Commission's report was the unflinching admission of guilt by the comuneros. That the comuneros never varied from their story, and that all of them stuck to the one official version was, for many, proof that they had been cowed into telling this story under duress and threat. Therefore, the critics reasoned, the comuneros of Uchuraccay had to be covering for others who had committed the crimes. What was most wanted by the opposition to Belaunde's government was an admission that it was the police or the army that had committed the killings. The comuneros have had many opportunities to recant their story, and such a recantation would have been jubilantly received in many sectors of society. But they never did.

Another possible explanation—that the Shining Path guerrillas had forced the comuneros to kill the journalists, or were materially involved—has not been properly explored. This is considered unlikely. Shining Path wanted all the publicity it could get, and killing those who best provide them with the opportunity to shock the nation seemed ridiculous. Moreover, among the journalists there were newspapers represented, which, at least at the beginning, took a less jaundiced view of Shining Path. However, such an action may look, in retrospect, to be more possible, given what we now know about how Shining Path uses assassinations and killings for shock value. If that is what they sought, they certainly got it.[14]

Many *senderólogos* also find the actions of Shining Path in Uchuraccay unbelievable. Following hallowed Maoist teachings, Senderistas have been taught never to antagonize the peasantry. Gorriti, the most respected among Sendero experts, describes how Shining Path is very selective and strategic in its assassinations. Senderistas have to learn to kill in systematic and depersonalized ways and also to be prepared to sacrifice their own lives for the cause. Killings are to be carefully calibrated to provoke blind raging reactions from the state. The higher the excesses of the reaction, the easier it is to transfer guilt to the state. Their principal targets thus are representatives of state activity and authority (electricity pilons, police, government officers, development projects and local authorities, landowners, and merchants). They also use the horror of killing to impose their authority over the villages. They gain the villagers' favor by summary trials of shopkeepers, adulterous husbands, abusive exploiters. They also intimidate the population by threatening and killing "informants" and "collaborators." Moreover, the Shining Path's Andeanized version of Mao's three rules and eight warnings on how to act among the peasants was stated clearly enough to the cadres.[15] The pattern of reported killings and thefts in the Vargas Llosa report diverges from other earlier actions known to have been undertaken by Shining Path. Yet, a distinction must be made between what Senderistas are taught and what they actually do.

There is now considerable evidence that the events in Uchuraccay coincided with a raging battle between Senderistas and comuneros, and that during those days, Shining Path was committing atrocities against villagers, and it has certainly done so after the events in Uchuraccay. Thus, the rules of how Senderistas were to impose their authority on comuneros may not invalidate the claims made by the people of Uchuraccay that the terroristas did indeed steal and kill and make themselves hated.[16] Portraying the Senderistas as wanton indiscriminate killers and pillagers was part of the government's agitprop.

Anthropological Authority

In his novel *El Hablador* (*The Storyteller,* 1987), fictionalized author/character Mario Vargas Llosa traces divergent career patterns between himself and Saul Zuratas, his friend from his student days at the University of San Marcos. Zuratas chooses to become an anthropologist and eventually (perhaps) "goes native" among a jungle tribe in the Amazon forest. Vargas Llosa becomes the writer, observer, and commentator of political reality.

Zuratas and Vargas Llosa (the character) sustain a debate throughout the novel about the role of anthropology in Peruvian society. In the novel, idealist Zuratas who argued that the Machiguenga tribe should be left alone loses out to realist Vargas Llosa, but it is the latter who feels the loss of Machiguenga cultural identity and the inevitable shoddy product that their integration into modernity implies. Vargas Llosa's (the author) position is summarized in his article in *Harper's* magazine (1990). This is not the only time that anthropologists appear in Vargas Llosa's novels. Constructed in similar fashion is *Historia de Mayta* (*The Real Life of Alejandro Mayta,* 1984), where author/character Vargas Llosa retraces the life and times of his erstwhile schoolfriend-turned-revolutionary, Alejandro Mayta. One of Mayta's early contacts, in those heady days of clandestine political party activity, is fictionalized social scientist Moises Barbi Leyva, director of a prestigious research institute, whom Vargas Llosa interviews to (re)construct Mayta's story.

Peruvian anthropologists, however, are not at all like fictionalized Saul Zuratas. Since the 1930s, anthropology as a new discipline with respectable credentials has lent authority to an intellectual movement known as *indigenismo,* which saw in the regeneration of exploited Indians a bright future for Peru. Prominent *indigenista* anthropologists such as Julio C. Tello and Luis Valcárcel had been ministers of education; novelist-ethnologist José María Arguedas headed the National Institute of Culture; and ethnologist Mario Vázquez was the architect of the Peruvian agrarian reform. Peruvian readers of *Mayta* can instantly identify Moises Barbi Leyva as a prominent anthropologist of the 1960s–1980s with the same political agenda. These professionals argued against "preserving" native cultures. They worked hard at achieving new ways of integrating the Indians into national society and at revitalizing Andean cultural patterns to make them compatible with a modern nation state. They considered themselves to be progressive and viewed the state as the primary agency to achieve these aims. The profession is also identified with expertise on "Indian" affairs. As we shall see, with the growth of the Left in Peru, anthropological discourse tended toward a more Marxist orientation for those on the Left, making the accusation that if a more culturalist structural functionalist framework is used, one is more closely identified with conservative positions.

These views are important elements of Peru's intellectual background and are necessary to understand the Vargas Llosa report, for it is not unusual that in Peru, in the investigation of the events in Uchuraccay, a writer and anthropologist should be so prominent. The result was an anthropological text rather than a fact-finding report. Historian Pablo Macera (1983) observed that, as the end product of an investigative commission, the report had serious deficiencies. It gave no names of people interviewed, nor dates, and no methodology or evidence of which facts were proven, et cetera.

Anthropological input into the Commission thus lent an aura of legitimate expertise concerning indigenous affairs. And anthropological expertise was also used to criticize the report. Thus, anthropologist Rodrigo Montoya bitterly commented that "the report lends political support to the government. . . . Such are the uses of anthropology as elements of analysis and decoration!" (Montoya 1983). Montoya criticized the report because the anthropological work was not serious. "A serious anthropological report about the events should not remain within the narrow limits of *lo andino* (the Andean) as a closed universe. It is fundamental to demonstrate, for example, the important atriculations and subordination of Indigenous authorities to the State." Luis Lumbreras, a native Ayacuchano, stated that "the people of Uchuraccay do not mistake the Senderistas with the devil nor are they afraid that they will stamp a myth out of their heads. Those people have food problems and boundary problems. . . . It is a grave error to have studied their [the comuneros of Uchuraccay] cultural and thought patterns instead of the reality in which they live" (Lumbreras 1983). Even Shining Path has its anthropologists. Sendero's second in command expert on strategy, Osman Morote (now in jail), was an anthropology professor at the University of Huamanga in Ayacucho, and numerous Senderistas arrested in the early days were anthropology students.

What interests me is the use of anthropological discourse in this text, for, after all, it is rare that anthropology gets so much press and, even more rare, support by distinguished writers. Why was this discourse so unacceptable, and even distasteful, to so many?

The Two Peru Argument

At the emotional level, which is much more problematic, Vargas Llosa appealed to anthropological discourse on the fractured nature of the Peruvian nation. This deserves careful scrutiny for it is here, really, that pernicious anthropological language infiltrates political discourse. As quoted above, Vargas Llosa appealed to the "two Peru" argument by citing impeccable and respected intellectual sources: historian Jorge Basadre who, in 1943, first used the phrase Peru profundo (deep Peru)[17].

As we shall see, Vargas Llosa's use of Basadre's notion is very different from the original formulation. Concerned as he was with problems of national identity and the notion of Peruvianess among its population, Basadre made a distinction between legal and profound Peru. For him, the distinction of the two Perus is between the state *(país legal)* and the nation composed of its people *(país profundo)*.[18] Basadre insists that the history of Peru is not only the history of the state but also that of the nation. He goes on to note that countries or nations exist even if they do not exhibit unity of race, territory, language, and economic interests among its populations. The historical process of forging a modern nation is relatively recent in the case of Peru, but is nevertheless present. It can be characterized, dated, and analyzed not only in the works of intellectuals but also in the popular uprisings that arose with immense hopes of achieving national transformations. He demolishes the popular belief that this nation is composed of a majority of Indians. He cites the results of the 1940 census that show a steady decline of ennumerated Indians and denies that there is a cultural abyss that separates Indians from mestizos or the highlands from the coast. He extolls *mestizaje* as the most important cultural process by giving a list of illustrious Peruvians of Indian, mestizo, European, and Asian descent who have actively contributed to the process of nation building.

Basadre's position on this has been challenged (see, for example, Bourricaud 1989, Mörner 1985; Szeminski 1987). But one must remember that his ideas were formulated during World War II, and that they were part of Basadre's self-conscious project of providing through his historical researches the very tools for nation building he so fervently expressed in the title of his most famous early work, *Peru Problema y Posibilidad* (1978b). Noting his own skill at finding apt phrases to summarize ideas, Basadre wryly remarked in 1978 that this celebrated essay was better known by its title than its contents until it had become a veritable myth (Basadre 1978:xx). The myth caught up with Vargas Llosa, for, over time, the phrase Peru profundo has become popular in academic usage (always with due attribution to Basadre), and has come to mean the historical roots of Indianness as a component of Peru's sense of nationhood. In Mexico, Bonfil Batalla (1987) has adopted the phrase as the title of his newest book extolling Indian identity.

When Vargas Llosa refers to the state as forming part of "official Peru," and only when he makes references to the distance between the state and its people, is he congruent with Basadre's original formulation. For Basadre, profound aspects of a people's sense of nationhood are present among all sectors of the population. Nowhere in his writings does he reserve the term profundo to refer exclusively to aspects of Indian culture or identity or sense of nationhood. In fact, in his colophon he quite explicitly denies it: "On the other hand, where is the Indian national consciousness? Who will be able to tie the Quechua, Aymara 'nationalities' to those of the Chancas, Huancas, Yungas and other races and subraces that co-exist at the same time, without even counting the tropical forest tribes?'' (Basadre 1947:273). For Vargas Llosa, non-Indian Spanish-speaking civilians and officials are members of ''official Peru,'' whereas for Basadre, everyone in the nation represents its profound embodiment.

But according to Vargas Llosa there are two Perus, one official and the other profound, separated by an enormous gulf that has its origins in the brutal conquest of the indigenous population and that continues to keep them apart from the rest of the nation. The two Perus are separated in space and time. Vargas Llosa stated in an interview: ''That there is a real nation completely separate from the official nation is, of course, the great Peruvian problem. That people can simultaneously live in a country who participate in the 20th century and people like the comuneros of Uchuraccay and all the Iquichano communities who live in the 19th—if not to say the 18th century.[19] This enormous distance which exists between the two Perus is behind the tragedy that we have just investigated'' (Vargas Llosa 1990:146).

Setting up polarities and dual oppositions, however, lends itself to ambiguous interpretations, multiple meanings, and disputable appropriations of concepts. The root metaphor of profundo apparently has appeal in intellectual disciplines (i.e., in psychoanalytic conceptualizations of deep currents of the collective unconsciousness; culturally, as in Geertz's ''deep play''; in literature where profound understandings of social conditions are the mark of good writing; or in more popularly accessible appeals such as Alex Haley's botanical derivation of deep to ''roots''). It is, nevertheless, a dangerous game. Dualistic distinctions bunch value judgments and lead to stereotyping. Metaphoric language permits the expression of prejudices. In Vargas Llosa's reading, the metaphor ''deep Peru'' stands for Indian Peru.

For Vargas Llosa deep Peru is ''archaic,'' ''primitive.'' It is economically depressed, with poor resources. The communities of the highlands of Huanta ''represent perhaps the most miserable, needy human conglomerate'' (Vargas Llosa et al. 1983:36). Deep Peru is defined by negatives and wants: ''Without water (i.e., faucets), light (i.e., that kind of light which can be turned on and off), without medical attention, without roads that link them to the rest of the world'' (1983:36). The people who live in deep Peru are isolated, malnourished (''condemned to survive on a meager diet of potatoes and lima beans''), and cannot read and write (in Spanish, a language they do not speak). The ''struggle for existence is very hard, where death through starvation, sickness, or natural catastrophe threatens at every step'' (1983:36). Deep Peru has only experienced official Peru through the ugliest expressions: ''Since republican times Iquichanos have known only *gamonal*,[20] exploitation, the cheating exactions of the tax collector and the backlashes of mutinies and civil wars by military authorities'' (1983:36). Deep Peru has not known progress: ''the very notion of progress must be difficult to conceive by the communities whose members never remember having experienced any improvement in the conditions of their lives, but rather, prolonged stasis with periods of regression'' (1983:36). Yet the Commission's report states that Uchuraccay was given land as a benefit of the Agrarian Reform (Ossio and Fuenzalida 1983:64).

The contrast is clear. Modernity, education, civilization, and the existence of other laws and customs characterize the ''other,'' or official, Hispanic and

Westernized Peru. All the positive valuations fill the compartment of official Peru; the negative ones are the properties ascribed to the other. Deep Peru evokes compassion. Compassion, a human quality that members of official Peru should have toward those of deep Peru, is needed to overcome another negative—but perhaps justified—feeling of resentment held by those who live in deep Peru. When pressed further in an interview, Vargas Llosa did mention positive qualities for Indian cultures. But listen to his adjectives: "There is a culture over there which has been *preserved,* which may be *archaic,* but which has permitted those compatriots of ours—*primitive* and *elemental*—to survive under conditions of extreme harshness" (Vargas Llosa 1990:154).

This view is also shared by some factions in the extreme Left, most notably by Sendero Luminoso. The discourse differs a bit, but essentially is the same. Semifeudal conditions of the peasants (in the Marxist language) have the same time and space distancing connotations, and both espouse the need for evolution and the need to work toward progress to achieve higher and better forms of life by adopting Western socialist customs and erasing any vestiges of the exploitative Andean past. In this view, too, traditionalism, archaism, non-capitalism, are more features of Andean culture than any trait that may have a positive content or valuation.[21]

Compassion and responsibility to narrow the gap between the two Perus is to be achieved through integration, modernization, and Westernization. Those in deep Peru are condemned ultimately to disappear in the name of progress, whether they want to or not. "The price they must pay for integration is high—renunciation of their culture, their language, their beliefs, their traditions and customs and the adoption of the culture of their ancient masters" (Vargas Llosa 1990:52). And both Left and Right agree that for this to happen, a degree of pressure, or more often coercion, has to be brought to bear to impose change on these people. Vargas Llosa and General Huaman[22] believe that can be achieved through the modernization process and development projects. Shining Path's conviction is that this can only be achieved through violent revolution as a precondition.

Another reading of the same issues provides a different view. In a recent article, Orin Starn (1991) accuses American anthropologists of being so engrossed in studying the Andean (lo andino) that they missed the war. Starn imputes the fascination American anthropologists have with Indian culture of the Andes to a false notion akin to Said's (1979) "Orientalism." "Andeanism is a representation that portrays contemporary highland peasants as outside the flow of modern history" (Starn 1991:64).

Viewed out of context, Starn seems to accuse American anthropologists of accepting Vargas Llosa's original dichotomy of deep (Indian) Peru vs. official (Hispanic) Peru, but inverting the signs; that is, they accept the dichotomy but value everything Andean positively and everything Hispanic negatively.[23] The same critique applied to Vargas Llosa is also applicable to this "romanticizing" view of Andean society, and Starn reiterates it. I agree with him. Andean society is not static, isolated, or restricted to the "remote" areas; rather it is a deeply enmeshed component of Peru's national fabric. Starn's attempt to demonstrate that American anthropologists were "romantics," however, fails dismally.

What is not acceptable is Starn's abysmally careless reading of the role of American anthropology in Peru.[24] Also, it is necessary to object to Starn's arbitrary selection of quotes and unfair portrayals of the authors mentioned as committing the errors he accuses them of. For example, omitted by Starn is any mention of a whole chapter in Billie Jean Isbell's (1978) book on migrants from the Andean Community of Chuschi in Lima. Omitted, too, is the subtitle ("Duality and Land Reform Among Quechua Indians of Highland Peru") and several chapters on land invasions and political conflict with Vanguardia Revolucionaria in Harald Skar's (1982) book. Skar is only quoted as saying that he chose that village because it was "where traditional Quechua culture seemed to be most intact" (Starn 1991:69). But Starn does not say that Skar chose it to evaluate the most fundamental social change that took place there as a result of the conflicts engendered by agrarian reform. These examples are accompanied by a host of other selective citations and misrepresentations of the authors cited, myself included.[25]

Starn, likewise, accuses American anthropologists of portraying timelessness and changelessness in Andean culture. Here his criticism is in tune with the archaism of Vargas Llosa. However, in real cultures things do change, some faster, some slowly, and some very slowly indeed, as Braudel has emphasized. Starn criticizes Zuidema and Quispe (1973) because they find similarities between dreams of a contemporary Quechua woman and Inca mythology. To me, this is as acceptable as seeing the contemporary U.S. practices of Christmas trees and Easter eggs in old European pagan traditions tacked on to a very old and slow changing Judeo-Christian tradition. Those who decorate pine trees while they "dream of a white Christmas" relate to a folk's *mentalités* and even *mythologiques* and also invest in Wall Street at the same time. I agree with Starn that the Andean world is made up of sharp breaks, but disagree with him that it is not valid to trace, along with these breaks, long-term continuities and persistences. Nor can cultural aspects of Andean peoples be easily dismissed in contemporary Peru, as the case of Uchuraccay so clearly shows.

But the so-called romantic position Starn attacks must also be seen in the Peruvian political context of the times. Given the anti-Andean prejudices of the two Peru argument (of which Vargas Llosa's version is but one in a long sequence in the intellectual tradition of Peru's elite), to search for, to demonstrate with ethnographic facts, and to portray a "living" culture rather than dead "survivals" seemed to those in my generation of fieldworkers to be a worthwhile task. Symbolism in fiestas carried out in the village of Chuschi was analyzed by Billie Jean Isbell. This is dismissed by Starn. Instead, he argues, one should focus on hunger, exploitation, and the poor's search for upward mobility. These fiestas continued during Shining Path's occupation of Chuschi. In fact, the villagers forced the Senderistas to dance with them and thereby felt that they had scored a victory over the Senderistas (Isbell 1991). Perhaps Andean anthropologists erred a bit in overstating the case, in drawing the lines all too sharply, and in not being "actor-oriented" or self-reflexive enough. But the enterprise was worth it as a counterweight to the prevailing Peruvian national ideology.

What is more interesting, and this is not discussed in Starn's article at all, is the fact that many Senderistas are young men and women who partake of traditional Andean and modern migratory life, flit in and out of Indian, mestizo, and *cholo*[26] status, and yet so profoundly reject their own Andean roots. Why "occidentalism," "evangelism," and "Maosim" (to a growing number of fervent followers of Presidente Gonzalo)[27] are so much more attractive to most young men and women than Andeanism needs to be explained. In Ecuador, Guatemala, Bolivia, Mexico, Iran, Palestinia, Eastern Europe, the U.S., and elsewhere, young revolutionaries have assumed with fanatical enthusiasm the defense of their own ethnic identity, and through such revitalization have succeeded in redefining the terms of hegemonic political discourse.[28] This is not the case with Shining Path.

Senderistas vehemently reject Andeanism. They refer to it as *"nacionalismo mágico quejumbroso,"*[29] which Poole and Rénique (1991:12) aptly translate as "magical-whining nationalism." José María Arguedas, the most coherent indigenista, is attacked in Sendero's newspaper *El Diario* as follows:

> Internationalism has to fight against magical-whining nationalism, whose fossilized remains we have had and continue to have in a chauvinist nationalism, whose promoter was none other than that writer who not only rejoiced in declaring himself purely apolitical, but who, during World War II, was proud of his little Hitler moustache. His name: José María Arguedas, affable disciple and animator in Peru of North American anthropology. In content, the Arguedian arguments lead us to believe that the Indio is the only being with virtuous dispositions, incapable of any fault; and that therefore, we should isolate him and care for him in order to avoid that he be contaminated. Such is *indiofilia zorra.* . . .[30]

The image of Zuratas again!

I do not think that Andean anthropologists "missed the war." At that time it was taking place in universities, and young Marxists attacked us all for our "romantic Andeanism" when we gave papers there. Social classes and modes of production held sway among Peru's newest thinkers. The atmosphere in these universities was truly defiant and aggressive, and this too was, and is being, studied by anthropologists.[31] But why our position has not found ears among Peru's youngest generation of activists is indeed food for thought.

The final turn of this debate: Is the Sendero Luminoso phenomenon—ultimately—one more Indian rebellion in rural Peru? (For example, "Sendero's aims in the establishment of its 'New Democracy' could succinctly be said to be expulsion from Peru of the white man and his mixed-race allies and all their works, and the reimposition of the primitive autarchic and paternalistic agricultural society which existed in Inca times" [Anderson 1987:60]. This is the Pol Pot comparison.) Or does the Sendero phenomenon constitute an imposition by a small minority of resentful lower-class mestizos desperate to restore their local power base at gun point? (For example, "[Sendero's] leadership has always been made up of *'mistis'*—small town mestizos—rooted in the Andean seignorial system" [Degregori 1991:12].) This may have been true in the early days. Today, as information on the PCP-SL grows, we learn that prominent middle-class Limeños are also implicated in Sendero leadership, including José María Arguedas's Chilean widow, Sybila Arredondo, and a support group of European and U.S. Maoists. A video recently captured by the Lima police shows the leadership of Sendero in comfortable upper middle-class surroundings in Lima. Middle- and upper-class infatuation with guerrillas is also prominent in the MRTA (Movimiento Revolucionario Tupac Amaru) and in the death squad movement "Rodrigo Franco," as it was in the 1965 Che Guevara-inspired guerrilla movement (Bejar 1973).

José Luis Rénique (1990) describes what has now become a mind-shattering experience for middle-class Peruvians: a visit to the prisons. The contrast between the chaotic and corrupt pavilions of the common criminal and the narco-criminal with the clean, orderly, disciplined, and self-organized Sendero quarters is remarkable. Rénique (1990:18) quotes one of them, "Paco": "As prisoners we have not lost our positions as soldiers in the popular army. We learn how to discuss, how to explain the party line without making concessions, how to be clear but strong. We practice physical and oral belligerence." Rénique's friend "Paco" was a "leftist in the 1970s, a potsmoker in the Woodstock era, a political activist in the '80s, a rock concert entrepreneur, and is now a prisoner in Canto Grande Security prison, singing 'All but power is illusion' in unison with the other political prisoners." Rénique also met comrade Pérez: ". . . in his late twenties and speaks with a heavy Quechua accent, but is very conversant and loquacious about the party line and current affairs. He is illiterate, so to participate in the discussions he asks somebody to read the documents over and over so he can keep every detail in mind."

A comparison of the sociological characteristics between people sentenced for common violent crimes and those sentenced for acts of political terrorism in the judicial records of Lima provides a profile of the rank-and-file revolutionaries of Peru. Chávez de Paz (1989) finds that 76% of those sentenced for terrorism are from the rural hinterland of Peru, and of these, 60% come from the impoverished highland areas. Overwhelmingly they are young (43% between the ages of 21 and 25), single, and better educated than the common criminals. Whereas most common criminals are high school dropouts (46%), 30% of those sentenced for terrorism tend to have pursued university studies (24% list their occupation as students). Only 2% of those sentenced for violent crimes have some university education, and 6% give their occupation as students. Overwhelmingly the sentenced terrorists are in occupations that sharply contradict their educational achievements. Eleven percent are in agricultural occupations, 22% work in proletarian situations, 10% are peddlers, and 15% have technical or white-collar occupations. Half of the men earn their living in occupational categories that are precarious and generate low incomes. In economic terms, there are similarities to the sentenced common criminals: 44% of the common criminals work in proletarian occupations; 11% as peddlers and 23% in technical or white-collar jobs. Revolutionaries are overwhelmingly young, highly mobile, better educated, provincial migrants earning a precarious living in occupations far below the levels that their education had led them to expect.

A high proportion of those sentenced for terrorism are women (16%), and of these, half have been in the university, compared to 28% of the men. Women play prominent roles in the guerrilla organization. They lead commando groups and they have masterminded daring raids. Maria Parado is said to have directed the assault on the Ayacucho prison on March 7, 1982, that freed hundreds of prisoners (Andreas 1990:21). Edith Lagos was a Senderista commander when she was killed by the military; she has since become a folk heroine. Carol Andreas (1990) is not unsympathetic to what Senderistas claim they do for women. In liberated villages, Shining Path overthrows village governing structures substituting them with "people's committees." Andreas says, "It is in these 'committees' that women's predominance is most evident. In effect, this has meant the overthrow of male-dominated local governments and the establishment of female-dominated structures, which has allowed women to 'settle accounts' in their own fashion as well as to organize social life in a manner they view as more equitable" (1990:21). Andreas also seems to approve of the Shining Path's system of justice. "Local cadres seem to have great latitude in carrying out *ajusticiamientos* (settling of accounts), sometimes by execution, against those who are considered to be enemies, spies, or traitors to the movement, including men accused of rape. Many women, who perhaps have more accounts to settle than do men, do not seem to find this disturbing" (1990:27). Whether this is true, or merely Sendero propaganda, needs, of course, to be established.

Settling accounts, authoritarianism, imposition, and extremist solutions pervade thinking among young Peruvians. Gonzalo Portocarrero and Patricia Oliart (1989) studied attitudes of schoolchildren and found that they admire *la mano dura* (authoritarian) approach to restoring order in a chaotic nation. In a chilling interview, a 17-year-old schoolboy in Puno disagrees with the Senderistas, but, nevertheless, believes in the need for a "complete" revolution for his school and the whole country. He is frustrated by strikes, school closings, teacher absenteeism, and disorder in the classroom. His solution: "Punishment right away for those who do not study. . . . It should no longer be permissible, for example, to have a student walking in the street during classroom hours. A policeman should come and say: 'Why are you here?' And if the student has no reason, two days of detention in the police station" (1989:169). He himself has attempted to lead a strike for a "complete revolution" in his school to rehabilitate the chemistry laboratory so he can learn better.

> The country needs a complete revolution so that everything will change. A complete communist revolution, so that everyone works. I say that there should not be thieves, delinquents . . . all those vices . . . drugs . . . and when there is a complete revolution, then there should not be any terrorism, nothing. All the armed forces should be in control. For example, if in Puno there would be a revolution, the guards should come to control everyone, house to house, no one should be left out. No one should be in the streets without a license that permits them to study, and all those who are capable should go to the jungle. Between rich and poor there should be no differences, and all should be equal. And the rich should not be choosing their foods. All should eat the same things . . . all should queue to receive the same dish. Everyone the same clothes. Everyone to work . . . [Portocarrero and Oliart 1989:181–182]

Suppose, however, that we shake up the elements we put into these dichotomies and see what the kaleidoscope of metaphors can bring toward a different kind of reading of the two Peru image. Let us mix Andean and Western together and disregard positive and negative valuations for a moment. Suppose—using metaphors again—that qualities that go into deep have longer persistence and deeper time depth and, thus, more "weight." The opposite of deep would then be "shallow" or "superficial." The elements in the superficial category would "float" to the surface.[32]

In this collage, deep Peru would include both Indian and mestizo. It would include Indian resistance and mestizo repression; it would include resentment and hate. It would have to describe the many cycles of rebellion and repression in Peruvian history as archaic, brutal, and savage. Modernity and underdevelopment (or dependent capitalism and functional dualism [De Janvri 1981]) are also rooted deeply in Peru. Police brutality, indiscriminate killings, and mass dumping of bodies with faces and fingers so disfigured that they cannot be identified also belong to the ethnography of death in deep Peru. The capacity to act "savagely" is not limited to lynchings by peasants but also includes mass assassinations of peasants by the army and by Sendero. Overreacting by beating the pulp out of people until they become totally submissive and lose any semblance of their own personae is as much a feature of deep Peru as is imposing one's will on peasant communities through calculated terrorism, dynamite, sabotage, and selective assassination. Deep Peru includes Kafkian judicial systems, which it calls its administration of justice, that systematically enmesh lower-class and Quechua-speaking citizens in complicated and unreal proceedings. And it created, along with other Latin American nations, a new transitive verb, *desaparecer* (someone), to circumvent its own judicial system. It is deep Peru because these behaviors are "rooted," and deeply so, in the culture. It is deep, because, seemingly, these practices cannot be that easily eradicated.

Superficial Peru would include the weaker aspects in this one society, such as the rule of law, but not the manipulation of law. It is wishful thinking. The state would, in this view, assure the respect for every citizen regardless of race, religion, or political conviction; the imposition of nonexploitative economic and social relations; opportunities for legal redress for those who have been injured; and the fining and punishing of those who break the law. The list goes on: the right to organize in defense of one's own interests without repression or terrorist destructiveness; equal access to all the benefits the society can offer without discrimination; the vigorous adherence to "civilized" methods of reaching consensus, negotiating agreements, and transacting disagreements; the conduct of "clean" political campaigns for those in government and those in the opposition; the acceptance of those elements of Hispanic and Andean culture that make for a civil society and a Peruvian Culture with a capital C. These, alas, are features of superficial Peru. Like orchids, they have real roots that are easily extirpated and substituted for deeper passions and shorter term economic and political interests. This formulation, chimerical and idealistic, is at least in concordance with Basadre's original formulation about the differences between deep and legal Peru.

One does not have to travel far to find the limits of superficial or official Peru. Deep Peru is present everywhere, not only in remote areas such as Uchuraccay. It is even present in Lima, as Hernando de Soto (1988) has shown in his study of how the informal sector constantly challenges official/superficial Peru. And were this not so, Senderistas would not be capable of hiding so successfully from official Peru.

The Kaleidoscope Metaphor Deconstructed

As an optical device that is closed at the viewing end, the kaleidoscope is singularly inept as a metaphor for conveying the notion that one wants to view things with clarity. It contains glass beads, colored pieces of paper, buttons, et cetera, which undergo multiple reflections through intersecting mirrors mounted lengthwise in the tube, producing endlessly transforming symmetrical patterns that can be seen through the eyepiece. The kaleidoscope metaphor imposes a changeless recombination of patterns, in which duality reproduces itself, depending on the number of mirrors used and how their planes intersect one another. To be useful as a metaphor one has to pay more attention to the position of the mirrors than to the illusionary patterns it creates. Its appeal as a metaphor is due to the many images it creates out of the same elements that are placed in the optical screen.

As such, the kaleidoscope has been used as an apt metaphor by Billie Jean Isbell to emphasize that no matter from which angle one observes social forms in the village of Chuschi, the patterns that tend to form reveal an underlying symmetry and order that structure Andean thought patterns.[33] Isbell pays attention not only to "turns" of the kaleidoscope but also to transformations. "The migrants' [of Chuschi to Lima] experiences have been such that they do not see the world as foreign and threatening and have redefined the term in accordance with their experiences. . . . Their notion of social space is still concentric and dual, but the organization has been rearranged" (Isbell 1978:188).

In this article I have used the kaleidoscope metaphor to illustrate the extent to which the two Peru argument is sterile. Fixing attention on the two Peru argument, as demonstrated above, has created so many possible permutations of the dual categories that they do indeed invalidate any use of the two Peru model for explanations. Although its metaphors may make for good text, literary discourse, and excellent fiction, they make for bad social science.

However, the kaleidoscope metaphor suggests other optical phenomena useful for an analysis of the emblematic character of the events sparked by Uchuraccay: polarization and condensation. A series of events has become compressed through a thought process that tends to polarize views of the events. And this implies a loss of perspective. The Vargas Llosa report contributed to the viewing of the events in Uchuraccay from lopsided perspectives. The report polarized positions by stressing the bravery of comuneros of Uchuraccay (albeit mistakenly applied) versus the savagery of the Senderistas. The opposition sought instead to focus attention on the savagery of the armed forces against civilians, thereby—

by implication—leaving an opening to label the actions of Sendero Luminoso as bravery (albeit mistakenly applied). All middle positions were eliminated.

For example, General Noel saw communist subversion everywhere—a subversion that necessitated persecuting an unspecified number of the 10,000 graduates from the Universidad San Cristóbal de Huamanga in Ayacucho, "who are identified with the postulates of communist doctrine which are now scattered through all the regional, departmental and district levels of the nation and conform the leadership of the subversion" (Noel 1989:81). He sees subversion in the actions of Peruvian journalists of the opposition press. They are "people of reproachable moral conduct who are the intellectual and material authors progressively poisoning and destroying the country" (Noel 1989:21). "Fantasy and hate" lie behind the journalists' hypothesis on Uchuraccay, a "hate they exhibit against men and institutions that sacrifice themselves for social and economic and political stability of the country" (Noel 1989:101). It is a hate he readily reciprocates. José María Salcedo, director of the newspaper *El Diario* also remembers that "a dividing line had been traced: government and opposition. To opt for the hypothesis of exclusive responsibility of the comuneros of Uchuraccay was a way to exculpate the regime. To question that hypothesis was a way to incriminate it" (Salcedo 1984:178). Objective facts (and witnesses) disappeared. The Vargas Llosa report, the comuneros of Uchuraccay, and the exploitable grief of the widows of the murdered journalists, soldiers, and policemen all became pawns in a sordid power play.

Long after the events in Uchuraccay, analysis of Sendero Luminoso continues to be plagued by polarization. Poole and Rénique (1991:28) severely critique the views of U.S. based "senderologists." They conclude that "the mechanistic and universalizing model leaves out all 'gray areas' between the essentialized poles of violence and democracy. . . . Democracy/legitimacy and violence/illegitimacy become equated finally and absolutely with the oppositions of center-periphery, Spanish-Indian, urban-rural. According to this calculus, as long as Peru remains divided between 'Indians' and 'Spaniards', 'traditional' and 'modern', the nation will never become a modern 'legitimate' state." Even as the mirrors of the kaleidoscope become increasingly bespattered with blood, we continue to insist on its use.

Judicial Farce and Popular Critique

After the Vargas Llosa report and the furor it engendered, judicial proceedings began in the courts of Ayacucho to determine guilt and punishment of those responsible for the death of the eight journalists. Preliminary investigations were entrusted to Judge Juan Flores. These dragged on for more than a year. During this time sensationalism reigned. There were mass demonstrations in Lima demanding a speedup in the procedings and accusations of deliberate foot-dragging. The case continued to be debated more in newspapers than in the court. Military personnel, journalists, and witnesses ignored orders to testify. Judge Flores was denied facilities to travel to Uchuraccay to conduct investigations. And the army, high judicial officials, and the press leaked information (such as newly "discovered" photographs) according to political convenience rather than as a response to court orders.

Toward the end of 1984 a formal case against three named cumuneros of Uchuraccay—Dionisio Morales, president of the community; Simeón Aucatoma; and Mario Ccasani—was opened under the presidency of Judge Hermenegildo Ventura Huayhua. Unlike most trials, this one included a public and oral part— Perry Mason style. But the trial had dragged on for months without any new revelations. General Noel had defied the court and refused to testify, and all known witnesses from Uchuraccay had been killed or had disappeared. The perpetrators of these murders were never known. Public opinion is strongly divided over whether these deaths were the responsibility of the military to cover up public knowledge of events they would prefer to keep secret, or whether they were Sendero reprisals. None of these later deaths was seriously investigated. Those who believe that the military killed these people also believe that it was, in fact, the military that killed the journalists. There also had been deaths when people from Uchuraccay refused to be dragged to Ayacucho to testify. Terrorist and antiterrorist violence in Ayacucho had reached unprecedented levels, veritably burying the case of the journalists under a mountain of bodies. But for the sake of democratic form, the judicial proceedings had to go on.

The only good citizens who readily agreed to testify were the members of the Vargas Llosa Commission. Mario Vargas Llosa's encounter with Judge Hermenegildo Ventura Huayhua took place in November of 1984. He appeared in court in an elegant beige suit. Vargas Llosa, framed by a huge crucifix, stood during the whole proceeding in front of the judge. There, he was subjected to more than 15 hours of intense and relentless questioning, to aggressive stances by Judge Ventura Huayhua. Overnight he was kept incommunicado; an armed guard was posted outside his bedroom in the Tourist Hotel. Many of Judge Ventura Huayhua's statements and questions were deemed insulting and offensive to the person of Vargas Llosa. Hints—none too subtle—were dropped that the writer had profited from the *New York Times* story, that he had lent his writer's gifts to serve the needs of the Belaunde government in a cover-up, and that his Commission had subverted the judiciary's ability to conduct a fair trial. He was asked by another member of the court, "When you refer to absolute truth do you refer to occidental or oriental Peru?" and "Do you support occidental Peru?" (Caretas 1984a).

There was immediate press reaction to Ventura Huayhua's offensive treatment of Vargas Llosa. The newsmagazine *Caretas* printed a vicious condemnation of Judge Ventura Huayhua and his court. However, the populace reacted differently. In bars, taxis, at work, everywhere, the common people celebrated how Judge Ventura Huayhua had brought the aristocratic Vargas Llosa down by two notches, scored a couple of points, and deflated the writer's urbane stuffiness. Ventura Huayhua's popularity was immense. *Serranos* (highlanders) in particular enjoyed the discomfort that one of their *paisanos* had inflicted on a coastal and urban Limeño.[34]

The press, however, embarked on an equally dirty campaign to besmirch Judge Ventura Huayhua's prestige. They dug into his humble provincial origins; they were disdainful of his affiliation with the lower echelons of the APRA party; they cruelly ridiculed his literary ambitions and underlined every grammatical mistake as they transcribed choice phrases from the proceedings. None of that, however, diminished the judge's popularity. Judge Ventura Huayhua, happily conceding interviews to the leftist and international press, disclosed his intended verdict before the trial was over. He hinted that his investigations and proceedings would soon reveal important evidence that would falsify the findings of the Commission. Neither was ever forthcoming. A few months later a mistrial was declared, and Judge Ventura Huayhua was dismissed from the case to sink back to the obscurity of provincial life he had been working so hard to overcome.

In May 1987, I interviewed Judge Ventura Huayhua in the Hostal Santa Rosa in Ayacucho. The Hostal Santa Rosa is a second-class hotel where the murdered journalists stayed, and where members of Peru's security forces, petty bureaucrats, anthropologists, traveling salesmen, and even Senderistas stay. It is an old converted house with inner patios and adjoining rooms. The judge received me in the hotel's living room. This room, with its windowpaned doors, high ceilings, painted plaster walls, kerosene soaked wood floors, and plastic-covered deep sofas, was the very same room where the eight journalists had planned their trip. Born in 1930 in a small town in the neighboring department of Huancavelica, Judge Hermenegildo Ventura Huayhua is single, suffers from bone pains, and cures himself with strict diets and herbal medicines recommended by local *curanderas* and *curiosas*.

I was curious why the judge had chosen instantaneous popularity by effectively mocking a famous personality over enduring glory by conducting an exemplary trial. After all, he had everything going for him. He could have attempted to falsify the findings of the Vargas Llosa Commission by producing new evidence of a cover-up. Even if there was no such evidence, surely he could have investigated the extent of police and military complicity in the events. So many aspects of the case that remained obscure could have been cleared up. Even if he ended with a ruling that found extenuating circumstances exonerating the three accused men from Uchuraccay he would have been appreciated. Instead, the judge scuttled his own prospects and chose to go down in a brief moment of glory? Why?

Newspaper editorials saw in this behavior obscure party maneuvers seeking to embarrass the government (Caretas 1984b). On the other hand, in Ventura Huayhua's defense, the progressive journal *Quehacer* hinted at the difficulties and obstructionism the judiciary had in pursuing a proper investigation, including a veiled reference that the judiciary in Ayacucho might have to be careful of the reaction from Shining Path (Rubio 1984:12–17). The judge compared the few resources he had with the helicopters, facilities, and experts Vargas Llosa had in his investigation. Was there official obstructionism as the judge wanted me to believe, or just incompetence? Legal experts in Vargas Llosa's camp delighted in pointing to procedural faults in the conduct of the trial. But one needs to remember that key witnesses, such as General Noel and the police captain who first arrived in Uchuraccay, never appeared in Ventura Huayhua's court.

To me, the judge came across as an eccentric, provincial intellectual, and the story he told was surprising indeed. The interview lasted for more than three hours because, like Mark Lane (the lawyer who still believes in Oswald's innocence), it all had to be built up with complex circumstantial suppositions. But the gist was that the journalists had been lured out of Ayacucho by members of Shining Path (some lived in the Hostal Santa Rosa) under the pretext that they would see something very important. To leave Ayacucho without arousing suspicions, the journalists claimed that they were going to investigate the cases of the killed Senderistas.[35] Once out of town, the journalists then met the guerrillas who showed them "this something" that was so tremendous, so frightening, and so damaging to the government that the army had no choice but to kill the journalists and then foist the bodies and the guilt onto the comuneros of Uchuraccay. Had "this something" come to light, the Belaunde government would have fallen. Judge Ventura Huayhua could not, of course, know what it was that the journalists saw, but he supposed that it must have been the latest and technically most advanced military installation put there under U.S. auspices. Darth Vader's spaceship had landed on the punas of Ayacucho! Judge Ventura Huayhua has told various versions of this story to foreign correspondents. In these, the unspeakable secret turns out to be: "torture centers run by the infantry or the marines," "communications centers," or "evidence of how the comuneros were being indoctrinated to eliminate any suspicious person who collaborates with the guerrillas" (Vargas Llosa 1990:221).

What also came through in the interview was the deep resentment the judge had toward Vargas Llosa the writer. Perhaps, ultimately, it was the frustration of the provincial intellectual, unable to convert his fictions into a credible story, who envied the other storyteller's successes. Isbell notes that, for peasants, events in this war are instantly transformed into a "mythohistory" that makes local sense (1991), and this may be true for the judge's own version, and all other versions, of the Uchuraccay incident.

There was a third trial of comuneros from Uchuraccay. It was quietly conducted in Lima in 1986. The same three men from Uchuraccay were accused and tried only because they were community members. Essentially they remained silent during the whole proceedings. As with the Ventura Huayhua court (de Trazegnies 1984), they answered questions but frequently contradicted themselves and adjusted their testimony to what they thought the judges wanted to hear. The comuneros were declared guilty of the murder of the journalists, and given ten-, eight-, and six-year prison sentences in March of 1987. General Noel was again summoned. He flew to Lima from Washington, D.C., where he was military attache with the Peruvian embassy. His testimony added nothing new. The court decision sentencing the three comuneros also instructed the provincial court in Huanta to begin investigations on General Noel and seven other military functionaries for possible charges of being the intellectual authors of the assassinations and for obstructing judicial inquiries.

In July of 1989, two comuneros from Uchuraccay were quietly released by President Alan García as part of the presidential amnesty program that is customary on the day Peru celebrates its independence anniversary. The older man, Simeón Aucatoma, had died in prison of tuberculosis.[36]

Missing Voices

In all the debate, publicity, opinions, and counter arguments, the voice of the comuneros of Uchuraccay was never once heard. Their point of view was always mediated by translators, interpreters, and experts. Although the testimony, given during the one meeting at Uchuraccay, that the Commission members had was carefully transcribed, not one single complete sentence has been reproduced in the printed final report. There are only three words from the comuneros that Vargas Llosa directly quotes: *"terrorista sua"* (terrorist thief), *"señor gobierno"* (Sir Government), and "ignorant." There is only one partial quote: "Could we ask the 'Honorable Mr. Government' to send them at least three rifles?" (Vargas Llosa et al. 1983:10). The quotes are not attributed to anyone.

The authenticity of their testimony is vouched for by Vargas Llosa alone. He says that "they did it naturally, without guilt, intrigued and surprised that people had come from so far away—that there was so much excitement—because of something like this" (1983:10).[37] There is no way to evaluate whether there were dissenting voices, no variant forms of saying the same things, no opportunities to look beyond the mediated message conveyed by the Commission's report. People in Uchuraccay come through to us in the third person plural and in indirect speech.[38] The dangers of imputing an identical collective identity to all comuneros are only too obvious when one considers that the army persistently has acted on the assumption that if there is one anonymous pro Sendero grafitti on a wall, all the villagers must be Senderistas.

The circumstances of the meeting that the members of the Commission had with the comuneros were unusual. The Commission members flew in by helicopter and ordered the people to assemble. Vargas Llosa distributed coca leaves (on the advice of the anthropologists), and then the questioning began. Lots of strangers with cameras, tape recorders, and modern equipment squatted on the ground on one side of a semicircle, the assembled comuneros on the other. Police and army were everywhere in evidence. It is said that some had flown in the afternoon before the meeting to make sure that everything was safe for the Commission. Apart from the linguistic experts, no one in the Commission spoke Quechua. Everything had to be carefully translated both ways.

The unanimity of the testimony is troublesome. The historical and literary precedent of Lope de Vega's play, "Fuenteovejuna,"[39] about peasant resistance in 15th-century Spain has struck more than one observer not only in terms of the plot of the play, but also the theatricality in the performance, as noted by Millones (1983:88): "The meeting we [members of the Commission] had with the community reached a level of the performance of a set drama in which the authorities acted as prompters in order to insure that the libretto was faithfully followed. Although it was occasionally departed from, it became a frame which clearly made explicit their internal solidarity with the committed crime and of a previous agreement to repeat one single version in the best interest of all.''

Anthropological testimony is usually based on protracted periods of fieldwork to permit long interactions in diverse contexts with people. In this case, fieldwork lasted half a day. More information on Uchuraccay comes from the schoolteacher Alejandrina de la Cruz than from the comuneros. The transcribed tapes of the inquest, which contain statements made by the comuneros, were not made available to Judge Ventura Huayhua until his court had talked to Vargas Llosa, and when they were delivered to him, he dismissed them (Caretas 1984c). Throughout the trials, the performance of the defense lawyers was so inept or uninteresting to the press that I have not been able to find one statement that, in some way, would represent the voice of the comuneros of Uchuraccay. During the trials, translation was only one-way, from Quechua to Spanish, and only when Spanish monolingual court officials wanted to ask questions of Quechua monolinguals. The accused comuneros never even understood the court proceedings.

In this, too, certain aspects of official Peru strongly reaffirmed themselves again. Comuneros, though citizens of this country, rarely have a voice or even personality of their own. It is time to provide them with the means to exercise their right to freedom of expression in their own terms, no matter how anthropologically legitimated or literary their interpreters and mediators may be.

As for Sendero Luminoso, the only direct reference to the events in Uchuraccay I was able to trace was a note in a newspaper stating that on the third of June of 1983, members of Shining Path captured the radio station in Huanta and broadcast a message. It rejected the Vargas Llosa report and supported the thesis that paramilitary personnel were responsible. It went on to say that Sendero would take revenge on those who perpetrated the death of several of their militants in Uchuraccay. ''The death of the martyrs of Uchuraccay will not remain unpunished, those guilty will fall prey to popular justice'' (DESCO Resumen Semanal 1983). On April 3, 1983, Senderistas attacked the town of Lucanamarca and murdered 80 people in the village square. On July 18, 1983, Shining Path killed eight people in Uchuraccay.

On the events in Lucanamarca, Abimael Guzman, chairman of the Communist Party of Peru-SL (Guzman 1988), made the following comment:

> Lucanamarca: Neither they nor we have forgotten it, to be sure, because there they saw an answer that they could not imagine. There more than 80 were annihilated, that is the truth. And we say it, there was an excess. . . . In some occasions, as in that one, it was the Central Leadership itself that planned the actions and gave the instructions, it had been that way. There the principal thing was that we dealt them an overwhelming blow and we checked them and they understood that they were dealing with another type of combatants of the people, that we were not the ones that they had combatted before, that was what they understood.

Zavala's Question

Santiago Zavala is the main character in Vargas Llosa's (1975) novel *Conversation in the Cathedral*. In the opening pages of the novel, Zavala asks himself, "At what moment did Peru get screwed?" This question provides the leit-motiv in the novel in which life in Lima and the doings of corrupt government officials are described along with Zavala's own disillusionment with the dreary 1950s. The question Zavala asked himself has become a popular phrase. In 1990, Carlos Milla Bartres edited a book (*¿En Qué Momento Se Jodió el Perú?*) in which distinguished intellectuals wrote essays that tried to answer that question. Most of the answers offered go back to Francisco Pizarro and the colonial period. The authors cite centuries-old racist attitudes and dissolute elite behavior patterns as the main cause. Is this a depressive escape into the past at a time when the country is in the midst of one of the worst economic, political, and social crises in its history? Does blaming events in the remote past signal an inability to do something about solving the country's serious contemporary problems?

Personally, I do not think that it is necessary to go back hundreds of years to find out when Peru screwed itself. Uchuraccay and all that happened afterward can easily be shown to be one of those times. Peru's inability to understand the Sendero Luminoso uprising and its inability to deal with Sendero Luminoso in realistic terms are at the heart of the emblematic events that took place after the incident at Uchuraccay.

Fernando Belaunde's government did not take the Sendero uprising seriously, probably because nobody in sophisticated Lima cares what happens in remote Andean provinces. Certain factions of the intellectual Left are also to blame for not clearly defining their positions regarding the deviations of the Senderistas and for not loudly ringing the alarm bells about the dangers of the uprising. The military's antiquated counterinsurgency strategy is another factor. Through persecution, torture, and disappearances they created a situation in which fears of military repression outweighed the Senderista threat to the civilian population. The military's refusal both to cooperate with civilian society in handling the uprising and to heed minimal rules of openness with the press (presumably because it did have things to hide) are chiefly to blame for the deterioration of civilian-military relations.

A farcical judicial system has closed off possibilities of conflict resolution through legally established mechanisms, as every sector of society bypasses the legal system. The Belaunde government investigating the events at Uchuraccay preferred a "Commission" to the judiciary; the military had nothing but disdain for the courts; the oligarchy heaped scorn on provincial lawyers; judges became circus performers; the press conducted trials in newspapers, and the comuneros never defended themselves in court.

The "blood and gore" sensationalist press as well as part of the left-wing press became more interested in scoring points and making life difficult for the government than establishing the truth and understanding the causes of the events. The right-wing press labeled any kind of criticism of the government as unpatriotic and pro-Sendero. Intellectuals, incapable of rising above the totally out-of-date and well-trodden clichés they used, constructed implausible explanations, which led to skepticism and cynicism instead of understanding. The generalized tendency to seek "experts" to speak for others instead of letting people express their own views produced a barrage of half-baked concepts and phrases that obfuscated rather than clarified the causes and character of this armed insurgency. Well-written but poorly researched reports produced literary critiques rather than critical confrontations with facts.

A progressive military group had directed one of Peru's most wide-ranging reformist efforts only 12 years before Sendero declared war. It had opened opportunities to many aspiring provincial young men and women whose hopes were then dashed when job opportunities drastically declined as Peru's economy virtually ground to a halt. The post-Velasco regimes closed their eyes to the rising expectations of new sectors in society. Elites shut them out as prosperity declined.

Peru screwed itself because an early option to effectively combat the Sendero Luminoso uprising in cooperation with the comuneros of the rural areas was never developed. Instead, the comuneros were repressed by an authoritarian system that denied their efforts any validity. Peruvian society could not recognize the contributions of its impoverished, illiterate, and inarticulate allies in the midst of the uprising. The civilian sectors of society never developed an effective response to neutralize the revolutionaries. By now it may be too late.

Epilogue

During these many years the comuneros of Uchuraccay and its neighboring villages have been removed from the area. The survivors are living in fortified refugee camps many miles away from their homes, unable to return home because of threats to their lives. After the events in Uchuraccay, the armed forces' feared "dirty war," which the Left was so intent on foisting onto the consciousness of the nation, did indeed take place. Amnesty International has reported numerous mass killings, disappearances, and uncountable cases of torture on all three sides: peasants, armed forces, and Senderistas (Amnesty International 1985, 1989). Prisons became strongholds of Sendero agitation and were then bombed by the airforce and stormed by the army in June of 1986. Shining Path has descended from the mountains into the cities, as have hundreds of thousands of refugees fleeing the war in the Andes. It is now a serious political contender, and its tactics of terrorism have escalated. Limeños now have first-hand experience with Shining Path. Assassinations against prominent Lima politicians are common, as are blackouts and bombings. Industry and business pay *cupos revolucionarios* (protection money). Rival police and army units fight each other. Dismissed corrupt police personnel have formed their own private kidnapping gangs.

The remaining comuneros throughout Peru continue to oscillate between army and Sendero domination. Occasionally they organize into self-defense groups (called *rondas campesinas*) and succeed in killing members of various guerrilla groups. The debate over whether rondas should be provided with arms continues unresolved. The army now also organizes peasant militias *(montoneras)* to do its dirty work (Jo-Marie Burt 1990:30–31). By controlling coca growing areas in the Upper Huallaga, Sendero now has a steady source of income (NACLA Report on the Americas 1989). The successes of Shining Path's terrorist tactics are emulated by other small political groups. So-called death squads have also appeared on the killing scene, as have organized criminal groups associated with the narcotics trade and kidnappings of prominent industrialists and financiers.

Legal recourse against abuses committed by all sides has become impossible to redress through judicial methods. Arrested suspects are hardly ever tried. Known Senderistas are released for lack of specific legally admissible evidence and because members of the legal system are under threat. Guerrilla leaders organize spectacular escapes from prison.

Uchuraccay itself is now a deserted place, and the grass has grown over the shallow graves of the journalists. Many Peruvians have shuddered that the murder of eight journalists generated such outrage and public display of government trials, commissions, and judicial mobilization, while thousands of humble peasants have simply disappeared without a trace, and those responsible cannot be ferreted out through any kind of legal actions. This continues to be true in today's one Peru. Arrests these days are few. The army and police shoot to kill, and the newspaper accounts quoting military sources endlessly repeat that "on the bodies of those killed in action, guns, dynamite and subversive propaganda was found." Not too many people really care anymore. A resigned population feels that it is now necessary to "kill them all and get it over with so we can live in peace" (Manrique 1990:37). The death toll in this war now stands at 18,000.[40]

Notes

Acknowledgments. I am grateful to the faculty of the Department of Anthropology at Yale University for initial comments and the opportunity to write this article during the time I was a visiting professor there in the spring semester of 1991. Helpful comments and suggestions were made by Richard Burger, William Kelly, Patricia Mathews, Irene Silverblatt, Billie Jean Isbell, Deborah Poole, Clodoaldo Soto, Janet Dixon Keller, Juan Ossio, and Helaine Silverman. Peter Johnson, Cesar Rodríguez, and Nelly Gonzalez (the Latin American bibliographers of Princeton University, Yale University, and the University of Illinois) were particularly helpful with references.

[1]In this article I use "terrorists," "Senderistas," "Shining Path," and *"terroristas"* interchangeably to refer to the political party Partido Communista del Perú-Sendero Luminoso (PCP-SL). I will not, however, use PCP-SL, as they would like to be called. In an article critical of U.S. scholars who analyze the "Shining Path phenomenon," Poole and Rénique (1991) remonstrate against the use of such terms as "terrorist" because they are part of the objectionable scholarly apparatus with which U.S. "senderologists" have hampered our understanding of this and other Third World political phenomena. Labeling them with such terms as "madmen, terrorists, war lords, drug barons, charismatic leaders and fundamentalist mass movements" (Poole & Rénique 1991:29) obfuscates rather than clarifies. The authors go on to say, "The PCP-SL is a political party which must be treated as such. It is neither a 'movement' nor a mystery, but rather an organization with a specific political and military rationality" (1991:43). I recognize Poole and Rénique's objections. Sendero must not be "mystyfied" or "satanized." But at the same time, there are minimum criteria that have to be fulfilled to be recognized as a political party, which the PCP-

SL chooses not to accept. They are not registered as a party, nor legitimated, and they refuse to participate with the minimum rules of electoral party politics. The status of revolutionary parties (in Lenin's sense) when they are in *clandestinidad* is, of course, problematic when their legitimacy is denied by official powers and its members are persecuted for ideological reasons, and also for crimes committed against legal and constitutional norms. In the case of PCP-SL it is they who chose to go underground and it is they who declared the "armed struggle." Until the PCP-SL chooses to emerge from its clandestine position and seek some official reconciliation with civil society. I will continue calling them terroristas for that is their weapon of choice.

[2] In all newspaper accounts he is named as General Clemente Noel Moral. In his own book he calls himself Roberto C. Noel Moral (Noel Moral 1989).

[3] I have tried to find as many quotes in English translation as possible. As indicated in the bibliography, all titles in Spanish imply that the quotes from these references are my translations into English.

[4] Studies have confirmed the way highland pastorialists have historically been struggling to become independent from the lower lying farming communities, and therefore had little patience for attempts by Senderistas (more associated with valley areas) to reassert control over them. See Favre (1984).

[5] Originally reported by Basadre (1947:226), wherein he established the stereotype that the Iquichanos are "particularly barbarous residents of Huanta and La Mar provinces, descendents of the Pokras, tribes of the Chanca race."

[6] See Pásara 1984 for a legal study of local justices of the peace and their relationship to higher courts and the application of written legal codes.

[7] As noted by Ossio and Fuenzalida (1983:73) in their report to the Commission.

[8] In some areas of the Andes these encounters have become part of their ritual life. *Tinkuys* are considered successful if they are wounded and blood is spilled (Platt 1986; Poole 1984).

[9] One notorious case occurred during the Velazco regime. As reported by the press, the comuneros of Huayanay (in the department of Huancavelica) had collectively killed an abusive ex *mayordomo*. They then signed a document stating that they had taken justice into their own hands and handed over the body to the authorities. The appeal of a story of exasperated comuneros finally killing a man who had twice bought himself free from prison convinced public opinion and cowed the judge of the case into absolving the comuneros for their act of informal justice. However, research conducted by Fernando de Trazegnies (1977, 1978) revealed that the killing had occurred as part of a long, drawn-out feud between two extended families. The victimizers had pressured the uninvolved comuneros of Huayanay into signing the collective document.

[10] Organization of peasant communities to defend themselves against cattle rustlers has gradually become the basis of anti-Sendero self-defense groups. They started in the department of Cajamarca and have gradually spread throughout the highlands. See Taylor (1983) and Brandt (1987).

[11] See Flores Galindo (1988) for a hair-raising denunciation of cotidian police practices anywhere in Peru, even before terrorism induced counterterrorism.

[12] "Testimony from the schoolteacher of Uchuraccay demonstrates that lately the community has been the object of intense evangelical preaching" (Ossio and Fuenzalida 1983:63).

The encounter with evangelical preachers among the Iquicha is also described by Salcedo (1984:145). Degregori (1990), Skar (1982), Berg (1987), and Quintanilla (1982) describe political activism in the Ayacucho countryside.

[13]In 1989 the Senate Commission on the causes of violence and alternatives toward peace devoted three chapters to study "structural violence" in Peruvian society (Comisión Especial 1990). The Commission saw structural violence as a historical, cumulative, and ingrained process ". . . to the extent that the very constituted order of things, its legality and the organization of power become expressions of a structural violence that accumulates, reproduces itself and tends to perpetuate itself, impelling under certain circumstances to actual violent behavior in its diverse manifestations" (1990:34). Two general trends are given as causes of structural violence. One is its gradual accumulation through historical discontinuities, displacement of people, disintegration, marginalization, incommunication, authoritarianism, centralism, and the absence of a national project. The second is found in the patterns of social relations between people and includes ascriptive asymmetric status, domination, racism, and gender domination (1990:120–130).

[14]See Gorriti (1990:Chap. 9) on how the leadership of Shining Path taught its militants to get the maximum value out of assassinations.

[15]The three rules: (1) Obey orders in all actions; (2) Do not take from the masses not even one needle nor a thread; (3) Hand over all captured things. The eight warnings: (1) Speak politely; (2) Pay honestly for whatever is brought; (3) Return borrowed things; (4) Compensate for every damage caused; (5) Do not hit or insult the people; (6) Do not damage standing crops; (7) Do not take liberties with their women; (8) Do not mistreat prisoners (Gorriti 1990:174).

[16]Gorriti promises to deal with this aspect in the second volume of his book: "As will be shown, the application of these directives was notoriously uneven in areas where Shining Path was disputing its supremacy, but constant in those where they had an influence" (Gorriti 1990:174).

[17]Vargas Llosa et al (1983:32), Vargas Llosa (1990:134). Though popular, Basadre's phrase Perú profundo is hard to trace among his voluminous writings. The earliest reference comes in his 1943 essay "1945" (reprinted in Basadre 1978a:489). A barely more extensive discussion appears as a nine-page colophon entitled Colofón sobre el país profundo in the 1947 edition of his La multitud, la ciudad y el campo en la historia del Perú (1929).

[18]Basadre (1978a:489) follows French writer Charles Pegúy in making this distinction.

[19]This insistence continues despite repeated negations of isolation made by members of his own commission. Examples: "The peasants of the Iquicha highlands had until 1826 an intense and constant participation in the political life of the region and the nation. Their isolation and stasis do not come in the 16th century but begin in the 19th century which appear to be associated to the general decline of economic and social life which accompanied republican centralization" (Ossio and Fuenzalida 1983:49–50).

[20]"The term gamonal derives from the name of a virtually indestructible perennial plant of the lily family, the gamón (asphodel). . . . As a metaphor for the particular class of bilingual, bicultural and horrendously abusive landlords it describes, this name could not be more precise" (Poole 1988:372).

[21]On "semifeudalidad," see Mariátegui (1971), Díaz Martinez (1969), J. C. F. (1988). On predominantly capitalist relations, see Montoya (1980), Claverías (n.d.), and Caballero (1980).

[22]General Adrian Huaman Centeno succeeded General Noel in the command of the army in Ayacucho. Toward the end of his period Centeno became the darling of progressive groups because he said that the only resolution of the Sendero uprising was through development work. For his open criticisms of the government he was relieved of his command. Few, however, mention that it was under this general that the most serious abuses of human rights occurred.

[23]In the Anglo-Saxon world, this is an old tendency, best reflected in William Prescott's historical works (1893). Since Queen Elizabeth and Phillip the II, the Anglo-Saxon world has been deeply prejudiced against anything Hispanic. And what better way to disparage the Spanish than by describing the viciousness of the conquest and the exploitation of the Indians during Hispanic colonialism. How easy it is to see the continuation of these practices in contemporary Peru. How gratifying to be able to document the survival of Indian cultures.

[24]A useful guide that would have got him going is Osterling and Martinez's "Notes for a History of Peruvian Social Anthropology" in *Current Anthropology* (1983). It even contains illustrative comments by American anthropologists who have worked in Peru. Also in Peru self-analysis has begun. The edited volumes by Peruvians Rodriguez Pastor (1985) and Luis Soberón (1986) are but the tip of the iceberg.

[25]Though minor, I would point out that all the practices described in the Alberti and Mayer book (1974) are there today, explained in functional and contemporary situations, pervasive and important. While Starn was at the Instituto de Estudios Peruanos he might also have looked for a book called *El Indio y el Poder* (Mayer 1970), in which, along with other authors, I had begun to explore the contextualized and shifting nature of Indian status and identity in Peru.

[26]*Cholo* is a descriptive term, insulting or endearing, ascribed to people of Andean cultural background who are rapidly trying to acculturate. The term connotes brashness, pushiness, innovativeness, as well as insufficient acculturation, by which cholos can always be identified and belittled. As a social science category, the term has had enormous difficulties, best reflected in Quijano's seminal work (1980). Quijano proposed that the emerging new "class" of cholos came from peasant Indians breaking away from the restrictive conditions in haciendas and communities to conquer new positions in a rapidly expanding capitalist economy. Unhappy with his own formulation, Quijano refused to let this work, originally written in 1964, be published until 1980 when he felt sure that his work would no longer be critiqued as "culturalist" and thereby minimize class conflict. The term has mostly been dropped from social science discourse, but not from the popular understanding of the phenomenon of highlanders aggressively invading social and economic niches from which they were previously excluded. In popular understanding, too, the term cholo, or *cholificación*, refers to a recognizable style of behavior, dress, language, and interpersonal behavior that challenges existing inter-group behavioral patterns (see also Matos Mar 1984).

[27]The *nom de guerre* of Abimael Guzman founder of the PCP-SL.

[28]On emerging Indianism as a political movement in Latin America, see Bonfil Batalla (1981), on Ecuador, see Whitten (1981, 1991) on Bolivia, see Albó (1987), on Guatemala,

see Arias (1990) and Smith (1990). In Peru the Movimiento Indígena has been singularly unsuccessful. During the years of the dirty war, Salvador Palomino became its president and protested that the Indians were "sandwiched" between Senderistas and the army. Because of that, he was lumped by General Noel with those who aid subversion (Noel 1989:137).

[29]First published in the pro-Sendero newspaper *El Diario* (JCF 1988).

[30]Cited in Degregori (1990:296). The word *zorra* is an incredibly vicious reference to Arguedas's last novel, *El Zorro de Arriba y el Zorro de Abajo* (1978).

[31]Krueger (1980), Lynch et al. (1990), and Degregori (1990). *Mayta* (Vargas Llosa 1984) and *Conversation in the Cathedral* (Vargas Llosa 1975) also cover the same ground. The ridicule and heavy irony with which he characterizes left-wing student politicians in *Mayta* is one source of enjoyment for readers. When the University of Piura was taken over by Opus Dei and all political discussion was banned, Vargas Llosa praised its reorganization.

[32]Even Basadre became aware of possible permutations of his original formulation. In 1978 he called for regional assemblies to elaborate a National Plan that would be representative of "profound" Peru, and not of "superficial" Peru (Basadre 1978c:563).

[33]"I have used the metaphor of 'a view through an Andean kaleidoscope' because of the process of my own reflections as I constructed an orderly presentation of my data" (Isbell 1978:11). The major themes (positions of the mirrors) Isbell highlights are: duality, complementarity, symmetry/assymmetry, and polarization between the foreign dominators and the members of the community (Isbell 1978:11).

[34]Judge Ventura Huayhua had exposed a weakness in Vargas Llosa that was to be exploited during the author's subsequent political campaign. This weakness cost him the presidency in 1990. During this campaign, the widows of the journalists sat in Fujimori camp among the audience during the televised presidential debate. One of them, however, declared herself for Vargas Llosa, whereupon the leftist newspapers accused her of being a "class traitor."

[35]General Noel believes this story, too (Noel 1989:56, 62, 92).

[36]Juan Ossio, having been a member of the Vargas Llosa Commission, circulated a petition that was published as a paid advertisement in a Lima newspaper pointing out that it is unfair to pass judgment on individuals for collective acts. It also mentioned that many terrorists had been released by the judicial system, and those who were sentenced had been given shorter prison terms than the three comuneros of Uchuraccay (Ossio 1988a). When Simeón Aucatoma died, Ossio published a moving obituary notice in a newspaper with the self-explanatory title "Is it a crime to be an Indian?" In it he said: "In the national context, Simeón Aucatoma's Indian condition, along with that of his companions, has caused him to become the scapegoat of a society that because it does not want to face reality has washed its conscience by sanctioning its weakest member" (Ossio 1988b).

[37]In his novel *The Real Life of Alejandro Mayta* (1986), Vargas Llosa conducts an inquest to reconstruct the revolutionaries' passage through Quero, an Andean community near Jauja. There, too, the narrator Vargas Llosa does not leave the village square, and there, too, he relies on the help of an interpreter and authority figure (the justice of the peace) to reconstruct events. In the novel, however, individual witnesses are named and described, and the novel's literary strength depends on the difficulty of sorting out different versions of "truth" and "lies."

[38]In the Quechua language it is necessary to add a suffix to every sentence to distinguish what is based on personal witness of the speaker from hearsay. Were the report ever to be translated into Quechua, every sentence would have to be qualified as ''hearsay.''

[39]Lope de Vega's play is based on a historical incident. In 1476, the people of Fuenteovejuna, Spain, killed the odious Fernán Gómez de Guzmán, Comendador of the Chivalric Order of Calatrava, their lord. ''He was killed by the villagers allegedly on account of the brutal treatment which he had inflicted on the community for a long period. When the royal authorities arrived to investigate the incident, all the villagers, even when tortured, refused to say more than 'Fuenteovejuna lo hizo,' with the result that no individual culprit for the killing could be identified, and nobody was eventually put on trial'' (Hall 1985: 11). Fuenteovejuna is taught in Peruvian high schools.

[40]Latest count in NACLA Report 1990 Vol XXIV, No. 4.

References Cited

Alberti, Giorgio, and Enrique Mayer, eds.
  1974   Reciprocidad e intercambio en los Andes peruanos. Lima: Instituto de Estudios Peruanos.
Albó, Xavier
  1987   From MNRistas to Kataristas to Katari. In Resistance, Rebellion, and Consciousness in the Andean Peasant World, 18th to 20th Centuries. Steve Stern, ed. Pp. 379–419. Madison: University of Wisconsin Press.
Anderson, James
  1987   Sendero Luminoso: A New Revolutionary Model? London: Institute for the Study of Terrorism.
Andreas, Carol
  1990   Women at War. NACLA Report on the Americas, Fatal Attraction: Peru's Shining Path XXIV(4):20–23.
Ansión, Juan, and Eudoisio Sifuentes
  1989   La imagen popular de la violencia, a través de los relatos de degolladores. In Pishtacos: de verdugos a sacaojos. Juan Ansión, ed. Pp. 61–105. Lima: Edición Tarea.
Amnesty International
  1985   Peru: Amnesty International Briefing. London: Amnesty International Publications.
  1989   Peru: Human Rights in a State of Emergency. London: Amnesty International Publications.
Arguedas, José María
  1978   El zorro de arriba y el zorro de abajo. Spain: CSIC.
Arias, Arturo
  1990   Changing Indian Identity: Guatemala's Violent Transition to Modernity. In Guatemalan Indians and the State: 1540 to 1988. Austin: University of Texas Press.
Basadre, Jorge
  1947[1929]   La multitud, la ciudad y el campo en la historia del Peru. Lima: Editorial Huascarán.
  1978a[1943] 1945.   In Apertura: Textos sobre temas de historia, educación, cultura y política, escritos entre 1924 y 1977. Patricio Ricketts, ed. Pp. 489–494.
  1978b[1931]   Perú problema y posibilidad: segunda edición con el apendice, algunas considetaciones 47 años despues. Lima: Banco Internacional del Peru.

1978c   Mentira of factibilidad del Perú. *In* Apertura: Textos sobre temas de historia, educación, cultura y política, escritos entre 1924 y 1977. Patricio Ricketts, ed. Pp. 549–565. Lima: Ediciones Taller.

Béjar, Hector

1973   Las guerrillas de 1965: balance y perspectiva. Lima: Ediciones PEISA.

Berg, Ronald

1987   Sendero Luminoso and the Peasantry of Andahuaylas. Journal of Inter-American Studies and World Affairs 28(4):165–196.

Bonfil Batalla, Guillermo

1981   Utopía y revolución: el pensamiento político contemporáneo de los indios en América Latina. Guillermo Bonfil Batalla, ed. Mexico: Editorial Nueva Imagen.

1987   Mexico profundo: una civilización negada. Mexico: CIESAS.

Bourricaud, François

1989   Poder y sociedad en el Perú. Lima: Instituto de Estudios Peruanos.

Brandt, Hans Jürgen, ed.

1987   Legalidad, derecho consuetudinario y administración de justicia en comunidades campesinas y zonas rurales andinas. *In* Justicia popular. Pp. 101–166. Lima: Centro de investigaciones judiciales de la corte suprema de justicia de la república.

Burt, Jo Marie

1990   Counterinsurgency = Impunity. *In* NACLA Report on the Americas, Fatal Attraction: Peru's Shining Path XXIV(4):30–31.

Caballero, José María

1980   Economía agraria de la sierra peruana antes de la reforma agraria de 1969. Lima: Instituto de Estudios Peruanos.

Caretas: Ilustración Peruana

1984a   Caso Uchuraccay: la tremenda corte. 828:21–23.

1984b   Esta también es el APRA ¿Que les Pareca? 828:23.

1984c   Huachuajasa el lugar de la masacre. 829:23–24.

Chávez de Paz, Denis

1989   Juventud y terrorismo: características sociales de los condenados por terrorismo y otros delitos. Lima: Instituto de Estudios Peruanos.

Claverías, Ricardo, Elizeo Zeballos, and Jesus Tumi

n.d.   Teorías sobre el capitalismo en la agricultura y el problema regional en el Perú: 1893–1983. El caso del movimiento regional de Puno. Puno: Instituto de Investigaciones para el Desarrollo Social del Altiplano.

Comisión Especial del Senado Sobre las Causas de la Violenia y Alternativas de Pacificación en el Perú

1990   Violencia y pacificación. Lima: DESCO and Comisión Andina de Juristas.

de Trazegnies, Fernando

1977   El caso Huayanay: el derecho en situacion límite. Cuadernos Agrarios, No. 1. Lima.

1978   El ocaso de los heroes. Cuadernos Agrarios, No. 2. Lima.

1983   Informe. *In* Informe de la comision investigadora de los sucesos de Uchuraccay, Anexo 1. Vargas Llosa et al., eds. Pp. 127–152. Lima: Editora Peru.

1984   Proceso de Uchuraccay: ¿Ritual de justicia? Caretas 821:45–66.

De Janvri, Alain

1981   The Agrarian Question and Reformism in Latin America. Baltimore: Johns Hopkins University Press.

Degregori, Carlos Iván
  1989   Entre los fuegos de sendero y el ejército: regreso de los pishtacos. *In* Pishtacos: de verduguos a sacaojos. Juan Ansión, ed. Pp. 109–114. Lima: Ediciones Taréa.
  1990   Ayacucho 1969–1979: el surgimiento de sendero luminoso. Lima: Instituto de Estudios Peruanos.
  1991   A Dwarf Star. NACLA Report on the American XXIV(4):10–17.
DESCO Resumen Semenal
  1983   Terrorismo 206(6):7.
Díaz Martinez, Antonio
  1969   Ayacucho, hambre y esperanza. Ayacucho: Ediciones Waman Puma.
Favre, Henri
  1984   Sentier lumineux et horizons obscurs. Problemes d'Amerique Latine 72:3–27.
Flores Galindo, Alberto
  1988   Pensando el horror. *In* Tiempo de plagas. Pp. 185–190. Lima: Ediciones Caballo Rojo.
Gorriti, Gustavo
  1990   Historia de la guerra milenaria en el Perú. Lima: Editorial Apoyo.
Guzman, Abimael
  1988   Presidente Gonzalo Rompe el silencio: entrevista en la clandestinidad. (Originally published in El Diario, July 24, 1988. English version available from Red Banner Editorial House.)
Hall, J. B.
  1985   Lope de Vega Fuenteovejuna. Critical Guides to Spanish Texts. London: Grant & Cutler Ltd.
Isbell, Billie Jean
  1978   To Defend Ourselves: Ecology and Ritual in an Andean Village. Austin: University of Texas Press.
  1991   Responses to Shining Path in Provincial Ayacucho in the 1980s. *In* The Shining Path of Peru. David Scott Palmer, ed. New York: St. Martin's Press (in press).
Kapsoli Escudero, Wilfredo
  1987   Los movimientos campesinos en el Perú 1879–1965. Lima: Editorial Atusparia.
Krueger, Christine E.
  1980   Pedro Ruiz Gallo National University, Peru: A Case Study in the Anthropology of University Organization. Ph.D. dissertation, University of Florida, Gainesville.
J. C. F.
  1988   Pensamiento Gonzalo: marxismo del nuevo siglo (VIII). El Diario, June 9:12.
Lope de Vega
  1982[1619]   Comedia famosa de Fuenteovejuna. Madrid: Ediciones Cátedra.
Lumbreras, Luis Guillermo
  1983   Declara el Dr. Luis Guillermo Lumbreras: Informe de Uchuraccay descriptivo e incompleto. El Observador. March 18, Pp. 15–16, and continued March 19, Pp. 15–16.
Lynch, Nicolas, et. al.
  1990   Los jóvenes rojos de San Marcos: radicalismo universitario de los años 70. Lima: El Zorro de Abajo Ediciones.
Macera, Pablo
  1983   Entrevista al Dr. Pablo Macera Uchuraccay: ¿Crimen sim castigo? La República. March 19, p. 11.

Manrique, Nelson
1990   Time of Fear. *In* NACLA Report on the Americas, Fatal Attraction: Peru's Shining Path XXIV(4):28–38.

Mariategui, José Carlos
1971[1928]   7 ensayos de interpretación de la realidad peruana. Lima: Empresa Editora
Amauta.

Matos Mar, José
1984   El desborde popular y crisis del estado. Lima: Instituto de Estudios Peruanos.

Mayer, Enrique
1970   Mestizo e Indio: el contexto social de las pelaciones interétnicas. *In* El Indio y
el Poder en el Peru. Fernando Fuenzalida, Enrique Mayer, Gabriel Escobar, François
Bourricaud, José Matos Mar, eds. Pp. 87–152. Lima: Instituto de Estudios Peruanos.

Milla Batres, Carlos, ed.
1990   En qué momento se jodió el Perú. Lima: Editorial Milla Batres.

Millones, Luis
1983   La tragedia de Uchuraccay: informe sobre sendero. *In* Informe de la comision
investigadora de lo sucesos de Uchuraccay, Anexo 2. Vargas Llosa et al., ed. Pp. 85–
102. Lima: Editora Peru.

Montoya, Rodrigo
1974   Capitalismo y no capitalismo en el Perú: un estudio histórico de su articulación
en un eje regional. Lima: Mosca Azul Editores.
1980   Lucha por la tierra, reformas agrarias y capitalismo en el Peru del siglo XX.
Lima: Mosca Azul Editores.
1983   Entrevista al Dr. Rodrigo Montoya: Uchuraccay ¿Crimen sim castigo? La República. March 19, p. 7.

Mörner, Magnus
1985   The Andean Past: Land, Societies and Conflicts. New York: Columbia University Press.

NACLA Report on the Americas
1989   Coca: The Real Green Revolution. Vol. XVII(6):12–40.

Noel Moral, Roberto C.
1989   Ayacucho: testimonio de un soldado. Lima: CONCYTEC.

O'Phelan Godoy, Scarlett
1988   Un siglo de rebeliones anticoloniales: Perú y Bolivia 1700–1783. Cusco: Centro
de Estudios Rurales Andinos ''Bartolomé de las Casas.''

Orlove, Benjamin
1980   The Position of Rustlers in Regional Society: Social Banditry in the Andes. *In*
Land and Power in Latin America: Agrarian Economies and Social Processes in the
Andes. Benjamin S. Orlove and G. Custred, eds. Pp. 170–194. New York: Holmes
and Meier Publishers Inc.

Ossio, Juan
1983a   Sobre el juicio de los comuneros de Uchuraccay. Expreso, Lima, July 31, 1983,
p. 9.
1983b   ¿El delito de ser indio en el Perú? Expreso, Lima, January 6, 1983, p. 2.

Ossio, Juan, and Fernando Fuenzalida
1983   Informe sobre Uchuraccay. *In* Informe de la comision investigadora de los sucesos de Uchuraccay, Anexo 1. Vargas Llosa et al., eds. Pp. 43–81. Lima: Editora
Peru.

Osterling, Jorge P., and Hector Martínez
    1983   Notes for a History of Peruvian Social Anthropology, 1940–80. Current Anthropology 24(3):343–360.
Pásara, Luis
    1984   Perú: ¿Administración de justica? In La administración de la justica en América Latina. Lima: Consejo Latinoamericano de Derecho y Desarrollo.
Platt, Tristan
    1986   Mirrors and Maize: The Concept of Yanantin Among the Macha of Bolivia. In Anthropological History Andean Polities. John V. Murra, Nathan Wachtel, and Jacques Revel, eds. Pp. 228–259. Cambridge: Cambridge University Press.
Poole, Deborah
    1984   Ritual-Economic Calendars in Paruro: The Structure of Representation in Andean Ethnography. Ph.D. dissertation, University of Illinois, Urbana-Champaign.
    1988   Landscape of Power in a Cattle-Rustling Culture of Southern Andean Peru. Dialectical Anthropology 12:367–398.
Poole, Deborah, and Gerardo Rénique
    1991   The New Chroniclers of Peru: U.S. Scholars and their "Shining Path" of Peasant Revolution. Bulletin of Latin American Research 10(1).
Portocarrero, Gonzalo, and Patricia Oliart
    1989   El Perú desde la escuela. Lima: Instituto de Apoyo Agrario.
Prescott, William H.
    1893   The History of the Conquest of Peru. Philadelphia: J. B. Lippincott, Co.
Quijano, Anibal
    1980   Dominación y cultura, lo cholo y el conflicto cultural en el Peru. Lima: Mosca Azul Editores.
Quintanilla, Lino
    1982   Andahuaylas: la lucha por la tierra. Lima: Mosca Azul Editores.
Rénique, José Luis
    1991   The Revolution Behind Bars. In NACLA Report on the Americas, Fatal Attraction: Peru's Shining Path XXIV(4):17–19.
Rodriguez Pastor, Humerto
    1985   La antropología en el Perú. Lima: Concejo National de Ciencia y Tecnologia.
Rubio Gorrea, Marcial
    1984   Testigos de "primera" y poderes de "Segunda" ¿Proceso en tela de juicio? Quehacer 32:12–17.
Said, Edward
    1979   Orientalism. New York: Vintage Books.
Salcedo, José María
    1984   Las tumbas de Uchuraccay. Lima: Cóndor Editores.
Scott, James C.
    1986   Weapons of the Weak. New Haven: Yale University Press.
Skar, Harald
    1982   Warm Valley People: Duality and Land Reform Among Quechua Indians of Highland Peru. Oslo: Universitetsforlaget.
Smith, Carol A.
    1990   History and Revolution in Guatemala. In Guatemalan Indians and the State: 1540–1988. Carol Smith, ed. Pp. 258–286. Austin: University of Texas Press.
Soberón, Luis
    1986   Las ciencias sociales y el desarrollo rural del Perú. Lima: FOMCIENCIAS.

Soto, Hernando de
   1988   The Other Path: The Invisible Revolution in the Third World. New York: Harper
      & Row.
Starn, Orin
   1991   Missing the Revolution: Anthropologists and the War in Peru. Cultural Anthro-
      pology 6(1):63–91.
Stern, Steve J.
   1987   Resistance, Rebellion, and Consciousness in the Andean Peasant World, 18th to
      20th Centuries. Madison: University of Wisconsin Press.
Szeminski, Jan
   1987   Why Kill the Spaniard? New Perspectives on Andean Insurrectionary Ideology
      in the 18th Century. *In* Resistance, Rebellion, and Consciousness in the Andean Peas-
      ant World, 18th to 20th Centuries. Steve J. Stern, ed. Pp. 166–193. Madison: Uni-
      versity of Wisconsin Press.
Taylor, Lewis
   1983   Maoism in the Andes: Sendero Luminoso and the Contemporary Guerrilla
      Movement in Peru. Working Paper 2, Centre for Latin American Studies, University
      of Liverpool, England.
Vargas Llosa, Mario
   1975   Conversation in the Cathedral. Gregory Rebasa, trans. New York: Harper &
      Row.
   1983   Inquest in the Andes. New York Times Magazine, July 31.
   1984   Historia de Mayta. Barcelona: Editorial Siex Barral.
   1986   The Real Life of Alejandro Mayta. New York: Farrar, Strauss, Grioux.
   1987   El Hablador. Barcelona: Editorial Siex Barral.
   1989   The Storyteller. New York: Farrar, Strauss, Grioux.
   1990   Questions of Conquest: What Columbus Wrought, and What He Did Not. Har-
      per's, December, 45–46.
   1991   Sangre y mugre en Uchuraccay. *In* Contra viento y marea III. Pp. 85–220. Bar-
      celona: Editorial Siex Barral.
Vargas Llosa, Mario, Abraham Guzman Figueroa, and Mario Castro Arenas
   1983   Informe de la comision investigadora de los sucesos de Uchuraccay. Lima: Ed-
      itora Peru.
Whitten, Norman
   1981   Cultural Transformations and Ethnicity in Modern Ecuador. Urbana: University
      of Illinois Press.
   1991   The Ecuadorian Levantamiento Indígena 1980 and the Epitomizing Symbol of
      1992 (in press).
Zuidema, R. T., and Ulpiano Quispe
   1973   A Visit to God: A Religious Experience in the Peruvian Community of Choque-
      Huarcaya. *In* People and Cultures of Native South America. Daniel R. Gross, ed. Pp.
      358–373. Garden City, N.Y.: Natural History Press.

"Speaking with Names": Language and Landscape Among the Western Apache

Keith H. Basso

> What we call the landscape is generally considered to be something "out there." But, while some aspects of the landscape are clearly external to both our bodies and our minds, what each of us actually experiences is selected, shaped, and colored by what we know.
>
> Barrie Greenbie, *Spaces*

An unfamiliar landscape, like an unfamiliar language, is always a little daunting, and when the two are encountered together—as they are, commonly enough, in those out-of-the-way communities where ethnographers have a tendency to crop up—the combination may be downright unsettling. From the outset, of course, neither landscape nor language can be ignored. On the contrary, the shapes and colors and contours of the land, together with the shifting sounds and cadences of native discourse, thrust themselves upon the newcomer with a force so vivid and direct as to be virtually inescapable. Yet for all of their sensory immediacy (and there are occasions, as any ethnographer will attest, when the sheer constancy of it grows to formidable proportions) landscape and discourse seem resolutely out of reach. Although close at hand and tangible in the extreme, each in its own way appears remote and inaccessible, anonymous and indistinct, and somehow, implausibly, a shade less than fully believable. And neither one, as if determined to accentuate these conflicting impressions, may seem the least bit interested in having them resolved. Emphatically "there" but conspicuously lacking in accustomed forms of order and arrangement, landscape and discourse confound the stranger's efforts to invest them with significance, and this uncommon predicament, which produces nothing if not uncertainty, can be keenly disconcerting.

Surrounded by foreign geographical objects and intractable acts of speech, even the most practiced ethnographers become diffident and cautious. For the meanings of objects and acts alike can only be guessed at, and once the guesses have been recognized for the arbitrary constructions they almost always are, one senses acutely that one's own experience of things and events "out there" cannot be used as a reliable guide to the experience of native people (Conklin 1962; Frake

1962). In other words, one must acknowledge that local understandings of external realities are ineluctably fashioned from local cultural materials, and that, knowing little or nothing of the latter, one's ability to make appropriate sense of "what is" and "what occurs" in one's environment is bound to be deficient (Goodenough 1964). For better or worse, the ethnographer sees, landscape and speech acts do not interpret their own significance. Initially at least, and typically for many months to come, this is a task that only members of the indigenous community are adequately equipped to accomplish; and accomplish it they do, day in and day out, with enviably little difficulty. For where native men and women are concerned the external world *is* as it appears to them to be—naturally, unproblematically, and more or less consistently—and rarely do they have reason to consider that the coherence it displays is an intricate product of their own collective manufacture (Schutz 1967). Cultures run deep, as the saying goes, and natives everywhere take their "natives' point of view" very much for granted.

In this way (or something roughly like it) the ethnographer comes to appreciate that features of the local landscape, no less than utterances exchanged in forms of daily discourse, acquire value and significance by virtue of the ideational systems with which they are apprehended and construed. Symbolically constituted, socially transmitted, and individually applied, such systems operate to place flexible constraints on how the physical environment can (and should) be known, how its occupants can (and should) be found to act, and how the doings of both can (and should) be discerned to affect each other (Sahlins 1976). Accordingly, each system delineates a distinctive way of being-in-the-world (Ricoeur 1979), an informal logic for engaging the world and thinking about the engagement (Geertz 1973), an array of conceptual frameworks for organizing experience and rendering it intelligible (Goffman 1974). In any community, the meanings assigned to geographical features and acts of speech will be influenced by the subjective determinations of the people who assign them, and these determinations, needless to say, will exhibit variation. But the character of the meanings—their steadier themes, their recurrent tonalities, and, above all, their conventionalized modes of expression—will bear the stamp of a common cast of mind. Constructions of reality that reflect conceptions of reality itself, the meanings of landscapes and acts of speech are personalized manifestations of a shared perspective on the human condition (Shutz 1967).

Mulling over these apparent truths, the ethnographer is likely to notice that members of the local community involve themselves with their geographical landscape in at least three distinct ways. First, they may simply observe the landscape, attending for reasons of their own to aspects of its appearance and to sundry goings-on within it. Second, they may utilize the landscape, engaging in a broad range of physical activities that, depending on their duration and extent, may leave portions of the landscape visibly modified. Third, native people may communicate about the landscape, formulating descriptions and other representations of it that they share in the course of social gatherings. On many occasions, community members can be observed to alternate freely among these different modes of involvement (they may also, of course, combine them), but it is obvious that events in the latter mode—communicative acts of topographic representation—will be most revealing of the conceptual instruments with which native people interpret their natural surroundings. And although such representations may be fashioned from a variety of semiotic materials (gestural, pictorial, musical, and others), it is equally plain that few will be more instructive in this regard than those that are wrought with words.

Ordinary talk, the ethnographer sees, provides a readily available window onto the structure and significance of other peoples' worlds, and so (slowly at first, by fits and starts, and never without protracted bouts of guessing) he or she begins to learn to listen. And also to freshly see. For as native concepts and beliefs find external purchase on specific features of the local topography, the entire landscape seems to acquire a crisp new dimension that moves it more surely into view. What earlier appeared as a circular sweep of undifferentiated natural architecture now starts to emerge as a precise arrangement of named sites and localities, each of which is distinguished by a set of physical attributes and cultural associations that marks it as unique. In native discourse, the local landscape falls neatly and repeatedly into *places*—and places, as Franz Boas (1934) emphasized some years ago, are social constructions *par excellence*.

It is excessive to claim, as George Trager (1968:537) has done, that "the way man talks about the physical universe is his only way of knowing anything about it." Nonetheless, most ethnographers would agree that Trager's claim contains a substantial amount of truth, and some have suggested that this can be seen with particular clarity where language and landscapes are concerned (Berndt 1976; Conklin 1957; Evans-Pritchard 1949; Malinowski 1920; Sapir 1912). For whenever the members of a community speak about their landscape—whenever they name it, or classify it, or evaluate it, or move to tell stories about it—they unthinkingly represent it in ways that are compatible with shared understandings of how, in the fullest sense, they know themselves to occupy it. Which is simply to note that in conversational encounters, trivial and otherwise, individuals exchange accounts and observations of the landscape that consistently presuppose (and therefore depend for both their credibility and appropriateness upon) mutually held ideas of what the landscape actually is, why its constituent places are important, and how it may intrude on the practical affairs of its inhabitants. Thus, if frequently by implication and allusion only, bits and pieces of a common worldview are given situated relevance and made temporarily accessible. In talk about the landscape, as Martin Heidegger (1977:323) so aptly put it, cultural conceptions of "dwelling together" are naively placed on oblique display.

At the same time, however, and often just as obliquely, persons who engage in this sort of talk will also exchange messages about aspects of the social encounter in which they are jointly involved, including their framings of the encounter itself (i.e, "what is going on here") and their morally guided assessments of the comportment of fellow participants. Consequently, the possibility arises that as speakers communicate about the landscape and the kinds of dealings they have with it, they may also communicate about themselves as social actors and the kinds of dealings they are having with one another. Stated more precisely, statements pertaining to the landscape may be employed strategically to convey indexical messages about the organization of face-to-face relationships and the normative footings on which these relationships are currently being negotiated. Indirectly perhaps, but tellingly all the same, participants in verbal encounters thus put their landscapes to work—interactional work—and how they choose to go about it may shed interesting light on matters other than geography (Basso 1984). For example, when a character in a short story by Paul Gallico (1954:69) says to his chronically unfaithful lover, "Go make a nest on Forty-Second Street," it is altogether clear that he is drawing upon the cultural meaning of a place to communicate something important about their disturbed and precarious relationship.

From the standpoint of the ethnographer, then, situated talk of geographical landscapes is more than a valuable resource for exploring local conceptions of the material universe. In addition, and surely just as basic, this sort of talk may be useful for interpreting forms of social action that regularly occur within it. For landscapes are always available to their seasoned inhabitants in other than material terms. Landscapes are available in symbolic terms as well, and so, chiefly through the manifold agencies of speech, they can be "detached" from their fixed spatial moorings and transformed into instruments of thought and vehicles of purposive behavior. Thus transformed, landscapes and the places that fill them become tools for the imagination, expressive means for accomplishing verbal deeds, and also, of course, eminently portable possessions to which individuals can maintain deep and abiding attachments, regardless of where they travel. In these ways, as N. Scott Momaday (1974) has observed, men and women learn to *appropriate* their landscapes, to think and act "with" them as well as about and upon them, and to weave them with spoken words into the very foundations of social life.[1] And in these ways, too, as every ethnographer eventually comes to appreciate, geographical landscapes are never culturally vacant. Filled to brimming with past and present significance, the trick is to try to fathom (and here, really, is where the ethnographic challenge lies) what it is that a particular landscape may be called upon to "say," and what, through the saying, it may be called upon to "do."

But where to begin and how to proceed? How, in any community, to identify the conceptual frameworks and verbal practices with which members appropriate their local geography? One promising approach, I want to suggest, is to attend to native placenames and the full variety of communicative functions served by acts of naming in different social contexts. It may be noted in this regard that placenames, or toponyms, comprise a distinct semantic domain in the lexicons of all known languages, and that the formal properties of placename systems, together with their spatial correlates and etymological histories, have long been objects of anthropological inquiry.[2] But the common activity of placenaming—the actual use of toponyms in concrete instances of everyday speech—has attracted little attention from linguists or ethnographers.[3] Less often still has placenaming been investigated as a universal means—and, it could well turn out, a universally primary means—for appropriating physical environments.

The reasons for this innocuous piece of scholarly neglect are undoubtedly several, but the main one arises from a widespread view of language in which proper names are assumed to have meaning solely in their capacity to refer and, as agents of reference, to enter into simple and complex predictions (Lyons 1977; Russell 1940). Many of the limitations imposed by this narrow conception of meaning have been exposed and criticized in recent years, most ably by linguistic anthropologists and philosophers of language who have shown that reference, though unquestionably a vital linguistic function, is but one of many that spoken utterances can be made to perform (Donnellan 1972; Hymes 1974; Searle 1958, 1969; Silverstein 1976; Strawson 1959; Tyler 1978). But despite these salutary developments, and unhappily for students who seek to understand linguistic meaning as an emergent property of verbal interaction, the idea persists in many quarters that proper names, including toponyms, serve as referential vehicles whose only purpose is to denote, or "pick out," objects in the world.[4]

If a certain myopia attaches to this position, there is irony as well, for place-names are arguably among the most highly charged and richly evocative of all linguistic symbols.[5] Because of their inseparable connection to specific localities, placenames may be used to summon forth an enormous range of mental and emotional associations—associations of time and space, of history and events, of persons and social activities, of oneself and stages in one's life. And in their capacity to evoke, in their compact power to muster and consolidate so much of what a landscape may be taken to represent in both personal and cultural terms, placenames acquire a functional value that easily matches their utility as instruments of reference. Most notably, as T. S. Eliot (1932) and Seamus Heany (1980) have remarked, placenames provide materials for resonating ellipsis, for speaking and writing in potent shorthand, for communicating much while saying very little. Poets and songwriters have long understood that economy of expression may enhance the quality and force of aesthetic discourse, and that placenames stand ready to be exploited for this purpose. Linguists and anthropologists would do well to understand that in many communities similar considerations may influence common forms of spoken interaction, and that, in this arena too, placenames may occupy a privileged position. For these and other reasons, an ethnographic approach to the activity of placenaming seems well worth pursuing. The present essay, which now takes a sharp ethnographic turn, is offered as an illustration of where such an approach may lead, and why, beyond the illumination of specific cases, it may also shed light on matters of general interest.

II

Of old names, old places.

—Edmond Rostand, *Cyrano de Bergerac*

The Western Apache residents of Cibecue, an isolated settlement located near the center of the Fort Apache Indian Reservation in east-central Arizona, are not adverse to talking about each other, and some of them—like Lola Machuse—

seem to enjoy it immensely.[6] "I'm intress in evybody!" Lola will exclaim in her distinctive variety of English, and everyone in Cibecue knows she speaks the truth. Just over fifty years old, she is a handsome woman with large brown eyes, a sharply defined nose, and splendidly shaped hands that are hardly ever still. The mother of seven children, she divides her time between caring for the needs of her family, collecting plants for use in herbal medicines, participating in ritual activities, and . . . well, gossiping. Which is, within certain limits, just as it should be. Middle-aged Apache women are expected to keep themselves informed at all times of what is going on in their communities, and those who have led exemplary lives, such as Lola Machuse, are also expected to comment on their findings. And comment Lola does—intelligently, incisively, usually sympathetically, and always with an unquenchable enthusiasm for nuance and detail that can be as amusing as it is sometimes overwhelming. Western Apache communities, like small communities everywhere, operate largely by word of mouth, and people from Cibecue have suggested more than once that Lola Machuse is practically a community unto herself.

It is a hot afternoon in the middle of July and Lola Machuse is working at home. Seated in the shade of a large brush-covered ramada, she is mending clothes in the company of her husband, Robert, two Apache women named Emily and Louise, and another visitor, myself, who has come by to settle a small debt and get a drink of water.[7] The heat of the afternoon is heavy and oppressive, and there is little to do but gaze at the landscape that stretches out before us: a narrow valley, bisected by a shallow stream lined with cottonwood trees, which rises abruptly to embrace a broken series of red sandstone bluffs, and, beyond the bluffs, a flat expanse of grassy plain ending in the distance at the base of a low range of mountains. Fearsome in the blazing sun, the country around Cibecue lies motionless and inert, thinly shrouded in patches of light bluish haze. Nothing stirs except for Clifford, the Machuse's ancient yellow dog, who shifts his position in the dust, groans fitfully, and snaps at the passing of a fly. Silence.

The silence is broken by Louise, who reaches into her oversized purse for a can of Pepsi-Cola, jerks it open with a loud snap, and begins to speak in the Cibecue dialect of Western Apache. She speaks softly, haltingly, and with long pauses to accentuate the seriousness of what she is saying. Late last night, she reports, sickness assailed her younger brother. Painful cramps gnawed at his stomach. Numbness crept up his legs and into his thighs. He vomitted three times in rapid succession. He looked extremely pale. In the morning, just before dawn, he was driven to the hospital at Whiteriver. The people who had gathered at his camp were worried and frightened and talked about what happened. One of them, Louise's cousin, recalled that several months ago, when her brother was working on a cattle roundup near a place named *tsibiyi'itin* ("trail extends into a grove of stick-like trees"), he had inadvertently stepped on a snakeskin that lay wedged in a crevice between some rocks. Another member of the roundup crew, who witnessed the incident, cautioned the young man that contact with snakes is always dangerous and urged him to immediately seek the services of a "snake medicine person" *(tł'iish diiyin)*. But Louise's younger brother had only smiled, remarking tersely that he was not alarmed and that no harm would befall him.

Louise, who is plainly worried and upset by these events, pauses and sips from her drink. After a minute or so, having regained her composure, she begins to speak again. But Lola Machuse quietly interrupts her. Emily and Robert will speak as well. What follows is a record of their discourse, together with English translations of the utterances.[8]

Louise:	*shidizhé . . .* ("My younger brother . . .")
Lola:	*tsé hadigaiyé yú 'ágodzaa.* ("It happened at line of white rocks extends upward and out, at this very place!")
	[Pause: 30–45 seconds]
Emily:	*ha'aa. túzhį' yahigaiyé yú'ágodzaa.* ("Yes. It happened at whiteness spreads out descending to water, at this very place!")
	[Pause: 30–45 seconds]
Lola:	*da'aníí. k'is deeschii'naaditiné yú'ágodzaa.* ("Truly. It happened a trail extends across a long red ridge with alder trees, at this very place!")
Louise:	[laughs softly]
Robert:	*gozhoo dooleeł* ("Pleasantness and goodness will be forthcoming.")
Lola:	*gozhoo dooleeł* ("Pleasantness and goodness will be forthcoming.")
Louise:	*shidizhé bíni'éshid ne góshé?* ("My younger brother is foolish, isn't he, dog?")

Following this brief exchange, talk ceases under the brush-covered ramada, and everyone retreats into the privacy of their own thoughts. Louise drinks again from her can of Pepsi-Cola and passes it on to Emily. Lola Machuse returns to her sewing, while Robert studies a horse in a nearby corral. Only Clifford, who has launched a feverish attack on an itch below his ear, seems unaffected by what has been said. Silence once again.

But what *has* been said? To what set of personal and social ends? And why in such a clipped and cryptic fashion? If these questions create problems for us (and that they do, I think, can be assumed), it is because we are dealing with a spate of conversation whose organization eludes us, a strip of Western Apache verbal doings whose animating aims and purposes seem obscure. But why? The problem is not that the literal meanings of utterances comprising the conversation are in any way difficult to grasp. On the contrary, anyone with a passing knowledge of Western Apache grammar could attest that each of the utterances, taken as a sentence type, is well-formed in all respects, and that each presents one or more simple claims whose positive truth-value no Apache would presume to dispute. It is not, then, on the surface of the utterances—or, as some linguists might prefer to say, at the level of their propositional content—where our interpretive difficulties lie.

What is puzzling about this snippet of Western Apache talk is that we are unable to account for the ways in which its constituent utterances are related to each other. Put more exactly, we lack the knowledge required to establish sequential relations among the utterances, the unstated premises and assumptions that order the utterances, just as they occur, into a piece of meaningful discourse. It is by no means evident, for example, how Lola Machuse's statement ("It happened at line of white rocks extends upward and out, at this very place!") should be related to Louise's narrative about her ailing brother. Neither is it clear how Emily's assertion ("Yes. It happened at whiteness spreads out descending to water, at this very place!") should be interpreted as a response to the narrative or to Lola's statement. What are we to make of Lola's response to Emily ("Truly. It happened at trail extends across a long red ridge with alder trees, at this very place!"), and why should it be, as things are coming to a close, that Louise sees fit to address the Machuse's dog? Our puzzlement persists throughout, causing us to experience the text of the conversation as fragmented and disjointed, as oddly unmotivated, as failing to come together as a whole. In short, we are unable to place a construction on the text that invests it with *coherence,* and so, in the end, we cannot know with any certainty what the conversation itself may have been about. Lola Machuse and her companions have surely accomplished something with their talk. But what?

The episode at Cibecue exemplifies a venerable practice with which Western Apache speakers exploit the evocative power of placenames to comment on the moral conduct of persons who are absent from the scene. Called "speaking with names" *(yałti' bee' ízhi),* this verbal routine also allows those who engage in it to register claims about their own moral worth, aspects of their social relationships with other people on hand, and a particular way of attending to the local landscape that is avowed to produce a beneficial form of heightened self-awareness. And as if this were not enough, much of what gets said and done is attributed to unseen "ancestors" *(nohwizą́' yé)* who are prompted by the voices of conversational participants to communicate in a collective voice that no one actually hears. All in all, "speaking with names" is a rather subtle and subterranean affair.

To reach an understanding of this practice and the sources of its coherence for Western Apache people, I shall assume that spoken discourse is a cooperative activity in which individuals seek, within the bounds of negotiated social proprieties, to accomplish a range of purposes. I shall also assume that participants in many kinds of discourse use language to explore with each other the significance of past and potential events, drawing from these examinations certain consequences for their past and future actions. Finally, I shall assume that speakers pursue such objectives by producing utterances that are intended to perform several speech acts simultaneously, and that hearers, making dexterous use of relevant bodies of cultural knowledge, react and respond to them at different levels of abstraction. Spoken discourse, then, is more than a chain of situated utterances. Rather, as Labov and Fanshel (1977:26–28) have shown, discourse consists in a developing matrix of utterances and actions, bound together by a web of shared understandings pertinent to both, which serves as an expanding context for interpreting the meanings of utterances and actions alike. More a matter of linguistic function than linguistic form, coherence in discourse is achieved when participants put their utterances to interlocking forms of mutually recognizable work

(Becker 1982; Labov and Fanshel 1977:65–81; Pike 1978). More a matter of implicit doings than explicit sayings, coherence is what participants hear (though generally they fail to notice hearing it) when their work is going well.

At Lola Machuse's somnolent camp, where the work of discourse went off without a hitch, coherence was never in question. Neither was the smooth implementation of a Western Apache technique for appropriating the natural landscape, a distinctive cultural framework for interpreting the landscape and turning it by means of speech to specific social ends. Never in question, that is, to anyone but myself—a superfluous, slightly stupefied, and keenly perplexed outsider. What the devil did Lola Machuse and those other Apaches imagine themselves to be up to as they sat around swapping placenames? How were they making sense, and what sort of sense were they making? What manner of thinking informed their utterances and the actions their utterances performed? What, in short, was the culture of their discourse?

III

In order to understand what another person is saying, you must assume it is true and try to imagine what it could be true of.

—George Miller, *The Imagination of Reality*

If the discourse at Lola Machuse's camp is to be usefully understood, if we are to grasp its coherence and appreciate the structure of its interactional design, steps must be taken to enter the conceptual world of the Western Apache people who produced it. Needless to say, we cannot recover their experience of their discourse as it actually occurred, what the phenomenologist Merleau-Ponty (1969:89) called the "inner experience of language-spoken-now." But we can explore, perforce retrospectively and therefore in reconstructive terms, what participants in the encounter took their discourse to be about, why they saw fit to contribute to it as they did, and how they interpreted the utterances and actions that comprised it. In addition, and certainly just as important, we can explore the culturally based assumptions and beliefs that made these interpretations possible, the "linguistic ideology" with which people from Cibecue rationalize for themselves and explain to others what spoken words are capable of doing when used in certain ways.[9] In short, we can construct an ethnographic account of the speech event itself, an interpretation of Apache interpretations that relates the event to the body of thought that made its occurrence meaningful and to the particular social circumstances that made its meaning unique.

All such undertakings profit from the guidance of experienced native instructors, and no one living at Cibecue is more capable or willing in this regard than Lola Machuse herself. So let us begin, as in fact I did shortly after the episode at her camp took place, by considering her own account of what transpired as the women drank their Pepsi and Clifford snapped at flies.

We gave that woman [i.e., Louise] pictures to work on in her mind. We didn't speak too much to her. We didn't hold her down. That way she could travel in her mind.

She could add on to them [i.e., the pictures] easily. We gave her clear pictures with placenames. So her mind went to those places, standing in front of them as our ancestors did long ago. That way she could see what happened there long ago. She could hear stories in her mind, perhaps hear our ancestors speaking. She could reknow the wisdom of our ancestors. We call it speaking with names. Placenames are all we need for that, speaking with names. We just fix them up. That woman was too sad. She was worried too much about her younger brother. So we tried to make her feel better. We tried to make her think good thoughts. That woman's younger brother acted stupidly. He was stupid and careless. He failed to show respect. No good! We said nothing critical about him to her. We talked around it. Those placenames are strong! After a while, I gave her a funny story. She didn't get mad. She was feeling better. She laughed. Then she had enough, I guess. She spoke to the dog about her younger brother, criticizing him, so we knew we had helped her out.[10]

Lola Machuse recorded this statement two days after the speech event at her camp took place, and four days later, having discussed her account with all parties involved, I determined to treat it as a guide for subsequent research. Everyone to whom I presented Lola's account agreed that it was encompassing and astute; it touched, they said, on everything that was essential for getting a proper sense of what "speaking with names" might be used to accomplish. But they also agreed that it was rather too highly condensed, a bare bones sort of interpretation (certainly adequate for persons already familiar with the practice, but understandably opaque to a neophyte such as myself) which could profit from explication and fleshing out. Never one to be outdone, Lola Machuse agreed instantly with the agreers, saying she was well aware of the problem, thank you very much, and had understood all along that further instruction would be necessary. Sometimes talk is complicated, she admonished, and one must move slowly to get to the bottom of it. So with all of us scrambling to agree with Lola, and with Lola herself firmly in charge, the fleshing out process began. Our work took longer than I expected, but now, with much of it done, Lola Machuse's original account seems better to me than ever; it provides, as one of my older Apache consultants told me it would, a "straight path to knowing." And so I have used Lola's interpretation here, partitioned into convenient segments, as a model, a path of a different kind, for organizing and presenting my own.

We gave that woman pictures to work on in her mind. We didn't speak too much to her. We didn't hold her down. That way she could travel in her mind. She could add on to them easily.

Western Apache conceptions of language and thought are cast in pervasively visual terms. Every occasion of "speaking" *(yałti')* provides tangible evidence of "thinking" *(natsíkees),* and thinking, which Apaches describe as an intermittent and variably intense activity, occurs in the form of "pictures" *(be' elzaahí)* that persons "see" *(yo'ii)* in their "minds" *(biini').* Prompted by a desire to "display thinking" *(nil'íínatsíkees),* speaking involves the use of language to "depict" *('e' ele')* and "carry" *(yo'ááł)* these mental images to the members of an audience, such that they, on "hearing" *(yidits' ag)* and "holding" *(yotá')* the speaker's words, can "view" *(yínel'ii')* facsimiles of the images in their own minds. Thinking, as the Apache conceive of it, consists in picturing to oneself and attending privately to the pictures. Speaking consists in depicting one's pictures for other people, who are thus invited to picture these depictions and respond to them with depictions of pictures of their own. Discourse, or "conversation" *('ilch'i̧' yádaach'ilti'),* consists in a running exchange of depicted pictures and pictured depictions, a reciprocal representation and visualization of the ongoing thoughts of participating speakers.

But matters are not really so neat and tidy. According to consultants from Cibecue, the depictions offered by Western Apache speakers are invariably incomplete. Even the most gifted and proficient speakers contrive to leave things out, and small children, who have not yet learned to indulge in such contrivances, leave out many things. Consequently, Apache hearers must always "add on" *('ínágoda'aah)* to depictions made available to them in conversation, augmenting and supplementing these spoken images with images they fashion for themselves. This process—the picturing, or viewing, of other people's verbal depictions—is commonly likened by Apaches to adding stones to a partially finished wall (or laying bricks upon the foundation of a house) because it is understood to involve a "piling up" *(łik'iyitł'ih)* of new materials onto like materials already in place. It is also said to resemble the rounding up of livestock: the "bringing together" *(dalaházhi̧'ch'indíít)* of cattle or horses from widely scattered locations to a central place where other animals have been previously gathered. These metaphors all point to the same general idea, which is that depictions provided by Apache speakers are treated by Apache hearers as bases on which to build, as projects to complete, as invitations to exercise the imagination.

The Western Apache regard spoken conversation as a form of "voluntary cooperation" *(łich'i̧' 'odaach'idii)* in which all participants, having presumably come together in the spirit of good will, are entitled to displays of "respect" *(yińtsih).* Accordingly, whenever people speak in cordial and affable tones, considerations of "kindness and politeness" *(bił goch'oba')* come centrally into play. Such considerations may influence Apache speech in a multitude of ways, but none is more basic than the courtesy speakers display by refraining from "speaking too much" *(łaago yałlti').* Although the effects of this injunction are most clearly evident in the spare verbal style employed by experienced Apache storytellers, people from Cibecue insist that all forms of narration stand to benefit from its application. And the reasons, they explain, are simple enough.

A person who speaks too much—someone who describes too busily, who supplies too many details, who repeats and qualifies too many times—presumes without warrant on the right of hearers to build freely and creatively on the speaker's own depictions. With too many words, such a speaker acts to "smother" *(biká' nyinłkaad)* his or her audience by seeming to say, arrogantly and coercively, "I *demand* that you see everything that happened, how it happened, and why it happened, *exactly* as I do." In other words, persons who speak too much insult the imaginative capabilities of other people, "blocking their thinking," as one of my consultants put it in English, and "holding down their minds." So Western Apache narrators consistently take a very different tack, implying by the economical manner of their speech, "I will depict just enough for you to see what happened, how it happened, and perhaps why it happened. Add on to these depictions however you see fit." Apache hearers consider this properly modest, properly polite, and just the way it should be. An effective narrator, people from Cibecue report, never speaks too much. An effective narrator, they say, takes steps to "open up thinking," thereby encouraging his or her listeners to "travel in their minds."[11]

> We gave her clear pictures with placenames. So her mind went to those places, standing in front of them as our ancestors did long ago. That way she could see what happened there long ago. She could hear stories in her mind, perhaps hear our ancestors speaking. She could reknow the wisdom of our ancestors.

Nothing is considered more basic to the effective telling of a Western Apache "story" or "narrative" *(nagodi'é)* than identifying the geographical locations at which events in the story unfold. For unless Apache listeners are able to picture a physical setting for narrated events (unless, as one of my consultants said, "your mind can travel to the place and really see it"), the events themselves will be difficult to imagine. This is because events in the narrative will seem to "happen nowhere" *(dohwaa 'ágodzaa da),* and such an idea, Apaches assert, is both preposterous and disquieting. Placeless events are an impossibility; everything that happens must happen somewhere. The location of an event is an integral aspect of the event itself, and therefore identifying the event's location is essential to properly depicting—and effectively picturing—the event's occurrence. For these reasons, people from Cibecue explain, placeless stories simply do not get told. Instead, to borrow a useful phrase from the linguist Harry Hoijer (1973), all Western Apache narratives are "spatially anchored" to points upon the land with precise depictions of specific locations. And what these depictions are accomplished with—what the primary spatial anchors of Apache narratives almost always turn out to be—are "placenames" *(ni'bízhi'*; literally, "land names").

The great majority of Western Apache placenames currently in use are believed to have been created long ago by the "ancestors" *(nohwizá'yé)* of the Apache people. The ancestors, who had to travel constantly in search of food, covered vast amounts of territory and needed to be able to remember and discuss many different locations.[12] This was facilitated by the invention of hundreds of descriptive placenames that were intended to depict their referents in close and exact detail.[13] In this important undertaking, as in many others, the ancestors were successful. Today, as undoubtedly for centuries before, Apaches observe with evident satisfaction that the mental pictures evoked by placenames are "accurate" *(da'áíyee)* and "correct" *(dábik'eh).* Again and again, people from Cibecue report, ancestral placenames bring graphically to mind the locations they depict.[14]

Some appreciation of the descriptive precision of Western Apache placenames can be gained by matching names with photographs of their referents. By way of illustration, consider the three names listed below, which have been seg-

mented into their gross morphological constituents and whose referents are shown
in Figures 1–3.

1. *t'iis bitł'áh tú 'olį́į́: t'iis* ("cottonwood tree") + *bitł'áh* ("below it"; "underneath
   it") + *tú* ("water") + o- ("inward") + *lį́į́'* ("it flows").
   Gloss: "Water flows inward underneath a cottonwood tree."

2. *tséłigaí dah sidil: tsé* ("rock"; "stone") + *łígaí* ("white") + *dah* ("above
   ground level") + *sidil* ("three or more form a compact cluster").
   Gloss: "White rocks lie above in a compact cluster."

3. *tsé biká' tú yahilį́į́': tsé* ("rock"; "stone") + *biká'* ("on top of it"; a flattish object) + *tú* ("water") + *ya-* ("downward") + *-hi-* ("linear succession of regularly repeated movements") + *-lį́į́'* ("it flows").
   Gloss: "Water flows down on top of a regular succession of flat rocks."

As shown by the photographs, Western Apache placenames provide more
than precise depictions of the sites to which the names may be used to refer. In
addition, placenames implicitly identify positions for viewing these locations: optimal vantage points, so to speak, from which the sites can be observed, clearly
and unmistakably, just as their names depict them. To picture a site from its name,
then, requires that one imagine it as if standing or sitting at a particular spot, and
it is to these privileged positions, Apaches say, that the images evoked by placenames cause them to travel in their minds.

Wherever the optimal vantage point for a named site may be located—east
of the site or west, above it or below, near it or at some distance away—the van-

Figure 1
t'iis bitł'áh tú 'olį́į́' ("**Water flows inward underneath a cottonwood tree**").

Figure 2
Tsé łigai dah sidil (**"White rocks lie above in a compact cluster"**).

tage point is described as being "in front of" *(bádnyú)* the site; and it is here, centuries ago, that ancestors of the Western Apache are believed to have stood when they gave the site its name. Accordingly, consultants from Cibecue explain that in positioning people's minds to look "forward" *(bidááh)* into space, a place-name also positions their minds to look "backward" *(t'aazhi')* into time. For as persons imagine themselves standing in front of a named site, they may imagine that they are standing in their "ancestors' tracks" *(nohwizą́'yé biké'é)*, and from this psychological perspective, which is sometimes described as an intense form of "daydreaming" *(bił 'onaagodah)*, traditional accounts of ancestral events associated with the site are said to be recalled with singular clarity and force. In other words, by evoking detailed pictures of places, together with specific vantage points from which to picture picturing them, placenames acquire a capacity to evoke stories and images of the people who knew the places first. When place-names are used by Apache speakers in certain ways, mental pictures of the ancestors come instantly and vividly alive.

The capacity of Western Apache placenames to situate people's minds in historical time and space is clearly apparent when names are used to anchor traditional narratives—"myths" *(godiyihgo nagoldi'é)*, "sagas" *(nłt'éégo nagoldi')*, and "historical tales" *('ágodzaahí nagoldi'é)*—which present depictions of "ancestral life" *(nohwizą́'yé zhineego)* and, in so doing, illustrate aspects of "ancestral wisdom" *(nohwizą́'yé bi kigoya'íí)*.[15] But the evocative power of placenames is most dramatically displayed when a name is used to substitute for

Figure 3
Tsé biká' tú yahilį́į́' ("Water flows down on top of a regular succession of flat rocks").

the narrative it anchors, "standing up alone" *('o'áá),* as Apaches say, to symbolize the narrative as well as the wisdom it contains. On such occasions, consultants from Cibecue report, a single placename may accomplish the communicative work of an entire saga or historical tale; and sometimes, depending on the immediate social circumstances, it may accomplish even more. For when placenames are employed in this isolated and autonomous fashion—when, in other words, Apache people practice "speaking with names"—their actions are interpreted as a recommendation to recall ancestral wisdom and apply it directly to matters of pressing personal concern. And in emotionally charged contexts like these, my consultants maintain, "ancestral voices" *(nohwizą́'yé bizhíí)* may seem to speak directly to the individuals involved.[16]

> *We call it speaking with names. Placenames are all we need for that, speaking with names. We just fix them up. That woman was too sad. She was worried too much about her younger brother. We tried to make her feel better. We tried to make her think good thoughts.*

"Speaking with names" is considered appropriate under certain conditions only, and these conditions, which Apaches describe as socially "taut" *(ndoh)* and "heavy" *(ndaaz),* tend to occur infrequently. Consequently, as people from Cibecue are quick to point out, placenames are usually put to other communicative ends. Most of the time, in the recurrent situations supplied by everyday life, placenames are called upon to perform simple verbal chores: to indicate where one is going, for example, or to announce where one has been; to make plans for a forthcoming hunt, or to pinpoint the latest happenings gleaned from local gossip. When placenames are used for ordinary purposes such as these, Apache speakers typically produce the names in shortened or contracted forms. Thus, the name *t'iis bitłah tú'olíí'* ("water flows inward underneath a cottonwood tree") is commonly heard as *t'iis tł'áh 'olíí'* or *t'iis tú 'olíí'*, the name *tsé biká' tú yahilíí* ("water flows down on top of a regular succession of flat rocks") as *tsé ká' yahilíí* or *tsé tú yahilíí'*, and so forth. In marked contrast to these abbreviated renderings, placenames intended to evoke mental pictures of the past are invariably spoken in full and are embellished, or "fixed up" *(náyidlé)*, with an optional suffix that imparts an emphatic force roughly equivalent to English "right here!" or "at this very place!" Accordingly, the placename *t'iis bitł'áh tú olíí'* is produced in traditional narratives as *t'iis bitł'áh tú 'olíné*, the name *tsé biká' tú yahilíí'* as *tsé biká' tú yahilíné*, etc. Although the optional suffix may be employed for purposes other than helping to summon ancestral images and voices, my consultants agree that this is one of its primary functions. And at no time is that function more readily apparent as when Apache men and women, bent upon "speaking with names," dispense with narratives completely and use placenames, fully encliticized, in the expression *X'ágodzaa yú* ("It happened at X, at this very place!").[17]

This expression is normally reserved for social situations in which speaking of absent parties to persons closely connected to them must be accomplished with delicacy and tact. More specifically, the expression is used when ancestral wisdom seems applicable to difficulties arising from serious errors in someone else's judgment, but when voicing one's thoughts on the matter—or, as one of my consultants said, "making wisdom too plain"—might be taken as evidence of moral conceit, critical disapproval, and a lack of sympathetic understanding. Instead, and ever so deftly, "speaking with names" enables those who engage in it to acknowledge a regrettable circumstance without explicitly judging it, to exhibit solicitude without openly proclaiming it, and to offer advice without appearing to do so.

But "speaking with names" accomplishes more than this. A traditional Apache narrative encapsulated in its own spatial anchor, the expression *X'agodzaa yú* is also a call to memory and imagination. Simultaneously, it is a call to persons burdened by worry and despair to take remedial action on behalf of themselves. "Travel in your mind," the expression urges those to whom it is addressed. "Travel in your mind to a point from which to view the place whose name has just been spoken. Imagine standing there, as if in the tracks of your ancestors, and recall stories of events that occurred at that place long ago. Picture these events in your mind and appreciate, as if the ancestors themselves were speaking, the wisdom the stories contain. Bring this wisdom to bear on your own disturbing situation. Allow the past to inform your understanding of the present. You will feel better if you do."

And Western Apache people report that sometimes they do feel better. Having pictured distant places and dwelled on distant events, their worries may become less plaguing and acute: less "sharp" *(ts'ik'ii),* less "rigid" *(ntł'iz),* less "noisy" *(gónch'add)* in their minds. Feelings of anxiety and emotional turbulence may give way to welcome sensations of "smoothness" *(dilkọọh)*, of "softness" *(dédi'ilé)*, of growing inner "quiet" *(doo hwaa gọńch'aad da)*. And when this actually happens—when ancestral wisdom works to give beneficial perspective and fresh recognition that trying times can be dealt with successfully and eventually overcome—persons thus heartened may announce that relationships characterized by "pleasantness and goodness" *(gozhọọ)* have been restored between themselves and their surroundings. A psychological balance has been reestablished, an optimistic outlook borne of strengthened confidence and rejuvenated hope, and people may also announce that a "sickness" *(nezgai)* has been "healed" *(nábilziih)*. "Bad thinking" *(ncho'go natsíkeẹs)* has been replaced by "good thinking" *(nzhọọgo natsíkeẹs)*, and at least for a while the exigencies of life can be met with replenished equanimity.

IV

No matter what else human beings may be communicating about, or may think they are communicating about, they are always communicating about themselves, about one another, and about the immediate context of communication.

—Robert Pittinger, Charles Hockett, John Danahy, *The First Five Minutes*

The foregoing account of aspects of Western Apache placename ideology supplies the basic conceptual framework with which to interpret the conversational encounter at Lola Machuse's camp in Cibecue. But because the account has been formulated as Apache people themselves insist upon doing—that is, in abstract normative terms—it fails to elucidate what the practice of "speaking with names" served to accomplish on that particular occasion. In other words, we have yet to identify the social actions that participants in the encounter used their utterances to perform, and thus, necessarily, we have yet to grasp the coherence of their talk. So let us be about it. Having fashioned an account of the cultural logic on which "speaking with names" is understood to operate, attention may now be directed to a functional interpretation of how, and with what sorts of interpersonal consequences, this mode of discourse was actually put to work. Once again, Lola Machuse.

That women's younger brother acted stupidly. He was stupid and careless. He failed to show respect. No good! We said nothing critical about him to her. We talked around it.

The social gathering at Lola Machuse's camp was uncomfortable for everyone involved, but especially for Louise. Troubled by her brother's sudden illness, she was troubled even more by his apparent lack of common sense. Having come into contact with the snakeskin near the roundup camp, he should have gone directly to a ritual specialist for assistance in dealing with his contaminated state. That he failed to do so was disturbing enough, but that he treated the incident in such a cavalier fashion was more disturbing still. Plainly, he was guilty of a grave lapse in judgment, and now, as surely he could have anticipated, he was suffering the painful consequences. Why had the young man acted so irresponsibly? In addition to being upset, Louise was bewildered and perplexed.

Louise's chronicle of her brother's misfortune created an opportunity for all on hand to comment on his conduct. But because her account portrayed him in a distinctly unfavorable light, it also presented him as a target for easy criticism. If criticism were to be forthcoming, it could only serve to embarrass Louise, for she would have no alternative but to try to defend her brother's actions—and this would be awkward and difficult at best. Yet refusing to defend him could be taken to mean that she was prepared to condemn him entirely, and condemning one's relatives, especially in the presence of nonrelatives, is a conspicuous violation of kinship loyalties that Western Apaches rarely see fit to excuse.[18]

For these reasons, Louise's candid statement placed her companions in a delicate dilemma. On the one hand, no one could assert that Louise's brother had not acted wrongly without casting serious doubt on his or her own good judgment. On the other hand, no one could openly censure the young man without adding to Louise's discomfort, thereby displaying a lack of considerateness for her aggravated feelings and a lack of concern for the circumstances that had produced them. How, then, to respond? How to speak the truth—or something that could be heard as not denying the truth—without exacerbating an already sensitive situation?

Those placenames really helped us out! We gave her pictures with placenames. That way she started feeling better. Those placenames are strong!

After finishing her account, Louise paused, took a long drink from her Pepsi-Cola, and started to speak again of her beleaguered brother. But Lola Machuse intervened at this point, saying softly but firmly, *"tsé hadigaiyé yú 'ágodzaa' "* ("It happened at line of white rocks extends upward and out, at this very place!"). Lola's utterance was intended to evoke a historical tale for Louise to picture in her mind, but it was also designed to change the topic of talk and set the conversation on a new and different course. Instead of Louise's brother, whom Lola was showing she had no desire to criticize, attention was shifted to Louise herself and her troubled reactions to her brother's unfortunate predicament. Instead of disapproval, Lola Machuse was exhibiting sympathy and concern.

As later told by herself, the historical tale that Lola Machuse wished to evoke is the following.[19]

It happened at line of white rocks extends upward and out.

Long ago, a girl lived alone with her maternal grandmother. Her grandmother sent her out regularly to collect firewood. She went to a place above her camp. She could get there quickly by climbing up through a rocky canyon. Many snakes lived there. So her grandmother told her always to go another way.

The girl went to collect firewood. The day was hot. Then the girl became thirsty. Then she thought, "This wood is heavy. I don't want to carry it too far." Then she started to walk down the rocky canyon. There were loose rocks where she walked. Then she slipped and fell down. The firewood she was carrying scattered everywhere! Then she started to pick it up. A snake bit her hand! Then she got scared. "My grandmother knew this would happen to me," she thought.

Then the girl returned to where she was living with her grandmother. Her arm and hand became badly swollen. Then they worked over her [i.e., performed a curing ceremony]. Later, the girl went to her grandmother. "My life is still my own," she said. Then her grandmother talked to her again. Now she knew how to live right.

It happened at line of white rocks extends upward and out.

As Lola Machuse had reason to suspect, Louise knew this story well. She had heard it many times and on several occasions had performed it for her own children. Consequently, Louise reported later, her mind traveled instantly to a spot from which to view the place named *tsé hadigai* ("'line of white rocks extends upward and out"), and images of the girl carrying firewood—and, most vividly of all, of the girl's scrambling attempts to retrieve it after she lost her footing—appeared just as quickly. As a lengthy silence descended on the Machuse camp at Cibecue, Louise's thoughts moved along these lines.

A bad thing happened at that place. Very bad! I saw that girl. She was impulsive. She forgot to be careful. She ceased showing respect. She was like my younger brother. She ceased thinking properly, so something bad happened to her. She became very scared but recovered from it. She almost died but held onto her own life.

Lola Machuse's evocative comment had a calming effect on everyone sitting beneath the ramada at her home. Her statement relieved Louise of any need to publicly defend her brother's conduct, and, at the same time, charted a conversational path that others could easily follow. Acknowledging the felicity of that path, and taking steps to pursue it, Emily produced a similar statement of her own—"'Ha'aa. Túzhí' yahigaiyé yú 'ágodzaa." ("'Yes. It happened at whiteness spreads out descending to water, at this very place!'")—and once again Louise was urged to travel in her mind and picture a historical tale.

Emily's version of this tale, which she said has been slightly abridged, is as follows.

It happened at whiteness spreads out descending to water.

Long ago, a boy went to hunt deer. He rode on horseback. Pretty soon he saw one [a deer], standing on the side of a canyon. Then he went closer and shot it. He killed it. Then the deer rolled all the way down to the bottom of the canyon.

Then the boy went down there. It was a buck, fat and muscular. Then he butchered it. The meat was heavy, so he had to carry it up in pieces. He had a hard time reaching the top of the canyon with each piece.

Now it was getting dark. One hindquarter was still laying at the bottom of the canyon. "I have enough meat already," he thought. So he left the hindquarter where it was lying. He left it there.

Then he packed his horse and started to ride home. Then the boy got dizzy and nearly fell off his horse. Then his nose twitched incontrollably, like Deer's nose does. Then pain shot up behind his eyes. Then he became scared.

Now he went back to the canyon. It was dark when he got there. He walked down to where the hindquarter was lying—but it was gone! Then he returned to his horse. He rode fast to where he was living with his relatives.

The boy was sick for a long time. The people prayed for him on four separate occasions. He got better slowly.

Some time after that, when the boy had grown to manhood, he always had bad luck in hunting. No deer would present themselves to him. He said to his children: "Look at me now. I failed to be careful when I was a boy and now I have a hard time getting meat for you to eat."

It happened at whiteness spreads out descending to water.

The actions performed by Emily's utterance were readily apparent to Louise. Emily, like Lola Machuse before her, was attempting to distract Louise with constructive thoughts and comfort her with expressions of support. But Louise was not intimately familiar with the story of the boy and the deer, and though her mind went swiftly to a point near *túzhi' yahigai* ("whiteness spreads out descending to water"), she had difficulty picturing all the events in the story. She did, however, have one vivid image—of the pain-ridden boy struggling to stay astride his horse—and this was sufficient to remind her of her brother. In addition, Louise said later, she could hear the boy, now an adult, as he spoke to his children about his fateful mistake.

It was like I could hear some old man talking. He was talking to his children. "I was impatient, so I left behind good meat from that deer. Then I became very sick and very scared. I failed to show respect." Even so, that boy lived on and grew up and had children. He learned to think right, so he talked to his children about it. Maybe my brother will learn to improve his thinking like that.

The historical tale evoked by Emily is similar in several respects to the tale evoked by Lola Machuse, and, at this point in the proceedings, Louise probably sensed that a definite pattern was starting to form. In both of the stories, young people are depicted as irresponsible and disrespectful, but for reasons having solely to do with their innocence and naïveté. In both stories, they suffer life-threatening consequences—serious illness and intense fright—from which they learn to avoid carelessness and impatience in the future. Finally, and most important of all, they regain their health and continue living, presumably for many years. Thus the unstated message for Louise, which is also a prominent aspect of Western Apache ancestral wisdom, was a distinctly positive one; in effect, "Take heart. These things will happen. Young people make foolish and dangerous mistakes, but they usually profit from them and the mistakes are seldom fatal. Be optimistic. There is reason to believe your brother will recover."

After a while, I gave her a funny story. She didn't get mad. She was feeling better. She laughed. Then she had enough, I guess. She talked to that dog about her younger brother, criticizing him, so we knew we had helped her out.

Following another lengthy silence inside the brush-covered ramada, Lola Machuse acted to affirm and consolidate the tacit messages communicated thus far with a placename intended to evoke a third historical tale with similarities to the previous two. But with this utterance—*"Da'aníí. K'is deeschii' naaditiné yú 'ágodzaa."* ("Truly. It happened at trail extends across a long red ridge with alder trees, at this very place!")—Lola took a moderate social risk. Although it deals with serious matters, the story Lola was thinking of presents a humorous aspect, and one of her purposes in evoking it was to lighten Louise's spirits (and everyone else's) by striking a note of reserved good cheer. The risk Lola ran was that her action would be perceived as intemperate, perhaps even playful, and thus inappropriate to the solemnity of Louise's circumstances.

This is the historical tale, as narrated by herself, that Lola Machuse had in mind.

It happened at trail extends across a long red ridge with alder trees.

A boy and a girl were newly married. He didn't know that he should stay away from her when her grandmother came to visit, [i.e., when she was having her menstrual period]. Then he tried to bother her. "Don't! I'm no good for that," she said. He was impatient. Then he tried to bother her again. Then she gave in.

Then the boy got sick, they say. It was hard for him to sit down. Then his penis became badly swollen. Pissing was painful for him, too. He walked around clutching his crotch. He was deeply embarrassed in front of his wife and her relatives. Then he got scared. "I wonder if I will be this way forever," he thought.

Then someone talked to him, saying "Don't bother your wife when her grandmother comes to visit. Stay away from her." Then that person gave the boy some medicine, saying "Drink this. It will make you well. Then you can stop being embarrassed. Then you can stop walking around clutching your crotch!" That is all.

It happened at trail extends across a long red ridge with alder trees.

Fortunately, Lola Machuse's lighthearted gamble did not misfire. Louise's mind traveled to a vantage point from which to picture *k'is deeschii' naaditiné* ("trail extends across a long red ridge with alder trees"), viewed the crestfallen lad with his hand where it should never be seen in public, and returned from the journey with Louise mildly amused. Afterwards, Louise made these comments.

Everyone knows that story. My mind went there. It's funny to see that boy in the story holding onto himself. He should have left his wife alone. He was impulsive. He didn't think right. Then he got scared. Then he was made well again with medicine. . . . I've heard that story often, but it's always funny to see that boy holding onto himself, so shy and embarrassed.

At the Machuse camp in Cibecue, Louise expressed her amusement by laughing softly. This was an auspicious sign! Though sorely worried still, Louise had been moved to levity and everyone could tell that her spirits had briefly improved. Here was evidence that the unspoken messages conveyed by Lola Machuse and Emily—messages of sympathy, consolation, and encouragement—had been beneficially received. Here was an indication that ancestral wisdom was providing Louise with a measure of comfort and hope. Seizing the moment, Robert Machuse acted to make elements of these messages explicit, compressing their dominant thrust into one succinct statement. *"Gozhǫǫ doleeł"* ("Pleasantness and goodness will be forthcoming"), said Robert with quiet conviction. And moments later, endorsing his sentiments and adding conviction of her own, Lola Machuse repeated the same phrase: *"Gozhǫǫ doleeł"* ("Pleasantness and goodness will be forthcoming").

Touched by this friendly display of goodwill, and well aware that some sort of acknowledgment of it would soon be in order, Louise responded by taking a deft and self-effacing step. In the form of a mock question addressed to Clifford, the Machuses' dog, she gently criticized her own brother: *"Shidizhé bíni' éshid ne góshé?"* ("My younger brother is foolish, isn't he, dog?"). This utterance accomplished several actions simultaneously. First, by drawing attention away from herself, Louise gave notice that further evocations of traditional narratives could be politely dispensed with; in effect, "You have all done enough." Also, by directing her question to one who could not answer it, Louise indicated that additional discussion of her brother and his difficulties would serve no useful purpose; in effect, "Let the matter rest. There is nothing more to say." Finally, and most adroitly of all, by voicing the thought that had been on everyone's mind from the beginning—that Louise's brother had indeed acted foolishly—she contrived to thank them for their tact in not having voiced it; in effect, "This is the discrediting truth about my relative. I know it and I know that you know it. You were polite and thoughtful to refrain from expressing it."

As could have been predicted, Clifford did not respond to Louise's bogus query. Neither did anyone else. The speech event was over. A few minutes later, Louise and Emily rose to their feet, complained to each other about a sudden plentitude of flies, and set off together in search of a cold can of Pepsi-Cola. Lola Machuse resumed her sewing and Robert Machuse went to water his horse. The day was beginning to cool, and the landscape beyond Cibecue, its rugged contours softened now by patches of lengthening shadow, looked somewhat more hospitable than before.

V

A society to exist at all must be incessantly reenacted; its basic communications must be repeatedly resaid.

—Edward Shils, *Tradition*

The possibilities of human language are variously conceived and variously understood. Every culture, whether literate or not, includes beliefs about how language works and what it is capable of accomplishing. Similarly, every culture contains beliefs about the kinds of social contexts in which these capabilities may be realized most effectively. That such beliefs are present in contemporary Western Apache culture should now be obvious, and that they may operate in direct and telling ways to influence patterns of verbal interaction should likewise be apparent. Moreover, it should now be possible to appreciate how aspects of Western Apache linguistic ideology contribute to perceptions of coherence in one form of Apache discourse, and also why, when contextual conditions are right, that same ideology may invest the briefest of utterances with ample meaning and substantial expressive force.

The episode at Lola Machuse's camp suggests that while coherence in Western Apache discourse can be usefully described as a product of interlocking utterances and actions, the expressive force of Apache discourse—what people from Cibecue call its "strength" *(nalwod)*—may be viewed as a product of multiple interlockings at different levels of abstraction. Put more exactly, it is my impression that those utterances that perform the broadest range of mutually compatible actions at once are those that Apaches experience as having the greatest communicative impact. In other words, the expressive force of an Apache utterance seems to be roughly proportionate to the number of separate but complementary functions it accomplishes simultaneously, or, as Alton Becker (1982) has intimated, to the number of distinguishable subject matters it successfully communicates "about."

The Western Apache practice of "speaking with names" manifests just this sort of functional range and versatility. Thus, as we have seen, an utterance such as *tsé hadigaiyé yú 'ágodzaa* ("It happened at line of white rocks extends upward and out, at this very place!") may be understood to accomplish all of the following actions: (1) produce a mental image of a particular geographical location; (2) evoke prior texts, such as historical tales and sagas; (3) affirm the value and validity of traditional moral precepts (i.e., ancestral wisdom); (4) display tactful and courteous attention to aspects of both positive and negative face; (5) convey sentiments of charitable concern and personal support; (6) offer practical advice for dealing with disturbing personal circumstances (i.e., apply ancestral wisdom); (7) transform distressing thoughts caused by excessive worry into more agreeable ones marked by optimism and hopefulness; (8) heal wounded spirits.

This is a substantial amount for any spoken utterance to be capable of accomplishing, and what provides for the capability—what the forceful activity of "speaking with names" always communicates most basically "about"—is the cultural importance of named locations within the Western Apache landscape. Named places have long been symbols of mythic significance for the Apache people, and placenames—symbols that designate these symbols—supply Apache speakers with a ready means for appropriating that significance and turning it with brisk efficiency to specialized social ends. By virtue of their role as spatial anchors in traditional Apache narratives, placenames can be made to represent the narratives themselves, summarizing them, as it were, and condensing into compact form their essential moral truths. As a result, narratives and truths alike can be swiftly "activated," foregrounded, and brought into focused awareness through the use of placenames alone. And so it happens, on those occasions when Apache people see fit to speak with placenames, that a vital part of their tribal heritage seems to speak to them as well. For on such occasions, as we have seen, participants may be moved and instructed by voices other than their own. In addition, persons to whom placenames are addressed may be affected by the voice of their ancestors, a voice that communicates in compelling silence with an inherent weight described by Mikhail Bakhtin as the "authoritative word":

> The authoritative word demands that we acknowledge it, that we make it our own; it binds us, quite independent of any power it might have to persuade us interally; we encounter it with its authority already fused on it. The authoritative word is located in a distanced zone, organically connected with a past that is felt to be hierarchically higher. Its authority was already acknowledged in the past. It is a prior discourse. . . . It is given (it sounds) in lofty spheres, not those of familiar contact. Its language is a special (as it were, hieratic) language. [Bakhtin 1981:342]

When Western Apache placenames are called upon to serve as vehicles of ancestral authority, the wisdom thus imparted is not so loftily given as to inhibit its utilization in the mundane spheres of everyday life. On the contrary, as the episode at the Machuse camp illustrates clearly, such knowledge exists to be applied, to be thought about and acted upon, to be incorporated (the more so the better, Lola Machuse would have us understand) into the smallest corners of personal and social experience. And insofar as this kind of incorporation occurs— insofar as places and placenames provide Apache people with symbolic reference points for the moral imagination and its practical bearing on the actualities of their lives—the landscape in which the people dwell can be said to dwell in them. For the constructions Apaches impose upon their landscape have been fashioned from the same cultural materials as constructions they impose upon themselves as members of society. Both give expression to the same set of values, standards, and ideals; both are manifestations of the same distinctive charter for being-in-the-world. Inhabitants of their landscape, the Western Apache are thus inhabited *by* it as well, and, in the timeless depth of that abiding reciprocity, the people and their landscape are virtually as one.[20]

This reciprocal relationship—a relationship in which individuals invest themselves in the landscape while incorporating its meanings into their own most fundamental experience—is the ultimate source of the rich sententious potential and functional versatility of Western Apache placenames. For when placenames are used in the manner exemplified by Lola Machuse and her friends, the landscape is appropriated in pointedly social terms and the authoritative word of Apache tribal tradition is brought squarely to bear on matters of importunate social concern. Concomitantly, persons in distress are reminded of what they already know but sometimes forget—that ancestral wisdom is a powerful ally in times of adversity, and that reflecting upon it, as countless generations of Apaches have learned, can produce expanded awareness, feelings of relief, and a fortified ability to cope. And because helping people to cope is regarded by Apaches as a gesture of compassion, the use of placenames for this purpose serves as well to communicate solicitude, reassurance, and personal solidarity. The primary reason that "speaking with names" can accomplish so much—the reason its expressive force is sometimes felt to be so "strong" *(nalwod)*—is that it facilitates reverberating acts of kindness and caring. And the effects of kindness and caring, especially when spirits are in need of healing, can be very strong indeed.

As must now be apparent, the ethnographic account presented in this essay has been shaped by a "pragmatic" view of spoken communication that rests on the premise that languages consist in shared economies of grammatical resources with which language users act to get things done.[21] The resources of a language, together with the varieties of action facilitated by their use, acquire meaning and force from the sociocultural contexts in which they are embedded, and therefore, as every linguist knows, the discourse of any speech community will exhibit a fundamental character—a genius, a spirit, an underlying personality—which is very much its own. Over a period of years, I have become convinced that one of the distinctive characteristics of Western Apache discourse is a predilection for performing a maximum of socially relevant actions with a minimum of linguistic means. Accordingly, I have been drawn to investigate instances of talk, like the one involving Lola and Robert Machuse, in which a few spoken words are made to accomplish large amounts of communicative work.[22] For it is just on such occasions, I believe, that elements of Apache culture and society fuse most completely with elements of grammar and the situated aims of individuals, such that very short utterances, like polished crystals refracting light, can be seen to contain them all. On these occasions, the Western Apache language is exploited to something near its full expressive potential, and even Apaches themselves, struck momentarily by the power of their discourse, may come away impressed.

Such powerful moments may not be commonplace in Western Apache speech communities, but they are certainly common enough—and when they occur, as on that hot and dusty day at Cibecue, robust worlds of meaning come vibrantly alive. Conveying these worlds, capturing with words both the richness of their content and the fullness of their spirit, requires an exacting effort at linguistic and cultural translation that can never be wholly successful. The problem, of course, is that verbally mediated realities are so densely textured and incorrigibly dynamic, and that one's own locutions for representing them—for drawing the reader, as James Fernandez (1983:327) has urged, into "the very center of the complex flow of communicative experience and activity"—fail to do justice to the numerous subtleties involved. Unavoidably, delicate proportions are altered and disturbed, intricate momentums halted and betrayed; and however much one explicates there is always more (or so one is tempted to suppose) that might usefully be done. Despite these persisting uncertainties, however, enough can be learned and understood—and, I would hope, effectively conveyed as well—so that we, like the Apaches of Cibecue, may come away from certain kinds of speech events instructed and impressed. And sometimes roundly moved. Following its more accentuated moments, moments shaped by graciousness and the resonating echoes of a fully present past, the minimalist genius of Western Apache discourse leaves us silent in its wake—traveling in our minds, listening for the ancestors, and studying the landscape with a new and different eye. On the pictorial wings of placenames imaginations soar.

Notes

Acknowledgments. This essay has benefitted from the good graces of a number of friends and colleagues. Thanks go first, as always, to my Western Apache consultants from the community at Cibecue, including Lola and Robert Machuse, Nick Thompson, Nashley Tessay, Morley Cromwell, Frances and Sarah DeHose, Calvert and Darlene Tessay, Charles Henry (now deceased), Jack Case, Alvin Quay, and Imogene Quay. For fruitful discussions, helpful correspondence, and other expressions of interest while the essay was being written, I am grateful to Alton Becker, Harold Conklin, Vine Deloria, Jr., Bill Douglas, Joseph Errington, Charles Frake, Philip Greenfeld, William Kelly, Sir Edmund Leach, Floyd Lounsbury, Ray McDermott, Scott Momaday, Harold Scheffler, John Searle, and Michael Silverstein. The penultimate version of my paper was presented at a multidisciplinary conference on "Discourse in Sociocultural Context" held at the University of Texas at Austin in April of 1987; on that occasion I received valuable comments and criticism from Aaron Cicourel, Susan Ervin-Tripp, Steven Feld, John Haviland, and Joel Sherzer. Other suggestions for improvement, for which I am equally grateful, come later from Richard Bauman, Larry Evers, William Hanks, Dell Hymes, George Marcus, Stephen Tyler, Anthony Woodbury, and Peter Whitely. Above all, I am indebted to Gayle Potter-Basso, partner in fieldwork as in everything else, whose steady encouragement, graceful acumen, and sheer good sense helped immeasurably in moving things along. The linguistic and ethnographic research on which the essay is based was financed by grants from the National Science Foundation and the Wenner-Gren Foundation for Anthropological Research; I am pleased to thank these institutions for their support. Needless to say, I am alone responsible for the contents of the essay, and thus for any and all flaws and errors it may be found to contain.

[1]Compatible views on environmental appropriation are expressed in Deloria (1975) and Silko (1986).

[2]A brief discussion of the history of placename research in American anthropology may be found in Basso (1983).

[3]Schegloff (1972) demonstrates nicely why placenaming, together with other conversational methods of "formulating place," warrants close investigation by students of language concerned with the organization of everyday talk.

[4]Silverstein (1976, 1979) argues that a preoccupation with the "semantico-referential" function of language has provided the basis for a uniquely biased Western linguistic ideology in which other functions, expecially indexical ones, are accorded secondary importance. In this regard, the views expressed in Tyler (1978, 1984) are also highly instructive.

[5]See, for example, recent ethnographic studies by Feld (1982), Rosaldo (1980), and Schieffelin (1979), all of which attest to the symbolic importance of placenames in non-Western cultural contexts. Other reports, similarly illustrative, include Berndt (1976), Cruikshnak (1983), Munn (1973), and Takaki (1984).

[6]A short ethnography of the Western Apache community at Cibecue, completed in 1968 and now increasingly out of date, is presented in Basso (1970).

[7]"Emily" and "Louise" are pseudonyms; Lola Machuse, Robert Machuse, and Clifford are not.

[8]This verbal exchange was not recorded on tape. I am satisfied, however, as are the Apache persons who participated in the exchange, that the text given here is essentially accurate. What is missing, of course, is information pertaining to prosodic phenomena, but none of the participants could recall anything in this regard that they considered out of the ordinary. Lola Machuse offered the following generalizaton: "When we talk like that [i.e., "speaking with names"] we just talk soft and slow, so that people know to listen real good."

[9]I follow here Silverstein's (1979:195) definition of linguistic ideologies as "any sets of beliefs about language as a rationalization or justification of perceived language structure and use." For an informative discussion of some of the perceptual and cognitive limits that may be inherent in linguistic ideologies, see Silverstein (1981).

[10]This statement by Lola Machuse was delivered in Western Apache; it was translated into English by Lola Machuse, Robert Machuse, Nashley Tessay, and myself.

[11]Refraining from speaking too much has pleasing aesthetic consequences that Apache people from Cibecue value and appreciate. It produces a lean narrative style, concise and somewhat stark, which is notably free of cursory embellishments—a kind of narrative minimalism in which less is held to be more. But it is a narrative style with definite moral underpinnings. Refraining from speaking too much results in effective depictions, and this, Apaches say, is all to the good. But economical speech also shows respect for the ample picturing abilities of other people, and this is better still.

[12]For a description of Western Apache territory in prereservation times [i.e., prior to 1872], together with a discussion of Apache seasonal movements, see Goodwin (1942).

[13]Several hundred placenames in current use among Apache people at Cibecue, accompanied by morphological analyses and semantic glosses in English, are presented in Basso et al. (n.d.); a more detailed investigation of morphological processes, focused primarily on the pictorial attributes of Apache placenames, is found in Basso et al. (n.d.).

[14]The pictorial character of Western Apache placenames is frequently remarked upon when Apache people are asked to compare their own placenames with familiar placenames in English. On such occasions, English names—such as Globe, Show Low, McNary, Phoenix, and other—are regularly found deficient for "not showing what those places look like" or for "not letting you see those places in your mind." Alternatively, Western Apache placenames—such as *gizh yaa'itin* ("trail leads down through a gap between two hills"), *ch'iłdiiyé cho sikaad ("cluster of big walnut trees stands bushing out")*, *and túzhi'yaahichii* ("redness spreads out extending down to water")—are consistently praised for "making you see those places like they really are" or for "putting those places in your mind so you can see them after you go away." One Apache from Cibecue put the difference succinctly: "The white man's names [are] no good. They don't give pictures to your mind." And a local wit said this: "Apaches don't need Polaroids. We've got good names!"

[15]The distinguishing features of these three traditional narrative genres as articulated by Western Apache people themselves are discussed in Basso (1984).

[16]Western Apaches readily acknowledge that "speaking with names" is possible only among persons who share knowledge of the same traditional narratives; otherwise, placenames would evoke stories for hearers that are different from those intended by speakers. But this, it seems, is rarely a problem among older people. Most adults living in Cibecue

maintain that they are familiar with the same corpus of narratives, and while any narrative is understood to have several versions (and different storytellers different ways of performing them), there is little confusion as to where events in the narrative are believed to have taken place. Consequently, the placename (or names) that anchor a narrative can function reliably to evoke comparable images of ancestral events and corresponding appreciations of ancestral wisdom. Younger Apache people, I was told, are ignorant of both placenames and traditional narratives in increasing numbers, so that for some of them "speaking with names" has become difficult or impossible. Although the instance of "speaking with names" discussed in the present essay features women conversing with women, I have been assured by consultants from Cibecue that the use of this verbal practice has never been, and is not today, restricted to female interlocutors. Apache men, I was informed, employ the practice when speaking to men, and persons of opposite sex may employ it when speaking to each other.

[17]Sapir's description of Algonkian words as "tiny imagist poems" applies nicely to Western Apache placenames, and there is little doubt in my mind that the practice of "speaking with names" exhibits poetic qualities. I have not pursued this line of thought in this essay because I remain uncertain as to what Apache conceptions of "poetic speech" might be. That such conceptions exist is certain, as evidenced by my consultants' observations that most forms of talk can be more or less "beautiful" *(diñzhoñé)*. But I was also informed that judgments concerning beauty in speech cannot be made in the abstract, suggesting that features of social context may inform such judgments as much as (and perhaps, in some cases, even more than) attributes of grammatical form and phonetic shape. For useful discussions of the poetic dimensions of speech in relation to discourse generally and to a recasting of the Sapir-Whorf hypothesis in particular, see Friedrich (1986) and Sherzer (1987).

[18]Louise, who is distantly related to Emily, is not related to Lola Machuse or Robert Machuse.

[19]The texts of the three historical tales presented in this essay were originally recorded in Western Apache; they were subsequently translated into English by Lola Machuse, Robert Machuse, Nashley Tessay, Morley Cromwell, Nick Thompson, Imogene Quay, and myself.

[20]A brief but informative discussion of the moral contours of Native American landscapes is found in Deloria (1975).

[21]This view of language and its suitability for an ethnographic approach to the study of discourse has been most fully articulated by Hymes (e.g., 1974). For extended applications of this approach, together with useful theoretical discussion, see Sherzer (1983) and Bauman (1984). Hymes's more recent work (e.g., 1981), is also illustrative in this regard, as are treatments by Bauman (1986), Feld (1982), and Friedrich (1986). Tyler (1978) presents a sweeping philosophical critique of formalism in modern linguistic theory, and, on grounds somewhat different than Hymes, argues persuasively for a more sensitive and sensible approach to the study of language use in its cultural and social contexts.

[22]Some other manifestations of the predilection for "mini-maxing" in Western Apache discourse are described and discussed in Basso (1969, 1976, 1984).

References Cited

Basso, K.
  1969   "To Give Up On Words": Silence in Western Apache Culture. Southwestern
    Journal of Anthropology 24(3):252–266.
  1970   The Cibecue Apache. New York: Holt, Rinehart, and Winston.
  1976   "Wise Words of the Western Apache": Metaphor and Semantic Theory. *In*
    Meaning in Anthropology. K. Basso and H. Selby, eds. Pp. 93–123. Albuquerque:
    University of New Mexico Press.
  1983   Western Apache Placenames Hierarchies. *In* Naming Systems. E. Tooker, ed.
    Pp. 78–94. Washington, D.C.: American Ethnological Society.
  1984   "Stalking with Stories": Names, Places, and Moral Narratives among the West-
    ern Apache. *In* Text, Play, and Story: The Construction and Reconstruction of Self
    and Society. E. Bruner, ed. Pp. 19–53. Washington, D.C.: American Ethnological
    Society.
  n.d.   Some Linguistic Principles for the Study of Western Apache Placenames. Un-
    published manuscript.
Basso, K., and N. Tessay, M. Cromwell, M. Graves, F. DeHose, N. Gregg, C. Henry,
R. Machuse, L. Machuse, G. Potter-Basso, N. Thompson
  n.d.   Placenames in the Cibecue Region of the Fort Apache Indian Reservation. Un-
    published manuscript and accompanying maps.
Bakhtin, M.
  1981   The Dialogic Imagination: Four Essays by M. M. Bakhtin. M. Holquist, ed.
    Austin: University of Texas Press.
Bauman, R.
  1984   Verbal Art as Performance. Chicago: Waveland Press.
  1986   Story, Performance, and Event: Contextual Studies of Oral Narrative. Cam-
    bridge: Cambridge University Press.
Becker, A.
  1982   Beyond Translation: Esthetics and Language Description. *In* Contemporary Per-
    ceptions of Language: Interdisciplinary Dimensions. H. Byrnes, ed. Pp. 124–137.
    Washington, D.C.: Georgetown University Press.
Berndt, R.
  1976   Territoriality and the Problem of Demarcating Sociocultural Space. *In* Tribes and
    Boundaries in Australia. N. Peterson, ed. Pp. 133–161. Atlantic Highlands: Human-
    ities Press.
Boas, F.
  1934   Geographical Names of the Kwakiutl Indians. Columbia University Contribu-
    tions in Anthropology, No. 20. New York.
Conklin, H.
  1957   Hanunóo Agriculture: A Report on an Integral System of Shifting Cultivation in
    the Philippines. Rome: Food and Agriculture Organization of the United Nations.
  1962   Comment on Frake. *In* Anthropology and Human Behavior. T. Gladwin and W.
    Sturtevant, eds. Pp. 86–91. Washington, D.C.: Anthropological Society of Washing-
    ton.
Cruikshank, J.
  1983   Getting the Words Right: A Perspective on Naming and Places in Athapaskan
    Oral History. Unpublished manuscript.
Deloria, V., Jr.
  1975   God is Red. New York: Dell.

Donnellan, K.
1972 Proper Names and Identifying Descriptions. *In* Semantics of Natural Languages. B. Davidson and G. Harman, eds. Pp. 356–379. Dordrecht: D. Reidel.

Eliot, T. S.
1932 The Sacred Wood. London: Methuen.

Evans-Pritchard, E.
1949 Topographical Names among the Bedouin of Cyrenaica. Journal of the Royal Anthropological Institute 76(2):177–188.

Feld, S.
1982 Sound and Sentiment: Birds, Weeping, Poetics, and Song in Kaluli Expression. Philadelphia: University of Pennsylvania Press.

Fernandez, J.
1983 Afterword: At the Center of the Human Condition. Semiotica 46(2/4):323–330.

Frake, C.
1962 The Ethnographic Study of Cognitive Systems. *In* Anthropology and Human Behavior. T. Gladwin and W. Sturtevant, eds. Pp. 72–93. Washington, D.C.: Anthropological Society of Washington.

Friedrich, P.
1986 The Language Parallax: Linguistic Relativism and Poetic Indeterminacy. Austin: University of Texas Press.

Gallico, P.
1954 Love of Seven Dolls. *In* Love of Seven Dolls and Other Stories. Garden City, New York: Doubleday.

Geertz, C.
1973 Thick Description: Toward an Interpretive Theory of Culture. *In* The Interpretation of Cultures: Selected Essays by Clifford Geertz. Pp. 3–30. New York: Basic Books.

Goffman, E.
1974 Frame Analysis: An Essay in the Organization of Experience. New York: Harper and Row.

Goodenough, W.
1964 Introduction. *In* Explorations in Cultural Anthropology. W. Goodenough, ed. Pp. 1–24. New York: McGraw-Hill.

Goodwin, G.
1942 The Social Organization of the Western Apache. Chicago: University of Chicago Press.

Heany, S.
1980 Preoccupations: Selected Prose, 1968–1978. London: Faber and Faber.

Heidegger, M.
1977 Building Dwelling Thinking. *In* Martin Heidegger: Basic Writings. D. Krell, ed. Pp. 319–339. New York: Harper and Row.

Hoijer, H.
1973 Personal Communication.

Hymes, D.
1974 Foundations in Sociolinguistics: An Ethnographic Approach. Philadelphia: University of Pennsylvania Press.
1981 In Vain I Tried To Tell You: Essays in Native American Ethnopoetics. Philadelphia: University of Pennsylvania Press.

Labov, W., and D. Fanshel
    1977   Therapeutic Discourse: Psychotherapy as Conversation. New York: Academic
        Press.
Lyons, J.
    1977   Semantics: Volume One. Cambridge: Cambridge University Press.
Malinowski, B.
    1920   The Language of Magic and Gardening. London: Allen and Unwin.
Merleau-Ponty, M.
    1969   On the Phenomenology of Language. *In* Problems in the Philosophy of Lan-
        guage. T. Dishewsky, ed. Pp. 89–101. New York: Holt, Rinehart, and Winston.
Momaday, N. Scott
    1974   Native American Attitudes to the Environment. *In* Seeing with a Native Eye:
        Essays on Native American Religion. W. Capps, ed. Pp. 79–85. New York: Harper
        and Row.
Munn, N.
    1973   Walbiri Iconography: Graphic Representation and Cultural Symbolism in a Cen-
        tral Australian Society. Ithaca: Cornell University Press.
Pike, K.
    1978   Here We Stand—Creative Observers of Language. *In* Approches du colloque
        interdisciplinaire tenu á Paris. Pp. 9–45. Paris: Sorbonne.
Ricoeur, P.
    1979   The Model of the Text: Meaningful Action Considered as a Text. *In* Interpretive
        Social Science: A Reader. P. Rabinow and W. Sullivan, eds. Pp. 92–123. Berkeley:
        University of California Press.
Rosaldo, Renato
    1980   Ilongot Headhunting, 1883–1974: A Study in Society and History. Palo Alto:
        Stanford University Press.
Russell, B.
    1940   An Inquiry into Meaning and Truth. London: Allen and Unwin.
Sahlins, M.
    1976   Culture and Practical Reason. Chicago: University of Chicago Press.
Sapir, E.
    1912   Language and Environment. American Anthropologist Vol. 14:226–242. Men-
        asha: American Anthropological Association.
Schegloff, E. A.
    1972   Notes on a Conversational Practice: Formulating Place. *In* Language and Social
        Context. P. P. Giglioli, ed. Pp. 95–135. Middlesex: Penguin.
Schieffelin, E.
    1979   Mediators as Metaphors: Moving a Man to Tears in Papua, New Guinea. *In* The
        Imagination of Reality: Essays in Southeast Asian Coherence Systems. A. Becker and
        A. Yengoyan, eds. Pp. 127–144. Norwood: Ablex.
Schutz, A.
    1967   The Phenomenology of the Social World. G. Walsh and F. Lehnert, trans. Ev-
        anston, Ill.: Northwestern University Press.
Sherzer, J.
    1983   Kuna Ways of Speaking: An Ethnographic Perspective. Austin: University of
        Texas Press.
    1987   A Discourse-Centered Approach to Language and Culture. American Anthro-
        pologist 89:295–309.

Searle, J.
1958 Proper Names. *In* Readings in the Philosophy of Language. J. Rosenberg and C. Travis, eds. Pp. 212–222. Englewood Cliffs: Prentice-Hall.
1969 Speech Acts: An Essay in the Philosophy of Language. Cambridge: Cambridge University Press.

Silko, L.
1986 Landscape, History, and the Pueblo Imagination. *In* Antaeus, Special Issue: On Nature. D. Halpern, ed. Pp. 85–94.

Silverstein, M.
1976 Shifters, Linguistic Categories, and Cultural Description. *In* Meaning in Anthropology. K. Basso and H. Selby, eds. Pp. 11–53. Albuquerque: University of New Mexico Press.
1979 Language Structure and Linguistic Ideology. *In* The Elements: A Parasession on Linguistic Units and Levels. P. Clyne, W. Hanks, and C. Hofbauer, eds. Pp. 193–247. Chicago: University of Chicago Press.
1981 The Limits of Awareness. Sociolinguistic Working Paper No. 84. Austin: Southwest Educational Development Laboratory.

Strawson, P.
1959 Individuals: An Essay in Descriptive Metaphysics. London: Methuen.

Takaki, M.
1984 Regional Names in Kalinga: Certain Social Dimensions of Placenames. *In* Naming Systems. E. Tooker, ed. Pp. 55–77. Washington, D.C.: American Ethnological Society.

Trager, G.
1968 Whorf, Benjamin L. International Encyclopedia of the Social Sciences, Vol. 16. D. Sills, ed. Pp. 536–537. New York: Cromwell Collier and MacMillian.

Tyler, S.
1978 The Said and the Unsaid: Mind, Meaning, and Culture. New York: Academic Press.
1984 The Vision in the Quest, or What the Mind's Eye Sees. Journal of Anthropological Research 40(1):23–40.

Nostalgia—A Polemic

Kathleen Stewart

This article attempts to objectify a cultural polemic between forms of nostalgia in the culture of "late capitalism" (Mandel 1978) or "the end of organized capitalism" (Lash and Urry 1987). Hegemonic and resistant nostalgias, "middle-class" and "working-class" nostalgias, the nostalgia of a "mass culture" and the nostalgia of and for local, nameable places are a three-ring circus of simultaneous images in the arenas of life-style, spectacle, and loss. The angst-ridden modern city is replaced by the delirious surround of consumer capitalism (Jameson 1983). Nostalgia, like the economy it runs with, is everywhere. But it is a cultural practice, not a given content; its forms, meanings, and effects shift with the context—it depends on where the speaker stands in the landscape of the present.

On one "level" there is no longer any place for *anyone* to stand and nostalgia takes on the generalized function to provide some kind (any kind) of cultural form. In positing a "once was" in relation to a "now" it creates a frame for meaning, a means of dramatizing aspects of an increasingly fluid and unnamed social life. Nostalgia is an essential, narrative, function of language that orders events temporally and dramatizes them (Stewart 1984) in the mode of "things that happened," that "could happen," that "threaten to erupt at any moment." By resurrecting time and place, and a subject *in* time and place, it shatters the surface of an atemporal order and a prefab cultural landscape. To narrate is to place oneself in an event and a scene—to make an interpretive space—and to relate something to someone: to make an interpretive space that is relational and in which meanings have direct social referents.

Nostalgia rises to importance as a cultural practice as culture becomes more and more diffuse, more and more a "structure of feeling" (Williams n.d.), as culture takes on the power of "distance" that comes of displacing speakers—the power to flatten distinctions, to blur genres, to unname the practices of the social world so that they look like nature (Barthes 1957). Culture is more and more unspoken and unnamed. Painted onto the surface of things, it passes us by as a blur of images and we "read" it instantaneously as if it is a photographic image already "written" and framed. As Jameson (1983) has argued, the cultural decentering and fragmentation of our present is experienced as a breakdown in our sense of time. As a result, the present rises before us in the ultravivid mode of fascination—a fascination that is experienced as a loss, an unreality (or what Baudrillard [1981] calls "hyperreality"). In a world of loss and unreality, nostalgia rises to importance as "the phantasmal, parodic rehabilitation of all lost frames of reference" (Foster 1985:90).

But it depends on where you stand: from one place in the cultural landscape nostalgia is a schizophrenic exhilaration (Jameson 1983) of a pure present that reads images for their own sake; from an other place it is a pained, watchful desire to frame the cultural present in relation to an "other" world—to make of the present a cultural object that can be seen, appropriated, refused, disrupted or "made something of." Culture is "seductive" only from the "point of view" of a "self" whose (polemical) cultural practice it is to construct codes of distinction and good taste—a pure aesthetic that is rooted in an ethos of elective distance from the contingency of the natural and social world (see Bourdieu 1984). Here the desire is to purify, reify, and miniaturize the social world and so to make a giant of the individual self (Stewart 1984). Here, individual life narratives dramatize acts of separation—freedom, choice, creativity, imagination, the power to model and plan and act *on* life. From here there is the danger of being drawn in by images that are "larger than life" or have "a life of their own."

But in an "other" place there are "others" whose practice it is to speak from "closeness" and contingency, to "talk back" to codes with the informality of anticodes and to back talk "distinction" with universalizing ethics of personhood. For these "others" on the "margins" the social world is not reified and fixed but thrown into flux and doubleness. Talk is double-voiced, codes are visible from one mode of attentiveness and quite invisible from another so that they refer, inescapably, to the context of their social use. Here it is recognized that everything "depends"; meaning can only be made and read in a "context" that is not just a "background" for the "text" but its very inspiration—its enabling condition. Here texts are contingent and they are *about* contingency. From here, nostalgia is a painful homesickness that generates desire and not, in itself, "seductive" or debased; it would be said that seduction and debasing are things that *people* do and not things inherent in a cultural form. Like other cultural practices in places like this, nostalgia sets in motion a dialectic of closeness and distantiation; its goal is not the creation of a code based on empty distinctions but the redemption of expressive images and speech. Bourdieu would say this is the "deliberate naïveté" of "popular culture"—a move to refuse the refusal to engage that characterizes the distancing pure aesthetic of "good taste.' But the nostalgia of "others" is not the good natured incredulity of a more natural people; it has its own "sophisticated," or self-conscious, sense of its cultural constructions. The difference is that the desire is not to act *on* "the world out there" but to act *in* a world that surrounds. So they retain, and continuously redeem, conventional cultural discourses and more and more they are on the one hand romanticized as those who can (still) speak and on the other hand coldly judged and dismissed because they speak "incorrectly" and "inefficiently."

Two Mirages

Postmodern culture is a wave we ride in the disorganizing and all pervasive economy of late capitalism. Awash in a sea of faces, we look back nostalgically to the shore in a sudden memory of a ground already lost. Once, where there was a time and a place for everything, there was also a time and a place for nostalgia. But now, threatened with a deadening pluralism that makes us all just an "other" among others (Ricoeur 1965), in which difference erases into an utter indifference (Foster 1983), and where the self is a pastiche of styles glued to a surface, nostalgia becomes the very lighthouse waving us back to shore—the one point on the landscape that gives hope of direction.

Across the dry expanse of water two mirages appear on the shore. The first is a grand hotel, representing the public space of a grandiose economy and state. It is a spectacle of riches—gold staircases, revolving elevators, waterfalls cascading down the walls around the guests. The guests are lunching in the grand hall amid hanging plants, afternoon candlelight, and classical music. Those who cannot afford to stay the night come as spectators and as customers for the nostalgia "shoppes" in the mall that ring the concourse overlooking the waterfall and the diners below. The diners in the grand concourse see themselves mirrored in the eyes of the spectators looking down/in on them from the outside and imagine themselves important, glamorous, somehow "above it all." For the (mere) shopper in the mall (more temporary even than an overnight guest) there is an exact replica of a '50s diner where overpriced burgers and malts are served to the strains of Frank Sinatra and Peggy Lee; perhaps here the experience of sitting is not so much the glamorous experience of being watched by an envious gaze but the doubled possibilities of "losing oneself" in the scene of a total (fantasy) world and/or of framing the illusion with the social sarcasm of Bakhtin's carnivalesque laughter.

Finally, in the grand hotel there is a "museum" of "modern life-styles," like the new museum in Henry Ford's Greenfield Village in Detroit or the futuristic scenic worlds at Disneyworld's Epcot Center. The museum is arranged by rooms, each a total world in itself—a '60s living room, a '30s kitchen, Archie Bunker's chair before the TV, father and son in the driveway shining the '52 Chevy, bride and bridesmaids in the bedroom dressing for the wedding. Visitors to the museum might imagine themselves in each scene or life-style (as a '50s father," a "working class bigot," a "bride" in a time when love worked out and when love was for life); they might take pleasure in choosing the (life) style they like best. They might read the scenes symbolically—a reading that refers to the self through the "content" of the image (what does it mean to me?). Or they might read the scenes in the mode of a carnivalesque laughter that degrades potentially weighted cultural forms (weighted with what—the "sacred"?, the "oppressive"?) into spectacles, making them empty objects before the festive gaze of the crowd which notices not naturalized absolute "meanings" but the play of forms, the traces of interpretive strategies to "make something of" life.

Now the rooms of the grand hotel (where the people stay) are ordinary and small. Next to the mall they seem claustrophobic and frighteningly empty. This is "home." As Raymond Williams dramatizes it, we create enclosed rooms,

> above all rooms . . . in which life is centered but inside which people wait for the knock on the door, the letter or the message, the shout from the street, to know what

will happen to them. . . . (We are) at home, in our own lives, but needing to watch what is happening, as we say, "out there": not there in a particular street or a specific community but in a complex and otherwise unfocused and unfocusable national and international life. . . . Yet our lives are still here, still substantially here, with the people we know, in our own rooms, in the similar rooms of our friends and neighbors, and they too are watching: not only for public events, or for distraction, but from a need for images, for representations, of what living is now like, for this kind of person and that, in this kind of situation and place and that. [n.d.:14]

In the suburbs we might walk down the street at night peering into lighted interiors as we pass. In the city the action is on the street in eccentric encounters. In the hotel we might notice the other people staying on our hall through glimpses in the elevator, sounds overheard, the hours of coming and going. We notice with the fascination of a search for our own "identities." What is it like to "live with the life-style" of a banker? Or of a mother? "The character of the self is already widely offered to be appropriated in one or another of these dramatized forms: producer or consumer, married or single, member or exile or vagrant" (Williams n.d.:18).

Next to the grand hotel is another mirage—a country cottage encircled with gables and gingerbread icing and a long porch filled with swings and rocking chairs—a filled and embodied interiority unlike the empty little rooms of the hotel. But the cottage has enormous, postmodern windows—walls of glass—and the inside is one large room of spacious light. The kitchen is of European design. Depending on the class of the property owners, the decor may be sparse and "natural" looking with a smattering of classical styles and austere looking wooden pitchforks captured at an auction and carried off to hang, at a strange angle, on the brick wall beside the fireplace. Or, more likely, the place is filled with the popular nostalgic "country" decor. The walls are covered with country print wallpaper, quilted country scenes, baskets, and miniaturized collections of ducks and cows. The walls are covered as if to shore them up against the flooding force of the sea, creating enclosure against the "real" world—that dream world afloat somewhere "out there."

As Susan Stewart (1984) argues, miniatures and collections exaggerate interiority—the space and time of the individual perceiving subject. But in the process they also exaggerate the enclosure of "style" so that these interiors are not just sanctuaries but also prisons, like the standardized rooms in the grand hotel. Or they are timeless tableaus, like the rooms in the museum of life-styles—each "moment" meant as a monument against instability, randomness, and vulgarity (Stewart 1984) but also crushed under the weight of a visual code that has been given the power to capture particular times, places, identities, and ways of life in a single silent image and without a moment's notice. Meaning hemorrhages out at the rate of a flood, leaving in its wake a cultural landscape littered with signs.

In the wake of a flood, we are "tourists" whose constituting practice it is to read things *as* signs (Culler 1981). Lovers kissing on the street in Paris (or on the street in Chelsea, Michigan) is a sign of a timeless "romantic Paris." A decaying farmhouse surrounded by rusting tractors in the midwestern wheat fields is a sign of the plight of "the small farmer" and "the country's" failure to respond to that plight. The grand hotel displays signs of life-styles and pasts collected in the shape of characteristic, or "typical," objects. The country cottage is the sign of a life-style read "as if" from the inside yet only through the imitation of what are already stereotypic representations of a self and a past. We are tourists who *know* we are tourists, or "post-tourists" (Urry 1987). We know that

> the glossy brochure is a piece of pop culture, that the "authentic" local entertainment is as socially contrived as is the "ethnic bar" and that the quaint "fishing village" preserved in aspic could not survive without the income from tourism. [Urry 1987:7]

The "post-tourist" knows that

> he is not a time traveler when he (sic) goes somewhere historic, not a noble savage when he stays on a tropical beach; not an invisible observer when he visits a native compound. Resolutely "realistic" he cannot evade his condition of outsider. [Feifer, as quoted in Urry 1987:7]

The (magical, ahistorical, asocial) "realism" of a distanced outsider locks into place on the "other side" of the room/mind from the naïve nostalgia of a "participant" in seductive fantasy worlds so that the two become a nauseating oscillation like the red and white stripes of a beach ball tossed into the ocean and slowly but continuously turning as it rides the waves. For the "post-tourist" there is no need to leave the living room to have a tourist experience—to view named scenes through a frame (Urry 1987). On the other hand there is an exhilaration with travel and commerce—a heroization of change and transience for their own sake, modeled as "progress" but experienced as the dizziness of hypertension.

Cultural production is driven back inside the mind. We cannot look out on the world as a referent. All we can do is to trace our own images of the world as we have inscribed them on the walls—as stuffed ducks and quilted barns. To the extent that the world is experienced as a succession of completed material substances—the full maturity of the process of mystifying social relations as things—we lose access to the sight of historical forces and cultural constructions (Jameson 1983). Worse, culture itself becomes reified and fetishistic so that we both play with it in gleeful, cynical abandon and stand in dread of its power to seduce consciousness and empty life.

The loss of a sense of time and place reorients people to a more literalizing attention to words—an attention to sound, appearance, voice, and accent (Jameson 1983) on the romantic side of the room and an obsession with efficiency, succinctness and categorical definitions on the realistic side. This "culture" is not a realm of collective discourses to mediate between us "in here" and the world "out there" but more a kind of tension on the surface of the water that both keeps us afloat and binds us to the surface. We see it as it is when we see it not as a symbolic system but as structures of feeling that have the quality of a wake that comes after a movement. There is no clear "inside" or "outside" anymore, no private and public spheres of life. We build public space as fantasy environments to roam around in—malls, theme parks, every town modeled as a postmodern village of the imagination. History is spatialized and space itself is a rationalized, universalized surface. "Historical societies" appropriate, preserve, rearrange, collect, and reproduce "history" as a symbolic enclosure embodied in handsome, well-kept buildings—a "history" exempted from the ravages, and freedoms, of history. Local, named places dissolve and "the country" becomes just an urban space with more room. There is no one in charge, no one to blame; social hierarchies are diffusely, perniciously encoded in a semiotics of everyday life. The self becomes a pure screen for networks of influence, and social categories that seemed familiar, if not "natural," ten years ago have become uncertain and elusive. We are "baby boomers" searching for a place and a past in Norman Rockwell's paintings and Walt Disney's main street and carried along on the wave of Wall Street.

If, in the modern age, the world became a picture and the person who pictured it became a unified subject through that representational act of mastery (Foster 1985:66), then in the postmodern age the form of hegemony lies in the power to master signs of styles and periods, the ability to read/construct "codes of distinction"—a reading that is still, most importantly, "from a distance." By now systems and rules are already inscribed in the objects arranged on the cultural landscape; order and power do not have to be imposed, or authored, but are already embodied in the very order of objects as they are presented (Fisher 1975:594). They are "taken" in the mode not of a "producer"/participant but of a consumer/observer. The continuing effort of "the individual" to "transcend" culture and contingency, to act *on* the world, continues to produce forms of cultural oppression—the overcoding of life, the appropriation of the self as life-style, and that peculiar vulnerability to culture as a seductive and demanding pure code stripped of signifying contexts, authors, and readers that comes to prominence when the interpretive subject is displaced and social locales obscured. It is not just power relations that are unnamed, made invisible, turned to the stone and apocalyptic power of "nature," but even "history," "society," and "the person" are infused with a petrified drama.

From here, resistance takes the form of making further inscriptions on the landscape of encoded things—inlays on the existing inscriptions—in an effort to fragment the enclosing, already finished order and reopen cultural forms to history. So, for instance, on the tip of Long Island's North Shore, a town called Orient has recently become a "new land" for "yuppies" from the city. They have built country dream houses in the nostalgic image of a remembered *feeling* of childhood. A picturesque square overlooking the bay has been pieced together with a collection of 18th- and 19th-century schoolhouses, inns, and white steepled churches that have been moved to the location from nearby sites or from their primitivist origin—New England itself. They are museums open to the public and each has a formal historical society sign in front that narrates some fragment of its history—"George Washington slept here on (some date) during (such and such a campaign)" or "from 1810 to 1860 the 'Oyster Bays' schoolhouse housed the children of slaves brought over as part of the great silk trade." During the summer the square is the exhilarating scene for "18th-century days" when townspeople dress in 18th-century replica costumes and collectively enact "a day in the marketplace" (in the morning) and a "battle with muskets" (in the afternoon).

But the (recently named) "locals" (who, ironically, are now leaving town because they can no longer afford the property), either ignore the effort to create "the look" and leave their snow plows and old trucks in the yard or, in a more contentious mode, they deliberately inscribe their disruptive, fragmenting signs on top of the look or in its midst. As in the case of the man whose body shop, he was told, needed painting. The message came, over and over again, in the looks of the passersby and finally in so many words. So one night in the dark, he painted it and in the morning people strolling down Main Street to pick up the *New York Times* and a bagel at "the village store" came upon the body shop graffitied from top to bottom in multiple, day-glo colors. The "locals," then, use the strategy of the inner city against the urban "country" dwellers, importing the form of graffiti that, as Foster has argued, resists both erasure and recuperation by the hegemonic coding because it is already in itself a written form. An empty play of signs, a code without a message, its "meaning" can only be understood by placing the form (scribbled, obscene words, out of place and transgressing ordinary frames) in the context of its production—the social and cultural conflict in the town (and of the times), the expression of a voice denied expression. Since it is "criminal" (ugly, antisocial) the graffiti is not easily redeemed by the code but remains a transgression and turns an enclosed, already finished space into spaces of response (Foster 1983:48–50). It remains a social expression (here, in the form of a "crude" joke) and cannot be reduced to a style. The "locals" are nostalgic for the (actual) place the way it was "before," before it became picture perfect, so it is satisfying to *them* to mark the place with a scar signifying (crude) "reality" and the *loss* of perfection. The graffitied body shop is read as an allegory—a ruin that has no immediate, symbolic significance captured in its very "look" but requires an interpreter to read meaning into it (Wolin 1982). And in this way the place is reconstituted for the "locals" as a place filled with significant ruins and emptied spots; more and more ruins become visible as the allegorical practice is taken up and eventually becomes the defining characteristic of the local culture. Or at least there is this possibility.

If cultural hegemonies and resistances are interpretive practices based in social uses rather than fixed contents of ideas, then a similarly alternate, allegorical reading is also possible through other, less obviously contentious forms of nostalgia. The "country decor" in the cottage, for instance, is not meant to *reproduce* country life "as it really was" but to *produce* a world made out of signs: the living room is made "whole," and a "worldview" expressed, through subtle distinctions in tints, nuance, and type; each "country" object refers with careful discrimination to its place within the system of signs of "country" things; every year the "country style" changes subtly so that things have to be added and removed. The (interpretive) practice of the decoration calls attention to the status of these "country" objects as signs and the point is not just to "decorate" in itself but to signify the production, or at least the possibility, of meaning.

What *kind* of meaning is another question. A "country" living room may signify subtle class distinctions or it may ignore, obscure, or attempt to transcend them in favor of more universalizing sensibilities of vulnerability and popular cultural efforts to create places. It may create the home as a total environment—a coded milieu embodying the enclosure of imaginary worlds. Or it may open private and imaginary space to history and the body. Clearly there is every sign of symbolic enclosure and the attempt to miniaturize contingency. But there are also signs of lost (and so hoped for) meanings. It depends on where you stand.

There may be a redemptive nostalgia in a distinction between the (active) production of "country crafts" and their (mere) consumption of their (passive) reproduction as empty styles. But it is certainly not the ideology itself that makes the difference but the social situations to which it attaches. The practice of making "traditional" country objects through the learned techniques of stenciling, tinsmithing, applique, quilting, refinishing, etc. will only enclose the self in a self-conscious image and wrap "the folk" and "history" in a primitivist cloak if the interpretive practice is one of reading action and events and products as symbolic examples or manifestations of an already fixed (symbolized) structure or time. This is interpretation that claims to have no situation. Then there is an "other" discourse of craft production that speaks specifically to situation; it constructs arts and crafts as "something to do" instead of, or while, watching television or "listening" to it; then it is meant as something to break the dulling pattern of "doing nothing" in the evening but not with the intention to withdraw from life as popularly lived in the present but rather to produce active ways of being in it. From there, there may be an exchange of the objects between family and friends that produces a network of living rooms marked by markedly produced objects. For the producers/exchangers each place where their objects are placed is added to the world of personally and culturally significant places. Again, there is a potential allegorical reading of the objects for those who made and exchanged them. My mother makes and paints wooden tulips that sit on windowsills; she gives them to all of her sisters, her daughters, her daughters-in-law, her friends, *my* friends if she meets them. As she says, she gives them to all of her women friends, and they all put them in their windows; there are these wooden tulips in (sometimes unexpected) windows all over the country.

Even consumption is a production—a production of class, privilege, the power to model reality, or a production of relationships or the carnivalesque, spectacle atmosphere of the country auction where the objects are laid out for collective display and their value marked as a social construction in a fast bid between characters. The scenes of consumption (malls, flea markets, auctions, nostalgia shoppes, K marts) frame either social situations or signs of (self) distinction.

Exiles

The "local" "Appalachians" (or "white trash") in Raleigh County, West Virginia, where the "local" economy of coal has collapsed and the unemployment in the area is total and final, live in the ruins and fragments of the old coal camps. Like the "locals" on Long Island, they resist the loss of a cultural home by continuously reinscribing places on a place whose meaning is emptying out. By inscribing the ruined and trashed landscape with allegorical ruins that embody the history of the place, that history, painful as it is, surrounds, overwhelms, becomes a living world to act *in* rather than a world of fixed objects and contents to act *on*. They are nostalgic not as tourists taking in framed scenes from a maintained and exercised distance but as exiles in their own homeland, painfully holding on to closeness in a world that has already deserted them. They live in the fragments and ruins of company camps that are now emptying, again, as they have before, in mass migrations set off by a wave of total unemployment that sweeps through the region like an act of God. The local landscape has been ravaged by history—strip-mined, deforested, the old family farms left to rot in the move down the hillsides into the company camps, and now even the camps fallen to ruin. But people roam from ruin to ruin reading out the absences they embody, reading out how "thangs have got down anymore," dwelling in the mournful desire they represent. People have "places" where they go and sit and stare at a ruin; as Benjamin argued, melancholy searches the past for an adequate object on which to stare itself out. In the camps, the cultural "ideal" is to "git out and go," to notice everything that happens and to dramatize it in a story (to "make something of things"), to "remember" people and events. It is a process of piling things up around the self until there is no border between inside and outside, no distance; from there it is necessary to "get things out" to get out and go—a bursting—and then they begin to pile things up again.

I am told that those wild roses ramble around the chimney in "the old Graham place" field *because* the house is gone, and the Graham family is gone and the ideal "used to" of the family farms is also gone. The vacancy of a lot in Rhodell "remembers" the fire that burned Johnny Millsap to death while he cried out for help (then follows the always graphic story of the cries and the flames and the lasting effect on those who were there at the time but could do nothing but watch). An exposed electrical wire in the hills above Amigo Mines #2 remembers that in 1980 Buddy Hall, a nine-year-old boy, was electrocuted on it. They point to the wire and dwell in the image of the boy hanging from it. "An when hit finally dropped im it had blowed his heel plum off. Blowed a hole right through his heel, tuk the meat out of it, buddy. They said there was the meat on the ground next to his foot."

It is a nostalgia of being inescapably haunted by the images they dwell in. A responsibility to remember what happens, especially those things that "try" to erase someone. (In a narrative culture, overstuffed with possible events and filled with the contingency that anything could happen, something is always "trying to happen.") "You cain't forgit people and these thangs that have happened. If you forgit, that's when you're really crazy." For them, having a culture is a matter of people leaving their mark on the place and, in turn, the place and its history leaves "marks" on the people, even as bodily scars. The interiors of the houses, like the hills outside, are crowded with signs remembering the past. Rooms are filled to overflowing with "whatnots" and walls are covered every inch with nostalgic pictures of the dead and souvenirs of lost moments. Their yards are overflowing with junked, broken, or decaying objects that they are constantly "foolin with"; they dis-member and re-member things, leaving them undeniably marked at every suture as a human construction. The continuity in life comes in always piecing together what is always falling apart. Their "high art" is a *bricolage*. The men take apart trucks and recombine them, marveling at the juxtapositions of parts and memorializing events and encounters in the stories that surround every scratch and dent. Women piece together quilts from scraps of clothing, and in every scrap a memory and so a story.

They live in the bodily realization of knowing one life and also another life that displaces the first. Theirs is at each moment a double vision—two cultures differentiated through a lived experience of loss (Said 1984). And the two worlds, nostalgically, narratively, juxtaposed, constitute their mode of representation. Not a "traditional" mode, but the thoroughly postmodern mode of the exile.

> Exile is predicated on the existence of, love for, and bond with, one's native place; what is true of all exile is not that home and love of home are lost, but that loss is inherent in the very existence of both.
> They regard experiences *as if* they were about to disappear. What is it that anchors them in reality? What would you save of them? What could you give up? . . . only someone whose homeland is "sweet" but whose circumstances make it impossible to recapture that sweetness can answer those questions. (Such a person would also find it impossible to derive satisfaction from substitutes furnished by illusion or dogma.) [Said 1984:55; emphasis in original]

The search for a past and a place leads them to reconstitute their lives in narrative form, a story designed to reassemble a broken history into a new whole. The world created there is a world unnatural and unreal; it resembles fiction or dream. They create an extreme subjectivism, an insatiable will to meaning (Said 1984) yet "meanings" are frozen as empty, allegorical signs on the landscape of loss and abject contingency. Everything is "just talk" and "talk" is an essential, valorized necessity. The culture becomes double-voiced, dialogic; it rejects that "realism" that is a mimetic approach to the representation of social reality. Instead, people develop as eccentric characters whose action is noted in story, not fact. For them, language is already distinct from "reality"; there is no chance for an illusion that what is said could be a simple mapping of what is. Nor is there any chance for taking some distance on life. They see themselves doubly—as they construct themselves in the local talk (and this is itself already masked and metaphoric) and as they are imaged by the distanced surround of "America" (whether nostalgically, as our "contemporary ancestors" or, in the ideology of "progress" and the "need to be realistic," as buffoons—holdovers from the 19th century living in a backwater of the country).

As migrants in the city, and now in the hills too, more and more, they have lived out schizophrenic images of themselves. But through the proliferation of inscriptions—both with objects and forms of "talk"—they still have the last word. What is more, their interpretation is, of necessity, a meta-interpretation; to recover a history that is either misrepresented or rendered invisible, they have to uncover the codes that covered it. As Said put it, "Only to those who are excluded from the social nexus comes the idea of raising a question about the limits of human nature because they need a human that includes them" (1984:53).

The first thing they do is to fragment the illusions of style and codes of respectability that characterize hegemonic "American" nostalgia. So Sissy "back talked" old man Henson when he tried to keep people from walking on his lawn. It was bad enough he already had a brick house (which is read as an imitation of the style of the rich and urban) but he went too far in trying to keep people off his lawn.

> Why, I'll tell you what.
> If I had to live in a place,
> where I had to have me a patch of grass like at
> and couldn't nobody git up on it.
> Well what good is it *for?*
> I'd just get me a *ce*ment truck—one a them *big* ones.
> And ah'd cover me th whole thang over with that *ce*ment.
> That way people could park their cars on it if they wanted to,
> I don't care.
> Buddy I'd turn it into a parkin lot fore I'd git high and mighty
> over some old patch a weeds.
> I tell you what, buddy,
> now when you git to where you got to watch your grass for
> fear somebody'll come and git up *on* it,
> Buddy that's when thangs is *really* got down.

Then nostalgic talk—the work of re-membering things—begins with a litany of mournful, embodied complaints of how thangs is got down, how "anymore" people treat each other like dogs and the old people have to eat out of cans of dog food, how no one visits like they used to, and people don't talk like they used to, and there ain't nothin here and nothin to do, don't nobody care about nobody but their own self, the mines is shet down and the young people is havin to leave— well, there ain't nothin here *for* em, you cain't *blame* em, and the rich people and the powerful people are a gloatin over the desperate pain of the poor and helpless, and the people leave for work and they are shunned and they won't give em water to drank nor a place to lie down, and comes a storm and blows away everythang they *had* in the *world,* and they had to come on back *home,* and their houses are gone, and they had to go to live with their mommie and daddy, and they live all piled up and fussin like cats and dogs in heat, and in the cities, buddy, they have people a dyin on the sidewalks and people walk right *over them*—"I said *they* walk right on *top* a *them* people, buddy."

By this time, in listening, I would be depressed. But for them the next sentence after the litany is cheerful, countering any realist reading of a hell on earth with a "satisfied" conclusion that "thangs'll git back up. Bound to." An "irrationally" utopian voice directly contradicts, or fragments, any simple nostalgia for a "dying culture" (as seen, enclosed, from a distance) or the "realistic" assimilationist claim to the necessity for change and adjustment. For them, there is no inevitability of "progress"; there is, rather "this place" and its allegorical history read into its ruins.

> In the ruin history has physically merged into the setting. And in this guise history does not assume the form of the process of an eternal life so much as that of irresistible decay . . . the events of history shrivel up and become absorbed in the setting. [Benjamin 1977:177, 179]

It is among these ruins, and behind them, that the storytellers stand. This is the "place" from which they speak. In this frame there is no other place to go "in this world," no future of assimilation into America, no need for an abstract notion of progress that would only distract attention from the present (filled with a past) that is being replaced. There is only the finality of this way of life that began in this place and ends here. It is a place that includes an other place—a nowhere utopia that is impregnable, cannot be appropriated, because it is a nowhere—an "outside" that provides the frame to see cultural forms as productions and history as human-made despite the postmodern or late capitalist fragmentations of social life (Said 1984).

Once the melancholic litany of how "thangs is got down" sets the frame for a story of history, they enter the spoken place of desire. They say "Well. I b'lieve thangs is gonna git back up, don't you? B'lieve the mines is a gonna come back and the people will git to go back to work" or they say "But you know, I love these people round here, ain't no better people in the world" or they say "But you know this is home to me and I wouldn't never want to leave it." Talk moves into the hallucinatory, contentious, parodic, dialogic voice of storying what happened on the way to the post office this morning. Or what Miss Lavender said when Bobby Johnson found her hauling 50-pound sacks of pig feed up the railroad tracks because her neighbor, playing out their long feud, had driven pilings into her access road to prevent her using her truck and then skipped away singing. Miss Lavender will use witchcraft against him because, as an older black woman, that is among her cultural tools.

Late capitalism and postmodernism are not predetermined forms; they are grotesques—unfinished forms, developing "out of control," disrupting encasing boundaries of "explanation." Economy and culture merge in one mode of representation that desituates us from any place from which to speak while seducing us with the tourist's nostalgia for style and enclosure. These are the cultural meanings of "taking distance." But at the same time, this system that is also an antisystem, this mode of representation that is both unspeakably coherent and utterly incoherent, also turns back on itself, undermining its own forms of realism and parodying its own faith in forms. Then the truly "reactionary" nostalgia is to imagine a life in the positivist "realism" that protects the beast from parody.

There is another form of realism—a social realism that depends on cultural access to the forces of change. Lukacs (1963) defined it as a literary mode in which characters are portrayed as part of a narrative that places them within the entire historical dynamics of their society—a historical reality revealed as a process in concrete individual experience, mediated by particular groups, institutions, classes, and so on. It is the loss of *this* realism that reduces culture to a flattened juxtaposition of disparate images. Without it the project that fascinates us is not history or possibility but the conflation of internal fantasy and external object. And it is this loss that Appalachians and other "local" cultures nostalgically resist when they re-encode their landscape, and their bodies, with a tortured past still lived, ironically, parodically, religiously, in their very postmodern present. A present based not on "fact" or "solid ground" but on a faith in human fictions that drives them to continuously dis-member and re-member the model of what it is to be "human" in order that it can include them and their lives as they now know them. Postmodern modes of representation—story, fragmentation, montage, juxtaposition—are necessary, not because they are aesthetically, stylistically "right" for a moment frozen in history but because built into their surfaces are the layers of history as they have been frozen there and the ruins of contemporary social relations as they lay in waste. A sense of history and collective reality may need to be built up through a montage of carefully juxtaposed nonlinear images if we are to suggest anything of its "totality." Historical and social redemption would be a work of allegory and *bricolage*—a piecing together of encompassing stories without recourse to the ideological notions of interiority and transcendence (see Foster 1985:75–85 and Haraway 1983).

So when Appalachians send the young people off as migrants to "the city" with the words "there ain't nothin here for em, thangs is got down" they are not mouthing a pragmatic ideology of the need to assimilate, but reproducing their own nostalgic genre of speech and the ideal world it constructs—an "other world" set apart from the city yet thoroughly in the citied world of the present. In their religious discourse, they are "in" the world but not "of" it. In the litany of loss they are reproducing a narrative speech—the power to construct worlds and the power to "talk back" to an overcoded order that depends on unnaming and distanced speechlessness. They are sending the young people off with the weight of the place behind them, piling the place up around them, almost as if to propel them out with the excess of feeling and meaning that builds until it threatens to burst the boundaries of "this world."

Those "left behind" in the hills will follow the young people's "progress" (which is usually a drifting back and forth from the city to the hills via heartbreak and windstorms). They follow this "progress" in dramatic story that poses the migrant as a martyr, though utterly human and moved by "foolishness" and "just talk" as much as by heroism and transcendent ideals, as much adrift in the sea and lost on the crossroads as they are captains of their own consciousness. The storytellers are "making something of" what is happening to them as a people, and so maintaining the place for the young people to come back to. The story is not assimilationist but revivalistic. And the "migrants," the exiles, drifting back and forth, coming close from desire and moving distant from necessity and "confusion," are allegorical references to the final desire/fear of leaving "this world" and to the melancholy of a desire that has to continuously fill in "this world"— a world that is always emptying itself out.

Those still "at home" in the hills follow the migrants' progress bodily, like the course of a disease, like the "spells" of "the dizzy" and "the nerves" that now inflict everyone, "every body." News of the migrants passes through the camps instantly and continuously, like a wave, and like the "fallin down spells" that now, on some days, pass through whole camps and counties in a wave that washes over the place but leaves people talking amidst the rubble.

References Cited

Barthes, Roland
    1957   Mythologies. New York: Hill and Wang.
Baudrillard, Jean
    1981   For a Critique of the Political Economy of the Sign. Charles Levin, trans. St. Louis: Telos Press.
Benjamin, Walter
    1977   The Origin of German Tragic Drama. J. Osborne, trans. London: New Left Books.
Bourdieu, Pierre
    1984   Distinction: A Social Critique of the Judgement of Taste. Cambridge: Harvard University Press.
Culler, Jonathan
    1981   Semiotics of Tourism. American Journal of Semiotics 1:127–140.
Fisher, Philip
    1975   The Future's Past. New Literary History 6:587–606.
Foster, Hal
    1985   Recodings: Art, Spectacle, Cultural Politics. Port Townsend, Wash.: Bay Press.
Foster, Hal, ed.
    1983   The Anti-Aesthetic: Essays on Postmodern Culture. Port Townsend, Wash.: Bay Press.
Haraway, Donna
    1983   A Manifesto for Cyborgs: Science, Technology, and Socialist Feminism in the 1980s. Socialist Review 80:65–107.
Jameson, Fredric
    1983   Postmodernism and Consumer Society. In The Anti-Aesthetic: Essays on Postmodern Culture. Hal Foster, ed. Pp. 111–125. Port Townsend, Wash.: Bay Press.
Lash, S., and John Urry
    1987   The End of Organized Capitalism. Madison: University of Wisconsin Press.
Lukacs, Georg
    1963[1957]   The Meaning of Contemporary Realism. London: Merlin Press.
Mandel, Ernst
    1978   Late Capitalism. London: New Left Books.
Ricoeur, Paul
    1965   Universal Civilization and National Cultures. In History and Truth. Charles Kelbley, trans. Pp. 273–287. Evanston, Ill.: Northwestern University Press.
Said, Edward
    1984   The Mind of Winter: Reflections on Life in Exile. Harpers 269:49–55.
Stewart, Susan
    1984   On Longing: Narratives of the Miniature, the Gigantic, the Souvenir, the Collection. Baltimore: Johns Hopkins University Press.

Williams, Raymond
    n.d. Drama in a Dramatized Society. *In* Writing in Society. New York: Schocken
    Books.
Wolin, Richard
    1982   Walter Benjamin: an Aesthetic of Redemption. New York: Columbia University
    Press.
Urry, John
    1987   Cultural Change and Contemporary Holiday-Making. Unpublished MS.

Fictions that Save: Migrants' Performance and Basotho National Culture

David B. Coplan

> . . . You know, my fathers, my parents,
> Why should I steal [reveal secrets] in this way?
> I feel I want to shake the nation. . . .
> —Majara Majara

Of all South Africa's neighbors, none has suffered more severely from expropriation and underdevelopment by white colonialism and supremacy than the Kingdom of Lesotho. In reality, Lesotho is not South Africa's neighbor but its backlot: an eroded, mountainous, Belgium-sized (11,716 square miles) remnant of a once expansive semifeudal African highveld state. The military depredations of the Free State Afrikaners, combined with successive betrayals of its erstwhile "protectors," the imperial British, transformed Basutoland from a largely self-sufficient agricultural exporter to an impoverished, dependent supplier of labor to South Africa (Murray 1980). While independence from Britain in 1966 did nothing to improve its economic position, Lesotho is one African nation whose citizens have never felt the slightest nostalgia for the colonial period. In the mid 19th century, the Basotho (sing.: Mosotho) were lauded by missionaries and resident British officials for their courtliness, ingenious adaptability, and eagerness for the "progress" they believed would come from the adoption of European ways. In the event, however, British and white settler colonialism deprived them of both autonomy and resources in virtually every sphere.

In response, the Basotho have retreated to the stubborn protection of their last existential redoubt, *Sesotho,* their unifying language and culture. Like a cultural correlative of the impassable but sheltering ranges of the Drakensburg up against which the Europeans drove them, the secrets *(likoma)* of *Sesotho* have become a defensible symbolic landscape, ringed by authoritative knowledge and identity. Connotatively and ideologically, *Sesotho* refers to anything, ideational, behavioral, or material, that Basotho regard as purely of their own devising, unadulterated by "external" influences. The impossibility of identifying the boundaries or content of *Sesotho* in this sense historically is not the point. The point is that the concept of *Sesotho* has long served as a cognitive and behavioral defense against the loss of Basotho national identity and the misappropriation of the resources to which this identity gives title. From varying and sometimes conflicting perspectives, *Sesotho* is spoken of by all classes of Basotho as vital to both social and "national" survival. With so much of the original Basotho territory irretrievably incorporated into the Orange Free State, and so many Basotho residing in South Africa, the most significant markers of national identity are cultural. Representations of such markers, however, are constructed on the basis of geographical origins and political allegiances within what remains of the autonomous monarchal state. As retired migrant Makeka Lihojane, a World War II veteran who spent forty years in the South African mines, sang in his autobiographical *sefela* song:

> I reside at Quthing Sebapala [in southern Lesotho];
> I was born there, I pay tax there,
> The brother of 'Mamphasa and 'Mamoitheri,
> I am the soldier of [Chieftainess] 'Mamokhesuoe's village. . . .

In this sense Lesotho's current borders enclose and anchor a more wide-ranging historical patrimony. But as South Africa enters a period of dramatic political change, Lesotho's independent existence, already a fiction in an economic sense, may cease to be worth the candle except to the small military, professional/bureaucratic, and aristocratic elites who have a vested interest in structures of government and patronage, land allocation, and the political economy of migrant labor. It is members of this class who most pointedly represent cultural and political identity as coterminous, bottling up *Sesotho* in Lesotho. As a prominent Mosotho professor of African Languages complained to me, "These things you are studying from the migrants and bars and prostitutes, they were never in Lesotho, they have been brought in from South Africa." Not surprisingly, the erstwhile "Sesotho Academy" of Basotho intellectuals locates the performance domain of *Sesotho* in much honored but seldom performed chiefly "praise poetry" (*lithoko;* see Kunene 1971), rural dance/song genres (Matsela 1987), and written Sesotho literature.

Yet it is the nature of culture to be suffocated by a too self-conscious and solicitous embrace. The continuing development of Sesotho (no italics) as a living symbolic structure guiding autonomous social action has passed in large degree from aristocratic retainers and "praise singers" (*liroki*) into the hands of people historically consigned to Lesotho's social margins. These are the disenfranchised, physically mobile and frequently absent, socially ambiguous yet economically indispensable migrant workers. As other Basotho educators have come to realize (Mokitimi 1982; Moletsane 1982, 1983) it is the performing artists and genres among migrants, both male and female, that have expanded and kept open the boundaries of Sesotho, while still reproducing its collective understandings and historical representations for the affective encoding of social experience. Migrant working men and women have created new performance genres that enlarge Basotho cultural boundaries and increase their permeability, challenging idealized or authoritative notions of what constitutes *Sesotho*.

From among the various categories of Basotho performers and performances, this article focuses on migrant tavern singers turned recording artists, to whom some of the task of making and remaking Basotho "national culture" has fallen. Their songs, long performed in wayside bars and now widely distributed on radio and audio cassette, reveal the dynamics of genre, gender, and expressive authority in the politics of performance. Their relation to Sesotho as emergent tradition embodies the layered contradictions created by the need for social solidarity in the face of competing positions and interests, and for historical continuity (re)presented in collective metaphors in the face of a radically transformed and fragmented social reality. In proposing the universality of the marginal as the defining condition and not merely the by-product of structuration, Babcock-Abrahams argues that marginality is not a structurally residual category, but "That which is socially peripheral or marginal is symbolically central and predominant" (Babcock-Abrahams 1975:155). Recognizing this, performers openly adopt "marginality" as a stance from which to address the tension between the impracticabilities of solidary structural ideals and the conflictual structure of real social practices.

In the larger sense in which Sesotho is a means of confronting, interpreting, and domesticating the external conditions that affect Basotho migrant life, the work of these performers represents what Raymond Williams (1977) called a "structure of feeling": an articulation of experience with broader social forces and expressions of ideology, of authoritative genres and metaphors with what Mikhail Bakhtin called "the common people's creative culture of laughter" (Holquist 1981:20). As Bakhtin argued, such articulations occur in some form in the cultural representations of every historical context. What Basotho migrant performers in particular are up to is a kind of organic rejection of apartheid-sponsored dualities of culture, in which historical and social identity is opposed to the pursuit of material interests and rationalized modes of social cooperation and agency. In the apartheid conception, colonial categories of African ethnicity are reified as an immemorial heritage indispensable to group autonomy and development, and so it follows that being a Mosotho is opposed to being an active member of the black National Union of Mineworkers. As what the mine companies once called "foreign natives" (!), citizens of Lesotho are not legally entitled to join the South African union, but Basotho from both countries do in fact comprise a large segment of both its members and leaders. One result of this situation was the repatriation of more than 5,000 Basotho mineworkers to Lesotho following their summary dismissal during the massive union mine strike of 1987.

Understandably, union leadership also regards ethnic loyalty as divisive and therefore inconsistent with worker militancy. Harriet Ngubane reports (personal communication, 1989) that when Mineworkers Union General Secretary Cyril Ramaphosa and President James Motlatsi urged workers at a union rally to put aside their identification as Basotho, Xhosa, or Shangaan in the interests of solidarity and united action, many were indignant. They protested that upholding Sesotho was not an expression of disrespect or hostility toward members of other ethnic groups as workers. Further they pointed out that whereas the leaders who spoke against Sesotho were educated and cosmopolitan professionals, invited to speechify before the mighty in Johannesburg, Europe, and America, mineworkers would still be in the South African mines with their attendant hardships no matter how successful the union's campaigns. Was it not then unfair for citizens of the world like Ramaphosa to ask mineworkers to downgrade the one thing that was inalienably theirs, their sociocultural and thus human identity as Basotho? This identity, moreover, is maintained as a defense against the continuing reinvention of Basotho "tradition" by the bureaucratic purveyors of apartheid ideology. Adding injury to insult, the culture of black workers is recreated in the image that dominant others make of it and thrown in their faces as either a confirmation of their lack of capacity and entitlement or a reproach to their rational methods toward amelioration.

Attempts like those of the Basotho to create forms that are qualitatively new yet invested with the authority of historically continuous cultural practices, a kind of cultural self-preservation through self-transformation, are widely characteristic of formerly colonized societies both in Africa and elsewhere. In the present instance we will follow both Bakhtin and Williams, showing how the ethnographic interpretation of oral genres in their contexts of construction can reveal the cultural ground of migrants' accommodation and resistance to the existing social order (Marcus and Fischer 1986:133). Carrying their accordions and *likhetsi* ("medicine bags") full of historical metaphors, popular Basotho musicians cross and recross cognitive boundaries in order "to tap the continued vitality of the mingled continuity and innovation which resides within indigenous cultures as they have continued to develop underneath the rigidities" of invented tradition (Ranger 1984:262).

Symbolic Dualities, Mediating Genres

There is no evidence that songmaking, much less anything comparable to our notion of musician, was ever an authoritative or functionally differentiated role in agrarian Basotho communities. Even the authoritative composers (liroki, sing.: *seroki*) of royal praise poetry (lithoko) residing at court performed this function irregularly and made a living by other means. Of the lexemes commonly used to refer to specialized abilities in composition and performance only a few others are of immediate relevance. These include *mosue* (pl.: *basoue,* from *ho sua*: "to make hides supple"), a teacher at boys' or girls' circumcision schools whose duties include instructing the initiates in sacred secret likoma and other songs, dances, and in the case of boys, the composition of their own praises. A more widely extended term is *kheleke,* "eloquent one," applied to any talented maker of musical texts in any genre, but suggesting extraordinary abilities in lyric/melodic/rhythmic extemporization.[1] In ordinary discourse, kheleke is most often associated with male migrant composer/performers of lengthy first-person extemporaneous songs known as *lifela tsa litsamaea-naha,* "inveterate travelers songs" (see Coplan 1987a, 1987b, 1988).

Operating metaphorically, the title *ngaka* (pl.: *linaka*), "spirit diviner and herbal healer" is extended as a recognition of expertise in any domain of cultural knowledge; hence *ngaka ea lipina* "doctor of songs," for any renowned song-smith. Such expressions gloss the Basotho prescription, taught by basoue at initiation, that adults should use whatever special talents the ancestors may have given them for the benefit of the community. Further, a productive ideal of social harmony or agreement lies at the center of Basotho moral ideology. The ancestor cult that comprises the essence of Basotho pre-Christian religion sanctions this ideology, frequently through the offices of the ngaka, who ritually mediates relations between ancestors and their descendants and among living members of the community. Such mediation can, of course, foster the disruption along with the reordering of social relations. Master *lingaka* are as much feared for their ability to confront and reveal witchcraft as they are needed to restore physical and moral composure to the sick and conflicted.

Praise poets enjoy a parallel license to criticize as well as eulogize their aristocratic subjects, while migrant *likheleke* disdain the need for any hierarchical or contextual legitimation in celebrating or satirizing chiefs or commoners, kith or kin, including themselves. A renowned singer of *lifela* (sing.: sefela) migrants' songs who is in demand among his juniors as a teacher of composition is known as a *ngaka ea lifela*. In bringing the causes of social disaffection to public attention through heightened modes of aesthetic discourse, the *seroki* turned kheleke shares in the ritual functions and authority of the ngaka, creating the opportunity for cognitive and social reassessment and reintegration through "illocutionary acts" both in and of performance. *Bongaka,* "traditional divination/healing," is a potentially full-time occupation in Basotho society and thus one of the few alternatives to labor migrancy open to landless, unschooled rural Basotho. Though traditional healers are still very widely employed in both the medical and ritual exigencies of everyday life, they have largely lost their historical position as seers and councillors to the powerful. Bongaka is a form of institutionalized liminality discredited by educated resident elites, and today shares in the categorical marginality of migrancy, though in Lesotho migrancy is a marginality that has overgrown the center. Likheleke and lingaka can also be compared to what Gramsci termed "organic intellectuals," purveying the knowledge underlying the historical continuity of Sesotho in respectively aesthetic or ritual performance and discourse. Like singers, traditional healers are classified not by their varied divinatory techniques but by personal reputation (Murray 1975:67). Both *bokheleke,* eloquence, and bongaka, healing, are repositories of *Sesotho,* and singer as traditional diviner/herbalist is one of the most popular metapoetic tropes by which a composer lays claim to authoritative knowledge. Beyond the spiritual powers of the ngaka, however, the singers exploit the historical status of aural poetry as a legitimate, contested medium for the expression of power relations in southern African chiefdoms (White 1982). The singers' reflective resonation of historical metaphors with personal experience is a flight of "moral imagination," because "To imagine another kind of world is always a judgement about this one" (Beidelman 1986:204). "Eloquent ones," like diviners, have the capacity to articulate the social realities and contradictions that lie beneath the surface of institutional and community life, and so to help reestablish the moral basis of productive and satisfying social relations.

From the point of view of male migrant workers and their women, more than a few of whom are migrants themselves, the moral system attributed to history is in dire need of reestablishment, for current Basotho social reality is disoriented and disaffected indeed. First there is the alienation and contradiction of migrancy, a system in which the survival of a patriarchal household depends upon the forced absence of its male head. Second there is Lesotho's dependent position in South Africa's political economy, and the society's resultant loss of patterns of production and exchange based on reciprocity and cooperation. That migrants use Sesotho performance to create an integrated, positive self-concept in the face of displacement, fragmentation, and dehumanization should not surprise us. On the other hand, the uses of *Sesotho* suggest that the once entrenched "dualist" economic model (Wallmann 1969) now so widely criticized in studies of southern African labor migrancy (Bardill and Cobbe 1985:28, 42n.; Murray 1981) is equally misleading when applied to the symbolic structure of the Basotho social universe.

Much writing based on this dualist view has depicted southern African migrants as "men of two worlds" (women migrants have been largely ignored); people who maintain a symbolistic discontinuity between the structure of social relations, patterns of interaction, and cultural norms encountered in South Africa, and those governing social participation in the home communities. Alverson (1978) and more recently John and Jean Comaroff (1987) have based their analyses of migrant consciousness in Botswana on this opposition. The Comaroffs have identified two Setswana verbs for the same apparent activity, "working," as representing this fundamental dichotomy. The first, *go dira,* refers to working as an autonomous, socially productive activity in the home community; while *go bereka,* derived, significantly, from Afrikaans *werk,* refers to working for whites: the proletarianized, unequal exchange of labor for wages on the farms and mines. The Basotho are ancient relatives of the Batswana and their languages were not recognizably distinct until the 19th century. Such a deliberately rigid, unreconcilable opposition would seem ideal for differentiating between *Sesotho* and *Sekhooa,* the culture of the whites, or *mtheto,* the unwritten code that governs life at the mines. Ideally, perhaps this is so. On closer ethnographic examination however, the discontinuity between Lesotho and *makhooeng,* the "whitemen's place" (the mines) appears as a putative representation, a fiction useful only in the defense of *Sesotho* and its attached situational entitlements. The term *ho lira* (for *go dira*) does not properly exist in Sesotho and is regarded as a South African synonym for *ho etsa,* "to make, do, create." The verb for working, *ho sebetsa,* can be used for any kind of work, in South Africa or Lesotho. *Ho bereka,* though less common, does have the connotation of "working for whites," but again is regarded as a South African loan word and is not categorically opposed to ho sebetsa.

There is evidence to show, moreover, that Basotho migrants no longer regard the environments of the mines and the home villages as two separate social fields. Labor migrancy is more firmly woven into the fabric of Basotho experience and more economically pervasive in Lesotho than in Botswana. The latter, with its

Texas-sized territory (275,000 square miles), thriving cattle and mineral production, and its backdoor to central Africa, is a place where significant numbers of rural household heads can "build up the homestead" by other means than labor migration, and thus the ideology of go dira and the opposition between it and go bereka can be maintained. This is not the case in Lesotho, where only 6% of average disposable household income comes from agriculture despite the employment of 92% of the *resident* workforce in farming and animal husbandry. A far greater proportion, two-thirds of Lesotho's gross domestic product, comes from the remittance of migrants' wages.

Sesotho, we might reemphasize, extends beyond the boundaries of Lesotho as a national state, and operates also among Basotho in the Free State, Transvaal, and Transkei. In another passage of the sefela quoted above, Makeka Lihojane, better known by his performance *nom de voix* "Ngoana Mokhalo," sings about a *thokolosi* (Ashton 1952:294–296), a witch's demon-familiar and poetic/ritual/medical symbol of social evil, sickness, and disruption. A ngaka can chase a thokolosi out of a village with powerful herbs and magic, but the traveler poet/healer must expel the demon, which physically resembles a monkey, by relentless pursuit over the countryside. Here, the chase brings Ngoana Mokhalo to his wife's natal village:

> . . . At Pechela's in the mountains
> I arrived in the morning
> (There) I discovered my wife's parents bewitching.
> I found them down in the river, beating out *seakhi,*
> The pastor was naked,
> Their monkey (thokolosi) sat by,
> Pointing with a barbed spear in silence.
> I saw them file past, the witches,
> They filed across the river. . . .

The thokolosi has taken refuge among the singer's in-laws, who are busy bewitching people, including our hero, while performing the seakhi dance. This seems peculiar, since the seakhi is a dance performed only by mineworkers in the dead of night in the mine compounds in South Africa. The focus of the seakhi is a competition in which the winning dancer is awarded the right to take a young newcomer, dressed as a girl for the occasion, as his homosexual "wife." Payments to black mine compound overseers (*lintona:* this office has recently been abolished) who sponsor the dances have been known to influence the outcome of seakhi. Why should a miner's rural in-laws perform it? Both witchcraft and homosexuality are considered inverted forms of social behavior. Miners insist that, with women available, homosexual liaisons contracted out of necessity at the mines are never continued at home. Witchcraft, however, can be practiced by and upon anyone, even white people, anywhere. The associated images of demon-familiar and witchcraft here unify the social field, since jealous in-laws are quite capable of sending a thokolosi to bewitch, afflict, injure, or kill a mineworker when he is down in the shaft. Further, witches, like seakhi performers, dance naked. South Africa and Lesotho thus become a single social world, full of evils and dangers that the migrant performer must uncover and overcome at every turning in his endless road. As one kheleke exhorted his comrades:

> Koete ha habo monna ke hohle; u nke molamu u k'u itekile.
> Gentlemen, a man's home is everywhere; take up your stick and ramble.
> [Mokitimi 1982:456]

In contrast to Alverson's (1978) suggestions about the Batswana, Basotho migrants' conformity to one code of conduct, *mtheto,* at the mines and to *Sesotho* at home does not imply any reformulation of his identity as a *Mosotho oa mankhonthe,* a true Mosotho. "Mosotho" is a unified concept that includes the willingness to face danger in the pursuit of family livelihood wherever the migrant finds himself.

Or herself: despite restrictions, 7% of registered (and many more unregistered) migrants to South Africa are women. Thousands more have migrated from rural homes to seek employment in the capital, Maseru, and other border towns (Wilkinson 1985). Up until 1962, 25% of known Basotho migrants were women, but then South African law made female migration from Basutoland illegal. Among the reasons for this bitterly resented restriction was the century-old fame of Basotho females in South Africa as independent suppliers of wine (beer), women, and song to urban and migrant black workingmen (Bonner 1988). It was these barflies and canteen-keepers—single, deserted, deserting, or married—who developed the dance and song genre that forms the basis of contemporary Basotho national popular music. The ramshackle illegal taverns called *shebeens* (Gaelic: "little shop," Coplan 1985:92–98) provided women not only with an independent albeit hard-won means of livelihood; they created a female-controlled arena for individuated performance.

Basotho women's rural choral songs, such as those for the famous *mokhibo* kneeling dance, provided little acknowledged scope for extended solo composition. We must be careful, though, to discriminate between normative and actual potentialities for self-expression in a culture where women's opportunities for social comment are protected by the useful fiction that there aren't any. Eventually the tragedy of women left in Lesotho or forced into migration themselves by absent and unsupportive husbands did find expression in village women's feast or party songs, such as the following recorded by Hugh Tracey in 1959:

> Aunt, stretch out the blanket
> There are two of us.
> Stretch out the blanket,
> I'll be coming; I'm going out to smoke [make love].
> When I leave here, going away,
> Montsala remain here and look after my children.
> Look after Mamotolo and Malerato and Toma.
> Toma, look after these children of mine
> Particularly Mamotolo and Malerato.
> It looks as if I'll be going away.

I feel I'm going.
I really feel I'll be crossing the [Caledon] river [into South Africa]
[Music of Africa Series, AMA. TR-103 (B-3)]

This potential migrant is perhaps luckier than many of her counterparts, for it appears she may be going to South Africa with her man, rather than in search for him or even to get away from him. The distorted social system that no longer provided social security in return for the continuing subordination of women made migration to South Africa an attractive, sometimes necessary alternative to exploitative local chiefs and in-laws. Local authorities attempted to deal with this problem by collaborating with South African attempts to prevent the flow of women across the Caledon river, but with little effect except to keep female migrants on the move, wherever they were. Women who migrated specifically to enter the liquor trade often returned along with their migrant menfolk, and established the shebeen as a fixture of both town and country life in Lesotho itself. Such women became known as *matekatse,* a term universally translated in Lesotho as "prostitutes," derived from *ho teka* "to roam about helplessly," and *ho tekatsa,* "to abandon one's husband."

The immediate sources for women's shebeen songs appear not to have been established women's genres, but the relatively new *lifela tsa litsamaea-naha* songs of their men. Textual evidence and oral testimony suggest that early in the 20th century, the shebeen setting provided women with the inspiration and compositional models of male lifela, along with acknowledged places to perform their own songs of moral assessment, self-justification, and affliction. Though they lack the cultural prestige and extended seminarrative elaboration of the typically unaccompanied lifela, shorter solos closely resembling truncated lifela are an integral feature of dance songs performed to the barrel-house Sesotho rhythms of accordion and drum in shebeens. Though men also take their solo turns, often as a retort or appreciation for a female singer's barbs or praises, the recognized virtuosos of this style are women, who will not perform without instrumental accompaniment.

Lifela are most often egocentric, reflecting the male migrant's existential self-concept as a contemporary hero in the traditional Sesotho mold (Kunene 1971:4), an ordinary man confronting extraordinary dangers in an alien place, exiled from the home, family, and community he is (thanklessly) fighting to preserve. Like black American bluesmen they sing of love affairs and faithlessness not marriage, doubt and danger not certainty, wage labor not agriculture, trains and trails not home and family. Once again "Ngoana Mokhalo":

I am the soldier of 'Mamokhesuoe's village.
When I was leaving to go to the place of whites [mines],
I spoke to my heart and we finished.
And my soul we understood each other.
My eyes cried I was not content,
I felt sick from eating nothing . . .

. . . The train is a taker and a returner,
Ours, that of the young men,
It came running from Rouxville, the white-faced carriage . . .
. . . It galloped like a white-spotted hare,
Like a hare of the uplands.
The train entered Bloomfontein at night,
At five o'clock in the evening.
It has taken men who are workers;
Chaile and 'Makhoana, those who survived the west shaft, . . .
. . . When it reached Moselekatse [Johannesburg labor depot]
It reached and gave birth to people for Moshoeshoe,
[Moshoeshoe II, reigning monarch and by extension Moshoeshoe I, dynastic founder,
    d. 1870]
It delivered of people in hundreds.
It's then I went off to the location [African township]:
Johannesburg, South Africa. . . .

Women's songs proclaim a resolute, individualistic, and adventurous spirit imitative of male itinerant heroism, and deliberately contrary to the stationary domestic commitment expected of adult women in Lesotho. Their flight from the normative is an enforced one, however, and the accompanying sense of displacement profound. Theirs is in an explicitly shared affliction, mourning the loss of kinship and marital security; friendship found, sundered, and betrayed; the anomic reality starkly outlined against the communal ideal.

Heee! the cruelty to my mother,
To my mother, an unfortunate woman, she cries daily,
Always my heart never forgets.
I am going away.
I am a person living in difficulties:
I live by cheating workers [taking advantage of migrants],
I am not working;
I am a wanderer, a divorced one;
Divorcer [philanderer], a little girl of Lesotho
Give me a ticket, gentlemen, a ticket and my stick
When I leave, I wander about—
I am going home, home to Lesotho.
When I leave, I move fast;
Chabane is a prostitute.
My father is looking for me,
My father or Teboho,
The man who begot me
They pass; my brother is coming.
Hele helele my sister Anna,
The misfortunes I am caught up in!
Why am I going?
I am a polygamist [I have many men] . . .
. . . These women, they speak about me girl,
About me at the corners of houses.
I look at them; they look away, yonder.
He-e you, my girl child, my father or Nthako,
I abandon my sisters [fellow barmaids];
Here they are at Hlotse camp [town], girls,

In whose trust do I leave them?
I have entrusted them to God eee! [they have no husbands]
I have left, pray for me,
Yes why? Because I am a prostitute.
I know where I live, girls:
They ask where I stay?
At Hlotse, the camp [town],
Helele, helelele, helehelele, helehelele
Father or Molefi helele,
I can leave my sister [friend], Tholinyana
My heart is fighting against my thoughts,
Me, a little girl of Masupha's (district).

Nthabiseng Nthako, the composer/performer of this passage, was 22 years old, an unmarried barmaid afraid that the miner who paid the rent on her tiny ramshackle bedroom might forsake her, but confident of attracting a replacement when he did so. The male dimension of her stance is exemplified by the rhetorical request: "Give me a ticket, gentlemen, a ticket and my stick," referring to the train ticket and heavy wooden fighting stick *(molamu)* that symbolize the intrepidity of the male migrant. Her friend and fellow shebeen singer Thakane Mahlasi (called Tholinyana in the passage above) performed the following admonition to "little boys" (reluctant migrants), reminding them of their responsibilities, and that women's struggles are equivalent to their own:

He ee oele oelele oele!
Dying at one's home, little boy,
Yes, one dying in his home
Is no meat for his relatives:
A man's home is everywhere.
Helo child of Mathopela;
A man is never overwhelmed by troubles:
Even women do overcome them,
Oh, little girl of (the) Kholokoe (clan). . . .

Their right to sing out was ensured by the intoxicated (literally) freedom of the "immoral" and illicit but indispensable shebeen, a setting whose social centrality is symbolized by the white or yellow flags *(phephesela)* that fly on poles outside these *libara* (Eng.: "bar") in every Lesotho community. Indeed, unlike the family homestead, the pastures and cropfields, or the distant workplace, which tend to segregate the sexes and limit social intercourse between them, the shebeen provides an environment for cross-gender communication, performance, and sociability; a change in relationships fostered by processes of proletarianization all over the world. Like male lifela . . . performers, the *chanteuses* can be called "eloquent ones," but their songs have no commonly accepted generic label. The most convenient way to refer to the song texts themselves is to say *seoeleoelele*, an ideophone representing the act of singing that serves as the universal introduction to shebeen songs in performance. It may be that, within the politics of performance in Lesotho, a women's genre whose texts are often fiercely critical of the behavior of men and governments is being denied a public identity:

> I wish my voice would ring like a bell,
> To let the miners know that I live in hardships here in Lesotho.
> I deeply fear the government in power! . . .
>
> . . . Go away from here,
> You with porridge between your teeth.
> Go away from here,
> You with your stinking body,
> Return to your cattle posts! . . .
> . . . Here in Hlotse town in bed I outstretch myself,
> But I do pay dearly for the rent. . . .
> [Thakane "Tholi" Mahlasi, from the film, *Songs of the Adventurers*, Costant
>   Springs Productions 1986]

Outside the shebeen, however, Basotho women characteristically express explicit disapproval in the presence of authority by affecting a stony, sullen silence that speaks more powerfully (and more safely) than angry words. Women have perhaps sought to preserve this new medium for expressing their social grievances and by collaborating in its anonymity. This genre that dare not speak its name achieves its purposes by traveling incognito—pointed commentary, emotional community, high art and low comedy—acceptable only if kept categorically outside the secret precincts of *Sesotho*. In this context, the contradiction of women usurping the expressive privileges of men is resolved not only by the ambiguous, "independent" social position of shebeen women, but also by the Sesotho metonymical principle whereby individuals performing unaccustomed roles can be reclassified with the category of persons who ordinarily perform them. Thus a singer may urge a prospective lover to come and "play the husband," or, urged on by shouts of *"Hela, ntate!"* ("Hey now father/sir!") belt out the following:

> . . . What do you say, you men of Lesotho?
> When I leave I clear out,
> I am the donkey stallion, girl!
> The donkey stallion, neck-bridle breaker:
> When I leave I travel. . . .
>   [Nthabiseng Nthako]

Pursuing the male metaphor from sung rhetoric into dance, it is only in shebeens, singing and moving to the music of accordion and drum, that I have seen women snatch up and wave (quite aggressively) the massive and beautifully decorated *melamu* fighting sticks carried by the men.

The provision of the shebeen or *sepoto* (Eng.: "spot") as a space for non-normative behavior, self-expression, and gender crossing on the part of women helps to reduce the stress caused by the need to maintain the more general operation of social norms, *molao* ("the law'), as useful fictions. This principle allows for the reproduction of social structure as both a moral and historical template for cultural identity and integrative behavior, while reducing the socially disruptive consequences of what people actually wish or have to do. The Basotho have a proverb *(maele): Leshano le pholosang le molemo,* "The lie that rescues is good,'' widely cited to sanction the white lies and inadmissions that smooth the surface of social interaction or prevent public injury to the feelings or pride of people "caught out." It is also much quoted by non-Basotho as proof that unapologetic prevarication is a normative quality of Basotho social character. The deeper meaning of this proverb, however, is that neither competing personal interests and loyalties, nor intractable social and material realities, nor even plain human frailty ought to be allowed to fracture the general acceptance of and attempts to approximate stabilizing structural ideals. Cynicism, an attitude bespeaking a lack of faith in social values in both motivation and conduct, is therefore an inappropriate alternative to social naïveté.

Moreover, their social practice reveals that Basotho are aware of and exploit the transformational potential embedded in structural contradictions. For example, the ideology of "cousin marriage" in this patrilineal society gives preference to unions with the mother's brother's daughter, based on values of cooperation and equality among affines. In practice, however, the preference is for marriage with a father's brother's daughter, which infuses these affinal behavioral norms and expectations into the hierarchical and competitive relations that inevitably undermine the solidarity expected among agnates. As Kuper explains (1975:74):

> This is not stressed in the ideology, and it does not appear in the ideal order of close-kin marriages, since a preference for this sort of marriage [FBD] implies that relationships with close agnates are fraught with difficulty and need to be translated into something else. The Sotho prefer to see their endemic fraternal conflicts as occasional and lamentable deviations from the ideal amity.

The concept of molao, the law, is further used to bring normative and actual patterns of behavior into greater harmony or agreement *(tumelano)*. Among the most striking examples is *bonyatsi,* a nonnormative but virtually institutionalized form of adultery in which married men or women contract extended extramarital relationships in the frequent and lengthy absences of a spouse (Spiegel 1990a). Bonyatsi for a man is condoned on the basis of the once-normative institution of polygyny, forbidden by the Christian denominations to which the vast majority of Basotho nominally belong. Bonyatsi among women is probably no less common, but may be overlooked rather than condoned since Basotho seek to prevent human weakness, however understandable or prevalent, from threatening the overall maintenance of social harmony and customary law. Women point to accepted notions of the universal human need for emotional and sexual satisfaction, and to beliefs about the harmful physiological and mental effects ("stagnant blood") of celibacy in justifying bonyatsi for themselves. There are, however, clear socioeconomic motivations for female bonyatsi, since the cattle paid as bridewealth for a woman by her husband go to her father and other consanguineal relatives, while the secret but mandatory gifts from a *nyatsi* ("lover") are hers alone, free even from the restrictions that a husband may place on the disposition of other family income (Spiegel 1990a:5–6).

Among the likoma (sing.: *koma*) secret lore taught to girls during the *bale* rites of initiation are instructions in how to conceal adultery from their future husbands and, in the event her transgressions are discovered but tolerated by an understanding or equally guilty spouse, how to keep her affairs from causing him intolerable public embarrassment. It is for such reasons, and not only because of their deep historical and cultural embeddedness and authority, that the Basotho say *koma ke nnete*, "a koma is truth" (Guma 1967:117). For most Basotho, marriage is an indispensable social and economic partnership, preserving the male migrant's investment and entitlements in his home community and providing distributive and reproductive security for women and children, more than an emotional and sexual union. Hence bonyatsi is virtually never discussed in public (why spoil things?) and the lie that rescues social structure is a higher truth than the truth that fosters stress and discord. Initiates are strictly enjoined from singing Likoma outside the bush lodge *(mophato)*. To tell these sacred secrets to noninitiates or to mention their specific content in public is sanctioned by beating and inspires the proverb *ho bolella koma hae*, "to tell a koma at home," which condemns inappropriate or socially hurtful revelations in everyday contexts. As the koma admonishes:

> The first *koma*,
> It is not sung at home,
> It is sung in the wilderness. . . .
> [Guma 1967:125; my revision]

The parties, music, and dancing that accompany shebeen singing go beyond bonyatsi into *botekatse* ("prostitution"), a publicly recognized (and rather less concealable) arena for "deviance" in which the very harshness and social fragmentation of migrant life becomes a basis for commiseration, commensality, and collective self-expression. The goings on are grouped under the terms *famo*, from *ho re famo*, "to throw up one's skirts," or *focho*, "wild, bawdy, or intoxicated dancing," from *fecha*, the pelvic movements of a woman during sexual intercourse. In the Basotho areas of South African towns, the original instrument for famo dancing was the pedal organ *(okono)*, which might even be loaded into a horsecart or taxi and moved when occasion demanded. In the smaller depots and country junctions, the portable German concertina *(korosetina)*, adopted from Afrikaner farmers, was the ubiquitous accompaniment. The term famo apparently originated as a term for the bawdy dance parties organized by the infamous Basotho "russian" gangsters around Johannesburg. Divided into regional factions of "Matsieng" from southern Lesotho, and "Ha-Molapo," from northern Lesotho, these gangs fought each other, the police, citified criminal predators called *tsotsis* (Eng.: "zoot suit"), and members of other ethnic groups in pitched battles in the ghetto streets (Motlatsi and Guy 1983). The name "russians" *(marashea)* apparently began in the early Cold War days of the late 1940s as an antonym to that of their major tsotsi foes, Johannesburg's feared "Americans" gang, and in identification with the Soviet Union, "the only nation feared by the whiteman in South Africa," as one retired russian explained. "Russianism" *(borashea)* was a sort of urban proletarian recrudescence of the tradition of fierce stickfighting between young herdboys of neighboring rural villages, and of the historical antagonism between the royalists of south Lesotho and the restive collateral nobility of north Lesotho, their activity a blend of vigilantism, social banditry, and blood sport.

The night before a prearranged battle, faction members would gather for a famo party at their favorite shebeen, where their women, *matekatse,* would brew, cook, sing, and dance for them in encouragement. The word famo refers to the rhythmic artfulness with which a woman would fecha her hips backward and throw up her skirt to reveal her naked derriere in a single fetching movement. At dawn the men would take up their formation outside the bar, performing a male traditional *mohobelo* dance and song. One such anthem of the Matsieng faction in Johannesburg praised the role of women in supporting the embattled men:

> My boy [lover] when I get out of here, I will depart,
> Leave carrying you on my back [like a baby],
> Boy, when I get out of here, I will depart,
> Fearful for you of the thief-men [tsotsis and rival russians].

It should be noted that rather than the *mokorotlo,* the dance songs of war in which each soldier prepared himself to meet death (not victory) through individualized, self-revealing, extemporaneous movements, the russians chose mohobelo, the highly stylized and synchronized dance of male fellowship, unity of purpose, and team display—a dance of social agreement—as entertainment in the bar and as preparation for the fray. Possibly of equal importance, however, is the sense of national unity symbolized by mokorotlo, "a song by which Basotho distinguish/ differentiate themselves from other peoples" (Adams 1974:172–173). Mohobelo, on the other hand, is performed in two distinct southern and northern Lesotho regional styles, "Leribe" and "Mohale," which originated in the civil conflicts between Moshoeshoe's sons in the 1890s, and which correspond to and express the opposition between Matsieng and Ha-Molapo russians (Adams 1974:170). Along with courage, loyalty is the preeminent value of *borashea,* guaranteed by the swearing of secret oaths by both male and female faction members.

As the enemy approached, a whistle was blown, and a brutal clash would commence, resulting on occasion in numerous deaths. A great many of the most stirring women's shebeen songs focus on the russians and provide harrowing and piteous evocations of famous faction fights. Perhaps the most renowned of all the shebeen singers is 'Malitaba, now retired in Lesotho, who attended her husband, a Matsieng faction leader, at numerous battles in the Johannesburg area during the 1950s and '60s. Asked what role she played during the actual fighting she replied, "Why, to carry on singing, to give them courage to win the fight!" Russians themselves insist that the gangs' operations were originally defensive, and have always been confined to the lawless and uncivilized South African environment, outside Lesotho. Perhaps, but today in tough Lesotho border towns like Hlotse, a major migrant labor recruitment center, it's easy to pick out the russians in any backstreet shebeen. Thus have the organizing values and historical oppositions of *Sesotho,* under a foreign name, been extended by embattled Basotho men to "humanize" (enculturate) an uncivilized environment. Identification with the russians and the marginal position to which they are both socially consigned leads female singers to express admiration for these stout-hearted men and to the appropriation of images of battle to express women's existential struggles:

> Hae oele oele! You, child of 'MaKhalemang [a male russian, friend and fellow bar singer],
> Blow the whistle so the russians may fight oe!
> When it's fought it is fearsome,
> When it's fought it is fearsome:
> I can fling off my blankets [in anguish, aggression, sympathy, excitement, desire?],
> He! I, the child 'Ma'tsepe oe!
> The loafers' [russians] whistle blower, Khalemang,
> Whistler of loafers, Khalemang, you, man of Mokotane's,
> Makotane's at Mantsonyane,
> Lead them into the way (of battle); they know it (well).
> Hee! (so) I seize the black (heavy) fighting stick;
> I'm fighting,
> I cannot be stopped; I am fighting.
>   [Alinah Tsekoa, "Malitsepe"]

Nevertheless a favorite verse of many women singers is overtly critical of the russian *likoata* ("uncultured ruffians") who frequent the shebeens. In the version sung by "Malitsepe" (Mother of "Springboks," a russian gang):

> What kind of people are you russians?
> Each time you meet one another, you fight.
> After greeting one another, you fight.
> Hello! You, my little young fellow,
> My sweet young Bonang. . . .

Interestingly, male shebeen singers and lifela . . . performers rarely give bor-ashea more than a mention, and almost never sing about russian battles, particularly if they themselves are russians. The women, who would never actually join such a fight, sing about them in detail, praising the valorous and handsome, mourning the fallen, projecting themselves into the fray. So these denizens of the labor depots on the Lesotho/South Africa border identify with each other. Just as the term for barmaids derives from the verb "to wander about," male migrant performers commonly refer to themselves as *lipapatlele*, "vagabonds," *likhutsana*, "orphans," *likeleme* (Afrikaans: "skelm"), "rogues," *melotsana*, "deceivers," *likempolara*, "gamblers," *makholoa*, "absconders," and most professionally as *litsamaea-naha le liparola-thota*, "inveterate travelers of the wilderness." In wildness is their salvation, and moreover, the salvation of *Sesotho* (see Taussig 1987:209–220). I do not use the term "salvation" randomly. As one older woman singer explained:

> . . . At that time I was associated with people whose manners were rough, wild. When I was deeply depressed and worried, in order to express myself and feel con-

tented, like a Christian would open a page in the bible, with me I went to the *shebeen* to sing these things. I had gone (to town) to visit my husband and I found him but we separated. I suffered alot because of that. So I had to go to these places and get some joy out of life and unburden myself. [Coplan 1985:101]

The Professionals: Studio Shebeen Singers and *Sesotho*

Local recording companies had been on the lookout for material for the growing African market since the 1920s. The Basotho concertina tradition was already highly developed, and in the 1940s a number of recordings of solo male singer/players appeared that featured astonishing virtuoso performances on that small instrument ("Tshetla" and "Kroonstad," T. Makala. Gallotone GB1604.Y591). Complex melodic runs that imitated the vocalic qualities of sung poetry were not suitable for dancing however, and thus lacked an important selling point. The rhythmic three-chord instrumental accompaniment made women's shebeen singing a good sales prospect, and by the 1950s migrants could buy *seoe-leoelele* recordings spiced up with tell-it-like-it-is female vocals (*Famo Ngoan-ana*, Mamapetle Makara koa Famong. Gallotone GB2012). In 1960, the great Malitaba was "discovered" singing in her Soweto shebeen by a talent scout and made several recordings which brought her fame throughout Lesotho and Sesotho-speaking South Africa. Her texts concentrate on the terrors and excitements of russian warfare, and her desire to return to Lesotho:

> I always tell them I was not born so [in hardship] but compound my mistakes, my
>   child Lenka [the accordionist].
> When she's there, 'Malitaba of Mphoso, you won't see hardships, things just go
>   smoothly.
> I am not afraid of a giant, even one full of cunning.
> Knives they can clean miss me,
> Sticks swing over my head,
> Cracking (together) over my head, man! the fighting sticks of men.
> Who can be asked bad news [whether she is dead]?
> They can be asked of Sanaha [her husband], the man jo! the master of love.
> I always tell them oe! The person from Chele's, well!
> I won't stay in Naledi [Soweto],
> Jo! A person of (Chief) Shale's, well oe!
> To your home [Lesotho] (you devil)!
> I won't stay in Naledi, Tlali, or Moletsane, my child [all townships in Soweto]
> I say, among cannibals [russians] yonder, in Mapetla or Senaoana [in Soweto],
> When the State of Emergency[2] was fought.
> It's finished I'm leaving, time up I am going,
> Time up I am going [to Lesotho]. . . .

It was also during the early '60s that the piano accordion *(koriana)* appeared in South African music stores and was adopted by Basotho instrumentalists in the mining compounds and shebeens in preference to the pedal organ. Combining the portability of the concertina with the musical range and full-textured volume of the organ, the piano accordion enabled its most serious exponents to make live performance something like a full-time profession. Shebeen owners could afford to buy accordions and supply them to musicians playing in various locations. The musicians could sling the instrument over their backs and tour by bus and foot from the black townships of urban South Africa to the remotest village shebeens in Lesotho. Others made long-term agreements modeled on mineworking contracts with female "shebeen queens" *(bo-mamosali)* in the border towns to stay and play daily for the patrons. Although many Basotho women found it easy enough to evade the antimigration statutes or establish legal South African residency by some means, the repatriation of thousands of them under the new regulations in 1963 brought a great many fine female singers back to the shebeens of Maseru, Lesotho's growing capital, and other smaller communities throughout the country. Ensembles were completed by the addition of a drum *(moropa)* constructed of a 20-liter tar can topped with a piece of tire inner-tubing, above which was fastened a row of bottlecaps or metal jangles *(manyenenyene)* to provide a jingling beat to alternate with the thump on stretched rubber of drumsticks made from slices of tire.

Famo and shebeen music was now everywhere that working-class Basotho gathered for drink and entertainment, with most of the singing provided by the brewers and customers themselves. What was needed to turn this neighborhood barrelhouse entertainment into a Basotho national music was the emergence of major recording personalities among composer/singers and accordionists. Among the first and most enduring of these professional recording ensembles was Tau ea Matsekha ("Lion of Matsekha," a district in northern Lesotho). Both the accordionist, Forere Motloheloa, and the vocalist/composer Apollo Ntabanyane, had acquired their performing skills and experience at the mines, where they entertained their fellow workers in their spare time, and played in shebeens for extra cash. Notably, now that enhanced financial rewards were possible, male likheleke were joining women in shebeen singing. The group's early albums, such as *Ha-Peete Kea Falla* ("Peete's Place I'm Quitting," EMI) were phenomenally successful, and their name became synonymous among many listeners with the form itself, so that this type of music was often called "Tau ea Matsekha." By the early 1970s Ntabanyane, a fine, athletically comic stage dancer as well as vocalist/composer, decided he could do better for himself by leading his own group. In 1974 he had himself proclaimed "King of Famo Music" at a major concert at Maseru's Airport Hotel, an occasion attended by Her Majesty 'MaMohato herself, the wife of Lesotho's King Moshoeshoe II.

Since then a number of well-known recording groups have emerged, including David Motaung's Tau ea Linare and the first from southern Lesotho, Mahosana Akaphamong. Only a very few can afford to give up nonmusical jobs to go on concert tours, and most must be satisfied with revenues from occasional recording sessions and royalties. The shebeens, however, provide an actual living for a significant number of itinerant accordion players. Good female singers are much respected and sought after, and shebeen owners in Maseru stage paid competitions between the top composer/singers among the *matekatse*. Of the women, the long-time and current champion is indisputably Puseletso Seema, who in forty-some years has suffered all the slings and arrows of outrageous fortune and every shock a Mosotho migrant woman's flesh is heir to.

Puseletso was born in Seteketekeng ("place of [drunken] staggering"), a fierce, shebeen-strewn section in Johannesburg's old Western Areas. In the early 1960s she was removed with her mother to the Soweto township of Orlando East, where they both presently reside. At 12 she was sent to stay with her grandmother in rural northern Lesotho, and put to a boy's tough task of herding cattle. The village proved no safer for the maturing girl than the city, and within a year she was kidnaped into marriage *(chobeliso)* and gave birth to her first child. Escape from her abusive in-laws did not prevent her husband from tracking her down and impregnating her once again, so at age 15 she was back in Soweto with two infants to care for. Working in her mother's shebeen, she developed her talents at composing and singing, and soon set off on a career as itinerant as any male migrant, brewing and singing in shantytowns throughout the Free State and Transvaal. The object of rivalry among "russian" commanders, she contracted lengthy liaisons with three of them, and attended numerous russian faction fights around Johannesburg. After the death of her last man in 1976, she began her professional recording career. In the mid-1980s she mysteriously suffered a loss of voice for an extended period. The diviner diagnosed "spirit sickness" and prescribed initiation as a traditional diviner and healer. During her training her voice returned, and she is now a medical as well as musical practitioner.

So has she achieved a *summa* of proletarian Basotho cultural knowledge, combining the three professions of migrant shebeen queen, kheleke, and ngaka. Her shield has been that powerful voice that sends *seoeleoelele!* chills down her listeners' spines, and led russian commanders to kidnap her just to sing for their side in famo dance-song competitions. The success of her recordings, backed by the superb accordionist Maele Phuthiang and studio singers, guitarists, and drummers, have enabled her to retire to stable single motherhood in Soweto. The studio process has affected her performances, forcing her to shorten solos to fit arrangements for popular singles. Perhaps as a result, each of her songs on record focuses on a different aspect of her experience, rather than concatenating experiences into a mutual resonance as is usually the case with extended shebeen texts. This song from an album she made in 1981 with Tau ea Linare, *He O Oe Oe!* (Globe Style ORB003), concerns a trip from Soweto home to Lesotho:

Hae! ha lele! lelele! lelele! ee! ho eoho ee!
Ho eoho! Men of Leribe, come so we depart, 'Molo ee!
So we tramp in silence going to Maputsoe at Ntate
Sekekete's! Hey! towards the "school" at Maputsoe,
Where we first take out (our) passports, at the home of my child Lerato.
I remember the infant child,
Khele! My child Lerato, 'Malerato ee!
'Me'Malerato you Motaung's wife, draw me water to slake my thirst oe!
I say Helele! Manchild oe!
I am not pleased I'm (so) angry I just pass by!
I, the sister of 'Maboy,
Hee! My mother and father, brothers and sisters, are still crying oe!
Hee! My mother you cry looking into the kraal;
My father you cry looking deep inside the house.

My friend, manchild, I have no dishes, I have no cattle ee!
No! No cattle, but I am mad about sour milk, I the little last born girl.
Hee! I remember the woman who brought me up girls ee!, 'Me'Mathabo of Nqabe's,
When I go to her home girls, which way should I take ee!
I leave Maputsoe still feeling angry,
I reach Hlotse [Leribe],
Even here at Hlotse I am still impatient oe!
As I head towards Khanyane I saw my fields of Likhakeng,
The low-lying fields of my home ee!
Hey! I saw the beautiful mountain of Litaung, my friend the manchild,
That's when I first started to laugh oe!

Here, Puseletso calls to her men friends, "homeboys" from Hlotse town, capital of Leribe District, to accompany her to Lesotho, even if it means a long and (uncharacteristic for Basotho travelers) sullen march. She crosses the border at Maputsoe, a rough boomtown, and passes the notorious Sekekete Hotel, a "school" of drinking and prostitution where migrants fresh from the mines find beer and willing but often predatory female companionship. She meets 'Ma-Lerato, wife of David Motaung (whose group is backing her on this recording), and asks her to bring some water before she gets angry, possibly indicating strained personal relations. Apropos of that, she recalls her own forced elopement by a man who never paid any bridewealth for her. So her mother cries, seeing the kraal empty of cattle; her father cries, seeing a house empty of possessions. Turning from the subject of her poverty and misfortune, she recalls her dear grandmother with whom she lived in the Lesotho village of Mohobong. So long has she been away she has to ask the way there. A car offers to take her, but she is irritable and suspicious until at last she spies the farmlands and mountains of her home. So strong is the identification of this *lekholoa* (one who has disappeared into South Africa) with her original family home that she feels only joy, forgetting the poverty, forced marriage, and mistreatment that drove her away. Puseletso's success has evoked some jealousy and gentle satire among Lesotho's shebeen singers, including Hlotse's Thakane Mahlasi:

We met at the crossroads,
We didn't recognize one another, jo, my darling girl!
Puseletso, little girl of Seema:
Her short stature is hers by nature;
Her light complexion is self-made [with skin-lighteners], Oh girl! . . .

Popular Song and *Sesotho:* Mutual Infusions, Emergent Tradition

To return to the theme of *Sesotho,* nothing is more central to the ideology of Basotho culture as a fixed tradition than *lebollo,* the circumcision schools that initiate boys and girls into adulthood. Lebollo was once an institution whose variant procedures and geographical focus served to differentiate politically independent communities and clans. Boys initiated in the company of the son of a sponsoring district chief were bound to him in political and military service. Lesotho's founder, King Moshoeshoe I, attempted to gain control of the educational and military system by transforming initiation into a fount of national unity; sending his sons to be initiated with those of his vassals, where they would become comrades-in-arms treated with the same local chief's medicine horn (Guma 1965:243). Although only a small proportion of Basotho children presently undergo these lengthy secluded rites, attendance seems to have been increasing since independence in 1966, and lebollo remains in any case one of the most powerful symbolic complexes of *Sesotho*. Certain ceremonies of the initiation take place in public, but most are guarded with the most extreme secrecy. Such secrecy is embodied and symbolized in the sacred, esoteric likoma songs:

> The corral of the ancestors
> Has no door:
> It is simply round.
> Call traditional healers
> To come and circle [doctor] it.
> While they circled it,
> Having circled (it) once,
> Inside it
> There arose a foal
> Of the hidden head . . .
> . . . It (foal) turned itself into a mountain
> A mountain of settlement,
> Of the settlement of villages,
> Those many villages
> That belong to our uncles,
> They do not belong to our forefathers.[3]
>   [Guma 1967:124; revised by Coplan]

Other important types of performance taught at male lebollo include *mangae* (sing.: *lengae*) songs, which provide a choral accompaniment to the recitation of self-composed initiates' praises, *lithoko tsa makoloane,* at graduation. Nowadays virtually everything associated with lebollo is regarded as secret, and the identification of these ceremonies as the essence of *Sesotho* has intensified to the point where in the minds of many, *Sesotho* itself is all likoma, knowledge both to be kept from outsiders and free of outside influences. But not so to the migrants, whose self-image as rural yeomen and keepers of the true cultural knowledge of Sesotho is tempered by their lack of benefit from or investment in the present boundaries and existence Lesotho as a political state. Thus the realities of migrant labor and the influence of South Africa affects performance in lebollo itself, through the words and music of lifela and *seoeleoelele.* Interestingly, Guma (1967:116–117) reports that his informants regarded lifela as another name for likoma, and offered that as the reason that the Christians had taken the term lifela to indicate sacred hymns, as in the famous hymnal, *Lifela Tsa Sione* (1843), "The Hymns of Zion." While my own informants denied this association, citing secrecy as the distinctive characteristic of initiation likoma, it is thought provoking to consider a possible association between the latter and the revelatory, rudely open "truths" *(linnete)* of the lifela songs of the profane migrant workers.

The mangae songs composed at lebollo today reveal the influence of South African popular culture. The following lengae was recorded at an initiation graduation at the village of Sephokong, Mafeteng District in March 1989, and was performed in two choral parts by younger and older initiates, respectively. Part one is the refrain of a currently popular song by recording star Apollo Ntabanyane:

Hey! Hey do you see him, that hardened criminal?:
"Somoria napau, napau napau" (twice).

The second line is not Sesotho, but replicates the slang street gangsters use so they cannot be overheard by others. The original lines come from one of the "cops and robbers" dramas frequently broadcast over Radio Sesotho, the South African government service from Johannesburg. Part two of the song, or the "response" continues:

Na mabele a butsuoe?	Has the sorghum ripened?
A bolilana se ka maeba.	It is distasteful to the rock doves,
Selemo se lekana le hlabula,	Spring is followed by summer,
Loetse e lekana le Mphalane.	September is followed by October.
Le Mafeteng ka fetella,	And Mafeteng compounds its vices,
Le ha Mojela ba ntjella,	And at (Chief) Mojela's they live off others' harvest,
Le Ntate Molimo oa khotso	And Father, God of peace,
Le rona likhutsana rapeleha,	And we, orphans, are moved to prayer,
Le rona litsamaea-naha,	And we, inveterate travelers,
Le manyeloi a matsoho.	And angels of hands (bless us).

I have included the Sesotho text here so that readers of this clever, sardonic lengae may note the typical homophonic wordplay on *Mafeteng/fetella* and *Mojela/ntjella*. The answer to the opening query is that it must be May, for this is the month when the sorghum grains are hard and ripe enough so that birds cannot eat them, thus the Sesotho name for May, *Motsehanong*, "Laughing-at-birds." As one season or month follows another, the wrongs committed by Mafeteng people mount up, the people of Chief Mojela (to the south Mafeteng town and the area where the song was recorded) still live off the labors of others, in particular the "orphans" and our ubiquitous sefela-singing "travelers," who must go to the mines and look only to God for assistance.

Among the most interesting male singer/composers today is David Sello Motaung, leader of Tau ea Linare. In 1986 Motaung, at the age of thirty eight, decided for the first time to attend lebollo and become an initiate. The reasons for this, he stated, were to immerse himself in Sesotho and to learn more deeply the variety of performance genres taught at the circumcision lodge. This would provide him with skills, techniques, and inspiration for composition, and enable him to relate the latter more directly to his own strong feelings of identity as a Mosotho. On his latest album, *Litaba Motaung* (CCP L4 RAIN (EO) 4062294; 1988), there are two songs which Motaung says directly resulted from his experience at lebollo. On one, *Makhooa*, "Whites," the chorus is performed by four male singers in the style of a lengae initiation song, though backed by the usual accordion, drum, and bass. The solo takes the place of an initiate's praises. The subject matter might seem rather surprising:

Chorus:

Whites, whites, hey! whites,
Hey, jo! Whites are of no use: (twice)
They don't appreciate a man who knows his work,
Whites are of no use. (twice)
Hela! Whites, whites, whites,
Hey! Those are whites, they have no use. (twice)
Pretoria is the final court, hey!
Those are whites, they have no use. (several repeats)

Solo:

Pretoria is the final court, (twice)
You, man, Seshoba,
Hee! You my child, drive we are leaving,
So we go to the place of Europeanism (the mines), Hey you ee!
Hee! We should take our tax receipts,
President Brand, President Steyn (mines); mine compounds are the same,
The child who slips away to join (the mines) does not complete (the contract),
Se jo'na! (alas) Hardships!
Many men, we fear *moghasheoa* [heat-tolerance test],
Jo! Manchild across (the river) in Johannesburg (the mines),
Hae oele! oelele! oelele! oelelele, man! [after the opening formula of female shebeen
   songs]
Pretoria, the far away lands,
Jo! My child, Jo! My child bo!

This blend of initiation song, praises, and seoeleoelele appears to mix categories and put the meaning of *Sesotho* in question. But it is clear that the postinitiation experience of migration to the hostile world of the mines, where indolent white mine team captains lord it over real workers (Basotho), backed up by the distant but inescapable authority of Pretoria, has crept into *Sesotho*.

Conclusion

> We use our mouth to crack palm-kernels on the surface of the road
> —''Song of Prostitution in Lagos,''
> Irewolede Denge, 1937
> [HMV, J. Z. 3/0AB.5.]

A good part of anthropology's particular value as a discipline, deriving from the methodological centrality of fieldwork, is the study of social groupings and their ''whole life process'' from the inside out, the ground up. To those who see the controlling hand of political or economic colonization in every African social and cultural form (cf. Ranger 1984; Wolpe 1972) anthropologists have demonstrated that Africans are agents in the making of their own history, using cultural resources to give meaning to life as a strategy for survival. Jean Comaroff

(1985:197–198), to cite a notable example, argues that syncretic reinterpretations of historical and experiential metaphors as well as microlevel continuities in cultural practices can be explained essentially as forms of resistance to incorporation in a capitalist political economy (Spiegel 1990b:8).

But as Christopher Waterman (1990) demonstrates in his recent study of Nigerian Yoruba popular *juju* music, cultural process is ideologically charged through productive mediation by social actors with particular values and experiences of power. So both continuity and syncretism can as easily mask empirical structural relations through the upholding of what Raymond Williams would call the "selective tradition," hegemonic social understandings, as they can serve subversively the interests of the oppressed (Waterman 1990:9). Performative signification encodes the social relations and contradictions of power as they arise in a particular history. These relations shape communicative interactions, just as their character is reflected in the constitution of symbols and meanings (Ulin 1984:118, 123).

In black African cultures, aural performance replicates and reinforces principles of social order (Waterman 1990:219–220), which serve to ground its inherent potential for social critique. Africans explicitly regard performance as a context for metacommentary, and the interpenetration of politics and art appears to them as both normative and demonstrable. Performance genres in black Africa are treated as neither independent of social and material forces nor epiphenomenal to them, but rather as thoroughly integrated modes of social action in political contexts. Realized through creative structures that legitimate its content, auriture both records and shapes the operation of social forces (Finnegan 1970:142). Its analysis depends upon an understanding of the association of expressive forms with the periods and structures of society that gave rise to them (White 1982:10).

As I hope the texts herein interpreted suggest, the study of popular performance is one significant way to address the problem of "how to represent the embedding of richly described local cultural worlds in larger impersonal systems of political economy" (Marcus and Fischer 1986:77). In contemporary Nigeria, *juju* music and its public performance mediate the disjunction between conceptions of precolonial polity and nation state, and help to maintain the postcolonial invention of a unitary, pan-Yoruba identity (Waterman 1990:147). This identity in turn serves to extend and reinforce the historically rooted moral economy of hierarchical but reciprocal patron-client relations in the face of ethnically unmarked processes of class formation. The juju metaphor, as Waterman puts it, "may help to transform the world by sustaining the illusion that it remains, in some deep and essential sense, the same" (Waterman 1990:227–228).

Among Basotho shebeen singers and their listeners, in contrast, there is no confidence whatever that the Basotho economic or political elite have any commitment to practicing or upholding precolonial values of hierarchical reciprocity or communal social exchange. Hence the assonantal parallelism '*khooana tsoana* ("little black whitemen") as a working-class term for the Basotho bourgeoisie is contemptuous rather than critical, suggesting a self-defeating abandonment of *Sesotho* while still falling short of European status. The army, who presently rule

Lesotho, fare even worse. Although the rank and file and many of the officers come from humble backgrounds, their exercise of power is more repressive than that of the most autocratic precolonial chief. "When you ask the soliders the reason for something," despaired an elderly wisehead, "they show you a gun." The contingent exception to these negative views about resident elites is that toward the traditional land-controlling aristocracy, chiefs who *are* weighed in the scales of the hierarchically reciprocal social values their hereditary offices embody. These offices comprise a political geography and a source of identity for aural composers, but as individuals chiefs are either disparaged or hailed to the extent that they are seen to violate or uphold the social morality of leadership in *Sesotho*. With formal and mass technological modes of communication closed to the migrants, urban workers, and resident "peasantariat," communal and popular song becomes a vital and significant medium for creatively reflecting on their experience and inserting it into public political discourse (Waterman 1990:10, 88).

Like the composers of Yoruba juju, Basotho migrant singers employ cultural metaphors by turns profound and comic to cross social boundaries and integrate opposing social domains. Both share a double identity as traditional bards and contemporary existential heroes, using their moral and creative cultural imagination to make one world of many in time and space. Their performances relate theories of power to theories of the person, shaping motive and action by images and ideals of what constitutes goodness in people, relations, and conditions of life. Such judgments are always made in reference to a process of rhetorical self-definition. Because culture is an essential constituent of the self, the operation of "local knowledge" (Geertz 1983) in performance contexts depends upon the emotions attached to reflections about the nature of persons and social relations (Marcus and Fischer 1986:46). In creating a "structure of feeling," sentiment is a primary constituent of performance as a social practice, a practice in which affect is essential to effect:

> . . . The day I decided to go to the mines,
> I had a talk with my heart, and we compromised.
> My eyes are crying, though nothing has got into them;
> I feel like vomiting, though nothing bad have I eaten . . .
> [Makeka Lihojane, "Ngoana Mokhalo"]

There is value in the effort to get at the "reciprocal determination of material forces and cultural forms" (Comaroff 1985:xii) through excavating the instrumentalities of symbolic structures enacted in metaphors of semantic opposition, but in so doing the Comaroffs (1987) have underestimated the tendency of these metaphors toward reversal and resolution. Home and exile, reciprocity and self-interest, secrecy and exposure, truths and lies, law and crime, culture and deracination turn into one another like the impersonating monsters in southern African folktales.

The indigenous concept of *Sesotho*, like any other reified and consciously mobilized notion of tradition, is composed of continuities, reinterpretations, syncretisms, and inventions that are alike situationally contested. As with Yoruba for the juju composer, *Sesotho* for the migrant aurator is the vehicle of what Benedict Anderson has called an "imagined community" of the Basotho, distinguished not by its sociological falsity or genuineness, but by the style in which it is imagined (Anderson 1983:15). Unlike the Yoruba performer, the Mosotho migrant kheleke may recognize that his people are today divided by social class, but in a deeper sense they all share *Sesotho,* just as they share the larger disabilities historically enforced by the predatory South African leviathan next door and its economic partners abroad. As one Mosotho university colleague reproved me gently in response to an impertinent cultural observation: "You don't know who we are."

Forms such as shebeen songs have long been extending Basotho culture into new domains of experience and across the borders of Lesotho. But never have the boundaries of what is regarded as *Sesotho 'nete 'nete,* true Basotho culture, been more strongly defended than they are today, when Lesotho has little economic or political autonomy. In such circumstances *Sesotho* becomes a precious resource, a reservoir of identity, self-expression, and social entitlement that appears crucial to any meaningful form of national survival. Moshoeshoe I understood this when he sent his sons to be initiated with the sons of his allies and vassals, and it is no accident that institutions such as lebollo initiation are not dying out, but are if anything increasing in attendance. Migrant workers and their women, without whose labor Lesotho cannot, even for a short time, survive, are producing elaborate forms of auriture which do not simply preserve but enlarge and revitalize Sesotho in direct confrontations with the social forces that threaten it. Basotho migrant performers do not cast aside historical Basotho culture but root themselves deeply within it. The resonant images and shared understandings of Sesotho are used to comprehend, assess, decry, and even celebrate the quality of Basotho participation in a world they cannot control, but which must not be allowed, at any cost, to control their collective and individual sense of self, their continuing reformulation of a national culture.

Today seoeleoelele music is popular to some extent with virtually all segments of Lesotho's resident and nonresident population. For the exclusively Sesotho speaking, this is their favorite music; but even the highly educated enjoy it, no longer look down upon it, and appreciate it's sagacity, humor, and Sesotho aesthetic and cultural qualities. Recorded in Johannesburg, seoeleoelele is the nearest thing to a contemporary popular Basotho national music. *Sesotho,* as an invented and guiding metatradition of useful fictions, would become not a saving but a patent falsehood without the infusions of performance from and through the border, the songs of its migrant vagabond orphan-like *lintho tsa molimo* ("creatures of God"), the healing efflorescence of its songs and dances of the wild(er)ness.

> Jo! Eloquence is not stuck on like a feather (in a cap):
> The year before last I should have been respected,
> For showing I know how to speak.
> The Lion is here, at the ridge on the plain
> It's eye shines with anger
> Heroes lost their minds

When they saw the Lion roaring. . . .
. . . These little creatures of God, men
People who speak by shells [behind cupped hands]
They whisper breathily
They fear to speak, they are noiseless, soundless:
Jo! evil words or innuendo.
Let unity be written; peace increase
Cases should cease to take up appeals
Let the guilty be forgiven at the courts here,
Men guilty of great crimes. . . .
. . . However well you may sing
I, Sporty, can never be beaten
The way I speak, travelers,
This eloquence runs in my family:
Father Mareka was born eloquent,
Mother Mary was born eloquent
My sisters and brothers were born with this eloquence,
Father surpasses in (singing) the *likoma* of the veld [initiation lodge]
Mother surpasses in ululation,
My sisters and brothers surpass in dancing,
The beautiful initiation girls, whose women are they?

[Majara Majara]

Notes

[1] Further developing the concept suggested in the term *orature* popularized by Kenyan author Ngugi wa Thiong'o as a replacement for the oxymoron "oral literature," I would propose the term *auriture* to represent vocal art in which verbal text, sonic qualities, and rhythm are interdependent expressive resources. This term does not, unfortunately, go far enough in glossing the synesthetic integration of performative media in African cultures, revealed for example in Sesotho terms such as *ho tlala,* "to dance praises."

[2] The singer is comparing this russian battle to the State of Emergency declared by Prime Minister Leabua Jonathan after his loss of the parliamentary elections of 1970. The winning party, to which the singer belongs, was the Basutoland Congress Party, whose protests and supporters were violently suppressed by Chief Jonathan's forces.

[3] These lines suggest the founding of the Basotho nation by King Moshoeshoe I of the invading Bakoena, whose mother Kholu was a member of the aboriginal Bafokeng, and thus her brothers and by extension of Bafokeng clan stand as maternal uncles to the royal house of the Basotho and the ruling Bakoena aristocracy.

References Cited

Adams, Charles
   1974   Ethnography of Basotho Evaluative Expression in the Cognitive Domain "Lipapali" (Games). Ph.D. dissertation, Indiana University.
Alverson, Hoyt
   1978   Mind in the Heart of Darkness. New Haven: Yale University Press.
Ashton, Hugh
   1952   The Basuto. London: Oxford University Press.

294   David B. Coplan

Babcock-Abrahams, Barbara
    1975   A Tolerated Margin of Mess: The Trickster and His Tales Reconsidered. Journal of the Folklore Institute XI(3):147–186.
Bardill, John, and James Cobbe
    1985   Lesotho: Dilemmas of Dependence in Southern Africa. Boulder, Colo.: Westview Press.
Beidelman, T. O.
    1986   Moral Imagination in Kaguru Modes of Thought. Bloomington: Indiana University Press.
Bonner, Philip
    1988   Desirable or Undesirable Women? Liquor, Prostitution, and the Migration of Basotho Women to the Rand, 1920–1945. Unpublished MS.
Comaroff, Jean
    1985   Body of Power, Spirit of Resistance. Chicago: University of Chicago Press.
Comaroff, John L., and Jean Comaroff
    1987   The Madman and the Migrant. American Ethnologist 14(2):187–209.
Coplan, David B.
    1985   In Township Tonight! South Africa's Black City Music and Theatre. New York: Longman.
    1987a   The Power of Oral Poetry: Narrative Songs of the Basotho Migrants. Research in African Literatures 18(1):1–35.
    1987b   Eloquent Knowledge: Lesotho Migrants' Songs and the Anthropology of Experience. American Ethnologist 14(3):413–433.
    1988   Musical Understanding: The Ethnoaesthetics of Migrant Workers' Poetic Song in Lesotho. Ethnomusicology 32(3):337–368.
Finnegan, Ruth
    1970   Oral Literature in Africa. Oxford: Clarendon Press.
Geertz, Clifford
    1983   Local Knowledge. New York: Basic Books.
Guma, S. M.
    1965   Aspects of Circumcision in Basutoland. African Studies 24(4):241–249.
    1967   The Form, Content, and Technique of Traditional Literature in Southern Sotho. Pretoria: J. L. van Schaik.
Hobsbawm, Eric
    1984   Introduction. *In* The Invention of Tradition. Terence O. Ranger and Eric Hobsbawm, eds. New York: Cambridge University Press.
Holquist, Michael, ed.
    1981   The Dialogic Imagination: Four Essays by M. M. Bakhtin. Austin: University of Texas Press.
Kunene, Daniel
    1971   Heroic Poetry of the Basotho. Oxford: Clarendon Press.
Kuper, Adam
    1975   The Social Structure of the Sotho-Speaking Peoples of Southern Africa. Africa XLV (Part I):67–82.
Matsela, F. Z. A.
    1987   Dipapadi Tsa Sesotho. Mazenod, Lesotho: Mazenod Printers.
Mokitimi, Makali I. P.
    1982   A Literary Analysis of Lifela tsa Litsamaea-Naha Poetry. M.A. thesis, Nairobi.

Moletsane, R. I. M.
  1982   A Literary Appreciation and Analysis of Collected and Documented Basotho
         Miners' Poetry. M. A. thesis, Orange Free State.
  1983   Liparola-Thota. Maseru: Longman.
Murray, Colin
  1975   Sex, Smoking and the Shades: A Sotho Symbolic Idiom. *In* Religion and Social
         Change in Southern Africa. M. Whisson and M. West, eds. Pp. 58–77. Cape Town:
         David Philip.
  1980   From Granary to Labour Reserve: An Economic History of Lesotho. South Af-
         rican Labour Bulletin 6(4):3–20.
  1981   Families Divided: The Impact of Migrant Labour in Lesotho. Cambridge: Cam-
         bridge University Press.
Ranger, Terence O.
  1984   The Invention of Tradition in Colonial Africa. *In* The Invention of Tradition.
         Terence Ranger and Eric Hobsbawm, eds. New York: Cambridge University Press.
Spiegel, Andrew
  1990a Polygyny as Myth: Towards Understanding Extra-marital Relations in Lesotho.
         Paper presented to the History Workshop, Johannesburg, 6–10 February.
  1990b Changing Continuities: Experiencing and Interpreting History, Population
         Movement and Material Differentiation in Matatiele, Transkei. Ph.D. dissertation,
         Cape Town.
Taussig, Michael
  1987   Shamanism, Colonialism, and the Wild Man: A Study in Terror and Healing.
         Chicago: University of Chicago Press.
Thabane, Motlatsi, and Jeff Guy
  1983   The *Ma-rashea,* a Participant's Perspective. *In* Town and Countryside in the
         Transvaal. Belinda Bozzoli, ed. Jhb: Ravan.
Ulin, Robert
  1984   Understanding Cultures. Austin: University of Texas Press.
Wallmann, Sandra
  1969   Take Out Hunger: Two Case Studies of Rural Development in Basutoland. Lon-
         don: Athlone.
Waterman, Christopher Alan
  1990   Juju: A Social History and Ethnography of an African Popular Music. Chicago:
         University of Chicago Press.
White, Landeg
  1982   Power and the Praise Poem. Journal of Southern African Studies 9(1):8–32.
Wilkinson, R. C.
  1985   Migration in Lesotho. Ph.D. dissertation, Newcastle upon Tyne.
Williams, Raymond
  1977   Marxism and Literature. London: Oxford University Press.
Wolpe, H.
  1972   Capitalism and Cheap Labour Power in South Africa: From Segregation to
         Apartheid. Economy and Society 1(4):425–456.

Race and Reflexivity: The Black Other in Contemporary Japanese Mass Culture

John Russell

Editor's Note

This manuscript was originally submitted with 11 figures. However, when the author contacted the various publishers to obtain permission to reprint certain images he was denied permission apparently because of the sensitivity of their subject matter in contemporary Japan. Where necessary the author has substituted narrative descriptions of the images *CA* was unable to reprint.

> Two Days before we left Loo Choo the commodore gave still another farewell banquet for Loo Choo's regent. Our "Ethiopian minstrels" put on an evening of theatrical entertainment afterward. The guests seemed well pleased—they laughed a lot—but why?
>
> —William Heine, brigadier general
> *With Perry to Japan* (1856)

> Why won't black mothers let their children play in the sandbox?
> Because the cats keep covering them up.
>
> —Dave Spector, *It's Only a Joke!* (1984),
> an anthology introducing Japanese
> to American humor, Tokyo: Ark.

On 22 September 1986 in remarks widely reported in the American press, Japanese Prime Minister Nakasone Yasuhiro, addressing a National Study Council meeting of his ruling Liberal Democratic Party, blamed the presence of blacks, Puerto Ricans, and Mexicans for declining "American intelligence levels." In the same address, Nakasone praised Japan as a "high-level information society" *(kōdo jōhō shakai)* on the cutting edge of the information age. Unfortunately, the prime minister was silent on the question of the source and quality of that information, as his comments on American intelligence levels and subsequent remarks by Watanabe Michio in 1988, at yet another party meeting accusing blacks of indifference to bankruptcy, strongly suggest. Whether callous or calumnious, these statements are not isolated incidents, for they are embedded in a negative view of the blacks that permeates virtually all aspects of Japanese discourse on the black Other.

American furor over these comments focused on Japanese arrogance, ethnocentrism and antiblack racism; almost overnight Americans came to see Japanese "homogeneity"—a myth embraced by many Japanese and Americans alike—as a weakness, with Op-Ed columns and advertisements singing self-congratulatory paeans to the strength of American racial diversity and problematizing Japan's shabby treatment of its own—suddenly visible—minorities. What many American commentators ignored was the contiguity of Japanese and Western antiblack racism.

As Marylin Ivy points out in her dissection of the speech, Nakasone's is a "classically paranoic attempt to confirm Japanese world parity in an increasingly fragmented international and domestic milieu, to restore the honor of the Japanese by comparing it to other races" (1989:23). It is worth noting that in these attempts the Japanese have been aided by a view of the world—particularly the nonwhite world—heavily indebted to Western discourse on the theme of race and difference. Nakasone's comments came as no surprise to those familiar with the theories of Arthur Jensen and William Shockley or purveyors of the Morton Downey, Jr., show and late-night radio talk programs where blacks (and other minorities) are cast as modern Vandals crashing the gates of the American Empire and whose growing visibility within those gates is treated as symbolic of a collapse of American social order. Nor, given the informational exchange between the United States and Japan, should it have surprised Americans that Nakasone would borrow this idiom as an omen of what would take place in Japan were it to replace its official ideology of "monoracialism" *(tan' itsu minzoku)* with American-style pluralism, and that he would merely recapitulate (apparently for domestic consumption only) the fears of the American bourgeoisie. Sakai's observations on the *nihonjin-ron* ("treatise on the Japanese") genre, of which Nakasone's statement is part, seem appropriate here, for Nakasone's insistence on asserting Japanese difference from the West "embodies a nagging urge to see the self from the viewpoint of the [white] Other." Not only does this "positing of Japan's identity in Western terms" establish "the centrality of the West as the universal point of reference" (Sakai 1989:105) in defining the parameters of Japanese difference, but also in privileging Western discourse on the black Other.

Japanese literary and visual representations of blacks rely heavily on imaginary Western conventions. Such representations function to familiarize Japanese with the black Other, to preserve its alienness by ascribing to it certain standardized traits which mark it as Other but which also serve the reflexive function of allowing Japanese to meditate on their racial and cultural identity in the face of challenges by Western modernity, cultural authority, and power.

An analysis of the visual and literary conventions used to represent blacks in Japan reveals their striking resemblance to those which have prevailed in the West and whose influence in shaping Japanese perceptions of blacks can be detected as

early as the 16th century. True, in Japan as in Europe the color black has traditionally carried negative symbolic connotations (e.g., corruption, death, evil, illness, impurity), and certainly neither Heian nor Nara Period aesthetics leave any
doubt as to the value associated with white skin. Japanese proverbs testify to the
positive aesthetic valuation of the color white as a marker of beauty: *iro no shiroi
wa shichinan kakusu* (a white [skin] compensates for many deficiencies), *kome
no meshi to onna wa shiroi hodo yoi* (in rice and women, the whiter the better),
and *Fujisan no mieru kuni ni bijin nashii*, the last conveying the notion that
women who live in the overcast, snowy northern prefectures of Shimane, Niigata,
and Akita are pale-skinned beauties compared to those who live in warmer, sun-
nier climes, a view that survives today in such expressions as *Akita bijin* (Akita
beauty).

Nonetheless, it does not follow that the *racial* characteristics Japanese ascribe to dark-complexioned races, particularly blacks, ought necessarily to parallel Western ones, which they do all too frequently. Indeed, the evidence suggests that in ascribing certain of these characteristics to blacks the Japanese have
been heavily influenced by Western values and racial paradigms, imported along
with Dutch learning and Western science in their rush to catch up with the West.
In a word, Japanese views of blacks have taken as their model distorted images
derived from Western ethnocentrism and cultural hegemony. That the Japanese
had, as Dower (1986) points out, their own indigenous racial paradigm based on
Tokugawa Confucian notions of "proper place" is not denied; what is suggested,
however, and conveniently overlooked by many Western commentators on Japanese antiblack racism, is that the position blacks have come to occupy in the
Japanese hierarchy of races not only echoes Western racist paradigms but borrows
from them. In the postwar period in particular, with the rise of American hegemony, these perduring stereotypes of the black Other have been in large part rein-
forced by the centrality of American discourse on the nonwhite Other in Japan
which, with the cultural authority and the distributive currency of American mass
media and popular culture, has resulted in Japan's uncritical acceptance and indigenization of the racial hierarchies they project. One sees in these representations of black Otherness a repetition of the discursive strategies (e.g., the domestication of the exotic, familiarization, stereotyped conceits) employed by the West
in its construction of the Orient. In both cases "[s]omething foreign and distant
acquires . . . a status more rather than less familiar . . . [and is seen] as a version
of things previous known" (Said 1978:55).

A Genealogy of the Black Other

Derogatory references to Africans appear early in Japanese contacts with
blacks. Metaphors equating blacks with animals and subhumans can be traced to
the 16th and 17th centuries and Japan's initial contacts with the African and East
Indian servants who accompanied Portuguese and Dutch traders to Japanese ports
in Dejima and Nagasaki. Japanese envoys dispatched to America in 1860 to establish ambassadorial relations accepted the institution of black slavery as a fact

of life and viewed the African slaves they encountered as timid apelike creatures or as subhumans whom they equated with Japan's own outcasts, the *burakumin* (Miyamoto 1979; Wagatsuma and Yoneyama 1980; Wagatsuma 1967). References to blacks in diaries kept by the delegation are more or less contemptuous and unsympathetic, describing them as pitifully stupid, grotesque, dirty, unmannered, and physically repulsive. In some cases, it appears these views were prompted by the comments of their white guides, as the following account from the diary of one member of the delegation suggests:

> The faces of these natives are black, as if painted with ink and resemble those of monkeys. According to the Americans, they are the incarnations of apes. [Wagatsuma and Yoneyama 1980:64]

Contemporary literary representation of the black Other has generally adhered to these early impressions. A brief survey of literary and visual representation of blacks in contemporary Japan reveals the persistence of racial stereotypes which ascribe to blacks the following characteristics: (1) infantilism, (2) primitivism, (3) hypersexuality, (4) bestiality, (5) natural athletic prowess or physical stamina, (6) mental inferiority, (7) psychological weakness, and (8) emotional volatility. But this tendency to dehumanize and belittle blacks disguises another tendency, particularly in literary works, to employ the black Other as a reflexive symbol through which Japanese attempt to deal with their own ambiguous raciocultural status in a Eurocentric world, where such hierarchies have been largely (and literally) conceived in terms of polarizations between black and white and in which Japanese as Asians have traditionally occupied a liminal state—a gray area—"betwixt and between" the "Civilized White" and the "Barbarous Black" Other.

For the most part, Japan's image of the black Other is deeply ensconced in the cushy deliriums of Euro-American supremacy. The dichotomy that the West had drawn between "European Culture and Civilization" on the one hand and "African Barbarity and Savagery" on the other, a paradigmatic hierarchy justified by the theological theory of the Great Chain of Being and the Social Darwinism of 19th-century anthropology and intellectual discourse, provided a conceptual base upon which Japan could erect its own hierarchy of racial otherness, but one in which its own position tenuously mediated color boundaries while maintaining Western centrality. The conventional wisdom, adopted by Japanese scholars, was to retain this hierarchy, placing Japan and its Asian neighbors between the two extremes. Thus Fukuzawa Yukichi in his *Bunmei-ron no Gairyaku* [Outline of Civilization] (1875), holds up an idealized West as the apex of "civilization" *(bunmei),* deems Japan and its Asian neighbors "semicivilized" *(hankai)* and positions the African continent at its nadir, as a land of naked "savages" *(yabanjin)* mired in barbarity. This hierarchy was consistent with contemporary Euro-American discourse that placed the "Mongol race" between, as one 19th-century scholar wrote, "the lowly blacks and the lofty whites." Such attitudes about Africa were replicated in the imaginative geographies and just so stories about Africa written by Japanese during the 19th and early 20th centuries, in which their authors, adopting the vocabulary of their colonial mentors, refer to Africa as the "Dark Continent" *(ankoku tairiku; ankoku Afurika)*, "primitive" *(mikai; genshi)* and Africans themselves as, variously, *dojin, mikaijin, genshijin, yamin, domin,* and *genjumin,* terms never applied to whites. (See Shiraishi [1983:171–197] for a discussion of the impact in Japan of the 19th- and early 20th-century Western discourse on Africa.)

Modern Japanese narratives reproduce these tropes. For example, Endō Shū-saku's *Kuronbō* [Nigger] (1973), set in 16th-century Japan, is the fictional tale of Tsumpa, an African brought to Japan by a Jesuit missionary who, out of compassion, has purchased him from slave traders and taken him on as a manservant. As the two make their way through the village of Kamo in Kyoto, the unfamiliar sight of a black man causes such a public uproar that daimyō Oda Nobunaga dispatches his retainers to investigate. Tsumpa and the missionary are brought before the daimyō and the African is made to perform for him.

> The missionaries were perplexed. Knowing the kind of man Nobunaga was, they knew they could not refuse his order. They knew that if the Negro humiliated Nobunaga, they would face his wrath. But they did not know what, if anything, the Negro could do. Until then they had only used him to carry their belongings and for his labor.
> "What can he do?" Nobunaga asked. Valegnani [one of the missionaries] was completely nonplussed. Organtin [another missionary] whispered Nobunaga's order to the Negro.
> Unexpectedly, the Negro laughed, revealing his white teeth. And beaming like a child, shouted . . .
> The Negro made tapping gestures with his hands. "Is it possible to borrow a drum. . . ?" Organtin asked.
> A retainer quickly ran to fetch one.
> The Negro took up the drum and gazed on it happily like a child. After tapping experimentally on it with his fingers two and three times, his body began to sway and he started to sing in an unfamiliar language.
> Nobunaga watched the strange dance. The Negro was violently swaying back and forth, jumping up, and then—and then suddenly in front of the powerful Nobunaga something unheard of happened.
> Bu, bu, bu
> Pu, pu, pu
> At first, no one knew where the sounds were coming from. But after a while, realization dawned. The two missionaries blanched. The sounds were being emitted from the Negro's buttocks. In rhythmic tones, high and low, strong and weak, [the Negro] was farting. [Endo 1973:20–21]

In the novel, the Japanese of the 16th century act just as diary accounts from the period suggest they did upon seeing Africans for the first time. They see Tsumpa as a dirty, semihuman creation, an *oni* ("demon")—though one strikingly different from and inferior to the "southern barbarians" *(nanbanjin)* to whom they have more or less grown accustomed. Indeed, upon first seeing the African, Nobunaga orders his retainers to bathe him to see whether his black skin will wash off.[1] What is problematic is not so much these depictions—which reflect contemporary narratives—as the character of Tsumpa as rendered by the modern day, omniscient third-person narrator, a narrative tone which resurrects in a Japanese setting the Western stereotype of the African as a primitive, if in some cases saintly, Noble Savage. Although Tsumpa is described as an adult (he is 25 years old), his behavior throughout the novel is consistently rendered as infantile. Though a powerful giant, Tsumpa seems more comfortable among the children he befriends; and the image Endō presents in these scenes is one of gentle playmate and clown. The modern, ironic sensibility, which pervades most of the novel and its depiction of feudal intrigue and political machinations, does not extend to its portrait of the African, who emerges in the end as little more than oversized child.

It is noteworthy that black characters often appear in Japanese stories in connection with children. Such juxtapositions are symbolically suggestive. On the one hand, the black Other is often employed as a symbol of childhood alienation. Like his adolescent companions, the black Other in these narratives is a tragic man-child and it is through their association and identification with him that the Japanese adolescents in these narratives attempt to resolve some internal crisis and assume the burden of adult responsibilities, as in Oe Kenzaburō's *Shiiku* [The Catch] (1958) and Itsuki Hiroyuki's *Umi o mite itta Joni* [Johnny who Saw the Sea] (1966), both of which describe relationships between Japanese male youths and black American GIs. These narratives, including Endō's *Kuronbō* (1973), the black Other would seem to borrow the American literary convention of introducing an adolescent nonblack protagonist to an unjust world of adults, marking their loss of innocence and naïveté, as, for example, in Twain's *Huckleberry Finn,* Faulkner's the *Rievers,* or Carson McCuller's *Member of the Wedding.*

However, on another level, these narratives depict the black Other as himself (black women rarely appear as major characters in Japanese fiction) childlike; as a weak, pitiful being whose confused and impotent attempts to master his environment are defeated in the end by forces beyond his control. This trope consistently appears in fictional works in which blacks appear, from Ariyoshi Sawako's *Hishoku* [Not Because of Color] (1967), to more recent works, such as Yamada Eimi's *Beddotaimu Aizu* [Bedtime Eyes] (1987), and Morimura Shōichi's *Ningen no Shōmei* [Proof of the Man] (1977). In short, the black Other as victim and underdog.

The equation of blacks with children is implicit in the use of the diminutizing suffixes -*bō* and -*chan* employed to belittle blacks, as in such expressions as *kuronbō* and *kurochan* ("nigger"), the suffixes themselves connoting emotional immaturity and less than full adult status.[2]

The popularity of child and animal tropes is not limited to literary narratives. The association of blacks with children as "playmates" also finds expression in consumer goods, such as the "Dakko-chan" *ningyō* (Figure 1) popular during the '60s and the recent line of Sambo products marketed here, products which often blur the boundary between human—or perhaps more accurately homunculoid— and animal. For example, black character dolls are sometimes placed next to stuffed apes and other stuffed animal toys in shops. Indeed, when shown photographs of some of these goods, some Japanese interviewed for this study con-

Figure 1
The Takara Company's *Dakko-chan* doll (center), a best-seller in the 1960s, a logo based on it served as the company's trademark until fear of American criticism prompted its recall. Takara refused permission to reprint the trademark illustration stating that it depicted "a healthy sun-tanned Japanese child" *("hi ni yaketa genki na nihonjin no kodomo")*. The explanation, however, fails to account for the fact that the doll wears a stylized grass skirt, a standard signature used to signify the black primitive. [Photo: Courtesy of Arita Toshiji]

tended they thought they were not blacks but animals, apes of some kind; few seemed disturbed by their admission. Boundary blurring is also suggested by a line of floor mats called "Animal Mats" that come in the shape of various animals, but which include two in the form of a black male and female domestic (Figure 2). Nor is popular media immune: In the Japanese-dubbed version of the television series "The A-Team" the black character played by Mr. T is renamed "Kong." Finally, there is the story of a black woman on a suburban Tokyo train where a little girl reportedly pointed to her in fascination and asked her father "Daddy, what is that?" The embarrassed father, trying to satisfy her curiosity by reminding her of the Chinese fable *Saiyuki,* prods her to recall Songoku, the simian hero of the tale (*Los Angeles Times,* 1 January 1990).

Japan, the West, and the Search for Identity

As I mentioned previously, Japanese images of the black are inextricably linked to Japan's unequal relationship with the West. With the importation of

Figure 2
Arita Hajime, who with his parents cofounded two years ago an Osaka-based organization to ban black stereotype merchandise poses with Animal Mats and other items from their private collection. [Photo: Arita Toshiji, the Association to Stop Discrimination Against Blacks]

Dutch learning, Japanese acquired not only taste for Western science but also for Western prejudices against blacks and other subjected races. The stereotype of the black as comic jester and quintessential entertainer was introduced to the Japanese as early as 1854 when Commodore Matthew Perry, returning to Edo Bay to conclude a trade treaty with Japan, treated Japanese negotiators to an "Ethiopian" minstrel show, performed by white crew members in black-face ("a serenade of pseudo-darkies" as one witness to the performance put it) aboard the flagship *Powhatan*. According to crew diaries, the Japanese were quite delighted by the comical, cavorting "blacks" (Barr 1965:37; Heine 1990:169).

European art trends and American films also influenced the way Japanese came to perceive and depict the black Other.[3] An example of the influence and longevity of Western stereotypes is the Calpis beverage company's popular "kuronbō minstrel" trademark (Figure 3), designed in 1923 by German artist Otto Dünkelsbühler, it adorned bottles of the soft drink in Japan until 1989.[4] While certainly more stylish than similar black caricatures, Dünkelsbühler's black minstrel evokes European modernism's fascination with "Negro primitivism." The influence of his design is evident in an illustration which appears in a 1987 English conversation text (Figure 4), though the original's fashionable black dandy has been replaced by a less sophisticated "aboriginal" cousin.

Popularly referred to as the "Calpis *kuronbō* ("nigger") minstrel," German artist Otto Dünkelsbühler's illustration depicts a dandified black minstrel in top hat and bow tie, with thick, wide lips and large expressive eyes, bent over a glass and contentedly sipping the company's soft-drink product through a straw. Calpis refused permission on the grounds that it had discontinued use of the trademark two years ago and its use would "tarnish the company's image" *("kaisha no imēji ga daun ni naru kara")*.

Figure 3
The original Calpis Negro minstrel trademark designed by German artist Otto Dünkelsbühler in 1923.

Figure 4
A "native" inspired by the popular trademark as it appears in an English conversation text, *Dogu Toshite no Eigo: Yomikata-hen* [English as a Tool: A Reader] (1987). [Reprinted here with the permission of the publisher, JICC Shuppan Kyokai]

The legacy of such Western conventions is further evident in the work of 20th-century Japanese illustrators. The black "primitives" *(bankō)* the child-king Dankichi encounters in Shimada Keizo's popular children's book *Boken Dankichi* [The Adventurous Dankichi] (serialized from July 1933 to February 1939 in the magazine *Shōnen Kurabu)* (Figure 5) are in the Sambo mode; comical entities with bulging eyes, misshapen ears, and bulbous white lips, a depiction not noticeably different from that which prevailed in American animated cartoons of the same period. A more direct influence can be observed in the work of Tezuka Osamu, the "Walt Disney of Japan," whose black "primitives" in such works as *Jungle Taitei* [Jungle Emperor] (serialized in *Manga Shonen* from February 1950 to April 1954) (Figure 6) show the stylistic signature of his namesake, as well as Shimada's, whose work he admired. Like Shimada, Tezuka follows the imaginary geography laid down by the Western view of Africa and its inhabitants, borrowing inspiration from the popularity of the Tarzan films of the 1930s and 1940s, a genre he attempted to imitate in such early works as *Jungle Makyō* [Jungle World of Devils] (1948), *Tarzan no Himitsu Kichi* [Tarzan's Secret Base] (1948), and in subsequent works.

In *Jungle Taitei* Tezuka replaces the Shimada's child-king Dankichi with Leo, the white lion cub protagonist. Like his predecessor, Tezuka's narrative condescends to the Africans; two of its recurring human protagonists—the Tarzan-like Japanese youth Ken'ichi and the white Mary, whom the Africans have en-

---

Two panels from the comic book, *Boken Dankichi* (The Adventurous Dankichi). In the top right panel, Dankichi instructs a group of black "natives" to line up in a row with their backs turned to him. The "natives" are depicted with thick, white lips, goggle eyes and small, triangular ears. The bottom left panel shows the young child-king, instructing two seated "natives" by using the backs of the natives whom he has ordered to line up in the previous panel as a makeshift blackboard. The publisher, Kodansha, refused to grant permission to use the panels because of "racial problems" *("jinshu mondai")* connected with the comic.

Figure 5
"Black" savages. Shimada Keizo's *Boken Dankichi* circa 1933.

Six panels from Tezuka Osamu's *Jungle Taitei,* showing fierce, spear-carrying, grass-skirted "natives" confronting Ken, the Tarzanlike Japanese youth, and Mary, the white Goddess Queen.

Figure 6
Angry Africans confront Ken'ichi and Mary in Tezuka Osamu's *Jungle Taitei,* circa 1950.

throned as their Queen/Goddess—are depicted as superior to the Africans. Within this fabulous landscape, the author combines three processes: (1) the anthropomorphization of the story's animal protagonist, (2) the deification of its nonblack protagonists, and (3) the subhumanization of the black Africans, who are depicted as less civilized and far more inept than the creatures with whom they share their jungle habitat.

Helen Bannerman's *The Story of Little Black Sambo* (1899) sees the continuation of this stylistic legacy, though it is important to note that while introduced to Japan during the Meiji Period (1868–1911), it did not obtain widespread recognition until 1953 when a new version, complete with "pickaninny" illustrations (Figure 7), was published by Iwanami Shoten (Bannerman 1953) as part of a new line of children's books. Although published well after the convention of representing blacks in the Western stereotypical mode had taken root, its popularity (120 versions have appeared since) and influence in shaping the Japanese image of the black Other should not be underestimated.

As I suggested earlier, the black Other serves as a repository for certain negatively sanctioned values ("impurity," "primitivism," "laziness," technocultural "underdevelopment" and "backwardness," etc.) yet it also serves as a convenient instrument in the search for Japanese racial identity. In some ways the black Other occupies the same symbolic space and function as *burakumin* and Koreans, two categories of other with which blacks are often equated (cf. Ohnuki-Tierney 1987). While the former serve reflexively to remind Japanese of their identity as Japanese, the black Other serves as a reflexive symbol through which Japanese attempt to reappraise their status vis-à-vis whites and the symbolic power (e.g., modernity, enlightenment, European-style civility and High Culture) they are seen to represent; that is, it is employed as a category mediating white Otherness and Japanese Selfhood, forcing Japanese, particularly those who have lived abroad, to rethink both their identification with whites and their valorization of Eurocentric aesthetic and cultural values. Such reflexive use of the blacks expresses itself in two ways: (1) The Japanese agent/narrator may continue to accept the racial status quo and see oneself as an excluded and inferior other

---

Cover from the 1953 Iwanami Shoten edition of Helen Bannerman's *The Story of Little Black Sambo (Chibikuro Sambo)* showing a bulbous-eyed, thick-lipped Sambo, an umbrella deployed over head, gaping incredulously as a circle of four tigers surrounds him. Iwanami did not give a reason for its refusal but suggested that other publishers be approached.

Figure 7
Iwanami Shoten's Japanese-language version of *Little Black Sambo, Chibikuro Sambo* (1953).

vis-à-vis Euro-American norms, but attempt to compensate for the perceived deficiencies by elevating him or herself above other "backward" groups; (2) He/she may identify with the black Other, asserting solidarity with nonwhites in general as a fellow *yūshokujin* (person of color), and reject the racial status quo.

An example of the former can be found in Endō Shūsaku's "Aden Made" [Up to Aden] (1971[1954]) which is noteworthy for the negative symbology it attaches to the color black and the author's frank admission of his own feelings of inferiority toward whites, as witness this scene where the narrator, returning home by ship from study abroad in France after an ill-fated love affair with a Frenchwoman, shares a fourth-class cabin with a dying African woman.

> Lying down in the fourth class cabin, I stare at the feverish brown body of the sick [African] woman before me. I truly feel her skin color is ugly. The color black is ugly, yellow even more so. This black woman and I both belong eternally to ugly races. I have no idea how or why only the skin of white people became the standard of beauty, nor how or why the standard of human beauty in sculpture and painting are all derived from the white bodies of the Greeks and remains so today. But I am certain that with regard to the body, those like myself and this black woman can never forget the miserable feelings of inferiority in front of white people, however disturbing such an admission may be. [Endo 1971:161]

An example of the latter is provided by the nonfiction works of photojournalist Yoshida Ruiko, particularly in her debut work *Hāremu no Atsui Hibi* [Hot Harlem Days] (1979[1967]), an account of her experiences living in New York's Harlem during the heyday of the Black Power movement and a provocative critique of American racial hierarchies.

> But why did I, a Japanese, want to continue to photograph blacks? Of course, the environment in which I happened to be placed was a factor, as well as the discovery that I could capture [their] beautiful images. But now back in Japan I realize that was not all. Their continued history of struggle and oppression and reawakening to their blackness, unconsciously compelled me to project my own identity as a yellow person placed among other races in a racist national state [*jinshushūgi-kokka*]. A desperate defiance as a yellow woman placed between black and white [*kuro to shiro no aida ni okareta kiiroi josei*] was also a factor. Whenever I took photographs of [their] dazzling, shiny black skin, I felt as if some yellow fluid like mustard were seeping from my skin. [Yoshida 1979:216]

Concluding her book, Yoshida writes:

> *Hāremu no Atsui Hibi* is a coming-of-age record of the maturation of one yellow-skinned woman's [*kiiroi hada no onna*] life in an American black ghetto in the 1960s. At the same time, it is also a journal of one person's search for self-identity, a person who—like blacks—is a minority in American society. [Yoshida 1979:226]

Yoshida's use of terms like *ōshokujin* (yellow person) and *hada no kiiroi onna* (yellow-skinned woman) and her identification of herself a "minority" is a deliberate statement of her solidarity with other people of color; a consciousness, she tells the reader, she did not possess until her experiences in America. In this and subsequent works, Yoshida rejects Western racial hierarchies, while criticizing her compatriots, particularly the Japanese intelligentsia, for their uncritical embrace of them and oppression of minorities at home.

Western hegemony and Japan's subordinate relation to the West has had a profound effect on the Japanese self-image as well as their image of the nonwhite Other. The West has played a pivotal role not only in introducing Japan to the black Other but in defining the parameters of culture and civilization in general. Given Western hegemony and cultural authority and its lavish display of modernity and material power in Japan and elsewhere, it is not surprising that in its attempt to catch up with the West, Japan began to identify with it and peripheralize cultural links with its Asian neighbors whose influence on Japan waned with the expansion of Euro-American power in the Pacific.

This alignment can be detected in the "Caucasianization" of Japanese as Western fashion and aesthetic sensibilities begin to take root, flowering in the Meiji Period and again in the 1920s in the form of *moga* and *mobo*, "modern girls and boys" (epitomized by the character of Naomi in Tanizaki Junichirō's *Chijin no Ai*, 1925)—who modeled their appearance on contemporary Western silent film stars. Nor did the anti-Western rhetoric of World War II prevent Japanese from depicting themselves as Caucasian in physical appearance, in effect, "(distancing) themselves physically from the 'darker' peoples of Asia" (Dower 1986:209), a convention that survives today in comics and animated cartoons. According to Dower, the antiwhite, anti-Western rhetoric of the war years was "reactive" and had "no clear counterpart in the racism of white supremacists" (1986:204). Japanese racism was preoccupied with elevating the Japanese and with "wrestling with what it really meant to be Japanese" (1986:205). While the "reactive" nature of Japanese racism may account in part for the antiwhite racism of the war years, neither it nor theories which link Japanese racial attitudes to culturally informed prejudices regarding skin color adequately explains antiblack racism in Japan. To account for the latter, one must recognize the impact of Western hegemony and the other factor Dower cites, specifically, the Japanese preoccupation with racial elevation and their desire to distance themselves from races subjected by Western power and whose plight Japan hoped to avoid by acquiring the accoutrements—material and intellectual—of a powerful, implacable colossus.

This attempt to distance the "Japanese" self from the darker Other is nicely described in Endō Shūsaku's autobiographical novel, *Ryūgaku* [Studies Abroad] (1968[1965]). Early in the novel the protagonist is invited to a party at a restaurant in Lyons, France, by a Japanese friend. Also in attendance are a Roman Catholic priest, several Frenchwomen and two black Morrocan students, Paulan and Magiro, who have been studying in Paris. Symbolically, Paulan represents what author V. S. Naipaul has termed a "mimic man," a nonwhite who attempts to ingratiate himself with whites by adopting Western ways as his own, but whom whites find humorous. Even the narrator finds the African, with his coarse hair slicked down with oil and parted in the middle in imitation of a French gentleman, a wretched, pitiful figure.

In one telling scene the priest introduces the protagonist's companion to Paulan, but the Japanese student is so startled by the contrast between the pink palms and black skin of the African's extended hand that he pulls back his own in an involuntary reflex of physical repulsion. Later, one of the women requests that one of the African students sing a "traditional" song for them. Both the Japanese protagonist and the French view the singing African as a miserable if unintentionally comic figure.

> Paulan spread his legs wide and began to clap out a beat. His body swayed as he sang. His voice was shrill and the exaggerated movements of his body were enough to embarrass the onlookers. The Catholic priest chewed his pipe stifling a laugh and the women, unable to bear it all, turned away. It was clear to Kudo that the women did not find his dancing and singing attractive. Yet Paulan continued to sing anyway. He was deliberately planning to endear himself with these women.
>
> Kudo, trying his best not to look in their direction, averted his eyes. As the student named Paulan sang, he knew almost too painfully what his true motives were. The Negro is singing that stupid song to ingratiate himself with the white women. He thinks that will endear them to him.
>
> After Paulan had finished singing, the priest, his pipe still fixed in his mouth, placed his hand on Paulan's shoulder. The brown brow and cheeks of the Negro student dripped with sweat, the sweat of a slave forced to perform hard labor.
>
> "Do the Japanese go in for such singing and dancing?"
>
> Kudo glared at the priest and blurted, "Absolutely not! We . . ."
>
> The priest had not understood Kudo's feelings. Somewhat nonplussed, he said quietly, "No, no, of course. I only meant we'd heard that Japanese songs are artistic."
> [Endō 1968:34–35]

Aside from the suggestion of an implicit sexual rivalry between the Japanese and the African for the attention of the white women, the scene suggests that for Kudo the black is an uncomfortable reminder of his own insecure status to whites. Kudo's strong reaction to the priest's innocent suggestion that Japanese might have something in common with these Africans prompts his angry outburst and would seem to indicate that the presence of these dark, unsophisticated interlopers has shattered his delusive identification with European culture.

A rather remarkable but by no means exceptional example of distancing in the form of racio-cultural one-upmanship—where Japanese hoist whites on their own supremacist petard by elevating themselves above whites but at the expense of other nonwhites—is evident in the following excerpt from psychiatrist Ohara Kenshirō's popular study of mental depression, *Utsubyō no Jidai* [The Age of Depression].

> It is well known that compared to America the number of suicides in our country is high and I have already touched upon the close relationship between depression and suicide. In fact, one cannot think of them without reference to self-punishment and guilt. Dr. Kraines, an authority on depression, in comparing the suicide and homicide rates of white and black Americans has suggested that suicide among whites is higher and that a reason for this is that whites tend to direct aggression internally upon the self in contrast to blacks who tend to direct their aggression externally and he has suggested that the level of culture of whites is higher than blacks. Following this

premise, the Japanese, who have a higher suicide rate than white Americans, have a higher level of culture than Americans. [1981:173–174]

In connection with distancing and elevation, I would like briefly to discuss two other related processes: "negrofic*tation*" and "primitization." In both, the image of the black Other is forced to conform to certain stylized, procrustean categories—preconditioned "pictures in the head," as Walter Lippman aptly referred to stereotypes—that serve to maintain a conceptual distance between Self and Other. In short, the integrity of the stereotype must be preserved despite contradictory evidence, external reality made to conform to the internal dictates of representational conceits so that the conceptual center holds.

In Japan, negrofiction manifests itself both visually and vocally. Visual negrofiction is evident in the caricatures of Carl Lewis, Ben Johnson, and the Tanzanian runner Jima Ikanga in an illustration that appeared in the 1984 Seoul Olympics edition of the television program guide *TelePal* (Figure 8) and in the grossly deformed black mannequins that appeared in front of a Tokyo department store in 1988 (Figure 9).

Such grotesqueries run the fine line between caricature and stereotype. Whereas caricatures exaggerate existing personal characteristics, negrofiction substitutes exaggerated racial features—here markers of pseudo-negritude (e.g., thick, bulbous lips, banjo-eyes, flaring nostrils)—where they do not objectively apply to the individual who serves as model, thus forcing a fit where one is absent. The distinction is a subtle one, but one which must be kept in mind given the proliferation and popularity in Japan of *monomane* (comical mimicry), caricature, and stylized portraiture in which popular Japanese celebrities are rendered in ways that might strike an outside observer as racist had a non-Japanese done them. The pervasiveness of these markers of pseudo-negritude has made it virtually impossible for some Japanese even to conceive of representing blacks nonstereotypically. For example, some Japanese informants interviewed for this study suggested that without them they would be unable to identify such figures as black; in such light, nonstereotyped representation seems to be regarded as oxymoronic. Visual negrofiction seems to be a 20th-century phenomenon. Edo and Meiji prints render black-skinned servants in the same Tengu mode (i.e., with long, narrow faces dominated by elongated phallic noses) used for white foreigners, distinguishing them from their white masters by costume (many are bare-footed),

---

Eight panels from the Seoul Olympics edition of *TelePal* depicting Carl Lewis, Ben Johnson, and the Tanzanian runner Jima Ikanga. All are depicted with grossly exaggerated thick lips and goggle eyes.

Figure 8
Carl Lewis, Ben Johnson, and Jima Ikanga as they appear in the Japanese magazine *TelePal*, 1984.

Figure 9
Black mannequins pose "stylishly" in front of a Tokyo department store.
These mannequins have now been removed from stores throughout Japan.
[Reprinted here from the *Washington Post*, 22 July 1988, p. A18, with the
permission of Shigehiko Togo of the *Washington Post*.]

hair texture, and black or grayish skin color. Indeed, the black Africans in the
Yokohama Prints of Meiji artist Hashimoto Sadahide are rendered with dignity
and sympathy (Figure 10). And it would appear that the convention of representing dark-skinned people in the Sambo-mold favored in the West is not standardized until the turn of the century.

Vocal negrofictation frequently occurs when the voices of blacks are dubbed
into Japanese. It is not an uncommon practice among Japanese TV producers to
substitute coarse, deep-throated, or high-pitched, whiney voices—often rich in
dialect—for those of black males even when the speakers' original voices are otherwise race-neutral and dialect-free. The standardization of voices to "fit" certain
categories of Other is not limited to blacks. One encounters it in quiz and news
programs where stylized vocalizations, substituting for the foreigner's original
voice, are used to impose essentialistic qualities *(rashi-sa)* based on the speaker's
perceived class, gender, and age.

Primitization of the black Other is a ubiquitous feature of Japanese docu-
mentaries/game shows. "Primitives" and rural villagers are frequently chosen as
objects for presentation and comparison and made to fill the role. A recent example is the case of N'Xkau the South African !Kung and "star" of *The Gods*

Hashimoto Sadehide's portrait of two black slaves in Yokohama circa 1860. The Meiji Period print shows two black slaves carrying wooden barrels on their backs. In the foreground a black woman washes clothing in a wooden tub. A written explanation of the scene by the artist appears in Japanese in the upper lefthand corner of the print. Significantly, the depiction of blacks here is devoid of the stereotyped conventions that have come to dominate the depiction of blacks in 20th-century Japanese illustration.

Figure 10
Yokohama print of black servants by Meiji artist Hashimoto Sadahide, circa 1860.

Must be Crazy who, following the popularity of the film in Japan and a subsequent Japanese television feature on his life in the South African "bush," was invited to Japan. Whatever the producer's intent, the result was to juxtapose the !Kung's "endearing primitiveness" against the "modernity" and "sophistication" of urban Tokyo. Indeed, N'Xkau's treatment and Japanese reaction to him recalls a scene from *Kuronbō* in which the Tsumpa becomes a sideshow attraction. Producers may also request that their "primitives" appear in traditional (i.e., "tribal") wear despite the fact that Western attire is not unknown to them. If genuine primitives are unavailable, they can be manufactured and their reactions orchestrated, as when a group from a Kenyan village (again, attired natively) were invited to Japan a few years back and directed by the studio sponsoring them to display before the cameras bemusement and wonder at the marvels of hi-tech Tokyo, since apparently that was what viewers should expect from *real* exotics.

Transvaluation

Recent trends in Japanese literary representation of the black Other tend to portray blacks as sexual objects, studs, fashion accessories (Figure 11) and quintessential performers, images that imported American media reinforce daily. Consider the following passage from a guidebook to New York's ethnic diversity:

> At parties thrown by whites, just having a fashionable black guest who dances skillfully adds life to party. This effect is so well known in New York that [whites] boast that they have stylish black friends. In fact, when [white] New Yorkers assemble with their friends to sing, dance, and drink, if there are just a few blacks the party will come to life. They may be natural entertainers. However, more than anything else the blacks themselves seem to enjoy playing the role of entertainer. [Nagasawa and Miyamoto 1986:136]

Just as the image of the black Other in the West as bumbling Stepin Fetchit and contented domestic was eventually replaced with the threatening superstuds

Figure 11
Jealous Japanese women guard their prized possessions, "Black People,"
Hiragana Times, **June 1990. [Reprinted here with the permission of the *Hiragana Times*]**

of '70s blaxploitation films, like *Shaft* and *Superfly,* a similar transvaluation seems to have taken place in Japanese mass culture. Though stereotypes of blacks as sexual athletes and born entertainers are not new, they were perhaps given greater distributive currency during the Occupation and the Korean War with the influx of black GIs and American popular culture, and through Japanese exposure to racist white GIs who were not above spreading the seeds of their racism overseas: once warned by government propaganda of the propensities of Americans for rape and carnage, Japanese were now being told similar horror stories about blacks by white American GIs.[5]

With the Vietnam War, the rise of the counterculture and the influx of black popular music and culture, disaffected Japanese youth came to see the African American as a counter to the values of the Japanese establishment, and the black

Other was adopted as a symbol of defiance, forbidden fruit, and their own alienation from the Japanese mainstream.

This change in attitude is suggested in Murakami Ryū's Akutagawa Prize-winning *Kagirinaku Tomei ni Chikai Burū* [Almost Transparent Blue] (1976), an explicit tale of decadence that graphically depicts the sexual exploits of a group of disaffected Japanese youths involved with black GIs stationed at Yokota Air Base. Drug use, orgies, and human debasement dominate this novel of sexual excess in which stereotypes of black sexuality abound.[6]

The trope of the African-American male as sexual athlete and priapic paramour acquires a masturbatory redundancy in the works of Yamada Eimi, a prolific, young writer whose sexually graphic fictions consistently take as their theme torrid love affairs between Japanese women and black GIs. The prize-winning *Beddotaimu Aizu* [Bedtime Eyes] (1987), Yamada's debut work, explores the relationship between Kim, a naïve Japanese club singer and Joseph "Spoon" Johnson, a Harlem-born GI who has gone AWOL and who is secretly selling military secrets to an unidentified foreign power.

"Spoon"—the nickname resonates with phallic symbolism—is the ultimate priapic stud, a smooth operator, and stylish hustler. Their relationship is a purely physical one. Some Japanese reviewers of the novel have praised Yamada for the frankness of her descriptions, her refusal to substitute flowery euphemisms for the sex act. Instead she invests her novel with Anglo-Saxon vulgarisms and a dry, almost clinical naturalism.

Yamada's virgin work and subsequent works and images of blacks projected in American films have sparked a renewed interest, bordering on preoccupation, with black sexuality in the Japanese media.[7] The result has been a breakdown of the boundaries between private and public culture. What had once been a taboo subject—the relation between black GIs and Japanese women—suddenly became a topic fit for open discussion, sensational serials in Japanese magazines, late-night television debate, and underground cinema. It is worth noting that only a few decades before the publication of *Beddotaimu Aizu,* Yoshida Ruiko complained of the preoccupation of her Japanese colleagues who would take her aside to ask whether she had slept with blacks or, assuming that she had, to ask that she rate their sexual performance. By 1984, however, TV stations were sending crews to Roppongi and American bases in Yokota and Yokotsuka to ask Japanese women dating black men the same questions and broadcasting their responses for inquiring minds at home.

Conclusion

The representation of blacks follows conventions largely derived from Western racial categories and hierarchies. Contemporary images—more old wine in new bottles, or more accurately, old stereotypes in new media—continue to rely on Western conventions, though some of these conventions, as in the case of the Sambo imagery, may have passed out of usage in the West itself. While Japanese themselves often fail to recognize these images as racist (a response not unlike whites when first confronted with their black stereotypes), Japanese representation of blacks tends to be condescending and to debase, dehumanize, exoticize, and peripheralize the black Other, who at once serves as a symbolic counterpoint to modernity, rationalism, and civility—and as an uncomfortable reminder of the insecurities and ambiguity of Japanese racial and cultural identity vis-à-vis an idealized West.

Notes

Acknowledgments. Research for this article was supported by a grant from the Japan Foundation, 1989–1990. All translations are mine. The Japanese convention of giving surname first is followed throughout for Japanese names.

[1] In many ways Tsumpa the African is a black counterpart to Gaston, the titular "wonderful fool" of Endō's *O-baka-san* (1959). Both are fish out of water, clown/mediators (see Ohnuki-Tierney 1987), whose misadventures in Japan satirize Japanese foibles, though Gaston's is the face of reasoned civilization, Tsumpa's is that of primitive, uncultured innocence. The African's black skin inspires scatological associations. Indeed, at the beginning of the novel Tsumpa's arrival is predicted by an old fortune-teller whose predictions are inspired by inspecting his client's feces. Upon inspecting the feces of a young woman client the fortune-teller informs her that she will soon meet a strange man who will pass in front of her house. The prediction proves correct, for the next day Tsumpa and company arrive in town. Shimada Keizo's *Boken Dankichi* (1933–39) offers a variation of the scene in *Kuronbō* where Tsumpa is ordered to bathe to demonstrate to Nobunaga that his skin color is natural and not a deception. In Shimada's inverted version, the Japanese child-king covers his body in mud to pass as a native in order to escape from cannibals, only to have his deception ruined, predictably, by a sudden rainstorm. In both the equation of blacks with dirt is obvious.

[2] One reason for the popularity in Japan of Bannerman's *The Story of Little Black* may owe, in part, to the coincidental affinity the character's name has with other terms which employ the diminutizing *-bō* suffix *(kuronbō,* nigger, a darkie, "little black one"; *akanbō,* a baby, "little red one"; *okorinbō,* a person who easily angers, "little petulant one"), and may explain why many Japanese, who are unaware of its racist etymology, regard the term as cute and endearing.

[3] Contemporary images of blacks in Japan are more or less variations of archetypes derived from American cinema. For example, Tarzan-like characters, complete with "savage natives," are a staple of Japanese animation. *Gone with the Wind (Kaze to tomo ni Saranu)* still enjoys tremendous popularity in Japan on video and in theatrical revival and a musical version is part of the repertoire of the all-woman Takarazuka musical revue. Donald Bogle, in his much overlooked *Toms, Coons, Mulattoes, Mammies and Bucks* (1973) notes that American cinematic stereotypes of blacks are multivalent and often contradictory; stereotypes of black as "pickaninnies," slow-witted "coons," and timorous "darkies," coexisting with those of threatening subhumans, lascivious rapists, and domesticated militants. These ambivalent images are presently embodied in the personas of the Child-Eunuch Michael Jackson and the Priapic Prince, both of whom fall within Bogle's tragic mulatto category. On the other hand, rap images revolt against the desexualization and mulattoization of the black male. Although on its surface the iconography of posturing black macho would

seem consistent with the stereotype of the threatening black male, the subtext is largely subversive, using it to promote a positive, uncompromising black self-image. However, the popularity of rap music among Japanese youth would seem to lie less in the subversive content of its sociopolitical message than its counterfashion *(han-seiso)* statements and danceability *(nori ga ii),* all of which ultimately serve to confirm black stereotypes.

[4]Negative American reaction and the efforts of Japanese activists prompted many Japanese companies to cease production of stereotypical black character goods and company trademarks. In 1988, Iwanami Shoten ceased publication of the Sambo book (Bannerman 1953); other publishers followed. Calpis and Takara (manufacturer of *Dakko-chan*) abandoned use of their black character trademarks in 1989.

[5]The Occupation not only helped export antiblack racism to Japan, it also gave the Japanese the means of reproducing it for white consumption back in the States by encouraging production of stereotyped black figurines under the "Made in Occupied Japan" label. Other stereotypes are not so benign. The image of the black GI as rapist has become something of a staple of Japanese pornography and films about the Occupation (Buruma 1984:57). The black rapist trope also appeared in Matsumoto Seichō's short story *Kuroji no Ei* [Picture on Black Cloth] (1965) and in adult comic books.

[6]The film version, directed by Murakami, soft-peddles the novel's explicit interracial sex scenes and is tame even by the censor-sensitive standards of Japanese visual pornography. Only one orgy scene survives; the partially clad black actors engage in stylized writhing atop their Japanese partners, yet never so much as even kiss them, as if the director believed such intimate contact contaminating.

[7]Reviewers frequently apply such terms as *mondai sakuhin, mondai shosetsu* (controversial novel) to Yamada's works, stressing their "shock value" and "taboo-breaking" content. Yet given the ubiquity of the black rapist trope, the shock value of her books would seem to owe less to their miscegenational themes than to the suggestion that Japanese women would *willfully* select blacks as sexual partners.

References Cited

Ariyoshi, Sawako
    1967   Hishoku [Not Because of Color]. Tokyo: Kadokawa Shoten.
Bannerman, Helen
    1899   The Story of Little Black Sambo. London: Grant Richards.
    1953   Chibikuro Sambo. Furasnku Dobieasu, trans. Tokyo: Iwanami Shoten.
Barr, Patricia
    1965   The Coming of the Barbarians. London: Penguin.
Bogle, Donald
    1973   Toms, Coons, Mulattoes, Mammies and Bucks. New York: Viking Press.
Buruma, Ian
    1984   Behind the Mask. New York: New American Library.
Dower, John W.
    1986   War without Mercy. New York: Pantheon.
Endō, Shūsaku
    1959   O-baka-san [The Wonderful Fool]. Tokyo: Chuko Bunko.
    1968 [1965]   Ryūgaku [Studies Abroad]. Tokyo: Shincho Bunko.
    1971 [1954]   Aden Made [Up to Aden]. *In* Shiroi Hito/Kiiroi Hito [White People/Yellow People], short story collection. Tokyo: Kodansha Bunko.

1973 [1971]   Kuronbō [Nigger]. Tokyo: Kadokawa Bunko.

Fukuzawa, Yukichi
1986[1875]   Bunmei-ron no Gairyaku [Outline of Civilization]. Tokyo: Iwanami Bunko.

Heine, William
1990 [1856]   With Perry to Japan. Honolulu: University of Hawaii Press.

Itsuki, Hiroyuki
1966   Umi o mite itta Joni [Johnny who Saw the Sea], short story collection. Tokyo: Kodansha Bunko.

Ivy, Marilyn
1989   Critical Texts, Mass Artifacts: The Consumption of Knowledge in Postmodern Japan. In Postmodernism and Japan. Masao Miyoshi and H. D. Harootunian, eds. Pp. 21–46. Durham: Duke University Press.

Matsumoto, Seichō
1965   Kuroji no Ei [Picture on Black Cloth], short story collection. Tokyo: Shincho Bunko.

Miyamoto, Masao
1979   As We Saw Them. Berkeley: University of California Press.

Morimura, Shōichi
1977   Ningen no Shōmei [Proof of the Man]. Tokyo: Kodansha Bunko.

Murakami, Ryū
1976   Kagirinaku Tomei ni Chikai Burū [Almost Transparent Blue]. Tokyo: Kodansha Bunko.

Nagasawa, Makoto, and Miyamoto Michiko
1986   I Love New York. Tokyo: Bunshun Bunko.

Naipaul, V. S.
1967   The Mimic Men. Harmondsworth: Penguin.

Oe, Kenzaburō
1958   Shisha no Ogori—Shiiku [The Extravagance of the Dead and The Catch], short story collection. Tokyo: Shincho Bunko.

Ohara, Kenshirō
1981   Utsubyō no Jidai [The Age of Depression]. Tokyo: Kodansha Gendai Shinsho.

Ohnuki-Tierney, Emiko
1987   The Monkey as Mirror. Princeton: Princeton University Press.

Said, Edward W.
1978   Orientalism. New York: Pantheon.

Sakai, Naoki
1989   Modernity and Its Critique: The Problem of Universalism and Particularism. In Postmodernism and Japan. Masao Miyoshi and H. D. Harootunian, eds. Pp. 93–122. Durham: Duke University Press.

Shimada, Keizo
1933–39   Boken Dankichi [The Adventurous Dankichi]. In Shonen Kurabu, July 1933–February 1939.

Shiraishi, Kenji
1983   Kindai Nihon no Afurika Ninshiki Shikiron [A Preliminary Essay on Modern Japan's Knowledge of Africa]. In Seio Afurika vs. Nippon [Western Europe-Africa vs. Japan]. Osaka Ni-Futsu Sentā, ed. Pp. 171–197. Tokyo: Daisan Shokan.

Tanizaki, Junichirō
1985[1925]   Chijin no Ai [A Fool's Love]. Tokyo: Shincho Bunko.

Wagatsuma, Hiroshi
    1967   The Social Perception of Skin Color in Japan. Daedalus, Spring:407–443.
Wagatsuma, Hiroshi, and Yoneyama Toshinao
    1980   Henken no Kōzō [The Structure of Prejudice]. Tokyo: NHK Books.
Yamada, Eimi
    1987   Beddotaimu Aizu [Bedtime Eyes]. Tokyo: Kawade Bunko.
Yoshida, Ruiko
    1979 [1967]   Hāremu no Atsui Hibi [Hot Harlem Days]. Tokyo: Kodansha.

Representing Culture: The Production of Discourse(s) for Aboriginal Acrylic Paintings

Fred Meyers

> To see something as art requires something the eye cannot descry—an atmosphere of artistic theory, a knowledge of the history of art: an artworld.
>
> —Arthur Danto, "The Artworld,"
> Journal of Philosophy 61:580, 1964

When I was returning to Central Australia in July of 1988, I noticed an unusual woman on the plane from Sydney to Alice Springs, the heart of Australia's "Outback" where the clothing tends to range from tourist sweat suits and reeboks, to country western style outfits with R. M. Williams stockman's boots, to hippie-traveler casual. Compared to most of the passengers, this woman was dramatically overdressed—wearing fine gold-colored Italian leather sandals, scarlet nailpolish, and a kaftan style designer jacket and trousers made of dark silk. She was accompanied by a man with long black hair drawn back in a ponytail, a black goatee and mustache, and a long black duster coat—the combined effect evoked a late 19th-century studio artist from the École des Beaux Arts in Paris. Leaving the plane, I wondered what these people, who seemed ready for a gallery party in Sydney, could be doing in the frontier town of Alice Springs, particularly since they seemed to know their way around.

An hour later, dressed in my uniform of choice, a denim shirt and jeans, I stopped in to greet old friends at the shop of the Papunya Tula Artists company, where I was introduced to the mystery woman. She was Gabrielle Pizzi, the Melbourne art dealer who is the principal distributor of the acrylic paintings produced by the Aboriginal people with whom I have been working since 1973. Our different ideas about attire for meeting Aboriginal artists in the Outback emphasized our differences. Ironically, my discomfort with *their* entry into a domain I had considered refreshingly remote from the pretensions of our own society's high culture lead me to examine the world from which *they* came.

Back in New York, in May of 1989 the John Weber Gallery in Soho had a show of Papunya Tula Artists' work, and as I waited there one afternoon to interview the gallery owner, I was jarred by hearing a visitor to the gallery talk with familiarity of Simon Tjakamarra's "colorism" and the decline of Clifford Possum's recent paintings. These are Aboriginal men I know from my fieldwork, where I was once threatened for merely having asked the name of a man's country!

Such cultural incongruity appears even when the emphasis is on the "Aboriginality," or distinctiveness, of their paintings. I find it dislocating to hear them repeatedly represented as "painters"or "artists." In Weber's gallery, the acrylics are hung to emphasize that role as defined by the West.[1] No information is presented about specific content: only the name of painter, the date, and title are given, although an accompanying catalog traces some of the general historical tradition related to the production of these images.

In short, the people whom the *Guinness Book of Records* inscribed as having the simplest material culture of any people on earth (the "Bindibu"[2]), representatives of a people regarded disparagingly by the dominant white majority in Australia, are now accorded international appreciation as producers of "high art," an appreciation rarely granted to Australia's white art producers.

A sign of the definitive success of Australian Aboriginal acrylic paintings in the United States was the exhibition at the Asia Society Galleries in New York City in late 1988. Entitled "Dreamings: The Art of Aboriginal Australia," this show drew the largest attendance (27,000 visitors) of any exhibit ever held at the Asia Society. Viewers came to see a display of 103 objects, of five types and from four different "cultural areas" in Australia. There were wood sculptures (from Cape York Peninsula), bark paintings (from Arnhem Land), acrylic paintings on canvas and shields (Central Australia), and small carved pieces known as *toas* or message sticks (from the Lake Eyre region) (see Sutton 1988).

For the Aborigines of Central Australia, the acrylic paintings on canvas (as well as the paintings on bark) are a *new* form, objects made for sale and not for their own ritual or practical use. They are attempting, nonetheless, to define these products in terms meaningful to them. While bark and acrylic paintings are produced as commodities for commercial sale to outsiders (see Bardon 1979; Kimber 1977; Megaw 1982; Morphy 1977, 1983; Myers 1989; Sutton 1988; N. Williams 1976), both artistic traditions draw largely on designs and stories embedded in indigenous religious activities and this constitutes—for Aborigines and probably for whites (although differently)—a major part of their value. Yet the significance of these objects and their activities—the meaning of their meanings, as it were— is not controlled by the Aboriginal painters as they move into the wider cultural arena in which they are displayed and sold.

Nobody in 1973 or 1974 would have expected to read about Papunya paintings in the *New York Times,* as we do (occasionally) now. Yet, from the beginning, their existence was defined in three differentiated cultural arenas—local, state, and art circles. Specifically, their production has provoked growing self-consciousness among the Aboriginal producers for whom the sales have had economic and cultural importance,[3] responses from those formulating "cultural policies" in the agencies of the Australian state—such as the government-funded Aboriginal Arts Board of the Australia Council and the Department of Aboriginal

Affairs (see Altman 1988:52–53; Altman, McGuigan, and Yu 1989)—and, increasingly, evaluations from the art markets.

The movement of the acrylic paintings into the "international art scene" has generated rising prices[4] and an inventory of articles and reviews from the art critical world. What is challenging for anthropologists about the presentation of Aboriginal art in the Asia Society exhibition—or in events like this exhibition in which images are exchanged internationally—is not just that ethnographic representations of Aboriginal culture play a visible part in the "constitution" of these objects; these anthropological representations, drawn from our own discourse, are contested by other representations as well.

My point in this article is to show that the production, circulation, and consumption of these objects constitutes an important dimension of self-production of Aboriginal people and of the processes of "representing culture" significant in what Appadurai and Breckinridge (1988:1) have described as the "global cultural ecumene" of the contemporary world. The task is to understand how these paintings have come to represent "Aboriginal culture" through a variety of practices and discourses: This is a hybrid process of cultural production, bringing together the Aboriginal painters, art critics, and ethnographers, in addition to curators, collectors and dealers: in short, an "artworld" (Becker 1982). I am particularly concerned with the attempts by critics to situate these art forms in cosmopolitan art circles. Such a situation places anthropologists in an unfamiliar relationship to their stock in trade—knowledge rooted in *local* constructions.

It seems to me, drawing upon my own experience, that anthropologists have been largely concerned to defend their own interpretations or to make them intelligible within the shadow of what they *take* to be the prevailing, culturally hegemonic notions of "art." In so doing, we have tended to reify our own culture's concepts into a more stable form than they actually have, and we fail to consider empirically (and critically) the processes in which we (and the art critics) are engaged as ethnographically important processes of cultural representation. This is ironic, I think, because the point of the struggle is almost entirely a question of how to represent others. Thus, if these antagonistic encounters (and I must admit to being a willing participant) about the imposition of Western art historical concepts often seem to be only so much turf warfare, they can also be conceived of as themselves forms of the social and cultural practices of representation. In reconceptualizing the relationship between art criticism and anthropology in this way, it may be possible to articulate more cogently the processes through which difference can be rendered intelligible.

To be sure, such ethnocentrism persists, despite the interventions of anthropologists and art critics. However, the discourse of art critics (and art historians) is not a univocal one, and cases like those discussed by Price (1989) represent what is now only a portion of the Western discourse of art. This discourse is as unsettled and multiple as our own. What I want to trace out here is the "engagement" (is it a military metaphor or a romantic one?) between anthropological and indigenous accountings of Australian Aboriginal acrylic paintings and those of art critics. In part, the choice of subject is accidental, owing much to my personal circumstances and history.

Disjunctions, I

My sense of disjunction in examining the representation of Aboriginal painting is both personal and professional. Since I began research with Western Desert—Pintupi-speaking—Aboriginal people, this work association has taken me to a number of local communities west of Alice Springs.[5] Although nearly all were living in more or less permanent settlements by 1973, many of them had been still living as hunter-gatherers until the 1960s (and one family until 1984). On government settlements in the 1960s, these Aboriginal people lived largely in conditions of administered welfare colonialism and began to exercise a significant degree of local self-determination with the election of Gough Whitlam's Labour Government in 1972—shortly before I arrived. The development of acrylic painting began at the settlement of Papunya in 1971 under the sponsorship of art teacher Geoff Bardon, whose own book (1979) chronicles the transformation of indigenous forms of graphic representation—signs and designs deployed in ceremony, body decoration, cave paintings, and sand stories—into paintings on masonite and canvas board for sale.

Even in communities as remote as Warlungurru, 250 miles west of Alice Springs in the Northern Territory, the Aboriginal producers of these paintings live in a world complexly related not only to the Australian state (through welfare payments and other forms of services) but also to an international world of images (films, videos, television), sounds (country western music, rock and roll, Gospel), and clothing (especially, for men the cowboy/stockman attire of jeans, boots, and western shirts). Evangelical activity competes with religious movements of cultural revival and intensification, but indigenous meanings continue to dominate local discourse. Such intermingling of culturally heterogeneous forms is, of course, one of the principal problems for contemporary cultural theory. A decade and a half after painting was first adopted as an activity, then, is it a means through which Central Desert people add their voices to the cultural discourses of the world? Or, is it more evidence of "cultural homogenization"? What is to be understood in Aboriginal claims that these very new forms are "authentic" and "traditional"—that is, that they are "from the Dreaming," "true," or "from the beginning"?

Disjunctions, II

To an anthropologist who has long been used to working his interpretations of a distant culture in some obscurity, one of the most important dimensions of the flurry of interest in Australian Aboriginal acrylic paintings is the very cultural production occasioned by these objects and their makers. There are many stories—both by Aboriginal people and others—involved in placing these objects meaningfully in a cultural order. Certainly, it should not be surprising to anthropologists either that new objects might require stories to place them meaningfully in a cultural order or that different stories might contest each other's accounts. Rarely, however, do we regard our accounts and their competitors from such a disengaged analytical perspective, but that is what I argue we should be doing.

These interpretive activities are of ethnographic interest for two reasons—first, because through them the acrylic paintings are being used to signify something about Aboriginal culture. Second, the way these representations contest each other provides an entry both into the disjunctions of local and global process, into the question of authoritative ethnographic representation, and the relationship between anthropological knowledge and art criticism.

My experience suggests that the disjunction between these arenas in which meanings are produced and circulate is more complex than commodification. There is not only the sense of spatial and cultural incongruity that is accompanying the globalization of cultural processes, when people in New York City discuss, debate, and evaluate the meanings of objects produced in small Aboriginal communities and the intentions and lives of their producers. There is also the disjoined relationship between the discourses of the art world and those of Aboriginal painters—the gap between how the producers account for their paintings and what significance they are made to have in other venues.

In all the interpretive activity devoted to Aboriginal paintings, Meyer Rubinstein's insightful review seems best to have grasped the elusive situation that I am labeling as disjunction:

> But for now, as our two worlds meet upon the site of these paintings, we and the Aborigines are in similar positions: neither knowing quite what to think. For both societies the appearance of these paintings is relatively recent and their nature and role is still being discovered. They are in limbo between two homes, sharing their functions and sense of belonging with both, but not fully explicable in either's language. They are, like those ancestral beings whose journeys they depict, traversing a featureless region and giving it form. In the words of an Aboriginal man trying to explain Dreamings to an anthropologist, "You listen! Something is there; we do not know what; *something*." [Rubinstein 1989:47][6]

We cannot understand these processes by attempting to transcend the gap. Rubinstein's discussion is important not merely because it draws attention so dramatically to the disjunction, however. While Rubinstein recognizes the incongruities, his statement conceives of the engagement of critical discourses with their subject as more than the encounter between reified, hypostasized cultural categories (''art'' and ''Dreaming''/*tjukurrpa*) but as human *activity* that should be examined.[7] Aboriginal objects are not simply or necessarily excluded by Western art critical categories; they may in fact contribute to or challenge these discourses for the interpretation of cultural activity in productive ways. They can hardly do so, however, if anthropological interpretation accepts a stable category of ''art'' as its horizon of translation.

There are several distinctive (discursive) levels involved in the social construction of the objects—ranging from the indigenous accountings to government cultural policies, art dealers, and art critics. The stories are numerous, and they are all interesting, but I cannot discuss them all here. They include, for example, the humanizing representation of Aboriginal culture as "artistic," of acrylic paintings as "cultural renewal," of their message as "spiritual wholeness" in contrast to a desolate modernity, and so on—representations all situated in the changing sociopolitical context of Aborigines in a settler society. In this article, I restrict my discussion principally to the constructions of anthropology and art critical reception.

Indigenous Discourse as Cultural Production

Before turning to the critical response(s) to the Asia Society exhibition as constructive and deconstructive activities involved in defining the significance of Aboriginal painting, I want to discuss the accountings provided most directly by the Aboriginal producers. I am concerned with the disjunction between ethno-graphic/local accountings and those issuing from venues of cultural production at a greater distance.

The evaluation of Aboriginal practices is not a simple interpretation of "some facts" existing out there. In these constructive activities, rather, one dis-cerns the properties of intertextuality or of what Bakhtin called the "dialogi-cal"—in which one "word" is addressed to, assumes, or is aware of other inter-pretations. Before the appearance of these reviews, for example, I was brought in most often as a translator and was asked to explain what these paintings "mean" to the Aborigines, as the way in which viewers might learn how to look at them, how to interpret their significance. This practice always tacitly assumed other readings, usually "ethnocentric" ones, that needed to be countered, but I rarely considered these worthy of analytic or ethnographic attention.

Anthropologists have tried—extending our role as translators—to stretch ourselves into a function usually allocated to critics: that is, to tell people what they should see in the paintings. This may be simply a promulgation of Aboriginal statements, but it does constitute a position—as authority, if you will—within the definition of meaning. This is where we have been challenged by others with a different understanding of what there is to know about a surface, with different questions to engage, and often with a more developed and critical vocabulary for discussing visual phenomena and their production. Moreover, the evaluation of Aboriginal image production is not based on a static Western notion of "art"— since the tradition of cultural criticism in which art practices are themselves embedded has been questioning precisely what this category is and should be.

Be this as it may, "Aboriginal art" could not exist without Aboriginal cul-ture(s), Aboriginal persons and traditions of body painting, sandpainting, and so on. We begin, therefore, with the practices through which Aboriginal producers assign significance to their productions. Nancy Munn's study of *Walbiri Iconog-raphy* (1973) and Howard Morphy's *Too Many Meanings* (1977) are well known for articulating the processes of producing and exchanging images in ritual in Cen-tral Australia and Arnhem Land respectively. Even though the acrylic images are not themselves produced for local consumption, these processes and coordinate social and cosmic identities represent the first level of organization and the basis for most Aboriginal evaluations of the objects. Nonetheless, most commentators gain access to these meanings not in the experience of daily life, but through some textualization.

My Textualization of Pintupi Practice:

Let me begin with my understanding of Pintupi explanations and practices. What the Pintupi painters continually stress is (1) that their paintings are "stories" *(turlku),* representations of the events in the mythological past of the Dreaming, and (2) that they are "true" *(mularrpa),* that they are not made up. Like all the other Central and Western Desert people who do acrylics, the Pintupi have a rich ceremonial and ritual life in which songs, myths, and elaborate, complex body decorations as well as constructed objects are combined in performances that reenact the somewhat mysterious events known as "the Dreaming" *(tjukurrpa)* which gave their world its form and order. The significance of the paintings in their own eyes is bound up with their ideas about the relationship between this world and the Dreaming. All paintings represent stories from one of many cycles that concern traveling, mythical ancestral beings (Dreamings), and Pintupi country is laced by the paths of their travels. The value of the Dreaming lies in the fact that the world as it now exists is conceived to be the results of the actions of these beings. Persons, customs, geographical features are all said to have originated in the Dreaming, or as Pintupi people regularly say, *tjukurrtjanu, mularrarringu* ("from the Dreaming, it became real"). Access to knowledge of these events, to tell the stories, and the rights to reenact the events and reproduce the designs and objects in ceremony are restricted, and transmitted through a variety of kinship links. Instruction in the most important details of esoteric knowledge takes place in ceremonies in which men (and women in their own ritual activities) reenact the stories of the Dreaming, constructing ritual objects and decorating the actors in designs said to be "from the Dreaming." These designs, often forbidden for men or women to see if produced by the opposite sex, are in some ways iconic representations of the event and the landscape that records it, but they are also said to come from the Dreaming (indexically) and to have been "revealed" *(yutinu).*

Finally, like the rituals of which they are considered to be part—the story-song-design complexes are "owned" by various groups of persons, and the rights to "show" them are in the hands of the owners of the place, especially those whose own "spirits" come from that Dreaming. The particular formulations of ownership vary throughout Aboriginal Australia, but the overall features of these relations of image production are fairly consistent at least in Central Australia. Thus, Pintupi continue to think of their commercial paintings as related to and derived from their ceremonial designs and rock paintings, associated with important myths, and therefore possessing value other than that merely established in the marketplace.

I want to point out that no single significance is entailed by the account above. What is critical to recognize, I believe, is that the display of ritual knowledge is both a revelation of something "from the Dreaming" and one's rights to a place, but it is also a performance of a central component of the identities of those who produce the display. Nonetheless, the further movements of these objects through the world suggest that instead of regarding this discourse for image production as intrinsically the *meaning* of the paintings, we should consider how this (or other) discourses are drawn on by painters in *accounts* of their acrylic images.

Other Textualizations:

Aboriginal people increasingly have the opportunity to deploy their meanings directly, and their versions circulate fairly widely now in the press and in exhibition catalogs (where they are partly mediated by interpretive accounts of "the Dreaming" like mine above). I will make my point from these self-presentations.

Consider, for example, how one woman painter—in New York for the first time and on stage at the Asia Society for a symposium in which Aboriginal paintings are being discussed (22 October 1988)—defined her production. Dolly Granites spoke in Warlpiri; her words were translated into English by the anthropologist Françoise Dussart. "Dolly," Dussart reported,

> says that she holds the Dreaming from her father. She holds the Dreaming from her father's father, and she holds many Dreamings in her country. She also holds the Dreaming from her mother. She holds the Dreaming from her father's father and from her father's mother.

This was what an Aboriginal painter thought needed to be explained. No background or interpretive framework was offered beforehand.[8] Indeed, the anthropologists and art adviser present on stage felt obliged to provide such a context in their comments.

An article in the *Sydney Morning Herald* (Kent 1987), on the occasion of a show at the Hogarth Gallery there, reports how Aboriginal painters in the Napperby Station community (northwest of Alice Springs) see their painting. "This dreaming," a painter named Cassidy says,

> is about the place where I was born. . . . This waterhole and this emu track are part of my Dreaming. It takes me two weeks to make. *One day my painting will make Napperby number one.* . . . I show the young fellas what we Aboriginal people can do for ourselves. [Kent 1987:48; emphasis added]

Like Dolly, Cassidy's comments combine a reference to the Aboriginal worldview[9] which is usually said to be embodied in the paintings—the Dreaming, as described above—with themes that are commonly part of Aboriginal thinking: usually the right to portray the designs of one's dreaming (that is, the ancestral/mythological being whose spirit animated one).

A good ethnographer might press further into what it could mean for Napperby to be "number one." At some level the quotation must generally be held to signify increasing self-esteem through external recognition—a form of self-production that is precisely what, one might argue, Aboriginal people typically accomplish in their traditional practices of "owning," producing and exchanging representations of the Dreaming (see Myers 1986, 1989). Most painters continue to think of their commercial paintings as related to and derived from their ceremonial designs and rock paintings, associated with important myths, and therefore possessing value other than that merely established in the marketplace.

The newspaper article, however, gave more prominence to another set of themes articulated by other Aboriginal painters in the Napperby community—about money, respect, self-esteem, and dignity. As Rita Nungala, a woman painter, put it:

> We have no grog here, on this station, because we don't want fights. We make that decision ourselves. We do have this painting, though and it gives us something to do. It is good that the youngsters see that, that they work and they get paid. [Rita Nungala in Kent 1987:48]

The painters made it clear that while money is a principal reason for painting, they regard the canvases as more than mere commodities.[10] Rita's statement of the positive effect the painting has on everyone reflects—in addition to the influence of government training programs on Aboriginal views of labor—an appreciation of how painting represents a cultural effect, an act of autonomy, self-esteem, and cultural reproduction. While her statement might seem more accessible than Dolly's, it too draws on a presumed context—in this case, the recent history of Australian government policies for what has been called "Aboriginal self-determination" (see Beckett 1985), which I discuss below.

Constructions similar to those delineated briefly above are commonly offered in public presentations by painters.[11] What these examples make clear is that these interpretations, those of the natives and others, are all accountings—constructions—each presuming a set of taken-for-granted givens which they also reproduce. The painters *presume* their own cultural discourses: they expect that those who see the paintings will recognize in them the assertion/demonstration of the ontological link between the painter, his/her Dreaming, the design, and the place represented. They also (tend to) presume the function these links will have. When Dolly Granites was at the Metropolitan Museum in New York, upon finding out that the Degas paintings were not "from the Dreaming," she classified them as "rubbish" (of no significance).

Clearly, the available meanings to Aborigines for this activity are many. To summarize briefly, they include painting as a source of income, painting as a source of cultural respect, painting as a meaningful activity defined by its relationship to indigenous values (in the context of "self-determination"), and also painting as an assertion of personal/sociopolitical identity expressed in rights to place.

Construction: Aboriginal Culture as Art

In this section, I want to explore how the representations of the acrylic paintings offered by whites, while basing themselves on remarks such as those I have described, have primarily constructed a *permissible* Aboriginal culture, that is, a representation that meets the approval of the dominant white society's notions of "common humanity." The reasons for this are complex and not possible to consider here,[12] but let me start with the initial framing devices. Most of the constructions of acrylic paintings interpret them within the rubric of "art." This occurs at two levels: (1) the assertion/demonstration that they have "art," value it, and that the tradition is very old (implying that they are able to preserve things of value) and that therefore their culture is vital and worthy of respect; and (2) that this "art" contributes something important—something different or challenging—to the world of art. It will be clear that much of the "construction" of Aboriginal activities as art draws heavily on a variety of themes in modernist discourse, ranging from visual invention to human creativity and the loss of spirituality with development. These constructions, then, can be seen as a kind of cultural production.

The presentation of the objects at the exhibition itself drew partly on such "humanistic" representations. According to the publicity circulated, the exhibition of these varied objects shows

the extraordinary vitality of Aboriginal art. It is the oldest continuous art tradition in the world, and is flourishing with new energy and creativity in contemporary media. The works in the exhibition represent the "Dreamings," the spiritual foundation of Aboriginal life.

There are many significations in this theme, but one bears immediate tracing. The scientifically reported 30,000-year history of visual culture on the Australian continent has considerable salience for contemporary urban Aboriginal people, who treat this history in much the same way that the French conceive of their prehistoric cave paintings. The appearance of "art" in the Australian archaeological record precedes that of the Ice Age in Europe, for example, of Lascaux, so often regarded popularly as the first evidence of civilization. This representation offers an image of cultivated Aboriginal ancestors while Europe still lacked aesthetic vision. Moreover, in stressing that this tradition of visual culture is continuous, the museum publicity can attest to the survival, renewal ("flourishing"), and contemporary creative potential ("extraordinary vitality," "creative energy") of Aboriginal culture. The roots of this potential lie in the Dreamings, identified as the "spiritual foundation of Aboriginal life."

The Spiritual Is Political:

Ordinary Australians, who may have had trouble dealing with the poverty, customs, and appearance of Aborigines, have finally been able to respect their artform. For Westerners, beautiful artifacts are the accepted currency of cultural accomplishment. [Pekarik 1988:52]

This construction is a step toward the synecdochic representation of Aboriginal culture itself by one form of its practice. Indeed, the significance or place of Aboriginal "art" in the representation of Aboriginal culture and identity owes much to motivations that are political, in the hope of improving the condition of Aboriginal people in Australia by gaining appreciation of their achievements.

The themes of Jane Cazdow's (1987a) article in the 1987 *Australian Weekend Magazine,* reporting on the art boom, are illustrative of the stories in which the paintings are embedded. She emphasizes three themes: (1) the financial and morale benefits to Aboriginal communities, (2) the controversy about the loss of "authentic" Aboriginal art as "the number of Aboriginals raised in traditional tribal societies is dwindling" (p. 15), according to one collector,[13] and (3) the significance of the art's success for black-white relations.

Cazdow (1987a:15) reports that the (then) Minister for Aboriginal Affairs, C. Holding, believes that the boom in Aboriginal art is important in gaining respect for Aboriginal culture, "in creating bridges of understanding between Aboriginal and white Australia" (an important goal of the Department of Aboriginal Affair's cultural policies, see above). According to Holding,

> Many Australians have been taught that Aboriginal people have no traditions, no culture. . . . When they come to understand the depth of tradition and skill that's involved in this area, it's a very significant factor in changing attitudes. [Cazdow 1987a:15]

The capacity of the success of these paintings to signify for black-white relations depends largely on art's standing for the generically (good) human.

Although largely a stranger himself to Australian shores, the Director of the Asia Society Galleries, Andrew Pekarik—who brought the show to New York—recognized a similar dimension and articulated (more self-consciously) some of its subtler political twists in the statement that begins this section (above). Many writers have drawn on explicit Aboriginal constructions about the political significance of their representation of places. The Australian fiction writer Thomas Keneally certainly drew on such statements and a wealth of anthropological material for his *New York Times* piece to place the paintings in a meaningful context for viewers. Keneally asked rhetorically what these men and women were "praising" in their work. This is something "we are entitled to ask . . ." he says. The answer he offers—that "Every stretch of land belongs to someone," that this is not art for art's sake (1988:52)—frames this work in the politics of Australia, the concern with land rights and the development of a movement of return to traditional homelands, and the need for money.

Visual Invention:

I like the way they move the paint around. [John Weber, personal communication]

Another important story, more recognizably "modernist," has been that they are "good" art, describable in the conventions of contemporary Western visual aesthetics. Art critic Kay Larson, in *New York Magazine,* wrote

> Modernism has allowed us to comprehend the Aboriginal point of view. . . . Aboriginal art at its best is as powerful as any abstract painting I can think of. I kept remembering Jackson Pollock, who also spread the emotional weight of thought and action throughout the empty spaces of his canvas. [Larson 1988]

Others, like John Weber, the Soho gallery dealer, also thought it was "good art" (Sutton 1988; Wallach 1989; but see Michaels 1988).

But, as the art critic Nicolas Baume (1989:112) notes, the Aboriginal paintings do not simply repeat the familiar for Larson. They assert their *differences,* their challenge to contemporary norms.

Roberta Smith (1988) builds a different story, deriving from features of this same discourse. In her review in the *New York Times,* Smith judges that the exhibition "can unsettle one's usual habits of viewing," presenting a "constantly shifting ratio of alien and familiar aspects, undermining the efficacy of designating any art outside the mainstream." But the judgment is that "This is not work that overwhelms you with its visual power or with its rage for power; it all seems *familiar* and *manageable*" (emphasis added).[14] Smith recognizes that the paintings are based on narratives and motifs handed down through generations, but for her,

> The more you read, the better things look, but they never look good enough. The accompanying material also suggests that these same motifs are more convincing in their original states . . . [Smith 1988]

Thus, Smith is open to the possibility of this art but falls back to formalist conventions, in weighing the enduring problem of "context" in relation to "art."

While critics disagree, the important point is their assimilation of these forms to a historically and culturally specific discourse that focuses on creative invention and the way a painting, essentially self-designating, organizes color and other values on a two-dimensional surface.[15] In some sense, the conventions of modernism suggest that the visual demonstrations of art can stand alone but that artifacts need contexts.[16]

"Artistry" and Human Creativity:

Some critics have focused on whether these works challenge Western conventions of the artist as individual producer either by their communal production, a feature stressed in several accounts (Cazdow 1987a; Michaels 1988), or notions of artistic specialty by virtue of the fact that "Traditionally, all people in the Aboriginal community are artists" (Stretton 1987:32; see also Isaacs 1987).

With his usual acerbic eye, Eric Michaels caught this ideologically transparent combination of romantic and modernist conceit in a newspaper account (Cazdow 1987b) of the journey of the curators of the Asia Society exhibition to the Aboriginal community of Yuendumu:

> These clever sorts managed to discover a whole tribe of Picassos in the desert, presumably a mysterious result of spontaneous cultural combustion. We're told of the

curator's astonishment at finding more painters per capita of population than in Manhattan's Soho! [Michaels 1988:62]

Spirituality and Modernity:

Other evaluations suggest that the acrylics offer a glimpse of the spiritual wholeness lost, variously, to "Western art," to "Western man," or to "modernity." Robert Hughes's (1988) glowing review of the Asia Society exhibition in *Time* draws precisely on this opposition:

> Tribal art is never free and does not want to be. The ancestors do not give one drop of goanna spit for "creativity." It is not a world, to put it mildly, that has much in common with a contemporary American's—or even a white Australian's. But it raises painful questions about the irreversible drainage from our own culture of spirituality, awe, and connection to nature. [Hughes 1988:80]

In Hughes's estimation, and he is himself an Australian expatriate in New York, their "otherness" occupies a world without much in common with ours; the artistic values of individual creativity and freedom are not relevant. But this otherness is itself meaningful for us. Another line of evaluation asks if they can be viewed as a conceptual return to our lost ("primitive") selves, as suggested in Amei Wallach's subtitle: "Aboriginal art as a kind of cosmic road map to the primeval" (Wallach 1989).[17] Many of the visitors to the Asia Society certainly embraced this sort of New Age spiritualism.

Creativity as Cultural Renewal:

Within the context of Australia more specifically, the significance of artistic activity among Aboriginal people is often embedded in a slightly different narrative of self-realization through aesthetic production—although still formulating potentially universalist meanings. Addressing conceptions of Aboriginal culture as inevitably on the course of assimilation, Westernization, or corruption, many observers ask whether these paintings are not evidence of cultural renewal, creativity, resistance, and survival (Isaacs 1987; Myers 1989; Sutton 1988; Warlukurlangu Artists 1987), whether they should be seen as an assertion of indigenous meanings rather than as homogenization.

Writing about an exhibition at the Blaxland Gallery in Sydney, for example, Jennifer Isaacs (1987) embraces more the pluralism compatible with postmodern art theory,[18] in emphasizing that the admixture of European materials and venues for Western Desert visual culture (i.e., canvas, acrylics, and exhibitions instead of bodies, ochres, and ceremonies) is not a loss of *authenticity* or cultural subordination (which means a product that is not an expression of inner spirit). The hybridization, she argues, represents an explosion of creativity even breaking the bounds of the wrongheaded (to her mind) restraints for cultural "purity" urged by some advisers in the use of traditional ochre colors only. Such policies—which she characterizes as "bureaucratic"—are reminiscent, in her construction, of earlier policies for Aborigines that advocated separate development and postulated an unchanging Aboriginal culture.

The rhetoric of Isaacs's article is of "cultural explosion" as creativity and strength in opposition to "purity" as restraint, governmental, and bureaucratic. Isaacs's construction also must be seen as an interpretation that implicitly counters commonly held views of "the Aboriginal" as tradition bound, incapable of change and innovation (as Strehlow [1947] emphasized), unable to enter into the 20th century, doomed to extinction.

The representation of Aboriginal paintings appears to be defined in relation to the political discourse of "nationalism," on the one hand, and the spiritual and aesthetic ones of "modernism," on the other. Moreover, as we shall see, these concerns are often themselves related.

Contexts

Aborigine as Sign:

These discourses that develop around Aboriginal acrylic painting intersect some of the recent theorizing about "national imaginaries" (Anderson 1983), especially because of the Australian concern to create a national identity in which, increasingly, Aboriginal people or culture have figured. Reflecting on the significance of "Aborigines" and "Asians" in Australia, Annette Hamilton (1990) has tried to specify the process historically: she suggests that a concern with "Others" emerges most clearly at the same time as the sense of national identity is most threatened by emergent trends of internationalization and new forms of internal cleavage.[19] Hamilton's analysis maintains that recent developments in Australia manifest not a rejection but an appropriation of—an identification with—certain features of the "Aborigine" as image.[20] The significance of the "Aboriginal" as a sign is established by its placement in these historical contexts, with Aboriginality participating in multiple circuits of meaning.

If Aborigines were no longer themselves a threat to national development, as Native Americans were in a vital period in the formulation of their image in the American national identity, the "Aboriginal problem" was a central concern for the Labour Government that took office in 1972 and was addressed through welfare subsidies and policies promoting "Aboriginal self-determination" and "multiculturalism" (see Beckett 1985, 1988). "Self-determination" is the principal discourse underwriting cultural policies, anticipating that local control and autonomy will have beneficent effects on people's confidence, self-esteem, and success in acting on the world.[21] The support of and recognition for Aboriginal art, for example, was seen by most of its promoters at this time as a way to promote appreciation for the accomplishments of Aboriginal culture. Such appreciation, it was believed, would not only provide a basis for self-esteem for a long-disenfranchised racial minority, but would also support recognition for the value of Aboriginal culture in a context of increasing struggle with interests opposed to Aboriginal land rights, a struggle evidenced in the mounting campaigns by the mining companies in Western Australia.

There was an important combination of interests here involved in promoting appreciation for Aboriginal "artistry"and "spirituality." Many white Australian artists who opposed the dominant, rationalistic, and materialistic white culture were attracted to Aboriginality as an indigenous, local form expressive of their opposition. Elkin's (1977) *Aboriginal Men of High Degree* was republished, for example, and its representation of Aboriginal mysticism met with considerable popular enthusiasm among those who also attempted to establish Australia's regional identification with Southeast Asia in opposition to the cultural domination of Europe/America. Another intersection between the identities of a "spiritual" and "natural" Aboriginality (that was seen as "respecting" the land) and oppositional Australian culture was forged in the environmental movement—opposed to uranium mining in Arnhem Land, hydroelectric development in Tasmania. These economic developments were derogated by some as serving primarily the interest of foreign national economic exploiters, by others as expressive of the continued devastation of environmental relations by a mechanico-rationalistic culture, and so on.

Through such significations, the mysterious interior of Australia, a place long resistant to the purposes of (white) man[22] in Australian lore, comes to stand for Australian identity as a spiritual/Aboriginal center on which to define an identity opposition to foreign, industrial control. Various meanings of Aboriginality are constituted in such processes of political incorporation. Hamilton's account is illuminating in showing that such significations draw on images of Aborigines constructed in earlier historical experience (see Hamilton 1990)—especially the dichotomizing ambivalent respect for the "wild bush black" and contempt for the "detribalized fringe campers," "mission blacks," and "half-castes." The "wildness" of the bush Aboriginal—an image focused on the bush, nature, mystic power and "tribalism"—while it "held a threat to the normal functioning of station life . . ."—"also marked Aborigines as somehow able to transcend everything which European civilization (itself a fragile flower on the frontier) was able to offer" (Hamilton 1990:18). Recent constructions draw on these previous images, manifesting a particular form of desire, according to Hamilton:

> the wish to move into the mystic space and spiritual power which has been retained from the earlier construction of "good" Aboriginality, and to somehow "become" the good Aborigine. [Hamilton 1990:18]

With an emphasis on "self-determination" through land rights and ultimately an ideology of "self-realization" in culture, these were bases for the inclusion of Aboriginal themes in the creation of a specifically Australian identity. Finally, the "difference" of Aborigines later allowed them to be figured as a symbol of exoticism and wildness (Morton 1988) to be sought out and consumed in a growing tourist industry, attempting to market the "true heart" of Australia.[23]

Aboriginal Painting:

Modernist art narratives need not imply that Aboriginal paintings are simply the equivalents of Western forms. Critical discourse, modernist or not, is not so simpleminded. The question is whether this placement of the acrylics "into the existing structures of popular art theory" (Weber 1989) is appropriate or whether, as the New York dealer John Weber holds, "A new vision demands a new system of critical thought" (Weber 1989).

Most writers on the art recognize it to be decoratively pleasing and fitting comfortably enough within the visual expectations of the Western tastes for kinds of formalism of the '60s and '70s and busy surfaced acrylic work of the '80s.[24] Thus, it not only suits the development of national identity, but it fits without discomfort on corporate walls and in the preexisting collections filled with such works.

John Weber—who is known for supporting conceptual and minimal art and exhibits the work of site-specific artists like Richard Long and political artists like Hans Haacke—is the first significant gallery owner in New York to take on the work, and he attempts to place the work's entry into the art market as demanding a *rupture* in critical constructions, as something more than 1970s formalism. He talks of the need for "an art dialogue sympathetic to the intent of this work . . . to engender a deeper understanding and appreciation of what the viewer sees and subsequently feels and thinks" (Weber 1989).[25] If a new set of art critical theory is necessary to elucidate this new art, Weber's discussion suggests it should engage four central features, (1) the vitality and compositional complexity of the paintings, (2) their site-specific quality, (3) their political message, and (4) their narrative subject matter.

Weber's comments are also revealing of the accommodations it takes for these paintings to enter into the "fine art" market. Referring to the appearance of fly-by-night dealers and galleries[26] and inflated prices, he argues that the current "commercial onslaught" in the marketing of the acrylic paintings threatens the continued existence of the movement. This is another institutional problem, in that, "as Australia has not previously generated an art movement of international significance, the art power structure is at a loss to deal professionally with the fast emerging Aboriginal scene" (Weber 1989). Only one commercial gallery—Gabrielle Pizzi's, which has exclusive rights to Papunya Tula Artists—has what he considers to be a "well thought out program of group and one person shows of this work" (Weber 1989).

There are more narratives for the paintings, but I want to turn my attention now to what are essentially responses to these initial constructions.

Disjunction as Discursive Incongruity

While anthropologists and Aboriginal painters have been inclined to emphasize the continuities between the paintings and indigenous Aboriginal *traditions*, emphasizing their *authenticity* as expressions of a particular worldview, these very terms—and their meanings—are among those most hotly contested in art critical circles. This discursive incongruity is a point that Eric Michaels, and others embracing a postmodern position, grasped immediately (and enthusiastically):

> traditionalism and authenticity are now completely false judgments to assign to contemporary Aboriginal painting practices. . . . The situation I worked in at Yuendumu

demonstrated unequivocally that the Warlpiri painting I saw, even if it accepts the label "traditional" as a marketing strategy, in fact arises out of conditions of historical struggle and expresses the contradictions of its production. . . . To make any other claims is to cheat this work of its position in the modernist tradition as well as to misappropriate it and misunderstand its context. [Michaels 1988:62]

From here, it seems possible to go on to discuss the practices of cultural appropriation by the West, the impact of the West's "gaze" in defining the "other." Indeed, there has been much critical writing that has explored and deplored such "representational practices."

Deconstruction

The "appreciation" of Aboriginal acrylic paintings and their placement comfortably *in* the art world are problematic for critical-pluralist postmodernism like that embodied in James Clifford's (1988a) criticism of the much publicized 1984 exhibition at the Museum of Modern Art that was called "Primitivism in 20th Century Art: Affinity of the Tribal and the Modern."[27] Clifford (1988a) and others (e.g., Moore and Muecke 1984) argue that the sort of humanism deployed in such representations makes the culturally different too familiar, when it should challenge the universality and natural status of Western categories.[28] Clifford writes, "we need exhibitions that question the boundaries of art and the art world, an influx of truly indigestible 'outside' artifacts . . ." (1988a:213). From this position, the acrylic paintings—as they are inserted in the art scene and gathered for exhibitions as "fine art"—are seen as confirming the power of the formerly colonial masters to determine what matters.

The postmodern critique of "humanism," one which points out the loose ends (i.e., deconstructing) in attempts to make "them" look more like "us," locates a weakness that is common in projects of "imagining" difference and one with which anthropologists are familiar (see Marcus and Fischer 1986).[29] Is it any wonder, therefore, that some anthropologists who have been engaged in the construction of Aboriginal culture have been surprised by the ferocity of the critique of *our* rhetoric (see Fry and Willis 1989; Michaels 1988; von Sturmer 1989; Sutton 1988)?

The generic critique of the "humanistic" does not compromise the full range of deconstruction's attack. In more specific and limited ways, the construction of the paintings as "art" has been undermined variously by "revealing" the essentially "economic motivation" of Aboriginal painting and/or the contrast between the supposed spirituality of the art and the destruction of its civilization by white settlement. Faced with other popular representations of Aboriginal people as drunks, as lazy, and/or as a morally dispirited remnant, many are critical of hopeful/poetic/romantic representations of Aboriginal cultural and spiritual renewal such as that offered by Isaacs (see above).

The Loss of the "Other"

Peter Schjeldahl's (1988) review in *7 Days* finds the acrylic paintings to be not "other" enough, too accessible, and thereby essentially representative of the domination and destruction of Aborigines by whites. He contrasts a visit he once made to Alice Springs—remembering the challenge that an Aboriginal presence (although brief and insubstantial) offered to his sense of the universal and real— with the show, attacking the basic constructions of art as somehow redeeming of Aboriginal subordination: "the paintings are seen as a means to build independent wealth and self-esteem for a people gravely lacking both." Sadly, he writes, "In problem-solving terms the idea is impeccable. But the paintings are no good." The domination is unfortunate, he says, and it is probably praiseworthy to attempt to show good benefits for Aboriginal people, but this liberal solution will not wash: the paintings exhibit the final domination of Western categories. Indeed, their very recognition of his realities (manifest in the materials and the straight lines of the canvas) appears to undermine their ability to challenge them. So, "Don't go looking for that power of strangeness at the Asia Society."

Once upon a time, the mere interest in things Aboriginal in a metropolitan center like New York would have been seen as a triumph over ethnocentrism. Yet Australian critics Fry and Willis (1989:159) criticize the emphasis on representing Aboriginal culture as the "spectacular primitive" because it diminishes "Aboriginals to a silenced and exoticized spectacle." They decry as "ethnocide" the manufacture of "Aboriginal culture" in the process through which "experts" who "trade in the knowledge of 'the other' " make their own careers (1989:159–160).[30] And, if anthropologists once railed against art critics for the imposition of Western aesthetic categories on objects produced in other cultural contexts, some critics (Rankin-Reid 1989) attack anthropologists and curators for their emphasis on the "ethnographic," for focusing on the narrative and "mythological" content of the acrylic paintings—as a primitivizing device that precludes appreciation of the "patently visual accomplishments of the work."[31] In the artists' home communities or traveling with the painters in New York, these positions seem terribly distant. They are artworld battles.

How is one to compare Schjeldahl's criticism with the self-esteem expressed in comments made to me by Michael Nelson, the Warlpiri painter, when he visited New York for the Asia Society show? The latter believes people are really interested in his work and the work of other "traditional" people. "They want to see paintings from the Centre," he said, contrasting this with the lack of white interest in the work of urban Aboriginal artists. This contrast makes sense to him in his own culture's terms in which religious knowledge is the basis for recognition:

> Urban Aboriginal people *ngurrpaya nyinanyi* ("unknowing/without knowledge— they sit down"). I feel sorry for them. We're lucky. We still have our Law (religious traditions), everything. [Michael Nelson, 1989][32]

Andrew Pekarik's reading of the relative popularity of the acrylic paintings (in comparison to the work of urban Aboriginal artists) follows this implicit contrast in another way, suggesting that the popularity of work like Nelson's owes much to a certain preservation of the cultural boundaries of the audience:

What people like is a safe way to incorporate an element of Aboriginality. They won't be as interested in what the urban [Aboriginal] artists do. There is too much pain. People don't like "accusatory art." They want something they can feel more positive about, they can feel good about. They see buying the paintings as helping to preserve these existing cultures. . . . This "traditional" Aboriginal art allows Australians to feel good about themselves. [Pekarik, personal communication]

That is, the "traditional" acrylics are not understood by audiences as challenging them where they live, so to speak, drawing the audience's accountability into the frame of the exchange. To follow Hamilton's (1990) terms, the acrylics of "traditional" people represent the "good" Aborigine—a spirituality, respect for land, and so on of people at a distance (see Fabian 1983) rather than people who are seen as contemporaries competing for the same life-space—which viewers or buyers can incorporate. In a sense, this incorporation of "difference" is possible by virtue of the very self-contained and cultural confidence of artists like Michael Nelson and Dolly Granites, men and women who still remain relatively secure in their own cultural traditions.

Despite *their* assurance, however, Aboriginal people's expectations that knowledge of their culture's foundation in the Dreaming will result in recognition of their rights are not entirely fulfilled. The answer to such a question rests not so much on the qualities of the object, or even in the structural relations between cultural groups, but in the capacity to make one or another set of meanings prevail or even visible.

Critical Practice: "Origins" and Destinations

Fry and Willis maintain a suspicious and deconstructive stance toward an emphasis they see on Aboriginal painters as "all traditional people who have little experiences of cities" (1989:159–160). They find the same emphasis on the theme of the "spectacular primitive" at the display of artists and their work from all over the world, *Magiciens de la Terre,* where Warlpiri men from Yuendumu built a ground painting in Paris in Spring 1989. However, while Schjeldahl is disappointed and angered at the domination of the authentic in the new medium and its recontextualization, they take an opposing position with respect to that theme:

The marketing of contemporary Aboriginal art can be seen as a form of soft neo-colonialism, through which Aboriginal people are incorporated into commodity production (with the attendant reorganization of social relations). One result is that traditional beliefs and practices have to be reconfigured according to the relative success or failure of the commodity. There is thus no continuity of tradition, no 40,000-year-old culture, no "time before time." There are only objects produced by a range of fragmented cultures with varying connections to tradition and economic necessity, posed against the homogenized readings of these objects according to the meaning systems of the culture of dominance. [Fry and Willis 1989:116]

At issue is the question of what one sees in these cultural productions, and Fry and Willis are concerned principally with the claim of the new art's "continuity" with (and renewal) of Aboriginal culture. Drawing on a "poststructural-ist" approach which is highly critical of presumed essences and continuities, for Fry and Willis,

> in Australia, the romantic recovery of the past as a pre-colonial life is impossible. . . . The return to the old culture is therefore really a new culture built upon the signs of the past . . . [Fry and Willis 1989:160]

For these critics, displays of art as indigenous culture cannot be the basis for Aboriginal self-identity, being oriented largely "for the gaze of the colonizer and on terms and conditions set by the dominant culture" (Fry and Willis 1989:160). Rather than providing forms for the development of Aboriginal self-determina-tion, "in the appropriation of Aboriginal culture, careers in 'white' society are being made." In this social field, moreover, the career advancement of these white experts depends upon the reproduction of "the primitive." Far from being a token of authenticity,

> In this process, "Aboriginal culture" is something manufactured within the param-eters of the professional norms of the careerists; it becomes a culture from which Ab-original people are excluded either literally or by having to assume subject positions made available only by "the oppressor." [Fry and Willis 1989:159]

Not surprisingly, therefore, Fry and Willis claim that they have no authority to speak on behalf of what Aboriginal people mean. This position has the ap-pearance of being politically more satisfactory in the avoidance of submitting "their" meanings to "our" categories, yet to hold such a position is still to as-sume one knows the impact of colonial practices on these subjects.[33] For all the perspicacity, here are the outsiders who know more than the participants, out-siders whose representational practices directly thwart the representations of Ab-original painters.

As we saw in the Schjeldahl and Smith reviews,[34] Fry and Willis are not alone in showing little interest in finding out what the Aboriginal people are doing, saying, or understanding in these events which are addressed partly to us. They presume, following Eric Michaels (1988) for instance, that "looking"—as in attending a Warlpiri ceremony—is the privilege of domination. This is not nec-essarily or simply so in Aboriginal cultures where the revelation of forms to the sight of the uninitiated is a gift that carries responsibilities. In showing their paint-ings, Aboriginal people may require that to have seen something is to be respon-sible for understanding it.

Nonetheless, such criticism's point is that the terms and conditions for the display of indigenous culture are always set by the dominant culture and that the exchange will be massively unequal. Is this, as Fry and Willis claim, "ethno-cide"—a cultural erasure accomplished by "obliging them to transform them-selves to the point of total identification, if possible, with the model proposed to or upon them" (Clastres 1974, in Fry and Willis 1989:116)? What do such dis-courses mean for Aborigines? It appears that Aborigines have to establish them-selves within or against these defining terms—or do they?

Controversy

My concern is this article is not so much to resolve the controversy about the acrylic paintings—to go beyond it in some way—but rather to present and understand it ethnographically as a form of cultural production.

Andrew Pekarik, the Director of the Asia Society Galleries during the show and a specialist in Asian art, sees the show as a success *because* of the controversy, but not just because any publicity is good. He explained this to a small group of collectors convened by the New Museum of Contemporary Art in February 1990, which I later asked him to articulate.

> This is a good thing. One of the worst things would be is if people said, ''Yes, that's cute.'' If there is no controversy, that means nobody is thinking about it.

What Pekarik said about the controversy offers a curator's more concrete appreciation of education. He offered that

> The real significance of the acrylic movement is its ability to be a point of cultural communication. There hasn't been a language in terms of which these two sides [i.e., white and Aboriginal] could communicate. They are so far apart that they can't help but misunderstand each other. And in these misunderstandings, the Aboriginal side has had the worst of it. These paintings are the first occasion for cross-cultural communication. For Aborigines they represent a way of dealing with the majority world. For outsiders, they represent a way of trying to hear what the other side is saying, because it is in a language that is not threatening . . .
>
> Roy Wagner says that cargo cults are a kind of New Guinea anthropology, their way of understanding what they are seeing on the outside. That's what is taking place in the paintings. Outsiders have to make an *effort* to try to understand. Obviously, [given the controversy and disagreements] they are working on it. [Andrew Pekarik, personal communication]

Pekarik's analysis reflects an art world insider's understanding of its processes—processes in which artists, gallery dealers, museums, collectors, and critics are a kind of network, ''all in it together.'' They produce meaning for objects and construct their place(s) in an overarching theory. The production of culture is a social process: the ideal-typical career course is for an artist to become taken up by a gallery, who shows his/her work and gets it placed with select collectors, gradually encouraging and establishing recognition of its sensibilities and gaining a reputation for it with reviews. After a series of exhibitions, the next step would usually be placement with collectors and then with museums. In the case of the Asia Society show, evidently, the initial establishing exhibition was a more *official* recognition or certification of the objects' worth than that of a dealer's gallery. The reviews of a show in New York were significant in drawing attention to the work, here and in Australia, in legitimating it: ''putting it on the map.''[35] Despite this flurry of attention, potential dealers for the acrylics in the United States realize that more shows are necessary to demonstrate the stability of the art as an object of interest. This is where the artworld network functions again: dealers need museums to show the paintings regularly in order to remind people such art is there.

Art worlds "make art," as Becker (1982) showed, and while one can view this cynically (as artists and dealers have been prone to do recently) or institutionally (as Becker did), it is also clear that the processes of "making art" require the establishing of a sensibility, a way of appreciating different forms of cultural activity. This is what the critic Clement Greenberg did for abstract art—focusing on "universal" aesthetic principles as an attempt to sustain modern art within a tradition, as not representing a radical break from the "Western tradition"—and what Lucy Lippard did for conceptual art (see Crane 1987). As an artist friend told me, "We all need a good scholar to write about our work: art and words, that's what you need." And art criticism—with its constant anticipation of the next movement, style, or fashion—partly is in the business of producing such styles and differences. Although criticized itself for such promotional/self-promotional celebration of certain trends and movements to the exclusion of the actual diversity of art (Alloway 1984), art criticism plays a significant role in this process of producing "difference" and rendering it intelligible.

From an outsider's vantage point, here is where the ambivalence and energetic responses of the art world seem to lie. Art critics produce their stories and sensibilities as part of larger, ideological concerns about art and the world—chiefly, it would appear, against the threat of "mass culture," "kitsch," "the market," and "commodification." Yet the work of critics is deeply embedded in a capitalist marketplace, fueled by novelty and "difference" to offer buyers.[36] In this sense, and this is the chief irony with which many artists contend, the art world (despite its claims to the opposite) may itself reflect—rather than transcend—the placelessness of late capitalism (Jameson 1984; Lash and Urry 1987). Thus, within the art world, artists and critics struggle with the recognition that new differences—the regional, the local, the challenging—are too easily drawn within the common, "international culture" that subverts the initial differences and incongruities:

> The way [global culture] works now is by diversifying. It has to work by making regional differences active, making them recognisable but not really disturbing. It has to keep the structures in play and change the details. So regionality is really absolutely essential news for global capital at the moment, absolutely essential. [artist Terry Smith, quoted in Nairne et al. 1987:212]

Conclusion

It is clear that the "acrylic movement" may not only compete with modern art on its own level, but can just as easily defeat it in those same terms. This apparent victory for Aboriginal art may, however, turn out to be pyrrhic. If our pseudo-humility before Aboriginal art is based on its confirmation of our own aesthetic values and spiritual aspirations, it will simply be subsumed by the reactive processes of cross-cultural projection. Instead of confining our understanding to the illusory tradition created by visual association, we might seek out the unseen differences. Interpretations that reduce art to a literal content and a structural grammar only tame it, make it comfortable.

What Aboriginal acrylics may offer, unlike most recent art, is precisely their potential to make us nervous. [Baume 1989:120]

Anthropology has been long concerned with the problem of interpreting or translating between the indigenous concepts and practices of other cultural orders and those of our own society. But we are not alone in our engagement in such interpretive activity. The easy authority of our interpretations has been questioned in frequently cited works. The best known of these, surely, is that of Clifford (1988a, 1988b), representing the general pluralist positions delineated by the band of cultural theory known as "postmodernism."

A significant domain in which the question of such interpretation has regularly been of interest is that of "art." This is a concept about which most scholars are now self-conscious. "Art" is long recognized to be a *cultural* domain in the West, one not necessarily shared or similar in all societies, and one which has been convincingly historicized (R. Williams 1977). This is a problem on which anthropologists have fought the "good fight." Indeed, a good deal of self-satisfied writing by anthropologists has focused on this problem, criticizing the imposition of Western categories on the practices of other peoples.[37]

These categorizations of "art," "creativity," or "humanity" matter in more than merely academic ways insofar as they can imply differing representations of cultures. To say that Aborigines do not have "art," however qualified by insisting that the category is a distinctively historical one in the west, without hierarchical and evaluative significance, can easily be read as "racism."[38] Any anthropologist with the experience of trying to explain this issue to nonspecialists should recognize the practical problem.

Anthropological translations may founder as much in their transparencies with respect to cultural boundaries as their opacities. In an important sense, what Aboriginal producers say about their work—their own discourse for its interpretation—draws primarily on an indigenous tradition of *accounting,* and it is this discourse (frequently) that anthropologists have sought to present as the authentic meaning. But as one must learn from the appearance of the acrylic paintings in New York and elsewhere, this knowledge of the Aboriginal culture, persons, and traditions of image making—knowledge of what Aboriginal painters say about their work—does not necessarily recognize the potential and significance of these forms to engage interest from those concerned with visual images in our own culture.

One asks, therefore, whether the engagement with art criticism as a competing practice of interpretation offers anything for anthropological understanding? Art theory's concern with the boundaries between art and nonart, both as a modernist evaluative process (i.e., is it art?) or as a postmodernist critically problematized/oppositional practice (i.e., what does it mean to define such boundaries?) is a critical part of the processes through which Aboriginal people are producing themselves in the contemporary world. Thus, the reception of the paintings raises the broader question of the capacity of indigenous people to objectify *their* meanings into the discourses for their reception.[39]

Can there genuinely be dialogue between their conventions and those of the art world? The examples I have presented suggest that Aborigines are triangulated by a series of discourses—which might represent positive benevolence, political support, sympathy, or renewed racism[40]—discourses in which Aborigines are central but usually absent. Aboriginal accounts enter more explicitly into that Derridean world in which all signification exists in a context of other representations, in which there is no transcendental signified outside of representation.[41] Are Aboriginal actors able to make their practices have just the meanings they claim?

To review briefly, I have delineated differences with three sets of critics.

1. There is Roberta Smith, who says we must hold these paintings up to standards of our own culture since they circulate in it now. In those terms, she says, "Too bad, they represent second rate neo-Expressionism." She rejects the paintings in terms of the art world.

2. Another set of critics, exemplified by Peter Schjeldahl, want the lost romance, and reject these paintings in terms of the West's nostalgia for some other that the Aboriginal paintings cannot represent by virtue of their "contamination" by Western forms.

3. The third set, Fry and Willis, treat the paintings in terms of commodity circulation and the inevitable corruption it entails. They reject the paintings, supposedly from an Aboriginal perspective.

Such criticisms are part of the discursive practices that define "high art." The *fact* of the debates, the very fact of them, is what has validated the acrylic paintings as objects worthy of broader consideration. This is exactly what John Weber desires in his plea for a "new art critical theory." He is, after all, a dealer and what he does is find paintings and transform them into "art" by selling them. The acrylic paintings not only have a meaning, they are being made to have a meaning about the nature of human creative activity, and made into saleable "fine art."

Those discourses fail to explain the meaning at the Aboriginal level. At best, the Aborigines are considered to be co-opted; at worst, they are not considered at all. It should be clear that my association with the painters makes it difficult to accept at face value criticisms of the acrylic movement which derogate the local focus on the "continuity" and "authenticity" themes as a "constructed primordialism"—to borrow a term from Arjun Appadurai (1990). Most Pintupi and Warlpiri painters have not constructed primordial identities, "origins," principally in opposition to wholly external "others," as in various nationalisms—not, that is, as an ethnic discourse of "Aboriginality."

Aboriginal people's primordialisms are constructed, of course, but they are frequently constructed and sustained in relation to processes different from colonial ones. They are constructed in complex systems of similarity and difference—"totemisms" if you will—in which larger collective identities are only temporary objectifications, shared identities produced for the moment (see Myers 1986; Sansom 1980). "Country" as most Aborigines would call the places represented in acrylic paintings, the token of the painter's identities, represent the basis for objectifications of shared identity through time.

A critical art theory struggles with the local message because of its own preoccupation with the global processes that suffocate it, threatening to make all the world the same, all processes and forms substitutable for each other. It is just such a fear of "cultural homogenization" at work—the incorporation of Aboriginal products into European fine art—that underlies much of the art critical writing. Such one-way narratives deny any "indigenization," despite the fact that the potential of such "indigenization" is what is ultimately of interest in Aboriginal paintings.[42] The identities that many acrylic painters produce on their canvases are not uprooted or deterritorialized; this is their very claim.[43] It is surely ironic that, as art theorists Deleuze and Guattari (1987) place their bets on "nomadology" as a way to find a path through this placeless rhyzomic world, so did the late Bruce Chatwin, a refugee from the art world on a romantic search for the "nomad" representing some imagined version of a ceaseless human urge for wandering, seek out Australian Aborigines (see Chatwin 1987).[44] However, Aboriginal Australians are precisely those who insist on not being *displaced*.

The situation of Fourth World people should not be so loosely compared with other postcolonial circumstances that currently inform cultural theory. Pintupi— or Warlpiri or Anmatjira—claims that the paintings are "from the Dreaming" or that they are expressive of an ontology in which human beings gain their identity from associations with place *do* express a historical struggle, but initially at least they have done so in their own right, not simply in recognition of a colonizing threat from outside. To see these claims—their identities—as "our" product (as from colonialism) is to colonize doubly by denying them their own histories.

If art theory fails to grasp what the activity means to the painters, their critical responses so far only skirt the question of its appeal. I want to conclude by considering what this appeal might be and what it suggests about the contribution Aboriginal acrylics might be making as "art." The appeal of the paintings is not, I suggest, as ineffable as the best critics suggest.

Ironically, the paintings have significance in art theory and for the buyer because of their local meanings for Aboriginal people, the association they represent for buyers between an artist and a place. As forms acceptable to the art world, Aboriginal acrylics offer a powerful link to particular locations in a world which is said—according to most postmodern theorists—to have "no sense of place" (see Meyrowitz 1985). What the acrylics represent to their makers resists this sort of commodification: all places are *not* the same. Painters can only produce images from their own local area, all conceived of as different.

In Warlpiri artist Michael Nelson's explication of the meaning of the paintings, one traces the "original meanings" in the emergence of something that is new: an "Aboriginality" that is also becoming defined in opposition to "Europeans":

> White people don't really fully appreciate these dreamings that we paint. These dreamings are part of this country that we all live in. Europeans don't understand this

> sacred ground and the law that constrains our interaction with it. We've been trying
> to explain it to them, to explain what it means to us. For the sake of all Australians,
> we try to show them that this is our land. We try to show them our dreamings which
> are part of this country that we all live in. But white people don't even recognize our
> ownership of it. We paint all these pictures and they still can't understand. They want
> them as souvenirs to hang on their walls but they don't realise that these paintings
> represent the country, all of this vast land.
>
>   In other countries, they're all right; the land belongs to them, it's their country.
> We belong to this country; that's why we keep saying that we want our land back.
> [Michael Nelson at the Sydney Biennale 1986, quoted in Nairne et al. (1987:221)]

Michael Nelson continues to deploy here the same principal discourses that
an anthropologist is most likely to encounter. His statement reminds us that these
discourses are not some intrinsic bottom line but that they take shape in the context
of contemporary politics in Australia: but their goal, their intent, is not displaced.

I do not mean to say that the "place-meaning" of acrylic paintings is the
totality of their signification or that the signification of this meaning is the same
for all consumers. Given the regular association of purchasing the paintings with
travel to the area in which they are produced and located, for instance, I suspect
some particular thrill accompanies knowing the place that is represented in such
utterly "other" (i.e., unfamiliar) graphic signs which hold a different meaning
for "others." For Westerners, this both valorizes the travel—to a place that is
genuinely different—and the painting as a sign of that difference.

Moreover, what is at stake in a "sense of place" in Australia is different
from what it is for consumers from overseas. In Australia, for some, the places
of Aboriginal people are places before history, a place in the Outback often coded
as more primeval—a frontier in which Australians are fascinated to know that
some *real* "stone age" hunting and gathering people still live (see Myers 1988).
This primordial spirituality at the heart of Australia, especially at Ayers Rock but
also (in a way) in each painting,[45] provides links with tourism and travel away
from the solid domesticity of suburban homes and rational order of "white science" (see Fiske, Hodge, and Turner [1987:119–130] for a discussion of these
themes). The Aboriginal and the Outback are, increasingly, the source of Australia's self-marketing for the international tourist industry, the "difference" they
have to offer. These constitute an important dialectical dimension of emerging
formulations of Australian national identity: something essential outside and before the nation that lies also at its heart, central to its identity,[46] these significations
give Aboriginal representations of place a particular value. The paintings represent this mystery, in a way, by being the token of what the place/country is prior
to or outside its appropriation into the uses and purposes of white society. Australians, therefore, can obtain such tokens and display them as representations of
some part of themselves on their wall.

Their appeal is the sense of their rootedness in the world—although this
"rootedness," the sense of place—is what appears to some of the critics to be
undermined by the apparent cosmopolitanism of the painters and the circulation
of their products. It is not that Western art critics understand the specific information or details of the Dreaming-places that are usually the subject of the paint-

ings, but rather that the fact of these relations fulfills a real or nostalgic sense of the loss of attachment to place. The specific understanding of a story is not so important as that it signifies so rich, complex and unself-conscious a sense of connection.

It is not accidental that this sense is what informs postmodernism so strongly. There is a great irony of historical accident in this: the paintings make their way into the art market by virtue of their strong formal similarity to abstract expressionism, a movement defined by its detachment from specificity and location! Postmodernism looks to the margins of a dominant culture and minority voices not only for a critique of oppression, but also out of a genuine concern to reroot high culture to sources of the sensory and the intellectual delight in everyday life. This is what can be found in the descriptions of the "creative process" in Aboriginal communities—a sense of the "cottage industry" with painters sitting out in the sun, making images without the European's requisite sturm and drang.

Postscript. Because I would develop a more dialectical conception of knowledge, I seek to question both the increasingly popular identifications of ethnographic knowledge as merely domination of our objects but also the defensive reaction, by many anthropologists, to the revelation of our project's placement within history. Recognition of the social and cultural place of interpretive projects—positioning ethnography, reflexively, within its own frame of consideration—is an essential step for contemporary anthropology to gain insight into the multiple circuits in which the representation of culture operates. In writing this article, my hope is to help place anthropological practices of interpretation more adequately—more ethnographically—within our (limited) perspectives as acting subjects and within the larger historical perspectives which define us.

Notes

Acknowledgments. A much truncated version of this article was originally given at the annual meeting for the Society for Cultural Anthropology in Santa Monica, California, 18–19 May 1990. For their direct help in understanding the process of Aboriginal art's movements, I want to thank Michael Nelson, Billy Stockman, Peter Sutton, Chris Anderson, Richard Kimber, Andrew Pekarik, Françoise Dussart, Felicity Wright, and Daphne Williams. This article has benefited from many conversations, readings, and criticisms, but most especially it would never have been written without the encouragement and imaginative engagement of Faye Ginsburg. For comments and criticisms on the article and general discussion, I thank Don Brenneis, Sandro Duranti, Faye Ginsburg, Annette Hamilton, Barbara Kirshenblatt-Gimblett, George Marcus, Bambi Schieffelin, Toby Volkman, and Annette Weiner.

[1] A trainee at the gallery told me that presenting the paintings in this minimal way allows "connoisseurs" to feel good about their knowledge.

[2] This is the name that the anthropologist Donald Thomson gave to Pintupi-speaking people when he encountered them in the 1950s; "Bindibu" is the term Warlpiri-speakers (who were Thomson's guides) often used.

[3]In 1988, for example, the artists in the Pintupi community at Warlungurru were receiving around $30,000 per month from their art cooperative, Papunya Tula Artists. For more details about the economic dimensions of acrylics in Western Desert communities, see Anderson and Dussart (1988), Megaw (1982), and Myers (1989).

[4]Reportedly, an important painting of Clifford Possum was sold by the collector Margaret Carnegie to the National Gallery of Victoria for $140,000. While entirely exceptional, the prices of the acrylics have created a boom market for speculators. For a discussion of the changing price structure, see Benjamin (1990).

[5]For a fuller account of this research and of Pintupi social life, see Myers (1986). Field research with Pintupi people—at Yayayi, Northern Territory (1973–75), at Yayayi and Yinyilingki (1979) and at New Bore and Papunya, Northern Territory (1980–81)—was supported by NSF Doctoral Dissertation Improvement Grant No. GS 37122, NIHM Fellowship No. 3F01MH57275-01, and research grants from the Australian Institute of Aboriginal Studies. Short visits with Pintupi in Kiwirrkura, W. A., and Warlungurru, N.T. (in 1983 and 1984) were undertaken under the auspices of the Central Land Council. A longer stay in 1988 was supported by the Australian Institute of Aboriginal Studies, National Geographic Society, and the John Simon Guggenheim Memorial Foundation. The bulk of this study and this article were done while I was a Fellow of the Guggenheim Foundation and of the National Endowment for the Humanities.

[6]More recently, Baume (1989, see especially page 120) has made a similarly cogent argument about the issue of critical disjunction, I draw on his discussion more fully in the conclusion of the article.

[7]For the conception of aesthetic theory as an activity, see also Becker (1982:131–137).

[8]Dolly Granites was not the only Aboriginal painter speaking, and the remarks of the Arnhem Land painters—Jimmy Wululu and David Malangi—were very similar. Unfortunately, space prevents me from considering them all here.

[9]This worldview, usually delineated in the concept of the Dreaming in Aboriginal English, has been extensively discussed in anthropological and other representations of Aboriginal cultures. The analysis below will address many of the issues, but for an entry into these descriptions, see also Myers (1986), Stanner (1956), and Sutton (1988).

[10]But this construction is not solely that of the article's writer nor a product of recent conditions of Aboriginal life. The function of image production in mediating Aboriginal autonomy, especially in ritual, is of long standing (see Myers 1988).

[11]When Billy Stockman, an Anmatjirri painter from Papunya, was visiting New York in conjunction with the Asia Society exhibition and was interviewed by the producer of the McNeill-Lehrer News Hour segment on the paintings, he explained all of this quite clearly—but they had not yet set up for videotaping. When the TV crew arrived in the hotel room, they tried to create a little rapport and communication, asking the men where they learned to speak English. Billy Stockman, at that point, actually told them most of what they would have wanted in an interview.

He said that he didn't learn to speak English in school but at stock camps. Before any of that, however, he had to learn ceremony, their own Law, from his father's Law—in the bush: "I didn't go to school . . . went to Aboriginal school, ceremony. Learned Aboriginal Law. Sort of Aboriginal high school, you know? Not white people's school. Learned ceremony, painting, there.'' Later, he learned white people's ways. Of course, this was not on camera, and it did not seem to me that the two women saw how much they were being informed about the value or priority of ''Aboriginal high school,'' of learning ''our law'' which is what Billy sees as the significance of his painting.

[12]In a hyperbolic and nasty but inspired comment on the repression that stands as an obstacle to grasping the internal life of Aboriginal people, the anthropologist John von Sturmer points to the problem of such tranquil notions of humanity:

> One senses that there is something of the same destructiveness [as that of the narrator of Dostoevsky's *Village of Stepanchikovo*, who in the name of certain ideals would destroy the whole household] directed at Aboriginal societies, that that they too can only be treated as spectacle, as tableau. Is it because they lie beyond the possibility of a truly lived engagement? It is still the case, as it has been from the very beginning, that they do not live according to ''civilised'' notions of society, refinement, propriety, group welfare or personal well-being. They fight too much, they drink too much, they fuck too much, they are too demanding, they waste their money and destroy property. But a lack of restraint, caution, or calculation is not necessarily an absence or a failing. It can be a superfluity. A refusal: a refusal to accept the repressive principle . . . [von Sturmer 1989:139]

[13]This theme, which I do not have time to elaborate here, is of relevance particularly to concerns of collectors. For them, the fact that there is a limited supply of ''authentic'' Aboriginal art is important—and that soon there will be no more—is critical in establishing the value of their collections.

[14]In other words, the paintings do not ''challenge'' Western conventions of the visual imagination. As ''outsider'' art, Smith sees the work in the Aboriginal show as ''for the most part quite weak,'' pale versions of 1970s neo-expressionist abstraction. Without question, most critics regard the formal resemblances between the acrylic paintings and recent art production in the West as a central condition for its acceptance. They have, nonetheless, different positions on this apparent resemblance.

[15]These modernist conceptions of painting as an art form are usually seen as developed most cogently by Clement Greenberg. The debates between ''modernism'' and ''postmodernism'' in the art world constitute one important background for the reception of Aboriginal acrylic paintings. These debates concern not only the nature of ''art'' as a category of understanding in our culture—that is, they are attempts to define what should be included as ''art'' and what should be excluded as peripheral to its ''essential'' function— but the debates also focus particularly on the applicability and/or criticism of such a concept as a ''universal'' one.

The positions are complex and I cannot describe them here; they will emerge more fully in the discussion of particular critiques, but I want to alert you to the relevance of these internal art debates for the reception of the acrylic paintings. I do think it is important to recognize that two classic positions in anthropology—the universalizing and the particularizing (interpretive)—intersect the art critical discourses of modernism and postmodernism in important ways that generate different stances.

[16]See Kirshenblatt-Gimblett (1991) for a discussion of these issues with respect to museums. It is also important to recognize that Clement Greenberg's oft-discussed preference for the visual in its own right, for looking at the object, did not really presume an experience entirely innocent of or uneducated context in the sense of art history (see Tillim 1987).

[17]The conventions of their differences have also been seen as morally instructive about some of our own associations, especially of our materialism. In his travels to Australia during the planning of the exhibition, Andrew Pekarik (Director of the Asia Society Gallery) is reported as saying, "that these people with practically zero material culture have one of the most complex social and intellectual cultures of any society" (in Cazdow 1987b:9). In this romantic construction, a critique of modernity, the paintings may represent the worthiness of Aboriginal survival and, consequently, the dilemma and indictment of modern Australia's history and treatment of their forebears as less than human (Hughes 1988; Keneally 1988).

[18]Ironically, few anthropologists who have stressed the vitality of the local to engage and assimilate the forces of Westernization, colonialism, or capitalism have seen compatibility with postmodern theory. The anthropological discourse reflects, instead, an emphasis on the defining capacity of culture.

[19]In writing about the National Imaginary, Hamilton writes as follows:

> I suggest that under world conditions of the past two hundred or so years, and more so recently, the problem of distinguishing a national self has moved to the forefront precisely as it is challenged by social economic and political mechanisms which undercut the prior senses of national, ethnic, local, class or trade-specific identities. [Hamilton 1990:5]

[20]More precisely, she writes

> although there is a fear of something in the heart and outside the boundaries, there is also a lure and fascination, which can be neutralised not by retreat, but by appropriation. This is not an appropriation of the "real," but an appropriation of commodified images which permit the Australian national imaginary to claim certain critical and valuable aspects of "the Other" as essentially part of itself, and thereby claim both a mythological and spiritual continuity of identity which is otherwise lacking. [Hamilton 1990:10]

[21]In a far-ranging critique, Morris (1987) discusses the hegemony of the state's domestication of social and cultural differences in policies of cultural pluralism that are limited and partial insofar as they seek to subordinate expressions of identity to the universal structures of the dominant society. For some explorations of the cultural dimensions of the discourse of self-determination as revealed in the perspectives of remote area Aborigines and their function in the larger system, see Beckett (1988), Hamilton (1987), Myers (1985), Peterson (1985), and Rowse (1988).

[22]The masculine reference is meant to be specific here.

[23]A number of writers have pointed out that tourists to Central Australia place a high value on the possibility of coming into contact with Aboriginal culture.

[24]A friend asked one New York artist to place the paintings in terms of current art movements, if a gallery had received a box of these paintings and was told they had been done in the last 30 years by a European or American artist. The answer: "Pattern painting of the late 1960s and early 1970s—the stuff Holly Solomon used to deal. Dots, stripes, ribbons. Value, not chroma, painting."

[25]Weber clearly understands the role of aesthetic theory in legitimating or justifying inclusion of work in an artworld, what Becker (1982) refers to as the institutional theory of art. The philosopher and critic Arthur Danto (1964) stated the problem succinctly in the well-known citation beginning this article.

[26]There were at least three different shows of "acrylic paintings" in Soho in 1989.

[27]This particular exhibition and critiques of it provide a model for the reception of many, quite different attempts at cross-cultural representations. In itself, I think, this shows something of the cultural significance of presentations and reviews in New York.

[28]Moore and Muecke (1984) criticized the growing pluralist representation of Aboriginal culture in terms of "art" as one which:

> allows for the acceptance of Aboriginal art, dance, language, etc. whilst simultaneously screening out aspects like extended family forms, aspects of Aboriginal law, "undesirable social habits," "unhealthy environments," and economic independence within a rigid harmony. In this sense, the notion of "common humanity" should be seen as a ruse.

[29]Any attempt to represent similarities between cultures, whether these be the "affinities" between "primitive art" and "modernism" decried by Clifford for its ethnocentrism or the apparent "similarities" in "kinship systems" similarly critiqued by the anthropologist David Schneider (1970), seems destined to fall short, to be attempts "to reconcile the irreconcilable" whose loose ends will show, as Fry and Willis (1989:113) judged Kay Larson's review of the Asia Society show. In this respect, more fully recognizing the dialectical nature of knowledge than most who embrace postmodernist positions, Clifford (1988a) recommends a complement of "surrealist" subversion, challenge and disruption of categories to balance the familiarizing comparisons of "humanistic" representations.

[30]They criticize particularly a loose passage in Peter Sutton's catalog for the Asia Society show in which Sutton talks about the development of a field of Aboriginal art scholarship (Sutton 1988:213–214). Fry and Willis claim that not only is such "unselfconscious prioritizing of conventional academic knowledge . . . ethnocide in action" (1989:160) but so also is the creation of what they call the "spectacular primitive" through the art establishment's management of the discourses of art (1989:160).

[31]"With all the hype about the 'dreaming' in these and other Aboriginal artists' acrylic paintings," Rankin-Reid writes,

> it was hard for viewers to look at these works of art without the textual references served up by self-styled field experts. . . . The point is . . . that the glamorisation and recontextualisation is beginning to have a negative effect and the Aboriginal work of art is being muffled by the very act of trying to raise it from its "earthy" origins into the "sophisticated" art world. For the viewer, the literal equations that claim to provide access to meaning in Aboriginal painting are sheer entrapment, perpetuating the myth of the narrative as the *raison d'être* of the Aboriginal work of art. . . . The likelihood that some Aboriginal artists possess talent beyond the telling of dreamings in their paintings is an idea that anthropologists, government art agencies, shopkeepers and self-styled international representatives of Aboriginal art have yet to convey officially. In their enthusiasm to promote the saleability of Aboriginal acrylic paintings, the mediocre is given the same billing as the sublime . . . [Rankin-Reid 1989:12]

[32]A more extensive explanation of Michael Nelson's perception is textualized in the following comments reported for him in a discussion of the Sydney Biennale of 1986:

> You must appreciate that we, my generation, were brought up in the bush, in our own country in the desert. We were instructed by the old people. We did go to school and learned something of the European way, but only to a limited extent. We were primarily brought up within our own Law. We became well versed in our own culture. Our culture was very much alive. We had our

dreaming places, our sacred sites, our song cycles and traditional dances and ceremonial regalia, like shields and so on.

We hadn't lost all of that; not like some people living here in Sydney. They've lost all their culture, they just follow the European way. But we still hold fast to our culture. North of us, south of us, west of us, our language and culture is still intact, right there in the middle of the desert, among the spinifex and the sand dunes. I still remember when we lived in bush shelters and travelled constantly, from Ngangaritja to Papunya and Yuendumu and then back again.

The designs I had learned from corroborees and from traditional ceremonial regalia I had been taught by my uncle, my father, and my grandfather. All of us—the young, the old and the middle-aged—we all knew this way. The designs were also painted on shields, usually little shields, sometimes big ones. The designs were derived from those we created in the sand. Now that we paint these designs on canvas, white people and other Aboriginal people can see them and appreciate them. They can be seen all the time, whereas the traditional forms of our art could only be seen at ceremonies. Those shields that we painted we only used them at certain times; for corroborees or related rituals. The designs we made in the sand were only seen occasionally. We use these designs still in corroborees and other ritual practices. *I still participate in ceremonies. It's embedded in my heart. Others may have lost it all but at Kintore, Papunya and Yuendumu, we still retain our culture. We cherish our traditions.* [emphasis added]

I cite this explanation at length here because such textualizations of Aboriginal commentary are not only rare but also much drawn upon by art critics—who usually lack extensive first-person experience of Aboriginal language, culture, and daily life. In that sense, given the art world's reliance on the textual, one might want to compare such textualized representations as having an even greater potential for alienation than is the case for ordinary ethnographic representations. In the case of this quotation, which does not appear to be entirely in the English that Michael Nelson would ordinarily use moreover, we do not know what language Nelson was speaking and how it was translated.

[33]See also Roger Benjamin's recent (1990:71) response to the Fry and Willis discussion, in which he considers how "their argument deprives Aboriginal culture of the dynamic capacity for adaptation and change which distinguishes it in the harsh environment of interaction with First World culture."

[34]The same can be said of Paul Taylor's (1989) article about the show at the John Weber Gallery in May 1989.

[35]The art magazines—in which most reviews are published and circulate—are heavily supported by dealers and collectors. Here lies part of the material basis of representational practice: the organizers of the Asia Society show worked long and hard, not only to obtain financial support to put on the show, but to gain timely publicity and reviews.

[36]The following statement represents a widely held position:

The market system works to make art "rare" (more original, more authentic) and to keep prices at the highest level. Maximum return is generally produced in a field of low technology . . . by controlling the supply and working to create an excess of demand. The art market trades on exciting a desire for the "touch" of the original hand. The glamorous aspects of the art world, the auctions featured in fashion magazines, the siting of art galleries among prestigious shops, the exclusivity of the opening or "private view" are features of the system. . . . Yet it is the market . . . that takes chances in bringing forward new work to wider public attention; much of that work is selected later by public museums and galleries. [Nairne et al. 1987:14]

[37]An important recent example of this intervention—and a step toward capturing the cultural formation of our own artistic values—is Price (1989), examining the barriers to the entry of Suriname Maroon patchwork cloth into the domain of "fine art."

[38]Such themes prevail in the recent debate in the Australian cultural journal, *Meanjin*, between art historians Donald Brooks and Bernard Smith.

[39]In a book extending this article, I will discuss several levels in the production and circulation of the paintings that I cannot consider here—such as the art advisers, the changing relationship of the Australian welfare state toward Aborigines and toward cultural issues, the support of community craft centers by government agencies pursuing a variety of cultural policies, and the practices of art dealers. Their practices all contribute to the fashioning of meaning for the paintings.

[40]The continuation of racist rhetoric is sufficiently documented in a particularly offensive remark by Auberon Waugh, cited by Robert Hughes (1988).

[41]In another publication I hope to take up more directly the significance of these critical positions in terms of theoretical questions about empiricism, deconstruction, and representation. Here I only mention that Derrida's *Of Grammatology* (1977), and his general criticisms of ethnology, have had a central influence on the critics' response to the language of "authenticity" and "origins."

[42]To capture some complex processes, in which the metropolis is no longer simply the center, Appadurai suggests that we

> begin to think of configuration of cultural forms in today's world as fundamentally fractal, that is, as possessing no Euclidean boundaries, structures or regularities. Second, [he] would suggest that these cultural forms . . . are also overlapping. [1990:21]

[43]And this is how, perhaps, they speak to what is said to be a "central problematic of cultural processes in today's world . . .":

> The world we live in now seems rhizomic (Deleuze and Guattari 1987), even schizophrenic, calling for theories of rootlessness, alienation and psychological distance between individuals and groups, on the one hand, and fantasies (or nightmares) of electronic propinquity on the other. [Appadurai 1990:2–3]

[44]Before becoming a famous travel writer, Chatwin worked for Sotheby's art auction house.

[45]And also in the interest in Asia—and its mystical spirituality—among Australia's young. These themes are represented in the Australian films like *Picnic at Hanging Rock, Walkabout, The Year of Living Dangerously, The Last Wave*.

[46]I do not have the time or expertise to go into Australian notions of the land in any depth, but the literature on the harshness of the interior—its resistance to white/human efforts—is well known. So also do most Australians know from school that Aborigines knew and understood the land (C. Strachan, personal communication; see Keneally 1988).

References Cited

Alloway, Lawrence
    1984   Network: Art and the Complex Present. Ann Arbor, Mich.: UMI Research Press.
Altman, J.
    1988   The Economic Basis for Cultural Reproduction. *In* The Inspired Dream: Life as Art in Aboriginal Australia. M. West, ed. Pp. 48–55. Brisbane: Queensland Art Gallery.

Altman, J., C. McGuigan, and P. Yu
    1989   The Aboriginal Arts and Crafts Industry. Report of the Review Committee. Department of Aboriginal Affairs. Canberra: Australian Government Publishing Service.
Anderson, B.
    1983   Imagined Communities. London: Verso Press.
Anderson, C., and F. Dussart
    1988   Dreaming in Acrylic: Western Desert Art. *In* Dreamings: The Art of Aboriginal Australia. P. Sutton, ed. Pp. 89–142. New York: George Braziller/Asia Society Galleries.
Appadurai, A.
    1990   Disjuncture and Difference in the Global Cultural Economy. Public Culture 2(2):1–24.
Appadurai, A., and C. Breckinridge
    1988   Why Public Culture? Public Culture 1(1):5–9.
Bardon, G.
    1979   Aboriginal Art of the Western Desert. Sydney: Rigby.
Baume, Nicholas
    1989   The Interpretation of Dreamings: The Australian Aboriginal Acrylic Movement. Art and Text 33:110–120.
Becker, Howard
    1982   Art Worlds. Berkeley: University of California Press.
Beckett, J.
    1985   Colonialism in a Welfare State: The Case of the Australian Aborigines. *In* The Future of Former Foragers. C. Schrire and R. Gordon, eds. Pp. 7–24. Cambridge: Cultural Survival.
    1988   Aboriginality, Citizenship and Nation State. Social Analysis 24(special issue: Aborigines and the State in Australia):3–18.
Benjamin, R.
    1990   Aboriginal Art: Exploitation or Empowerment? Art in America 78(July):73–81.
Cazdow, J.
    1987a   The Art Boom of Dreamtime. The Australian Weekend Magazine, 14–15 March:1–2.
    1987b   The Art of Desert Dreaming. The Australian Weekend Magazine, 8–9 August:6.
Chatwin, B.
    1987   The Songlines. New York: Viking.
Clastres, Pierre
    1974   Society Against the State. New York: Urizen Books.
Clifford, James
    1988a   Histories of the Tribal and the Modern. *In* The Predicament of Culture. Pp. 189–214. Cambridge: Harvard University Press.
    1988b   On Ethnographic Authority. *In* The Predicament of Culture. Pp. 21–54. Cambridge: Harvard University Press.
Crane, Diana
    1987   The Transformation of the Avant-Garde. Chicago: University of Chicago Press.
Danto, Arthur
    1964   The Artworld. Journal of Philosophy 61:571–584.

Deleuze, G., and F. Guattari

    1987   A Thousand Plateaus: Capitalism and Schizophrenia. B. Massumi, trans. Minneapolis: University of Minnesota Press.

Derrida, J.

    1977   Of Grammatology. G. Spivak, trans. Baltimore: Johns Hopkins University Press.

Elkin, A. P.

    1977 [1945]   Aboriginal Men of High Degree. St. Lucia, Queensland: University of Queensland Press.

Fabian, Johannes

    1983   Time and the Other. New York: Columbia University Press.

Fiske, J., B. Hodge, and G. Turner

    1987   Myths of Oz: Reading Australian Popular Culture. Boston: Allen & Unwin.

Fry, T., and A. Willis

    1989   Aboriginal Art: Symptom or Success? Art in America 77 (July):109–117, 159–160, 163.

Hamilton, Annette

    1987   Equal to Whom? Visions of Destiny and the Aboriginal Aristocracy. Mankind 17:129–139.

    1990   Fear and Desire: Aborigines, Asians and the National Imaginary. Australian Cultural History (July). (in press).

Hughes, R.

    1988   Evoking the Spirit Ancestors. Time, 31 October:79–80.

Isaacs, J.

    1987   Waiting for the Mob from Balgo. Australian and International Art Monthly, June:20–22.

Jameson, F.

    1984   Postmodernism: or, The Cultural Logic of Late Capital. New Left Review 146:53–93.

Keneally, T.

    1988   Dreamscapes: Acrylics Lend New Life to an Ancient Art of Australian Desert. New York Times Sunday Magazine, vol. 138, 13 November:52.

Kent, S.

    1987   A Burst of Colour in the Western Desert. Sydney Morning Herald, 11 July:48.

Kimber, R.

    1977   Mosaics You Can Move. Hemisphere 21(1):2–7, 29–30.

Kirshenblatt-Gimblett, Barbara

    1991   Objects of Ethnography. In Exhibiting Culture: The Poetics and Politics of Museum Display. I. Karp and S. Lavine, eds. Washington, D.C.: Smithsonian Institution Press. (in press).

Larson, K.

    1988   Their Brilliant Careers. New York Magazine, 4 October:148–150.

Lash, S., and J. Urry

    1987   The End of Organized Capitalism. Madison: University of Wisconsin Press.

Marcus, G., and M. Fischer

    1986   Anthropology as Cultural Critique. Chicago: University of Chicago Press.

Megaw, V.

    1982   Western Desert Acrylic Painting—Artefact or Art? Art History 5:205–218.

Meyrowitz, J.
    1985   No Sense of Place: The Impact of Electronic Media on Social Behavior. New
            York: Oxford University Press.
Michaels, E.
    1988   Bad Aboriginal Art. Art and Text 28:59–73.
Moore, C., and S. Muecke
    1984   Racism, Aborigines and Film. Australian Journal of Cultural Studies 2:36–53.
Morphy, H.
    1977   Too Many Meanings. Ph.D. dissertation, Department of Prehistory and Anthro-
            pology, Australian National University, Canberra.
    1983   "Now You Understand"—An Analysis of the Way Yolngu Have Used Sacred
            Knowledge to Retain their Autonomy. In Aborigines, Land and Land Rights. N. Pe-
            terson and M. Langton, eds. Pp. 110–133. Canberra: Australian Institute of Aborig-
            inal Studies.
Morris, B.
    1987   The Politics of Identity: From Aborigines to the First Australian. In Past and
            Present: The Construction of Aboriginality. J. Beckett, ed. Pp. 63–86. Canberra:
            Australian Institute of Aboriginal Studies.
Morton, John
    1988   Black and White Totemism: Conservation, Animal Symbolism and Human Iden-
            tification in Aboriginal and Non-Aboriginal Australia. Unpublished MS.
Munn, N.
    1973   Walbiri Iconography. Ithaca, N.Y.: Cornell University Press.
Myers, F.
    1985   Illusion and Reality: Aboriginal Self-Determination in Central Australia. In The
            Future of Former Foragers. C. Schrire and R. Gordon, eds. Pp. 109–122. Cambridge:
            Cultural Survival.
    1986   Pintupi Country, Pintupi Self: Sentiment, Place, and Politics among Western
            Desert Aborigines. Washington, D.C. and Canberra: Smithsonian Institution Press
            and Aboriginal Studies Press.
    1988   Locating Ethnographic Practice: Romance, Reality and Politics in the Outback.
            American Ethnologist 15:609–624.
    1989   Truth, Beauty and Pintupi Painting. Visual Anthropology 2:163–195.
Nairne, S., Geoff Dunlop, and John Wyver
    1987   State of the Art. London: Chatto and Windus.
Pekarik, A.
    1988   Journeys in the Dreamtime. World Archaeology, Nov.–Dec.:46–52.
Peterson, Nicolas
    1985   Capitalism, Culture, and Land Rights. Social Analysis 18:85–101.
Price, Sally
    1989   Primitive Art in Civilized Places. Chicago: University of Chicago Press.
Rankin-Reid, J.
    1989   Colonial Foreplay. Artscribe International, Sept.–Oct.:12–13.
Rowse, Tim
    1988   Paternalism's Changing Reputation. Mankind 18:57–73.
Rubinstein, M. R.
    1989   Outstations of the Postmodern: Aboriginal Acrylic Paintings of the Australian
            Western Desert. Arts Magazine, March:40–47.

Sansom, B.
1980   The Camp at Wallaby Cross. Canberra: Australian Institute of Aboriginal Studies.

Schjeldahl, P.
1988   Patronizing Primitives. 7 Days, November 16:13–15.

Schneider, D.
1970   What is Kinship All About? *In* Kinship Studies in the Morgan Centennial Year. P. Reining, ed. Pp. 32–63. Washington, D.C.: Anthropological Society of Washington.

Smith, R.
1988   From Alien to Familiar. The New York Times, 16 December:C32.

Stanner, W. E. H.
1956   The Dreaming. *In* Australian Signpost. T. A. G. Hungerford, ed. Pp. 51–65. Melbourne: F. W. Cheshire.

Strehlow, T. G. H.
1947   Aranda Traditions. Melbourne: Melbourne University Press.

Stretton, R.
1987   Aboriginal Art on the Move. The Weekend Australian, 5–6 September:32.

Sturmer, J. von
1989   Aborigines, Representation, Necrophilia. Art and Text 32:127–139.

Sutton, P., ed.
1988   Dreamings: The Art of Aboriginal Australia. New York: George Braziller/Asia Society Galleries.

Taylor, P.
1989   Primitive Dreams are Hitting the Big Time. New York Times, 21 May:H31, 35.

Tillim, S.
1987   Criticism and Culture, or Greenberg's Doubt. Art in America 46(May):122–127.

Wallach, A.
1989   Beautiful Dreamings. Ms., March:60–64.

Warlukurlangu Artists
1987   Yuendumu Doors: Kuruwarri. Canberra: Aboriginal Studies Press.

Weber, J.
1989   Papunya Tula: Contemporary Paintings from Australia's Western Desert. *In* Papunya Tula, catalog for show at John Weber Gallery, 25 May–17 June 1989.

Williams, N.
1976   Australian Aboriginal Art at Yirrkala: Introduction and Development of Marketing. *In* Ethnic and Tourist Arts. N. Graburn, ed. Pp. 266–284. Berkeley: University of California Press.

Williams, Raymond
1977   Marxism and Literature. Oxford: Oxford University Press.

Indigenous Media: Faustian Contract or Global Village?

Faye Ginsburg

> And tomorrow? . . . The dreams of Vertov and Flaherty will be combined into a mechanical "cine-eye-ear" which is such a "participant" camera that it will pass automatically into the hands of those who were, up to now, always in front of it. Then the anthropologist will no longer monopolize the observation of things.
>
> —Jean Rouch, "The Camera and Man,"
> in Principles of Visual Anthropology, 1975, p. 102

> Aboriginal communities are ensuring the continuity of their languages and cultures and representation of their views. By making their own films and videos, they speak for themselves, no longer aliens in an industry which for a century has used them for its own ends.
>
> —Michael Leigh (1988:88)

Over the last ten years, indigenous and minority people have been using a variety of media, including film and video, as new vehicles for internal and external communication, for self-determination, and for resistance to outside cultural domination.[1] The new media forms they are creating are innovations in both filmic representation and social process, expressive of transformations in cultural identities in terms shaped by local and global conditions of the late 20th century. Such alternative "multicultural media" have become both fashionable and more visible in the latter part of the 1980s: museum shows in the United States,[2] the Black Film workshop sector in the United Kingdom,[3] and a Special Broadcasting Service (SBS) in Australia are just a few examples of this increased interest.[4] Until quite recently, support for and exhibition of such work focused on productions by ethnic minorities, rather than indigenous groups.[5] While many of the issues they contend with are shared concerns, I will focus in this essay on specific dilemmas posed to indigenous people by the introduction of video and television, grounding my discussion in recent developments in Australian Aboriginal media.

Efforts to produce indigenous media worldwide[6] are generally small-scale, low budget and locally based; because of this, their existence is politically and economically fragile, while their significance is largely invisible outside of occasional festivals or circles of specialists.[7] There is very little written on these developments, and what exists comes mostly in the form of newsletters and reports, which are useful, but do not address directly broader theoretical questions regarding how these developments alter understandings of media, politics, and representation. It is particularly surprising that there is so little discussion of such phenomena in contemporary anthropological work, despite the fact that video cassette recorders (VCRs), video cameras, and mass media are now present in even the most remote locales. This is due in part to the theoretical foci anthropologists carry into the field that have not expanded to keep up with such changes. The lack of analysis of such media as both cultural product and social process may also be due to our own culture's enduring positivist belief that the camera provides a "window" on reality, a simple expansion of our powers of observation, as opposed to a creative tool in the service of a new signifying practice.

I want to argue that it is of particular importance, now, that these most contemporary of indigenous forms of self-representation and their creators be considered seriously. They are of critical theoretical and empirical significance for current debates in several fields regarding the politics and poetics of representation, the development of media in Third and Fourth World settings, and the expansion of ethnographic film theory and the canon associated with it.

The first part of this essay addresses how indigenous media challenges the conventions and very categories of both "traditional culture" and "ethnographic film." The second part explores the specific cases of several media groups in Central Australia that I have been studying since 1988. These are Warlpiri Media Association in the Central Desert Aboriginal community of Yuendumu; CAAMA—the acronym for the Central Australian Aboriginal Media Association located just outside the town of Alice Springs; and Imparja Television based in Alice Springs, but serving all of the Northern Territory and large parts of South Australia as well.

The developments I discuss are the most recent manifestation of the ever-increasing involvement of Australian Aboriginal people in media production over the last two decades. Different aspects of this involvement are summarized nicely in essays by film historian Michael Leigh (1988) and filmmaker David MacDougall (1987). As Leigh points out, the upsurge of collaborative productions with Australian Aboriginal people began during the Labor government in 1972–75, in part enacting its liberal left policy toward Aboriginal "self-determination."[8] For example, since the early 1970s, at the Australian Institute for Aboriginal and Torres Straits Islanders Studies Film Unit (the Institute), new projects were based increasingly on interest expressed by Aboriginal communities, resulting in outstanding films such as *Waiting for Harry* (McKenzie 1980) or *Goodbye Old Man* (MacDougall 1977). Paralleling a similar shift in ethnographic writing, these changes in ethnographic film practice to accommodate indigenous interests were, according to David MacDougall, a shift away from

> reconstruction of pre-contact situations towards an examination of the realities of contemporary Aboriginal experience. Initially this took the form of supporting and documenting Aboriginal moves for cultural reassertion . . . [1987:55]

In 1979, the Institute began taking on occasional Aboriginal trainees in film and video. That same year saw the debut of *My Survival As An Aboriginal*, the first film directed by an Aboriginal woman, Essie Coffey of Brewarrina (made with Martha Ansara and Alec Morgan of the Sydney Filmmakers Co-operative).

Such "participatory cinema" (MacDougall 1975) is part of the increasingly collaborative approach to ethnographic filmmaking which foreshadowed and encouraged the development of indigenous media. Because all this work has been particularly innovative in the filmmaking *processes* as much as product, it seems appropriate that analysis should shift as well: I am concerned less with the usual focus on the formal qualities of film as text and more with the cultural *mediations* that occur through film and video works.

Given my concern with mediation, I want to call attention to the use of quotations and interviews as "data" in this article. They are intended to locate indigenous media at the intersection of a number of discourses, since part of what I am trying to understand is how this work gets positioned by those practicing it and by those in the dominant culture with some interest in it. So, for example, Australian art critics Tony Fry and Ann-Marie Willis greet Aboriginal media with a postmodern embrace, as they search for a disruptive and positive response on the part of Aborigines to the oppressive legacy of colonialism. Perhaps because of this intellectual commitment, they have a rather utopian view of television's potential for Aboriginal social relations and consciousness, particularly in comparison with the circulation of Aboriginal paintings in the world art market:

> [Aboriginal] Video trades on the assumption that its application and cultural production are a form of resistance. This is not because of its content, but rather because it is *occupied* as a cultural space from which the right to speak is asserted—a late-modern space to address the present and the future. Television's cultural and economic usefulness to Aboriginal people is great. For one thing, it is less easily accommodated into the international exchange of cultural commodities than are art works. More importantly, it can't be classified as easily and in the same ways as the 'spectacular primitive' (which isn't to say it is invulnerable). [Fry and Willis 1989:160; emphasis in original]

This perspective, shared by a number of contemporary art critics, is a bit naïve in its disregard for the destructive effects of television; since this is a concern voiced by many Aborigines themselves, it suggests the important contribution that grounded anthropological research can make to this critical discourse.[9] Nonetheless, I would like to take an optimistic view as well, tempered by my awareness of compromises and problems that are more visible from an "on-the-ground" (rather than distant) vantage point.

I am proposing that when other forms are no longer effective, indigenous media offers a possible means—social, cultural, and political—for reproducing and transforming cultural identity among people who have experienced massive political, geographic, and economic disruption. The capabilities of media to transcend boundaries of time, space, and even language are being used effectively to mediate, literally, historically produced social ruptures and to help construct identities that link past and present in ways appropriate to contemporary conditions. Before exploring these ideas further, I first want to address the general questions indigenous media raises for the genre of ethnographic film.

Indigenous Media and Ethnographic Film

Ethnographic film was originally conceived as a broad project of documenting on film the "disappearing" life-worlds of those "others"—non-Western, small-scale, kinship-based societies—who had initially been the objects of anthropology as it developed in the early 20th century. Ironically, the field of ethnographic film took on definition and shape as a genre during a critical period, the 1960s and '70s, when efforts to "reinvent anthropology" (Hymes 1972) were produced by a variety of historical, intellectual, and political developments. Briefly stated, these include:

- The end of the colonial era with the assertions of self-determination by native peoples.

- The radicalization of young scholars in the 1960s and the replacing of positivist models of knowledge with more interpretive and politically self-conscious approaches.

- A reconceptualization of "the native voice" as one that should be in more direct dialogue with anthropological interpretation.

Some have called this constellation of events "a crisis in representation" for the field that required new, experimental strategies for transmitting anthropological understandings (e.g., Marcus and Fischer 1986). It is not sufficiently appreciated that many people working in ethnographic film had, in fact, already responded to this "crisis." Often less constrained by the academy than those working in written ethnography, ethnographic filmmakers offered a variety of creative solutions, following the experimental turns in the arts and sciences in general. For example, questions of epistemology, ethics, and the position of the native interlocutor were being addressed in the 1950s by ethnographic filmmaker Jean Rouch, in works such as *Les Maîtres Fous* (1954), *Jaguar* (1955), or *Chronicle of a Summer* (1960). By the mid 1970s, the list included (to name a few) Tim Asch, David and Judith MacDougall, John Marshall, Gary Kildea, Barbara Myerhoff, and Jorge Preloran. A number of these people also articulated arguments in print for what David MacDougall has called more participatory methods and styles of representation (1975).

In addition to these more dialogical approaches in ethnographic film, an early attempt to put the camera directly into native hands was carried out by Sol Worth and John Adair in the 1960s. Their project, discussed in the book *Through Navajo Eyes* (1972), attempted to teach film technology to Navajos without the conventions of Western production and editing, to see if their films would be based on a different film "grammar" based on Navajo worldview. However, the experiment focused overmuch on the filmic rather than the social frame. Worth and Adair failed to consider seriously potential cultural differences in the social relations around image-making and viewing, even though these concerns were brought up clearly in the initial negotiations with Sam Yazzie, a leading medicine man and elder.

Adair explained that he wanted to teach some Navajo to make movies. . . . When Adair finished, Sam thought for a while and then . . . asked a lengthy question which was interpreted as, "Will making movies do sheep any harm?"

Worth was happy to explain that as far as he knew, there was no chance that making movies would harm the sheep.

Sam thought this over and then asked, "Will making movies do the sheep good?" Worth was forced to reply that as far as he knew making movies wouldn't do the sheep any good.

Sam thought this over, then, looking around at us he said, "Then why make movies?" [Worth and Adair 1972:5]

The lack of consideration for how movies might "do the sheep good" meant that the Navajo Eyes project was rather short lived and, retrospectively, is seen as a somewhat sterile and patronizing experiment. Still, the notion of distinct indigenous concerns for cinematic and narrative representation was prescient. By the 1970s, indigenous groups and some ethnographic filmmakers were questioning not only how conventions of representation are culture bound; they also concerned themselves with central issues of power regarding who controls the production and distribution of imagery. Indigenous peoples who had been the exotic objects of many films were concerned increasingly with producing their own images, either by working with accomplished and sympathetic filmmakers[10] or by entering into film and video production themselves, for example Hopi artist Victor Masayesva, or Inuit producer/director Zacharias Kunuk.[11]

These developments were part of a more general decentralization, democratization, and widespread penetration of media that emerged with the growth of new technologies that simultaneously worked the local and global fronts. On the one hand, inexpensive portable video cameras, and cable channels open to a spectrum of producers and viewers gave new meaning to notions of access and multicultural expression. On the other hand, the broad marketing of VCRs and the launching of communications satellites over Canada in the 1970s and Australia in the 1980s suddenly brought the possibility or menace, depending on one's point of view, of a mixture of minority/indigenous and mainstream Western programming entering into the daily lives of people living in remote settlements, especially those in the Canadian Arctic and central Australian desert.

Thus, indigenous and minority people have faced a kind of Faustian dilemma. On the one hand, they are finding new modes for expressing indigenous identity through media and gaining access to film and video to serve their own needs and ends. On the other hand, the spread of communications technology such as home video and satellite downlinks threatens to be a final assault on culture, language, imagery, relationship between generations, and respect for traditional knowledge. Freda Glynn, the Aboriginal director of CAAMA and chair of Imparja's board, articulates this sense of dilemma. As an Aboriginal woman who was taken from her family in childhood to be educated in Western schools, she is keenly aware of the impact of such interventions and sees television as part of a continuum of assaults on Aboriginal life that must be dealt with in as positive a manner as possible. Her words are instructive.

TV is like an invasion. We have had grog, guns and diseases, but we have been really fortunate that people outside the major communities have had no communication like radio or TV. Language and culture have been protected by neglect. Now, they are not going to be. They need protection because TV will be going into those communities 24 hours a day in a foreign language—English. It only takes a few months and the kids start changing. . . . We're trying to teach kids you can be Aboriginal and keep your language and still mix in the wider community and have English as well. At least they will be seeing black faces on the magic box that sits in the corner, instead of seeing white faces all day long. [Interview with author, 6 July 1988]

Some scholars of Third World broadcasting (following on the gloomy predictions of the Frankfurt school theorists) believe that people like Freda, at best, are simply bargaining with Mephistopheles. They conclude that the content and hegemonic control of mass media irreversibly erode traditional languages and cultures, replacing them with alien social values and an attraction to Western consumer goods. Such concerns, for example, have been the basis for debates in Papua New Guinea over the introduction of commercial television (Crossette 1986). Others argue that the very *form* of Western narratives may undermine traditional modes. As David MacDougall recently pointed out,

The dominant conflict structure of Western fictional narratives, and the didacticism of much of Western documentary, may be at odds with traditional modes of discourse. The division into fiction and documentary may itself be subversive. Or differences may arise in the conventions of narrative and imagery. At a film conference in 1978, Wiyendji, an Aboriginal man from Roper River, argued against the Western preoccupation with close-ups and fast cutting, saying that Aborigines preferred to see whole bodies and whole events. This may not be borne out by Aboriginal preferences when viewing non-Aboriginal material, but it is a common complaint about films by outsiders which portray Aboriginal subjects.
Such objections obviously cry out for more Aboriginal filmmaking. [1987:54]

Taking a similar perspective, indigenous people, scholars, and policymakers have been advocating indigenous use of media technology as a new opportunity for influence and self-expression. In this view, television technology offers unique potential for the expansion of community-generated production, and the construction of viewing conditions and audiences shaped by indigenous interests, and ultimately, cultural regeneration. Art critics Fry and Willis express this position in the language of postmodernism, updating Lévi-Strauss's image of *bricolage* with more contemporary metaphors, combining popular understandings of recombinant DNA and telecommunications.

Making a new culture which knowingly embraces the future is a more viable form of cultural bricolage (by this we mean the making of a culture by a process of the selection and assembly of combined and recombined cultural forms). Resistance to ethnocide is not seen as trying simply to defend an existent cultural identity but the forging of a new one which rejects the models sought to be imposed. Radio, television and video have become significant media in this cultural strategy. And what is particularly significant is that these media break the circuit of producing products for circulation and consumption within the culture of dominance (as opposed to works of art). Aboriginal radio, video and TV producers are producing ideas and images that circulate in their own cultures. [Fry and Willis 1989:160]

Finally, as John Lent noted in his collection *Case Studies of Mass Media in the Third World,* "The hard work of empirically done case studies on individual media in particular countries remains to be done" (1979:v). A 1986 report for the Australian Institute of Aboriginal Studies by researcher Eric Michaels on the introduction of local video production and low-power broadcast at a Warlpiri community, Yuendumu, in Central Australia presents one such case, demonstrating the possibilities and limits of these sorts of innovations. Making a case for the local control of media, the author argues that the substance and formal qualities of the tapes have a distinctly Warlpiri sensibility, marked, for example by an intense interest in the landscape as filled with specific meaning. But, he goes on to point out, of equal if not more importance is the social organization of media production; the ways in which tapes are made, shown, and used reflect Warlpiri understandings of kinship and group responsibilities for display and access to traditional knowledge (Michaels 1984).

The last point, regarding transmission of information, has been the subject of much recent ethnographic inquiry (Myers 1986), which demonstrates how ceremonial and other kinds of knowledge ("law") critical to cultural identity are transmitted. Elders impart their knowledge at appropriate times over the life cycle, most dramatically through initiation rituals. Thus, in traditional communities, knowing, seeing, hearing, speaking, and performing certain kinds of information are highly regulated; violation of norms can meet with severe sanctions. In addition, Aboriginal knowledge is made meaningful by associations with particular geographic locations, in contrast to the free-floating signifiers that characterize much of Western semiotics, particularly in television. As one communications scholar points out:

> European mass media with its homogenized messages transmitted from a central source is at odds with Aboriginal information patterns. Aborigines see their local areas as the centre from which information emanates. Their information/communications model is completely the reverse of the European model which sees the urban cities as the centre and the remote communities as the periphery. The mass media not only ignores local boundaries (Aboriginal countries), it also makes information accessible to all viewers. [Molnar 1989:8]

Indeed, the question of media reception is complex in such settings. And, as others have noted, such practice is significant not only to their own communities.

> Aboriginal people, both individually and collectively, are turning to film, video and television as the media almost likely to carry their messages to one another and into the consciousness of white Australia. [MacDougall 1987:58]

Transmitting Identity: Aboriginal Media

In the following discussion of particular instances of indigenous media production, I propose an analysis of how Aboriginal video practice is engaged in the construction of their contemporary identity that integrates historical and contemporary lifeworlds.

The Warlpiri Media Association[12] grew out of a project initiated by the Australian Institute of Aboriginal Studies in 1982, emerging from a concern over the possible deleterious impact of the AUSSAT satellite. Its launching in 1985 was to bring the possibility of television to remote areas, including many Aboriginal settlements and communities, for the first time. While Yuendumu and many other Aboriginal communities had not received the steady flow of broadcast television, it is important to point out that they were acquainted with Western filmmaking practice through community viewings of rented films, attending cinemas in towns, and most recently, through the circulation and viewing of materials through their own or resident whites' video cassette recorders.

American researcher Eric Michaels was hired to work with Warlpiri-speaking Aboriginal people at the Yuendumu community in the Central Desert to develop video based on Aboriginal concerns that might be programmed instead of the imagery of standard commercial television. The fifty tapes produced by Warlpiri videomakers between 1982 and 1984 demonstrated how media could be fashioned and used in ways appropriate to native social organization, narrative conventions, and communicative strategies. Originally intended for use in their school, the works covered subjects ranging from traditional dances, to a piece memorializing a massacre of Warlpiri people by whites, to recording of local sports events.

When I was there in 1988, the activities of Warlpiri Media Association had expanded from production and irregular broadcast of a Warlpiri evening news program to include the operation of a local low-power television station via a homemade transmitter since April 1985. (This operation as well as a more recent government-funded Aboriginal media scheme, in a Kafkaesque twist of bureaucracy, are considered illegal because the state had not managed to authorize a new, appropriate licensing category [Molnar 1989:34]!) The development of media similar to Yuendumu is happening in other remote communities such as Aurukun and Ernabella (Molnar 1989:25ff.; N. Turner 1990), while other production units in cities such as Perth, Sydney, Darwin, reflect the distinctive interests of urban Aboriginals.

The Central Australian Aboriginal Media Association, or CAAMA, is one of the most successful of Aboriginally controlled media projects. It was started as an FM radio station in 1980 by two Aboriginal people and one ''whitefella'' whose private record collection was the basis of most of the original programming. CAAMA quickly became one of the most popular radio shows for both blacks and whites in the Northern Territory. Its format combines country western, Aboriginal rock, call-ins, and discussion of news of concern to Aborigines in six native languages and English for nearly fifteen hours a day. It later expanded to AM and shortwave broadcasts, a prizewinning educational show called ''Bushfire,'' and a recording studio for Aboriginal bands whose tapes are sold along with other Aboriginal art products in the CAAMA shop. In addition, a video unit was established in 1984; originally, it produced a series of one-hour video newsletters in English and other major Aboriginal languages to circulate to communities without radio access.

In 1985, when the Australian government launched its communications satellite, AUSSAT, it was clear that eventually commercial television was going to be available to the remote Aboriginal settlements in CAAMA's radio broadcast area. Out of concern for the potential negative impact of this on traditional Aboriginal languages and culture, CAAMA made a bid for the satellite's downlink license to Central Australia, as a symbolic assertion of the presence and concerns of that region's Aboriginal people. Much to their surprise, their proposal for taking on this multimillion-dollar operation was taken seriously. In January 1987, after a prolonged battle against bigger commercial interests and opposition from the Northern Territory government, CAAMA won the Regional Commercial Television Services (RCTS) license for the television downlink to the Central Australian "footprint," (so named because it describes the general shape of the signal patterns to earth given off by satellites). They were able to make the acquisition with financial assistance from a variety of government sources.[13]

The private commercial station they now run, Imparja (which means "tracks" or "footprint" in the Central Australian language Arrernte), began broadcasting in January 1988, serving approximately 100,000 viewers in Central Australia, over a quarter of them Aboriginal (though some put that figure as high as 40%) (Goddard 1987). Thus far, in addition to public service announcements, logos, wraparounds, and the like which are directed to Aboriginal concerns such as bush foods or the Central Land Council, Imparja has been broadcasting regular Aboriginal programs. In 1988, they carried 26 30-minute current affairs programs, broadcast twice a week in prime time: "Urrpye" [messenger] a "magazine and current affairs style program helping to promote awareness about the concerns and issues of Aboriginal people" (in English);[14] and "Nganampa—Anwernekenhe" or "ours") a news show in different Aboriginal languages—Arrernte, Luritja, Pitjantjajara, Warlpiri—with English subtitles, intended to help maintain Aboriginal language and culture through art, music, stories, and dances. In 1989, Imparja developed a 13-part language series, an Aboriginal music program, and a late-night show featuring Aborigines talking in their own languages, telling their history and "dreaming" stories (Molnar 1989:23). As part of their support for Aboriginal health concerns, they refuse to sell commercials for alcohol.

There have been complaints, especially from other Aboriginal people, that 2 to 3 hours out of 70 hours a week, even at prime time, is insufficient Aboriginal programming. Others are concerned about Imparja's stress on "broadcast quality"—an elusive and problematic term for somewhat arbitrary technical standards for productions used by television stations, that effectively keeps low-budget and unconventional work off the air. In this case, the result has been to limit Imparja's use of material produced by Yuendumu, Ernabella, and other local Aboriginal media associations. It also restricts CAAMA's ability to produce programming for Imparja because of the costs involved in "broadcast quality" work. A 30-minute piece could cost between $10,000 and $20,000, while imported American shows can be purchased inexpensively (Molnar 1989:23).

The question of advertising also has an impact on programming content for any commercial television outlet. Imparja, like the other Australian satellite downlinks, struggles to meet the $4.5-million satellite rental fee (rising at 12% per year) via advertising revenues which will never rise significantly because the population numbers (and therefore potential consumers) are low. Aboriginal programming is particularly not lucrative because there is a dropoff in European viewers, and advertisers—who are mostly local business people—don't view Aborigines as consumers.

As one possible solution, in addition to their own Aboriginal productions, CAAMA is trying to correct for the homogenizing top-down flow of commercial television by providing "windows" which would allow the insertion of community-made video programs in language for local broadcast at places such as Ali Curung, Barunga, Borroloola, Ernabella, Galiwinku, Ntaria, Hermannsburg, Oenpelli, Wadeye, Port Keats, Santa Teresa, and Yuendumu.

Finally, while Imparja is the only large-scale commercial television station owned by Australian Aboriginal people, just 10% of the television staff is Aboriginal, because of a lack of skilled personnel. To help correct for this problem, in 1988, CAAMA and Imparja made a three-year training agreement with the Department of Education, Employment and Training to train 33 Aboriginal people as videotape operators, editors, recording assistants, television presenters, radio journalists and broadcasters, translator/interpreters, sales representatives, researchers, and bookkeepers. All trainees are supposed to be taken on as permanent employees by CAAMA and Imparja when they finish their training.

Some sympathetic white Australians, assessing Imparja at some distance from its internal difficulties, are hopeful. For example, Tony Fry and Ann-Marie Willis recently writing in *Art in America,* see Imparja as claiming

> a cultural space in which innovation is possible; it has a future. This is a new symbol of power in a culture dominated by the media. It doesn't override the effects of the damaged culture in which it functions, but creates a fissure in which a new set of perceptions can seep in. Such comments do not imply such an operation is free from either the reach of ethnocidal agency or of more direct effects of unequal exchange— it is not judged by authority as a mainstream commercial channel and is dependent on government funding. It is neither beyond nor lacking in criticism, especially over the nature and quantity of Aboriginal-made content. [1989:163]

While they and other critics at a distance focus on Imparja, it is important to look at the *range* of indigenous media projects and how they relate to each other. The Aboriginal cases I have been discussing are particularly interesting from this perspective because each video and television project is being introduced at a distinct level of social, political, and economic organization, yet they intersect each other. Together, Warlpiri Media Association, CAAMA, and Imparja (and there are more of course) might instruct us as to the costs and benefits of the introduction of media technologies.

While small groups such as Warlpiri Media Association have maintained community control artistically and politically (for example by setting up their own "illegal" satellite downlink and then inserting their own programming into the signal as they desired), they have developed a production style (both aesthetically and in work relations) that is embedded in local concerns and traditions. But such groups are fragile both economically *and* because they rely heavily on the unique talents of a few individuals. For example, Warlpiri Media's central figures, Francis Jupurrurla Kelly and Andrew Japaljarri Spencer, are able to juggle and use both Australian and traditional Aboriginal language and knowledge; they have the motivation, skills, and legitimacy to graft this Western form onto traditional sensibilities and concerns. Eric Michaels captured a sense of this in his description of Francis:

> Jupurrurla, in his Bob Marley T-shirt and Adidas runners, armed with his video portapak, resists identification as a savage updating some archaic technology to produce curiosities of a primitive tradition for the jaded modern gaze. Jupurrurla is indisputably a sophisticated cultural broker who employs videotape and modern technology to express and resolve political, theological, and aesthetic contradictions that arise in uniquely contemporary circumstances. [1987:26]

Such individuals, however, occupy a historically unique intergenerational position that is unlikely to be replicated unless a conscious effort is made to do so. So, the departure of just one of them—as when Andrew Japaljarri Spencer moved on—is a serious blow to the operation of these small-scale media groups.

At the other end of the spectrum from Warlpiri Media, Imparja is a large multimillion-dollar commercial interest. While it is owned and managed by an Aboriginal organization, and has initiated a three-year training program for young Aboriginal people, it is still 90% white and European in its staffing and programming. In between these two falls CAAMA. Perhaps it presents the golden mean between flexibility and sensitivity to local-level needs, but with sufficient institutional infrastructure to withstand the vagaries of funding and personal changes that plague the smaller media associations.

Positioning Indigenous Media

Given all this, how does one place such work in relation to the enterprise of ethnographic film? While many of us—myself included—might prefer to toss the term out altogether, I leave that concern aside momentarily for the sake of moving discussion forward in ways that are important to larger goals. I would like to consider briefly how indigenous media challenge the conventions and very categories of both "traditional" identity construction and "ethnographic film."

One response some Westerners have to indigenous media in relation to ethnographic film is to simply abandon or declare "colonialist" any attempt to film "the other"; indigenous media production makes it clear that they are capable of representing themselves. This response is common to those interested in ethnographic film, for example, who confront for the first time the possibility that such activity is not necessarily the "white man's burden." Underlying these responses, of course, is the idea that "we" and "they" are separate, which in turn is built on the trope and mystique of the noble savage living in a traditional, bounded world, for whom all knowledge, objects, values originating elsewhere are polluting of some reified notion of culture and innocence. The movie *Crocodile Dundee* presented a witty commentary on such misapprehension, in an encounter between New York journalist Sue Charlton (Linda Kozlowski) and Dundee's (Paul Hogan) Aboriginal friend Neville Bell (David Gulpilil).

> Creeping through the bush, looking authentic but sounding up-to-date, he is painted from the waist up but wears jeans and a watch. Sue then wants to take his photo. He solemnly tells her she can't. She wonders whether it is because it will steal his spirit. "No," he informs her, "the lens cap's on." [Malone 1987:114]

Questions about the legitimacy of one's presence in a foreign setting (especially in which power relations are unequal) as an outsider with a camera should *always* be raised, and generally have been in most successful projects. The fact that the people one is dealing with also have cameras and choose to represent themselves with them should not diminish that concern, nor does it make the act of taking those images by outsiders illegitimate. Filming others and filming one's own group are related but distinct parts of a larger project of reflecting upon the particulars of the human condition, and therefore each approach raises its own sets of issues regarding ethics, social and power relations. In fact, much of current postmodern theory, while raising important points about the politics of representation, is so critical of all "gazes" at the so-called "other" that to follow the program set forth by some, we would all be paralyzed into an alienated universe, with no engagement across the boundaries of difference that for better or worse exist.

Another response considers indigenous production as an altogether separate category from ethnographic film, with different intentions and audiences. The sense of differences is exacerbated by the academic or media positions of one set of producers, as opposed to the community-based locations of the other, a point raised cogently by Marcia Langton, an anthropologist of Aboriginal descent, regarding more academic anthropology (1982). One might, for example, view indigenous work as not intended to cross over so-called cultural boundaries, but rather as made for intracultural consumption and therefore not satisfying some minimal definition of ethnographic film as images of some "other" b, taken by people identified as "a" presented back to people "a." However, "ethnographic film" has never been bounded by its potential audience. To name only one prominent example, for nearly half a century, Jean Rouch has made a practice of taking his films back to those filmed, the people he considers to be his primary audience.[15] And recently, native groups all over the world have been reappropriating colonial photography and films for purposes of cultural revival and political reclamation (identifying relatives, land sites, designs, dances, etc.).

While I reject arguments for separating indigenous media from ethnographic film, I also recognize that they are quite distinct projects. *Because* of the differences, I believe it is crucial that those interested in ethnographic film be informed of and aware of developments in media being produced by those who might be their subjects. But beyond this ethical/political concern, I would like to propose a different frame that incorporates both kinds of productions in some analytically meaningful way.

Mediating Culture

I would like to propose expanding the field of ethnographic film to include what I call ethnographic media. I use media not simply because that term also embraces video and television which play an ever-increasing role in these concerns. I would like to draw attention to other uses of the word media. The *American College Dictionary* defines it as

> an intervening substance, through which a force acts or an effect is produced, [2] an agency, means or instrument.

related to mediate:

> to act between parties to effect an understanding, compromise, reconciliation.

Using these meanings, ethnographic media as a term points to the common (and perhaps most significant) characteristic that the works I have been describing share with more traditional understandings of ethnographic film. They are all intended to communicate something about that social or collective identity we call "culture," in order to mediate (one hopes) across gaps of space, time, knowledge, and prejudice. The films most closely associated with the genre (ideally) work toward creating understanding between two groups separated by space and social practice (though increasingly, they are calling attention to what might be the impossibility of knowing, for example, Dennis O'Rourke's *Cannibal Tours*).

Work being produced by minorities about themselves, I suggest, is *also* concerned with mediating across boundaries, but rather than space and cultural difference they are directed more to the mediation of ruptures of time and history—to heal disruptions in cultural knowledge, historical memory, and identity between generations due to the tragic but familiar litany of assaults—taking of lands, political violence, introduced diseases, expansion of capitalist interests and tourism, and unemployment coupled with loss of traditional bases of subsistence. Unfortunately, these abuses apply equally to the three most active centers of indigenous media production—native (especially Arctic) North Americans, Indians of the Amazon Basin, and Aboriginal Australians. Whether it be Inuit, Yup'ik, Hopi, Nambiquara, Kayapo, Warlpiri, or Pitjanjajara (to name a few)—almost always, the initial activities engaged in with the camera are simultaneously assertive and conservative of identity: documenting injustices and claiming reparations, making records of the lives and knowledge of elders who witnessed the often violent destruction of life as they had known it—from dramatizing mythic stories, to recreating historically traumatic events for the camera, to the always popular recording of food gathering and hunting techniques.

What these works share with the current practices of ethnographic filmmakers such as David and Judith MacDougall, Gary Kildea, Dennis O'Rourke, and Jean Rouch is that they are not about recreating a preexistent and untroubled cultural identity "out there." Rather they are about the *processes* of identity construction. They are not based on some retrieval of an idealized past, but create and assert a position for the present that attempts to accommodate the inconsistencies and contradictions of contemporary life. For Aboriginal Australians, these encompass the powerful relationships to land, myth, and ritual, the fragmented history of contact with Europeans and continued threats to language, health, culture, and social life, and positive efforts in the present to deal with problems stemming from these assaults.

Yet, as in Worth's study with the Navajo, perhaps the real question remains, "will it do the sheep good?" Or, in the case of satellites and VCRs, the question might be, "Can the sheep be kept alive?" As Rosemarie Kuptana, president of the Inuit Broadcasting Corporation succinctly phrased it:

> As you know, the history of the Inuit people is a history of adaptation; to climatic change, to cultural threat, to technological innovation. Television had clearly arrived to stay; a way had to be found to turn this threat to our culture into a tool for its preservation. [1988:39]

In central Australia, Imparja's Aboriginal programs "Urrpye" and "Nganampa" borrow the studio interview format of dominant television; yet, Aboriginal people, news, and languages are heard and seen twice weekly on commercial television in Central Australia. Do the formal conventions of Western television turn off more traditional Aboriginal viewers, or seduce them into watching other non-Aboriginal programs? Or conversely, are more European viewers inclined to attend to things Aboriginal when they appear in the "flow" of broadcast?

In Aboriginal media, the work is not simply an assertion of existing identity, but also a means of cultural invention that refracts and recombines elements from both the dominant and minority societies. This sort of cultural positioning via the creation of new expressive forms has been noted by others. In his essay on ethnic autobiography, Michael Fischer offers insights that seem appropriate to understanding indigenous media as well (recognizing that Aboriginal identity and ethnic identity are not to be equated into a depoliticized domain of multiculturalism):

> What the newer works bring home forcefully is, *first,* the paradoxical sense that ethnicity is something reinvented and reinterpreted in each generation . . . the search or struggle for a sense of ethnic identity is a (re-)invention and discovery of a vision, both ethical and future-oriented. Whereas the search for coherence is grounded in a connection to the past, the meaning abstracted from that past, an important criteria of coherence, is an ethic workable for the future. [1986:195–196; emphasis in original]

With these insights on ethnic autobiographies in mind, what are we to make of MTV-inspired indigenous productions with well-known Aboriginal rock groups? These are perhaps the metalanguage, the poetry of indigenous media, *performing* what is implicit in other kinds of productions that might follow more conventional lines. In one particularly popular segment featuring a band led by Aboriginal singer Ned Hargraves, the MTV style, clearly a Western form, might be interpreted as contradicting the message of the song the group sings:

> Look at us, Look at the price we have paid.
> Keep your culture, keep your land.
> Will you stop before your ways are dead?

As the group performs against a dramatic desert background, visions of men doing traditional dances, images of desert animals and sites, fade in and out. By the end of the piece, the lead singer, Ned Hargraves, falls down, apparently dead. It seems to be the fitting image to the end of the piece as the last line is repeated: "Will you stop before your ways are dead?" Then, suddenly, Ned revives with a wink and a "thumb's up" signal to the audience, suggesting a different perspective that inverts the usual jeremiad over cultural loss. Such unexpected bricolage borrows freely from a range of available expressive resources (rock music, video, Aboriginal language, and landscape) in the service of Aboriginal cultural assertion.

This piece represents the hopeful dimension of Aboriginal response to this new form introduced from the dominant culture, suggesting a more positive model of exchange than the Faustian contract. Still, in some remote Aboriginal communities, television retains its original nickname, "the third invader"; first were Europeans, then alcohol (McGregor 1988:35). In the range of media generated with and by Australian Aborigines in the 1980s one can see both sides of the bargain: the imposition of European commercial television (uninvited) into relatively isolated rural, intact, Aboriginal communities also catalyzed locally controlled, innovative, community-supported video production that has a revitalizing effect in some venues.

Indigenous media, like the ethnic autobiographies that Fischer discusses as well as other contemporary multicultural artistic production, is a cultural process and product. It is exemplary of the construction of contemporary identity of Fourth World people in the late 20th century, in which historical and cultural ruptures are addressed, and reflections of "us" and "them" to each other are increasingly juxtaposed. In that sense, indigenous media is a hybrid, and (to extend the metaphor), perhaps more vigorous and able to flower and reproduce in the altered environment that Aborigines live in today. Young Aboriginal people who are or will be entering into production are not growing up in a pristine world, untouched by the dominant culture; they are juggling the multiple sets of experiences that make them contemporary Aboriginal Australians. Many in this generation want to engage in image-making that offers a face and a narrative that reflects them in the present, connects them to a history, and directs them toward a future as well.

Notes

Acknowledgments. I received support from the Research Challenge Fund of New York University for six weeks of field research in Australia during the summer of 1988. During that time, I conducted interviews and spent time at the Central Australian Aboriginal Media Association (CAAMA), Imparja Television, and Warlpiri Media Association, and also did library research at the Australian Institute for Aboriginal Studies for background on these groups. This article is based on a piece I wrote as a Visiting Conference Fellow for a conference on "Film and the Humanities" convened in September 1989 at the Australian National University's Humanities Research Center, during which time I was able to update some of my information. I consider this all to be a preliminary inquiry for what I hope will be a larger research project. This piece could not have been written without the help of Fred Myers, who assisted me in the logistics and languages of Aboriginal research in the field and out, and offered insightful comments on this essay. I would also like to thank George Marcus, Jay Ruby, and Terry Turner for their helpful readings and encouragement of this project.

[1]In this essay, I am defining indigenous/minority media as that work produced by indigenous peoples, sometimes called the "Fourth World," whose societies have been dominated by encompassing states, such as the United States, Canada, and Australia. This is to distinguish such work from the national and independent cinemas of non-Western Third World nations in Africa, Latin America, and Asia, which have developed under different conditions, and for which there is considerable scholarship. For a recent comprehensive work, see Roy Armes, *Third World Filmmaking and the West* (1987).

[2]For example, in the summer of 1990, "The Decade Show: Frameworks of Identity in the 1980s," was hosted by a consortium of three New York City museums: the New Museum of Contemporary Art, the Studio Museum in Harlem, and the Museum of Contemporary Hispanic Art. The accompanying brochure to the show describes the issues uniting the diverse visual, video, and performing artists in the exhibition:

> Through their examination of familiar issues—homelessness, gender, racism, sexism, AIDS, homophobia, media politics, the environment, and war—these artists demonstrate that identity is a hybrid and fluid notion that reflects the diversity of American society . . .
>
> The work included in this exhibition may be seen as material evidence of alternate viewpoints. Many artists of color, for example, in their philosophical, aesthetic, and spiritual linkages to precolonial societies of Asia, Africa, and America, legitimize diversity, resist Eurocentric domination and create a foundation from which to analyze and explain contemporary social phenomena. Feminist, gay, and lesbian artists similarly affirm that there are other ways of seeing, ways equal to existing cultural dictates.

[3]As part of a commitment to multicultural awareness, Britain's Channel 4 and the British Film Institute, developed the Workshop Declaration of 1981, which gave nonprofit media-production units with four or more salaried members the right to be franchised and eligible for nonprofit production and operation money. These Workshops are expected to provide innovative media and educational programs in the communities where they are situated.

In the racially tense climate of Britain in the early 1980s, and especially after the 1981 Brixton riots, the Labour Party initiated progressive cultural policy through the establishment of a race relations unit and Ethnic Minorities Committee. Money was made available for film and video from the Greater London Council and local borough councils. Based on these funds, the future members of two influential and ground-breaking black film groups, Sankofa and Black Audio Film, financed their first works and organized workshops (Fusco 1988:10–11).

⁴The Special Broadcast Service (SBS) in Australia was set up initially as an ethnic broadcasting service. Until 1989, it viewed Aborigines as outside its mandate because they are indigenous rather than ethnic minorities.

⁵In April 1989, SBS initiated a 13-part TV series devoted to Aboriginal issues, called "First In Line," broadcast Tuesday nights at 7:30 P.M. The producers and crew were primarily Aboriginal, and consulted with communities throughout Australia for items stressing the positive achievements of Aborigines (Molnar 1989:38–39).

The ABC in Australia set up an Aboriginal Program Unit in 1987 to develop and purchase Aboriginal programs, but it was run by a white person and is regarded as underfunded. The Unit's first Aboriginally produced and presented program, "Blackout," began broadcasting in May of 1989, on a Friday 10:40 P.M. time slot. To its credit, the ABC has been training Aborigines since 1980. However, by 1987, there were only seven Aborigines employed by the ABC. That same year, the Prime Minister established the Aboriginal Employment and Development Policy (AEDP) which requires all industries to have 2% Aboriginal employment by 1991, which lead to a new more successful ABC training program (Molnar 1989:36–38).

In the Spring of 1990, the New Museum hosted "Satellite Cultures," a showcase of experimental and alternative video from Australia that included screenings of work by Tracey Moffat, an urban Aboriginal filmmaker and artist who is relatively well known in art circles, as well as a reel of work by CAAMA, and a documentary on Aboriginal land rights, "Extinct But Going Home." Unfortunately, the video was poorly contextualized and badly exhibited. Lacking any background, most American observers watching the CAAMA programs in that context seemed intrigued but bewildered.

⁶The main centers of indigenous media production (besides Australia) are among the Indians of the Amazon Basin, especially the Kayapo (T. Turner 1990), and among Native North American Indians (Weatherford 1981; Weatherford and Seubert 1988) and the Arctic Inuit (Murin 1988).

⁷Even with the increase in and significance of indigenous media, only occasionally is such work seen in independent film or Third World cinema circuits such as the Native American Film Festivals held regularly in San Francisco and New York City; the Pincher Creek World Festival of Aboriginal Motion Pictures held every summer in Alberta, Canada; and the Arctic Cultures and Media Conference, held in Montreal 1987.

Latin American "Fourth World" media has had a growth spurt in the last few years, due to the work of dedicated young activists such as Vincent Carelli in Brazil. The Instituto Nacional Indigenista in Mexico City, and the cross-national Instituto Indigenisto Interamericano, headed by Alejandro Camino, initiated a Latin American Film Festival of Indigenous Peoples in Mexico City. In 1988, the Festival was held in Rio, where, under the guidance of Claudia Menezes of the Museo de Indio, workshops were held to train indigenous groups in low-format media. In October 1989, the festival was held in Venezuela.

These developments are less well known here, although anthropologist Terry Turner has worked with Disappearing World to produce two excellent documentaries in 1988 and 1989 on the positive political and cultural uses of video made by the Kayapo. Documentary maker George Stoney has been making community video to make the political case for land claims for the Kraho Indians, north of the Amazon. These works were shown at the 1989 Native American Film and Video Festival, programmed by Elizabeth Weatherford and Mildred Seubert, for the Museum of the American Indian in New York City. They were also included with other journalistic and experimental works during a film festival and panel, "Representing the Amazon on Film and Video" that were part of "Amazon Week," held at New York University, 26 March–1 April 1990.

[8]For anthropological analyses of Aboriginal "self-determination" and the production of Aboriginal identity in relation to the state, see "Aborigines and the State in Australia," a special issue of *Social Analysis* (1988), edited by Jeremy Beckett.

[9]In fact, almost all this writing, as well as my own work, is based on the work of Eric Michaels whose analyses of Aboriginal media were based on applied anthropological field-work in Central Australia.

[10]These projects include works such as *Familiar Places* (1980), *Goodbye Old Man* (1977), *The House Opening* (1980), *Takeover* (1980) by David and Judith MacDougall with various Aboriginal groups in Australia; *Two Laws* (1983) made by Alessandro Cavadini and Carolyn Strachan with Aboriginal people in Boroloola; *Ileksen* (1978) and *Yumi Yet* (1976) made by Dennis O'Rourke in New Guinea; and Sarah Elder and Leonard Kamerling's work with the Alaska Native Heritage Project, including *At the Time of Whaling* (1973), *From the First People* (1976), *On the Spring Ice* (1976), *Tununeremiut* (1973), and *The Drums of Winter* (1988).

[11]Hopi video artist Victor Masayesva's works include *Itam Hakim, Hopiit* (1984) and *Ritual Clowns* (1988), Inuit producer Zach Kanuck's work includes *From Inuit Point of View* (1987) and *Quaggig* (1989).

[12]Most of this information is compiled from interviews with Philip Batty, and Freda Glynn, and Eric Michaels's report *The Aboriginal Invention of Television* (1986).

[13]Imparja's initial funding came from the Australian Bicentennial Authority ($2.5 million), the Aboriginal Development Commission ($1.8 million), the National Aboriginal Education Commission ($1.5 million), and the South Australian Government ($1 million) [Bellamy 1987:1].

[14]"Urrpye" was cancelled by the end of 1989 in favor of more programs in Aboriginal languages.

[15]Rouch (1975), p. 99:

> what reason could we as anthropologists give for the glances we cast over the wall at others?
> Without a doubt, this word of interrogation must be addressed to all anthropologists, but none of their books or articles has ever been questioned as much as have anthropological films . . . film is the only method I have to show another just how I see him. In other words, for me, my prime audience is . . . the other person, the one I am filming.

References Cited

Arnes, Roy
    1987   Third World Filmmaking and the West. Berkeley: University of California Press.
Beckett, Jeremy, ed.
    1988   Aborigines and the State in Australia. Social Analysis, Special Issue Series, no. 24, December.

Bellamy, Louise
    1987   Black and White TV From the Heart. The Age Green Guide, 22 October.
Crossette, Barbara
    1986   TV Comes to the Pacific. New York Times, 8 May:86
Fischer, Michael
    1986   Ethnicity and the Post-Modern Arts of Memory. *In* Writing Culture: The Poetics
        and Politics of Ethnography. James Clifford and George Marcus, eds. Pp. 194–233.
        Berkeley: University of California Press.
Fry, Tony, and Anne-Marie Willis
    1989   Aboriginal Art: Symptom or Success? Art in America 77(7):108–117, 160, 163.
Fusco, Coco
    1988   A Black Avant-Garde? Notes on Black Audio Film Collective and Sankofa. *In*
        Young, British and Black. Coco Fusco, ed. Pp. 7–22. Buffalo: Hallwalls Contem-
        porary Arts Center.
Goddard, Cliff
    1987   Imparja Gears up to bring TV to the Bush. Land Rights News 2(4):12.
Hymes, Dell
    1972   The Use of Anthropology: Critical, Political, Personal. *In* Reinventing Anthro-
        pology. Dell Hymes, ed. Pp. 3–79. New York: Pantheon.
Kuptana, Rosemarie
    1988   Inuit Broadcasting Corporation. Commission on Visual Anthropology Newslet-
        ter May:39–41.
Langton, Marcia
    1982   Some Comments on Consultative Anthropology in Aboriginal Australia. Pre-
        sented at the Australian Anthropological Society.
Leigh, Michael
    1988   Curiouser and Curiouser. *In* Back of Beyond: Discovering Australian Film and
        Television. Scott Murray, ed. Pp. 70–89. Sydney: Australian Film Commission.
Lent, John
    1979   Preface. *In* Case Studies of Mass Media in the Third World. John Lent, ed. Pp.
        v–vi. Williamsburg, Va.: Studies in Third World Societies.
MacDougall, David
    1975   Beyond Observational Cinema. *In* Principles of Visual Anthropology. Paul
        Hockings, ed. Pp. 109–124. Chicago: Aldine.
    1987   Media Friend or Media Foe. Visual Anthropology 1(1):54–58.
Malone, Peter
    1987   In Black and White and Colour: A Survey of Aborigines in Recent Feature Films.
        Jabiru, N.T. Australia: Nelen Yubu.
Marcus, George, and Michael Fischer
    1986   Anthropology as Cultural Critique: An Experimental Moment in the Human Sci-
        ences. Chicago: University of Chicago Press.
McGregor, Alexander
    1988   Black and White Television. Rolling Stone 415:35ff.
Michaels, Eric
    1984   The Social Organisation of an Aboriginal Video Workplace. Australian Aborig-
        inal Studies 1:26–34.
    1986   Aboriginal Invention of Television: Central Australia 1982–86. Canberra: Aus-
        tralian Institute for Aboriginal Studies.

1987   For A Cultural Future: Francis Jupurrurla Makes TV at Yuendumu. Melbourne: Art and Criticism Monograph Series.

Molnar, Helen

1989   Aboriginal Broadcasting in Australia: Challenges and Promises. Paper presented at the International Communication Association Conference, March.

Murin, Deborah Lee

1988   Northern Native Broadcasting. Canada: The Runge Press.

Myers, Fred

1986   The Politics of Representation: Anthropological Discourse and Australian Aborigines. American Ethnologist 13:138–153.

Turner, Neil

1990   Pitchat and Beyond. Artlink 10(1–2):43–45.

Turner, Terence

1990   Visual Media, Cultural Politics, and Anthropological Practice: Some Implications of Recent Uses of Film and Video Among the Kayapo of Brazil. Commission on Visual Anthropology Review Spring:8–13.

Weatherford, Elizabeth, ed.

1981   Native Americans On Film and Video: Volume I. New York: Museum of the American Indian.

Weatherford, Elizabeth, and Emelia Seubert

1988   Native Americans On Film and Video: Volume II. New York: Museum of the American Indian.

Worth, Sol, and John Adair

1972   Through Navajo Eyes. Bloomington: Indiana University Press.

Films Cited

Cavadini, Alessandro, and Carolyn Strachan

1981   Two Laws.

Coffey, Essie, with Martha Ansara and Alec Morgan

1979   My Survival As An Aboriginal.

Elder, Sarah, and Leonard Kamerling

1973   At the Time of Whaling.

1973   Tununeremiut.

1976   From the First People.

1976   On the Spring Ice.

1988   The Drums of Winter.

Kanuck, Zacharias

1987   From Inuit Point of View.

1989   Quaggig.

MacDougall, David, and Judith MacDougall

1977   Goodbye Old Man.

1980   Familiar Places.

1980   The House Opening.

1980   Takeover.

Masayesva, Victor

1984   Itam Hakim, Hopiit.

1988   Ritual Clowns.

McKenzie, Kim

1980   Waiting For Harry.

O'Rourke, Dennis
   1976   Yumi Yet.
   1978   Ileksen.
   1987   Cannibal Tours.
Rouch, Jean
   1954   Les Maîtres Fous.
   1955   Jaguar.
   1960   Chronicle of a Summer.

Tango

Julie Taylor

Ethos of Melancholy

Para la familia Dickinson, que siempro estuvo.

What the tango says about Argentina, the nation that created it, illuminates aspects of Argentine behavior that have long puzzled outsiders. In many foreign minds, the Argentine tourist, the Argentine military, or Argentine politicians and their followers conjure up images that at first glance seem to convey arrogant aggressiveness often carried to extremes outsiders find inconceivable. What foreigners do not realize is that both public posture and private introspection constantly confront Argentines with excruciating questions about their own identity. Are they civilized or barbarian? European or Latin American? a respected nation or a banana republic? an independent agent or a pawn?

Answers to these questions would not seem to be forthcoming from a dance defined as the tango is by the world outside of Latin America. In the popular image of the tango, Valentino or a counterpart, dramatically dashing in bolero, frilled shirt, and cummerbund, flings a partner backward over the ruffled train of her flamenco costume. One or another holds a rose. Out of this Andalucian vignette of total surrender to music and passion emerges the idea that tango lyrics express similar exuberance. Even when the words tell of lost love, treacherous fate, and an unjust world, a romantic hero supposedly sings them, gesturing flamboyantly to broadcast his sensitivity.

In dramatic contrast, in the classic Argentine tango, closed-faced men practiced the dance with each other and then, fedoras pulled down like masks, gripped women against rigid torsos sheathed in sober double-breasted jackets. Their feet, though subject to the same grim control, executed intricate figures all but independent from the rest of their bodies. Far from flamenco ruffles and roses, Argentines had invented the tango in the brothels on the edges of Buenos Aires as it thrust its slums ever further into the pampas at the turn of the century. The dancers demonstrated their skill by being able to perform like somber automatons, providing them with psychic space to contemplate a bitter destiny that had driven them into themselves.

The tango reflects this Argentine ambivalence. Although a major symbol of the Argentines' national identity, its themes emphasize a painful uncertainty as to the precise nature of that identity. For Argentines, this dance is deadly serious. In the tango, as in their personal lives and their politics, they tend to dwell on real or imagined affronts. In response, they attempt to seek out and affirm self-definition. They resort to elaborately staged behavior as a way of confronting the result of their search—a self-definition whose very essence is doubt. The tango proclaims this doubt and reveals the intensity and depth of Argentine feelings of insecurity, but it also insists that an aggressive facade should betray no hint that it could have arisen from an anguished sense of vulnerability.

Argentines who sing, dance, or listen to the tango today use it to think; hence its intimate, reflective quality. Argentine reflection is bleak. "We are a gray nation," they say, often wistfully. Why this should be the case, making them so different from the neighboring Brazilians with their happy samba, the contrast Argentines most often evoke, they do not understand. Their literature and conversation endlessly pose the problem of identity, and they examine the tango from all angles in search of a solution. Sociologists study it, popular essayists scrutinize it, the intelligentsia listen to it in concert and debate it in lecture. Major writers such as Ernesto Sábato and Martínez Estrada have analyzed it, and Jorge Luís Borges not only studied tango themes but wrote tangos himself. The lack of roots in a preconquest indigenous culture, the post-1880 wave of immigration that left three foreign-born people for every native Argentine in Buenos Aires streets, the continually high proportions of men to women that contributed to Buenos Aires' position as a world-renowned depot of the white slave trade, the nostalgia and resentment of newcomers when dreams of owning land became impossible to realize and other forms of success remained elusive—all these factors contributed to a bitter and insecure melancholy that Argentines recognize as a deep current in their culture.

Argentines know they are not given to exuberant emotion, much less to its display. Proudly in control, yet sometimes, for precisely this reason, trapped in themselves, Argentines channel their characteristic combination of inhibitions and introspection into a particular form of moping that amounts to a national institution: *el mufarse*. The mood relates closely to the tango. Mufarse involves bitter introspection, but beyond this, Argentines have a clear sense of self-indulgence when they give in to a *mufa*. It is a depression, but with a cynicism about the depression itself, an awareness that it can feel good to throw practicalities aside, have one of the demitasse coffees over which many a tango was written, and contemplate one's bad luck and its universal implications. Tango fans in particular pass time constructing complex personal philosophies of life, suffering, and love—philosophies that surprise outsiders who do not expect such elaborate abstractions as common themes of popular culture.

A man discusses such philosophy or sings tangos about it with the understanding that he is an essentially sensitive and vulnerable being in a life that forces him to cover up these qualities with the facade of the experienced, polished, suave, and clever man of the world. The man of the tango, *el hombre tanguero*, is idealistic, but he is not *gil*, the argot for the stupidly innocent. He tries to avoid revealing the naïveté inherent in the male sex, but the *quedirán,* the "what-they-will-say," obsesses him and he sees the rest of the world as mocking observers. He devotes himself to constructing the front that will obviate a smothered laugh or a wink behind his back. By contrast, the gil foolishly acts upon ideas that, if he had learned anything at all from experience, should long ago have been destroyed and relegated to their place as useless though forever-cherished childhood dreams.

The city and the women who live there most often waken the man of the tango from his dreams to the real nature of the world. The city center represents wealth, success, fame—a chance to climb the social ladder at the price of the human values left behind. But the emptiness of these goals provokes the tango's lament for the lost neighborhood or *barrio* on the edge of Buenos Aires, where the sophisticated but disillusioned tango singer spent his youth. The tango developed during the years when Buenos Aires began to demolish barrio life as it pushed out onto the pampas, where no geographical limits stood in its way. Through the first decades of the 20th century, construction was the city's major industry. Time after time the burgeoning city center obliterated its old limits. Asphalt and concrete covered the barrios, the neighborhoods that were half-city and half-country, where local soccer teams played in empty fields on weekend afternoons while families drank *mate* under grape arbors, and sweethearts arranged to meet in the evenings in entryways beneath the streetlamps. Tangos often sing of the man who comes back to his barrio with the hope that it might have escaped change.

Most of all, such a man returns to search for his mother and the values he deserted along with her when he was seduced by the city and its women. Ironically, the mother to whom entire tangos sing homage is in fact the first of the women to betray a man, by her very insistence on ideals that can never apply to reality outside her tiny home in the remembered barrio. So many tangos sing of betrayal by a woman, Argentines observe, that in Mexico the tango is known as "the lament of the cuckold." Man, the idealistic, dreaming innocent, is deceived and thus initiated in the ways of the world by Woman, the wily, unfeeling, vastly experienced traitor.

Women of the tango were themselves betrayed by the promise of better life in the city and often longed to return to the innocent cotton dresses they had worn in the barrio of their past. But many such women could reach for material success and fame only in the cabaret, a world from which there was no turning back to decent society.

Inevitably, men put their faith in these women, who became independent, powerful, and calculating creatures out for their own selfish ends. Inevitably, these beautiful but deadly women abandon the men they choose to exploit and move on to others who offer greater wealth and shallower spirits. The victims of the female sex find themselves helpless, destitute, and alone with no recourse but to sing the tangos that muse on their downfall.

You know it is the nature
  of man to suffer.
The woman whom I loved with
  all my heart
Left me with the man who knew
  how to seduce her
	Sabe que es condición de varón
	  el sufrir.
	La mujer que yo quería con
	  todo mi corazón
	Se me ha ido con el hombre
	  que la supo seducir

. . . all the love which I
  felt for her
She cut off with one slash of the
  blade of her treachery.
	. . . todo aquel amor que
	  por ella yo sentí
	lo cortó de un solo tajo con el
	  filo de su traición.

And if perhaps one day she
  might wish to return
To my side once more, I will
  have to pardon her.
If a man can kill another for
  jealousy
He forgives when love for any
  woman speaks powerfully.
	Y si acaso algún día quisiera
	  volver
	a mi lado otra vez, yo la he de
	  perdonar.
	Si por celos un hombre a otro
	  puede matar
	se perdona cuando habla muy
	  fuerte el querer a cualquier
	  mujer.

—J. A. Carusso
"Sentimiento Gaucho"

The only man who could resist city women and hold onto barrio values while conquering the sophistication of Buenos Aires and other world capitals was Carlos Gardel, whom Argentines unanimously praise as the greatest tango singer of all time. The features of "Carlitos," who was killed in a plane crash in 1935, are still as familiar as the Argentine national colors, which often surround the face that smiles down on passengers from decals in taxis and buses. That face was one of Gardel's greatest achievements. The illegitimate son of an immigrant washerwoman had taken care to leave no trace of his humble background or foreign origins in the calculated combination of dazzling smile, tilted hat, and impeccably arranged tuxedo. He incarnated the ideal of the Argentine as quintessentially urban. But he never allowed his urbane elegance to undermine his values or his loyalties. From the pinnacle of his success in the city center, he remembered the neighborhood friends of his youth, and he longed for Argentina while he triumphed in European capitals. Even more important, he resisted the glamour of the women surrounding him and remained faithful to his mother: Gardel never married, and his mother's tomb adjoins his. Carlitos took the tango as song to its apogee, yet he restates more than an aesthetic ideal each time an Argentine listens to his recorded voice and pronounces the familiar saying, "He sings better every year."

As both artist and man, Gardel commands special concentration on his rendering of tango lyrics. But tango enthusiasts pay special attention to other singers' renditions as well, even though the lines are often already so well known that all Argentines quote them as proverbs relevant to daily situations. Traditionally, Argentines will not dance to a tango that is sung. If they danced they could not attend properly to the music and lyrics, or hear their own experience and identity revealed in the singer's and musicians' rendering of quintessential Argentine emotions. The singer of the tango shares his personal encounter with experiences common to them all. He does not need bold pronouncement or flamboyant gesture. His audience knows what he means and his feelings are familiar ones. They listen for the nuances—emotional and philosophical subtleties that will tell them something new about their guarded interior worlds.

When they dance to tangos, Argentines contemplate themes akin to those of tango lyrics, stimulating emotions that, despite an apparently contradictory choreography, are the same as those behind the songs. The choreography also reflects the world of the lyrics, but indirectly. The dance portrays an encounter between the powerful and completely dominant male and the passive, docile, completely submissive female. The passive woman and the rigidly controlled but physically aggressive man contrast poignantly with the roles of the sexes depicted in the tango lyrics. This contrast between two statements of relations between the sexes aptly mirrors the insecurities of life and identity.

An Argentine philosophy of bitterness, resentment, and pessimism has the same goal as a danced statement of machismo, confidence, and sexual optimism. The philosopher elaborates his schemes to demonstrate that he is a man of the world—that he is neither stupid nor naive. In the dance, the dancer acts as though he has none of the fears he cannot show—again proving that he is not gil. When an Argentine talks of the way he feels when dancing a tango, he describes an experience of total aggressive dominance over the girl, the situation, the world— an experience in which he vents his resentment and expresses his bitterness against a destiny that denied him this dominance. Beyond this, it gives him a moment behind the protection of this facade to ponder the history and the land that have formed him, the hopes he has treasured and lost. Sábato echoes widespread feeling in Argentina when he says "Only a gringo would make a clown of himself by taking advantage of a tango for a chat or amusement."

While thus dancing a statement of invulnerability, the somber tanguero sees himself, because of his sensitivity, his great capacity to love, and his fidelity to the true ideals of his childhood years, as basically vulnerable. As he protects himself with a facade of steps that demonstrate perfect control, he contemplates his absolute lack of control in the face of history and destiny. The nature of the world has doomed him to disillusionment, to a solitary existence in the face of the impossibility of perfect love and the intimacy this implies. If by chance the girl with whom he dances feels the same sadness, remembering similar disillusion, the partners do not dance sharing the sentiment. They dance together to relive their disillusion alone. In a Buenos Aires dance hall, a young man turned to me from the fiancee he had just relinquished to her chaperoning mother and explained, "In the tango, together with the girl—and it does not matter who she is—a man remembers the bitter moments of his life, and he, she, and all who are dancing contemplate a universal emotion. I do not like the woman to talk to me while I dance tango. And if she speaks I do not answer. Only when she says to me, 'Omar, I am speaking,' I answer, 'And I, I am dancing.' "

Paper Tangos

Here we will sing, así no más,
the tangos of the exile of Gardel.
And we will recount, así no más,
the history of some paper tangos.
The tangos of the exile of Gardel
are tangos that are acted out in life—
tanguedias that never come down from the marquee.

We will begin
with letters of exile and of our country
. . . Letters of exile come and go,
bringing us emotions like daily bread:
errands and news that give us
the proof that everyone is still there

These notes try as well to recall San Martín
and the exile of the great unfinished nation.
All Latin American peoples have lived exiled
inside or outside of their land

Exile is absence, and death, a prolonged absence.
Who amongst us has not died a little?

The country we left no longer exists.

"How did it occur to you to make a tanguedia, as you call it?"

"He said to me, 'If you play the saxophone, stay here in Buenos Aires. But if you
play the tango on the bandoneon, go to Paris.' "

"What am I going to do in Paris?"

"The tanguedia. The Exile of Gardel."

"But what is the tanguedia?"

"Something that tells what is happening to us here in Buenos Aires."
"I said to him, 'But that is an enormous risk. . . .' "

"He said, 'The decision to be is always a risk. To live in Buenos Aires is a risk. But
to leave is also a risk. The triumph is to hold out, to remain united here as well as
there.' "

"And so his strategy of risk began to develop: It is necessary to invent a culture, a
poetics of risk."

—Fernando Solanas
from *The Exile of Gardel*

The arrival of two new statements of the tango, the film *The Exile of Gardel*
and the Broadway sensation, *Tango Argentino,* provided a special focus of self-
reflection for expatriate Argentines in mid-1987. *The Exile of Gardel,* in which
Argentines exiles sing and dance out fragments of their broken lives in Paris, was
directed in 1985 by Fernando Solanas, famed in Argentina as director of one of
the most controversial political films in Argentine history, *The Hour of the Fur-
naces,* which was clandestinely shown during the Argentine civil war of the
1970s. *Tango Argentino* displayed a history of tango dance and song that has

proved a surprise international hit. For Argentines, *Tango Argentino* brought together their most evocative tangos and became a statement both of their unique heritage and of its emotional and artistic hold on audiences worldwide.

Expatriate Argentines insisted that I see the film and took care that I met singers and dancers from the review. The film's tanguedia—with its paper tangos and letters of exile—like the classic tangos themselves, has no end. All call for a response that in itself is a cultural configuration of thought. How could I best evoke the density of accruing and changing cultural meanings in these new statements of the tango and responses to them? How better than to structure my thought into one of the responses demanded by the cultural form itself? The danger of self-indulgent reflection is recognized by Argentines themselves as inherent in the form, but it is the form and its responses—and their meditations on exile, identity, cultural vitality, gender, and the various forms of death—that I intend to explore, not by analysis of the form but through an enactment of a response.

A Paper Tango

For many years I have been sending and receiving letters of exile; as I write this, the last has come under the door: I do not want to open it. Under the door, the way letters come in Buenos Aires. I am writing a letter of exile for those who told me of a film of exile that speaks of the fate abroad of the tango, their song of loneliness and frustration, written after one exile, during another, and before yet another. These letters of exile become equated in the film with paper tangos. Paper tangos form tanguedias, rather than tragedias; they are parts of other tanguedias that will never find an end while our children confront yet another exile in their life without a country. Like the rest of the world, but our glimpse of our exile, fragmentation, lack of form and lack of an end to our story came early.

You made enormous efforts to contact me about the *Exile of Gardel,* but because we could find no time together, it was alone that I finally screened the tape. It seemed nevertheless particularly appropriate to be alone as I watched image after image of person after person turned thing by the denuded solitude of exile. This is the exile of the tango, the song to loneliness, the exile of everything deeply Argentine, the exile of the solitude of the South. But the song has sung not only of an exile outside but also inside, an exile that already existed before the exile: the exile left his country for the third time when we left Argentina. As children of immigrants unsettled in our lives or selves, Argentines find themselves in exile three times distant from themselves, and they can no longer remember when they did not exist in an enormous tunnel of mirrors. I made notes. I had to write very rapidly: with no time to stop to recast phrases to speak of "them," the notes like the film talk of "us." Or they are fragments without subjects, where "the tango," and "letters of exile," and the parents and "children of exile," and the exile itself are presupposed to exist in the context of Argentine experience that we share and in reference to those who do not understand but on whom we rely for media, space, and the confrontation of their misunderstanding in order to express ourselves.

I took the notes home. I looked at them just like that, as the film says, *así no más,* on paper. And *así no más,* I saw suddenly that they were and were not my own life. With the difference that I went to Argentina to study its culture and, passing for an Argentine, I confused even myself. At first we were all students, I just one among many, who were exploring our Argentine identity. The university closed the night I arrived, and we formulated our questions together. Everything I heard served me finally, as it served you, to analyze, again with the difference that this was not only my personal life but my professional task. Yet, after ten years surrounded always by Argentine life, slowly on the edges of my mind my analysis became my experience. And so I studied the tango, but also I danced it in the provinces and I listened to it in the capital, and I used it as a language to think and communicate my Argentine experience.

I, like you, lived years whose only continuity consisted in receiving and sending Argentine letters. Like many of you I studied abroad, in Oxford with Argentines and taught by Argentines, all of us bringing our minds to bear on Argentina. Like many of you I also married a member of a community that called itself foreign, regional, and Argentine, all at the same time. Tied to the Asturian Patagonian Argentines, I struggled to keep contact with Hungarian Argentines and Jewish Argentines and English Argentines who "came from" the capital: *porteños.* Or perhaps it was only our enormous families that kept us apart. The only one of all our friends who did not have the backing of such an identity was I myself, and so I wanted my child to have the only identity of which I could conceive: we returned to Buenos Aires so that the child of two foreigners with flimsy documents would be born on Argentine soil, by law irrevocably Argentine.

Argentina was our country, Patagonia, our home where the child was taken to "know" [*conocer*], but our work, like that of almost everyone else, took us "outside." So all of us began again to write letters from different points on the globe, and we met in London, in Los Angeles, in Mexico, in the airport in Rio, in congresses in Paris, in order to exchange *dulce de leche* in its blue cans, Sugus candies for the children, and shoes for letters and photos that began their long journey back. And, carrying *dulce de leche,* Sugus, and shoes whose leather above all permeated our suitcases with Buenos Aires, we came to know friends and uncles and grandparents and great-grandparents and children of Argentines in Asturias, in Italy, in Valencia, in Miami, in Rochester where other photos were on show in which children already grown had once looked at a camera from Tucumán, or Río Gallegos, or, of course, Buenos Aires. Bit by bit the interchange began to include rumors and memories and fears of terror in the country, and for all of us, in our minds flickered moments of fear that had touched us in Buenos Aires: when someone stopped momentarily in the gesture of serving wine as the sound of machine guns reached us—and then without knowing what to do, continued serving the wine in silence; or when a baby was in danger with no way through the police cordon that had us trapped inside a city block with a bomb no one knew where; or when there was no more news of a friend.

Sometime in those years as I came and went from Argentina, still asking the same questions—sometime in those years I stopped expecting answers, although always expecting letters, from Argentina. The second exile began for me as it had begun for others in other years and other generations. For me and for other Argentines, who had been children of immigrants, the second exile came after a first. In the first exile we had left one reality for another reality in Argentina. The second exile in Argentina itself was the growing consciousness that Argentina did not offer a reality: Argentina itself reflected back to us our doubts. The tango of the film and the tango in Argentina sings to the vast doubt, the *sin sentido* of the culture—which, as it negates, can also affirm the task of inventing life anew, offering all possible options and with them the exhilarating sensation of crisis. It is, I used to say, a culture of doubt; we needed to build monuments to doubt. In the film, as in the third exile, where we are alienated in many painful ways from Argentina itself and even at times from each other, our culture has become one of risk—the risk that the exile always relives, searching for a reply, an ending that may not exist, inside or outside Argentina.

So we were all exiled two times, and then three. Each of us confronts yet another exile in our children: What does my son remember of Buenos Aires? When will he return? What will it be like if he speaks in a language other *t*han the Spanish I speak to him? What will I tell him when he learns other words, another history, another music? But then all Argentines have always learned ''another'' language, ''another'' history, ''another'' music. For all of us our exile is our mirror.

All of this is in the notes. But what can I do with these notes, these reflections in another mirror where I suddenly see myself and you? Now we are no longer students. Now I ask questions of the questions that we posed together, we are perhaps no longer looking for the answer together. If we are not, what right do I have to say that I understood what I have just seen? My dilemma, my life, is the continuous frustrated attempt of the exiles, like us years back and like the film today, to get a dial tone in the public telephones to speak from Paris to the River Plate. I have been in those telephones in Paris. One said, in blue letters over the French graffiti, in the booth in 1979, *Las Malvinas son nuestras.*

Tango Argentino: Ballad for my Death

All of this, then, is what I think, at the same time that it is what I have learned I should think, when I hear the tango. But the mix of the profound and absurd that Argentines recognize as appropriate reactions to tango music, song, and dance implies beyond shared reality, highly personal experience. *Tango Argentino* confronted us with many of the most beloved tangos of all, performed one after the other and culminating, surely not by chance, in *Ballad for my Death*. Tangos are as different as listeners. But tangos, particularly this canon of tangos, present parameters for thought. The tango mines certain experiences and poses certain unanswered questions, but does so in the context of certain lives and certain historical moments. In order to communicate about the tango and about these tangos as ways of thinking about an individual life, I need to use an evocative strategy. This is no longer a letter: these are not thoughts addressed to anyone. They were of interest to me in thinking through my life, as I understand reactions to tango often are to those who take them seriously. The communication of the thoughts that occurred to me upon hearing *Ballad for my Death* enacts the dynamic involved in this experience, the quintessential Argentine reconstruction of an individual confrontation with life. Better than any dissection of this reconstruction is its evocation through the one individual case I can best know, my own. Precisely because this case is not only highly individual but ultimately that of a foreigner in Argentina, it illuminates, again by parallel, the way Argentines can think about their own stories with their tango.

Why should it be that the sense that the tango makes has become so urgent to me as a person? Sometimes I think that I recognize myself in you because you first recognized me. How otherwise did it happen not only that for the most part I was mistaken for an Argentine but that when I received any notice at all it was because one or another or whole groups of you thought you saw in me quintessences of yourselves? At the very least you remembered a model you thought you must have seen somewhere recently, or often a doll that might have existed in your past. Sometimes you realized, apparently quite suddenly as you made an aside to someone that I was not supposed to overhear, that you recognized what had always been for you the ideal face. Others felt it clearly natural I ask about the tango as you concluded time after time that I had the appearance of a dancer. Sometimes an anonymous person who did not quite comprehend what it was that I was doing would nod in grave accord that it made sense to study Eva Perón because "you even look like her." More sophisticated acquaintances would make a joke of this, or only tell me much later. Children still blurt it out to my face. Even worse, acknowledgeable now only because none of these experiences will ever occur again, were the repeated times in the provinces and even in the capital when people would expect me to know what to do when they, fishing in the past and the present to understand what it was that I evoked, would finally exclaim that after all they were seeing again just one more of the images of the Virgin Mary that had peopled their lives. I still carry with me the religious medals given to me because they looked like me. I don't know what to do with them.

What kind of curious concatenation of physiological and psychological happenstance could have allowed this to happen? Perhaps the physiological coincidence would never have been noticed had it not been for the psychological circumstance: I was happy in Argentina. People told me that this was evident: my radiance evoked images of Madonnas, of Evita who looked like them, of models, of dancers and of dolls. And to this another physiological accident added: at 21 I seemed to the Argentines to be 15 at the most, and at 26, they guessed I was 18. People treated me accordingly. Possibly this would have happened to me in any country—possibly; I can only know that when it did happen to me, it happened in Buenos Aires. I was a favorite child of the city: it was the only moment in my life when merely by existing (in Argentine Spanish one *is* existentially [*ser*] rather than temporarily [*estar*] a scholarship holder; and at the same time, sometimes to my woe, one *is* a doll or the ideal girl child woman), I was continually *regalada*, "given." People gave me banquets and gifts and offers of everything from flowers in the street to marriage.

So I recuperated a childhood that I could never know in what seemed a rather distant country that had never after all claimed me as its own. I could be taken in by family after family that fed me and dressed me and showed me off until I melted into one final family and disappeared.

As anthropologist, girl child, and madonna it was perfectly expectable that I should not know details and rules of earthly matters and that I should need instruction in them. So for a very long time very many people, whom on one level I knew I did not take seriously, laughed at what they admired but knew could not last, my simplicity. "This is wonderful," I was told once upon breaking yet another bit of protocol of a rather formal culture, "You are totally uncivilized." The less attention I paid to rules the more they liked it—to a point. At that point they gently took up the task of my education in their culture, because, after all, although I might be uncivilized I was asking for education in this culture that knew that I could not grow up without learning the rules, someday. Among the first things I learned was that I was by nature educated and refined, something recognizable in my mere physical presence and mannerisms. Stripped of the credentials of Harvard, Oxford, Fulbright, Ford, I carefully and literally took note that education is not learned, it is taken in with mother's milk, and that what nature does not bestow, Salamanca cannot make up for.

And then I learned that certain political responsibility, certain family loyalties, certain human goals and expectations would be attributed to me as an adult. No one had ever gotten around to this in my own country—or perhaps I paid less attention there where I had not been a successful daughter and where I was not an anthropologist. But when I wanted to take account of matters—*cuando quise darme cuenta*—in Argentina, I was no longer an anthropologist there, either, I was a bride.

Along the way, and perhaps significantly for my new status, my mother had died. She died in California, but I lived out her death in Argentina. I remember the systematic reassurances of the dozens of relatives and acquaintances as they evoked the many deaths they themselves had lived. As I waited to cross the Straits of Magellan and then to continue North, as days ground by in Buenos Aires while the family and its contacts searched out a place for me on the overloaded planes taking Argentine tourists to their summer destinations, on the 36-hour flight that would finally take me landing in Santiago, in Lima, in Guayaquil, in Bogotá, in Panamá, in Tegucigalpa, in Guatemala City, in Mexico—during all this time I learned not to be afraid, to remember that all children see the death of their parents, to know that there were many people who knew how this happened and what to do. They were waiting for me in Argentina—very different from the bewildered, dumbstruck fragmented little group that my American family made while it waited two days more for my mother's death and then dispersed again. All of this seemed to have occurred in Buenos Aires: the last comforting words I remembered hearing were those of an unknowing airline official, consoling me for what she thought was my natural reaction to leaving my country, "May your voyage not be a burden. You will come back to Argentina."

So one by one I learned the lessons of adult life, before it closed over me, in Buenos Aires. The tango reminded me once again that I have lived so much of life in Argentina that it seems more a state of mind than a country. The *Ballad for my Death* evoked this time around, in its music and its repeated names of places and experiences taken for granted in Buenos Aires, the sudden realization of human mortality that must come to everyone at some time or in some place. That realization came to me for the first time—in that sense really its only time because afterward I could recognize it—in Buenos Aires. It *was* in Buenos Aires; it *was* crossing and going away along a white street; it *was* crossing Santa Fé, la Plaza Francia a few blocks away in the dark; it *was* at dawn and at six—everything clear in my mind: the tea house, *el, Five O'Clock Tea,* one block from Santa Fé and another from Callao the last thing that I saw before entering the clinic where Martín was born. So that in this sense, in some real sense, I *will* always die in Buenos Aires just as I will always give birth in Buenos Aires. Second times for me are already imprinted with Buenos Aires. As I listened I had what must be a primordial sensation of recognizing something profound and commonplace that all human beings must feel but that I happened to feel in Buenos Aires.

> I will die in Buenos Aires
> it will be at dawn which is the hour of the death of those who know how to die
> I will put away in my silence perfumed bitterness *[mufa]*
> of that verse that I was never able to tell you
> I will go a few blocks and there, there in the Plaza Francia like shadows fled from a tired ballet
> repeating your name along a white street, my memories will tiptoe away from me
> I will die in Buenos Aires
> it will be at dawn
> I will tamely put away the things of life
> my small poem of good-byes and
> my tobacco, my tango
> I will put over my shoulders to be warm all of the dawn
> my next to last whisky will not be drunk
> Tangoly, my elaborated death will arrive
> I will be dead on the dot when it is six o'clock
> In Santa Fé
> I know that on our street corner you are dressed in sadness down to your feet
> Alma mía, let us go, the day is coming, do not cry
> I will die in Buenos Aires
> It will be dawn
> I will be dead at six.
>
> —H. Ferrer and A. Piazzolla
> from *Ballad for my Death*

Buenos Aires. Arbitrary city like all cities. My mother used to say that as a little girl she thought about all those Argentines going up and down streets so far away and she wondered if some day her life would have anything to do with them. Arbitrary city. But seen from Argentina, once there, a definitive point on the map. A point that made itself definitive on my map, the map I bought for my first journey south. That map is now covered with lines, coming and going in and out of Buenos Aires, erasing the city. Is it that my life erases Buenos Aires or that Buenos Aires became my life? Arbitrary point, but not absurd. Not absurd like Villazón, Bolivia or La Quiaca, Argentina—where once I thought I might die, and where the thought made me desperate at the absurdity of dying for nothing in no place. It was not that I thought I might die in Buenos Aires: rather, it was in Buenos Aires that I knew for the first time that I shall die.

—translated from the Spanish by the author.

Index

George E. Marcus is Professor of Anthropology at Rice University.
He is the author of *Lives in Trust*, co-author, with Michael Fischer,
of *Anthropology as Cultural Critique* and editor, with James Clifford,
of *Writing Culture*. He was the editor of *Cultural Anthropology* from
1986–1991.

Library of Congress Cataloging-in-Publication Data
Rereading cultural anthropology / edited by George E. Marcus.
p.   cm.
Includes index.
ISBN 0-8223-1279-4.—ISBN 0-8223-1297-2 (pbk.)
1. Culture.   2. Ethnology.   I. Marcus, George E.
GN357.R47   1992
306—dc20   92-21908 CIP